THE FOLLOWING IS A LIST OF **NETS-T** FOR THE CHAPTERS
THE END-OF-CHAPTER

Chapter	NETS-T for Chapter	NETS-T for Portfolio
1.	I-B; VI-D, E	Activity 1: I-B; V-A, B
2.	II-A, B, D, E; IV-A, C	Activity 1: I-A, B Activity 2: II-B
3.	II-A, C; III-A-D; IV-A, C; VI-B	Activity 1: IV-A Activity 2: II-A, C Activity 3: II-A-E
4.	I-A; II-A, D, E; II-A-D; III-A-D; IV-A, B; V-C, D	Activity 1: I-A, B Activity 2: II-A, C Activity 3: II-A-E
5.	I-A, B; II-A, C-E; III-A-D; IV-A-C; V-A, C, D; VI-B	Activity 1: I-A Activity 2: II-A, C Activity 3: II-A-E
6.	I-A, B; II-A, C-E; III-A-D; IV-A, C; V- C, D; VI-B	Activity 1: I-B Activity 2: II-A, C Activity 3: II-A-E
7.	I-A, B; II-A-E; III-A-D; IV-A, C; V-A, D; VI-A, B, D, E	Activity 1: IV-B Activity 2: II-A, C Activity 3: II-A-E
8.	I-B; 11-A-E; III-A-D; IV-A, C; V-D; VI- B, D, E	Activity 1: III-A, C Activity 2: II-A, C Activity 3: II-A-E
9.	I-A; II-A-E; III-A-D; IV-A, C; V-B; VI- B, C, E	Activity 1: I-B; III-A Activity 2: II-A, C Activity 3: II-A-E
10.	I-A; II-A-E; III-A-D; IV-A, C; V-B; VI- B, C, E	Activity 1: I-A Activity 2: II-A, C Activity 3: II-A-E
11.	I-A; II-A-E; III-A-D; IV-A, C; V-B; VI- B, C, E	Activity 1: I-A; IV-B Activity 2: II-A, C Activity 3: II-A-E
12.	I-A; II-A-E; III-A-D; IV-A, C; V-B; VI- B, C, E	Activity 1: I-A; V-D Activity 2: II-A, C Activity 3: II-A-E
13.	I-A; II-A-E; 111-A-D; IV-A, C; V-B-, Vl- B, C, E	Activity 1: IV-A Activity 2: II-A, C Activity 3: II-A-E
14.	I-A; II-A-E; 111-A-D; IV-A, C; V-B; Vl- B, C, E	Activity 1: I-B; III-C Activity 2: II-A, C Activity 3: II-A-E
15.	I-A; II-A-E; III-A-D; IV-A, C; V-B; VI- B, C, E	Activity 1: I-B; IV-B Activity 2: II-A, C Activity 3: II-A-E

ISTE NATIONAL EDUCATIONAL TECHNOLOGY STANDARDS FOR TEACHERS

NETS FOR TEACHERS

Educational Technology Standards and Performance Indicators for All Teachers

Building on the NETS for Students, the ISTE NETS for Teachers (NETS•T), which focus on preservice teacher education, define the fundamental concepts, knowledge, skills, and attitudes for applying technology in educational settings. All candidates seeking certification or endorsements in teacher preparation should meet these educational technology standards. It is the responsibility of faculty across the university and at cooperating schools to provide opportunities for teacher candidates to meet these standards.

The six standards areas with performance indicators listed below are designed to be general enough to be customized to fit state, university, or district guidelines and yet specific enough to define the scope of the topic. Performance indicators for each standard provide specific outcomes to be measured when developing a set of assessment tools. The standards and the performance indicators also provide guidelines for teachers currently in the classroom.

1. TECHNOLOGY OPERATIONS AND CONCEPTS.

   Teachers demonstrate a sound understanding of technology operations and concepts. Teachers:

   A. demonstrate introductory knowledge, skills, and understanding of concepts related to technology (as described in the ISTE National Education Technology Standards for Students).

   B. demonstrate continual growth in technology knowledge and skills to stay abreast of current and emerging technologies.

2. PLANNING AND DESIGNING LEARNING ENVIRONMENTS AND EXPERIENCES.

   Teachers plan and design effective learning environments and experiences supported by technology. Teachers:

   A. design developmentally appropriate learning opportunities that apply technology-enhanced instructional strategies to support the diverse needs of learners.

   B. apply current research on teaching and learning with technology when planning learning environments and experiences.

   C. identify and locate technology resources and evaluate them for accuracy and suitability.

   D. plan for the management of technology resources within the context of learning activities.

   E. plan strategies to manage student learning in a technology-enhanced environment.

3. TEACHING, LEARNING, AND THE CURRICULUM.

   Teachers implement curriculum plans that include methods and strategies for applying technology to maximize student learning. Teachers:

   A. facilitate technology-enhanced experiences that address content standards and student technology standards.

   B. use technology to support learner-centered strategies that address the diverse needs of students.

   C. apply technology to develop students' higher order skills and creativity.

   D. manage student learning activities in a technology-enhanced environment.

4. ASSESSMENT AND EVALUATION.

   Teachers apply technology to facilitate a variety of effective assessment and evaluation strategies. Teachers:

   A. apply technology in assessing student learning of subject matter using a variety of assessment techniques.

   B. use technology resources to collect and analyze data, interpret results, and communicate findings to improve instructional practice and maximize student learning.

   C. apply multiple methods of evaluation to determine students' appropriate use of technology resources for learning, communication, and productivity.

5. PRODUCTIVITY AND PROFESSIONAL PRACTICE.

   Teachers use technology to enhance their productivity and professional practice. Teachers:

   A. use technology resources to engage in ongoing professional development and lifelong learning.

   B. continually evaluate and reflect on professional practice to make informed decisions regarding the use of technology in support of student learning.

   C. apply technology to increase productivity.

   D. use technology to communicate and collaborate with peers, parents, and the larger community in order to nurture student learning.

6. SOCIAL, ETHICAL, LEGAL, AND HUMAN ISSUES.

   Teachers understand the social, ethical, legal, and human issues surrounding the use of technology in PK-12 schools and apply those principles in practice. Teachers:

   A. model and teach legal and ethical practice related to technology use.

   B. apply technology resources to enable and empower learners with diverse backgrounds, characteristics, and abilities.

   C. identify and use technology resources that affirm diversity.

   D. promote safe and healthy use of technology resources.

   E. facilitate equitable access to technology resources for all students.

INTEGRATING EDUCATIONAL TECHNOLOGY INTO TEACHING

FOURTH EDITION

M.D. Roblyer
University of Maryland University College

PEARSON

Merrill
Prentice Hall

Upper Saddle River, New Jersey
Columbus, Ohio

Library of Congress Cataloging-in-Publication Data
Roblyer, M. D.
  Integrating educational technology into teaching / M.D. Roblyer.—4th ed.
    p. cm.
  ISBN 0-13-119572-7
  1. Educational technology—United States. 2. Computer-assisted instruction—
United States. 3. Curriculum planning—United States. I. Title.
  LB1028.3.R595 2006
  371.33—dc22   2005001244

Vice President and Executive Publisher: Jeffery W. Johnston
Executive Editor: Debra A. Stollenwerk
Development Editor: Amy Nelson
Editorial Assistant: Mary Morrill
Production Editors: Kris Roach and Jo Ellen Gohr
Production Coordination: Carlisle Publishers Services
Design Coordinator: Diane C. Lorenzo
Photo Coordinator: Sandy Schaefer
Cover Designer: Ali Mohrman
Cover Image: Corbis
Production Manager: Pam Bennett
Director of Marketing: Ann Castel Davis
Marketing Manager: Darcy Betts Prybella
Marketing Coordinator: Brian Mounts

This book was set in Garamond by Carlisle Communications, Ltd. It was printed and bound by Courier Kendallville, Inc. The cover was printed by Phoenix Color Corp.

Photo Credits: Peter Anderson © Dorling Kindersley, p. 19 (bottom); Apple Computer, Inc., pp. 11 (top left), 197; Bill Aron/PhotoEdit, p. 185; Laura Bolesta/Merrill, p. 144; K_Britten/Getty Images Inc.–Hulton Archive Photos, p. 10 (bottom); courtesy of Jerome Bruner, p. 39 (second from right); Bill Burlingham/Prentice Hall School Division, p. 11 (bottom right); Corbis/Bettmann, pp. 38 (left), 39 (center), 93; Scott Cunningham/Merrill, pp. 367, 407, 418; Mary Kate Denny/Getty Images Inc.–Stone Allstock, p. 50; Mary Kate Denny/PhotoEdit, pp. 15 (bottom), 89; © Dorling Kindersley, p. 373; courtesy of Robert Gagné, p. 38 (right); Jay Gardner/Basic Books, Inc. p. 39 (right); Garmin International, Inc., p. 178; Spencer Grant/PhotoEdit, p. 215; Walter Hodges/Getty Images, Inc.–Stone Allstock, p. 213; courtesy of International Business Machines Corporation. Unauthorized use not permitted, p. 10 (top right); Zigy Kaluzny/Getty Images Inc.–Stone Allstock, p. 285; Bonnie Kamin/PhotoEdit, p. 177; Ken Karp Photography/PH Photo, p. 183; Frank La Bua/PH College, p. 16 (bottom); courtesy of the Library of Congress, p. 39 (left, second from left); David Mager/Pearson Learning Photo Studio, p. 15 (top); Anthony Magnacca/Merrill, pp. 11 (top left), 17 (top), 20 (center, bottom), 192, 249, 287, 409; Jeff Maloney/Getty Images, Inc.–Photodisc, p. 315; Phil Martin/PhotoEdit, p. 151; Modern Curriculum Press/Pearson Learning, p. 17 (bottom); courtesy of Bonnie Mohnsen, pp. 399, 401 (left, right); Liz Moore/Merrill, pp. 19 (top), 20 (top), 55, 56, 59, 60, 61, 81 (bottom), 108, 391; Michael Newman/PhotoEdit, pp. 307, 334; Pearson Learning Photo Studio, p. 11 (bottom center); PhotoEdit, p. 274; Prentice Hall School Division, p. 16 (center); A. Ramey/PhotoEdit, pp. 102, 325; Seth Resnick/Getty Images, Inc.–Liaison, p. 11 (bottom left); Valerie Schultz/Merrill, p. 3; Ellen Senisi/The Image Works, p. 357; Ariel Skelley/Corbis/Stock Market, p. 73; © 2005 SMART Technologies Inc. Used with permission, pp. 33, 347; SuperStock, Inc., p. 16 (top); SW Productions/Getty Images, Inc.–Photodisc, p. 1; Olaf Tiedie/Getty Images, Inc.–Taxi, p. 71; Official U.S. Air Force Photo, p. 10 (top left); Tom Watson/Merrill, p. 11 (top center); Patrick White/Merrill, pp. 49, 222, 292; Georgia Tech Communications, p. 207; © David Young-Wolff/PhotoEdit, pp. 17 (center), 81 (top), 117, 323.

Pearson Education Ltd.
Pearson Education Singapore Pte. Ltd.
Pearson Education Canada, Ltd.
Pearson Education—Japan

Pearson Education Australia PTY. Limited
Pearson Education North Asia Ltd.
Pearson Educacíon de Mexico, S.A. de C.V.
Pearson Education Malaysia Pte. Ltd.

PEARSON
Merrill
Prentice Hall

10 9 8 7 6 5 4 3 2
ISBN: 0-13-119572-7

DEDICATION

*For Bill and Paige Wiencke,
whose love is, as Arthur Clarke
said of advanced technology,
indistinguishable from magic*

PREFACE

A man is searching for lost keys in a pool of light. A policeman asks him where he lost them. "Out there," says the man, gesturing vaguely into the darkness. "Then why are you looking here?" asks the policeman. "Because the light's better," says the man. If we are scientifically honest, the real mysteries of human consciousness are still shrouded in darkness ... And suppose the real keys to our future are not in the pool of light, but somewhere out there?

John Davy, "Mindstorms in the Lamplight"
From *The Computer in Education: A Critical Perspective* (1985)

The first decades of electronic technologies in classrooms were a heady and hopeful time. In the warm glow of the computer monitor, we seemed to see the future of education itself, and the promise of unprecedented insights into the true nature of learning beckoned. Yet with each new scientific survey and study of technology use in schools, it has become increasingly clear that the technology itself provides only the raw materials for enhanced educational strategies. Now we know that everything depends on how teachers plan for and use these powerful devices.

We have more questions now than ever before about how to meet the varying needs of individual students so that none are left behind, but we also have some clearly defined guidelines on what works best when it comes to matching these needs with technology's capabilities. What have we learned so far that enlightens our use of technology in education? The following are some of our findings:

- **Good teaching comes first** — Recent innovations in distance resources gave renewed support to those who predicted, as did their predecessors in the 1960s, that technology would eliminate the personality of teachers from the instructional equation. However, our experience with Web-based learning in the past ten years has shown that interaction with teachers, flawed and variable as it may be, is more important than ever before. This textbook proposes that technology is, above all, a channel for helping teachers communicate better with students. It can make good teaching even better, but it cannot make bad teaching good. Conse-

quently, technology-using teachers never can be a force for improved education unless they are first and foremost informed, knowledgeable shapers of their craft. Before integrating technology into their teaching, educators must know a great deal, for example, about why there are different views on appropriate teaching strategies, how societal factors and learning theories have shaped these views, and how each strategy can address differing needs.

- **Technology is us** — Rather than seeing technology as some foreign invader here to confuse and complicate the simple life of the past, we can recognize that technology is very much our own response to overcoming obstacles that stand in the way of a better, more productive way of life. As Walt Kelly's "profound 'possum" Pogo said, "We has met the enemy, and he is us." Technology is us—our tools, our methods, and our own creative attempts to solve problems in our environment. Turmoil will accompany the transitions as we adapt to the new environment we ourselves have created. But technology is, by definition, intended to be part of our path to a better life, rather than an obstacle in its way.

- **We control how technology is used in education** — As a follow-up to our recognition that "technology is us," we must recognize the truth of Peter Drucker's statement: "The best way to predict the future is to create it." Both individual teachers and teaching organizations must see themselves as enlightened shapers of our future. Each teacher must help to articulate the vision for what the future of education should look like; each should acquire skills to help work toward realizing that vision.

The purpose of this book is to show how we are challenged to shape the future of technology in education. How we respond to this challenge is guided by how we see it helping us accomplish our own informed vision of what teaching and learning should be. Our approach to accomplishing this purpose rests on three premises:

- **Technology-based methods should be based in both learning theory and teaching practice** — There is no shortage of innovative ideas in the field of instructional technology; new and interesting methods come forward about as often as new and improved gadgets. Those who would build on the knowledge of the past should know why they do what they do, as well as how to do it. Thus, we have linked various technology-based integration strategies to well-researched theories of learning, and we have illustrated them with examples of successful practices based on these theories.

- **Uses of technology should match specific teaching and learning needs** — Technology has the power to improve teaching and learning, but it can also make a teacher's life more complicated. Therefore, each resource should be examined for its unique qualities and its potential benefits for teachers and students. Teachers should not use a tool simply because it is new and available—each integration strategy should be matched to a recognized need. We do not oppose experimentation, but we do advocate informed use.

- **Old integration strategies are not necessarily bad; new strategies are not necessarily good** — As technologies change and evolve at lightning speed, there is a tendency to throw out older teaching methods with the older machines. Sometimes this is a good idea; sometimes it would be a shame. Each of the integration strategies recommended in this book is based on methods with proven usefulness to teachers and students. Some of the strategies are based on directed methods that have been used for some time; other strategies are based on the newer, constructivist learning models. Each is recommended on the basis of its usefulness rather than its age.

This edition differs in structural ways from the first three, but its goal remains the same: to help teachers see more clearly their role in shaping the future of technology in education. This book illustrates that the real keys to great education lie not in the reflected light of a computer screen, but in the darker, less well-defined region "out there" that both encompasses and transcends it: the interplay of teacher, student, content, and tools.

THE FOURTH EDITION

Best known for its technology integration strategies grounded in strong research, the fourth edition of *Integrating Educational Technology into Teaching* now offers your students increased opportunities for practical application of these integration strategies. This new edition—*a total technology integration package*—will give your students hands-on practice with technology tools as they learn how to incorporate technology into the curriculum to support and shape

learning. The fourth edition also includes the author's five-part Technology Integration Planning (TIP) Model that shows teachers how to create an environment in which technology can effectively enhance learning.

WHAT'S NEW!

For the fourth edition, the author has developed a cohesive, comprehensive **technology integration framework** that builds on the strong research and numerous integration strategies of previous editions. This framework is designed to **introduce** your students to technology integration, help them effectively **plan** for technology integration, and give them numerous opportunities to **practice** technology skills and technology integration. This framework connects the four pieces of this integrated package: chapter content, the end-of-chapter Technology Integration Workshop, the *Technology Integration Workshop* DVD that is packaged with every copy of the book, and the Companion Website located at http://www.prenhall.com/roblyer.

THE TECHNOLOGY INTEGRATION FRAMEWORK

Introduces Your Students to Technology Integration

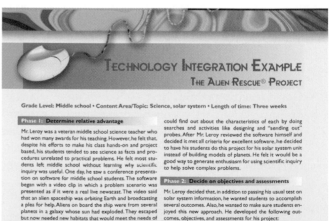

Technology Integration Examples (NEW!) Located at the beginning of Chapters 2–15, these classroom-based scenarios are linked to the end-of-chapter Technology Integration Workshop and tied to chapter objectives. Each example provides a classroom context for chapter content by focusing on the selection and use of specific technology within a classroom environment, and each walks the reader through the steps of the TIP Model.

Making the Case for Technology Integration (NEW!) In each chapter, this feature asks students to consider the issues regarding chapter content by reflecting on and considering the bigger picture of technology integration. Connected to the text's Companion Website, students can post their thoughts and respond to classmates through an online message board or click on the *Making the Case* module.

Top Ten (NEW!) This feature highlights and describes the best software features, uses, and strategies for teachers to apply and is located in Chapters 1 and 3–15.

Interactive Summary (NEW!) A study aid at the end of each chapter, this section summarizes critical chapter content and extends student learning through online examples and activities located on the Companion Website.

Helps Your Students *Plan* for Effective Technology Integration

Adapting for Special Needs (NEW!) This feature gives your students alternative software and technology materials to consider for use in helping students with special needs. This feature is located in Chapters 3–14.

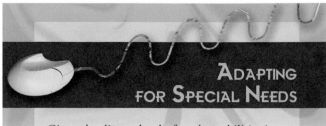

Technology Integration Ideas. Located in every chapter, this feature introduces technology lesson plan ideas. ISTE National Educational Technology Standards for Students (NETS•S) are identified.

TECHNOLOGY INTEGRATION IDEA 3.1

EXAMPLE STRATEGY FOR USING PROGRAMMING LANGUAGES
Title: A Window on Learning Logo
Content Area/Topic: Logic and analysis skills
Grade Level: Middle school
NETS for Students: Standards 1, 6
Description: Logo's graphic qualities make it a natural choice to explore the design qualities of symmetry, repetition, and precision. By using Logo variables, students can change their designs quickly and dramatically. With other methods, modifications would be more time consuming, and students would not be able to pinpoint the exact reasons and ways that designs were made different.
Instruction: Begin by reviewing basic Logo commands and exploring the Logo programming environment. Make sure students know that designs are programmed using the "turtle's" on-screen perspective and not their own. Have them practice developing simple procedures, and review debugging procedures line by line to determine how designs are drawn. Begin with an easy problem such as analyzing the steps in drawing a simple square to get children used to the logistics. Give students pictures of the Gothic rose window from the Notre Dame Cathedral. Ask them to analyze it, looking for patterns, shapes, and structures. Help them see that complicated designs are made up of simple geometric shapes. Then assign them the task of drawing their own window using three such shapes. Show them how to adjust basic designs by changing variable numbers. The best moments in the project occur when a student displays a "window" for the first time and a gasp of delight fills the room. (See example below.)
Assessment: Use rubric on programming language use and creativity.

Helps Your Students *Practice* Technology Integration

Technology Integration Workshop (NEW!) Located at the end of every chapter and on the DVD packaged in the back of the text, this extensive workshop includes hands-on, interactive features that connect chapter content to real-life practice.

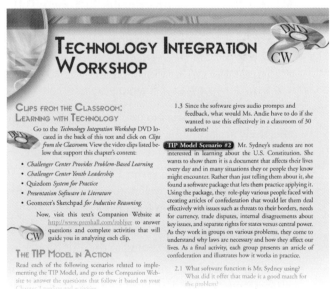

TECHNOLOGY INTEGRATION WORKSHOP

CLIPS FROM THE CLASSROOM: LEARNING WITH TECHNOLOGY
Go to the *Technology Integration Workshop* DVD located in the back of this text and click on *Clips from the Classroom*. View the video clips listed below that support this chapter's content:

• *Challenger Center Provides Problem-Based Learning*
• *Challenger Center Youth Leadership*
• Quizdom *System for Practice*
• *Presentation Software in Literature*
• Geometer's Sketchpad *for Inductive Reasoning*.

Now, visit this text's Companion Website at http://www.prenhall.com/roblyer to answer questions and complete activities that will guide you in analyzing each clip.

THE TIP MODEL IN ACTION
Read each of the following scenarios related to implementing the TIP Model, and go to the Companion Website to answer the questions that follow it based on your Chapter 3 reading and activities.

1.3 Since the software gives audio prompts and feedback, what would Ms. Andie have to do if she wanted to use this effectively in a classroom of 30 students?

TIP Model Scenario #2 Mr. Sydney's students are not interested in learning about the U.S. Constitution. She wants to show them it is a document that affects their lives every day and in many situations they or people they know might encounter. Rather than just telling them about it, she found a software package that lets them practice applying it. Using the package, they role-play various people faced with creating articles of confederation that would let them deal effectively with issues such as threats to their borders, needs for currency, trade disputes, internal disagreements about key issues, and separate rights for states versus central power. As they work in groups on various problems, they come to understand why laws are necessary and how they affect our lives. As a final activity, each group presents an article of confederation and illustrates how it works in practice.

2.1 What software function is Mr. Sydney using? What did it offer that made it a good match for the problem?

• **Clips from the Classroom: Learning with Technology** — These video clips provide students with immediate access to real classrooms where effective technology integration is happening. Students can watch teachers as they use technology in their classrooms to shape and support learning. Questions located on the Companion Website allow students to analyze scenarios presented in the video clips, which are based on chapter content.

- **The TIP Model in Action** — This activity deepens students' understanding of how to plan for effective technology integration by having them use the TIP Model to analyze classroom scenarios. Discussion questions in the text can also be answered on the Companion Website.

- **TIE into Practice** — Connected to the chapter-opening *Technology Integration Example (TIE)*, this hands-on activity extends student understanding and experience by giving students the opportunity to use **software tutorials** described in the Technology Integration Example. Students can click on the *Hands-On with Technology* section of the text's DVD to find the following tutorials:

  - Chapter 3: Rubric using *Rubistar*
  - Chapter 4: Spreadsheet on buying a car
  - Chapter 5: Microsoft *Publisher* desktop publishing to create an anthology
  - Chapter 6: Interactive storybook sample with *HyperStudio*
  - Chapter 7: Creating a Bookmarks/Favorites file
  - Chapter 8: Presidents Webquest using Netscape *Composer*
  - Chapter 9: *PowerPoint* book report
  - Chapter 10: French menu with Microsoft *Word*
  - Chapter 11: Spreadsheet graph in a *PowerPoint* presentation
  - Chapter 12: TrackStar website
  - Chapter 13: *Adobe Photoshop* graphic collage
  - Chapter 14: *iMovie* Video Record
  - Chapter 15: *Adobe Acrobat* survey

  - Answer questions related to implementing technology effectively in classrooms. Students can respond to these questions online through the Companion Website.

- **Technology Integration Lesson Planning** — Aligned to the ISTE Standards as well as the content standards for each area, this hands-on feature:

  - Gives students the ability to evaluate a set of technology integration ideas according to the TIP Model;

  - Provides modifiable measurement tools such as rubrics and checklists so students can evaluate the lesson plans and software and save their evaluations;

  - Allows students to search over 300 lesson plans aligned to ISTE standards by key search terms, including grade level, content area, technology, etc.; and

  - Allows students to modify lesson plans to meet their own needs and add new lessons to the collection.

- **For Your Teaching Portfolio** — This feature directs students to save the material they created in each chapter in a personal portfolio.

New Design

The fourth edition also features:

- **A four-color design** — With a new design that stimulates reader interest and includes more than five full-color photos per chapter, the fourth edition is now even more appealing to students.

- **Visual study aids** — Multiple new tables and summary figures in each chapter support student learning, synthesize chapter content for students to use as study aids, and provide at-a-glance outlines of essential information.

Integrated Supplements for Students

Technology Integration Workshop DVD

This DVD, which is packaged in the back of the book, contains:

- *Clips from the Classroom: Learning with Technology*
- *Hands-On with Technology*
  - *The TIP Model in Action*
  - *TIE into Practice*
  - *Technology Integration Lesson Planning*
  - *For Your Teaching Portfolio*

Companion Website: http://www.prenhall.com/roblyer

The Companion Website (CW) provides students with resources and immediate feedback on exercises and other activites linked to the text. These activities, projects, and resources enhance and extend chapter content to real-world issues and concepts. Each chapter on the CW contains the following modules or sections:

Technology Integration Workshop. This module includes a variety of hands-on activities including:

- **Clips from the Classroom: Learning with Technology** — Activities and questions give students the ability to analyze the video to gain an understanding of how to integrate technology into the classroom.

- **The TIP Model in Action** — Questions align with the scenarios at the end of each chapter.

- **TIE into Practice: Technology Integration Example** — Practical tutorial and skill-building activities as well as hands-on experiences build students' skills using popular software and hardware applications.

- **For Your Teaching Portfolio** — This feature directs students to save the material they created in each chapter in a personal portfolio.

Chapter Objectives. Outlines key concepts and issues in the chapter.

Interactive Summary. Summarizes chapter content and allows students to click on links to view examples.

Self-Assessment. Includes multiple-choice, true/false, and short-answer questions with automatic grading to provide immediate feedback to students.

Web Enrichment Activities. Includes meaningful activities that connect to chapter content and provide Web-based resources for students to use when completing the activities.

Key Terms. Provides students with chapter key terms and links to Web sites where they can explore additional information.

Website Resources. Links to World Wide Web sites that relate to and enhance chapter content.

Downloadable Resource Evaluations. Provides downloadable chapter rubrics, checklists, and evaluation forms to assist students with lesson planning, software and technology evaluation, and other chapter activities.

Making the Case for Technology Integration. This feature provides students the opportunity to explore issues and ideas they read about in the chapter.

Software Skill Builder Tutorials. Practical tutorial and skill-building activities give students hands-on experiences that build their skills using popular software and hardware.

Other Resources. Gives students access to *PowerPoint* slides, the ISTE Standards for students and teachers, and the user manual for the Technology Integration Workshop DVD.

OneKey

OneKey is Prentice Hall's exclusive new resource for students and instructors. This integrated online course management resource features everything students and instructors need for work in or outside of the classroom and is available in the nationally hosted CourseCompass platform, as well as WebCT and Blackboard.

SafariX

SafariX is Prentice Hall's exciting new digital platform where students can subscribe to textbooks at savings of up to 50% over the suggested list price of print editions. SafariX will help meet the needs of students who are looking for lower-cost alternatives to print editions.

For more information about OneKey or SafariX, please contact your local Merrill/Prentice Hall representative prior to placing your textbook order.

SUPPLEMENTAL MATERIALS FOR THE INSTRUCTOR

Instructor's DVD

Instructor's Manual and Media Guide. This manual provides concrete suggestions to promote interactive teaching and actively involve students in learning. Each chapter contains chapter objectives, key terms, key concepts, and group activities, as well as a comprehensive test bank containing multiple choice, true/false, short-answer, and essay questions.

Computerized Test Bank Software. This software gives instructors electronic access to the test questions printed in the Instructor's Manual, allowing them to create and customize exams on their computer. The software can help professors manage their courses and gain insight into their students' progress and performance. Computerized test bank software is available on a dual platform CD-ROM for MacIntosh and PC/Windows users.

PowerPoint Slides. Designed as an instructional tool, the *PowerPoint* presentations for each chapter can be used to present and elaborate on chapter content.

To access the above supplements click on the link on the Roblyer companion Website homepage. Then click *instructor* on the left-hand menu and get instructions on how to obtain the access code to download this material.

A TOTAL TECHNOLOGY INTEGRATION LEARNING PACKAGE

We recommend the following Prentice Hall supplements to enhance your teaching package when using *Integrating Educational Technology into Teaching*, Fourth Edition:

> *Technology Tools for Teachers: A Microsoft Office Tutorial,* Second Edition by Steven C. Mills and M.D. Roblyer (2006). ISBN 0-13-118727-9.
>
> *Linking Technology and Curriculum: Integrating the ISTE NETS Standards into Teaching and Learning,* Second Edition, Jeri A. Carroll and Tonya L. Witherspoon (2002). ISBN 0-13-0971081.

Educator Learning Center

Merrill Education and the Association for Supervision and Curriculum Development (ASCD) invite you to take advantage of a new online resource, one that provides access to the top research and proven strategies associated with ASCD and Merrill—the Educator Learning Center. At www.educatorlearningcenter.com you will find resources that will enhance your students' understanding of course topics and of current educational issues, in addition to being invaluable for further research.

How the Educator Learning Center Will Help Your Students Become Better Teachers. With the combined resources of Merrill Education and ASCD, you and your students will find a wealth of tools and materials to better prepare them for the classroom.

Look into the Value of Educator Learning Center Yourself. A four-month subscription to Educator Learning Center is $25 but is **FREE** when packaged with *Integrating Educational Technology into Teaching,* Fourth Edition. In order for your students to have access to this site, you must use this special value-pack ISBN number **WHEN** placing your textbook order with the bookstore: 0-13-168661-5. To preview the value of this Web site to you and your students, please go to www.educatorlearningcenter.com and click on "Demo."

ACKNOWLEDGMENTS

Monitoring the winds of change in technology is exciting, but often neverwracking, work. Educational technology is not only evolving rapidly, it is also expanding swiftly and in unpredictable directions. It is an ever more challenging task to capture and communicate its scope and essence. However, as has been the case with the last three editions, many people helped me meet this challenge.

The following reviewers provided insightful and practical critiques and advice, all of which helped to clarify the prose and sharpen the focus: Donna J. Baumbach, University of Central Florida; David Carbonara, Duquesne University; Cathy Cavanaugh, University of North Florida; Carrie Dale, Baker College of Flint; Lorana A. Jinkerson, Northern Michigan University; Valerie Larsen, University of Notre Dame; Nancy Maushak, Texas Tech University; Robert Perkins, College of Charleston; Barbara Rosenfeld, Brooklyn College; and Richard Allen Smith, University of Houston–Clear Lake.

As usual, the enormous professional and personal support given by the Merrill editorial staff is impossible to measure. The firm vision and competent direction of my editor and friend Debbie Stollenwerk helped me conceptualize and carry out the work on this edition, and the editorial and production team members (JoEllen Gohr, Kris Roach, Mary Morrill, and Amy Nelson) made sure this edition was attractive as well as useful.

As usual, I am in perpetual debt to my family and friends for taking second place for so many nights, weekends, and holidays while I made the commitment required for a good revision. I would like to recognize the enduring love and patience of my family, Bill and Paige Wiencke, and the tenacious loyalty of friends across the country and around the world. Also, I would like to continue to remember and acknowledge the enduring contributions of those who are with us now only in memory: S. L. Roblyer and Catherine Pryor Roblyer, and Raymond and Marjorie Wiencke.

And, as always, I recognize the contributions of all the educators who have worked so long and so hard to make it possible for us to fashion the education system of the future.

M. D. Roblyer

BRIEF CONTENTS

CONTENTS

PART 2

INTEGRATING SOFTWARE TUTORS AND TOOLS INTO TEACHING AND LEARNING 71

Note: Every effort has been made to provide accurate and current Internet information in this book. However, the Internet and information posted on it are constantly changing, so it is inevitable that some of the Internet addresses listed in this text book will change.

SPECIAL FEATURES

TECHNOLOGY INTEGRATION WORKSHOP

HANDS-ON WITH TECHNOLOGY TUTORIALS FOR TIE INTO PRACTICE

INTERACTIVE ASSESSMENTS FROM DVD

List of Special Features

ABOUT THE AUTHOR

M.D. Roblyer has been a technology-using teacher, professor, and contributor to the field of educational technology for over 35 years. She began her exploration of technology's benefits for teaching in 1971 as a graduate student at one of the country's first successful instructional computer training sites, Pennsylvania State University, where she helped write tutorial literacy lessons in the Coursewriter II authoring language on an IBM 1500 dedicated instructional mainframe computer. While obtaining a Ph.D. in instructional systems at Florida State University, she worked on several major courseware development and training projects with Control Data Corporation's PLATO system. In 1981–1982, she de-signed one of the early microcomputer software series, *Grammar Problems for Practice,* in conjunction with the Milliken Publishing Company.

She has written extensively and served as contributing editor and reviewer for numerous educational technology publications. Her other books for Merrill/Prentice Hall include *Starting Out on the Internet: A Learning Journey for Teachers* (3rd ed., 2006), *Technology Tools for Teachers: A Microsoft Office Tutorial* (with Steven C. Mills, 2nd ed., 2006), and *Educational Technology in Action: Problem-based Exercises for Technology Integration* (2004). Her recent research has focused on defining and measuring interaction in distance learning courses and creating and testing instruments to predict success for virtual school students.

Currently, she is Adjunct Professor of Educational Technology, teaching online for the University of Maryland University College's web-based graduate programs from her home in Carrollton, Georgia. She is married to William R. Wiencke and is the mother of a daughter, Paige.

CONTRIBUTORS

Rebecca Anderson,
University of Memphis
Chapter 9

Adrienne Herrell,
Florida State University–
Panama City
Chapter 10

Michael Jordan,
California State
University–Fresno
Chapter 10

Ed Dickey, University
of South Carolina
Chapter 11

Michael Odell,
University of Idaho
Chapter 11

Michael Berson,
University of South
Florida
Chapter 12

Dan Newson, Berklee
School of Music
Chapter 13

Barbara Houghton,
Northern Kentucky
University
Chapter 13

Bonnie Mohnsen,
Bonnie's Fitware
Chapter 14

Dave Edyburn,
University of
Wisconsin–Madison
Chapter 15

PART 1

INTRODUCTION AND BACKGROUND ON INTEGRATING TECHNOLOGY IN EDUCATION

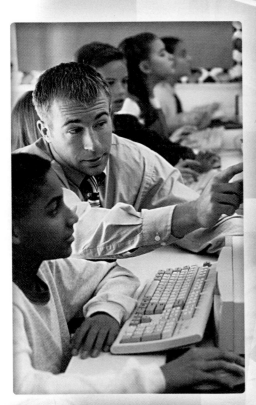

Chapter 1   **Educational Technology in Context: The Big Picture**

Chapter 2   **Foundations of Effective Technology Integration Models: Theory and Practice**

As we look today at what technology is doing—and what it promises to do—in classrooms across the country, we see that some of the most innovative and promising practices in education involve technology, and the promise of even more exciting capabilities foreshadows great benefits for teachers. This book presents some of the most powerful and capable educational technology resources available today and demonstrates how teachers can take advantage of them.

However, teachers must make a considerable investment of their time to prepare themselves to use technology resources well. The first two chapters introduce the world of educational technology and review the knowledge and skills teachers need to prepare themselves to apply educational technology—especially computer technology—effectively in classrooms.

PART 1

REQUIRED BACKGROUND FOR TEACHERS

In Part 1, two chapters provide important foundation information and skills to help teachers take the first steps to using technology in classrooms.

Chapter 1 Educational Technology in Context: The Big Picture

Computer technology in education has a history that spans some 50 years, and other kinds of technology have been in use for much longer. Classroom technology resources have changed dramatically over time, but a broad perspective of the field helps illuminate many of today's concepts, terms, and activities. Chapter 1 gives both an historical and current context for applications of educational technology in order to show how they have evolved—and are still evolving—into the tools described later in this book. The chapter also describes current resources, issues, and trends that shape today's educational technology.

Chapter 2 Foundations of Effective Technology Integration Models: Theory and Practice

This chapter emphasizes the need to reach beyond the "nuts and bolts" of how technology resources work by emphasizing links among three critical factors: learning theories, integration models, and essential conditions for effective integration. Successful integration requires a connection between how people learn and how teachers employ technology to assist and enhance this learning. Thus, this chapter begins with an overview of learning theories and how they have generated two different perspectives on how to integrate technology into teaching and learning activities: directed models and constructivist models. Secondly, this chapter introduces the Technology Integration Planning (TIP) Model, a systematic procedure for identifying problems and implementing and evaluating technology-based solutions. Finally, the chapter describes a series of conditions that offer essential support for teachers' technology integration.

CHAPTER 1

EDUCATIONAL TECHNOLOGY IN CONTEXT: THE BIG PICTURE

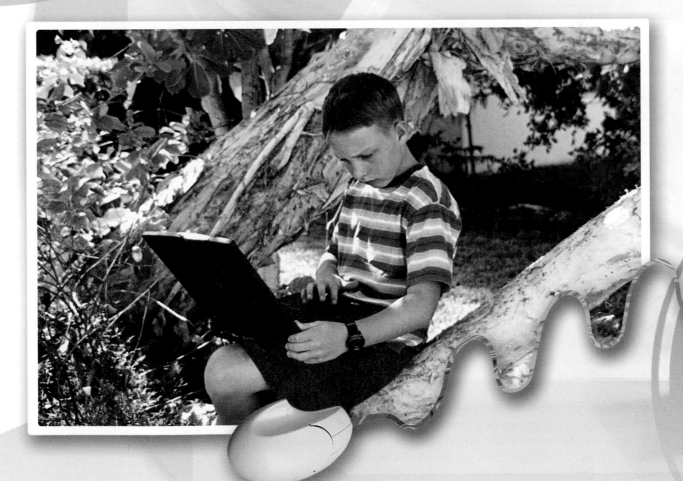

It is clear that educational technology is essentially the product of a great historical stream consisting of trial and error, long practice and imitation, and sporadic manifestations of unusual individual creativity and persuasion.

Paul Saettler, in *The Evolution of American Educational Technology* (1990)

THEN...

Anna was almost as proud of her new classroom computers as she was of her new teaching degree. She had high hopes for the 1978–1979 school year in her first teaching position, especially since the principal had asked her if she could use two brand new Apple computer systems that had been donated to the school. As a student teacher, she had helped children use computer-assisted instruction (CAI) on terminals that were located in the school's computer lab and connected by telephone lines to her university's big mainframe computer, but this would be much different. Now the computers would be located right in her own classroom, and how she used them would be completely up to her. With her new skills and these marvelous devices at her disposal, she felt a heady sense of power and anticipation.

She found some free and "shareware" drill-and-practice and instructional game software packages, and successfully lobbied the principal to buy others. She planned to buy more with money she would raise from bake sales. All the students wanted to use the computers, but with only two machines, Anna quickly devised activities that allowed everyone to have a turn. She had "relay-race math practices" to help them prepare for tests, and she created a computer workstation where students could play math games as a reward for completing other activities and where she could send students in pairs to practice basic skills.

As Anna used her new computers, she coped with a variety of technical problems. Some of the software was designed for an earlier version of the Apple operating system, and each disk required a format adjustment every time it was used. Programs would stall when students entered something the programmers had not anticipated; students either had to adjust the code or restart the programs. Despite these and other difficulties, by the end of the year Anna was still enthusiastic about her hopes, plans, and expectations. She felt she had seen a glimpse of a time when computers would be an integral part of everyday teaching activities. She planned to be ready for the future.

NOW...

As she prepared to begin another school year, Anna found it difficult to believe it had been almost 30 years since that first pioneering work with her Apple microcomputers. When she moved to a new school building in 2000, each classroom had a five-computer workstation connected to the school network. Teachers downloaded software and media from the school server, and dozens of titles were available across content areas. Her students used the Internet to do research projects and collaborate with students in other locations. Her class's favorite activity this year was working with students around the state to gather and compare data on prices for various products and services, but they also liked the spreadsheet software's "Buy a Car" activity.

She also marveled at how many other teachers in the school were using technology now. Everyone communicated via e-mail, and many, like herself, had their own web pages so students and parents could check homework assignments and view class projects. In other classes, students were using graphing calculators and handheld computers to solve problems, and she often heard them talking about the simulations they were doing in science and social studies. A video project to interview war veterans had drawn a lot of local attention, and the student projects displayed on school bulletin boards were ablaze with screen captures from websites and images students had taken with digital cameras.

There were still problems, of course. Computer viruses sometimes shut down the school server, and there was a growing issue with students plagiarizing work from Internet sources. The firewall that the district had put in place to prevent students from accessing undesirable Internet sites also prevented access to many other, perfectly good sites. Some teachers complained that they had no time for the technology-based group projects students loved because they were too busy preparing them for the new state and national tests.

Yet despite these concerns, Anna was amazed at how far they had come from those first, hesitant steps with technology in the classroom, and how much more there was to try. She knew other teachers her age who were retiring, but she was too interested in what she was doing to think about that. She had been asked to help design a virtual course for home-bound students. Not a day went by that a teacher didn't come to her for help on a new Internet page or video project. She couldn't wait to see what challenges lay ahead. She looked forward to the future.

OBJECTIVES

After reading this chapter and completing the learning activities for it, you should be able to:

1. Describe four different views on how to define the term *educational technology,* and identify professional associations that represent each view.

2. Identify periods in the history of educational computing and describe what we have learned from past applications and decisions.

3. Generate a personal rationale for using technology in education based on findings from research and practice.

4. Place a given educational technology resource in one of the following general hardware (stand-alone computer, network, and related device/system) or software (instructional, productivity, or administrative) categories.

5. Identify which one of the following technology resource configurations would be appropriate for a given educational need: laboratories, mobile workstations, mobile PCs (e.g., laptops or *handheld computers*), classroom workstations, and/or single classroom PCs.

6. Identify the general categories of educational technology instructional/productivity resources: instructional software, software tool, multimedia, distance learning, or a virtual reality environment.

7. Explain the impact of each of the following types of issues on current uses of technology in education: societal, educational, cultural/equity, and legal/ethical.

8. Identify trends in emerging technologies and implications they may have for teaching and learning.

9. Identify technology skills teachers and their students need to have to be prepared for future learning and work tasks.

KEY TERMS

- artificial intelligence
- Center for Applied Research in Educational Technology (CARET)
- Digital Divide
- educational technology
- electronic portfolio
- firewall
- global positioning system (GPS)
- hacker
- handheld computer
- hardware
- instructional technology
- laptop computer
- National Educational Technology Standards (NETS)
- No Child Left Behind (NCLB) Act
- radio-frequency identification (RFID)
- software
- software piracy
- tablet PC
- technology education
- virtual reality (VR)
- virtual system
- virus
- virus protection software
- wireless connectivity

For more information on Key Terms, go to the *Key Terms* module for this chapter of the Companion Website at http://www.prenhall.com/roblyer.

INTRODUCTION: WHY DO WE NEED THE "BIG PICTURE"?

When a classroom teacher like Anna browses the Internet for new teaching materials or has students use handheld computers to take notes, that teacher is using some of the latest and best of what is commonly called *technology in ed-*ucation or **educational technology.** But, as Saettler (1990) noted in this chapter's opening quote, educational technology is not new at all, and it is by no means limited to the use of equipment, let alone computer equipment. Modern tools and techniques are simply the latest developments in a field that some believe is as old as education itself.

This chapter explores the link between the early applications of educational technology and those of today and tomorrow. This review serves an important purpose. It helps new learners develop mental pictures of the field, what Ausubel (1968) might call *cognitive frameworks,* through which to view all applications and consider best courses of action. Several kinds of information help form this framework:

- **Key terminology** — Talking about a topic requires knowing the vocabulary. Yet the term *educational technology* and many related terms are not defined the same way by everyone. Educators who want to study the field must realize that language used to describe technology reflects differing views by various groups on appropriate uses of educational technology.

- **Reflecting on the past** — Showing where the field began helps us understand where it is headed and why. Reviewing changes in goals and methods in the field over time provides a foundation on which to build even more successful and useful structures to respond to the challenges of modern education.

- **Considering the present** — The current role of educational technology is shaped primarily by two kinds of factors: available technology resources and our perspectives on how to make use of them. Available technologies dictate what is possible, while a combination of social, instructional, cultural, and legal issues influence the directions we choose to take.

- **Looking ahead to the future** — Technology resources and societal conditions change so rapidly that today's choices are always influenced as much by emerging trends as by current conditions. To be informed citizens of an Information Society, teachers must be futurists.

WHAT IS "EDUCATIONAL TECHNOLOGY"?
Origins and Definitions of Key Terms

References to educational technology and **instructional technology** pervade professional journals and magazines throughout education. Yet no single, acceptable definition for these terms serves the field, and there is uncertainty even about the origins of the terms. Educational technology historian Paul Saettler (1990) says that the earliest reference for educational technology seems to have been made by radio instruction pioneer W. W. Charters in 1948, and instructional technology was first used by audiovisual expert James Finn in 1963. Even in those early days, definitions for these terms focused on more than just devices and materials. Saettler notes that a 1970 Commission on Instructional Technology defined it as both "the media born of the communication revolution which can be used for instructional purposes … "(p. 6) and "a sys-

tematic way of designing, carrying out, and evaluating the total process of learning and teaching …" (p. 6).

While today's educators tend to think of educational or instructional technology as equipment—particularly electronic equipment—Saettler (1990) reminds us that such a limited definition would have to change over time as resources change. Only about 20 years ago, Cuban's history of technology in education since 1920 (1986) placed the emphasis on radio and television, with computers as an afterthought. If such a description were written now, the focus might be on the Internet, while 20 years from now it might be on intelligent computer-assisted instruction or virtual reality or whatever these technologies are called then. As the 1970 commission concluded, a broader definition of educational technology that encompasses both tools and processes "belongs to the future" (Saettler, 1990, p. 6).

Therefore, in the view of most writers, researchers, and practitioners in the field, useful definitions of educational technology must focus on the process of applying tools for educational purposes as well as the tools and materials used. As Muffoletto (1994) puts it, "Technology … is not a collection of machines and devices, but a way of acting" (p. 25).

Four Perspectives That Define Educational Technology: Media, Instructional Systems, Vocational Training, and Computer Systems

If educational technology is viewed as both processes and tools, it is important to begin by examining four different historical perspectives on these processes and tools, all of which have helped shape current practices in the field. These influences come to us from four groups of education professionals. Because each of these groups emerged from a different area of education and/or society, each has a unique outlook on what "educational technology" is, and each defines it in a slightly different way. To some degree, these views have merged over time, but each retains a focus that tends to shape the integration practices it considers important. These four views and the professional organizations that represent them are summarized in Figure 1.1.

- **Perspective #1: Educational technology as media and audiovisual communications** — This perspective grew out of the audiovisual (AV) movement in the 1930s when higher education instructors proposed that media such as slides and films delivered information in more concrete, and therefore more effective, ways than through lectures and books. This movement produced audiovisual communications or the "branch of educational theory and practice concerned primarily with the design and use of messages that control the learning process" (Saettler, 1990, p. 9). The view of educational technology as media to deliver information continues to dominate areas of education and the communica-

Figure 1.1 Four Perspectives That Shaped Educational Technology

Perspectives: Educational Technology as ...	Organization and Members	Historical View	Current View
#1: Media and AV communications	Association for Educational Communications and Technology (AECT) *http://www.aect.org* Serves library-media educators	Began with focus on delivering information as alternatives to lectures and books, using devices to carry messages (e.g., films, TV) during instruction. Later added an emphasis on online and computer/information systems as "media."	Still focuses on technologies as media. Most AECT divisions still focus on concerns of library-media educators; AECT state affiliates usually refer to themselves as "media associations."
#2: Instructional systems and instructional design	International Society for Performance Improvement (ISPI) *http://www.ispi.org* Serves higher education and industry instructional designers, trainers	Originally National Society for Programmed Instruction. Emphasized making instruction and training more efficient.	Focus is on creating and validating instructional systems to improve productivity and competence in the workplace.
#3: Vocational training (a.k.a. technology education)	International Technology Education Association (ITEA) *http://www.iteawww.org* Serves technology education teachers	Until the 1980s was the American Industrial Arts Association. Focused on skills with manufacturing, printing, woodworking, and metals.	Now focuses on technology-related careers and promoting technological literacy through hands-on experiences that use technology in the context of learning mathematics, science, humanities, and engineering concepts.
#4: Computer systems (a.k.a. educational/ instructional computing)	International Society for Technology in Education (ISTE) *http://www.iste.org* Serves technology-using teachers, administrators, and higher education personnel	Until the 1980s, was the International Council for Computers in Education (ICCE). Focused on computer systems to support and deliver instruction.	Merged with the International Association for Computers in Education (IACE; formerly the Association for Educational Data Systems, or AEDS). Advances uses of technology in K–12 education and teacher education and technology skill standards for teachers and students.

tions industry. As late as 1986, the National Task Force on Educational Technology equated educational technology with media, treating computers simply as another medium (Saettler, 1990).

• **Perspective #2: Educational technology as instructional systems and instructional design** — This view originated with post–World War II military and indus-

trial trainers who were faced with the problem of preparing large numbers of personnel quickly. Based on efficiency studies and learning theories from educational psychology, they advocated using more planned, systematic approaches to developing uniform, effective materials and training procedures. Their view was based on the belief that both human (teachers) and nonhuman (media) resources could be parts of an efficient system for addressing any instructional need. Therefore, they equated "educational technology" with "educational problem solutions." As these training personnel began to work with both university research and development projects and K–12 schools, they also influenced practices in both of these areas. Behaviorist theories initially dominated and cognitive theories later gained precedence. In the 1990s, popular learning theories criticized systems approaches as too rigid to foster some kinds of learning, particularly higher order ones. Thus, the current view of educational technology as instructional systems is continually evolving. (See Chapter 2 for more information on two approaches to educational technology as instructional systems and how each influences methods of integration.)

- **Perspective #3: Educational technology as vocational training** — Also known as **technology education,** this perspective originated with industry trainers and vocational educators in the 1980s. They believed (1) that an important function of school learning is to prepare students for the world of work in which they will use technology, and (2) that vocational training can be a practical means of teaching all content areas such as math, science, and language. This view brought about a major paradigm shift in vocational training in K–12 schools from industrial arts curricula centered in woodworking/metals and graphics/printing shops to technology education courses taught in labs equipped with high-technology stations such as desktop publishing, computer-assisted design (CAD), and robotics systems.

- **Perspective #4: Educational technology as computer systems (a.k.a. educational computing and instructional computing)** — This view began in the 1950s with the advent of computers and gained momentum when they began to be used instructionally in the 1960s As computers began to transform business and industry practices, both trainers and teachers began to see that computers also had the potential to aid instruction. From the time computers came into classrooms in the 1960s until about 1990, this perspective was known as *educational computing* and encompassed both instructional and administrative support applications. At first, programmers and systems analysts created all applications. But by the 1970s, many of the same educators involved with media, AV communications, and instructional systems also were researching and developing computer applications. By the 1990s, educators began to see computers as part of a combination of technology resources, including media, instructional systems, and computer-based support systems. At that point, educational computing became known as educational technology.

How This Textbook Defines Technology in Education

Each of these four perspectives on technology in education has contributed to the current body of knowledge about processes and tools to address educational needs. But, as Saettler (1990) points out, no single paradigm that attempts to describe educational technology can characterize satisfactorily what is happening with technology in education today and what will happen in the future. Furthermore, all of the organizations described here seem to be engaged in a struggle to claim the high-profile term *educational technology.* However, their often-conflicting views of the role of technology in education confuse newcomers to the field and make it difficult for them to learn the role of technology; the resources and issues differ depending on whose descriptions teachers hear and which publications they read. This textbook attempts to address the disparate views on this topic in the following ways:

- **Processes** — For the processes, or instructional procedures for applying tools, we look to (1) learning theories based on the sciences of human behavior and (2) applications of technology that help prepare students for future jobs by teaching them skills in using current tools as well as skills in "learning to learn" for tools of the future that have not yet been invented—or even imagined.

- **Tools** — Although this textbook looks at technology tools as an overlapping combination of media, instructional systems, and computer-based support systems, it emphasizes a subset of all of these resources, focusing primarily on computers and their roles in instructional systems. There are three reasons for this focus:

  1. **Capabilities** Computers as media are more complex and more capable than other media such as films or overheads and require more technical knowledge to operate.

  2. **Convergence** Computer systems are currently moving toward subsuming many other media within their own resources. For example, CD-ROMs and DVDs now store images that once were shown on filmstrips, slides, and videotape. Presentation software (e.g., *PowerPoint)* has largely replaced overhead transparencies.

  3. **Complexity** Computer-based materials such as software lessons and computer-driven media traditionally have been more complicated for educators to integrate into other classroom activities. Educators can see much more easily—some would say even intuitively—how to integrate less technical media such as films or overheads.

It is with this rationale in mind that this text assigns the following "evolving" definitions:

Educational technology is a combination of the processes and tools involved in addressing educational needs and problems, with an emphasis on applying the most current tools: computers and other electronic technologies.

Integrating educational technology refers to the process of determining which electronic tools and which methods for implementing them are appropriate responses to given classroom situations and problems.

Instructional technology is the subset of educational technology that deals directly with teaching and learning applications (as opposed to educational administrative applications).

LOOKING BACK: HOW HAS THE PAST INFLUENCED TODAY'S EDUCATIONAL TECHNOLOGY?

A Brief History of Educational Computing Activities and Resources

Many of today's technology-oriented teachers have been using computer systems only since microcomputers came into common use, but as the timeline in Figure 1.2 shows, a thriving educational computing culture predated microcomputers by 20 years. When integrated circuits made computers both smaller and more accessible to teachers and students, microcomputers became a major turning point in the history of the field. Thus, most of the history of computer technology in education is told in two periods: before and after the introduction of microcomputers (Niemiec & Walberg, 1989; Roblyer, 1992). In 1994, yet another technological development, the World Wide Web, transformed educational technology. This development marked the beginning of the third and current era of computers in education.

Pre-microcomputer era. Although this era's computer resources were very different from those of today, both computer companies and educators learned much at this time about the role technology was destined to play in education and who could best shape that role. IBM was a pioneer in this field, producing the first instructional mainframe with multimedia learning stations: the IBM 1500. By the time IBM discontinued it in 1975, some 25 universities were using this system to develop CAI materials. The most prominent of these was led by Stanford University professor and "Grandfather of CAI" Patrick Suppes, who developed the Coursewriter language to create reading and mathematics drill-and-practice lessons. Other similar company- and university-led instructional initiatives ensued: Suppes founded the Computer Curriculum Corporation (CCC); the Digital Equipment Corporation created the PDP-1, the first instructional minicomputer; and the Control Data Corporation (CDC) created the Programmed Logic for Automatic Teaching Operations (PLATO) system and the *Tutor* CAI authoring language.

For about 15 years, these mainframe and minicomputer CAI systems dominated the field. Universities also developed instructional applications for use on these systems. Among these were Brigham Young University's Timeshared Interactive Computer-Controlled Information Television or TICCIT system and computer managed instruction (CMI) systems based on mastery learning models, such as the American Institutes for Research's Program for Learning in Accordance with Needs (PLAN) and Pittsburgh's individually prescribed instruction (IPI). However, these systems were both expensive to buy and complex to operate and maintain, and school district offices began to control their purchase and use. But by the late 1970s, it was apparent that teachers disliked the control of CAI/CMI applications by both district data processing and industry personnel; they began to reject the idea that computers would revolutionize instruction on a business office model.

Microcomputer era. The entire picture changed in the late 1970s with the invention of small, stand-alone desktop microcomputers, which wrested control of educational computers from companies, universities, and school districts and placed them in the hands of teachers and schools. Several different initiatives emerged to shape this new teacher-centered control. A software publishing movement that catered to educators quickly sprang up. With National Science Foundation funding, the Minnesota Educational Computing Consortium (MECC) become the single largest microcomputer software provider, and a multitude of other companies and cottage industries soon followed. To offer advice on how to select quality products, organizations emerged to review software (e.g., Northwest Regional Education Laboratory's MicroSIFT Project, the Educational Products Information Exchange or EPIE), and professional organizations, journals, and magazines all began to publish software reviews. As teachers clamored for more input into courseware design, companies created authoring languages (e.g., PILOT, SuperPILOT) and menu-based authoring systems (e.g., GENIS, PASS), but teacher authoring soon proved too time consuming, and interest faded. As schools searched for a way to make CAI more cost effective, districts began to purchase networked integrated learning systems (ILSs) with predeveloped curriculum to help teachers address required standards. Control of computer resources moved once again to central servers controlled by school district offices.

Figure 1.2 Computer Technology in Education Timeline

First computer used for instruction

Computer-driven flight simulator trains MIT pilots

1950

University time-sharing systems

Faculty/students in universities across the country use mainframe systems for programming and shared utilities

1960–1970

Mainframe and minicomputer applications dominate field

Schools begin using computers for instruction and administration. CDC President William Norris (1977) announces PLATO will revolutionize instruction

Mid-to-late 1970s

1959

First computer used with schoolchildren

IBM 650 computer teaches binary arithmetic in NYC

Early 1970s

Computer-assisted instruction (CAI) movement emerges

Large-scale, federally funded university projects use mainframe/minicomputer systems with schools

Late 1970s

CAI movement declines; computer literacy movement begins

Arthur Luehrmann coins term *computer literacy* for skills in programming and using software tools (e.g., word processing). Molnar (1978) warns that non–computer literate students will be educationally disadvantaged

---

Also at this time, *computer literacy* skills began to be required school and state curricula, spurred on by computer education experts like Arthur Luehrmann. However, this emphasis was soon dropped due to difficulties in defining and measuring these skills. As a result of Seymour Papert's work (1987), products and research based on the Logo programming language became the focus of the field. The Logo view of technology—that computers should be used as an aid to teach problem solving—began to replace traditional instructional computer uses (e.g., drills, tutorials) as the "best use" of technology. Yet despite its popularity and research showing it could be useful in some contexts, researchers could capture no impact from Logo use on mathematics or other curriculum skills, and interest in Logo, too, waned by the beginning of the 1990s.

Internet era. Just as teachers seemed to be losing interest once again in technology's potential for instruction, the first browser software (*Mosaic*) transformed a formerly text-based Internet into a combination of text and graphics. By the last

First microcomputers enter schools

Using desktop systems, classroom teachers begin to take back control of instructional and administrative applications from district data processing offices

1977

Integrated learning systems (ILSs) emerge

Schools begin to see ILS networked systems as cost-effective solutions for instruction to address required standards; marks movement away from stand-alone systems and toward central server with connected computers

Mid 1980s–1990s

International Society for Technology in Education (ISTE) creates standards

ISTE sponsors creation of National Educational Technology Standards (NETS) to guide technology skills, first for students, then for teachers and administrators

1998

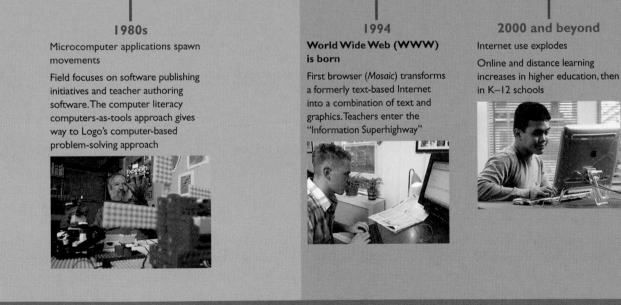

1980s

Microcomputer applications spawn movements

Field focuses on software publishing initiatives and teacher authoring software. The computer literacy computers-as-tools approach gives way to Logo's computer-based problem-solving approach

1994

World Wide Web (WWW) is born

First browser (*Mosaic*) transforms a formerly text-based Internet into a combination of text and graphics. Teachers enter the "Information Superhighway"

2000 and beyond

Internet use explodes

Online and distance learning increases in higher education, then in K–12 schools

part of the 1990s, teachers and students joined the throng of users on the "Information Superhighway." By the beginning of the 2000s, email, online (i.e., web-based) multimedia, and videoconferencing became standard tools of Internet users, and portable devices made Internet access ubiquitous. The ease of access to online resources and communications drove a dramatic increase in distance learning offerings, first in higher education, then in K–12 schools. As interest in technology in education began to expand once more, the International Society for Technology in Education (ISTE) developed **National Educational Technology Standards (NETS)** for teachers, students, and administrators.

What Have We Learned from the Past?

In no small part, developments in computer technology have shaped the history of educational technology. However, knowing the history of educational technology is useful only if we apply what we know about the past to future decisions and actions. What have we learned from more than 50 years of applying technology to educational problems that can improve our strategies now? Educators are encouraged to draw their own conclusions from these and other descriptions they might read. However, the following points also are important:

- **No technology is a panacea for education** — Great expectations for products such as Logo and ILSs have taught us that even the most current, capable technology resources offer no quick, easy, or universal solutions. Computer-based materials and strategies are usually tools in a larger system and must be integrated carefully with other resources and with teacher activities. Cuban (2001) proposes that technology was "oversold" from the beginning and is not having the system-changing impact many thought it would. Trend (2001) proposes that overuse of distance learning can create more problems than it solves. If we begin with more realistic expectations in mind, we have more potential for success and impact on teaching and learning. Planning must always begin with this question: What specific needs do my students and I have that (any given) resources can help meet?

- **Computer/technological literacy offers a limited integration rationale** — Many parents and educators want technology tools in the classroom primarily because they feel technical skills will give students the technological literacy required to prepare them for the workplace. But an employability rationale provides limited guidelines for how and where to integrate technology. The capabilities of technology resources and methods must be matched to skills that display an obvious need for application in our current system of education, for example, reading, writing, and mathematics skills; research and information gathering; and problem solving and analysis.

- **Teachers usually do not develop technology materials or curriculum** — Teaching is one of the most time- and labor-intensive jobs in our society. With so many demands on their time, most teachers cannot be expected to develop software or create complex technology-based teaching materials. In the past, publishers, school or district developers, or personnel in funded projects have provided this assistance; this seems unlikely to change in the future.

- **Technically possible does not equal desirable, feasible, or inevitable** — A popular saying is that today's technology is yesterday's science fiction. But science fiction also shows us that technology brings undesirable—as well as desirable—changes. For example, distance technologies have allowed people to attend professional conferences online, rather than by traveling to another location; however, people continue to want to travel and meet face to face. Procedures for human cloning are becoming available, and genetic engineering is increasingly feasible. In education, we can simulate face-to-face communication to an increasingly realistic degree. All of these new technological horizons make it evident that it is time to analyze carefully the implications of each implementation decision. Better technology demands that we become critical consumers of its power and capability. We are responsible for deciding just which science fiction becomes reality.

- **Things change faster than teachers can keep up** — History in this field has shown that resources and accepted methods of applying them will change, often quickly and dramatically. This places a special burden on already overworked teachers to continue learning new resources and changing their teaching methods. Gone are the days—if, indeed, they ever existed—when a teacher could rely on the same handouts, homework, or lecture notes from year to year. Educators may not be able to predict the future of educational technology, but they know that it will be different from the present; that is, they must anticipate and accept the inevitability of change and the need for a continual investment of their time.

- **Older technologies can be useful** — Technology in education is an area especially prone to what Roblyer (1990) called the "glitz factor." With so little emphasis on finding out what actually works, anyone can propose dramatic improvements. When they fail to appear, educators move on to the next fad. This approach fails to solve real problems and it draws attention away from the effort to find legitimate solutions. Worse, teachers sometimes throw out methods that had potential if only they had realistic expectations. The past has shown that teachers must be careful, analytical consumers of technological innovation, looking to what has worked in the past to guide their decisions and measure their expectations. Educational practice tends to move in cycles, and "new" methods often are old methods in new guise. In short, teachers must be as informed and analytical as they want their students to become.

- **Teachers always will be more important than technology** — With each new technological development that appears on the horizon, the old question seems to resurface: Will computers replace teachers? The developers of the first instructional computer systems in the 1960s foresaw them replacing many teacher positions; some advocates of today's distance learning methods envision a similar impact on future education. Yet the answer to the old question is the same and is likely to remain so: Good teachers are more essential than ever. One reason for this was described in

Naisbitt's (1984) *MegaTrends:* "…whenever new technology is introduced into society, there must be a counterbalancing human response … the more high tech (it is), the more high touch (is needed)" (p. 35). We need more teachers who understand the role technology plays in society and in education, who are prepared to take advantage of its power, and who recognize its limitation. In an increasingly technological society, we need more teachers who are both technology savvy and child centered.

Why Use Technology? Using Past Research and Practice to Develop a Sound Rationale

The history of educational technology also teaches us the importance of the "Why use technology?" question. Educators will use new methods if they can see clearly compelling reasons to do so. (See the discussion of "relative advantage" in Chapter 2.) Many educators look to educational research for evidence of technology's present and potential benefits. However, even though electronic technologies have been in use in education since the 1950s, research results have not made a strong case for its impact on teaching and learning. The number and quality of studies on educational impact have been disappointing (Cradler, 2003; Roblyer, Castine, & King, 1988), and researchers such as Clark (1983, 1985, 1991, 1994) have openly criticized "computer-based effectiveness" research such as meta-analyses to summarize results across studies comparing computer-based and traditional methods. Clark concluded that most such studies suffered from confounding variables that could either increase or decrease achievement. They attempt to show a greater impact on achievement of one delivery method over the other without controlling for other factors such as different instructors, instructional methods, curriculum contents, or novelty. Kozma (1991, 1994) responded to these challenges by proposing that research should look at technology not as an information delivery medium but as "the learner actively collaborating with the medium to construct knowledge" (1991, p. 179).

Although the lack of agreement on integration methods and benefits makes it challenging to state a clear and compelling case for using technology in education, four current conditions combine to make it essential that we do so:

- **Increasing costs of keeping up with technology** — The process of integrating technology effectively into education requires substantial investments in technology infrastructure and teacher training. Educators and policy makers need a solid rationale for why these funds are well spent (Ringstaff & Kelley, 2002).
- **Attacks by technology critics** — Justifying technology expenditures by confirming technology's benefits is increasingly important in light of recent volleys of criticisms from noneducators (Healey, 1998; Oppenheimer,

MAKING THE CASE FOR TECHNOLOGY INTEGRATION

Discuss these issues online with other students by selecting the *Making the Case* module for Chapter 1 of the Companion Website (http://www.prenhall.com/roblyer) or choose the *Message Board* module.

1. In his book *High Tech Heretic,* Clifford Stoll (1999) says, "You certainly can get an excellent education without a computer" (p. 32), and "When every student … is pressed to become a computer maven, and only the incompetent are allowed to become plumbers, neither our programs nor our pipes will hold water" (p. 123). After reading Chapter 1, how would you respond to this position?

2. Saettler (1990) said, "Computer information systems are not just objective recording devices. They also reflect concepts, hopes, beliefs, attitudes" (p. 539). What concepts, hopes, beliefs, and attitudes do you think our past and current uses of technology in education reflect?

3. Richard Clark's now-famous comment about the impact of computers on learning was that the best current evidence is that media are mere vehicles that deliver instruction but do not influence student achievement any more than the truck that delivers our groceries causes change in our nutrition (Clark, 1983, p. 445). Why do you think this statement has had such a dramatic impact on the field of educational technology? How would you respond to it?

4. In his article on "cybercheating," Gardiner (2001) says, "…I understand that the temptation of exchanging hours of research and writing for a few minutes of searching seems like a good deal as the deadline looms. …I wondered how I could ever overcome the power of the Internet and the lure of cheating" (p. 174). Can you suggest arguments that would help persuade students that cybercheating, while easy and quick, is not in their best interests?

Figure 1.3 Results from CARET's Reviews of Research

WHY USE TECHNOLOGY?	WHEN DOES TECHNOLOGY WORK BEST?
Studies show that it can: • Influence student academic performance; • Develop higher order thinking and problem solving; • Improve student motivation, attitude, and interest in learning; • Help to prepare students for the workforce; and • Address the needs of low-performing and at-risk students and those with learning handicaps.	**Studies show that it works best when it:** • Directly supports the curriculum objectives being assessed; • Provides opportunities for student collaboration; • Adjusts for student ability and prior experience, and provides feedback to the student and teacher about student performance or progress with the application; • Is integrated into the typical instructional day; • Provides opportunities for students to design and implement projects that extend the curriculum content being assessed by a particular standardized test; and • Is used in environments where teachers, the school community, and school and district administrators support the use of technology.

Source: The Center for Applied Research in Educational Technology (CARET), http://caret.iste.edu.

2003). These highly publicized attacks focus on the lack of evidence that technology's benefits outweigh the problems it causes (e.g., high costs of updating resources, implementation difficulties, potential dangers to students).

• **Low teacher use** — Recent surveys indicate that even teachers who have sufficient training and access to resources are not using technology as much as expected (Cuban, Kirkpatrick, & Peck, 2001; Norris, Sullivan, Poirot, & Soloway, 2003). Clearly, teachers are not hearing a convincing case for technology's benefits.

• **The influence of the accountability movement and the No Child Left Behind (NCLB) Act** — Passed in 2001, the federal NCLB act is predicted to dominate policy and drive funding for some time to come. One of its most controversial requirements is that funding for proposed expenditures must be tied to "scientifically based research" on effectiveness. Like many educational initiatives, technology integration currently lacks this kind of research base.

Research evidence. The **Center for Applied Research in Educational Technology (CARET),** a funded project of the International Society for Technology in Education (ISTE), has the most comprehensive review of research evidence available on the impact of technology in education (see http://caret.iste.edu). The What Works Clearinghouse (http://w-w-c.org/), established by the U.S. Department of Education's Institute of Education Sciences to provide "high-quality reviews of scientific evidence of the effectiveness of replicable educational interventions," is also a source for this research evidence.

CARET's approach to the technology use rationale is based on what educators have been saying for years: Simply having students use technology does not raise achievement. The impact depends on the ways the technology is used and the conditions under which applications are implemented. For example, CARET poses the question, "How can technology influence student academic performance?" It answers this question by citing studies that indicate the application influences performance, not as a delivery system, but as instruction that works under certain circumstances. Figure 1.3 summarizes research CARET has found about how and under what conditions technology can enhance teaching and learning.

As the CARET project illustrates, the case for using technology in teaching is one that must be made not just by isolating variables that make a difference, but by combining them. Figures 1.4 through 1.7 provide a summary of reasons practitioners have cited over the years for why we should integrate technology into teaching. When viewed together with research findings, they pose a powerful rationale for why technology must become as commonplace in education as it is in other areas of society. They also help point out specific ways to integrate technology into teaching and learning. A summary of the elements underlying a rationale for using technology in teaching is given in Figure 1.8.

LOOKING AROUND: WHAT FACTORS SHAPE THE CURRENT CLIMATE FOR TECHNOLOGY IN EDUCATION?

The history of educational technology shows us that two general characteristics shape the field's direction and the impact it will have on teaching and learning: (1) the capabilities of

Figure 1.4   Why Use Technology? To Motivate Students

Practitioners Say That Technology Can Motivate Students By:

- **Gaining their attention**—Capturing students' attention is the first of Robert Gagné's nine essential "events of instruction." Teachers say technology's visual and interactive qualities can direct students' attention toward learning tasks.

- **Supporting manual operations during high-level learning**—Students are more motivated to learn complex skills (e.g., writing compositions and solving algebraic equations) when technology tools help them do the low-level skills involved (e.g., making corrections to written drafts or doing arithmetic calculations).

  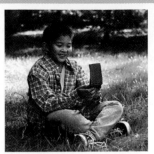

  They used to consider writing a loathsome, tedious chore, could find any number of reasons to procrastinate over a writing assignment, and dreaded having to rework edited assignments. But all that changed . . . thanks to creative assignments, cooperative activities, and the addition of handheld computers. (Furger, 2003; p. 5)

- **Illustrating real-world relevance through highly visual presentations**—When students can see that high-level math and science skills have real-life application, it is no longer just "school work"; they are more willing to learn skills that have clear value to their future life and work.

- **Engaging them through production work**—Students who learn by creating word-processed, hypermedia, and other technology products report higher engagement in learning and a greater sense of pride in their achievements (Franklin, 1991; Taylor, 1989; Tibbs, 1989; Volker, 1992).

- **Connecting them with audiences for their writing**—Educators say that students are much more motivated to write and do their best production work when they publish it on the web, since others outside the classroom will see their work (Cohen & Riel, 1989).

  Each day, a different student is assigned the job of roving reporter . . . (who) captures the day's activities in text and pictures . . . and reloads it to the class web site the next day. Because the daily log is widely read by parents and members of the school community, the activity is not only relevant, but provides students an opportunity to write for a broader audience—both of which contribute to their interest and enthusiasm. . . . As one student put it, "My parents read the daily log every day. I think it makes me write a lot better because I know my parents are reading it" (Furger, 2003, p. 5)

---

resources available at a given time in the evolution of technology; and (2) the combination of current societal influences, educational trends and priorities, economic factors, and company marketing initiatives. This section gives an overview of current technology resources, how they are used, and prevailing factors and issues that are shaping their impact.

Current Educational Technology Systems, Configurations, and Applications

Figure 1.9 gives a graphical overview of the technical resources available for teachers to use. Note that all technology integration strategies require a combination of **hardware** or equipment (desktop, **laptop,** or handheld computer, along with appropriate input/output devices such as printers and scanners) and **software** or programs written to perform various kinds of educational applications. As Figure 1.10 shows, computer equipment can be arranged or configured in various ways, each of which is suited to supporting specific types

of integration strategies. Software to support educational technology applications includes these types:

- **Instructional** — Programs designed to teach students skills or information through demonstrations, examples, explanation, or problem solving

- **Productivity** — Programs designed to help teachers and students plan, develop materials, and keep records

- **Administrative** — Programs that administrators at school, state, and district levels use to support record keeping and exchanges of information among various agencies.

Integration strategies described in this textbook focus on instructional and productivity applications that teachers implement. Administrative technology activities (e.g., student and faculty records, report card generation) are covered in other Prentice Hall texts.

Figure 1.5   Why Use Technology? To Enhance Instruction

Practitioners Say That Technology Can Enhance Instructional Methods By:

- **Supplying interaction and immediate feedback to support skill practice**—Software such as the drill-and-practice type offers many students the privacy, self-pacing, and immediate feedback they need to comprehend and retain lower level skills.

- **Helping students visualize underlying concepts in unfamiliar or abstract topics**—Simulations and other interactive software tools have unique abilities to illustrate science and mathematics concepts. Highly trained principles become easier to understand.

- **Illustrating connections between skills and real-life applications**—Technology tools support problem-based learning to help students see where high-level math and science skills apply. Students are less likely to have "inert knowledge," i.e., knowing how to do a skill but not recognizing where to use it.

  > Project-based learning (PBL) re-defines the boundaries of the classroom. The PBL classroom can be a forest or stream, an office or lab, a museum or zoo. The Digital Age is now bringing these environments to students virtually, permitting (them) to travel via the Internet to lava flows in Hawaii or to the Library of Congress. (Chen, 2001, p. 2)

- **Letting students study systems in unique ways**—Students use tools such as spreadsheets and simulations to answer "what if" questions they would not be able to do easily by hand or would not be feasible at all without the benefits of technology.

- **Giving access to unique information sources and populations**—The Internet connects students with information, research, data, and expertise not available locally. Multicultural awareness can increase when students of different cultures interact online (Roblyer, 1991).

  > One of the great things about teaching art history is that there's always going to be new content in the field. What the Web has done is allowed for better access to that new content. And museums, even the smaller ones, are going to have to put their collections online. (Cavallo, 2003, p. 18)

- **Supplying self-paced learning for capable students**—Self-directed students can learn on their own often with software tutorials and/or distance education materials. They can surge ahead of the class or tackle topics not offered by the school.

  > High schooler Rachel of Forks, Washington, loves Virtual High School classes. . . . She takes two VHS classes per semester, along with regular face-to-face classes. "I like the combination and I like the freedom of working on my own anytime I want." It all comes down to self-motivation and whether or not a student can work independently. (Furger, 2002, p. 17)

- **Allowing access to learning opportunities**—Students with disabilities depend on technology to compensate for vision, hearing, and/or manual dexterity they need in order to read, interact in class, and do products to show what they have learned.

- **Providing opportunities and support for cooperative learning**—Although students can do small group work without technology, teachers report that students are often more motivated to work cooperatively on hypermedia, database, and web page production projects.

Figure 1.6   Why Use Technology? To Make Student and Teacher Work More Productively

Practitioners Say That Technology Makes Teacher and Student Work More Productively by:

- **Saving time on production tasks**—Software tools such as word processing, desktop publishing, and spreadsheets allow quick and easy corrections to reports, presentations, budgets, and publications.

  > Systems are difficult to change. . . . Technology, however, often demonstrates a better, faster way of doing things and . . . can lead to transforming systems. (Lucas, 2003, p. 2)

- **Grading and tracking student work**—Integrated learning systems and handheld computers help teachers quickly assess and track student progress.

- **Providing faster access to information sources**—Students use the Internet and e-mail to do research and collect data that would take much longer to receive by traditional delivery methods.

  > Trying to find information about cultures and religions can be a daunting experience, particularly if you are from a region with limited library service. Filling the void is KidsConnect, which pairs 84 volunteer school librarians like me on the Internet with students from around the world who need answers to questions. (Brangwin, 2002, p. 13)

- **Saving money on consumable materials**—Software tools such as drill and practice and simulations save schools by taking the place of many materials (e.g., worksheets, handouts, dissection animals) that are used and replaced each year.

Figure 1.7   Why Use Technology? To Help Students Learn and Sharpen Their Information Age Skills

Practitioners Say That Technology Can Help Students Learn and Sharpen Information Age Skills in:

- **Technological literacy**—Technologies such as word processing, spreadsheets, simulations, multimedia, and the Internet have become increasingly essential to many job areas. Students who use these in school have a head start on what to do in the workplace.

  > "Technology should be a natural component of everything [students] do," says Heather Sinclair, district director of secondary curriculum and staff development for Lake Washington. "It should be a natural tool they use on a day-to-day basis. It shouldn't be something that is scary or contrived. It should be authentic and realistic." *PowerPoint®* is becoming routine. Students also make videos using digital cameras and movie editing software. They burn their own CDs. They use the Internet to converse with their mentors and conduct research. One student created a steam engine out of Plexiglas; another used computer-aided design (CAD) software to design a sailboat. (GLEF Staff, 2003, p. 9)

- **Information literacy**—Students learn skills that Johnson and Eisenberg (1996) call the "Big Six" (task definition, information-seeking strategies, location and access, use of information, synthesis, and evaluation).

- **Visual literacy**—Images continue to replace text as communication media. Students must learn to interpret, understand, and appreciate the meaning of visual messages; communicate more effectively through applying the basic principles and concepts of visual design; produce visual messages using the computer and other technology; and use visual thinking to conceptualize solutions to problems (Christopherson, 1997, p. 173). Some research correlates visual literacy with higher scores on intelligence tests (Roblyer, 1986).

Edutopia is the newsletter for the George Lucas Educational Foundation. It is available online at *http://www.glef.org*.

Figure 1.8 Why Use Technology? A Summary of Elements Underlying a Rationale

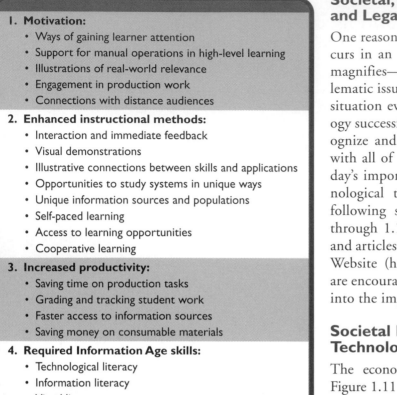

1. **Motivation:**
   - Ways of gaining learner attention
   - Support for manual operations in high-level learning
   - Illustrations of real-world relevance
   - Engagement in production work
   - Connections with distance audiences

2. **Enhanced instructional methods:**
   - Interaction and immediate feedback
   - Visual demonstrations
   - Illustrative connections between skills and applications
   - Opportunities to study systems in unique ways
   - Unique information sources and populations
   - Self-paced learning
   - Access to learning opportunities
   - Cooperative learning

3. **Increased productivity:**
   - Saving time on production tasks
   - Grading and tracking student work
   - Faster access to information sources
   - Saving money on consumable materials

4. **Required Information Age skills:**
   - Technological literacy
   - Information literacy
   - Visual literacy

An Overview of Today's Big Issues in Education and Technology: Societal, Educational, Cultural/Equity, and Legal/Ethical

One reason that teaching is so challenging is that it occurs in an environment that mirrors—and sometimes magnifies—some of society's most profound and problematic issues. Adding computers to this mix makes the situation even more complex. Yet to integrate technology successfully into their teaching, educators must recognize and be prepared to work in this environment with all of its subtleties and complexities. Some of today's important issues and their implications for technological trends in education are described in the following sections and summarized in Figures 1.11 through 1.14. The full URLs for many of the reports and articles in these figures are given on the Companion Website (http://www.prenhall.com/roblyer). Readers are encouraged to review them to broaden their insights into the impact of these issues.

Societal Issues Shaping Current Technology Uses

The economic, political, and social trends listed in Figure 1.11 have a great impact on whether or not innovations take hold, or have limited acceptance, or are ignored completely. Societal issues that are helping to shape

Figure 1.9 The Educational Technology "Tree of Knowledge"

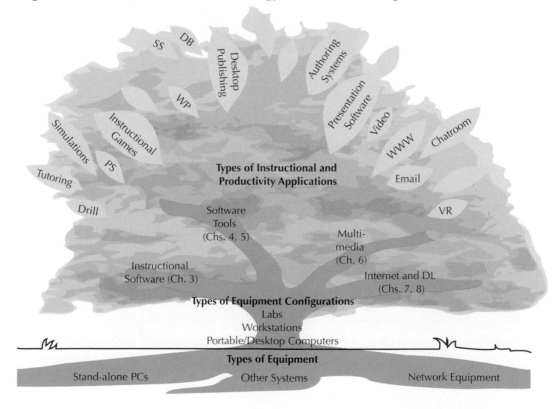

Figure 1.10 Types of Technology Facilities and How They Are Used

Types of Facilities	Uses	Benefits	Limitations/ Problems
Laboratories (usually 20–30 networked computers)			
All labs		Centralized resources are easier to maintain and secure; networking software can monitor individual performance in groups	Need permanent staff to supervise and maintain resources. Students must leave their classrooms to use them.
Special-purpose labs	• Programming or technical courses • Technology education/ vocational courses (e.g., with CAD, robotics, desktop publishing stations) • MIDI music labs • Labs dedicated to content area(s), e.g., mathematics/science, foreign languages • For use by Chapter or Title III students • Multimedia production work • Teacher work labs	Permanent setups of group resources specific to the needs of certain content areas or types of students.	Usually exclude groups who do not meet special purpose. Isolate resources.
General-use computer labs (open to all school groups)	Student productivity tasks (e.g., word processing, multimedia production); class demonstrations; student project work	Accommodate varied uses by different groups.	Difficult to schedule specific uses. Usually available to only one class at a time.
Library/media center labs	Same as for general-use labs	Same as for general-use labs, but permanent staff are already present. Ready access to all materials to promote integration of computer and noncomputer resources.	Same as for general-use labs. Staff members need special training. Classes cannot usually do production or group work that may bother other users of the library/media center.
Mobile Computers (a.k.a. computers on wheels or COWs)			
Mobile workstations	Demonstrations, short-term uses	Stretch resources by sharing them among many users; supply on-demand access.	Moving equipment can cause breakage and other maintenance problems. Sometimes difficult to get through doors or up stairs. Can increase security problems.

(continued)

Figure 1.10 (continued)

Types of Facilities	Uses	Benefits	Limitations/ Problems
Mobile Computers (continued)			
Mobile labs (complete set of computers, usually 15–30 handhelds or laptops on carts)	Individual student or teacher production and data gathering tasks; teacher assessment tasks (e.g., with handheld devices)	Same as for mobile workstations, but serve more students at one time.	Same as for mobile workstations.
Classroom Computers			
Classroom workstations (usually 2–5 computers with a printer)	Learning stations with individual tutoring and drills; whole-class demonstrations; Internet research and production tasks for cooperative learning groups	Easily accessible to teachers and students.	No immediate technical assistance available to teachers. Only part of class can use at one time.
Stand-alone classroom computer (one computer, often connected by network to school server)	Whole-class demonstrations; teacher e-mail; small group tasks	Same as for classroom workstations.	Same as for classroom workstations.

the current climate for educational technology include the following:

- **Economic conditions** — Recent economic downturns in the U.S. economy have meant decreased education funding. Experts predict that funds will not return to previous levels when the economy improves.

- **Anti-technology positions** — Some critics say that ubiquitous technology interferes with privacy and complicates daily life. Others feel that teaching/learning benefits have not been clearly established, and that technology is not as important as other programs that are being cut (e.g., music, arts). Still others say that computer use poses potential health hazards and that Internet cyberporn and predators pose other risks, especially to young users.

- **Impact of the NCLB Act of 2001** — Among other things, the NCLB act requires that all government-funded programs demonstrate benefits with "scientifically based research," and schools must demonstrate that all students are meeting standards.

Figure 1.11   Current Societal Trends and Issues Shaping the Use of Technology in Education

Economic conditions	• Budget ax falls on school tech programs (Murray, 2003a) • *The Learning Return on Our Technology Investment: A Review of Findings from Research* (Ringstaff & Kelley, 2002) (http://www.wested.org/cs/wew/view/rs/619) • *The What Works Clearinghouse*—a summary of scientific evidence on education strategies and products that work (http://w-w-c.org/)
Anti-technology positions	• *Fool's Gold: A Critical Look at Computers and Childhood* (Alliance for Childhood, 1999) (http://www.allianceforchildhood.net/projects/computers/computers_reports.htm) • *Failure to Connect: How Computers Affect Our Children's Minds—for Better or Worse* (Healey, 1998) • In Search of Appropriate Usage Guidelines (McNabb, 2001). • *The Flickering Mind: The False Promise of Technology in the Classroom and How Learning Can Be Saved* (Oppenheimer, 2003) • *The Age of Access* (Rifkin, 2000)
Impact of the No Child Left Behind (NCLB) Act of 2001	• Scientific Culture and Educational Research (Feuer, Towne, & Shavelson, 2002) • Accountability systems: Implications of requirements of the No Child Left Behind Act (Linn, Baker, & Betebenner, 2002)

Figure 1.12   Current Education Trends and Issues Shaping the Use of Technology in Education

Standards movement	• Getting our NETS worth: The Role of ISTE's National Educational Technology Standards (NETS) (Roblyer, 2003a) • *Understanding University Success: A Report from the Standards for Success Project* (Center for Educational Policy Research, 2003) (http://www.s4s.org/understanding.php)
Reliance on Internet and on distance education	• *Entering the Mainstream: The Quality and Extent of Online Education in the United States, 2003 and 2004* (http://www.sloan-c.org/resources/survey.asp) • *Virtual Schools: Trends and Issues* (Clark, 2001) (http://www.dlrn.org/trends.html) • *The Virtual High School: Teaching Generation V* (Zucker & Kozma, 2003) • Predicting Success of Virtual High School Distance Learners: Preliminary Results from an Educational Success Prediction Instrument (ESPRI) (Roblyer & Marshall, 2002–2003) • Liberal Arts for All, Not Just the Rich (Durden, 2001)
Debate over directed vs. inquiry-based, constructivist instructional methods	• The Constructivist/Objectivist Debate: Implications for Instructional Technology Research (Roblyer, 1996)

This combination of social conditions means that educators increasingly are forced to set priorities for scarce education dollars. In light of this and recent attacks on technology by those outside education, it is ever more important to use research results and best practice findings to establish a sound rationale for technology use and justify technology expenses and potential risks to student users. Increasingly, funding for technology-based strategies will be dependent on these results and findings. In light of increasing accountability requirements, it also seems likely that schools will begin emphasizing the use of computer systems to track student progress.

Educational Issues Shaping Current Technology Uses

Trends in the educational system are intertwined with trends in technology and society. The three kinds of educational issues shown in Figure 1.12 and listed next have special implications for the ways technology will be used in teaching and learning:

• **Standards movement** — All content areas and states have skill standards students must meet to pass courses and to get degrees and certification. High-stakes tests on standards determine success. This movement may drive a trend toward using technology

Figure 1.13 Current Cultural/Equity Trends and Issues Shaping the Use of Technology in Education

Digital Divide: Racial and economic equity	• *Bridging the Racial Divide on the Internet* (Hoffman & Novak, 1998) • *Losing Ground Bit by Bit* (Goslee, 1998) (http://www.benton.org/publibrary/losing-ground/home.html) • *Connected to the Future* (Corporation for Public Broadcasting, 2003) • Becker's 1986 studies • *Internet Access in U.S. Public Schools and Classrooms: 1994–2002* (Kleiner & Lewis, 2003) • No Access, No Use, No Impact: Snapshot Surveys of Educational Technology in K–12 (Norris et al., 2003) • Digital Desperation: Research Reports on a Growing Technology and Equity Crisis (Roblyer, 2000)
Gender equity	• *Tech-Savvy: Educating Girls in the New Computer Age* (AAUW, 2000) (www.aauw.org/research/girls_education/techsavvy.cfm) • *Unlocking the Clubhouse: Women and Computing* (Margolis & Fisher, 2002)
Special needs	• ABLEDATA website for information on assistive technologies (http://www.abledata.com) • Assistive Technology for Students with Mild Disabilities (Behrmann & Jerome, 2002)

in ways that help teachers and students pass tests and meet required standards.

• **Reliance on the Internet and on distance education** — Increasing numbers of virtual K–12 courses are being offered, and virtual high schools are becoming commonplace in U.S. education. This means that students could have increased access to high-quality courses and degrees. However, virtual learning takes special skills not all students have, and dropout rates from distance courses are higher, which could further widen the **Digital Divide.** Some critics say that distance learning is not as empowering as a face-to-face educational experience.

• **Debate over directed vs. inquiry-based, constructivist instructional methods** — Educators disagree on the proper roles of traditional, teacher-directed learning versus student-led, inquiry-based methods. Long-used and well-validated directed uses of technology have been shown to be effective for addressing standards, but many educators see them as passé. Inquiry-based, constructivist methods are considered more modern, but it is less clear how they could address required standards.

Cultural and Equity Issues Shaping Current Technology Uses

The three factors shown in Figure 1.13 and listed next reflect the complex racial and cultural fabric of our society, and they continue to have a great impact on technology use:

• **Digital Divide** — A phrase coined by Lloyd Morrisett, former president of the Markle Foundation, the Digital Divide refers to a discrepancy in access to technology resources among socioeconomic groups. The single greatest factor determining access is economic status, although race and gender may also play a role, depending on the type of technology. Recent studies (Corporation for Public Broadcasting, 2003) find that while children from all income levels have greatly increased their Internet use, children from underserved populations (e.g., low-income and minority students) still lag far behind other students in home and school access.

• **Racial and gender equity** — Technology remains dominated by males and certain ethnic groups. Studies show that when compared with males and whites, females, African Americans, and Hispanic minorities use computers less and enter careers in math, science, and technology areas at lower rates. Many educators believe these two findings are correlated: Lower use of technology leads to lower entrance to technical careers. Even where computers are available in schools, there tends to be unequal access to certain kinds of activities. For example, children in Title I programs may have access to computers, but use them mainly for remedial work rather than for email, multimedia production, and other personal empowerment activities.

• **Special needs** — Devices and methods are available to help students compensate for their physical and mental deficits and allow them equal access to technology and to learning opportunities. However, technological interventions that could help students with special needs are difficult to purchase and implement and often go unused. Parents clamor for the technology resources guaranteed their children by federal laws, but schools often claim insufficient funding to address these special needs.

Figure 1.14 Current Legal/Ethical Trends and Issues Shaping the Use of Technology in Education

Viruses/hacking	• Microsoft, Schools Mull Security Improvements (2003) • Computer Ethics Institute (http://www.brook.edu/its/cei/cei_hp.htm)
The new plagiarism	• Cybercheating: A New Twist on an Old Problem (Gardiner, 2001) • Teachers use: —Essay Verification Engine (http://www.canexus.com/eve/) —Turnitin.com (http://turnitin.com) —Plagiarism.org (http://plagiarism.org)
Privacy/safety	• Risk Factors For and Impact of Online Sexual Solicitation of Youth (Mitchell, Finkelhor, & Wolak, 2001)
Copyright	• Copyright and Distance Education: Making Sense of the Teach Act (Crews, 2003)
Illegal downloads/ software piracy	• University of Delaware website—*Writing an Acceptable Use Policy* (http://www.ash.udel.edu/ash/teacher/AUP.html) • Online Ethics. What's a Teacher to Do? (Carpenter, 1996)

As Molnar pointed out n his landmark 1978 article "The Next Great Crisis in American Education: Computer Literacy," the power of technology is a two-edged sword, especially for education. While it presents obvious potential for changing education and empowering teachers and students, technology also may further divide members of our society along socioeconomic, ethnic, and cultural lines and widen the gender gap. Teachers will lead the struggle to make sure technology use promotes, rather than conflicts with, the goals of a democratic society.

Legal and Ethical Issues Shaping Current Technology Uses

In many ways, technology users represent the society in a microcosm. The legal and ethical issues educators face reflect those of the larger society. The three major kinds of ethical and legal issues shown in Figure 1.14 and discussed next have great impact on how technology activities are implemented:

- **Viruses/hacking** — Illegal activities of two kinds are on the rise: (1) **Viruses,** or programs written to cause damage or do mischief, cause problems ranging from lost files to systems being shut down for weeks. (2) **Hackers** are breaking into online systems in order to access personal data on students, accomplish identify theft, and do other malicious acts. To combat these problems, schools are forced to install **firewalls** and **virus protection software** to safeguard classroom computers, and to spend larger portions of technology funds each year on preventing and cleaning up after illegal activities.

- **The new plagiarism** — Greater online access to full-text documents has resulted in increased "cybercheating," or students using materials they have found on the Internet as their own. Sites have emerged to help teachers catch plagiarizers, and the number of educational organizations and teachers using them is increasing.

- **Privacy/safety** — Increasing amounts of students' personal information are being placed online and students are spending more time using online resources. At the same time, studies show a high incidence of attempts by online predators to contact students, and objectionable material is readily available and easy to access. To address these concerns, schools are requiring students/parents to sign an Authorized Use Policy (AUP) and putting procedures in place to safeguard access to students' personal information. Schools have also been put on notice to supervise carefully all student use of the Internet, and to install filtering software to prevent access to objectionable materials.

- **Copyright** — Online availability of full-text publications is increasing, and distance courses are posting more materials in online course management systems. To make sure they comply with copyright laws, schools are making teachers and students aware of policies about copyright/AUP and fair use of published materials.

- **Illegal downloads/software piracy** — An increasing number of sites offer ways to download copies of software or other media without paying for them, and software and media companies are prosecuting more offenders. Despite the ease of copying or downloading free materials, teachers are tasked with modeling and teaching ethical behaviors with software and media.

The culture, language, and problems of the larger society also emerge among technology users, and their activities reflect many of the rules of conduct and values of society in general. Teachers who use technology are faced

1. **Accountability and the standards movement** — Educators want to know (a) how technology can help students meet required curriculum standards and (b) what role technology skills play in children's education.

2. **Funding for educational technology** — As technology costs grow and education funds wane, policy makers ask, "How can we justify spending scarce education dollars on technology?"

3. **The Digital Divide** — Since technology access differs between wealthy and poorer schools, people want to know if technology is deepening the economic chasm between rich and poor.

4. **Racial and gender equity** — Science, technology, and engineering careers remain dominated by males and certain ethnic groups; educators say more student involvement in technology at earlier levels could change this picture.

5. **The role of distance education** — Virtual schools are springing up around the country. Parents wonder: (a) Can all students succeed in online environments? (b) Will students learn as much as in face-to-face classrooms?

6. **Privacy and safety** — As more student data go online and students spend more time on the Internet, measures have to be put into place to limit access to personal data and to protect students from online predators.

7. **Viruses and hacking** — The online community is seeing an unprecedented number of viruses and illegal entries into networks. Schools are forced to spend precious funds on measures to protect themselves.

8. **Online plagiarism** — Students have easy access to papers and projects they can turn in as their own work. Teachers have to be on the alert for plagiarism and use online sources to check suspicious work.

9. **Anti-Technology sentiments** — In light of the scarcity of research on technology's impact on indicators of education quality, critics of educational technology are on the attack.

10. **Information literacy** — Society's increasing dependence on technology to communicate information means that students must learn skills to use information technologies effectively.

with addressing the problems that will arise when people try to work outside those values and rules.

The most important of these issues in terms of their impact in shaping what we can and must do with technology in education are summarized in the *Top Ten* feature shown above. What we are able to do to apply the power of technology to enhance education will be shaped primarily by how we are able to respond to these major issues.

Looking Ahead: What Developments in Technology Integration Are Emerging?

Emerging Trends in Hardware and Software Development

Visions of the future are suffused with images of technologies that may seem magical and far-fetched now, just as cellular phones and fax machines seemed only a few decades ago. And, although the technology images we see when we look into the future of education are murky and ill defined, we know that they will mirror current technical trends and the goals and priorities we set today for tomorrow's education. As with so many "miraculous" technologies, the question is how we will take advantage of their capabilities to bring about the kind of future education systems our society wants and our economy needs.

Future technological developments will have such a profound impact on education that the federally funded Institute for the Advancement of Emerging Technologies in Education (IAETE) at the Appalachian Educational Laboratory (AEL) was founded specifically to study and document leading-edge technologies with promising educational practices. IAETE's latest findings on innovations in education and the emerging technologies associated with them are documented at its website (http://www.iaete.org) and in its annual publication, *INSIGHT.*

Just as the Internet changed communications capabilities in ways that shaped educational practices, other technological developments will have equally dramatic consequences for schools. One such technology may be **radio-frequency identification (RFID),** which consists of a computer chip and an electronic monitoring system that tracks the location of the chip and can update information on it. First introduced in department stores to monitor inventory and prevent theft of goods, RFID is already being proposed to track student attendance, increase school security, and monitor the location of library resources (Murray, 2003b). Some educators envision even more school-related RFID uses and say it has the potential to save time that can be redirected to teaching activities. However, six other trends in technological developments, summarized in Figure 1.15, promise to have even more direct impact on teaching and learning activities: **wireless connectivity,** merged technologies, handheld devices, high-speed communications, **artificial intelligence,** and **virtual systems.**

- **Trend #1: Wireless connectivity** — A universal trend across computer systems, wireless connections are simplifying computer networks by reducing the number of required cables and allowing greater freedom of movement. Instead of each computer having a "drop" or cabled access point to the network, wireless networks have one drop through which many computer devices can access the network. One result is mobile labs on a cart that contains from 10 to 30 laptops and a wireless access point that can be plugged into a network jack. Some schools have "hot spots" or drops around the building, so that students can use a portable computer anywhere in the school.

- **Trend #2: Merging of technologies** — An ever-increasing number of devices combine communications capabilities that were once housed in individual devices. For example, cellular phones now allow not only voice communications, but also can create and send digital images and text messages. Handheld devices often incorporate the power of desktop computers and the capabilities of digital cameras.

- **Trend #3: Developments in portable devices** — Computers are becoming increasingly portable, which allows teachers and students greater flexibility in learning environments. Laptops are becoming more popular, along with **handheld computers** (a.k.a "palms") and **tablet PCs.** Many schools are replacing their desktop computers with these portable devices so that learning activities need not be confined to classrooms or school buildings.

- **Trend #4: Availability of high-speed communications** — Imitating the gradual spread of electrical power and telephone access into all parts of the United States during the early 1900s, high-speed Internet connections are becoming increasingly ubiquitous in the 2000s. Faster connections made possible by Digital Subscriber Lines (DSLs) and cable modems mean higher quality, more reliable voice and video communications, which are the necessary ingredients to make distance learning environments emulate face-to-face ones.

- **Trend #5: Visual immersion systems** — Once only dreamed of in science fiction, computer-generated environments that immerse students in simulated worlds are becoming increasingly available. Current applications include full immersion systems with head-mounted displays, augmented reality systems, and 3-D models on computer screens. Although full-immersion systems are still too expensive for most schools, experimental applications continue to appear sporadically. Virtual 3-D models on computer screens are becoming more prevalent (Parham, 2003; Thatcher, 2003). Some experts predict increased use of augmented reality systems, which allow people with computer-powered goggles to view real-world images with overlays from **global positioning system (GPS)** satellites (Augmented reality, 2002).

- **Trend #6: Intelligent applications** — Artificial intelligence (AI) has never had the same level of impact on education as it has had on activities such as chess playing and industrial training and problem solving. However, applications of so-called "intelligent programs" (software that emulates human thought processes and responses to situations) continue to appear in education as researchers explore ways to use AI-type capabilities to solve persistent problems in instruction and assessment.

Implications of New Technologies for Teachers and Students

The six trends just discussed promise significant changes in the way education is carried out. The changes in educational practices are gradual, and current examples are usually limited to pilot programs and studies. However, the technologies described here are advancing so quickly in other areas of society, it is easy to imagine a future where they are commonplace in education.

- **Flexible learning environments** — No longer do students have to leave classrooms for "pull-out" activities in labs. With wireless communications and portable devices, now the lab comes to the students, and learning environments can be located beyond the walls of classrooms and schools. Students can take notes, gather data, or do research from wherever they are and have easy, fast access to resources such as writing labs and digital production labs. Tinker, Staudt, and Walton (2002) describe an example of the power this flexibility offers on a field trip to do scientific observations, and Curtis, Williams, Norris, O'Leary, and Soloway (2003) describe

Figure 1.15   Emerging Technology Trends and Implications for Education

Emerging Trends	Examples	Implications for Technology Integration Strategies
Wireless connectivity Motorola and the stylized M Logo are registered in the US Patent & Trademark Office. All other product or service names are the property of their respective owners. © Motorola Inc. 2005. http://www.motorola.com	• Mobile labs • School-wide hot spots (wireless connections to networks)	• Mobility makes it easier for teachers to plan for and implement activities. • Easier access to networks makes it easier to obtain materials, update assessments.
Merging of technologies palmOne® is a registered trademark of palmOne, Inc.. http://www.palmone.com/	• Handheld devices with built-in communications and digital imaging capabilities	• Combined capabilities mean fewer devices to buy and keep track of during instruction.
Developments in portable devices	• Laptops • Multiple-function handheld devices • Tablet PCs	• Portability makes it easier for each student to have a computer, thus allowing individualized strategies. • Students can write and do research from any location. • Teachers can do continuous monitoring and assessment.
Availability of high-speed communications Courtesy of Westell. http://www.westell.com	• In homes: Digital Subscriber Lines (DSL) and cable modems • In schools: T1 lines, DSL, and cable modems	• High-quality, reliable voice and visual communications make distance learning more like face-to-face classrooms. • More students have access to virtual courses and degree programs.
Visual immersion systems	• Head-mounted VR systems. • Augmented reality systems • 3-D imaging systems	• Students with physical limitations can simulate movement in real situations. • Simulated systems allow more realistic and authentic presentations of information.
Intelligent applications	• Intelligent grading systems • Intelligent tutors	• Computer systems grade complex performances (e.g., writing) more quickly and reliably than teachers. • Computer tutors adapt more quickly to individual students' learning needs.

how to manage and carry out lessons that maximize the flexibility of handheld devices. One study has already indicated that teachers find handheld devices easy to integrate into classroom activities (Branigan, 2002a).

- **Adaptable assessment options** — New technologies are already having an impact on how educators assess students, and more changes seem likely in the future. Teachers are beginning to use handheld devices to make monitoring students' progress more immediate and continuous (Hudgins, 2001). As standards and accountability loom ever larger on the horizon, continuous assessment becomes more important, making it easier to guide student progress and ensure success on tests. The Pennsylvania Department of Education found that an intelligent system for scoring the essay portion of state-mandated tests matched an expert reviewer's scores more often than reviewers matched each other (Branigan, 2000). This indicates that faster, cheaper updates to current methods of assessing complex performances such as writing may not be far away.

- **Reliance on distance learning** — As high-speed connections become more readily available to schools and homes, the number of students learning through virtual systems is steadily increasing (Zucker & Kozma, 2003). Many states sponsor a virtual high school, and many organizations offer courses for junior high and even elementary students (Roblyer, 2003b). Though currently fraught with controversy, distance learning for K–12 students eventually will have the same degree of impact on reshaping schools as it has had on redefining higher education.

- **Support for people with disabilities** — New technologies continue to make the most dramatic advances in opportunities for people with disabilities. Kurzweil (2003) describes immersion systems and intelligent programs that help people with sensory impairments and physical disabilities function effectively in learning situations. Branigan (2002b) describes a **virtual reality** project that has dramatically improved the performance of students with hearing impairments. Because the No Child Left Behind Act requires that all students, including those with disabilities, meet high standards of achievement, it seems likely that schools will increase their investments in new assistive technologies (Assistive technologies, 2003).

Skills for the Future: ISTE NETS for Students, Teachers, and Administrators

Clearly, 21st-century educators will have to deal with issues that their predecessors could not even have imagined. Both they and the students they teach must have skills and knowledge that will prepare them to meet these new challenges.

The National Council for the Accreditation of Teacher Education (NCATE), the agency responsible for accrediting colleges of education, has joined with ISTE in not only establishing standards for teaching about technology in education, but also in saying that schools of education should increase their emphasis on the use of technology in teacher training (NCATE, 1997). Thus, the ISTE National Educational Technology Standards (NETS) for Teachers have become the benchmark for technology infusion in teacher education programs. NETS for Teachers are specified for each chapter and all end-of-chapter portfolio activities in this text. The student version of these standards is also shown at the front of this book. It is important to note the relationship between these sets of standards. NETS for Students are considered basic skills that students—and their teachers—should meet.

How Teachers Can Demonstrate Their Skills: Electronic Portfolios

Many teacher preparation programs require their candidates to develop a teaching *portfolio* as they go through the program. Portfolios are a collection of student's work products over time, arranged so that they and others can see how their skills have developed and progressed. They also include criteria for selecting and judging content. The portfolio concept originated in higher education with colleges of arts, music, and architecture. Work in these areas could not be measured well through traditional tests. Instead of final exams, these students had to have a professional portfolio when they graduated to demonstrate their level of accomplishment in their field. For today's technology-integrated curriculum, which often calls for multimedia work products, many teachers are turning to student **electronic portfolios** as the assessment strategy of choice. Although older students could decide on their own portfolio format, teachers usually provide the portfolio structure and tell students how to fill in the content. Teachers can choose from several kinds of resources for these structures:

- **"Ready-made" software packages** — These include *Learner Profile* (Sunburst), *Grady Profile* (Auerbach), and *My ePortfolio* (Learning Quest). Teachers can use these instead of creating their own structure. These systems usually are built on database software, with fields to attach files of written and visual products.

- **PDF documents** — To store and display documents (with or without graphics), teachers can use *Adobe Acrobat* software to create electronic versions of pages. These are essentially "pictures of pages" and are easy to store and share with others.

Figure 1.16 Electronic Teaching Portfolios: How to Create and Use Them

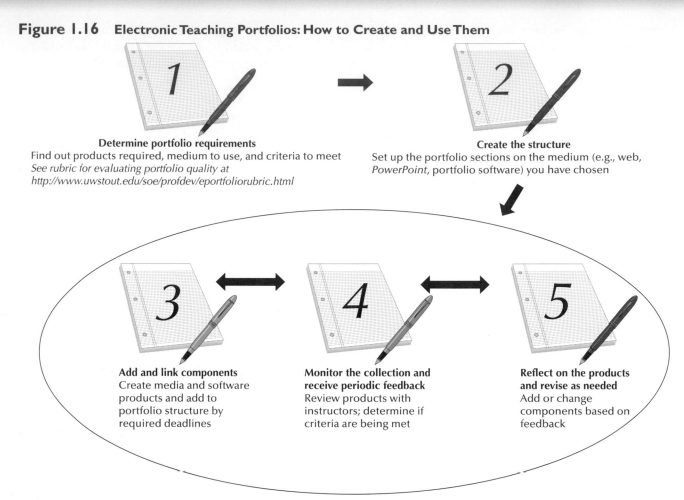

Determine portfolio requirements
Find out products required, medium to use, and criteria to meet
See rubric for evaluating portfolio quality at
http://www.uwstout.edu/soe/profdev/eportfoliorubric.html

Create the structure
Set up the portfolio sections on the medium (e.g., web, *PowerPoint*, portfolio software) you have chosen

Add and link components
Create media and software products and add to portfolio structure by required deadlines

Monitor the collection and receive periodic feedback
Review products with instructors; determine if criteria are being met

Reflect on the products and revise as needed
Add or change components based on feedback

NOTE: The American Association for Higher Education (AAHE) has developed a book on how to create electronic portfolios (*Electronic Portfolios: Emerging Practices in Student, Faculty, and Institutional Learning*, AAHE, 2002) and a searchable database of sample e-portfolios. For more information, see http://aahe.ital.utexas.edu/electronicportfolios/index. html.

Sources: Barrett, H. C. (2000). Create your own electronic portfolio. *Learning and Leading with Technology, 27*(7), 14–21; and Hanfland, P. (1999). Electronic portfolios. *Learning and Leading with Technology, 26*(6), 54–57.

- **Multimedia authoring software** — Early multimedia structures were in *HyperCard* or *HyperStudio,* but some teachers now structure portfolios with packages such as Microsoft *PowerPoint*, Macromedia *Director,* Travantis *Lectora,* or eZedia's *eZediaQTI.* These packages allow for advanced and sophisticated video and audio presentations.
- **Databases** — Relational database software such as *FileMaker Pro* is helpful to teachers who must keep track of many students' work. They offer teachers the advantage of cataloguing work and creating profiles of achievement across groups of students.
- **Websites** — Portfolios also may be posted on the Internet, where they can be more easily shared with others. Like multimedia packages, these portfolios can offer sophisticated video and audio presentations. Companies that act as hosts for electronic portfolios are listed at http://electronicportfolios.com/portfolios/bookmarks .html#vendors.

- **Video** — Although analog video offered only a low-cost, linear format, digital video offers much more flexible, interactive formats to display portfolio elements.

Figure 1.16 shows a suggested sequence to follow to create an electronic portfolio. Also see Barrett (2000) and her collection of portfolio resources at http:// electronicportfolios.com/ for more advice on portfolio development, and Hanfland (1999) for tips on portfolio development for young children.

INTERACTIVE SUMMARY

The following is a summary of the main points covered in this chapter. To see additional examples and information on these points, go to this textbook's Companion Website at http://www.prenhall.com/roblyer and click on the Chapter 1 *Interactive Summary* module to visit each of the recommended websites.

1. **Four perspectives that define educational technology:** The following educational technology organizations represent the four views of educational technology described in this chapter:

   - AECT — Technology as media and AV communications

   - ISPI — Technology as instructional systems and instructional design

   - ITEA — Technology as vocational training (a.k.a., technology education)

   - ISTE — Technology as computer systems.

2. **History of educational computing technology and what we have learned from it:** The three eras in the history of educational computing/technology were:

   - **Pre-Microcomputer Era (1950–late 1970s)** — University projects use mainframe and minicomputer systems to deliver instruction in schools; the computer literacy movement begins.

   - **Microcomputer Era (late 1970s–1994)** — Microcomputers enter schools and spawn the software publishing, Logo, and ILS movements.

   - **Internet Era (1994–present)** — The first web browser (*Mosaic*) makes possible travel on the Information Superhighway.

3. **A rationale for using educational technology:** Elements of a rationale for using technology in education include increased motivation, unique instructional capabilities, support for new instructional approaches, increased productivity, and required skills for an information age (technological literacy, information literacy, and visual literacy). The research rationale for using technology in teaching is documented at the CARET website.

4. **Current educational technology systems, configurations, and applications:** Get some ideas on designs for computer labs and what factors you should consider as you purchase and set up labs. Also, look at pictures of computers on wheels (COWs) and mobile labs. Remember that one of the primary concerns in setting up and maintaining any computer lab is accessibility for all users. Review this accessibility checklist for all the factors that should be considered.

5. **Factors shaping the climate for technology integration:** These include current educational technology systems, configurations, and applications. Issues include

   - Societal (economic, anti-technology positions, impact of the No Child Left Behind Act

   - Educational (standards movement, reliance on Internet and distance education, and debate over directed vs. constructivist methods)

   - Cultural and equity (Digital Divide, racial and gender equity, special needs)

   - Legal and ethical (viruses/hacking, online plagiarism, privacy/safety, copyright, illegal downloads/ software piracy).

6. **Emerging trends in hardware/software development:** These include:

   - Wireless connectivity

   - Merging of technologies

   - Developments in portable devices

   - Increasingly high-speed communications (e.g., through cable modem and DSL)

   - Visual immersion systems

   - Intelligent applications

7. **New skills for the future:** The International Society for Technology in Education established the National Educational Technology Skills (NETS) for students, teachers, and administrators. These standards document skills that will be essential in order to take advantage of emerging technology capabilities. People often use electronic portfolios to demonstrate technology and other skills they have attained.

Online Activities

Visit this text's Companion Website at http://www. prenhall.com/roblyer to gain access to a variety of questions, activities, and exercises to help build your knowledge of this chapter's content.

Online Chapter I Self-Test

To review terms and concepts for this chapter, click on the *Self-Test* module for this chapter of the Companion Website.

Software Skill-Builder Tutorials

To access practical tutorial and skill-building activities that will help you build skills using popular software and hardware, click on the *Software Skill-Builder Tutorials* module for this chapter of the Companion Website.

Web-Enrichment Activities

To complete activities that connect to chapter content and provide web-based resources, click on the *Web-Enrichment Activities* module for this chapter of the Companion Website.

TECHNOLOGY INTEGRATION WORKSHOP

CLIPS FROM THE CLASSROOM: LEARNING WITH TECHNOLOGY

Go to the *Technology Integration Workshop* DVD located in the back of this text and click on *Clips from the Classroom.* View the video clips listed below that support this chapter's content:

- *Assessment Examples Illustrated*
- SmartBoards *for Students with Hearing Impairments*
- *Tablet Computers Facilitate Learning*
- *Students Discuss Tablet Use*
- *Tablet Computers in Spanish*
- *Secondary Students Respond Positively*
- *Student Achievement Increases*

Now, visit this text's Companion Website at http://www.prenhall.com/roblyer to answer questions and complete activities that will guide you in analyzing each clip.

TIE INTO PRACTICE: TECHNOLOGY INTEGRATION EXAMPLES

Read each of the following scenarios related to implementing the TIP Model, and go to the Companion Website to answer the questions that follow it based on your Chapter 1 reading activities.

TIE-In #1: Perspectives on Educational Technology

A federal grant that the Paradigm School District wanted to apply for required that applicants have a district-wide technology plan in place. The superintendent appointed a Technology Committee to develop the plan. In the first meeting, veteran high school computer-assisted design (CAD) teacher Redd Borders said, "Of course, it's obvious that our plan must be structured around the technology education skills students need to learn in order to get a job. We can justify all the materials and equipment we'll need by listing them under the job skills." Curriculum coordinator Edna Gaines said, "Wait a minute, what about using computers for teaching and for helping students learn better?" "Oh, that stuff is just frills," said Redd. "What we really need to focus on is how technology can help our stu-

dents get a job after they graduate!" "Well, personally, I think we should let the audiovisual department develop this plan," said media specialist Twyla Jennings. "They're the ones who have always helped schools use all our equipment." When the meeting adjourned 2 hours later, the committee was still arguing abut what the plan's focus should be and who should be in charge of it.

1.1 Based on what you read in this chapter about the four perspectives on educational technology, explain what could have caused this disagreement on the basics of the technology plan.

1.2 Was one of the members' perspectives most correct? Explain why.

TIE-In #2: History

Ruie Frey was the social studies coordinator for a large urban school district. After attending a state workshop on using videos to help teach social studies, she proposed to the superintendent that the district develop its own set of video-based materials to support high school social studies instruction. She said that the district social studies teacher council could meet and outline a series of videos to support the district's required curriculum, and district media center personnel could train teachers to develop the videos. She requested that the district budget funds to award a stipend to each social studies teacher who agreed to develop one or more of the videos. She said this plan would be cost effective because it would be far cheaper to have teachers develop their own video materials than to buy the ones commercially available, and the district would be more certain that the videos were what the teachers would need, want, and use in their classrooms.

2.1 Describe what we have learned from the history of technology in education that could help the superintendent react appropriately to this proposal.

2.2 Based on what you read in Chapter 1, propose a more workable way to meet the needs of the district's social studies teachers.

TIE-In #3: A "Why Use Technology" Rationale

A school district instructional technology coordinator wanted the district to buy a new computer lab for a local foreign languages magnet school. She asked the magnet school coordinator to give her a summary of "hard research" to show how various technologies improve achievement and attendance in high school language learning courses, which she felt would help her "sell" this purchase to the school board.

3.1 Describe the assumption the coordinator is making about the benefits of technology for instruction. Based on what you read at the CARET website about educational technology research, explain why this "selling strategy" may not be a sufficient rationale.

3.2 What societal and economic conditions described in Chapter 1 may have led to the coordinator's requiring "hard research" of this kind? How does the NCLB act refer to "hard research"?

TIE-In #4: Current Technology Resources Lennie, a high school journalism teacher, was contemplating how to justify five multimedia production stations (each consisting of a computer and multimedia production software) he wanted to purchase for the journalism lab. This year, the district had funds available for instructional materials but not equipment. Lennie felt he could justify the stations as instructional materials, because they couldn't do the task of multimedia production without the multimedia software. Therefore, he reasoned that his purchase justification statement to buy the five stations could list the purchase category as "instructional materials."

4.1 Explain how and why the purchasing agent in the district business office would probably react to this justification statement.

4.2 Find out and explain why it is necessary for schools to divide technology purchases into equipment and materials.

TIE-In #5: Societal Issues Over the summer, the Empire School District installed computers connected to the Internet in every school classroom. In the district-wide faculty meeting at the beginning of the year, the district technology coordinator made a pitch to teachers to allow students to use their classroom computers after school whenever possible. He said that this would help give students access to computers they might not get at home and may help lessen the "Digital Divide." When one teacher asked who could help these students use the computers, he replied, "These kids know more about computers than we do. They will do just fine helping each other." One teacher remarked that, since each school has a computer

club, they might call on the members to help supervise after-school uses.

5.1 Based on what you read in Chapter 1, describe the kinds of problems that could arise from the kind of access the technology coordinator was advocating.

5.2 Explain why this strategy would or would not help address the Digital Divide.

TIE-In #6: Legal/Ethical Issues One of the school board members in your district has become alarmed at the increasing number of stories in the news about students using the Internet to plagiarize other people's work. She has asked for a district-wide policy that students not be permitted to access the Internet in schools unless it is in a library media center and they are under the supervision of a trained library media specialist. The board has asked you, the district technology coordinator, to react to this proposal.

6.1 After reading Gardiner's article (2001) about online plagiarism and McNabb's article (2001) on appropriate usage guidelines, what would you say about the feasibility and desirability of the school board member's proposal?

6.2 What other ways could you propose to the board to address the potential problem of online plagiarism in your district?

TIE-In #7: Equity Issues You are a math/science resource teacher in an elementary school. Your principal just returned from a seminar on gender equity issues, where she learned about the long-standing trend of females entering science and engineering fields in far fewer numbers than males. She also learned that girls' opinions on career options begin to be shaped at early levels of school. She asks you to recommend some hardware, software, and materials she could purchase that would encourage girls to consider going into technical fields and some additional hands-on activities such as science simulations that might interest girls at this age.

7.1 After reading the AAUW report *Tech-Savvy: Educating Girls in the New Computer Age* (2000) and the Margolis and Fisher article (2002), what positives and negatives could you tell her about the approach she has recommended?

7.2 What other, perhaps more effective, strategies could you suggest to address the problems she has identified?

TIE-In #8: Distance Education Issues The superintendent of the large school district in which you are a high school math teacher has been talking to administrators of a virtual high school consortium. He has decided the district should offer its high-level math and science courses, especially the advanced placement courses, in a "virtual" environment. He feels this will save money and offer more equitable access to the courses, since qualified teachers for all schools are hard to find. Most courses have already been developed by the virtual school consortium and are available for students to use. He has asked all the high school math and science teachers to come to a meeting to discuss how to replace the current course offerings with online ones.

8.1 After reading the articles and reports on virtual high schools listed in Figure 1.12, what would you recommend the superintendent consider before going ahead with this plan?

8.2 If the decision is made to do what he has recommended, what could you suggest to make the proposed change work more effectively for students?

TIE-In #9: Anti-Technology Issues A parent of a child in your school has read a report called *Fool's Gold: A Critical Look at Computers in Childhood* by the Alliance for Childhood (1999), which is highly critical of using computers in schools. Another parent has read Oppenheimer's *The Flickering Mind* (2003). The parents passed the report and book on to all of the school board members, who found them very disconcerting. They were especially upset since a bond issue had just been placed on the ballot to pay for technology upgrades and Internet connections for the schools. One board member suggested that perhaps the bond issue should be removed from the ballot until the question of the benefits of using computers in education could be clarified. The issue was put on the agenda for discussion at the next school board meeting. Your superintendent knows you are an advocate for using technology in education and asks you to speak to the board.

9.1 What could you tell the school board that might give them a context for understanding this and other similar reports?

9.2 What evidence could you provide to support your belief that technology has an important role to play in education? (Limit your comments to the three strongest points.)

TIE-In #10: Privacy/Safety Issues One of the teachers in your school told you about a project in which his students were doing research on the Internet. One of the students said he had "met" someone in a chat room who was an astronaut in the NASA program. The teacher encouraged several other students who were interested in space careers to contact that same person in the chat room and do a group presentation of their findings.

10.1 Does this sound like a good strategy to you? Why or why not?

10.2 After looking at the information at the University of Delaware website on writing an AUP, what should a school be sure to include in its AUP that addresses situations like this?

For Your Teaching Portfolio

At the end of each of Chapters 2 through 15 in this textbook, you will have an opportunity to add products to your teaching portfolio to show what you know and what you are able to do with technology in education. In this introductory chapter, review the information on teaching portfolios in the section titled How Teachers Can Demonstrate Their Skills: Electronic Portfolios (page 27); determine the portfolio requirements for your program; and begin creating your portfolio structure.

CHAPTER 2

FOUNDATIONS OF EFFECTIVE TECHNOLOGY INTEGRATION MODELS: THEORY AND PRACTICE

A theme in [American education] is that natural, real-world simulations . . . are superior to the artificial, step-by-step methods of traditional schooling. . . . Should students be immersed right away in complex situations that simulate real life . . . or should they first be provided with explicit modes of instruction that focus on small chunks deliberately isolated from the complexities of actual situations?

E. D. Hirsch, in *Classroom Research and Cargo Cults* (2002)

A Tale of Two Technology Integration Strategies

Which Strategy Works Best?

Strategy A: Preparing students for state tests

One of Bill's responsibilities as Mathematics Department chair was helping all teachers make sure their students did well on the mathematics portion of the state's Test of Essential Skills for Success (TESS). Because students could not go on to high school unless they passed the TESS, Bill and the other math teachers were determined that every student in the school would pass TESS-M, the math portion. They were also determined that they would not just "teach to the test." They wanted the students to have a good grounding in math skills that would serve them well in their future education.

From practice test scores he had seen, Bill realized that there were too many students who needed help to provide individual coaches or tutors for each one, and he disliked the idea of making all students work on skills only some of them needed. At a school he had visited in another district, Bill had been impressed with how teachers relied on a computer-based system that included drills, tutorials, simulations, and problem-solving activities that they could access in their rooms or from the computer lab.

One of the benefits of the system was that students could take practice tests and teachers could get a list of skills on which they were having problems. Then the system would recommend specific activities, on and off the system, matched to each child's needs. The activities ranged from practice in very basic math skills to solving "real-life" problems that required algebra and other math skills. Bill persuaded the principal to purchase a year's subscription to this system, and he and the other math teachers agreed on ways they would use it to supplement their classroom instruction.

That year, every student at the school passed TESS-M. The math teachers agreed that the computer-based activities had played a key role in students' preparation. They liked the way it helped them be more efficient at targeting students' specific needs while not overemphasizing test-taking. Bill asked the principal to make the system a permanent part of the school's budget.

Strategy B: A simulated family project

Mayda's seventh-grade math students are usually fairly good at math skills; almost none of them have any trouble passing the state's criterion-referenced test. However, she likes to do at least one ongoing project each year to show them how their math skills apply to real-life situations. She also wants them to learn to work together to solve problems just as they would be doing in college and in work situations when they graduated.

The first activity she does at the beginning of each year is have her students work in small groups to simulate "families." They select a type of "job" their "wage earner" will have, create a monthly budget in a spreadsheet template she has set up, showing income earned from an imaginary job versus estimated monthly expenses for each of them and for the "family." To select jobs, the groups consult online newspaper Help Wanted sections to get an idea of what positions are available and how much they pay.

To estimate expenses, they look at online newspaper and real estate ads to see how much it costs to rent a house or an apartment in an area they would like to live. Throughout the year, she gives each group unexpected monthly expenses (e.g., the dog gets sick, the roof is leaking) and they must adjust their spreadsheet budget to compensate for the extra expenses. If they get too far out of line with their budgeted expenses, she makes the group get a "loan," by researching available interest rates and adding a loan payment to their spreadsheet budgets that will pay off their "debt."

Toward the end of the year, she has them download a 1040 tax return form from the IRS website and do estimated taxes. Finally, they do a report using *PowerPoint* software to show charts of their spending and what they learned about "making ends meet." The students always tell her this is the most meaningful math activity they have ever done.

OBJECTIVES

After reading this chapter and completing the learning activities for it, you should be able to:

1. Match directed and constructivist integration strategies with their learning theory foundations.

2. Identify technology integration strategies as directed, constructivist, or combinations of these.

3. Describe the five phases of the Technology Integration Planning (TIP) Model.

4. Match descriptions of instructional problems with technology-based solutions that have the potential for high relative advantage to teachers and students.

5. Create outcome objectives and assessment plans for technology integration strategies.

6. For a given technology integration strategy, create an instructional plan that is pedagogically sound and addresses equity and classroom implementation needs.

7. For a given technology integration plan, create a logistical plan that addresses ethical, legal, equipment, scheduling, and technical issues.

8. Develop a plan to evaluate the impact of a given technology integration strategy.

9. Describe essential conditions to support effective classroom integration of technology.

10. Use the five-phase TIP Model to develop a sample classroom technology integration strategy.

KEY TERMS

- acceptable use policy (AUP)
- accommodation
- anchored instruction
- assimilation
- automaticity
- classical conditioning
- constructivist learning
- constructivists
- contingencies of reinforcement
- directed instruction
- discovery learning
- Events of Instruction
- firewall software
- inquiry-based learning
- learning hierarchies
- Likert scale
- long-term memory (LTM)
- mastery learning
- multiple intelligences
- objectivists
- operant conditioning
- programmed learning
- relative advantage
- rubric
- scaffolding
- semantic differential
- sensory registers
- short-term memory (STM)
- social activism
- systems approaches to instructional design
- zone of proximal development (ZPD)

For more information on Key Terms, go to the *Key Terms* module for this chapter of the Companion Website at http://www.prenhall.com/roblyer.

THEORETICAL AND PROCEDURAL FOUNDATIONS OF TECHNOLOGY INTEGRATION

As the opening scenario illustrates, the answer to Hirsch's question in the opening quote about "what kind of learning works best" is fundamental to understanding when technology works best. As Hirsch himself acknowledges later in his article, the answer is "The right method depends on the situation." Just as different learning needs call for different teaching methods, effective technology integration depends on a well-planned match of needs with resources and teaching strategies, along with classroom conditions that support them.

Figure 2.1 **An Enlightened Approach to Technology Integration**

This chapter describes the three factors that create the enlightened approach to effective technology integration strategies depicted in Figure 2.1:

- **Learning theory bases** — Since technologies are used to carry out learning strategies, it is important to begin with a look at two very different, competing theories of how learning should take place and examine how various kinds of integration strategies were derived from them.

- **Planning model** — For the procedural and "people" issues involved in technology integration, we look to a five-phase planning model and how teachers use it to plan technology-based lessons.

- **Essential conditions** — The International Society for Technology in Education (ISTE) emphasizes that technology-based strategies work best when optimal conditions are in place to support them. Thus, a review of these conditions is the final piece in the foundation.

Learning Theories as Bases for Integration Models

Directed and Constructivist Instruction Models: How Two Worlds Evolved

Prior to about 1980, there seemed little question about the appropriate instructional role for technology, particularly computer technology. According to respected writers of the time (Taylor, 1980), there were three acceptable roles: computers as tools to support learning (e.g., word processing, calculations), as tutors to deliver instruction (e.g., drill and practice, tutorials), and as "tutees" (e.g., learning to program computers).

However, as technology has become more capable and complex, everyday life has changed, and with it, our views of education and appropriate teaching strategies. In the past, educational goals reflected society's emphasis on the need for basic skills—such as reading, writing, and arithmetic—and an agreed-on body of information considered essential for everyone. Many educators now believe that the world is changing too quickly to define education in terms of specific information or skills; they believe it should focus on more general capabilities such as "learning to learn" skills that will help future citizens cope with inevitable technological change.

While everyone seems to agree that changes are needed to respond to modern challenges, they seem to disagree on which strategies will serve today's educational goals. As Hirsch (2002) points out in the opening quote, this controversy has been a catalyst for crystalizing two different views on teaching and learning. One view, which we will call **directed instruction,** is grounded primarily in behaviorist learning theory and the information-processing branch of the cognitive learning theories. The other view, which we will refer to as **constructivist** or **inquiry-based learning,** evolved from other branches of thinking in cognitive learning theory. A few technology applications such as drill and practice and tutorials are associated only with directed instruction; most others (problem solving, multimedia production, web-based learning) can enhance either directed instruction or constructivist learning, depending on how they are used.

This book is based on the premise that there are meaningful roles for both directed instruction and constructivist strategies and the technology applications associated with them. Both can help teachers and students meet the many and varied requirements of learning in today's Information Age society.

Theoretical Foundations of Directed and Constructivist Models

Like most people with radically different views on the same issue, **objectivists** and **constructivists** frequently use different terms to describe essentially the same things. Sfard (1998) says that differences in the language used to describe learning spring from two different metaphors used for learning: the acquisition metaphor and the participation metaphor. She notes that "…the acquisition metaphor is likely to be more prominent in older writings, [and] more recent studies are often

Figure 2.2 Two Epistemological "Planets": Objectivism and Constructivism

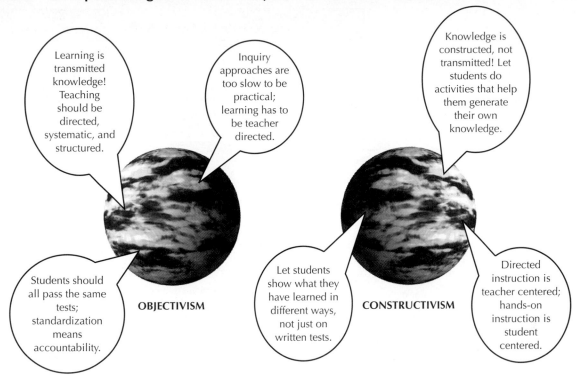

dominated by the participation metaphor" (p. 5). These differences in language signal fundamental differences in thinking about how learning takes place and how we can foster it. Figure 2.2 gives examples of how educators use different terms to describe the same things because of their differing views.

How did these differences come about? It is important to recognize that people who espouse both directed instruction and constructivist approaches are attempting to identify what Gagné (1985)called the *conditions of learning* or the "sets of circumstances that obtain when learning occurs" (p. 2). Both approaches are based on the work of respected learning theorists and psychologists who have studied both the behavior of human beings as learning organisms and the behavior of students in schools and classrooms.

Educators' views diverge, however, in the ways they define learning, how they identify the conditions required to make learning happen, and how they perceive the problems that interfere most with learning. They disagree because they attend to different philosophies and learning theories and, consequently, they take different perspectives on improving current educational practice. Figures 2.3 and 2.4 show the learning theories that underlie each perspective.

As Figures 2.3 and 2.4 show, the two sets of learning theories have very different underlying epistemologies: beliefs about the nature of human knowledge, as well as how

to develop it. *Constructivists* (those who espouse inquiry-based methods based on cognitive, developmental, and generative/discovery theories) and *objectivists* (those who espouse directed methods based on behavioral, cognitive-behavioral, and information processing theories) come from separate and different epistemological "planets," although both nurture many different tribes or cultures (Molenda, 1991; Phillips, 1995). The characteristics and theoretical origins of these philosophical differences can be summarized in the following way:

- **Objectivists** — *Knowledge has a separate, real existence of its own outside the human mind.* Learning happens when this knowledge is transmitted to people and they store it in their minds.

- **Constructivists** — *Humans construct all knowledge in their minds by participating in certain experiences.* Learning occurs when one constructs both mechanisms for learning and his or her own unique version of the knowledge, colored by background, experiences, and aptitudes.

Learning theories underlying objectivist methods. As Figure 2.3 shows, objectivists attend to concepts that evolved from behavioral, information-processing, and cognitive behaviorist learning theories and the **systems approaches to instructional design** that were based on them. The basic concepts of these theories are described

Figure 2.3   Theories Underlying Directed Technology Integration Strategies

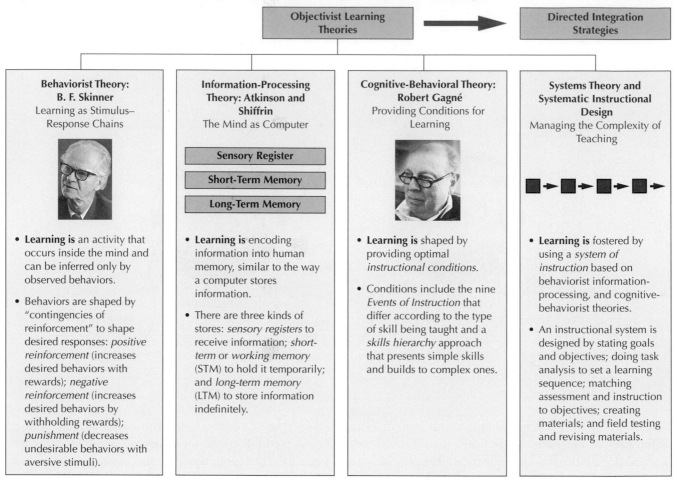

Objectivist Learning Theories → Directed Integration Strategies

Behaviorist Theory: B. F. Skinner
Learning as Stimulus–Response Chains

- **Learning is** an activity that occurs inside the mind and can be inferred only by observed behaviors.
- Behaviors are shaped by "contingencies of reinforcement" to shape desired responses: *positive reinforcement* (increases desired behaviors with rewards); *negative reinforcement* (increases desired behaviors by withholding rewards); *punishment* (decreases undesirable behaviors with aversive stimuli).

Information-Processing Theory: Atkinson and Shiffrin
The Mind as Computer

Sensory Register
Short-Term Memory
Long-Term Memory

- **Learning is** encoding information into human memory, similar to the way a computer stores information.
- There are three kinds of stores: *sensory registers* to receive information; *short-term* or *working memory* (STM) to hold it temporarily; and *long-term memory* (LTM) to store information indefinitely.

Cognitive-Behavioral Theory: Robert Gagné
Providing Conditions for Learning

- **Learning is** shaped by providing optimal *instructional conditions*.
- Conditions include the nine *Events of Instruction* that differ according to the type of skill being taught and a *skills hierarchy* approach that presents simple skills and builds to complex ones.

Systems Theory and Systematic Instructional Design
Managing the Complexity of Teaching

- **Learning is** fostered by using a *system of instruction* based on behaviorist information-processing, and cognitive-behaviorist theories.
- An instructional system is designed by stating goals and objectives; doing task analysis to set a learning sequence; matching assessment and instruction to objectives; creating materials; and field testing and revising materials.

---

briefly here, and their implications for education and for technology integration are summarized in Figure 2.5.

- **Behaviorist theories: B. F. Skinner** — Called by some "the most influential psychologist of the 20th century" (Eggen & Kauchak, 2004, p. 200), Skinner's **operant conditioning** concepts built on the **classical conditioning** concepts of Russian physiologist Ivan Pavlov. While Pavlov viewed learning as involuntary *physical* responses to outside stimuli (e.g., dogs salivate at the sight of a dog food can), Skinner said that people can have voluntary *mental* control over their responses and that the consequences of their past actions can act as stimuli to shape future behaviors. He said that since learning processes occur inside the mind and we cannot see them directly, learning can only be inferred by observing behaviors. He believed learned behaviors could be shaped by **contingencies of reinforcement** set up to shape desired responses: positive reinforcement (e.g., praise for correct answers) and negative reinforcement (e.g., avoiding detention by being on time to school) increase

behaviors, while punishment decreases behaviors (e.g., refraining from violence after being expelled for fighting). Skinner used reinforcement principles to develop **programmed learning** techniques, for training and instruction. Later, Benjamin Bloom used Skinner's principles in his **mastery learning** concepts, an approach that gave students a sequence of objectives that defined mastery of the subject. Students had to pass tests on each objective to demonstrate they had mastered a skill before proceeding to the next one. Today, many classroom management techniques are based on behavior modification principles derived from Skinner's reinforcement principles (e.g., students get praise or an entertaining graphic for correct answers; students memorize important basic skills by increasing the frequency of correct responses to problems).

- **Information-processing theories** — Because many people found Skinner's "learning as behavior-shaping concepts" insufficient to guide instruction, the first cognitive (as opposed to behavioral) learning theorists began to hypothesize processes *inside the brain* that al-

Figure 2.4 Theories Underlying Inquiry-Based Technology Integration Strategies

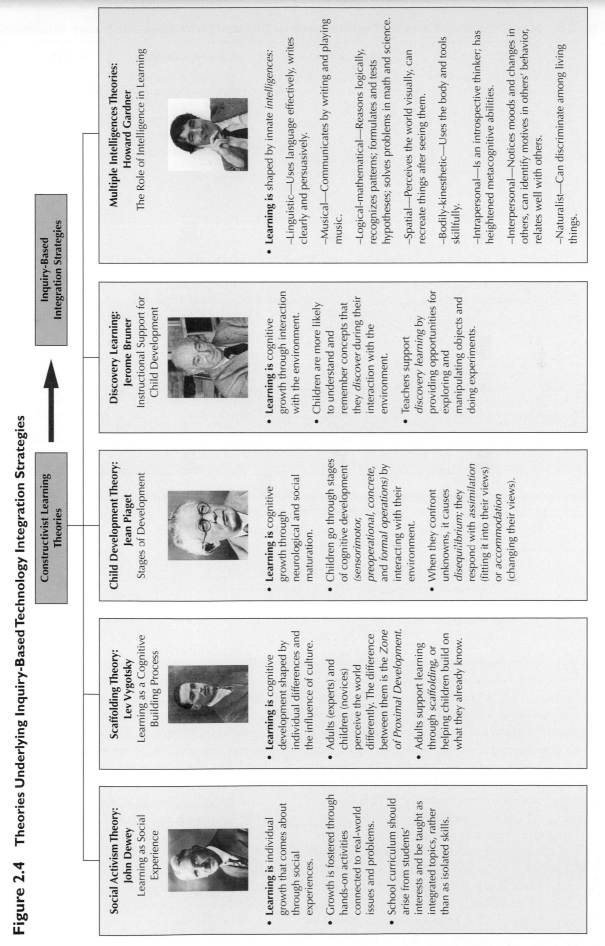

Figure 2.5   How Objectivist Learning Theories Lead to Directed Technology Integration Strategies

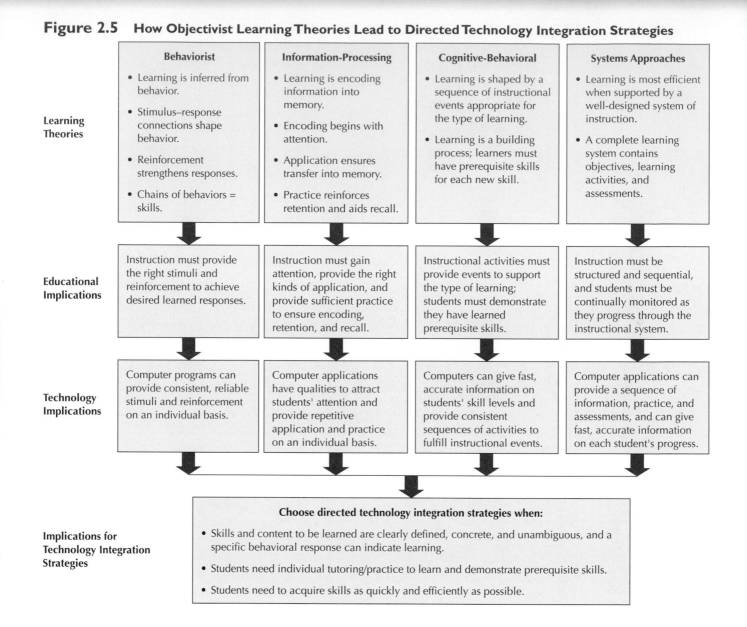

low human beings to learn and remember. Much of the work of the information-processing theorists is based on a model of memory and storage proposed by Atkinson and Shiffrin (1968), who said that the brain contains three kinds of memory or "stores," to process information—much like a computer. **Sensory registers** receive information a person senses through receptors (i.e., eyes, ears, nose, mouth, and/or hands). After a second or so, the information is either lost or transferred to **short-term memory (STM)** or working memory. STM holds new information for about 5 to 20 seconds. Unless it is processed or practiced in a way that causes it to transfer to **long-term memory (LTM),** it also is lost. LTM can hold information indefinitely, but for new information to be transferred to LTM, it must be linked in some way to prior knowledge already in LTM. Common teaching practices

based on these concepts include the use of (1) interesting questions and eye-catching material to help students pay attention to a new topic; (2) instructions that point out important points in new material to help students remember them by linking them to information they already know; and (3) practice exercises to help transfer information from STM to LTM. Guidelines for enhancing attention, encoding, and storage processes include (1) Gagné's hierarchical "bottom-up" approach, in which students learn lower order or prerequisite skills first (e.g., multiplication skills required to learn long-division skills) and build on them; and (2) Ausubel's "top-down" approach, in which "advance organizers" or topic overviews give students mental frameworks on which to "hang" new information. Computer programs provide ideal environments for the highly structured cueing, attention-getting, and practice features that information-processing theorists have found so essential to learning.

- **Cognitive-behavioral theory: Robert Gagné** — An educational psychologist who translated principles from behavioral and information-processing theories into practical instructional strategies for teachers and trainers, Gagné used research on information-processing models of learning to derive guidelines for arranging optimal "conditions of learning." Guidelines included **learning hierarchies** and the nine **Events of Instruction** for several types of learning: gaining attention, informing the learner of the objective, stimulating recall of prerequisite learning, presenting new material, providing learning guidance, eliciting performance, providing feedback about correctness, assessing performance, and enhancing retention and recall. Gagné also identified several types of learned behaviors and showed how teachers would use the Events of Instruction slightly differently to foster each type of learning. Types of learned behaviors are (1) intellectual skills, which included problem solving, higher order rules, defined concepts, concrete concepts, and discriminations; (2) cognitive strategies, or novel problem solutions and complex product; (3) verbal information or rote learning; (4) motor skills, or physical abilities; and (5) attitudes. The development of "intellectual skills" called for a building process: Lower level skills provide a necessary foundation for higher level ones. For example, to learn to work long-division problems, students first have to learn all the prerequisite math skills: number recognition, number facts, simple addition and subtraction, multiplication, and simple division. Therefore, to teach a higher level skill, a teacher must teach this learning hierarchy or set of building block skills. Gagné, Wager, and Rojas (1981) showed how Gagné's Events of Instruction could be used to plan lessons using each kind of instructional software (drill, tutorial, simulation). They said that only a tutorial could "stand by itself" and accomplish all of the necessary Events of Instruction; the other kinds of software required teacher-led activities to accomplish events before and after software use.

- **Systems approaches: instructional design models** — These methods have their roots in the collaborative work of educational psychologists Robert Gagné and Leslie Briggs, who developed a way to apply principles learned from military and industrial training to developing curriculum and instruction for schools. They believed that learning was most efficient when it was supported by a carefully designed system of instruction. Gagné promoted *instructional task analysis* to identify required learning hierarchy subskills and conditions of learning for them. Briggs offered systematic methods of designing training programs to save companies time and money in training their personnel. When combined, these areas of expertise became a set of step-by-step processes known as a *systems approach to instructional design,* or *systematic instructional design,* which came into common use in the 1970s and 1980s. Other names associated with this era include Robert Mager (instructional objectives), Glaser (criterion-referenced testing), Cronbach and Scriven (formative and summative evaluation), David Merrill (component display theory), and Charles Reigeluth (elaboration theory). Since instructional design results in a highly structured sequence of instruction, computer tutorials and self-paced distance learning courses offer ideal delivery systems for instruction design through these approaches.

Teaching methods and technology integration strategies that reflect objectivist theories. A considerable body of research indicates that directed methods work well for addressing certain kinds of teaching/learning problems. For example, Carnine, Silbert, and Kameenui (1997) and Stein, Silbert, and Carnine (1997) found that drill and practice can help teach basic reading and mathematics skills. Spence and Hively (1993) found that increased fluency practice supports precision teaching of basic reading and math skills to young learners. Mallott (1993) found that using reinforcement principles can improve the study habits and achievement of college students, and Carnine (1993) found that structured, teacher-directed techniques were effective in teaching problem-solving and higher order thinking skills to at-risk students. Hirsch (2002) says that studies show that "one minute of explicit (directed) learning can be more effective than a month of implicit (exploratory) learning."

Objectivists focus primarily on technology integration strategies for systematically designed, structured learning products such as drills, tutorials, and integrated learning systems (ILSs; discussed in Chapter 3). When they do use other, more open-ended materials such as simulations and problem-solving software, the integration strategies are very structured, focusing on providing a step-by-step sequence of learning activities matched to specific performance objectives. When objectivists evaluate these products, they typically look for a match among objectives, methods, and assessment strategies and how well they help teachers and students meet curriculum standards. To reflect objectivist principles, materials and integration strategies must have clearly defined objectives and a set sequence for their use.

Learning theories underlying constructivist methods. Figure 2.4 shows that constructivist beliefs and methods were derived from a combination of concepts in **social activism, scaffolding,** stages of development, and **multiple intelligences** theories. The basic concepts of these theories are described briefly here, and their implications for education and for technology integration are summarized in Figure 2.6.

- **Social activism theory: John Dewey** — An early proponent of racial equality and women's suffrage, John Dewey's radical activism shaped his beliefs about education. Identified closely with the Progressive Education reform initiative popular in the first half of the 1990s, many of his principles of education were in direct opposition to those of that period. Dewey deplored standardization and believed that curriculum should arise from students' interests. He also believed that curriculum topics should be integrated, rather than isolated, since teaching isolated topics prevented learners from grasping the whole of knowledge. He felt that education is growth, rather than an end in itself and that the common view that education is preparation for work separated society into social classes. Instead, Dewey believed education should be a way of helping individuals understand their culture and develop their relationship to and unique roles in society. Since he felt that social consciousness was the ultimate aim of all education, learning was useful only in the context of social experience. He found reading and mathematics had become ends in themselves, disconnected from any meaningful social context. Dewey believed that learning should be hands-on and experience-based, and that meaningful learning resulted from students working together on tasks related to their interests. Though considered by many the Grandfather of Constructivism, Dewey also advocated a merging of "absolutism" and "experimentalism," just as this chapter calls for combining directed and constructivist methods. Although he probably would deplore the current standards movement and the use of high-stakes testing programs, today's interdisciplinary curriculum and hands-on, experience-based learning are in tune with Dewey's lifelong message. Bruce (2000) says that Dewey would approve of technologies like the Internet to help students communicate with each other and learn more about their society. Dewey's call for cooperative learning would mesh well with technology-based group projects and presentations.

- **Scaffolding theories: Lev Semenovich Vygotsky** — Until the end of the Cold War in the 1990s, the writings of Russian philosopher and educational psychologist Lev Vygotsky had more influence on educational theory and practice in the United States than in his own country. His landmark book, *Pedagogical Psychology,* written in 1926, was not published in Russia until 1991 (Davydov, 1995). Since he viewed learners as individuals rather than as part of a "collective," his educational concepts were threatening to a communistic state, but found a warm reception in a democracy. He felt that how children learn and think derives directly from the culture around them. An adult perceives things much differently than a child, but this difference decreases as children translate their social views into personal/psychological ones. Vygotsky used the term **Zone of Proximal Development (ZPD)** to refer to the difference between adult/expert and child/novice levels of cognitive functioning. He felt that teachers could provide good instruction by finding out where each child was in his or her development and building on the child's experiences, a process he called *scaffolding.* Ormrod (2001) said that teachers promote students' cognitive development by presenting some classroom tasks that "they can complete only with assistance, that is, within each student's Zone of Proximal Development" (p. 59). Many of the visual technology tools from video-based scenarios to virtual reality are designed to scaffold students' understanding through graphic examples and real-life experiences relevant to their individual needs.

- **Child development theory: Jean Piaget** — Piaget referred to himself as a "genetic epistemologist," or a scientist who studies how knowledge begins and develops in individuals. He believed that, while the ages at which children mature vary somewhat, all children go through four stages of cognitive development, that each stage occurs only after certain genetically controlled neurological changes, and that all children develop higher reasoning abilities in the same sequence:

  - **Sensorimotor stage (birth–2 years)** — They explore the world around them through their senses and motor activity.

  - **Preoperational stage (2–7 years)** — They develop speech and symbolic activities (e.g., drawing objects, pretending, imagining), numerical abilities (e.g., assigning numbers and counting), increased self-control, and ability to delay gratification, but cannot do conservation tasks (recognizing that shape is not related to quantity).

  - **Concrete operational stage (7–11 years)** — They increase abstract reasoning, can generalize from concrete experiences, and can do conservation tasks.

Figure 2.6   How Constructivist Learning Theories Lead to Inquiry-Based Technology Integration Strategies

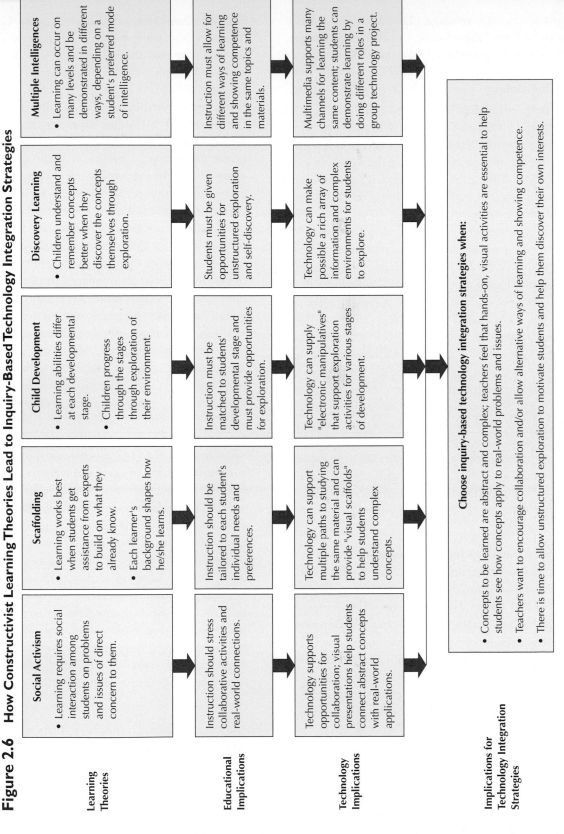

	Social Activism	Scaffolding	Child Development	Discovery Learning	Multiple Intelligences
Learning Theories	• Learning requires social interaction among students on problems and issues of direct concern to them.	• Learning works best when students get assistance from experts to build on what they already know. • Each learner's background shapes how he/she learns.	• Learning abilities differ at each developmental stage. • Children progress through the stages through exploration of their environment.	• Children understand and remember concepts better when they discover the concepts themselves through exploration.	• Learning can occur on many levels and be demonstrated in different ways, depending on a student's preferred mode of intelligence.
Educational Implications	Instruction should stress collaborative activities and real-world connections.	Instruction should be tailored to each student's individual needs and preferences.	Instruction must be matched to students' developmental stage and must provide opportunities for exploration.	Students must be given opportunities for unstructured exploration and self-discovery.	Instruction must allow for different ways of learning and showing competence in the same topics and materials.
Technology Implications	Technology supports opportunities for collaboration; visual presentations help students connect abstract concepts with real-world applications.	Technology can support multiple paths to studying the same material and can provide "visual scaffolds" to help students understand complex concepts.	Technology can supply "electronic manipulatives" that support exploration activities for various stages of development.	Technology can make possible a rich array of information and complex environments for students to explore.	Multimedia supports many channels for learning the same content; students can demonstrate learning by doing different roles in a group technology project.

Choose inquiry-based technology integration strategies when:

• Concepts to be learned are abstract and complex; teachers feel that hands-on, visual activities are essential to help students see how concepts apply to real-world problems and issues.

• Teachers want to encourage collaboration and/or allow alternative ways of learning and showing competence.

• There is time to allow unstructured exploration to motivate students and help them discover their own interests.

Implications for Technology Integration Strategies

43

- **Formal operations stage (12–15 years)** — They form and test hypotheses, organize information, and reason scientifically; they can show results of abstract thinking with symbolic materials (e.g., writing, drama).

Piaget believed children develop through these stages by interacting with the environment. When they confront new and unfamiliar features of their environment that do not fit with their current views of the world, they experience "disequilibrium." They learn by fitting the new experiences into the existing view of the world (i.e., **assimilation**) or change their views of the world to incorporate the new experiences (i.e., **accommodation**). He felt that children are active and motivated learners whose knowledge of the world becomes more integrated and organized over time. Although Piaget himself repeatedly expressed a lack of interest in how his work applied to school-based education, calling it "the American question," his pupil MIT mathematician Seymour Papert (1980) used Piaget's theories as the basis of his work with Logo, a language designed to let young students solve design problems using an on-screen "turtle." This environment provided the vital link that Papert felt would allow children to move more easily from the concrete operations of earlier stages of Piaget's hypothesis to more abstract (formal) ones. Papert's 1980 book *Mindstorms* challenged then-current instructional goals and methods for mathematics and became the first constructivist statement of educational practice with technology.

- **Discovery learning: Jerome Bruner** — Some of the principles associated with educational theorist Jerome Bruner seem to coincide with those of Vygotsky and Piaget. Like Piaget, Bruner believed children go through various stages of intellectual development. But unlike Piaget, Bruner supported intervention. He was primarily concerned with making education more relevant to student needs at each stage, and he believed that teachers could accomplish this by encouraging active participation in the learning process. Active participation, he felt, was best achieved by providing **discovery learning** environments that would let children explore alternatives and recognize relationships between ideas (Bruner, 1973). Bruner felt that students were more likely to understand and remember concepts they had discovered in the course of their own exploration. However, research findings have yielded mixed results for discovery learning, and the relatively unstructured methods recommended by Bruner have not found widespread support. Teachers have found that discovery learning is most successful when they provide some structured experiences first.

- **Multiple intelligences theory: Howard Gardner** — The only learning-developmental theory that attempts to define the role of intelligence in learning, Gardner's work is based on Guilford's pioneering work on the structure of intellect (Eggen & Kauchak, 2004) and on Sternberg's view of intelligence as influenced by culture (Ormrod, 2001). Gardner says there are at least eight different and relatively independent types of intelligence: *linguistic* (e.g., writers, journalists, poets use language effectively, are sensitive to the uses of language, and write clearly and persuasively); *musical* (e.g., composers, pianists, conductors understand musical structure and composition, communicate by writing or playing music); *logical-mathematical* (e.g., scientists, mathematicians, doctors reason logically in math terms, recognize patters in phenomena, formulate and test hypotheses, and solve problems in math and science); *spatial* (e.g., artists, sculptors, graphic artists receive the world in visual terms, notice and remember visual details, can recreate things after seeing them); *bodily-kinesthetic* (e.g., dancers, athletes, watchmakers see the body skillfully, manipulate things well with hands, use tools skillfully); *intrapersonal* (e.g., self-aware/self-motivated persons who are introspective thinkers, aware of their own motives, have heightened metacognitive abilities); *interpersonal* (e.g., psychologists, therapists, salespersons who notice moods and changes in others, can identify motives in others' behavior, relate well with others); and *naturalist* (e.g., botanist, biologists who can discriminate well among living things). According to Gardner's theory, IQ tests (which tend to stress linguistic/logical-mathematical abilities) cannot judge all students' ability to learn, and traditional academic tasks may not reflect true ability. This theory supports doing group work on multimedia products, assigning students group roles based on their type of intelligence (e.g., those with high interpersonal intelligence are project coordinators, those with high logical-mathematical ability are technical experts, and those with spatial ability are designers).

Teaching methods and technology integration strategies that reflect constructivist theories. As Figure 2.6 illustrates, constructivist methods are designed to make learning more visual and experiential and to allow students more flexibility in how they learn and demonstrate competence. These qualities were designed to address a problem John Seely Brown called *inert knowledge,* a term introduced by Whitehead in 1929 to mean skills that students learned but did not know how to transfer later to problems that required them (Brown, Collins, & Duguid, 1989). Brown said that inert knowledge resulted from learning skills in isolation from each other and from real-life application;

thus, he advocated *cognitive apprenticeships,* or activities that called for authentic problem solving, that is, solving problems in settings that are familiar and meaningful to students (CTGV, 1990). These ideas were based on the theories of Dewey, Vygotsky, Piaget, and Bruner.

The first technology integration strategies based on these ideas were Papert's Logo-supported "microworlds," in which children worked with a very visual programming language to create on-screen designs. Later, other technology-based materials such as the *Jasper Woodberry Problem Solving Series,* videodisc-based mathematics materials, were created by the now-disbanded Cognition and Technology Group at Vanderbilt (CTGV). These were designed to provide learning environments that reflected *situated cognition,* or instruction **anchored** in experiences that learners considered authentic because they emulated the behavior of adults. The CTGV felt that, with these materials, teachers could help students build on or "scaffold" from experiences they already had to generate their own knowledge in an active hands-on way, rather than receiving it passively. Today's constructivist integration strategies often focus on having students use data-gathering tools (e.g., handheld computers) to study problems and issues in their locale and creating multimedia products to present their new knowledge and insights.

Conflicting Views of Directed and Constructivist Methods

Not surprisingly, educators who attend to objectivist theories have dramatically different ideas about curriculum and teaching/learning methods than those who espouse constructivist theories. Sometimes these differences of opinion have generated strident debate in the literature (Baines & Stanley, 2000; *Educational Technology,* 1991a, 1991b). The debate continues because proponents of directed and constructivist views of learning focus on different kinds of problems (or different aspects of the same problems) confronting teachers and students in today's schools. Like the blind men trying to describe the elephant, each focuses on a different part of the problem, and each is correct in its own way.

Problems and needs addressed by directed and constructivist integration strategies. As Figure 2.7 illustrates, the characteristics of each model are specifically targeted to certain teaching and learning problems. Directed models stress individual work using traditional teaching and learning methods because they are designed to address problems of accountability and quality assurance in our educational system. Constructivist models, on the other hand, stress cooperative work and nontraditional exploration methods because they are designed to help students think on their own, work with diverse groups, and see the relevance of skills in their daily lives.

Assessment measures and grading strategies for directed and constructivist integration strategies. Figure 2.7 also shows the contrast in assessment methods used to support directed and constructivist methods. Because directed strategies are also mastery learning strategies, and teachers require clear, easily observable evidence that students have adequately mastered the skills, typical assessments for directed models are written objective tests (e.g., multiple choice, true/false, matching, short answer) and essays. Essays often are used to assess higher level performances such as writing a composition. Measures are graded according to preset criteria for what constitutes acceptable performance. Very often, a software package includes tests and built-in criteria for passing them. Essays usually are graded with a criteria checklist or writing **rubric,** an instrument consisting of a set of descriptions that define important components and qualities of the work.

Constructivists tend to eschew traditional assessment strategies as being too limiting to measure real progress in complex learning and too removed from real-life tasks to be authentic. However, teachers recognize that even the most innovative activities require a reliable and valid means of measuring student progress. Commonly used assessment strategies are project assignments (e.g., web pages, multimedia products, desktop-published publications), self-report instruments (e.g., student-prepared journals or other descriptions), and portfolio entries.

Electronic portfolios often are used as products in themselves or as organizing devices for products created over time. Rubrics and performance checklists are frequently used to grade these products. Usually, teachers design their own rubrics and checklists to match the specific performances in their curricula. However, some generic measures (e.g., those shown on the Technology Integration Workshop DVD and Companion Website at http://www.prenhall.com/roblyer for this text) are becoming more commonly used.

Criticisms of each model. It is because they have such different views of reality and theory bases that educators who espouse objectivist and constructivist beliefs take very different views of appropriate technology-based methods. Each tends to criticize the other. Objectivists say constructivist methods are unrealistic; constructivists say directed methods are outmoded. Figure 2.8 (p. 47) summarizes these criticisms.

The Future of Technology Integration: Merging the Two Approaches

As Molenda (1991) observed, an *either-or* stance to teaching models gains us little. Rather, we must find a way to merge the two approaches in a way that will benefit learners and teachers. A link between the two epistemological planets must be forged so that teachers and students can travel freely

Figure 2.7   A Comparison of Directed and Constructivist Models and the Problems They Address

	Directed Instructional Models	Constructivist Models
Characteristics	**Teaching/Learning Methods:** • Stress individualized work. • Have specific skill-based instructional goals and objectives; same for all students. • Teachers transmit a set body of skills and/or knowledge to students. • Students learn prerequisite skills required for each new skill. • Sequences of carefully structured presentations and activities to help students understand (process), remember (encode and store), and transfer (retrieve) information and skills. • Traditional teacher-directed methods and materials are used: lectures, skill worksheets.	**Teaching/Learning Methods:** • Stress group-based, cooperative work. • Have global goals such as problem solving and critical thinking; sometimes differ for each student. • Have students generate their own knowledge through experiences anchored in real-life situations. • Students learn lower order skills in the context of higher order problems that require them. • Learning through problem-oriented activities (e.g., "what if" situations); visual formats and mental models; rich, complex learning environments; and learning through exploration. • Nontraditional materials are used to promote student-driven exploration and problem solving.
	Assessment Methods: • Traditional assessments (e.g., multiple choice, short answer) with specific expected responses; student products (e.g., essays) graded with checklists or rubrics.	**Assessment Methods:** • Nontraditional assessments (e.g., group products such as web pages, multimedia projects) with varying contents or portfolios; students products graded with self-report instruments, rubrics.
Instructional Needs and Problems Targeted	• *Accountability:* All students must meet required education standards to be considered educated. • *Individualization:* Help meet individual needs of students working at many levels. • *Quality assurance:* Quality of instruction must be consistently high across teachers and schools in various locations. • *Convergent thinking:* All students must have the same skills.	• *Higher level skills:* All students must be able to think critically and creatively and solve problems. • *Cooperative group skills:* Help students learn to work with others to solve problems. • *Increase relevancy:* Students must have active, visual, authentic learning experiences that relate to their own lives. • *Divergent thinking:* Students must think on their own and solve novel problems as they occur.

from one to the other, depending on the characteristics of the topics at hand and individual learning needs.

Clearly, instructional problems identified by objectivists and constructivists are common to most schools or classrooms, regardless of grade level, type of students, or content. Teachers will always use some directed instruction as the most efficient means of teaching students required skills; teachers will always need motivating, cooperative learning activities to ensure that students want to learn and that they can transfer what they learn to problems they encounter. Tinker (1998) warns that "It is a fallacy to think that technology will make traditional content outdated. . . . The corollary to this thinking that traditional content is less

important than learning to learn … is a dangerous doctrine" (p. 2). Proficient technology-oriented teachers must learn to combine directed instruction and constructivist approaches and select technology resources and integration methods that are best suited to their specific needs.

Together, the two ostensibly different views of reality will merge to form a new and powerful approach to solving some of the major problems of the educational system, each contributing an essential element of the new instructional formula. Some theorists and practitioners believe that constructivism will eventually dominate overall educational goals and objectives such as learning to apply scientific methods, while systematic approaches will ensure that specific pre-

Figure 2.8   Criticisms of Directed and Constructivist Instructional Models

Limitations of Directed Instructional Models	Limitations of Constructivist Models
Critics say that:	*Critics say that:*
• Breaking topics into discrete skills and teaching them in isolation from each other is directed more at basic skills than at higher level ones; students cannot apply skills later (i.e., knowledge is inert). • Learning is repetitive and predictable; students often find it uninteresting and irrelevant; lack of motivation leads to lower achievement and higher dropout rates. • Not all topics lend themselves to directed approaches. • Students cannot solve novel problems or work cooperatively with others to solve problems.	• When students are allowed to demonstrate knowledge in varying ways, teachers cannot certify students' individual skill levels, as required by today's accountability standards. • Letting students generate their own knowledge is time consuming and inefficient; students may lack prerequisite skills to handle constructivist problem-solving environments effectively. • Not all topics lend themselves to constructivist approaches. • Despite learning being anchored in authentic problems, students may not transfer skills to real-life situations.

requisite skills are learned. Tennyson (1990) suggested, for example, that about 30% of learning time be spent on what he terms acquiring knowledge—verbal information and procedural knowledge. The remaining 70% should be spent on the employment of knowledge (contextual skills, cognitive strategies, and creative processes). As Hirsch (2002) says in the article from which the quote at the beginning of this chapter was taken, explicit (directed) learning is best for providing a foundation of skills, while implicit (inquiry-based) learning is probably best for developing global skills slowly over time.

Technology Integration Strategies Based on Each Model

Subsequent chapters in this book describe and give examples of integration strategies for various types of courseware materials and technology media. However, all of these strategies implement a group of general integration principles. Some strategies draw on the unique characteristics of a technology resource to meet certain kinds of learning needs. Others take advantage of a resource's ability to substitute for materials lacking in schools or classrooms. Teachers may use many or all of these strategies at the same time.

It is important to recognize that each of the integration strategies described here addresses specific instructional needs identified by educational theorists and practitioners. Strategies are not employed because technology is the wave of the future or because students should occasionally use computers because it is good for them. This text advocates making a conscious effort to match technology resources to problems that educators cannot address in other, easier ways.

As Figure 2.9 (p. 48) shows, four technology integration strategies are based primarily on directed models, four on constructivist ones, and four are strategies that could help address either model.

Technology integration strategies based on directed models. As Figure 2.10 and the following list show, the four integration strategies based on directed methods are all designed to address individual instruction and practice:

• **Integration to remedy identified weaknesses or skill deficits** — Constructivists say that students should learn prerequisite skills as they see the need for them in a group or individual project. However, experienced teachers know that even motivated students do not always learn skills as expected. These failures occur for a variety of reasons, many of which are related to learners' internal capabilities and not all of which are thoroughly understood. When the absence of prerequisite skills presents a barrier to higher level learning or to passing tests, directed instruction usually is the most efficient way of providing them. For example, if a student does not learn to read when it is developmentally appropriate, research has shown great success in identifying and remedying specific weaknesses among the component skills (Torgeson, 1986; Torgeson, Waters, Cohen, & Torgeson, 1988). Materials such as drill-and-practice and tutorial software have proven to be valuable resources that help teachers provide this kind of individualized instruction. When students have failed to learn required skills, they frequently find technology-based materials more motivating and less threatening than teacher-delivered instruction.

• **Integration to promote skill fluency or automaticity** — Some prerequisite skills must be applied quickly and without conscious effort in order to be most useful. Gagné (1982) and Bloom (1986) referred to this automatic recall as **automaticity.** Students need rapid recall and performance of a wide range of skills throughout the curriculum, including simple math facts,

Figure 2.9 Technology Integration Strategies for Directed, Constructivist, or Both Models

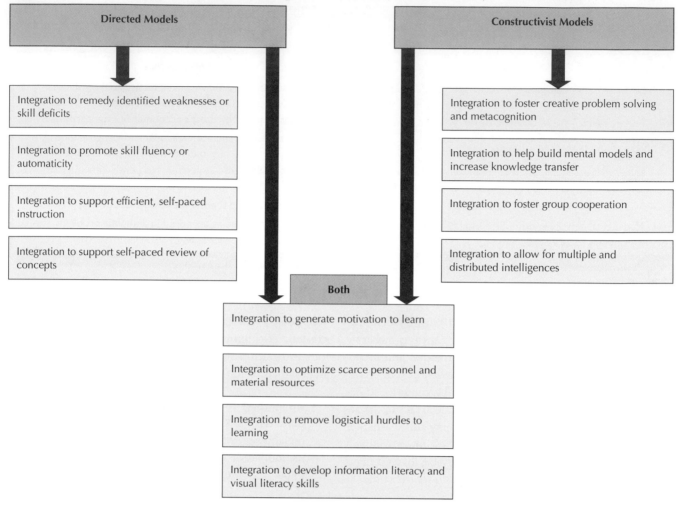

Directed Models	Constructivist Models
Integration to remedy identified weaknesses or skill deficits	Integration to foster creative problem solving and metacognition
Integration to promote skill fluency or automaticity	Integration to help build mental models and increase knowledge transfer
Integration to support efficient, self-paced instruction	Integration to foster group cooperation
Integration to support self-paced review of concepts	Integration to allow for multiple and distributed intelligences

Both

Integration to generate motivation to learn

Integration to optimize scarce personnel and material resources

Integration to remove logistical hurdles to learning

Integration to develop information literacy and visual literacy skills

Figure 2.10 Technology Integration Strategies Based on Directed Teaching Models

Integration Strategy	Needs/Problems Addressed	Example Activities
To remedy identified weaknesses or skill deficits	• At-risk students need individual instruction and practice. • Students fail parts of high-stakes tests.	Tutorial or drill-and-practice software is targeted to identified skills.
To promote skill fluency/automaticity	• Students need to be able to recall and apply lower level skills quickly, automatically. • Students need review for upcoming tests.	Drill-and-practice or instructional game software lets students practice math facts, vocabulary, or spelling words.
To support efficient, self-paced learning	• Students are motivated and able to learn on their own. • No teacher is available for the content area.	Use tutorial software or distance learning courses for foreign languages, higher level science or math, or other elective subjects.
To support self-paced review of concepts	• Students need help studying for tests. • Students need make-up instruction for missed work.	Use tutorial, drill-and-practice, or simulation software to cover specific concepts.

Directed technology integration strategies let students master skills at their own pace.

grammar and usage rules, and spelling. Some students acquire automaticity through repeated use of the skills in practical situations. Others acquire it more efficiently through isolated practice. Drill-and-practice, instructional games, and sometimes simulation courseware can provide practice tailored to individual skill needs and learning pace.

- **Integration to support efficient, self-paced learning** — When students are self-motivated and have the ability to structure their own learning, the most desirable method is often the one that offers the fastest and most efficient path. Sometimes these students are interested in topics not being covered in class or for which there is no instructor available. Directed instruction for these students can frequently be supported by well-designed self-instructional tutorials and self-paced distance learning workshops and courses.

- **Integration to support self-paced review of concepts** — When students cover a number of topics over time, they usually need a review prior to taking a test to help them remember and consolidate concepts. Sometimes students are absent when in-class instruction was given or need additional time going over the material to understand and remember it. In these situations, drill-and-practice and tutorial software materials are a good way to provide these kinds of self-paced reviews.

Technology integration strategies based on constructivist models. Figure 2.11 and the following list summarize the four integration strategies identified with constructivist methods:

- **Integration to foster creative problem solving and metacognition** — Although most people acknowl-

edge the importance of students having a knowledge base of specific skills and information, it is also becoming evident that our world is too complex and technical for students to learn everything ahead of time that they may need for the future. Thus, our society is beginning to place a high value on the ability to solve novel problems in creative ways. If students are conscious of the procedures they use to go about solving problems, they often can more easily improve on their strategies and become more effective, creative problem solvers. Consequently, teachers often try to present students with novel problems to solve and get them to analyze how they learn to solve them. Resources such as problem-solving courseware and multimedia applications often are considered ideal environments for getting students to think about how they think and to offer opportunities to challenge their creativity and problem-solving abilities.

- **Integration to help build mental models and increase knowledge transfer** — The problem of inert knowledge is believed to occur when students learn skills in isolation from problem applications. When students later encounter problems that require the skills, they do not realize how the skills could be relevant. Problem-solving materials in highly visual formats allow students to build rich mental models of problems to be solved (CTGV, 1991). Students need not depend on reading skills, which may be deficient, to build these mental models. Thus, supporters hypothesize that teaching skills in these highly visual, problem-solving environments helps to ensure that knowledge will transfer to higher order skills. These technology-based methods are especially desirable for teachers who work with

Figure 2.11 Technology Integration Strategies Based on Constructivist Models

Integration Strategy	Needs/Problems Addressed	Example Activities
To foster creative problem solving and metacognition	• Students need to be able to solve complex, novel problems as they occur. • Teachers want to encourage students' self-awareness of their own learning strategies.	• Video-based scenarios pose problems, help support student problem solving. • Graphic tools illustrate concepts and support student manipulation of variables. • Simulations allow exploration of how systems work.
To help build mental models and increase knowledge transfer	• Students have trouble understanding complex and/or abstract concepts. • Students have trouble seeing where skills apply to real-life problems.	• Video-based scenarios pose problems. • Students create multimedia products to illustrate and report on their research. • Simulations, problem-solving software illustrate and let students explore complex systems.
To foster group cooperation skills	• Students need to be able to work with others to solve problems and create products.	Students collaborate to: • Do Internet research. • Create multimedia/web page products. • Compete in instructional games.
To allow for multiple and distributed intelligences	• Teachers want to allow students multiple ways to learn and to demonstrate achievement.	Students have varying roles in group work to create: • Multimedia products. • Web pages. • Desktop-published newsletters, brochures.

Constructivist technology integration strategies can foster creative problem solving.

students in areas such as mathematics and science, where concepts are abstract and complex and where inert knowledge is frequently a problem.

• **Integration to foster group cooperation** — One skill area currently identified as an important focus for schools' efforts to restructure curriculum (U.S. Department of Labor, 1992) is the ability to work cooperatively in a group to solve problems and develop products. Although schools certainly can teach cooperative work without technology resources, a growing body of evidence documents students' appreciation of cooperative work as both more motivating and easier to accomplish when it uses technology. For example, descriptions of students who develop their own multimedia products and presentations are more common in current literature on teaching cooperative skills to at-risk students.

• **Integration to allow for multiple and distributed intelligences** — Integration strategies with group cooperative activities also give teachers a way to allow students of widely varying abilities to make valuable contributions on their own terms. Since each student is seen as an important member of the group in these activities, the activities themselves are viewed as problems for group—

Figure 2.12 Technology Integration Strategies to Support Either Model

Integration Strategy	Needs/Problems Addressed	Example Activities
To generate motivation to learn	• Due to past failures, at-risk students need more than usual motivation.	• Visual and interactive qualities of the Internet and multimedia resources draw and hold students' attention. • Drill-and-practice/tutorial materials give students private environments for learning and practice.
	• Students need to see the relevance of new concepts and skills to their lives.	• Video-based scenarios, simulations show relevance of science and math skills.
	• Students need to be active, rather than passive, learners.	• Hands-on production work (e.g., multimedia, web pages) gives students an active role in learning.
To optimize scarce personnel and materials resources	• Schools have limited budgets, must save money on consumables. • Teachers are in short supply in some subject areas.	• Simulations allow repeated science experiments at no additional cost. • Distance courses can offer subjects for which schools lack teachers.
To remove logistical hurdles to learning	• Students find repetitive tasks (handwriting, calculations) boring and tedious.	Students can use: • Word processing to make quick, easy revisions and corrections to written work.
	• Students lack motor skills to show their designs.	• Calculators and spreadsheets to do low-level calculations involved in math/science problem solving. • Computer-assisted design (CAD) and drawing software to try out and change designs.
	• Students cannot travel to places to learn about them. • Some physical and social phenomena occur too slowly, too quickly, or at too great a distance to allow observation.	• Virtual tours to see places they could not go physically. • Simulations to allow study of social systems (e.g., voting) and physical systems (chemical reactions).
To develop information literacy/visual literacy skills	Students need to learn: • Modern methods of communicating information. • How to analyze the quality of visual presentations.	Students can: • Do research reports as multimedia products or web pages. • Become media savvy by using information on the Internet and video.

rather than individual—solution. This strategy has implications for enhancing students' self-esteem and for increasing their willingness to spend more time on learning tasks. It also helps students see that they can help each other accomplish tasks and can learn from each other as well as from the teacher or from media.

Enabling integration strategies useful with either model. Some integration strategies have a more general support role for instruction and can address the needs of either model. These "enabling" strategies seem to be appearing with increasing frequency in combination with other directed or constructivist strategies described in this chapter. They seem to support the other strategies and make them more feasible and practical. The four strategies are summarized in Figure 2.12 and the following list:

• **Integration to generate motivation to learn** — Teachers who work with at-risk students say that capturing students' interest and enthusiasm is a key to success; frequently, they cite it as their most difficult challenge. Some educators assert that today's television-oriented students are increasingly likely to demand more motivational qualities in their instruction than students in previous generations. Constructivists argue that instruction must address students' affective needs as well as their cognitive ones, saying that students will learn more if what they are learning is interesting and relevant to their needs. They recommend the highly visual and interactive qualities of Internet and multimedia resources as the basis of these strategies. However, proponents of directed methods make similar claims about highly structured, self-instructional learning environments. They say that some students find it very motivating to learn at their own pace, in a private environment, because they receive immediate feedback on their progress. It seems evident that appropriate integration strategies to address motivation problems depend on the needs of the student; either constructivist or directed integration strategies can be used to increase motivation to learn.

- **Integration to optimize scarce resources** — Current resources and numbers of personnel in schools are rarely optimal. Many of the courseware materials described in later chapters can help make up for the lack of required resources in the school or classroom—from consumable supplies to qualified teachers. For example, drill-and-practice programs can replace worksheets, a good distance program can offer instruction in topics for which local teachers are in short supply, and a simulation can let students repeat experiments without depleting chemical supplies or other materials.

- **Integration to remove logistical hurdles to learning** — Some technology tools offer no instructional sequence or tasks but help students complete learning tasks more efficiently. These tools support directed instruction by removing or reducing logistical hurdles to learning. For example, word processing programs do not teach students how to write but let students write and rewrite more quickly, without the labor of handwriting. CAD software does not teach students how to design a house but allows them to try out designs and features to see what they look like before building models or structures. A calculator lets students do lower level calculations so they may focus on the high-level concepts of math problems. A CD-ROM may contain only a set of pictures of sea life but lets a teacher illustrate concepts about sea creatures more quickly and easily than with books.

- **Integration to develop information literacy and visual literacy skills** — A rationale underlying many of the most popular directed and constructivist integration strategies is the need to give students practice in using modern methods of communicating information. For example, when students use presentation software instead of cardboard charts to give a report, they gain experience for college classrooms and business offices, where computer-based presentations are the norm. Using technology to communicate visually represents Information Age skills that students will need both for higher education and in the workplace.

A Technology Integration Planning (TIP) Model for Teachers

An Overview of the TIP Model

Regardless of the integration strategy they use, teachers need a planning approach to ensure their strategy will be successful. The Technology Integration Planning (TIP) Model, shown in Figure 2.13, gives teachers a general approach to addressing challenges involved in integrating technology into teaching. Each of the model's five phases outlines a set of planning and implementation steps that help ensure technology use will be efficient and successful in meeting needs. Experienced technology-using teachers tend to do these steps intuitively. However, for new teachers or those just beginning to integrate technology, the TIP Model provides a helpful guide on procedures and issues to address. After an overview of the model, each phase is discussed here, along with a classroom example (the "Online Multicultural Project") of how to implement the tasks at each phase.

MAKING THE CASE FOR TECHNOLOGY INTEGRATION

Discuss these issues online with other students by selecting the *Making the Case* module for Chapter 2 of the Companion Website (http://www.prenhall.com/roblyer) or choose the *Message Board* module.

1. Sheingold (1991) said that teachers will have to confront squarely the difficult problem of creating a school environment that is fundamentally different from the one they themselves experienced (p. 23). In what ways is the current K–12 environment different from the one you experienced? Do you feel this presents an obstacle to effective use of technology in your teaching? What are some strategies you feel might help teachers overcome this obstacle?

2. NCATE's document *Technology and the New Professional Teacher* (1997) said that, in addition to technology skills, teachers need an attitude that is fearless in the use of technology, encourages them to take risks, and inspires them to be lifelong learners. What current factors and activities can help teachers develop such an attitude? What factors make it difficult for them to acquire it?

Figure 2.13   The Technology Integration Planning (TIP) Model

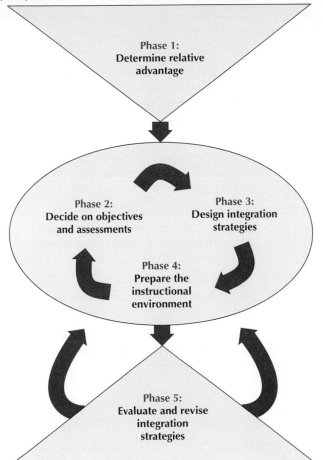

- **Phase 1 focus:** *Why should I use a technology-based method?* — Teachers look at their current teaching problems and identify technology-based methods that may offer good solutions. In his best-selling book on how and why innovations get adopted, Everett Rogers (2004) says that people resist changing how they do things, even if new ways are better. However, people are more likely to change if they see clearly the benefits of a new method over an old one. He calls this seeing a **relative advantage.**

- **Phase 2 focus:** *How will I know students have learned?* — Teachers decide skills they want students to learn from the technology-integrated lesson(s) and design ways to assess how well students have learned and how effectively the activity has been carried out.

- **Phase 3 focus:** *What teaching strategies and activities will work best?* — Teachers decide on instructional strategies and how to carry them out. When teachers create an instructional design for technology integration, they consider the characteristics of their topic and the needs of their students and decide on an instructional course of action that addresses both within the constraints of their classroom environment.

- **Phase 4 focus:** *Are essential conditions in place to support technology integration?* — Teachers organize the teaching environment so technology plans can be carried out effectively. Since research on effective technology uses shows that teachers can integrate technology successfully *only* if they have adequate hardware, software, and technical support available to them, the ISTE (2000) lists a set of *essential conditions* that are necessary to unleash the potential power of technology tools and methods. The school and district must provide many of these essential conditions, but for each technology integration strategy, the teacher considers which conditions are in place and to what degree. This helps shape the kind of integration possible for the situation.

- **Phase 5 focus:** *What worked well? What could be improved?* — Teachers review outcome data and information on technology-integrated methods and determine what should be changed to make them work better next time. In addition to collecting formal data on instructional and other outcomes, teachers sometimes interview students and observers to ask what they think could be improved. Some teachers keep daily notes or logs on implementation problems and issues. As they review all the information, teachers can use the *Technology Impact Checklist* (see the accompanying DVD or the Companion Website for this chapter at http://www.prenhall.com/roblyer) to help them reflect on whether the problems they identified in Phase 1 have, indeed, been addressed successfully.

Phase 1: Determine Relative Advantage

Every teacher has topics—and sometimes whole subject areas—that he or she finds especially challenging to teach. Some concepts are so abstract or foreign to students that they struggle to understand them; some topics students find so boring, tedious, or irrelevant that they have trouble attending to them. Some learning requires time-consuming tasks that students resist doing. Good teachers spend much time trying to meet these challenges and make concepts more engaging or easier to grasp, or make tasks more efficient to accomplish.

Recognizing relative advantage. Technology-based strategies offer many unique benefits to teachers as they look for instructional solutions to these problems. However, time and effort are required to plan and carry out technology-based methods, and sometimes additional expense is involved. Teachers have to consider the benefits of using such a method compared to their current ones and decide if the benefits are worth the additional effort and cost.

As mentioned earlier, Everett Rogers (2004) refers to this decision as seeing the *relative advantage* of using a new method. Figure 2.14 lists several kinds of learning problems

Figure 2.14 Technology Solutions with Potential for High Relative Advantage

Learning Problem	Technology Solutions	Relative Advantage
Concepts are new, foreign (e.g., mathematics, physics principles).	Graphic tools, simulations, video-based problem scenarios	Visual examples clarify concepts and applications.
Concepts are abstract, complex (e.g, physics principles, biology systems).	Math tools (Geometer's *SketchPad*), simulations, problem-solving software, spreadsheet exercises, graphing calculators	Graphics displays make abstract concepts more concrete; students can manipulate systems to see how they work.
Time-consuming manual skills (e.g., handwriting, calculations, data collection) interfere with learning high-level skills.	Tool software (e.g., word processing, spreadsheets) and probeware	Takes low-level labor out of high-level tasks; students can focus on learning high-level concepts and skills.
Students find practice boring (e.g., basic math skills, spelling, vocabulary, test preparation).	Drill-and-practice software, instructional games	Attention-getting displays, immediate feedback, and interaction combine to create motivating practice.
Students cannot see relevance of concepts to their lives (e.g., history, social studies).	Simulations, Internet activities, video-based problem scenarios	Visual, interactive activities help teachers demonstrate relevance.
Skills are "inert," i.e., students can do them but do not see where they apply (e.g., mathematics, physics).	Simulations, problem-solving software, video-based problem scenarios, student development of web pages, multimedia products	Project-based learning using these tools establishes clear links between skills and real-world problems.
Students dislike preparing research reports, presentations.	Student development of desktop-published and web page/multimedia products	Students like products that look polished, professional.
Students need skills in working collaboratively, opportunities to demonstrate learning in alternative ways.	Student development of desktop-published and web page/multimedia products	Provides format in which group work makes sense; students can work together "virtually"; students make different contributions to one product based on their strengths.
Students need technological competence in preparation for the workplace.	All software and productivity tools; all communications, presentation, and multimedia software	Illustrates and provides practice in skills and tools students will need in work situations.
Teachers have limited time for correcting students' individual practice items.	Drill-and-practice software, handheld computers with assessment software	Feedback to students is immediate; frees teachers for work with students.
No teachers available for advanced courses.	Self-instructional multimedia, distance courses	Provides structured, self-paced learning environments.
Students need individual reviews of missed work.	Tutorial or multimedia software	Provides structured, self-paced environments for individual review of missed concepts.
Schools have insufficient consumable materials (e.g., science labs, workbooks).	Simulations, CD-ROM-based texts, ebooks	Materials are reusable, saves money on purchasing new copies.
Students need quick access to information and people not locally available.	Internet and email projects; multimedia encyclopedias and atlases	Information is faster to access; people are easier, less expensive to contact.

CLASSROOM EXAMPLE: ONLINE MULTICULTURAL PROJECT

Phase 1: Determine relative advantage. Mia wanted to include more meaningful multicultural activities in the social studies curriculum. She and the other social studies teachers in her school focused primarily on studying various holidays and foods from other cultures. They sponsored an annual International Foods smorgasbord event that was very popular with the students, but she doubted it taught them much about the richness of other cultures or why they should respect and appreciate cultures that were different from their own. She sometimes overheard her students making disparaging comments about people of other nationalities. She felt a better approach to multicultural education might help. The previous summer, she had attended a workshop in another school district in which they described an online project with partner schools in countries around the world. One teacher told about her partners in Israel and Spain. She said students exchanged information with designated partners and answered assigned questions to research each other's backgrounds and locales. Then they worked in groups on travel brochures or booklets to email each other. They even took digital photos of themselves to send. It sounded like a great way for kids to learn about other cultures in a meaningful way while also learning some geography and civics. The teachers in the workshop remarked that it was difficult to demean people who look and talk differently from you when you've really worked with them and gotten to know them. Mia was so impressed with the online project they described that she decided to try it out in her own classroom.

Analysis Questions — Answer these questions online at the Companion Website (http://www.prenhall.com/roblyer). Select Chapter 2.
1. What is the problem Mia wants to address?
2. What evidence does she have that there is a problem?
3. What would be the relative advantage of the method she is proposing?
4. How does she hope this method will be better than previous ones?

---

and technology solutions with potential for high relative advantage to teachers. However, these lists are really just general guidelines. Being able to recognize specific instances of these problems in a classroom context and knowing how to match them with an appropriate technology solution require knowledge of classroom problems, practice in addressing them, and an in-depth knowledge of the characteristics of each technology. Chapters 3 through 15 of this textbook provide the latter information, as well as many examples of matching technology to various needs.

Phase 1 questions. The first phase in integrating technology requires answering two questions about technology's relative advantage in a given situation:

- **What is the problem I am addressing?** — To make sure a technology application is a good solution, begin with a clear statement of a teaching and learning problem. This is sometimes difficult to do. It is a natural human tendency to jump to a quick solution rather than recognize the real problem. Also, everyone may not see a problem the same way. Use the following guidelines to answer the question of "What is the problem?"

  - **Do not focus on technologies** — Remember that knowing how to use a technology appropriately is part

of a solution, and is not in itself a problem to solve. Therefore, avoid problem statements like "Students do not know how to use spreadsheets efficiently" or "Teachers are not having their students use the Internet." Not having the skills to use a technology (e.g., a spreadsheet or the Internet) is an instructional problem, but not the kind of teaching/learning problem to consider here. It is sometimes true that teachers are given a technology and told to implement it. In these situations, they must decide if there is a real teaching or learning problem the new resource can help meet. However, if teachers have a technology available and choose not to use it, it may mean they can see no relative advantage to using it; nonuse of a technology is not in itself a problem to address with the TIP Model.

- **Look for evidence** — Look for observable indications that there really is a problem. Examples of evidence include the following: Students consistently achieve lower grades on a skill area, a formal or informal survey shows that teachers have trouble getting students to attend to learning tasks, or teachers observe that students are refusing to turn in required assignments in a certain area.

- **Do technology-based methods offer a solution with sufficient relative advantage?** — Analyze the benefits of the technology-based method in light of the effort and cost to implement it and make a final decision. Use the following guidelines to answer the question of "Is technology a good solution?"

- **Estimate the impact** — Consider the benefits others have gained from using a technology as a solution. Is it likely you will realize similar benefits?

- **Consider the required effort and expense** — How much time and work will it take to implement the technology solution? Is it likely to be worth it?

Phase 2: Decide on Objectives and Assessments

Writing objectives is a good way of setting clear expectations for what technology-based methods will accomplish. Usually, teachers expect a new method will improve *student behaviors,* for example, better achievement, more on-task behaviors, improved attitudes. Sometimes, however, changes in *teacher behaviors* are important, for example, saving time on a task. In either case, objectives should focus on *outcomes* that are observable (e.g., demonstrating, writing, completing), rather than on internal ones that

cannot be seen or measured (e.g., being aware, knowing, understanding, or appreciating).

After stating objectives, teachers create ways to assess how well outcomes have been accomplished. Sometimes, they can use existing tests and rubrics. For others, they have to create instruments or methods to measure the behaviors.

Example outcomes, objectives, and assessments. Here are a few examples of outcomes; objectives, which are used to state outcomes in a measurable form; and assessment methods matched to the outcomes:

- **Higher achievement outcome** — Overall average performance on an end-of-chapter test will improve by 20%. (Assess achievement with a test.)

- **Cooperative work outcome** — All students will score at least 15 out of 20 on the cooperative group skill rubric. (Use an existing rubric to grade skills.)

- **Attitude outcome** — Students will indicate satisfaction with the simulation lesson by an overall average score of 20 of 25 points. (Create an attitude survey to assess satisfaction.)

Figure 2.15 Sample Brochure Rubric

Category	(4) Excellent	(3) Good	(2) Almost	(1) Not Yet
Attractiveness & Organization (Organization)	The brochure has exceptionally attractive formatting and well-organized information.	The brochure has attractive formatting and well-organized information.	The brochure has well-organized information.	The brochure's formatting and organization of material are confusing to the reader.
Content–Accuracy (Ideas)	The brochure has all of the required information (see checklist) and some additional information.	The brochure has all of the required information (see checklist).	The brochure has most of the required information (see checklist).	The brochure has little of the required information (see checklist).
Writing–Mechanics (Conventions)	All of the writing is done in complete sentences. Capitalization and punctuation are correct throughout the brochure.	Most of the writing is done in complete sentences. Most of the capitalization and punctuation are correct throughout the brochure.	Some of the writing is done in complete sentences. Some of the capitalization and punctuation are correct throughout the brochure.	Most of the writing is not done in complete sentences. Most of the capitalization and punctuation are not correct throughout the brochure.
Graphics/Pictures	The graphics go well in the text and there is a good mix of text and graphics.	The graphics go well with the text, but there are so many that they distract from the text.	The graphics go well with the text, but there are too few.	The graphics do not go with the accompanying text or appear to be randomly chosen.
Sources	There are many citations from a variety of sources accurately listed.	There are some citations from a variety of sources accurately listed.	There are a few citations accurately listed on the brochure.	Incomplete citations are listed on the brochure.

Source: Reprinted by permission of Kent School District, 12033 SE 256 St., Kent, WA 98030, (253) 373-7000 (http://www.kent.k12.wa.us/curriculum/tech/K6/3/puget_sound/brochure_rubric.htm)

- **Improved motivation** — Teachers will observe better on-task behavior in at least 75% of the students. (Create and use an observation sheet.)

Phase 2 questions. This phase in integrating technology requires answering two questions about outcomes and assessment strategies:

- **What outcomes do I expect from using the new methods?** — Think about problems you are trying to solve and what would be acceptable indications that the technology solution has succeeded in resolving them. Use the following guidelines:

  - *Focus on results, not processes* — Think about the *end results* you want to achieve, rather than the *processes* to help you get there. Avoid statements like "Students will learn cooperative group skills," which tells a process students use to achieve the outcome (improved cooperative group skills). Instead, state what you want students to be able to do as a result of the multimedia

project, for example, "90% of students will score 4 out of 5 on a cooperative groups skills rubric."

  - *Make statements observable and measurable* — Avoid vague statements like "Students will understand how to work cooperatively" that cannot be measured.

- **What are the best ways of assessing these outcomes?** — The choice of assessment depends on the nature of the outcome. See the following guidelines:

  - *Use written tests to assess skill achievement outcomes* — Written cognitive tests (e.g., short answer, multiple choice, true/false, matching) and essay exams remain the most common classroom assessment strategy for many formal knowledge skills.

  - *Use evaluation criteria checklists to assess complex tasks or products* — When students must create complex products such as multimedia presentations, reports, or web pages, teachers may give students a set of criteria that specify requirements each product must meet. Points are awarded for meeting each criterion.

- **Use rubrics to assess complex tasks or products** — Rubrics fulfill the same role as evaluation criteria checklists and are sometimes used in addition to them (see Figure 2.15). Their added value is giving students descriptions of various levels of quality. Teachers usually associate a letter grade with each level of quality (Level 5 = A, Level 4 = B, etc.).

- **Use Likert scale–type surveys or semantic differentials to assess attitude outcomes** — When the outcome is improved attitudes, teachers design a survey in **Likert scale** format or with a **semantic differential**. A Likert scale is a series of statements that students use to indicate their degree of agreement or disagreement. For example:

  I like writing more when I use word processing. (Circle one of the following numbers)

Strongly Agree	Agree	No Opinion	Disagree	Strongly Disagree
1	2	3	4	5

  In a semantic differential, students respond to a question by checking a line between each of several sets of bipolar adjectives to indicate their level of feeling about it. For example:

  "How do you feel about math?"

  Warm __ __ __ __ __ Cold?

  Happy __ __ __ __ __ Sad?

- **Use observation instruments to measure frequency of behaviors** — For example, if teachers wanted to see an increase in students' use of scientific language, they could create a chart to keep track of this use on a daily basis.

Phase 3: Design Integration Strategies

Teachers make many design decisions as they integrate technologies into teaching, including single-subject vs. interdisciplinary approach, grouping strategies, and sequence of learning activities. What usually drives these design decisions is whether the learning environment will be primarily directed (a teacher or expert source presents information for students to absorb) or primarily inquiry based or constructivist (students do activities to generate their own learning). To make this decision, examine the needs and integration strategies described in Figures 2.10 through 2.12 and determine which one(s) apply for the situation.

Deciding on teaching/learning methods. Use the following guidelines to help determine whether methods should be primarily directed or constructivist:

- **Use directed strategies** — when students need an efficient way to learn specific skills that must be assessed with traditional tests.

- **Use constructivist strategies** — when students need to develop global skills and insights over time (e.g., cooperative group skills, approaches to solving novel problems, mental models of highly complex topics) and when learning may be assessed with alternative measures such as portfolios and group products.

Phase 3 questions. This phase in integrating technology requires answering three questions about instructional strategies, technology materials, and implementation strategies. These questions are listed here with suggestions for answering them in actual classroom situations:

- **What kinds of instructional methods are needed in light of content objectives and student characteristics?** — After determining whether integration strategies will be primarily directed or constructivist, also consider the following:

  - **Content approach** — Should the approach be single subject or interdisciplinary? Sometimes school or district requirements dictate this decision, and sometimes teachers combine subjects into a single unit of instruction as a way to cover concepts and topics that they may not otherwise have time to teach. Most often, however, interdisciplinary approaches are used to model how real-life activities require the use of a combination of skills from several content areas.

  - **Grouping approach** — Should the students work as individuals, in pairs, in small groups, or as a whole class? These decisions are made in light of how many computers or software copies are available, as well as the following guidelines:

    - Whole class: For demonstrations or to guide whole-class discussion prior to student work
    - Individual: When students have to demonstrate individual mastery of skills at the end of the lesson or project
    - Pairs: For peer tutoring; higher ability students work with those of lesser ability
    - Small group: To model real-world work skills by giving students experience in cooperative group work

- **How can technology best support these methods?** — Think about the steps that will be required to carry out the technology-based solution you identified in Phase 2.

- **How can I prepare students adequately to use technologies?** — When designing a sequence of activities that incorporates technology tools, be sure to

CLASSROOM EXAMPLE: ONLINE MULTICULTURAL PROJECT

Phase 3: Design integration strategies. Mia knew that students would not achieve the insights she had in mind through telling them information and testing them on it. They would need to draw their own conclusions by working and communicating with people from other cultures. However, she felt she could use a directed approach to teach the Internet and email skills they would need to carry out project activities. The project website had good suggestions on how to set up groups of four with designated tasks for each group member. It also suggested the following sequence of activities for introducing and carrying out the project.

Step 1: Sign up on project website; obtain partner school assignments.

Step 2: Teachers in partner schools make contact and set a timeline.

Step 3: Teachers organize classroom resources for work on project.

Step 4: Introduce project to students: Display project information from project website and discuss previous products done by other sites.

Step 5: Assign students to groups; discuss task assignments with all members.

Step 6: Determine students' email and Internet skills; begin teaching skills.

Step 7: Students do initial email contacts/chats and introduce each other.

Step 8: Teacher works with groups to identify information for final product.

Step 9: Students do Internet searches to locate required information; take digital photos and scan required images; exchange information with partner sites.

Step 10: Students do production work; exchange final products with partners.

Step 11: Do debriefing and assessments of student work.

Analysis Questions — Answer these questions online at the Companion Website (http://www.prenhall.com/roblyer). Select Chapter 2.

1. Is Mia's approach primarily directed or constructivist?
2. Why did she decide to take this approach?
3. At which point should Mia do the preassessments to measure students' skills and attitudes prior to the project?
4. How should Mia determine students' levels of required Internet and email skills?

leave enough time for demonstrating tools to students and allowing them to become comfortable using them before they do a graded product.

Phase 4: Prepare the Instructional Environment

If teachers could obtain all of the teaching resources they needed whenever they wanted them, they would make all Phase 4 planning decisions after they had decided on the best instructional strategies in Phase 3. In practice, teachers make many Phase 3 and 4 decisions at the same time. Most teachers usually decide how they will teach something in light of what they have available to teach it.

Essential conditions for effective technology uses. In Phase 4, teachers make sure their instructional environment meets all of the following essential conditions required for successful technology integration:

- **Adequate hardware, software, and media** — Enough computers are available and there are sufficient legal copies of instructional resources.

- **Time to use resources** — Hardware and enough legal copies of software have been obtained or scheduled for the time needed.

- **Special needs of students** — Provisions have been made for access by students with disabilities and for all students' privacy and safety.

- **Planning for technology use** — Teachers are familiar enough with the hardware and software to use it efficiently and do necessary troubleshooting; they have

Phase 4: Prepare the instructional environment. As soon as Mia knew that her students would be able to participate in the Internet project, she began to get organized. First, she examined the timeline of project activities, so she would know when her students needed to use computers. She made sure to build in enough time to demonstrate the project site and get students used to using the browser and search engine. Then she began the following planning and preparation activities:

• Handouts for students — To make sure groups knew tasks each member should do, Mia created handouts of timelines and what should be accomplished at each stage of the project. She also made a checklist of information students were to collect and made copies so students could check off what they had done as they went. She wanted to make sure everyone knew how she would grade work, so she made copies of the assessments (rubric and description of country information test), handed them out, and discussed them with the students.

• Computer schedule — She had a classroom workstation consisting of five networked computers, each with an Internet connection, so she set up a schedule for small groups to use the computers. She knew some students would need to scan pictures, download image files from the digital camera, and process them for sending to their partner schools, so she scheduled some additional time in the computer lab for this work. She thought that students could also do other work in the library/media center after school, if they needed still more time.

Analysis Questions — Answer these questions online at the Companion Website (http://www.prenhall.com/roblyer). Select Chapter 2.

1. If Mia wanted to do a demonstration and display of the project website to the whole class at one time, what resource would she have to arrange to do this?

2. Mia was concerned about students revealing too much personal information about themselves to their partner schools. What guidelines should she give them about information exchanges to protect their privacy and security?

3. If the network or Internet access were interrupted for a day, what could Mia have the students do to make good use of their time during this delay?

---

allowed time for testing and backup of files; they have a backup plan in the event technology resources fail to work as planned.

Phase 4 questions. This phase in integrating technology requires answering three questions about preparing an instructional environment that will support technology integration:

• **What equipment, software, media, and materials will I need to carry out the instructional strategies?** — As you create ways to stretch scarce resources, be sure that your strategies are ethical and in keeping with the reasons you chose a technology-based solution in the first place. Some guidelines:

• *Computers* — If enough computers aren't available to support the individual format you wanted, consider organizing the integration plan around student pairs or small groups. Also consider having computer and noncomputer learning stations that individuals or groups cycle through, completing various activities at each one. However, if students must master skills on an individual basis, consider scheduling time in a computer lab when all students in the class can use resources at once.

• *Copies of software and media* — Unless a software or media package specifically allows it, making copies of published software or media is illegal, even if copies are used on a temporary basis. Inquire about education-priced lab packs and site licenses.

• *Access to peripherals* — In addition to computers, remember to plan for adequate access to printers, printer paper, and any other needed peripherals (e.g., probes, handhelds).

• *Handouts and other materials* — Prepare and copy (or post) necessary support materials. Unless learning to use the software without guidance is a goal of the project, consider creating summary sheets to remind students how to do basic operations.

CLASSROOM EXAMPLE: ONLINE MULTICULTURAL PROJECT

Phase 5: Evaluate and revise integration strategies. Mia was generally pleased with the results of the multicultural project. According to the semantic differential, most students showed a major improvement in how they perceived people from the country they were studying. Students she had spoken with were very enthusiastic about their chats and email exchanges. Some group brochures and booklets were more polished than others, but they all showed good insights into the similarities and differences between cultures, and every group had met the rubric criteria on content. The web searches they had done seemed to have helped a lot. One thing that became clear was that production work on their published products was very time consuming; the schedule would have to be changed to allow more time. Mia also realized she had to stress more that the deadlines are firm. Students would search and take digital photos forever, if she let them, and that put them behind on doing their products, and left little time to discuss their findings on comparisons of cultures. Results varied on the short-answer test on the government and geography of the country being studied. Only about half the students met the 80% criterion. Mia realized she would have to schedule a review of this information before the test. She decided to make this a final group task after the production work was done.

Analysis Questions — Answer these questions online at the Companion Website (http://www.prenhall.com/roblyer). Select Chapter 2.

1. Although all of Mia's groups did well on context overall, rubric scores revealed that most groups scored lower on one area: spelling, grammar, and punctuation of products. What steps could Mia add to the production work checklist that may improve this outcome next time?

2. If you found that only five of the seven groups in the class were doing well on their final products, what might be one way to find out more about why this was happening?

3. One teacher who observed the project told Mia it might be good to have the school district media/materials production office do the final work on the products for the students. Does this seem like a good idea? Why or why not?

- **How should resources be arranged to support instruction and learning?**

  - *Access by students with disabilities* — For students with visual or hearing deficits, consider software or adaptive devices created especially to address these disabilities.

  - *Privacy and safety issues* — Students should never use the Internet without adult supervision and should never do unplanned chat sessions. If possible, **firewall software** should be used to prevent accidental access to inappropriate sites.

- **What planning is required to make sure technology resources work well?**

  - *Troubleshooting* — Computers, like all machines, will occasionally break down. Learn simple diagnostic procedures so you can correct some problems without assistance.

  - *Test-runs and backup plans* — Leave sufficient time to learn and practice using resources before students use them, but also try out the resources again just before class begins. Have a backup plan in case something goes wrong at the last minute.

Phase 5: Evaluate and Revise Integration Strategies

As teachers complete a technology-based project with students, they begin reviewing evidence on how successful the strategies and plans were in solving the problems they identified. They use this information to decide what should be changed in objectives, strategies, and implementation tasks to ensure even more success next time.

Evaluation issues. In Phase 5, teachers look at the following kinds of issues:

- **Were objectives achieved?** — This is the primary criterion of success for the activity. Teachers review achievement, attitude, and observation data they have collected and decide if the technology-based method solved the problem(s) they had in mind. These data help them determine what should be changed to make the activity work better.

- **What do students say?** — Some of the best suggestions on needed improvements come from students. Informal discussions with them yield a unique "consumer" focus on the activity.

- **Could improving instructional strategies improve results?** — Technologies in themselves usually improve little; it is the way teachers use them that is critical. Look at the design of both the technology use and the learning activities surrounding it.

- **Could improving the environment improve results?** — Sometimes a small change such as better scheduling or access to a printer can make a big difference in a project's success.

- **Have I integrated technology well?** — Use the *Technology Impact Checklist* (see the Technology Integration Workshop DVD accompanying this text or the Companion Website for this chapter at http:// www.prenhall. com/roblyer) to determine if the activity has been "worth it."

Phase 5 questions. This phase in integrating technology requires answering two summary questions about evaluating and revising technology integration strategies:

- **How well has the technology integration strategy worked?** — Review the collected data to answer this question.

  - ***Achievement data*** — If the problem was low student achievement, do data show students are achieving better than they were before? If the goal was improved motivation or attitudes, are they achieving at least as well as they did before? Is higher achievement consistent across the class, or did some students seem to profit more than others?

  - ***Attitude data*** — If the problem was low motivation or students refusing to do required work, are there indications this behavior has improved? Has it improved for everyone or just for certain students?

  - ***Students' comments*** — Be sure to ask both lower achieving and higher achieving students for their opinions. Even if achievement and motivation seem to be improved, what do students say about the activity? Do they want to do similar activities again?

- **What could be improved to make it work better?** — The first time you do a technology-based activity, you can expect it will take longer and you will encounter more errors than in subsequent uses. The following areas are most often cited as needing improvement:

  - ***Scheduling*** — If students request any change, it is usually for more time. This may or may not be feasible, but you can review the schedule to determine if additional time can be built in for learning software and/or for production work.

  - ***Technical skills*** — It usually takes longer than expected for students to learn the technology tools. How can this learning be expedited or supported better?

- ***Efficiency*** — The teacher complaint is usually that the activity took longer than expected to plan and carry out. Review the schedule to see if there is any way this can be expedited.

Figure 2.16 summarizes the steps to consider in all five phases of the TIP Model.

WHEN TECHNOLOGY WORKS BEST: ESSENTIAL CONDITIONS FOR TECHNOLOGY INTEGRATION

When ISTE established National Education Technology Standards (NETS) for teachers, students, and administrators, they also described conditions that are necessary for teachers to exploit the potential power of technology. As ISTE leaders introduced NETS in forums around the country, teachers spoke of barriers they had encountered when they attempted to implement technology in their schools or classrooms. The essential conditions were distilled from these comments. These conditions are summarized in ISTE's 2002 *NETS for Teachers* book. Once teachers complete an effective preparation program and take positions in schools, their ability to use technology to good advantage is determined in large part by whether or not the school district and/or school have provided the conditions described here.

Essential Condition: A Shared Vision for Technology Integration

Teachers need system-wide support to implement technology. This means that the school, district, local community, and the state share with teachers a commitment to using technology to support teaching and learning. As Kwajewski (1997b) says, educational leaders must view technology as a "core value." Usually, this commitment is documented in the form of a statewide and/or district-wide plan created as a cooperative effort of teachers, administrators, and community business partners. The National Center for Technology Planning (http://www. nctp.com/) offers guidelines for planning strategies and examples of school and district plans. Kimball and Sibley (1997–1998) have provided a comprehensive rubric for assessing these plans. To ensure that teachers and administrators have a shared vision for how technology should be supported, all technology plans should reflect the qualities discussed next.

Coordinate school and district planning and involve teachers and other personnel at all levels. Plans at school and district levels should be coordinated with each other. It is helpful if each school has a technology liaison/coordinator to act as the school's representative in a district-wide planning committee. To obtain widespread support for a

Figure 2.16   The Technology Integration Planning Checklist

Phase 1:   Determine Relative Advantage—Why Use Technology?

_____ Do I have topics, curriculum objectives, or insights I have difficulty teaching?

_____ Are any of the above a good match for a technology-based solution?

_____ What is the relative advantage of the technology-based solution?

_____ Is relative advantage sufficient to justify the effort and expense of using these solutions?

Phase 2:   Decide on Objectives and Assessments—How Will I Know Students Have Learned?

_____ What outcomes do I expect of students after instruction to show me they have learned?

_____ What is the best way for me to assess students' learning (e.g., written tests, products)?

_____ Do the assessment instruments (e.g., tests, rubrics) exist or do I have to develop them?

Phase 3:   Design Integration Strategies—What Teaching Strategies Will Work Best?

_____ Will the instruction be single subject or interdisciplinary?

_____ Will students work as individuals, pairs, small or large groups, whole class, a combination?

_____ Should activities be directed, constructivist, or a combination of these?

_____ What strategies should I use to encourage female and minority student involvement?

_____ What sequence of activities should I teach?

_____ Will students have enough time to learn the technologies before I begin grading?

_____ Do I have demonstrations of equipment and the software skills students will need?

Phase 4:   Prepare the Instructional Environment—Are Essential Conditions in Place to Support Technology Integration?

_____ How many computers and copies of software do I need to carry out the activities?

_____ How many computers and copies of software are available?

_____ Over what time period and for how long will technology resources be needed?

_____ Do I need to schedule time in a lab or media center?

_____ Do I need to schedule projection devices or large-screen monitors for demos?

_____ What other equipment, software, media, and resources will I need?

_____ Are the uses I am planning legal according to copyright laws?

_____ Have I provided for students' privacy and safety?

_____ Have I made all necessary access provisions for students with physical disabilities?

_____ Am I familiar with troubleshooting procedures specific to the hardware or software?

_____ Have I built in time to test-run an equipment setup before students arrive?

_____ Have I built in time to back up important files? Have I trained students to back up theirs?

_____ Do I have a backup plan if I cannot use the resources as I had planned?

Phase 5:   Evaluate and Revise Integration Strategies—What Worked Well? What Should Be Improved?

_____ Were objectives achieved? What evidence do I have to indicate success?

_____ Have I solicited feedback from students about how to improve activities?

_____ Do data and comments indicate changes are needed to improve outcomes?

_____ Are there other ways to arrange technology resources or activities to improve results?

See a modifiable copy of this checklist on the Companion Website and the DVD.

---

plan, planning should involve parents, community leaders, school and district administrators, and teachers.

Budget yearly amounts for technology purchases and make funding incremental. Technology changes too rapidly for schools to expect one-time purchases of equipment or software to suffice. A technology plan should allow for yearly upgrades and additions to keep resources current and useful. A plan should identify a specific amount to spend each year and a priority list of activities to fund over the life of the plan.

Emphasize teacher training. Knowledgeable people are as important to a technology plan as up-to-date technology resources. Successful technology programs hinge on well-trained, motivated teachers. A technology plan should acknowledge and address this need with appropriate training activities.

Match technology to curriculum needs. Rather than asking, "How can we use this equipment and software?" an effective vision focuses on questions such as these:

- What are our current unmet needs and can technology address them?
- What are we teaching now that we can teach better with technology?
- What can we teach with technology that we could not teach before but that should be taught?

It is difficult to identify unmet needs since the emergence of new technology has a way of changing them. Many educators did not realize they needed faster communications until the fax machine, email, and cellular telephones became available. However, technology should become an integral part of new methods to make education more efficient, exciting, and successful.

Keep current and build in flexibility. Leading-edge technology solutions can quickly become outdated as new resources and applications emerge. To keep up with these changes, educators must constantly read and attend conferences, workshops, and meetings. School and district technology plans should address how schools will obtain and use technology resources over a 3- to 5-year period, but should also incorporate new information through annual reviews.

Essential Condition: Standards and Curriculum Support

The NETS for Students are technology knowledge and skills that students must acquire in order to "live, learn, and work successfully, in an increasingly complex and information-rich society" (ISTE, 2000, p. 2). However, as the example lessons throughout this textbook indicate, students do not learn these standards as a separate subject area. Rather, they achieve them in the context of their work in content-area courses. Therefore, it is critical to situate NETS for Students in content-area curriculum in ways that support both the subject-area content and the technology skills. Fortunately, many content-area standards already address appropriate technology resources and applications, and others seem poised to do so. Thus, this essential condition is best met when technology and content-area standards are designed to support each other.

Essential Condition: Required Policies

As discussed in Chapter 1, legal, ethical, and equity conditions in our society profoundly affect educational uses of technology in schools. Effective technology integration that supports student learning requires school and district policies to ensure the appropriate behavior, safety, and equitable treatment of all students.

Internet use policies. The increasing use of the Internet for communications and research also means increased risks for students. A recent national survey reported that 19% of all young people using the Internet had been approached by predators. The situation is so alarming that the U.S. Congress passed the Children's Internet Protection Act to encourage schools to take measures that will keep children away from Internet materials that could be harmful to them (McNabb, 2001). Most schools have students sign an **acceptable use policy (AUP)** that stipulates the risks involved in Internet use; outlines appropriate, safe student behavior on the Internet; and asks students if they agree to use the Internet under these conditions and if they agree to certain information about themselves being posted on the school's website. Example AUPs and guidelines for how to prepare them are available on the University of Delaware website at http://www.ash.udel.edu/. (See the Companion Website at www.prenhall.com/roblyer for the exact URL.)

Legal/ethical use polices. Schools also have policies and materials in place to address several common issues: illegal access to school servers (hacking), viruses, and software/media piracy. Districts usually address illegal access problems by placing *firewall software* on district and school networks. Firewall software prevents access to specific website addresses or to websites that contain certain keywords or phrases. (Unfortunately, firewalls and filtering software also create a new set of problems for schools by preventing their users from connecting to many legitimate educational sites.) Other districts or schools choose to use commercially available filtering software. Districts and schools also safeguard computers by using virus protection software and posting warnings to students and teachers about the hazards of opening downloaded files. Simpson (2001) gives an excellent summary of laws related to software copying, recommendations on publicizing software policies, and example copyright statements that schools and districts can use. He emphasizes that software companies are serious about enforcing software copyright laws and that districts and schools can protect themselves against copyright infringement lawsuits by stating and publicizing a policy regarding software copying, by requiring teacher and staff training on the topic, by requiring hard drive and network programs that discourage users from making illegal copies, and by providing adequate numbers of copies for their users (e.g., site licenses, lab packs, or networkable versions).

Policies to ensure equity. Schools are also responsible for ensuring equitable access and use of technology resources by all students, especially those who are traditionally underserved or underrepresented in mathematics, science, and technology occupations. This includes females, Hispanic and African American students, and students with disabilities.

Essential Condition: Access to Hardware, Software, and Other Resources

Finding funding. Experts agree that adequate funding can determine the success or failure of even the best technology plans. The summary of guidelines on funding shown in Figure 2.17 is based on recommendations from Ritchie and Boyle (1998) and Soloman (2001). Schools will never have the budgets for technology that they want or need. Strategies for optimizing available funds include requiring competitive bids, scheduling hardware and software upgrades, using donated equipment, and using broken computers for spare parts.

Purchasing hardware and software. Although teachers depend on their schools and district offices to take leadership in providing necessary resources, teacher input in this process is critically important. When schools and districts make hardware and software purchases, they are making curricular decisions. Therefore, it is important for purchases to begin with the curriculum needs for which teachers most need technology support.

Setting up and maintaining physical facilities. Schools have developed several arrangements for computer equipment to support teachers' various curriculum needs. (See Figure 1.10 in Chapter 1.) Schools can minimize technology repair problems if users follow good usage rules and conduct preventive maintenance procedures. In addition, education organizations usually choose one of the following maintenance options: maintenance contracts with outside suppliers, in-house maintenance office, built-in maintenance with each equipment purchase, or a repair and maintenance budget. Each of these methods has its problems and limitations and debate continues over which method or combination of methods is most cost effective depending on an organization's size and its number of computers and peripherals. Securing equipment is an equally important maintenance issue. Loss of equipment from vandalism and theft is a common problem in schools. Again, several options are available to deal with this problem: monitoring and alarm systems, security cabinets, and lock-down systems.

Essential Condition: Trained Personnel

As a result of the high-profile U.S. DOE initiative Preparing Tomorrow's Teachers to Use Technology (PT3), most preservice teacher training programs include at least some training in how to integrate technology effectively into teaching. However, because technology resources and applications change so quickly, continuing staff development in technology resources and applications remains an essential condition. Roblyer and Erlanger (1998) summa-

rize findings from the literature on what makes teacher training programs most effective in helping teachers get to higher stages of awareness about technology:

- **Hands-on, integration emphasis** — Technology integration skills cannot be learned by sitting passively in a classroom, listening to an instructor, or watching demonstrations. Participants must have an opportunity to navigate through a program and complete a set of steps to create a new product. The focus must be on how to use the technology resources in classrooms, rather than just technical skills.

- **Training over time** — Many schools are discovering that traditional models of staff development, particularly "one-shot" inservice training for the entire faculty, are ineffective for teaching skills and for helping teachers develop methods to use computers as instructional tools (Benson, 1997). Technology inservice training must be ongoing.

- **Modeling, mentoring, and coaching** — Instructors who model the use of technology in their own teaching long have been acknowledged as the most effective teacher trainers (Handler, 1992; Wetzel, 1993). Research also indicates that one-to-one mentoring and coaching programs are effective for new teachers (Benson, 1997). Linking teachers to each other and to staff developers has also been shown to be effective (Office of Technology Assessment, 1995; Ringstaff & Yocam, 1995). Most teachers seem to learn computer skills through colleague interaction and information sharing (Oliver, 1994).

- **Post-training access** — Teachers not only need adequate access to technology to accomplish training, they also need access after training to practice and use what they have learned.

Essential Condition: Technical Assistance

Each teacher needs training in simple troubleshooting procedures, such as what to do if a computer says a disk is "unreadable." However, teachers should not be expected to address more complicated diagnostic and maintenance problems. Nothing is more frustrating than depending on access to a computer to complete an important student project only to discover it is broken or malfunctioning. Cuban, Kirkpatrick, and Peck (2001) cite equipment problems as a major obstacle to effective technology integration. Schools must support teachers by replacing and repairing equipment designated for classroom use.

Essential Condition: Appropriate Teaching and Assessment Approaches

As Chapters 3 through 15 in this textbook illustrate, models of technology integration range from relatively passive

Figure 2.17   Finding Funding for Technology

Funding Sources

Hundreds of sources can be found under each of these five categories: *federal, state, corporate, private,* and *community.* The first four usually have budgets for funding larger projects. Schools and teachers usually have smaller projects and seek funding from community sources (e.g., companies, individuals, and groups). General funding sources include:

- **Federal funding sources:** http://www.grants.gov
- **Sources specific to your state:** Links from your state Department of Education website
- **Foundations of large companies:** Look for links from company websites
- **Issues of professional education magazines**
- **Issues of educational technology:** Columns on funding sources and deadlines.

Writing Successful Proposals

1. **Read and follow the guidelines.** Your idea MUST address directly the primary goals of the agency (e.g., some agencies cannot fund equipment; some accept only proposals from K–12 groups, and some only from higher education).
2. **Organize the proposal.** Have these components: a concise overview (one to two pages maximum), a statement of needs the proposal addresses, statements of specific goals and objectives, a narrative summary (as brief as possible), a budget spreadsheet that identifies costs in categories, and a budget narrative that explains the costs.
3. **Write in clear and compelling language.** Ask as many people as possible to read it and suggest changes before you submit the proposal.

Online Grant Writing Guides

Take a "short course" on how to write effective proposals. Most of these courses have links to sources, as well as basics on how to write proposals.

- About.com's Advice for Secondary School Educators (http://www.7-12educators.about.com/education/7-12educators/cs/grantwriting/)
- Eisenhower National Clearinghouse Guidelines and Opportunities (http://www.enc.org/professional/funding/)
- Grant Writing for Educators (http://capecod.net/~dkeefe/Grantwriting_for_Educators.htm)
- Guide for Proposal Writing Created at Michigan State University (http://www.LearnerAssociates.net/proposal)
- Guidelines for Beginners—An Educator's Guide (http://www.uml.edu/College/Education/Faculty/lebaron/GRANTBEGIN)
- National Science Foundation Proposal Writing Guide (http://www.her.nsf.gov/HER/DUE/documents/general/9783/proposal.htm)
- Proposal Writing Short Course (http://www.fdncenter.org/grants/grantwriting.html)
- TERC Grant Writing Guide (http://www.ra.terc.edu/publications/TERC/pubs/TERCGrantManual/TOC)
- West Ed's Proposal Writing Tips (http://www.wested.org/tie/granttips.html)

Characteristics of Successful Applicants

Schools and projects that obtain funding have several characteristics in common:

- They have ideas for how to make things better.
- They keep in constant touch with funding opportunities.
- They have things already written up so they are able to respond quickly when opportunities arise.
- They have one or more good writers handy.
- They are passionate about their work and know how to describe what they do.

Building on Success

To continue receiving outside funding, educators who have a funded project must do three things on a continuing basis:

1. **Carry out what you proposed.** Show you did good things with what you already received.
2. **Publicize your success.** Publicize through school and district public relations personnel. Create publications and websites to document accomplishments. Ask the local newspaper or TV and radio stations to come for a show-and-tell session. Give talks and presentations to local groups, and get your project on the agendas of school meetings.
3. **Generate new funding opportunities.** View funded projects as seeds for new opportunities, rather than one-time activities.

Sources: Ritchie, D., & Boyle, K. (1998). Finding the bucks for technology. *Learning and Leading with Technology, 26*(2), 46–50; and Soloman, G. (2001). Deconstructing a grant. *Technology & Learning, 21*(11), 44–52.

Figure 2.18 Summary of Essential Conditions for Effective Technology Integration

Effective Technology Integration			
Trained Personnel	Access to Hardware, Software, and Other Resources	Appropriate Teaching and Assessment Approaches	Technical Assistance
Shared Vision for Technology Integration	Standards and Curriculum Support		Required Policies

uses (e.g., teachers reviewing a topic with a *PowerPoint* presentation) to more interactive, hands-on ones (e.g., students using word processing for student reports or calculators for supporting mathematics problem solving, doing Internet searches for research, or creating hypermedia products to communicate research findings). Each of these models is appropriate, depending on the instructional need, and teachers should be encouraged to use all of them. Assessment practices also will vary with the technology integration model. The critical factor is matching the teaching strategy with an appropriate assessment strategy. For example, if students are creating web pages, a grading rubric would measure their achievement better than a traditional written test. Depending on the integration model, teachers may want to use a combination of assessment strategies (e.g., written tests, as well as products evaluated with a rubric).

A summary of these essential conditions for effective technology integration is shown in Figure 2.18.

INTERACTIVE SUMMARY

The following is a summary of the main points covered in this chapter. To see additional examples and information on these points, go to this textbook's Companion Website at http://www.prenhall.com/roblyer and click on the Chapter 2 *Interactive Summary* module to visit each of the recommended websites.

1. **Learning theories as bases for integration models:** Two lines of learning theories have given rise to two kinds of integration models: directed and constructivist.

   • *Directed models* were shaped by objectivist theories: behaviorist (Skinner), information-processing, cognitive-behavioral (Gagné), and systems theories.

   • *Constructivist models* were shaped by constructivist theories: social activism (Dewey), scaffolding (Vygotsky), child development (Piaget and Bruner), and multiple intelligences (Gardner) theories.

Review these learning theories at the Em Tech and Theory into Practice Database websites.

2. **The Technology Integration Planning Model:** This model is designed to help teachers (especially those new to technology) plan for effective classroom uses of technology. The model consists of five phases:

   • **TIP Model Phase 1: Relative advantage** — Deciding on instructional problems and whether or not a technology-based solution would be better than other ways of addressing the problems. (See five questions at the CARET website that teachers can ask to determine if technology-based methods have the potential to impact student learning.)

   • **Tip Model Phase 2: Objectives and assessments** — Stating desired outcomes in terms of better student achievement, attitudes, and performance; matching appropriate assessment strategies to each outcome. (See especially Kathy Schrock's Guide for Educators for good samples of assessment instruments.)

   • **TIP Model Phase 3: Integration strategies** — Deciding on teaching activities that incorporate technology resources to enhance student learning. (For some ideas for directed, constructivist, and combination strategies, look at the Blue Web 'N website, a collection of links to outstanding online lessons.)

   • **TIP Model Phase 4: Instructional environment** — Deciding on resources and conditions to put into place to support the activities.

   • **TIP Model Phase 5: Evaluation and revision** — Collecting achievement data and other information to determine if the activities were successful in meeting desired outcomes, and what could be improved next time.

3. **Essential conditions for technology integration** —For technology to have the desired impact on improved teaching and learning, several conditions must be in place:

   • **Shared vision for technology integration** — This requires coordinated school and district planning with teachers and other personnel at all levels, budgeting yearly amounts for technology purchases with incremental funding, emphasizing teacher training, matching technology to curriculum needs, and keeping current and building in flexibility.

- **Standards and curriculum support** — Technology and content-area standards are designed to support each other.

- **Required policies** — Policies are in place to ensure legal/ethical use, safe Internet use, and equity.

- **Access to hardware, software, and other resources** — There is adequate funding, purchasing procedures are organized and effective, and procedures are in place to set up and maintain technology resources.

- **Trained personnel** — Staff development that includes hands-on, integration emphasis; training over time; modeling, mentoring, and coaching; and post-training access to technology resources.

- **Technical assistance** — Continuing support for diagnostic and maintenance problems for teachers' and students' computers

- **Appropriate teaching and assessment approaches** — Teaching strategies that are matched to needs, and assessment strategies that are matched to the type of learning being measured See the ISTE website for more explanation of essential conditions for teachers' optimal use of technologies.

Online Activities

Visit this text's Companion Website at http://www.prenhall.com/roblyer to gain access to a variety of questions, activities, and exercises to help build your knowledge of this chapter's content.

Online Chapter 2 Self-Test

To review terms and concepts for this chapter, click on the *Self-Test* module for this chapter of the Companion Website.

Software Skill-Builder Tutorials CW

To access practical tutorial and skill-building activities that will help you build skills using popular software and hardware, click on the *Software Skill-Builder Tutorials* module for this chapter of the Companion Website.

Web-Enrichment Activities CW

To complete activities that connect to chapter content and provide web-based resources, click on the *Web-Enrichment Activities* module for this chapter of the Companion Website.

TECHNOLOGY INTEGRATION WORKSHOP

CLIPS FROM THE CLASSROOM: LEARNING WITH TECHNOLOGY

Go to the *Technology Integration Workshop* DVD located in the back of this text and click on *Clips from the Classroom*. View the video clips listed below that support this chapter's content:

- Geometer's Sketchpad *for Inductive Reasoning*
- *Parent Pleased with Son's Opportunities*
- *Technology Improves Teaching Skills*
- *Technology Manages Flow of Activities*
- PowerPoint *Guides and Prompts Teaching*

Now, visit this text's Companion Website at http://www.prenhall.com/roblyer to answer questions and complete activities that will guide you in analyzing each clip.

TIE INTO PRACTICE: TECHNOLOGY INTEGRATION EXAMPLES

Read each of the following scenarios related to implementing the TIP Model, and go to the Companion Website to answer the questions that follow it based on your Chapter 2 reading activities.

TIE-In #1: Phase 1—Determining the Relative Advantage

The superintendent of the Wellmade School District felt that every student should be "connected to the Information Superhighway," so he decided to install Internet connections in every school classroom in the district. The hardware and installations were funded through a federal grant and local business sponsors. Two years later, it became apparent that only about 25% of the teachers were using the Internet with students, and most uses were "casual surfing."

1.1 Why do you think the teachers did not see the relative advantage of this technology?

1.2 If you were made responsible for integrating this technology into instructional activities, how would you translate the superintendent's rationale into problems and solutions for which the relative advantage would be clear to teachers?

TIE-In #2: Phase 2—Deciding on Objectives and Assessments

As a school district science coordinator, you would like the high school biology teachers to begin using a dissection simulation program in lieu of actual dissections of pigs, which has always been done in the past. You feel this will save both time and money for materials. Some biology teachers are reluctant to make this change; they say that students cannot learn as much about anatomy and dissection techniques from a simulation as they can from the "real thing." However, they agree to a test of the software in a couple of classes.

2.1 What would be the expectations of the simulation method in terms of general outcomes?

2.2 If you were one of the biology teachers, how would you state objectives matched to these outcomes?

2.3 What instruments or information would you use to assess the "saving time and money" objective?

TIE-In #3: Phase 3—Designing Integration Strategies

Luella is a language arts teacher who uses a software package with vocabulary practice items to improve students' performance on a college entrance exam. Before she has the students use the software, she describes test-taking tips and strategies and then shows them how to use the software. Since she feels students can help each other with difficult words, she has them work in groups of three to practice the software. They take turns practicing for about 15 minutes at the end of each class period for the last 2 weeks of the grading period.

3.1 Are Luella's methods primarily directed or inquiry based?

3.2 Do you think this group-based strategy is a good one for the activity? Why or why not?

3.3 Do you think 15 minutes of group practice at the end of each class period will be enough to increase students' performance? Why or why not?

TIE-In #4: Phase 4—Preparing the Instructional Environment

Esmerelda is having her students do a social studies project in which they do "virtual interviews" of experts on various periods in U.S. history. She schedules time in the computer lab and has them locate experts by searching Internet sites. She gives them an initial list of sites, but encourages them to branch out from there, looking for additional sites on their own. There is no lab manager and she has to go back to the classroom for periods of time as they work, but she knows they are competent Internet users and can be trusted not to leave the lab without permission. For their contacts with experts, she has them prepare a standard email with the school name; their names, ages, addresses, and personal email addresses, if they have one; and a description of what they would like to know.

4.1 Assuming she is correct that students will not leave the lab with permission, is Esmeralda's plan for having students use the Internet a good one? Why or why not?

4.2 Do you see any problems with the email she is having them send?

4.3 How would you change her plan to improve it?

TIE-In #5: Phase 5—Evaluating and Revising Integration Strategies Wilfred was a special education resource teacher who wanted to give students with dysgraphia (nonwriting behavior) an alternative way to do homework and class assignments. He showed a couple of the students how to use a small portable "computer companion" with a keyboard and word processing program. They did their work wherever they were and downloaded it to a computer later and printed it out. Students quickly learned how to do the activity and were delighted with their new ability. For the first time, they turned in all assignments on time. However, on a brief survey he gave to the special education teachers, four of the five teachers indicated they would not use it for their own students with dysgraphia.

5.1 Would you say findings indicate the project was a success? Why or why not?

5.2 What should he do to find out why teachers responded in this way?

5.3 What other data or information could he gather about the quality of students' written assignments that could help him decide how to improve the strategy?

FOR YOUR TEACHING PORTFOLIO

For this chapter's contribution to your teaching portfolio, do the following and add them to your portfolio:

- Teachers choose technology-based methods over other methods when they see the "relative advantage, " that is, when the new method offers enough benefits to convince them to use it instead of the old one. Relative advantage is a perception or belief shaped by teachers' experience and by information they receive. One way teachers learn that a technology-based method has relative advantage is through reading research results. The Center for Applied Research in Educational Technology (CARET) website (http://caret.iste.org) summarizes "best evidence" research results on the impact of technology in education. Look at the results for the Student Learning area. List the five questions CARET says teachers can ask to determine if technology-based methods have an impact on student learning. Describe two or more studies at the CARET website that offer convincing evidence that a technology-based method has more impact on student learning than another method.

- Go to the ISTE website (http://cnets.iste.org /teachers/tprofile-gen.html) and make a chart of your own General Performance profile, based on the essential conditions at this level. (ISTE NETS-T, I-A, B)

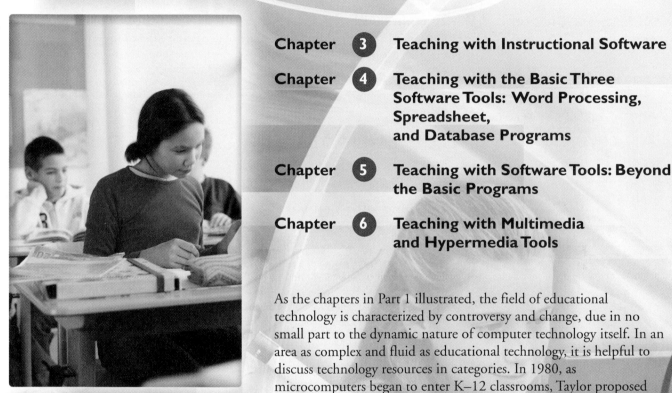

PART 2

INTEGRATING SOFTWARE TUTORS AND TOOLS INTO TEACHING AND LEARNING

As the chapters in Part 1 illustrated, the field of educational technology is characterized by controversy and change, due in no small part to the dynamic nature of computer technology itself. In an area as complex and fluid as educational technology, it is helpful to discuss technology resources in categories. In 1980, as microcomputers began to enter K–12 classrooms, Taylor proposed categorizing computer resources as "tutor, tool, and tutee" functions. The tutor functions included those in which the "computer [was] programmed by experts in both programming and in a subject matter . . . and the student [was] then tutored by the computer" (p. 3). In its tool functions, the computer "had some useful capability programmed into it such as statistical analysis . . . or word processing" (p. 3). Tutee functions helped the student learn about logic processes or how computers worked by "teaching" (programming) computers to perform various activities in languages like BASIC or Logo.

Many educators still use this function-based classification system. Because many resources can serve more than one function, those new to the field often find it helpful to supplement and overlay this classification system with one based on technical characteristics. This text adopts such a system, classifying resources as software (Part 2) and Internet based (Part 3). Part 2 chapters deal with technology resources that revolve around using a computer program (software). Software resources are grouped as instructional software (Chapter 3), software tools (Chapters 4 and 5), and multimedia/hypermedia (Chapter 6).

PART 2

REQUIRED BACKGROUND FOR TEACHERS

In Part 2, four chapters help teachers build technology skills they will need to take advantage of software resources.

Chapter 3   Teaching with Instructional Software

Most people think of instructional software (or courseware) as performing a "tutor" function common to directed instruction models. However, some software also can function as a tool in integration strategies that are based on constructivist models. Software described in this chapter fulfills the following instructional roles: tutorial, drill and practice, simulation, instructional games, and problem solving. Chapter 3 also covers networked delivery systems called integrated learning systems (ILSs) that provide these software functions and keep track of students' usage of them.

Chapter 4   Teaching with the Basic Three Software Tools: Word Processing, Spreadsheet, and Database Programs

Chapter 4 describes and gives integration strategies for three of the most commonly discussed computer programs under the category of classroom technology tools: word processing, spreadsheet, and database software. These tools were among the first tools to be developed and used in education, especially with microcomputers; thus, the literature documents more uses and classroom integration strategies for them than for most of the tools developed later. Also, these three functions are commonly found as components of so-called integrated software packages or software suites. (These are different from the integrated learning systems, or ILSs, discussed in Chapter 3.) Even though these three tools have come to be known as "productivity software," Chapter 4 describes and illustrates both productivity and instructional applications for them.

Chapter 5   Teaching with Software Tools: Beyond the Basic Programs

Since computers came into common use outside of the business office, software tools have emerged to fill a variety of functions. They support students with many repetitive and/or mechanical operations involved in learning, for example, handwriting (when the focus of instruction is writing a story or a composition); arithmetic calculations (for lessons on solving algebra problems); organizing information (for lessons on how to classify animals according to common features); and presenting information clearly and attractively (for presentations on the results of a research project). Software tools contribute to teaching in the same way that power tools contribute to designing and building a house as compared to using hand tools. They make it easier to carry out the mechanics of building the house, but they can also profoundly affect the complexity of the designs that builders may attempt. Similarly, technology tools not only make learning faster and easier, they also make possible more complex, higher level methods than would be achievable without such tools.

Chapter 6   Teaching with Multimedia and Hypermedia Tools

The final chapter in Part 2 focuses on some of the most exciting technology resources in education today. Multimedia and hypermedia applications can be done with a variety of different hardware and software combinations ranging from simple uses of presentation software to sophisticated multimedia authoring systems. Perhaps more than any other technology resources, these applications help teachers and students reflect on and draw from the diversity of images and motion that characterize the world around us. This chapter describes each of the configurations that can be used in classrooms, including commercial multimedia software and three kinds of authoring software: presentation software, digital video editing systems, and multimedia/hypermedia authoring systems.

REFERENCE

Taylor, R. (1980). *The computer in the school: Tutor, tool, and tutee.* New York: Teachers College Press.

CHAPTER 3
TEACHING WITH INSTRUCTIONAL SOFTWARE

The fact that individuals bind themselves
with strong emotional ties to machines ought
not to be surprising. The instruments [we] use become ...
extensions of [our] bodies.

Joseph Weizenbaum, in *Computer Power and Human Reason* (1976, p. 9)

Grade Level: Middle school • Content Area/Topic: Science, solar system • Length of time: Three weeks

Phase 1: Determine relative advantage

Mr. Leroy was a veteran middle school science teacher who had won many awards for his teaching. However, he felt that, despite his efforts to make his class hands-on and project based, his students tended to see science as facts and procedures unrelated to practical problems. He felt most students left middle school without learning why scientific inquiry was useful. One day, he saw a conference presentation on software for middle school students. The software began with a video clip in which a problem scenario was presented as if it were a real live newscast. The video said that an alien spaceship was orbiting Earth and broadcasting a plea for help. Aliens on board the ship were from several planets in a galaxy whose sun had exploded. They escaped but now needed new habitats that would meet the needs of their various species. They asked Earth for help in matching them with planets and moons each might find habitable. The software provided an array of information and images on the planets and moons in our solar system, and students could find out about the characteristics of each by doing searches and activities like designing and "sending out" probes. After Mr. Leroy reviewed the software himself and decided it met all criteria for excellent software, he decided to have his students do this project for his solar system unit instead of building models of planets. He felt it would be a good way to generate enthusiasm for using scientific inquiry to help solve complex problems.

Phase 2: Decide on objectives and assessments

Mr. Leroy decided that, in addition to passing his usual test on solar system information, he wanted students to accomplish several outcomes. Also, he wanted to make sure students enjoyed this new approach. He developed the following outcomes, objectives, and assessments for his project:

- **Outcome:** Demonstrate a problem-solving approach to assigned problems. **Objective:** All students working in small groups will create well-designed problem statements, solutions steps, and workable solutions for at least one of three problems assigned. **Assessment:** A checklist based on steps and criteria from the *Alien Rescue Teacher Manual (TM)*.

- **Outcome:** Create and present new problems and methods to solve them. **Objective:** All groups will achieve a rubric score of at least 80% on presentations of a new problem and solution related to the alien simulation software. **Assessment:** A rubric to assess the content and quality of the presentation.

- **Outcome:** Use scientific inquiry language outside the unit. **Objective:** At least 80% of students will use the language of scientific inquiry outside of the unit. **Assessment:** An observation checklist.

- **Outcome:** Enjoy using inquiry methods. **Objective:** At least 90% of students will demonstrate positive attitudes toward the work. **Assessment:** A five-item survey that students will complete anonymously.

Source: Screen from *Alien Rescue Software* © The Alien Rescue Team 2001–2004 (http://www.alienrescue.com). Reprinted by permission.

Phase 3: Design integration strategies

Mr. Leroy realized that his students would learn inquiry-based methods only by seeing them in action and practicing them over time. He would have to facilitate, rather than direct, student learning, which would take more time than usual. He also realized that students had to answer questions about the solar system on the state's required exams, so he would have to provide diagnostic testing over these concepts and facts and, if necessary, remedial practice. Luckily, the *TM* provided test items like this to cover background information, which he could supplement with his own. With these things in mind, he created the following activity sequence:

- **Day 1:** Show the opening video to the whole class. Assign students to groups and let them log on to computers. Allow them to explore the software environment on their own.
- **Day 2:** Have the class review the problem presented in the video by asking the probing questions listed in the *Alien Rescue TM*. Let groups explore software further to answer any additional questions they might have.
- **Days 3–5:** Hold discussions about how to work in groups and use inquiry approaches to solve problems. Ask students to develop their own problem statements and discuss procedures they will use to solve them. Students will demonstrate software features they will need. Students practice using the software features and define lists of alien needs.
- **Days 6–10:** Students use software features to explore planets and moons and develop hypotheses about best matches for each alien species. They use word processing software to document their notes so they can update them easily throughout the activity.
- **Days 11–13:** Groups present their findings on best places for each species and write up final selections in the required format. Individual students complete the fact worksheets and get remedial practice, if necessary.
- **Days 14–16:** Final reflections, assessments, and remedial practice, where necessary.

Phase 4: Prepare the instructional environment

Mr. Leroy decided to take the *TM*'s advice and resist the tendency to overdirect students. He knew he had to keep to a timeline to complete the project on schedule, but he also realized that the software designers were warning that too much structure would work against the purpose and design of the software. Keeping this in mind, he began his planning:

- **Software skills:** The software was quite rich with features, tools, and resources, but it was so complex that Mr. Leroy knew he couldn't be expert on everything in it

and that some of his students would probably become more expert than he in a very short time. However, he wanted to become as familiar with it as possible so he could answer students' initial questions, so he went through it carefully and took notes.

- **Handouts:** The *TM* provided a chart to help students keep track of each species' needs. Mr. Leroy prepared a group task sheet and inserted this and other helpful notes.
- **Lesson planning:** Mr. Leroy was such a veteran science teacher that he usually didn't use lesson plans. But this project was so new and different from his usual methods that he felt he needed to prepare a written sequence. He left space for items he would add as his class progressed, so he would be even more prepared when he taught it next time.
- **Software copies:** He knew the software was available to teachers only from the university where it was developed. It was free, but he had to sign an agreement that only his class would be using it. He completed the paperwork and obtained the software. He made sure each copy worked on the equipment they had available.
- **Computer scheduling:** The trickiest part would be scheduling time on computers in the computer lab, since he had only one computer in his room. Mr. Leroy arranged with the lab coordinator to have the lab on the days he needed it. He also spoke with the principal, who agreed to give him an extra computer for his room so that more students could work there, if needed.

Phase 5: Evaluate and revise

Mr. Leroy was impressed with the impact the project had on his students' enthusiasm for inquiry skills. Rubric scores indicated they did better with each probe they designed and each set of data they analyzed. Perhaps best of all, Mr. Leroy documented that about half of the students were talking like scientists, using "inquiry-speak" in other work. Some girls asked about careers in space exploration, so Mr. Leroy sent them to look at the NASA and Space Camp sites on the Internet. The problem-solving checklists reflected good progress, too. Scores on the first ones they did were a little low, but the last ones were really fine in all groups. Mr. Leroy observed only two real problems. One was when some group members had to leave for special school events, which left a "hole" in the group, and they had to improvise. The other problem was access to computers. Mr. Leroy resolved to ask the principal for a five-computer workstation and printer like the English teacher had. Students' scores on the solar system test varied a lot, so he interviewed students informally to determine why some students did so much better than others. In general, attitudes toward science seemed way up, and students were more on task than he had ever seen them.

OBJECTIVES

After reading this chapter and completing the learning activities for it, you should be able to:

1. Define five software functions (drill and practice, tutorial, simulation, instructional game, and problem solving) according to their unique features, benefits, and limitations, and identify examples of each.

2. Define integrated learning systems (ILSs) according to their unique features, benefits, and limitations, and identify examples of ILS products.

3. Identify one or more types of instructional software functions that could meet classroom needs.

4. Plan lesson activities that integrate instructional software using a directed learning strategy.

5. Plan lesson activities that integrate instructional software using a constructivist or combination learning strategy.

6. Use appropriate methods to evaluate instructional software according to essential criteria.

KEY TERMS

- applications programs
- applications software
- computer-assisted instruction (CAI)
- computer programs
- courseware
- drill and practice
- instructional game
- instructional software
- integrated learning systems (ILSs)
- Logo
- problem solving
- simulation
- software
- systems software
- tutorial

CW For more information on Key Terms, go to the *Key Terms* module for this chapter of the Companion Website at http://www.prenhall.com/roblyer.

WHAT IS INSTRUCTIONAL SOFTWARE?

The *Alien Rescue®* lesson illustrates an example of what Weizenbaum (1976) called using computers as "extensions of [our] bodies." Such uses have a long history in education. At the same time as people began to realize that computers could help them do many clerical tasks more quickly and accurately, they also began thinking, "If **computer programs** (instructions written for the computer) can be created to do essentially anything, why not program computers to teach?" Educators and developers alike began to pursue this idea in the 1960s and 1970s. Some, like William Norris (1977) who developed Control Data's PLATO teaching system, believed that computer-based education was the only logical alternative to education's "outdated, labor-intensive ways" (p. 451). He believed that education would be more efficient if computers took over the traditional role of teachers.

Today, after about 30 years of development and experimentation, there is less talk of computers replacing teachers, but computer programs still help perform various teaching functions. This chapter shows how programs like the one in the *Alien Rescue* lesson and others empower teachers, rather than replace them.

Software is another word for programs written in computer languages (e.g., Basic, Assembler, C++, Java). Software designed and developed to make computers function is called **systems software,** but programs written to perform tasks such as word processing or tutoring are called **applications software** or **applications programs. Instructional software** (or **courseware**) is applications software that is designed specifically to deliver or assist with student instruction on a topic. Although applications software such as word processing and spreadsheets can also enhance instructional activities, this textbook differentiates between applications software and instructional software. Software tools serve many purposes other than teaching; instructional software packages are programs developed for the *sole* purpose of delivering instruction or supporting learning.

In the early days—when instructional software was used primarily to tutor students—it was called **computer assisted instruction (CAI).** The term is still in common use, but some kinds of instructional software are designed with more constructivist purposes in mind; they support, rather than actually deliver, instruction. Therefore, many people consider the term CAI outdated and misleading. Teachers may hear instructional software referred to as computer-based instruction (CBI), computer-based learning (CBL), or computer-assisted learning (CAL), or in more generic terms such as software learning tools.

Instructional Roles for Software: Past and Present

It used to be easy to name a software package by the type of teaching function it served. It was a **drill-and-practice, tutorial, simulation, instructional game,** or **problem solving** program. (See descriptions and examples of these in Figure 3.1.) These terms originated because each package had clearly different characteristics and served a different instructional purpose. In contrast, much of today's software defies easy classification, because many software packages contain several different activities, each of which may perform a different function. For example, a program like *Reader Rabbit* has a number of straight drill activities along with activities that fulfill problem-solving and game functions. Also, developers use the terms interchangeably; there seems to be no consensus among developers for terms used to describe various types of programs. Some developers refer to a drill program that gives extensive feedback as a tutorial. Others refer to simulations or problem-solving functions as games.

Software still reflects the same five functions, but in light of current trends toward multiple-function software packages, teachers have to analyze a package and determine which instructional function(s) it serves. They may not be able to refer to an entire package as a drill or a simulation, but it is possible and desirable to identify whether it provides, for example, science vocabulary skill practice and/or opportunities for studying plant growth in action. As this chapter will show, each software function serves a different purpose during learning and, consequently, has its own appropriate integration strategies.

Learning Theory Connections

The first instructional software reflected the behavioral and cognitive learning theories that were popular at the time. Some software functions (i.e., drill and practice, tutorial) remain focused on *directed* strategies that grew out of these theories, delivering information to help students acquire and retain information and skills. Later instructional software was designed to support the more *constructivist* aims of helping students explore topics and generate their own knowledge. Therefore, some software functions (e.g., simulation, games) can be used in either directed or constructivist ways, depending on how they are designed. Figure 3.2 (p. 79) summarizes the strategies underlying each of the five software functions described in this chapter.

Gagné, Wager, and Rojas (1981) suggested a way to look at software that can help educators analyze a given product with respect to its instructional function(s) and design appropriate integration strategies that make use of these functions. Gagné et al. said that drills, tutorials, and simulations each accomplish a different combination of the Events of Instruction (see them described in Chapter 2). The nine events are guidelines identified by Gagné that can help teachers arrange optimal "conditions for learning" for various types of knowledge and skills. By determining which of the events a software package fulfills, he said, educators can determine the teaching role it serves and where it might fit in the instructional process. However, Gagné's approach was primarily for directed uses, rather than constructivist ones. This chapter describes both kinds of strategies for instructional software.

Programming Languages as Instructional Software

This chapter focuses on software designed solely for instructional purposes (see Figure 3.1 for descriptions and examples of drill and practice, tutorials, simulations, instructional games, and problem solving), while Chapters 4 and 5 address the uses of tool software in education. Unlike instructional software described in this chapter, the uses of tool software (e.g., word processing, computer-assisted design or CAD software) are not limited to education. However, a few programming languages were designed especially for educational purposes and, thus, may be considered hybrid software, since they merge the capabilities of both instructional and tool software. One of the most widely known of the programming languages used for instruction is **Logo.** Logo is used to introduce young children to problem solving through programming and to explore concepts in content areas such as mathematics, science, and language arts (Galas, 1998; Gonsalves & Lopez, 1998; Weinstein, 1999). See Technology Integration Idea 3.1 (p. 80) for a sample use of Logo as instructional software.

The work of Seymour Papert (1980) (see Chapter 2) and his colleagues at the Massachusetts Institute of Technology made Logo "widely used throughout the world as an introductory programming language and mathematical learning environment for students in elementary and secondary schools" (Watt, 1992, p. 615). Although not as popular as it was in the 1980s, Logo and its derivative materials such as *Microworlds* software are still used for instructional purposes. Logo also led the way for other programming resources to be used in the same instructional ways. For example, Ploger and Vedova (1999) describe a "programming system" called *Boxer*, which combines a programming language with text processing and graphics capabilities to help students learn number-sense concepts.

Figure 3.1 **Five Instructional Software Functions**

Samples	Function/Examples	Description
http://www.transparent.com/	**Drill and Practice** Example: *Spanish Before You Know It*® (Transparent Language)	Allows learners to work problems or answer questions and get feedback on correctness.
http://www.poynterextra.org	**Tutorial** Example: *Color, Contrast,* and *Dimension in News Design*® (Poynter Online)	Acts like a human tutor by providing all the information and instructional activities a learner needs to master a topic: information summaries, explanation, practice routines, feedback, and assessment.
http://www.digitalfrog.com	**Simulation** Example: *The Digital Frog Dissection*® (The Digital Frog)	Models real or imaginary systems to show how those systems or similar ones work or to demonstrate underlying concepts.
http://www.riverdeep.com	**Instructional Game** Example: *Arthur's*® *Math Games*™ (Riverdeep, Inc.)	Increases motivation by adding game rules to drills or simulations.
http://www.riverdeep.com	**Problem Solving** Example: *Thinkin' Things*® (Riverdeep, Inc.)	(a) Teaches directly (through explanation and/or practice) the steps involved in solving problems or (b) helps learners acquire problem-solving skills by giving them opportunities to solve problems.

Figure 3.2 Types of Integration Strategies for Each Instructional Software Function

Software Function	Instructional Uses	Strategy	
		Directed	Constructivist
Drill and practice	Skill practice	X	
Tutorial	Information delivery	X	
Simulation	Demonstration	X	
	Exploration		X
Instructional game	Skill practice	X	
	Exploration		X
Problem solving	Skill practice	X	
	Exploration		X

Recent Trends in Software Design and Delivery

Although instructional software resources have been around since the 1960s, the following are the most recent developments in their features and uses:

- **Multimedia design elements** — In 1998, Tergan noted that more software was incorporating hypermedia and multimedia environments (including Internet links). This trend has accelerated in recent years. Although many instructional software functions need not have features such as audio, video, and animations in order to be effective, many of the recently developed software products seem to reflect these features. Developers seem to feel that instructional software will be more popular if it reflects the interactive, eye-catching characteristics educators and students see in video games and on the Internet.

- **Online access and components** — The Internet is playing an increasingly prominent role in software. Much software on disc contains Internet links to additional activities or information. Also, educators and students often use instructional software directly on the Internet or obtain copies online by downloading them from websites to their computers.

- **Renewed emphasis on directed strategies and networked systems** — The recent emphasis on educational accountability as reflected in the No Child Left Behind (NCLB) Act has breathed new life into strategies that were once considered passé. As constructivist methods became more popular in the 1980s and 1990s, the demand for drill-and-practice and tutorial instructional software waned and use of simulation and problem-solving software increased. Now directed strategies made possible by drills and tutorials—which are ideal for preparing students for tests—are once

again on the rise. The same accountability emphasis has created new demand for networked instructional software products called **integrated learning systems** (ILSs), networked or online systems that provide both computer-based instruction and summary reports of student progress, which are described later in this chapter. These systems became popular in the late 1980s and early 1990s as an efficient way for many students to access instructional software from a central source (e.g., a school or district server), and educators often employed them to support directed instruction for remedial programs (e.g., Title III programs that provide special resources for disadvantaged students). Although de-emphasized in the late 1990s, today's ILSs are becoming valued not only for their centralized access, but also for their ability to track and report on student progress. Data on individual and group progress in a given classroom, school, or district is a central feature of the new NCLB Act accountability requirements.

DRILL-AND-PRACTICE SOFTWARE FUNCTIONS

Drill and Practice: Definition and Characteristics

Drill-and-practice software provides exercises in which students work example items, usually one at a time, and receive feedback on their correctness. Programs vary considerably in the kind of feedback they provide in response to student input. Feedback can range from a simple display like "OK" or "No, try again" to elaborate animated displays or verbal explanations. Some programs simply present the next item if the student answers correctly.

Types of drill and practice are sometimes distinguished by how the program tailors the practice session to student needs (Merrill & Salisbury, 1984). Types of drill functions,

TECHNOLOGY INTEGRATION IDEA 3.1

EXAMPLE STRATEGY FOR USING PROGRAMMING LANGUAGES

Title: A Window on Learning Logo

Content Area/Topic: Logic and analysis skills

Grade Level: Middle school

NETS for Students: Standards 1, 6

Description: Logo's graphic qualities make it a natural choice to explore the design qualities of symmetry, repetition, and precision. By using Logo variables, students can change their designs quickly and dramatically. With other methods, modifications would be more time consuming, and students would not be able to pinpoint the exact reasons and ways that designs were made different.

Instruction: Begin by reviewing basic Logo commands and exploring the Logo programming environment. Make sure students know that designs are programmed using the "turtle's" on-screen perspective and not their own. Have them practice developing simple procedures, and review debugging procedures line by line to determine how designs are drawn. Begin with an easy problem such as analyzing the steps in drawing a simple square to get children used to the logistics. Give students pictures of the Gothic rose window from the Notre Dame Cathedral. Ask them to analyze it, looking for patterns, shapes, and structures. Help them see that complicated designs are made up of simple geometric shapes. Then assign them the task of drawing their own window using three such shapes. Show them how to adjust basic designs by changing variable numbers. The best moments in the project occur when a student displays a "window" for the first time and a gasp of delight fills the room. (See example below.)

Assessment: Use rubric on programming language use and creativity.

Source: Image reprinted with permission from Dulsky, D. (1993). Logo rose windows. *The Computing Teacher, 20*(7), 16–19. Copyright © 1993 ISTE (International Society for Technology in Education), iste@iste.org, www.iste.org. All rights reserved.

which are described below, include flash card activities, branching drills, and extensive feedback activities.

- **Flash card activity** — This is the most basic drill-and-practice function. A student sees a set number of questions or problems, presented one at a time. The student chooses or types an answer, and the program responds with positive or negative feedback, depending on whether or not the student answered correctly.
- **Branching drill** — This is a more sophisticated form of drill and practice. In branching, the software moves students on to advanced questions after they get a number

of questions correct at some predetermined mastery level; it may also send them back to lower levels if they answer a certain number wrong. Some programs automatically review questions that students get wrong before going on to other levels. Students may not realize that branching is happening, since the program may do it automatically without alerting them to this fact. Sometimes, however, the program may congratulate students on good progress before proceeding to the next level, or it may allow them to choose their next activities.

- **Extensive feedback activities** — In these drills, students get more than just correct/incorrect feedback.

Students are using more instructional software online.

Some programs give detailed feedback on why the student got a problem wrong. This feedback is sometimes so thorough that the software function is often mistaken for a tutorial, which provides instruction. (See the next section for a description of tutorial functions.) However, the function of a drill is not instruction, but practice. Consequently, the integration strategies for drill and tutorial functions differ.

Criteria for Selecting Good Drill-and-Practice Software

In addition to meeting general criteria for good instructional software (see listing and discussion of software criteria in Figures 3.11 and 3.12 later in this chapter), well-designed drill-and-practice programs should also meet specific criteria:

- **Control over the presentation rate** — Unless the questions are part of a timed review, students should have as much time as they wish to answer and examine the feedback before proceeding to later questions. A student usually signals readiness to go to the next question by simply pressing a key.

- **Answer judging** — If programs allow students to enter a short answer rather than simply choosing one, a good drill program must be able to discriminate between correct and incorrect answers.

- **Appropriate feedback for correct and incorrect answers** — If students' responses are timed, or if their session time is limited, they may find it more motivating simply to move quickly to the next question. When drills do give feedback, they must avoid two common errors. First, feedback must be simple and display quickly. Students rapidly tire of elaborate displays, and the feedback ceases to motivate them. Second, some programs inadvertently motivate students to get wrong answers by giving more exciting or interesting feedback for wrong answers than for correct ones. The most famous example of this design error occurred in an early version of a popular microcomputer-based math drill series. Each correct answer got a smiling face, but two or more wrong answers produced a full-screen, animated

A popular use of drill software is preparing for important tests.

crying face that students found very amusing. Consequently, many students tried to answer incorrectly to see it. The company corrected this flaw, but this classic error still exists today in other programs.

Benefits of Drill and Practice

Research has shown that drill-and-practice software activities can allow the effective rehearsal students need to transfer newly learned information into long-term memory (Merrill & Salisbury, 1984; Salisbury, 1990). Many teachers feel that such practice gives students more rapid recall and use of basic skills as prerequisites to advanced concepts. They like students to have what Gagné (1982) and Bloom (1986) call *automaticity*, or automatic recall of these lower order skills to help them master higher order ones faster and more easily. The usefulness of drill programs in providing this kind of practice has been well documented, but the programs seem especially popular among teachers of students with learning disabilities (Hasselbring, 1988; Higgins & Boone, 1993; Okolo, 1992).

Although curriculum increasingly emphasizes problem solving and higher order skills, teachers still give students on-paper practice (e.g., worksheets or exercises) for many skills to help them learn and remember correct procedures. Drill software provides the following acknowledged benefits as compared to paper exercises (Kahn, 1998–1999):

- **Immediate feedback** — When students practice skills on paper, they frequently do not know until much later whether or not they did their work correctly. To quote a common saying, "Practice does not make perfect; practice makes permanent." As they complete work incorrectly, students may actually be memorizing the wrong skills. Drill-and-practice software informs them immediately whether or not their responses are accurate, so they can make quick corrections. This helps both "debugging" (identifying errors in their procedures) and retention (placing the skills in long-term memory for ready access later).

- **Motivation** — Many students refuse to do the practice they need on paper, either because they have failed so much that the whole idea is abhorrent, they have poor handwriting skills, or they simply dislike writing. In these cases, computer-based practice may motivate students to do the practice they need. Computers don't get impatient or give disgusted looks when a student gives a wrong answer.

- **Saving teacher time** — Since teachers do not have to present or grade drill and practice, students can practice on their own while the teacher addresses other

Adapting for Special Needs

Given the diverse level of student abilities in every classroom, teachers need products that anticipate and engage a broad range of skills. Early learning products like *Bailey's Book House*, *Sammy's Science House*, and *Millie's Math House* (all from Riverdeep) give students opportunities to play, explore, and interact with a variety of pre-academic instructional skills.

Also, many instructional software products support special access devices like switches and alternative keyboards. These are useful to students who have disabilities that prevent them from using instructional software via the standard keyboard.

Contributed by Dave Edyburn

student needs. The curriculum has dozens of examples of where the benefits of drill and practice apply. Some of these are:

- Math facts
- Typing skills
- English and foreign language vocabulary
- States and capitals
- SAT skills
- Musical keys and notations.

Limitations and Problems Related to Drill and Practice

Although drill and practice can be extremely useful to both students and teachers, it is also the most maligned of the software activities, sometimes informally referred to among its critics as "drill and kill." This criticism comes from the following two sources:

- **Perceived misuses** — Some authors have criticized teachers for presenting drills for overly long periods or for teaching functions that drills are ill suited to accomplish. For example, teachers may give students drill-and-practice software as a way of introducing new concepts rather than just for practicing and reinforcing familiar ones.

- **Criticism by constructivists** — Since it is identified so closely with traditional instructional methods, drill-and-practice software has become an icon for what many people consider an outmoded approach to teaching. Critics claim that introducing isolated skills and directing students to practice them contradicts the trend toward restructured curriculum in which students learn and use skills in an integrated way within the context of their own projects that specifically require the skills.

Despite these criticisms, it is likely that some form of drill-and-practice software probably will be useful in many classrooms for some time to come. Rather than ignoring drill-and-practice software or criticizing it as outmoded, teachers should seek to identify needs that drills can meet and use the software in ways that take advantage of its capabilities. See Figure 3.3 for examples of drill software and a summary of drill features.

How to Use Drill and Practice in Teaching: Integration Strategies and Guidelines

Classroom integration strategies for drill functions. Drill-and-practice programs may be used whenever teachers feel the need for on-paper exercises such as worksheets. On some occasions, even the most creative and innovative teacher may take advantage of the benefits of drill-and-practice software to have students practice using isolated skills. Integration strategies include:

- **Supplement or replace worksheets and homework exercises** — Whenever students have difficulty with higher order tasks ranging from reading and writing to mathematics, teachers may have to stop and identify specific prerequisite skills that these students lack and provide the instruction and practice they need to go forward. In these cases, learning may require a rehearsal activity to make sure information is stored in long-term memory so students can retrieve it easily.

Figure 3.3   Drill-and-Practice Summary Information

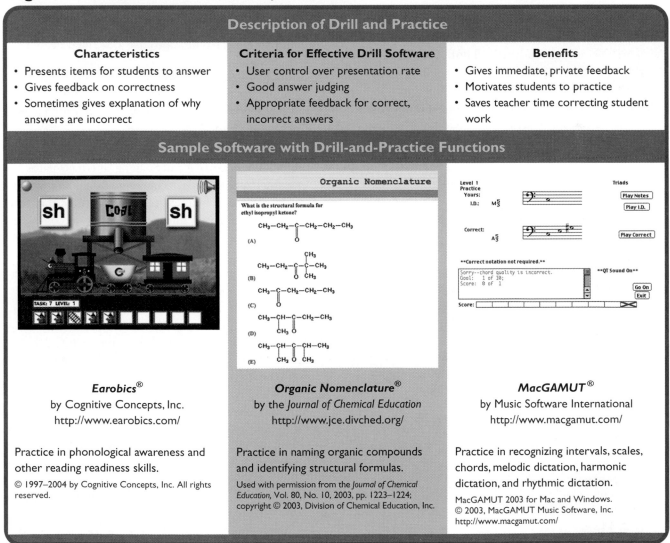

Description of Drill and Practice

Characteristics	Criteria for Effective Drill Software	Benefits
• Presents items for students to answer	• User control over presentation rate	• Gives immediate, private feedback
• Gives feedback on correctness	• Good answer judging	• Motivates students to practice
• Sometimes gives explanation of why answers are incorrect	• Appropriate feedback for correct, incorrect answers	• Saves teacher time correcting student work

Sample Software with Drill-and-Practice Functions

Earobics®
by Cognitive Concepts, Inc.
http://www.earobics.com/

Practice in phonological awareness and other reading readiness skills.

Organic Nomenclature®
by the *Journal of Chemical Education*
http://www.jce.divched.org/

Practice in naming organic compounds and identifying structural formulas.

MacGAMUT®
by Music Software International
http://www.macgamut.com/

Practice in recognizing intervals, scales, chords, melodic dictation, harmonic dictation, and rhythmic dictation.

Drills' motivation, immediate feedback, and self-pacing can make it more productive for students to practice required skills on the computer rather than on paper.

- **Prepare for tests** — Despite the new emphasis on student portfolios and other authentic assessment measures, students can expect to take several kinds of objective examinations in their education careers. When they need to prepare to demonstrate mastery of specific skills in important examinations (e.g., for end-of-year grades or for college entrance), drill-and-practice software can help them focus on their deficiencies and correct them. An example integration strategy for drill functions is shown in Technology Integration Idea 3.2.

Guidelines for using drill and practice. Use the following guidelines to make best use of drill capabilities when designing integration strategies for drill-and-practice functions:

- **Set time limits** — Teachers should limit the time devoted to drill assignments to 10 to 15 minutes per day. This ensures that students will not become bored and that the drill-and-practice strategy will retain its effectiveness. Also, teachers should be sure students have been introduced previously to the concepts underlying the drills. Drill software should serve mainly to debug and to help students retain their grasp of familiar concepts.

- **Assign individually** — Most drills are designed to allow self-pacing and personalized feedback. Therefore, these activities usually work best for individual computer use. However, some teachers with limited technology resources have found other, ingenious ways to capitalize on the motivational and immediate feedback capabilities of drills. If all students in a class benefit from practice in a skill using a drill program, the teacher may divide them into small groups to compete with each other for the best group scores. The class could even be divided into two groups for a "relay race" competition to see which group can complete the assignment the fastest with the most correct answers.

- **Use learning stations** — If not all students need the kind of practice that a drill provides, the teacher may make software one of several learning stations to serve students with identified weaknesses in one or more key skills. Drill-and-practice functions are used best when matched to the specific learning needs of individual students.

TUTORIAL SOFTWARE FUNCTIONS

Tutorials: Definition and Characteristics

Tutorial software is an entire instructional sequence similar to a teacher's classroom instruction on a topic. This instruction usually is expected to be a self-contained instructional unit, rather than a supplement to other instruction. Students should be able to learn the topic without any help or other materials. Unlike other types of instructional software, tutorials are true teaching materials. Gagné et al. (1981) said that good tutorial software should address all nine instructional events. (See the discussion of Gagné's Events of Instruction in Chapter 2.)

People may confuse tutorial and drill activities for two reasons. First, drill software may provide elaborate feedback that reviewers may mistake for tutorial explanations. Even software developers may claim that a package is a tutorial when it is, in fact, a drill activity with detailed feedback. Second, a good tutorial should include one or more practice sequences to check students' comprehension. Since this is a drill-and-practice function, reviewers can become confused about the primary purpose of the activity.

Tutorials often are categorized as linear and branching tutorials (Alessi & Trollip, 2001), as described below:

- **Linear tutorials** — A simple, linear tutorial gives the same instructional sequence of explanation, practice, and feedback to all learners regardless of differences in their performance.

- **Branching tutorials** — A more sophisticated branching tutorial directs learners along alternate paths depending on how they respond to questions and whether or not they show mastery of certain parts of the material. Even branching tutorials can range in complexity by the number of paths they allow and how fully they diagnose the kinds of instruction a student needs. More complex tutorials may also have computer-management capabilities; teachers may place each student at an appropriate level and get progress reports as each one goes through the instruction. Although a tutorial program does not necessarily need these components, data collection and management features can make it more useful to teachers.

Tutorials are usually geared toward learners who can read fairly well and who are usually older students or adults. Since tutorial instruction is expected to stand alone, it is difficult to explain or give appropriate guidance on-screen to a nonreader. However, some tutorials aimed at younger learners have found clever ways to explain and demonstrate concepts with graphics, succinct phrases or sentences, or audio directions coupled with screen displays.

EXAMPLE STRATEGY FOR DRILL-AND-PRACTICE SOFTWARE

Title: Organic Nomenclature

Content Area/Topic: Chemistry

Grade Level: High school

NETS for Students: Standard I

Description: This software gives students practice in naming organic compounds and identifying structural compounds.

Instruction: The teacher begins by introducing the topic of organic compounds and how they are represented by the formulas that show how their components combine. The teacher demonstrates to the whole class how to do these formulas by showing how to do formulas for one or two compounds. Then the teacher asks students to respond to others as a whole-class exercise. Next, the teacher turns around the problem by presenting one or two formulas and asking students to name the compound. Since it is important for each student to be able to identify and do formulas for these compounds quickly as a prerequisite to further work on organic compounds, the software is designed for use by individual students. The software presents a name or a formula, and the student selects the correct formula or name from the list of five options. Students do a set of these, and the software gives them feedback on their correctness. They do as many sets as needed to master the concept. Both students and teachers can use these exercises to gauge their readiness to proceed with other work.

Assessment: Uses a multiple-choice test formatted similar to items in software.

Software available from the *Journal of Chemical Education,* http://www.jce.divched.org/

Source: From Shaw, D. B., & Yindra, L. (2003). Organic nomenclature. *Journal of Chemical Education, 80*(10), 1223–1224. Used with permission from the *Journal of Chemical Education;* copyright © 2003, Division of Chemical Education, Inc.

Criteria for Selecting Good Tutorial Software

Being a good teacher is a difficult assignment for any human, let alone a computer. However, software must accomplish this task to fulfill tutorial functions. In addition to meeting general criteria for good instructional software, well-designed tutorial programs should also meet the following additional standards:

- **Extensive interactivity** — Good tutorials, like good teachers, should require students to give frequent and thoughtful responses to questions and problems and supply appropriate practice and feedback to guide students' learning. The most frequent criticism of tutorials is that they are "page-turners," that is, they ask students to do very little other than read.

- **Thorough user control** — User control refers to several aspects of the program. First, students should always be able to control the rate at which text appears on the screen. The program should not go on to the next information or activity screen until the user presses a key or gives some other indication of having completed the necessary reading. Next, the program should offer students the flexibility to review explanations, examples, or sequences of instruction or move ahead to other instruction. The program should also provide frequent opportunities for students to exit the program, if they like.

- **Appropriate pedagogy** — The program's structure should provide a suggested or required sequence of instruction that builds on concepts and covers the content adequately. It should provide sufficient explanation and examples in both original and remedial sequences. In sum, it should compare favorably to an expert teacher's presentation sequence for the topic.

- **Adequate answer-judging and feedback capabilities** — Whenever possible, programs should allow students to answer in natural language and should accept all correct answers and possible variations of correct answers. They should also give appropriate corrective feedback when needed, supplying this feedback after only one or two tries rather than frustrating students by making them keep trying indefinitely to answer something they may not know.

- **Appropriate graphics** — Although some authors insist that graphics form part of tutorial instruction (Baek & Layne, 1988), others warn that graphics should be used sparingly and not interfere with the purpose of the instruction (Eiser, 1988).

- **Adequate recordkeeping** — Depending on the purpose of the tutorial, teachers may need to keep track of student progress. If the program does keep records on student work, teachers should be able to get progress summaries quickly and easily.

Benefits of Tutorials

Since a tutorial includes drill-and-practice activities, helpful features include the same ones as for drills (immediate feedback to learners and time savings) plus the additional benefit of offering a self-contained, self-paced unit of instruction. Many successful uses of tutorials have been documented over the years. For examples, see Arnett (2000), CAI in Music (1994), Cann and Seale (1999), Graham (1994, 1998), Kraemer (1990), Murray et al. (1988), and Steinberg and Oberem (2000).

Limitations and Problems Related to Tutorials

Tutorials can fulfill many much-needed instructional functions but, like drill and practice, they also attract their share of criticism, including:

- **Criticism by constructivists** — Constructivists criticize tutorials because they deliver directed instruction, rather than letting students generate their own knowledge through hands-on projects. Thus, they feel tutorials are trivial uses of the computer.

- **Lack of good products** — Software publishers describe fewer packages as tutorials than any other kind of microcomputer software. This is partly due to the difficulty and expense of designing and developing them. A well-designed tutorial sequence emerges from extensive research into how to teach the topic well. Designers must know what learning tasks the topic requires, the best sequence for students to follow, how best to explain and demonstrate essential concepts, common errors that students are likely to make, and how to provide instruction and feedback to correct those errors. Therefore, programming and graphics can become fairly involved.

- **Reflect only one instructional approach** — These problems become still more difficult because teachers frequently disagree about what they should teach for a given topic, how to teach it most effectively, and in what order to present learning tasks. A teacher may choose not to purchase a tutorial with a sound instructional sequence because it does not cover the topic the way he or she presents it. Not surprisingly, software companies tend to avoid programs that are difficult to develop and market.

Although tutorials have considerable value and are popular in military and industrial training, schools and

Figure 3.4 Tutorial Summary Information

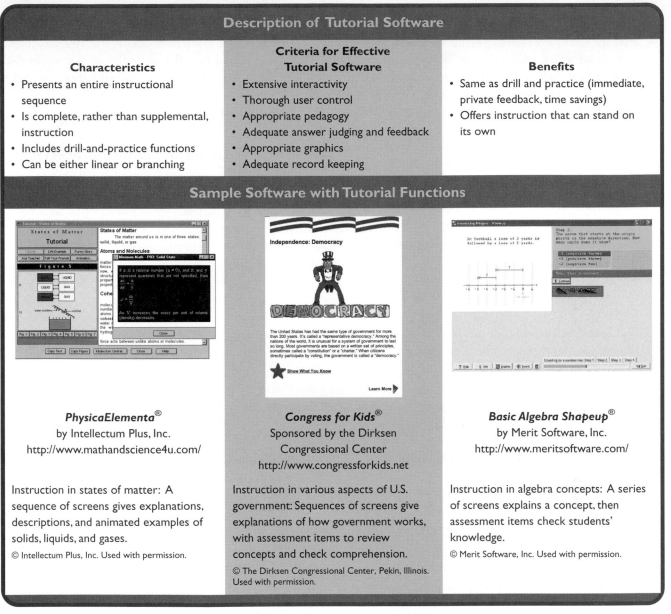

Description of Tutorial Software

Characteristics
- Presents an entire instructional sequence
- Is complete, rather than supplemental, instruction
- Includes drill-and-practice functions
- Can be either linear or branching

Criteria for Effective Tutorial Software
- Extensive interactivity
- Thorough user control
- Appropriate pedagogy
- Adequate answer judging and feedback
- Appropriate graphics
- Adequate record keeping

Benefits
- Same as drill and practice (immediate, private feedback, time savings)
- Offers instruction that can stand on its own

Sample Software with Tutorial Functions

PhysicaElementa®
by Intellectum Plus, Inc.
http://www.mathandscience4u.com/

Instruction in states of matter: A sequence of screens gives explanations, descriptions, and animated examples of solids, liquids, and gases.

© Intellectum Plus, Inc. Used with permission.

Congress for Kids®
Sponsored by the Dirksen Congressional Center
http://www.congressforkids.net

Instruction in various aspects of U.S. government: Sequences of screens give explanations of how government works, with assessment items to review concepts and check comprehension.

© The Dirksen Congressional Center, Pekin, Illinois. Used with permission.

Basic Algebra Shapeup®
by Merit Software, Inc.
http://www.meritsoftware.com/

Instruction in algebra concepts: A series of screens explains a concept, then assessment items check students' knowledge.

© Merit Software, Inc. Used with permission.

---

colleges have never fully tapped their potential as teaching resources. However, recent trends toward combining tutorial software with video media and distance education may bring tutorial functions into more common use. See Figure 3.4 for examples of tutorial software and a summary of tutorial features.

How to Use Tutorials in Teaching: Integration Strategies and Guidelines

Classroom integration strategies for tutorial functions. Self-instructional tutorials should in no way threaten teachers, since few conceivable situations make a computer preferable to an expert teacher. However, the tutorial's unique capability of presenting an entire interactive instructional sequence can assist in several classroom situations such as these:

- **Self-paced reviews of instruction** — Students often need to repeat instruction on a topic after the teacher's initial presentation. Some students may be slower to understand concepts and need additional time on them. Others seem to learn better in a self-paced mode without the pressure to move at the same pace as the rest of the class. Still others may need review before a test. Tutorials can provide self-paced instruction to address all these needs.

- **Alternative learning strategies** — Some students, typically those at advanced levels, prefer to structure their own learning activities and proceed at their own pace. With a good tutorial, advanced students can glean much background material prior to meeting with a teacher or others to do assessment and/or further work assignments.

- **Instruction when teachers are unavailable** — Some students have problems when they surge ahead of their class rather than falling behind it. The teacher cannot leave the rest of the class to provide the instruction that such an advanced student needs. Many schools, especially those in rural areas, may not offer certain courses because they cannot justify the expense of hiring a teacher for comparatively few students who will need physics, German, trigonometry, or other lower demand courses. Well-designed tutorial courses, especially in combination with other methods such as distance learning, can help meet these students' needs.

Guidelines for using tutorials. Use the following guidelines to make the best use of tutorial capabilities when designing integration strategies for tutorial functions:

- **Assign individually** — Like drill-and-practice functions, tutorial functions are designed for use by individuals, rather than by groups of students.
- **Use learning stations or individual checkout** — Depending on which of the above strategies it promotes, a tutorial may form a classroom learning station or may be available for checkout at any time in a library/media center. Sometimes teachers send students to learning stations with tutorials in order to review previously presented material while the teacher works with other students. (See Technology Integration Idea 3.3.)

SIMULATION SOFTWARE FUNCTIONS

Simulations: Definition and Characteristics

A simulation is a computerized model of a real or imagined system that is designed to teach how the system works. Unlike tutorial and drill-and-practice activities in which the teaching structure is built into the package, learners usually must choose tasks to do and the order in which to do them. Alessi and Trollip (2001) identify two main types of simulations: those that teach *about* something and those that teach *how to do* something. They further divide the "about" simulations into physical and iterative types and they divide the "how to" simulations into procedural and situational types.

TECHNOLOGY INTEGRATION IDEA 3.3

EXAMPLE STRATEGY FOR TUTORIAL SOFTWARE

Title: *ActivStats* Statistics Tutorial

Content Area/Topic: Advanced placement statistics

Grade Level: High school

NETS for Students: Standards 1, 6

Description: The *ActivStats* tutorial software has 26 lessons that cover the basics of introductory statistics.

Instruction: A teacher can use the short animated clips at the beginning of each lesson to introduce the topic to the whole class. The teacher continues the introduction with a review of the lesson's basic concepts by using an animation to illustrate the uses of the statistic and how changing the raw data can alter it. After this demo, students work individually on the remaining lesson activities. For example, most lessons allow the user to import pre-existing data files and provide instructions on how to plot them in a chart or in three dimensions.

Assessment: Students use the built-in quizzes to gauge their comprehension and determine if they are ready to take the teacher's final test over the topic.

Software available from Addison-Wesley, http://www.aw-bc.com/activstats/

Source: Based on Ashbacher, C. (2003). ActivStats. *Mathematics and Computer Education, 37*(2), 254–255. Reprinted with permission of *Mathematics and Computer Education* journal.

Source: P. Velleman, www.aw-bc.com/activstats/splash.html © Pearson Education, Inc. Reproduced by permission of Pearson Education, Inc., publishing as Addison Wesley.

Simulations That Teach About Something

- **Physical simulations** — These allow users to manipulate things or processes represented on the screen. For example, students see selections of chemicals with instructions on how to combine them to see the result, or they may see how various electrical circuits operate.

- **Iterative simulations** — These simulations speed up or slow down processes that usually happen either so slowly or so quickly that students could not ordinarily see the events unfold. For example, software may show the effects of changes in demographic variables on population growth or the effects of environmental factors on ecosystems. Alessi and Trollip (2001) refer to this type as "iterative" because the student can run it over and over again with different values, observing the results each time. Biological simulations such as those on genetics are popular, since they help students experiment with natural processes. Genetics simulations let students pair animals with given characteristics and see the resulting offspring.

Simulations That Teach How to Do Something

- **Procedural simulations** — These activities teach the appropriate sequences of steps to perform certain procedures. They include diagnostic programs, in which students try to identify the sources of medical or mechanical problems, and flight simulators, in which students simulate piloting an airplane or other vehicle.

- **Situational simulations** — These programs give students hypothetical problem situations and ask them to react. Some simulations allow for various successful strategies such as letting students play the stock market or operate businesses. Others have most desirable and least desirable options such as choices when encountering a potentially volatile classroom situation.

The preceding descriptions serve to clarify the various forms a simulation might take, but teachers need not feel they should be able to classify a given simulation into one of these categories. Simulations usually emphasize learning about the system itself, rather than learning general problem-solving strategies. For example, a program called *The Factory* has students build products by selecting machines and placing them in the correct sequence. Since the program emphasizes solving problems in correct sequence rather than manufacturing in factories, it should probably be called a problem-solving activity rather than a simulation. Programs such as *SimCity*™ (Electronic Arts), which let students design their own cities, provide more accurate examples of building-type simulations (Adams, 1998). (See Technology Integration Idea 3.4 for a classroom example using *SimCity*.)

Criteria for Selecting Good Simulation Software

Simulations vary in type and purpose, so a uniform set of criteria is not possible. For some simulations, a realistic and accurate representation of a system is essential (Reigeluth & Schwartz, 1989), but for others, it is important

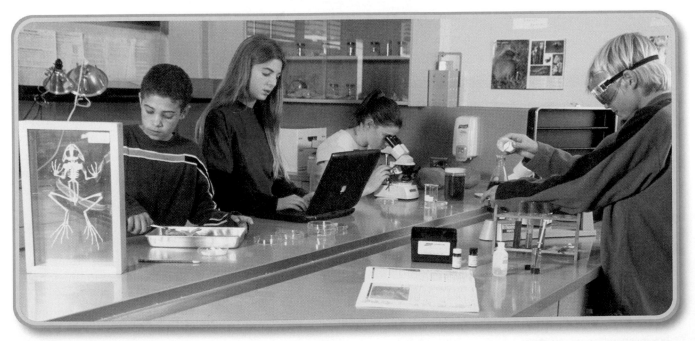

Simulations are often used for science activities such as dissections.

Figure 3.5 Simulation Summary Information

Description of Simulation Software

Characteristics

- Models a real or imaginary system
- Can model physical phenomena (e.g., growth), procedures (e.g., dissections), and hypothetical situations (e.g., stock market)
- Users can see the impact of their actions

Criteria for Effective Simulation Software

- System fidelity and accuracy (for some simulations)
- Good documentation to explain system characteristics and uses

Benefits

- Compresses time or slows down processes
- Gets students involved
- Makes experimentation safe
- Makes the impossible possible
- Saves money and other resources
- Allows repetition with variations
- Allows observation of complex processes

Sample Software with Simulation Functions

Virtual Labs: Electricity®
by Riverdeep, Inc.
http://www.riverdeep.com

Simulated electrical circuit board: Provides a safe means for students to apply electrical concepts to simulated devices.

Oregon Trail®
by Riverdeep, Inc.
http://www.riverdeep.com

Simulated trip in the Old West of the 1890s: Students learn about pioneer days by taking roles in a simulated wagon train journey.

SimCity 3000®
by Electronic Arts, Inc.
http://www.maxis.com/

Simulated city: Lets users build their own cities, create a budget for them, populate them, and run them, including responding to intermittent disasters.

only to know what the screen elements represent. Since the screen often presents no set sequence of steps, simulations need good accompanying documentation more than most software. A set of clear directions helps the teacher learn how to use the program and show the students how to use it rapidly and easily. See Figure 3.5 for examples of simulation software and a summary of simulation features.

Benefits of Simulations

The field of science seems to include more simulations than any other area (Andaloro, 1991; Mintz, 1993; Richards, 1992; Ronen, 1992; Simmons & Lunetta, 1993; Smith, 1992), but the use of simulations is also popular in social science topics (Adams, 1998; Allen, 1993;

Clinton, 1991; Estes, 1994). However, more simulations are currently in development and feature online delivery or supplements to combine the control, safety, and interactive features of computer simulations with the visual impact of pictures of real-life devices and processes. Depending on the topic, a simulation can provide one or more of the following benefits (Alessi & Trollip, 2001):

- **Compress time** — This feature is important whenever students study the growth or development of living things (e.g., pairing animals to observe the characteristics of their offspring) or other processes that take a long time (e.g., the movement of a glacier). A simulation can make something happen in seconds

EXAMPLE STRATEGY FOR SIMULATION SOFTWARE

Title: Building a Simulated City

Content Area/Topic: Social studies—citizenship/group cooperation in social projects

Grade Level: Middle school

NETS for Students: Standards 3, 5, 6

Description: This lesson helps raise students' awareness of their responsibility to become informed citizens, shows how they can participate in local decision making, and gives practice in working cooperatively with a group to carry out a social project. The software allows the development of a comprehensive plan for the township.

Instruction: Have a representative from the county planning and zoning office talk with the students about factors of concern to community development. The teacher then introduces students to the *SimCity*™ software. They form teams of four to five students each and start their own community planning projects with *SimCity*. Each group meets every week to discuss and develop its plan. As a group, they decide how to select and place features such as roads, homes, and utilities. After recording their decisions on paper, they enter them into the program and observe the results. The groups discuss feedback that the program provides on areas such as taxes, crime rates, and public opinion. After their plans are complete, each group presents its plan to the teacher and explains and defends their choices.

Assessment: Papers are graded by a rubric.

Source: From Jacobson, P. (1992). Save the cities! *SimCity* in grades 2–5. *The Computing Teacher, 20*(2), 14–15.

---

that normally takes days, months, or longer, so students can cover more variations of the activity in a shorter time.

- **Slow down processes** — Conversely, a simulation can also model processes normally invisible to the human eye because they happen so quickly. For example, physical education students can study the sloweddown movement of muscles and limbs as a simulated athlete throws a ball or swings a golf club.

- **Get students involved** — Simulations can capture students' attention by placing them in charge of things and asking, "What would you do?" The results of their choices can be immediate and graphic. It also allows users to interact with the program instead of just seeing its output.

- **Make experimentation safe** — Whenever learning involves physical danger, simulations are the strategy of choice. This is true any time students are learning to drive vehicles, handle volatile substances, or react to potentially dangerous situations. They can experiment with strategies in simulated environments that might result in personal injury to themselves or others in real life.

- **Make the impossible possible** — Very often, teachers simply cannot give students access to the resources

or the situations that simulations can. Simulations can show students what it would be like to walk on the moon or to react to emergencies in a nuclear power plant. They can see cells mutating or hold countrywide elections. They can even design new societies or planets and see the results of their choices.

- **Save money and other resources** — Many school systems are finding dissections of animals on a computer screen much less expensive than on real frogs or cats and just as instructional. (It is also easier on the animals!) Depending on the subject, a simulated experiment may be just as effective as a learning experience, but at a fraction of the cost.

- **Allow repetition with variations** — Unlike real life, simulations let students repeat events as many times as they wish and with unlimited variations. They can pair any number of cats or make endless airplane landings in a variety of conditions to compare the results of each set of choices.

- **Allow observation of complex processes** — Real-life events often are so complex that they are confusing, especially to those seeing them for the first time. When many things happen at once, students find it difficult to focus on the operation of individual components. Who could understand the operation of a stock market by looking at the real thing without some introduction? Simulations can isolate parts of activities and control background noise. This makes it easier for students to see what is happening later when all the parts come together in the actual activity.

Limitations and Problems Related to Simulations

Most educators acknowledge the instructional usefulness of simulations; however, there are some concerns, which include the following

- **Accuracy of models** — When students see simplified versions of these systems in a controlled situation, they may get inaccurate or imprecise perspectives on the systems' complexity. For example, students may feel they know all about how to react to driving situations because they have experienced simulated versions of them. Many educators feel especially strongly that situational simulations must be followed at some point by real experiences. Many teachers of very young children feel that learners at early stages of their cognitive development should experience things first with their five senses rather than on computer screens.

- **Misuse of simulations** — Sometimes, simulations are used to teach concepts that could just as easily be demonstrated on paper, with manipulatives, or with real objects. For example, students usually are delighted with the simulation of the food chain called *Odell Lakes*, a program that lets students see which animals prey on other animals in a hypothetical lake. However, some educators wonder whether such a computer simulation is necessary or even desirable to teach this concept. Hasselbring and Goin (1993) point out that students can often master the activities of a simulation without actually developing effective problem-solving skills; on the contrary, such applications actually can encourage counterproductive behaviors. For example, some simulations initially provide little information with which to solve problems, and students are reduced to "trial-and-error guessing rather than systematic analysis of available information" (p. 156). Teachers must carefully structure integration strategies so that students will not use simulations in inappropriate ways.

How to Use Simulations in Teaching: Integration Strategies and Guidelines

Simulations are considered among the most potentially powerful computer software resources; however, as with most software, their usefulness depends largely on the program's purpose and how well it fits in with the purpose of the lesson and student needs. Teachers are responsible for

recognizing the unique instructional value of each simulation and using it to its best advantage.

Classroom applications of simulation functions. Real systems are usually preferable to simulations, but a simulation is useful when the real situation is too time consuming, dangerous, expensive, or unrealistic for a classroom presentation. Simulations should be considered in the following situations:

- **In place of or as supplements to lab experiments** — When adequate lab materials are not available, teachers should try to locate computer simulations of the required experiments. Many teachers find that simulations offer effective supplements to real labs, either to prepare students for making good use of the actual labs, or as follow-ups with variations on the original experiments without using consumable materials. Some simulations actually allow users to perform experiments that they could not otherwise manage or that would be too dangerous for students.

- **In place of or as supplements to role-playing** — Many students either refuse to role play in front of a class or get too enthusiastic and disrupt the classroom. Computerized simulations can take the personal embarrassment and logistical problems out of the learning experience, make classroom role playing more controllable, and spark students' imagination and interest in the activities.

- **In place of or as supplements to field trips** — Seeing an activity in the real setting can be a valuable experience, especially for young children. Sometimes, however, desired locations are not within reach of the school, and a simulated experience of all or part of the process is the next best thing. As with labs, simulations provide good introductions or follow-ups to field trips.

- **Introducing and/or clarifying a new topic** — Software that allows students to explore the elements of an environment in a hands-on manner frequently provides students' first in-depth contact with a topic. This seems to accomplish several purposes. First, it is a nonthreatening way to introduce new terms and unfamiliar settings. Students know that they are not being graded, so they feel less pressure than usual to learn everything right away. A simulation can become simply a get-acquainted look at a topic. Simulations can also build students' initial interest in a topic. Highly graphic, hands-on activities draw them into the topic and whet their appetite to learn more. Finally, some software helps students see how certain prerequisite skills relate to the topic; this may motivate students more strongly to learn the skills than if the skills were introduced in isolation from the problems to which they apply. For example, Tom Snyder's *Decisions! Decisions!* software helps students see the relevance of topics such as the U.S. Constitution and elections.

- **Fostering exploration and process learning** — Teachers often use content-free simulation/problem-solving software (e.g., *The Factory*) as motivation for students to explore their own cognitive processes. Since this kind of software requires students to learn no specific content, it is easier to get them to concentrate on problem-solving steps and strategies. However, with content-free products, it is even more important than usual that teachers draw comparisons between skills from the software activities and those in the content areas to which they want to transfer the experience. For example, *Virtual Lab* (Riverdeep) presents an implicit emphasis on science process skills that the teacher may want to point out. It seems best to use these kinds of activities just prior to content-area activities that will require the same processes.

- **Encouraging cooperation and group work** — Sometimes a simulated demonstration can capture students' attention quickly and effectively and interest them in working together on a product. For example, a simulation on immigration or colonization might be the "grabber" a teacher needs to launch a group project in a social studies unit.

Guidelines for using simulation functions. Simulations offer more versatile implementation than tutorials or drills. They usually work equally effectively with a whole class, small groups, or individuals. A teacher may choose to introduce a lesson to the class by displaying a simulation or divide the class into small groups and let each solve problems. Because they instigate discussion and cooperative work so well, simulations usually are considered more appropriate for pairs and small groups than for individuals. However, individual use certainly is not precluded.

INSTRUCTIONAL GAME SOFTWARE FUNCTIONS

Instructional Games: Definition and Characteristics

Instructional games are software designed to increase motivation by adding game rules and/or competition to learning activities. Even though teachers often use them in the same way as drill-and-practice or simulation software, games usually are listed as a separate software activity because their instructional connotation to students is slightly different. When students know they will be playing a game, they expect a fun and entertaining activity because of the challenge of the competition and the potential for

Instructional games are one way to engage students in learning.

winning (Randel, Morris, Wetzel, & Whitehill, 1992). Naturally, classroom instruction should not consist entirely of these kinds of activities, no matter how instructional or motivational they are. Teachers intersperse games with other activities to hold students' attention or as a reward for accomplishing other activities.

It is important to recognize the common characteristics that set instructional games apart from other types of software: game rules, elements of competition or challenge, and amusing or entertaining formats. These elements generate a set of mental and emotional expectations in students that make game-based instructional activities different from nongame ones.

Criteria for Selecting Good Instructional Games

Since instructional games often amount to drills or simulations overlaid with game rules, these three types of software often share many of the same criteria (e.g., better reinforcement for correct answers than for incorrect ones). Teachers should use the following criteria to choose instructional games:

- **Appealing formats and activities** — When Malone (1980) examined the evidence on what makes things fun to learn, he found that the most popular games included elements of adventure and uncertainty and levels of complexity matched to learners' abilities.

- **Instructional value** — Teachers should examine instructional games carefully for their value as both educational and motivational tools.

- **Physical dexterity is reasonable** — Teachers should also ensure that students will be motivated rather than frustrated by the activities. For example, a game that requires shooting at an alien spaceship by pressing certain keys quickly before answering an item may prove difficult for some students.

- **Minimum violence/aggression** — Games that call for violence or combat require careful screening, not only to avoid modeling this behavior, but also because girls often perceive the attraction of these activities differently than boys, and because such games sometimes depict females as targets of violence.

Benefits of Instructional Games

A classroom without elements of games and fun would be a dry, barren landscape for students to traverse. In their review of the effectiveness of games for educational purposes, Randel et al. (1992) found "[the fact] that games are more interesting than traditional instruction is both a basis for using them as well as a consistent finding" (p. 270). They also observed that retention over time favors the use of simulations/games. Successful uses of games have been reported in many content areas (Flowers, 1993; Muckerheide, Mogill, & Mogill, 1999; Trotter, 1991). The appeal of games seems to center around students' desire to compete and play. Games provide teachers with opportunities for taking advantage of this innate desire to get students to focus on a curriculum topic. See Figure 3.6 for examples of instructional game software and a summary of game features.

Limitations and Problems Related to Instructional Games

Some teachers believe that any time they can sneak in learning under the guise of a game, it is altogether a good thing (McGinley, 1991). However, games are also frequently criticized from several standpoints:

Figure 3.6 **Instructional Game Summary Information**

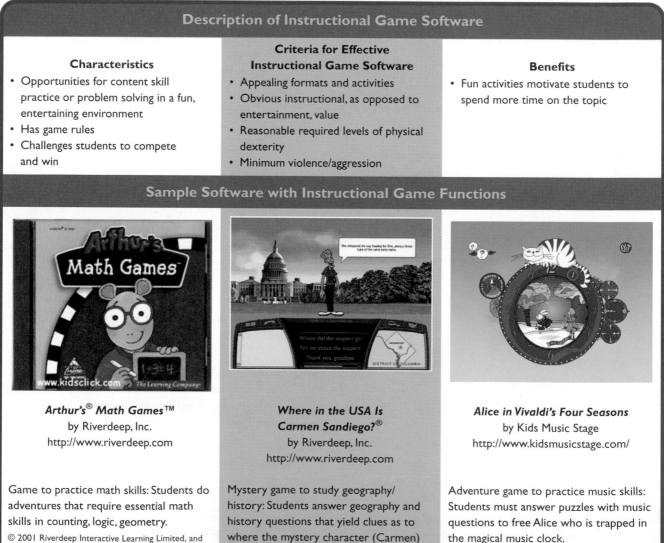

Description of Instructional Game Software

Characteristics
- Opportunities for content skill practice or problem solving in a fun, entertaining environment
- Has game rules
- Challenges students to compete and win

Criteria for Effective Instructional Game Software
- Appealing formats and activities
- Obvious instructional, as opposed to entertainment, value
- Reasonable required levels of physical dexterity
- Minimum violence/aggression

Benefits
- Fun activities motivate students to spend more time on the topic

Sample Software with Instructional Game Functions

Arthur's® Math Games™
by Riverdeep, Inc.
http://www.riverdeep.com

Game to practice math skills: Students do adventures that require essential math skills in counting, logic, geometry.
© 2001 Riverdeep Interactive Learning Limited, and its Licensors. All rights reserved.

Where in the USA Is Carmen Sandiego?®
by Riverdeep, Inc.
http://www.riverdeep.com

Mystery game to study geography/history: Students answer geography and history questions that yield clues as to where the mystery character (Carmen) is hiding.
© 2001 Riverdeep Interactive Learning Limited, and its Licensors. All rights reserved.

Alice in Vivaldi's Four Seasons
by Kids Music Stage
http://www.kidsmusicstage.com/

Adventure game to practice music skills: Students must answer puzzles with music questions to free Alice who is trapped in the magical music clock.
© Music Games International. Used with permission.

- **Learning versus having fun** — Some schools forbid any use of games because they believe games convince students that they are escaping from learning, thus drawing attention away from the intrinsic value and motivation of learning. Critics also feel that winning the game becomes a student's primary focus and that the instructional purpose is lost in the pursuit of this goal. Observers disagree about whether getting lost in the game is a benefit or a problem.

- **Confusion of game rules and real-life rules** — Some teachers have observed that students can become confused about which part of the activity is the game and which part is the skill; they may then have difficulty transferring their skill to later nongame situations. For example, the teacher's manual for Sunburst's *How the West Was One + Three × Four* reminds teachers that some students can confuse the math operations rules with the game rules and that teachers must help them recognize the need to focus on math rules and use them outside the game. Recent studies seem to indicate that instructional games can be useful in fostering higher order skills, but that their usefulness hinges on how teachers employ them (Henderson, Klemes, & Eshet, 2000; Rieber, Smith, & Noah, 1998).

- **Inefficient learning** — Although students obviously find many computer games exciting and stimulating, it is sometimes difficult to pinpoint their educational value. Teachers must try to balance the motivation that instructional games bring to learning against the classroom time they take away from nongame strategies. For example, students may become immersed in the challenge of the *Carmen Sandiego* series, but more efficient ways to teach geography may be just as motivating.

How to Use Instructional Games in Teaching: Integration Strategies and Guidelines

Classroom applications for instructional games. Several kinds of instructional opportunities invite teachers to take advantage of the motivational qualities of games. Instructional games should be considered in the following situations:

- **In place of worksheets and exercises** — As with drill-and-practice software, teachers can use games to help students acquire automatic recall of prerequisite skills.
- **To teach cooperative group working skills** — Like simulations, many instructional games serve as the basis

TECHNOLOGY INTEGRATION IDEA 3.5

EXAMPLE STRATEGY FOR INSTRUCTIONAL GAME SOFTWARE

Title: Problem-Solving and Geography

Content Area/Topic: Geography

Grade Level: Elementary to middle school

NETS for Students: Standards 1, 3, 6

Description: *Carmen Sandiego* (Riverdeep) can be used as the basis for learning geography and research skills. The game becomes a more powerful activity for improving research and reference skills when it is paired with use of an on-disc or online atlas.

Instruction: The class is divided into teams, and each team member is assigned a role: Field operative (runs the game software), Researcher (runs the atlas software), or Recorder (records information and coordinates team activities). Members switch roles every class period to give everyone a turn at each. A bar graph is posted in the classroom to show how many "cases" each class has solved. Within the class, teams are encouraged to help and coach each other. Thus, competition is fostered between classes, but collaboration is fostered within each class. To guide their work, the students receive data sheets and maps similar to those provided with the game software. The Recorder uses the map to circle each city the team "goes through" and draws a line indicating the direction they traveled from one city to the next. This information is recorded on another sheet, which the Researcher uses to try to find the next location to track the thief. At the end of each case, information is filled in on a matrix on a final sheet.

Assessment: The teacher checks the final sheet to grade each group's work.

Source: Greenman, M. (1991). A computer-based problem solving geography unit. *The Computing Teacher, 18*(2), 22–24.

MAKING THE CASE FOR TECHNOLOGY INTEGRATION

CW

Discuss these issues online with other students by selecting the *Making the Case* module for Chapter 3 of the Companion Website (http://www.prenhall.com/roblyer) or choose the *Message Board* module.

1. Drill-and-practice software is often referred to by the derogatory term "drill and kill." Do you believe this happens because the number of situations is diminishing in which drill-and-practice software would be the strategy of choice, or because people fail to recognize appropriate situations for using it? Explain your reasoning.

2. Some schools, such as those with a college preparatory focus, do not allow the use of instructional games of any kind. Is there a compelling case to be made for allowing the use of instructional game software to achieve specific educational goals? That is, can games do something in an instructional situation that no other strategy is able to do? If so, what? Can you give examples?

for or introductions to group work. A game's competitive qualities can present opportunities for competition among groups. (See Technology Integration Idea 3.5.)

- **As a reward** — Perhaps the most common use of games is to reward good work. This is a valid role for instructional software, but teachers should avoid overuse of it. Otherwise, the game can lose its motivational value and become an "electronic babysitter." Some schools actually bar games from classrooms for fear that they will overemphasize the need for students to be entertained.

Guidelines for using instructional games. Use the following guidelines to make the best use of game capabilities when designing integration strategies for game functions:

- **Use sparingly** — Some educators believe that games—especially computer-based ones—are overused and misused (McGinley, 1991). Some students may be unmotivated, or even threatened, by competition.

- **Involve all students** — Make sure that girls and boys alike are participating, and that all students have a meaningful role.

- **Emphasize the content-area skills** — Before students begin playing, make sure they know the relationship between game rules and content-area (e.g., math) rules. Students should recognize which rules they will be using in their later work and which are merely part of the game environment.

PROBLEM-SOLVING SOFTWARE FUNCTIONS

Problem-Solving Software: Definition and Characteristics

Although simulations and instructional games are often used to help teach problem-solving skills, problem-solving software is designed especially for this purpose. Problem-solving software functions may focus on fostering component skills in or approaches to general problem-solving ability, or it may provide opportunities to practice solving various kinds of content area problems. However, everyone has difficulty defining the activity of problem solving. Funkhouser and Dennis (1992) quoted an earlier author as saying that "Problem solving [means] the behaviors that researchers who say they are studying problem solving, study" (p. 338). Sherman (1987–1988) was somewhat more specific, claiming that all problem solving involves three components: recognition of a goal (an opportunity for solving a problem), a process (a sequence of physical activities or operations), and mental activity (cognitive operations to pursue a solution).

Problem solving covers a wide variety of desired component behaviors. The literature mentions such varied subskills for problem solving as metacognition, observing, recalling information, sequencing, analyzing, finding and organizing information, inferring, predicting outcomes, making analogies, and formulating ideas. Although there are many opinions about the proper role of instructional software in fostering these abilities, there seem to be two main approaches:

- **Content-area skills** — Some problem-solving software focuses on teaching content-area skills, primarily in mathematics and science. For example, *The Geometric Supposer* by Sunburst encourages students to learn strategies for solving geometry problems by drawing and manipulating geometric figures. Others, like *Alien Rescue* developed by the University of Texas, are what might be called problem-solving "environments." These complex, multifaceted packages offer a variety of tools that allow students to create solutions to science-related problems presented by a scenario. Still others provide opportunities to practice solving specific kinds of math or science problems.

- **Content-free skills** — Some educators feel that general problem-solving ability can be taught directly by specific instruction and practice in its component strategies and subskills (e.g., recalling facts, breaking a problem into a sequence of steps, or predicting outcomes). Others suggest placing students in problem-solving environments and, with some coaching and guidance, letting them develop their own heuristics for attacking and solving problems.

Although the purposes of the two views overlap somewhat, the first is directed more toward supplying prerequisite skills for specific kinds of problem solving, while the second view aims more toward motivating students to attack problems and to recognize solving problems as an integral part of everyday life.

Criteria for Selecting Good Problem-Solving Software

Qualities to look for in good problem-solving software depend on the purpose of the software. In general, problem formats should be interesting and challenging, and software should have a clear link to developing a specific problem-solving ability. Software documentation should state clearly which specific problem-solving skills students will learn and how the software fosters them. See Figure 3.7

Figure 3.7 **Problem-Solving Summary Information**

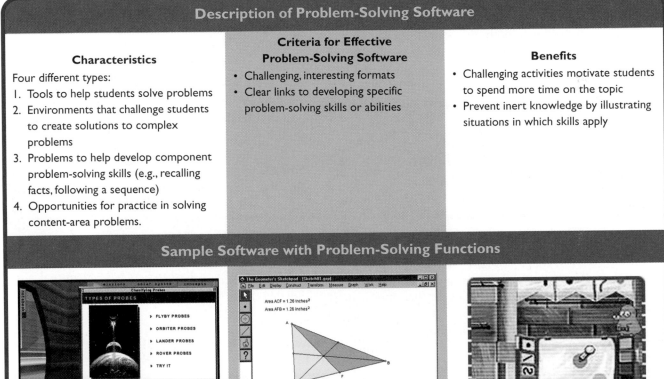

Description of Problem-Solving Software

Characteristics

Four different types:
1. Tools to help students solve problems
2. Environments that challenge students to create solutions to complex problems
3. Problems to help develop component problem-solving skills (e.g., recalling facts, following a sequence)
4. Opportunities for practice in solving content-area problems.

Criteria for Effective Problem-Solving Software
- Challenging, interesting formats
- Clear links to developing specific problem-solving skills or abilities

Benefits
- Challenging activities motivate students to spend more time on the topic
- Prevent inert knowledge by illustrating situations in which skills apply

Sample Software with Problem-Solving Functions

***Alien Rescue*®**
by The Alien Rescue Team
http://www.alienrescue.com

Challenge activity to teach scientific inquiry: Students must use software tools and information to locate new home planets in the solar system to match the needs of various aliens.

Screens from *Alien Rescue Software* © The Alien Rescue Team 2001–2004

***The Geometer's Sketchpad*®**
by Key Curriculum Press, Inc.
http://www.keypress.com/sketchpad

A dynamic construction and exploration tool: Students use software features to draw objects, investigate their mathematical properties, analyze problems, propose solutions, and do proofs to test their hypotheses.

The Geometer's Sketchpad®, Key Curriculum Press, 1150 65th Street, Emeryville, CA 94608, 1-800-995-MATH, www.keypress.com/sketchpad

***Frippletown*®**
by Riverdeep, Inc.
http://www.riverdeep.com

Activities to teach analysis and logical thinking: Students explore and practice various thinking strategies, including analyzing attributes, using logic, working backwards, identifying multiple solutions, and practicing creativity.

© 1999 Riverdeep Interactive Learning Limited, and its Licensors. All rights reserved.

for examples of problem-solving software and a summary of problem-solving features.

Benefits of Problem-Solving Software

Problem-solving software can help students in the following ways:

- **Improved interest and motivation** — Students are more likely to practice solving problems in activities they find interesting and motivating. Some educators also feel that students will become more active, spontaneous problem solvers if they experience success in their initial problem-solving efforts.

- **Prevents inert knowledge** — Content-area problem-solving environments can make knowledge and skills more meaningful to students, because they illustrate how and where information applies to actual problems. Students learn both the knowledge and its application at the same time. Also, students gain opportunities to discover concepts themselves, which they frequently find more motivating than being told or, as constructivists might say, programmed with, the information (McCoy, 1990).

Limitations and Problems Related to Problem-Solving Software

Problem-solving software packages are among the most popular of all software functions; however, the following issues are still of concern to educators:

- **Names versus skills** — Software packages use many terms to describe problem solving, and their exact meanings are not always clear. Terms that appear in software catalogs as synonyms for problem solving include thinking skills, critical thinking, higher level thinking, higher order cognitive outcomes, reasoning, use of logic, and decision making. In light of this diversity of language, teachers must identify the skills that a software package addresses by looking at its activities. For example, a software package may claim to teach inference skills. One would have to see how it defines inference by examining the tasks it presents, which may range from determining the next number in a sequence to using visual clues to predict a pattern.

- **Software claims versus effectiveness** — It would be difficult to find a software catalog that did not claim that its products foster problem solving, yet few publishers of software packages that purport to teach specific problem-solving skills have data to support their claims. When students play a game that requires skills related to problem solving, they do not necessarily learn these skills. They may enjoy the game thoroughly and even be successful at it without learning

any of the intended skills. Teachers may have to use problem-solving software themselves to confirm that it is achieving the results they want.

- **Possible negative effects of directed instruction** — Some researchers believe that direct attempts to teach problem-solving strategies can actually be counterproductive for some students. Mayes (1992) reports on studies that found "teaching sequenced planning to solve problems to high ability learners could interfere with their own effective processing" (p. 243). In a review of research on problem solving in science, Blosser (1988) also found indications that problem-solving instruction may not have the desired results if the instructional strategy does not suit certain kinds of students. For example, students with high math anxiety and low visual preference or proportional reasoning abilities will profit from instruction in problem solving only if it employs visual approaches.

- **Transfer** — Although some educators feel that general problem-solving skills such as inference and pattern recognition will transfer to content-area skills, scant evidence supports this view. In the 1970s and 1980s, for example, many schools taught programming in mathematics classes under the hypothesis that the planning and sequencing skills required for programming would transfer to problem-solving skills in math. Research results never supported this hypothesis. In general, research tends to show that skill in one kind of problem solving will transfer primarily to similar kinds of problems that use the same solution strategies. Researchers have identified nothing like "general thinking skills," except in relation to intelligence (IQ) variables.

How to Use Problem-Solving Software in Teaching: Integration Strategies and Guidelines

Classroom integration strategies for problem-solving software. Integration strategies for problem-solving software vary considerably depending on whether the desired approach is a directed or constructivist one. The following are guidelines for both kinds of integration strategies. Problem-solving software is appropriate for the following instructional needs:

- **To teach component skills in problem-solving strategies** — Many problem-solving packages provide good, hands-on experience with one or more of the skills required to use a problem-solving approach. These include identifying and following a logical sequence, identifying relevant information to solve problems, not jumping to conclusions too quickly, and remembering relevant information.

- **To provide support in solving problems** — Some software packages are specifically designed to serve a tool function as students practice solving complex problems. For example, *Geometer's Sketchpad* helps students draw objects and investigate their mathematical properties.

- **To encourage group problem solving** — Some software provides environments that lend themselves to solving problems in small groups. For example, *Alien Rescue*, the software described in the example at the beginning of this chapter, is designed specifically for collaborative problem solving.

Guidelines for directed teaching. Usually, teachers want to teach clearly defined skills. To teach problem solving, they must decide which particular kind of problem-solving ability students need to acquire and how best to foster it. For example, Stokes (1999) recommends that students use a teacher-designed reflection sheet and keep a log of problem-solving strategies and outcomes. (See Figure 3.8 for Stokes' example log.) With clearly identified skills and a definite teaching strategy, problem solving software has unique abilities to help focus students' attention on required activities. This kind of software can get students to apply and practice desired behaviors specific to a content area or more general abilities in problem solving.

The following six steps can help teachers to integrate software for directed teaching:

1. Identify problem-solving skills or general capabilities to build or foster skills in

   - solving one or more kinds of content-area problems (e.g., building algebra equations);

   - using a scientific approach to problem solving (identifying the problem, posing hypotheses, planning a systematic approach); and

   - components of problem solving such as following a sequence of steps or recalling facts.

2. Decide on an activity or a series of activities that would help teach the desired skills.

3. Examine software to locate materials that closely match the desired abilities, remembering to not judge capabilities on the basis of vendor claims alone.

4. Determine where the software fits into the teaching sequence (for example, to introduce the skill and gain attention, as a practice activity after demonstrating problem solving, or both).

5. Demonstrate the software and the steps to follow in solving problems.

6. Build in transfer activities and make students aware of the skills they are using in the software.

Guidelines for using constructivist strategies. Like many technology resources, some software with problem-solving functions is designed for more constructivist approaches to learning. These models give students no direct training in or introduction to solving problems; rather, they place students in highly motivational problem-solving environments and encourage them to work in groups to solve problems. Bearden and Martin (1998) describe such a strategy using problem-solving software combined with a listserv email (an email feature that allows a message to be sent to a group) for students to share their results. (Also see Martin and Bearden, 1998.) The following seven steps help teachers integrate problem-solving software according to constructivist models:

1. Allow students sufficient time to explore and interact with the software, but provide some structure in the form of directions, goals, a work schedule, and organized times for sharing and discussing results.

2. Vary the amount of direction and assistance provided, depending on each student's needs.

3. Promote a reflective learning environment; let students talk about the methods they use.

4. Stress thinking processes rather than correct answers.

5. Point out the relationship between software activities and other kinds of problem solving.

6. Let students work together in pairs or small groups.

7. For assessments, use alternatives to traditional paper-and-pencil tests.

Figure 3.8 **Problem-Solving Log for the Logical Journey of the Zoombinis**

Role/Date	Problem	Solution Tried	Outcome	Strategy
Monitor	What to do?	Click on screen	Not much happens	Trial-and-error
12.10.05			When click on dice, Zs appear	
		Quit and start again	Listen to introduction for clues!	Pay attention to detail

Source: Reprinted with permission from Stokes, J. (1999). Problem solving software, equity, and allocation of roles. *Learning and Leading with Technology, 26*(5), 9. Copyright © 1999 ISTE (International Society for Technology in Education), iste@iste.org, www.iste.org. All rights reserved.

TECHNOLOGY INTEGRATION IDEA 3.6

EXAMPLE STRATEGY FOR PROBLEM-SOLVING SOFTWARE

Title: Geometry with *Geometer's Sketchpad*

Content Area/Topic: Beginning geometry

Grade Level: Middle school

NETS for Students: Standards 3, 5, 6

Description: This software supports many kinds of learning activities ranging from highly structured student work to free exploration.

Instruction: An example of a structured activity with a pre-made sketch requires a teacher to demonstrate a *Sketchpad* sketch and lead students to understand the underlying concepts with guided observations and questions. A more open-ended, constructivist approach to the same objective would have students exploring the sketch themselves using guidelines the teacher provides (e.g., they make measurements of it and/or add new constructions). *Sketchpad* also supports activities called "black box tasks" for students with more sophisticated knowledge of the software. In these activities, students use the software tools to recreate a given figure or deduce the underlying properties that two or more objects have in common. Worksheets and templates to support these activities are available at http://math.nie.edu.sg/skteong/framework.htm.

The Geometer's Sketchpad®, Key Curriculum Press, 1150 65th Street, Emeryville, CA 94608, 1-800-995-MATH, www.keypress.com/sketchpad.

Source: From Ng, K., & Teong, S. (2003). The Geometer's Sketchpad for primary geometry: A framework. *Micromath 19*(3), 5–9. Used with permission.

For an example of a problem-solving software that supports both directed and constructivist applications, see Technology Integration Idea 3.6.

INTEGRATED LEARNING SYSTEMS

Integrated Learning Systems: Definition and Characteristics

Integrated learning systems (ILSs) are systems that offer computer-based instruction and other resources to support instruction, along with summary reports of student progress through the instruction; all are provided through networked or online sources. The most powerful—and the most expensive—of available software products, ILSs were introduced in the early 1970s and, until recently, were delivered via computer network from a central computer (server), usually located in the school. Initially, students and teachers used the instructional and management systems from terminals or microcomputers connected to the server. More recently ILS-type capability is provided by offering the curriculum online via the Internet, rather than through a local network.

Regardless of the delivery system, an ILS is characterized by a "one-stop shopping" approach to providing software. Each ILS offers a variety of instructional techniques in one place, usually as a curriculum package complete with technical maintenance and teacher training. In addition to providing a combination of drill-and-practice, tutorial, simulation, problem-solving, reference, and tool software, an ILS is capable of maintaining detailed records on individual student assignments and performance and supplying printouts of this information to teachers. Bailey and Lumley (1991, p. 21) include the following as characteristics of an ILS:

- Instructional objectives specified, with each lesson tied to those objectives
- Lessons integrated into the standard curriculum
- Software that spans several grade levels in comprehensive fashion
- A management system that collects and records results of student performance.

The teacher usually makes initial assignments for work on the system, monitors student progress by reviewing ILS reports, and provides additional instruction or support where needed. As each student signs onto a microcomputer connected to the server or Internet, the file server sends (or downloads) student assignments and software to the station and proceeds to keep records on what the students do during time spent on the system.

TOP TEN INTEGRATION STRATEGIES FOR INSTRUCTIONAL SOFTWARE

The best kinds and uses of instructional software depend on the content area and skills teachers need to address. The ten uses given here are among the most popular ones described in the literature.

1. Use simulation software such as Tom Snyder's *Operation Frog* http://www.tomsnyder.com or The Digital Frog International's online *Digital Frog* http://www.digitalfrog.com to replace or supplement hands-on dissections to help teach anatomy.

2. Use ExploreLearning's *Mouse Genetics* online simulation software http://www.explorelearning.com to let students explore basic principles of genetics and heredity.

3. Use Maxis Software's *SimCity* simulation software http://www.maxis.com to give students hands-on opportunities to see environmental and other consequences of city policy and planning decisions.

4. Use Tom Snyder's *Decisions, Decisions: The Constitution* http://www.tomsnyder.com to let students take a scenario approach to learning how separation and balance of power works in the U.S. federal government.

5. Use Key Curriculum Press's *Geometer's Sketchpad* http://www.keypress.com or the Center for Educational Technology's *Geometric Supposer* problem-solving software http://www.cet.ac.il/math-international/software5.htm to let students explore geometric principles and proofs.

6. Use Sunburst's *The Factory Deluxe* http://www.sunburst.com problem-solving software to give young children a visual environment for analyzing processes, predicting outcomes, and learning the importance of sequence in solving complex problems.

7. Use Sunburst's *How the West Was One + Three x Four* http://www.sunburst.com instructional game software to give students a highly motivating format for practicing the correct mathematical order of operations when solving math problems.

8. Use SAT preparation drill-and-practice software to help students prepare for taking the Scholastic Aptitude Test and other college entrance exams. (See the SuperKids website at http://www.superkids.com for a rating of the top five SAT Prep packages.)

9. Use drill-and-practice software like that available from Transparent Software http://www.transparent.com to let students practice foreign language vocabulary and phrase translations.

10. Use tutorial instructional sequences available from Renaissance Learning http://www.renlearn.com/ or CompassLearning http://www.compasslearning.com/ to give students detailed reviews of basic math or science topics or to let advanced students surge ahead.

CW

To visit these web links online, go to this text's Companion Website at http://www.prenhall.com/roblyer.

The software component of an ILS. Instructional activities available on an ILS range from simple drill and practice to extensive tutorials. Many ILSs are moving toward complete tutorial systems intended to replace teachers in delivering entire instructional sequences. An ILS usually includes instruction on the entire scope and sequence of skills in a given content area; for example, it may cover all discrete mathematics skills typically presented in grades 1 through 6.

The management system component of an ILS. The capability that differentiates ILSs from other networked systems is the emphasis on individualized instruction tied to records of student progress. A typical ILS gives teachers progress reports across groups of students as well as the following kinds of information on individual performance:

- Lessons and tests completed
- Questions missed on each lesson by numbers and percentages
- Numbers of correct and incorrect tries
- Time spent on each lesson and test
- Pretest and post-test data.

Integrated learning systems software is even more accessible with portable computers.

Criteria for Selecting ILSs

One way to ensure the appropriate use of ILSs is to have a careful, well-planned review process that involves both teachers and school administrators. Criteria for the selection process are usually based on the curriculum coverage and pedagogical strategies in the ILS, as well as perceptions about the usefulness of the reports that the system produces and how much they meet the needs of the district. See Figure 3.9 for examples of ILSs and a summary of ILS features.

Benefits of ILSs

Brush (1998) estimated that as of 1998, between 11% and 25% of all U.S. schools owned ILSs. Two recent developments have caused a rapid rise in these numbers (Readers' Choice Awards, 2004):

- **District- and state-adopted academic standards —** An increased emphasis on educational accountability in the 1990s caused states to set curriculum standards and create tests to measure students' progress on them. Integrated software and management assessments aligned with these standards helps schools prepare for meeting these standards.

- **Accountability requirements of the No Child Left Behind (NCLB) Act —** The NCLB Act stipulated that schools who fail to meet Adequate Yearly Progress (AYP) for 3 years in a row must use a portion of their Title I funds for out-of-school tutoring, which the NCLB Act refers to as Supplemental Educational Ser-

vices (Readers' Choice Awards, 2004). ILS materials are ideal for providing these services.

Since an ILS provides a combination of the materials described previously in this chapter, its potential benefits duplicate the benefits of these functions. In addition, networked or online materials are easier for teachers and students to access and can provide entire curricula from one location. Prepared curricula and ease of use mean that school personnel need not know a great deal about technology to use an ILS. Consequently, they usually simplify integration decisions by defining schoolwide curriculum rather than individual lessons. When teachers assign some students to use ILS activities, it frees more time for them to help other students who need their personal assistance. Also, teachers can personalize instructional activities for each student by reviewing the extensive information on student and class progress provided by the ILS management system.

Limitations and Problems Related to ILSs

Teachers should note that although many educators still refer to these multifaceted systems as "integrated learning systems," the vendors of the systems tend to refer to them as "educational solutions," "accountability solutions," or "supplemental educational services" (Readers' Choice Awards, 2004). By whatever name they are called, several items are ongoing concerns:

- **The costs of ILSs —** The primary criticism of ILSs centers on their expense compared to their impact on

Figure 3.9 Integrated Learning Systems Summary Information

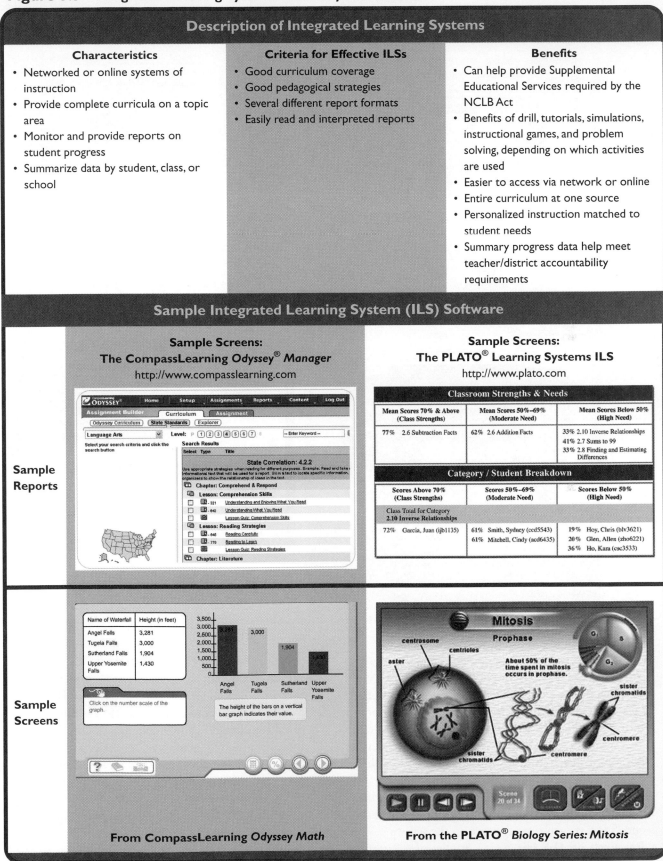

Description of Integrated Learning Systems

Characteristics
- Networked or online systems of instruction
- Provide complete curricula on a topic area
- Monitor and provide reports on student progress
- Summarize data by student, class, or school

Criteria for Effective ILSs
- Good curriculum coverage
- Good pedagogical strategies
- Several different report formats
- Easily read and interpreted reports

Benefits
- Can help provide Supplemental Educational Services required by the NCLB Act
- Benefits of drill, tutorials, simulations, instructional games, and problem solving, depending on which activities are used
- Easier to access via network or online
- Entire curriculum at one source
- Personalized instruction matched to student needs
- Summary progress data help meet teacher/district accountability requirements

Sample Integrated Learning System (ILS) Software

Sample Reports

Sample Screens: The CompassLearning Odyssey® Manager
http://www.compasslearning.com

Sample Screens: The PLATO® Learning Systems ILS
http://www.plato.com

Sample Screens

From CompassLearning Odyssey Math

From the PLATO® Biology Series: Mitosis

Figure 3.9 (continued)

Sample Integrated Learning System (ILS) Software

Sample Screens

From CompassLearning
Odyssey Reading/Language Arts

From the PLATO® Math Expeditions Series

From CompassLearning
Odyssey Social Studies

From the PLATO®
Focus Reading and Language Series

improving learning. ILS proponents feel that the students who experience the most success with ILSs are those whose needs are typically most difficult to meet (Becker, 1994; Bender, 1991; Bracy, 1992; Shore & Johnson, 1992). ILS proponents say there is value in any system that can help potential dropouts stay in school or help students with learning disabilities. They point to studies and personal testimony from teachers over the years that ILSs motivate students by allowing them to work at their own pace and experience success each time they are on the system.

- **Research on ILS impact** — Studies of a variety of ILSs in a number of different locations reached generally the same conclusion as Van Dusen and Worthen (1995): The impact of an ILS on student achievement varies greatly with implementation methods. Kulik's (2003) meta-analysis of ILS studies published between 1990 and 1997 shows modest gains for schools using ILSs. Becker's (1992) summary of some 30 studies of ILS effectiveness found wide variation in results with various implementation methods and systems. Students generally tend to do somewhat better with ILSs than with other methods, and results were sometimes substantially superior to non-ILS methods. But Becker found no predictable pattern for successful and unsuccessful ILSs. Subsequent large-scale studies of ILS use in the United Kingdom (Wood, Underwood, & Avis,

1999), Indiana (Estep, McInerney, & Vockell, 1999–2000), and New York (Miller, 1997; Paterson, Henry, & O'Quin, 2003) duplicated this finding. However, Brush, Armstrong, and Barbrow (1999) found that two different resources offered in the same ILS had different impacts on achievement. Individualized software designed to provide foundations instruction had less impact than software that could be selected by teachers to supplement their own instruction.

- **Concerns about the role of ILSs** — In a follow-up to his literature review on ILS uses, Becker (1994) criticized uses of ILSs that encourage "mindless adherence to the principle of individualized instruction" (p. 78). Brush (1998) agreed with Becker, finding that "...lack of teacher involvement (in ILS use) has led to improper coordination between classroom-based and computer-based instructional activities ... and lack of teacher understanding regarding effective strategies and procedures for using ILSs" (p. 7). An early concern expressed by many educators (White, 1992) that the cost of ILSs combined with the comprehensive nature of their curricula might cause schools to view them as replacements for teachers has not yet proven to be a real problem.

How to Use ILSs in Teaching: Integration Strategies and Guidelines

When used only as a teacher replacement to provide individual student instruction, ILSs seem to be less effective. When viewed as a supplement to other teacher methods and carefully integrated into a total teaching program, they seem more likely to have the desired impact on raising achievement. One way to ensure appropriate and cost-effective uses of ILS products may be through a careful, well-planned purchasing process that involves both teachers and administrators. One such process was developed by the California Department of Education (Armstrong, 1999). This five-stage process (planning, pre-evaluation, evaluation, selection, and implementation/post-evaluation) is designed to "establish selection procedures that ensure that ... curricular goals remain at the heart of the selection process" (p. 3). Guidelines for potential ILS purchasers based on those offered by Smith and Sclafani (1989), Chrisman (1992), and Vaille and Hall (1998) are summarized here:

- Clearly identify the problem the ILS is supposed to solve and understand the instructional theory on which the system is based.
- Determine whether the ILS is a closed system (one that provides 80% or more of the instruction for a given course) or an open system (one linked to the school's resources).
- Find out if the system's scope and sequence are matched to that of the school.
- Determine the target population for which the system was designed and whether or not it closely matches the characteristics of students with whom the ILS will be used.
- Consider the adequacy of the reporting and management system for the school's needs.
- Consider how much of its resources the school must spend on hardware and software.
- Project the educational benefits to the school from the system and compare them with the costs.
- Request that vendors inform the school on ILS updates.
- Carefully evaluate the grade-level software, management system, customization, and online tools and be sure that they match the school's expectations.
- Set up reasonable terms of procurement and calculate the personnel and fiscal impact of the ILS.

Successful uses of ILSs have been reported for both directed and constructivist teaching approaches.

Directed applications for ILSs. In a directed teaching approach, an ILS system can be used for remediation and as a mainstream delivery system. In either of these uses, teachers still have important roles to play. Teachers must assign initial levels of work, follow up on student activities on the system, and give additional personal instruction when needed.

- **For remediation** — Although ILSs are expensive alternatives to other kinds of delivery systems, the requirements of the NCLB Act have provided new motivation—as well as new funding sources—for using them. Even with new funding and motivation to use them, schools still must determine how ILS functions coordinate and complement those of the classroom teacher. ILS uses serve target populations that have typically presented the most difficult problems for traditional classroom activities: Title I groups, English for Speakers of Other Languages (ESOL) students, special education students, and at-risk students. Schools have tried and usually failed to reach these students with other methods.
- **As a mainstream delivery system** — Rather than using an ILS only as a backup system to address educational problems, a school may let an ILS do the initial job of teaching whole courses for all students in a grade level. In light of the expense of ILSs, these uses

are more rare. However, some alternative projects, like the Edison Project (Walsh, 1999), predict that the costs of using technology in this way will amount to substantially less over time than teacher salaries. Using ILSs to increase student-to-teacher ratios has stimulated ongoing debate and study.

Constructivist applications for ILSs. An ILS can also combine several kinds of technology resources to support constructivist learning approaches. This kind of ILS can provide what Perkins (1991) called a "rich environment" that students can use to construct their own knowledge. ILS products useful for constructivist purposes typically have an information bank (electronic encyclopedias), symbol pads (word processing and/or desktop publishing software), construction kits (Logo or other graphic languages or tools), and phenomenaria (computer simulations and/or problem-solving resources). They also usually have data-collection systems to track student usage of the system (Mageau, 1990).

A SUMMARY OF INSTRUCTIONAL SOFTWARE INTEGRATION STRATEGIES

Although descriptions of instructional software in the literature are changing, many references to software evaluation criteria and evaluation methods focus on products to be used with directed instruction. While many criteria are appropriate for software designed for both kinds of uses, additional details are often lacking on what to look for in software that will be used with constructivist methods.

Constructivist activities tend to emphasize multimedia and distance learning products rather than drill or tutorial software. For example, Litchfield (1992) lists criteria for "inquiry-based science software and interactive multimedia programs." Checklists by Hoffman and Lyons (1997) and Vaille and Hall (1998) are among those that include criteria for more open-ended products. Further criteria and methods for evaluating multimedia and online multimedia products will be discussed in Chapters 6 through 8. For a summary of all instructional software uses matched to directed and constructivist integration strategies, see the matrix in Figure 3.10.

EVALUATING AND SELECTING INSTRUCTIONAL SOFTWARE

In the 1980s, microcomputer software began to flood the educational market from such diverse sources as state projects, major publishing houses, and even cottage industries. Educators increasingly became aware that simply putting instruction on the computer was no guarantee of its quality or usefulness. Indeed, some of the products were so bad

that they could be worse than no instruction at all. Software quality became a major issue in education, and software evaluation evolved into a popular and highly publicized practice in magazines and in educational and professional organizations.

As the field of educational technology matured and educators refined their attitudes toward computer use, the mystique of software faded and the issues involved in selecting software became the same as those for choosing any good instructional material. During the 1980s, teachers primarily evaluated and selected their own software. Now, state- and school district-level personnel increasingly control these purchases. Thus, the evaluation procedures and criteria have changed considerably from the early days of microcomputers. Regardless of who chooses the products, teachers should recognize that just because software addresses certain topics or skills, it does not mean that it will meet their needs.

The Need for Software Evaluation

Software quality is less troublesome now than it was in the early days of microcomputers, when there were frequent technical problems. Software producers have obviously learned much from their early errors and problems, and overall technical and appearance quality has improved considerably. But educators still have good reasons for spending some time reviewing and/or evaluating software before selecting it for classroom use. Computerized instruction is not necessarily effective instruction, and eye-catching screen displays should not be the primary criteria for selecting materials.

Teachers should review software even after prescreening by committees or experts. Very often, state- or district-level committees are responsible only for selecting software that does not have gross problems and is aligned with a content or topic area. Each teacher must then determine which specific curriculum needs and specific grade levels the package addresses and whether or not software functions fit with planned teaching strategies. It cannot be emphasized enough that software must match clearly identified instructional needs. It should not be used simply because it is available at a discount or supplied free by the state or district.

Although there is no substitute for personal reviews, several organizations can help with selecting good software to review. Among these are:

- **SREB EvaluTech** (http://www.evalutech.sreb.org) — An initiative of the Southern Regional Education Board's (SREB) Educational Technology Cooperative, the EvaluTech website includes more than 10,000 recommended reviews of software and print resources.

Figure 3.10 Technology Integration Strategies for Directed, Constructivist, or Either Models

Integration Strategies for Instructional Software		Directed Models				Constructivist Models					Either Model		
		Remedy identified weaknesses or skill deficits	Promote skill fluency or automaticity	Provide efficient, self-paced instruction	Support self-paced review of concepts	Foster creative problem solving and metacognition	Build mental models, increase knowledge transfer	Foster group cooperation	Allow for multiple intelligences	Generate motivation to learn	Optimize scarce personnel and material resources	Remove logistical hurdles to learning	Develop information literacy and visual literacy skills
Drill and Practice	Supplement or replace worksheets, homework exercises	X	X										
	Prepare for tests	X	X										
Tutorials	Self-paced reviews			X	X								
	Alternative learning strategies			X	X								
	Instruction when teachers are unavailable			X	X								
Simulations	Replace or supplement labs										X	X	X
	Replace or supplement role playing								X	X			
	Replace or supplement field trips						X			X	X	X	
	Introduce a new topic						X			X			
	Foster exploration, process learning					X	X	X					
	Encourage cooperation and group work							X	X	X			
Instructional Games	Supplement or replace worksheets, homework exercises	X	X										
	Teach cooperative skills							X	X	X			
	As a reward									X			
Problem-solving	Teach component skills in problem-solving strategies					X	X						
	Provide support in solving problems		X			X							
	Encourage group problem solving					X		X	X				

Teachers evaluate software to select the best materials for their students.

- **California Learning Resource Network** (http://www. clrn.org/home) — This site includes a searchable database with hundreds of learning resource reviews.
- **SuperKids** (http://www.superkids.com) — Reviews for teachers are published on this resource site for teachers and parents.
- **Education World** (http://www.educationworld. com) — Reviews for teachers are published as part of a resource site for teachers.

Software Evaluation Procedures: A Recommended Sequence

Evaluation procedures and criteria vary dramatically depending on whether a teacher is selecting software for a single classroom or working as part of a district-level committee screening materials for use by many schools. One major difference is that committees generally must justify decisions to purchase one package over another by using weighted criteria checklists and assigning total point scores to individual packages. Small groups or individual teachers use much less formal procedures and criteria.

This section is designed primarily for individual teachers or small organizations such as individual schools that (1) do not have large organizations purchasing software for them, (2) wish to supplement resources purchased for them by others, or (3) want to review preselected software to determine its usefulness for their immediate needs. These procedures are intended to help teachers anticipate and deal with problems related to software quality and to

assist them in matching software to their classroom needs. The following sequence is recommended when selecting software for classroom use:

Step 1: Begin with an identified need — Know what topics and skills you want to address and how you think you will use technology. This will require some knowledge of what kinds of instructional support technology has to offer.

Step 2: Locate titles — As mentioned earlier in this section, teachers should probably not base their software purchasing decisions on descriptive reviews. Recommendations from colleagues and professional magazines and journals should serve primarily as leads. Once teachers discover a package they find interesting, they should use one or both of the next two general procedures to determine its usefulness.

Step 3: Complete hands-on reviews — There is no substitute for seeing the software working. Avoid reviewing demo packages (abbreviated versions of actual software), which can be misleading substitutes for the real thing. A typical hands-on review consists of two to three phases:

- An initial run-through to assess the package's capabilities and what it covers,
- A second, more comprehensive run-through to make incorrect responses and press keys that aren't supposed to be pressed in order to determine the program's ability to handle typical student use, and
- An optional third pass to review the usefulness and/or quality of particular demonstrations or presentations.

Evaluation checklists such as those shown in Figures 3.11 and 3.12 are helpful to guide teachers in a hands-on review. Tergan (1998) says that, given the number of packages teachers have to choose from and the time it takes to review each one, checklists can be useful tools if the evaluator knows what to look for. He advocates that teachers either develop their own checklist or adopt one that seems thorough and well designed. Though many checklists are based on rating software and assigning points to various aspects, teachers usually are much less concerned with a total score than with making sure they have looked at all relevant characteristics.

Step 4: Assign and collect student reviews — Experienced teachers usually can tell from their own hands-on reviews when instructional materials are appropriate for their students. Even so, they are sometimes surprised at student reactions to software. Students sometimes encounter unexpected problems, or they may not seem to get out of the activity what the teacher expected they would. If possible, field test software with students. Gill, Dick, Reiser, and Zahner (1992) describe a detailed method for evaluating software that involves collecting data on student use.

Figure 3.11   Essential Criteria Checklist for Evaluating Instructional Software

*The following checklist includes four sets of essential qualities used to discriminate between acceptable and unacceptable software material as well as criteria for specific software functions. If software does not meet all these criteria, it probably should not be considered for purchase. For each item, circle **Y** for yes if it meets the criterion, or **N** for no if it does not.*

Title _____ Publisher _____

Content Area _____ Grade level(s) _____

Hardware Required _____

Cost Information and Pricing Options Available _____

Courseware Functions:

_____ Drill and practice _____ Instructional game

_____ Tutorial _____ Problem solving

_____ Simulation _____ Other: _____

Objectives: _____

_____

_____

Set 1. Instructional Design and Pedagogical Soundness

Y   N   Teaching strategy is matched to student needs/levels and is based on accepted methods

Y   N   Presentation on screen contains nothing that misleads or confuses students

Y   N   Comments to students are not abusive or insulting

Y   N   Readability and learning difficulty are at an appropriate level for target students

Y   N   Graphics fulfill an important purpose (motivation, information) and are not distracting to learners

Comments: _____

_____

_____

Criteria specific to drill-and-practice functions

Y   N   High degree of control over presentation rate (unless the method is timed review)

Y   N   Appropriate feedback for correct answers (not elaborate or time consuming; none for timed review)

Y   N   Feedback is more reinforcing for correct than for incorrect reponses

Comments: _____

_____

_____

Criteria specific to tutorial functions

Y   N   High degree of interactivity (not just reading information)

Y   N   High degree of user control (forward and backward movement; branching upon request)

Y   N   Comprehensive teaching sequence so instruction is self-contained and stand-alone

Y   N   Adequate answer-judging capabilities for student-constructed answers to questions

Comments: _____

_____

_____

Criteria specific to simulation functions

Y   N   Appropriate degree of fidelity (accurate depiction of system being modeled)

Y   N   Good documentation available on how program works (if not intuitive)

Comments: _____

_____

_____

Criteria specific to instructional game functions

Y   N   Low quotient of violence or combat-type activities

Y   N   Amount of physical dexterity required is appropriate for students who will use it

Comments: _____

_____

_____

Set 2. Content

Y   N   No grammar, spelling, or punctuation errors on the screen

Y   N   All content accurate and up to date

Y   N   No racial or gender stereotypes; not geared toward only one sex or to certain races

Y   N   Exhibits a sensitive treatment of moral and/or social issues (e.g., perspectives on war)

Y   N   Content matches required curriculum objectives

Comments: _____

_____

_____

Set 3. User Flexibility

Y   N   User normally has some control of movement within the program (e.g., can go from screen to screen at desired rate; can read text at desired rate; can exit program when desired)

Y   N   Can turn off sound, if desired

Y   N   Interface is easy to use (e.g., similar format from screen-to-screen for forward and backward movement in program)

Comments: _____

_____

_____

Set 4. Technical Soundness

Y   N   Program loads consistently, without error

Y   N   Program does not break (i.e., stop working), no matter what the student enters

Y   N   Program does what the screen says it should do

Y   N   Program works on desired platform

Y   N   If included, online links work as indicated

Y   N   If included, animations and videos work as indicated

Comments: _____

_____

Decision: _____ Is recommended for purchase and use

_____ Is not recommended

Figure 3.12 Optional Criteria Checklist for Evaluating Instructional Software

The following checklist is based on criteria that may help teachers decide between two or more packages on the same topic, if all meet the essential criteria. This checklist may be used as a follow up to the **Essential Criteria Checklist.** *For each item, circle* **Y** *for yes if it meets the criterion, or* **N** *for no if it does not.*

Title _____ Publisher _____
Content Area _____ Grade level(s) _____
Hardware Required _____
Cost Information and Pricing Options Available _____
Functions:
_____ Drill and practice _____ Instructional game
_____ Tutorial _____ Problem solving
_____ Simulation _____ Other: _____
Objectives: _____
_____

Optional Instructional Design Criteria

Y   N   **Stated objectives:** Does the software state its objectives clearly?

Y   N   **Prerequisite skills:** Are skills specified that students will need in order to use the software activities, and are students likely to have the required skills?

Y   N   **Interest quotient:** Are examples and strategies likely to interest students at the targeted level?

Y   N   **Presentation logic:** Do instructional topics follow a logical sequence based on a skill hierarchy or commonly accepted curriculum sequences?

Y   N   **Tests:** Do tests match stated skills and are they good measures of the skills?

Y   N   **Significance:** Are stated skills "educationally significant" (e.g., in the curriculum)?

Y   N   **Use of medium:** Does software make good use of computer capabilities (e.g., highly interactive)?

Y   N   **Field testing:** Is there evidence that the software has been used with students and revised based on their feedback before its release?

Comments: _____
_____

Optional Interface/Navigation Criteria

Y   N   **Student ease-of-use:** Is the program easy to use for the intended students? Is a lot of typing required?

Y   N   **Required procedures:** Are the procedures required to input answers easy to remember (e.g., pressing "B" to go "back")?

Y   N   **Input devices:** Are alternate input devices allowed to make software more usable for special populations?

Y   N   **Directions:** Are there on-screen directions on how to use it?

Y   N   **Shortcuts:** Can users bypass lengthy introductory screens or directions, if desired?

Y   N   **Support materials:** Are there print support materials to support on-screen activities?

Y   N   **Optional assistance:** Is a "HELP" feature available if the student runs into difficulty?

Y   N   **Creativity:** Do materials foster creativity rather than just rote learning?

Y   N   **Summary feedback:** Are students given an on-screen summary of performance when they finish working?

Comments: _____
_____

Optional Teacher Use Criteria

Y   N   **Teacher ease of use:** Can teachers figure out, with minimum effort, how to work the program?

Y   N   **Management:** Does software contain adequate record-keeping and management capabilities?

Y   N   **Teacher manuals:** Are clear, nontechnical teacher manuals available with the software? Are manuals well produced and include a good Table of Contents and index?

Y   N   **Ease of integration:** Are software materials designed to integrate easily into other activities the teacher is doing?

Y   N   **Teacher assistance:** Does software improve the teacher's ability to teach the subject?

Y   N   **Adaptability:** Can teachers modify and adapt the software for their needs by changing content (e.g., spelling words) or format (e.g., animated versus written feedback)?

Comments: _____
_____

Optional Presentation Criteria

Y   N   **Graphics features:** Are graphics, animation, and color used for instructional purposes rather than decoration?

Y   N   **Screen layout:** Are screens so "busy" or cluttered that they may interfere with reading?

Y   N   **Audio and speech capabilities:** Is audio and speech of adequate quality so students can understand it easily?

Y   N   **Video and animation:** Do moving graphics display clearly, quickly, and without jerkiness? Are they in a high enough resolution to be useful?

Y   N   **Required peripherals:** Does the program require peripherals the schools are likely to have (e.g., speech synthesizers)?

Y   N   **Screen printing:** Can key screens from the software (e.g., summary performances) be printed?

Comments: _____
_____

Optional Technical Criteria

Y   N   **Response judging:** Does the response judging allow for ALL possible correct answers and disallow ALL possible incorrect ones?

Y   N   **Timing:** Does the program present itself quickly so displays and responses are accomplished without noticeable delays?

Y   N   **Web resources:** If online, are websites working most of the time and are they updated frequently, as needed?

Y   N   **Portability:** Can teachers transfer the software from one machine to another?

Y   N   **Compatibility:** Does software run on more than one platform?

Y   N   **Components:** Are all required drivers and plug-ins identified and either provided or easily downloadable online?

Y   N   **Technical manuals:** Do teacher or user manuals contain technical documentation on program operation and any technical features or options? Does the manual tell how to install and uninstall the program?

Comments: _____
_____

Optional Publisher Support

Y   N   **Cost effectiveness:** Is the price of the package appropriate in light of what it accomplishes?

Y   N   **Available versions:** Is the program available in desired versions (e.g., network or site license)? Does the company provide for free or discounted upgrades later?

Y   N   **Preview allowed:** Does the company allow free previews? Will they refund the purchase price or supply a replacement if user is not satisfied or if software is lost, stolen, or damaged?

Y   N   **Backup:** Is a backup disk provided or can user make one?

Y   N   **Training:** For more complicated course packages, is on-site or web-based training provided to buyers, and is there a newsletter or other way to communicate applications and updates?

Y   N   **Packaging:** Is it made to stand up to normal school and classroom wear? Are discs labeled clearly as to program part and platform?

Y   N   **Ongoing support:** Does the company answer questions and provide help for problems via local representatives, a toll-free telephone line, and/or a website?

Comments: _____
_____

Software Evaluation Procedures: Essential and Optional Criteria

Many sets of software criteria are available, but they tend to vary widely depending on the educational philosophy of the evaluator and the software functions being reviewed. Software criteria may be divided into two types: those that confirm *essential characteristics* are present and criteria that review *optional* or *situational characteristics* and are sometimes applicable and sometimes not, depending on the user's needs.

The discussion that follows presents four sets of *essential criteria* based on many sources (ISTE website; SREB website; Comer & Geissler, 1998; Hoffman & Lyons, 1997; Lockard & Abrams, 2001; Roblyer, 1983; Vaille & Hall, 1998). Teachers may find these criteria (summarized in the checklist shown in Figure 3.11) helpful for their first-pass review of the software's content and capabilities.

In addition to the essential criteria, teachers reviewing software may consider many additional characteristics depending on their needs, the program's purpose and cost, and the intended audience. Figure 3.12 presents a more comprehensive checklist summarizing optional criteria teachers may wish to use during a second pass through the program. Many of the criteria in the Figure 3.12 checklist are subjective in nature or dependent on teacher needs; it is up to the teacher to decide whether or not the software meets those needs and/or whether or not they are important enough to affect selection decisions. Optional criteria may make the difference when teachers locate two or more packages that meet the essential criteria.

Set 1: essential instructional design and pedagogy characteristics: does it teach?

- **Appropriate teaching strategy, based on best known methods** — This covers a wide range of needs related to teaching methodology, for example, providing enough examples for concept development, presenting ideas in a logical order, and including various components required for learning.

- **Presentation on screen contains nothing that misleads or confuses students** — For example, one particularly blatant error of this type was in a software package intended to teach young children about how the human body works. It depicted the human heart as a square box. Another, a math program, displayed a number of objects based on what the student answered, but never bothered to change the number of objects if it was a wrong answer. Thus, the student could be seeing the corrected numeral but the wrong number of objects.

- **Comments to students not abusive or insulting** — Programs must be sensitive to students' feelings, even if comments are intended humorously. One program based on a well-known cartoon cat with an acerbic personality belittled the student's name, saying "What kind of name is that for a worthy opponent?" It also commented on the student's "lack of mental ability" when a wrong answer was supplied. Although this was in keeping with the cat's comic persona, it was still inappropriate.

- **Readability at an appropriate level for students who will use it** — Although this may apply to any use of language in any program, it is particularly applicable to tutorials, which may require many explanations. For example, one tutorial for math skills at about second-grade level had many explanations written at about a fourth-grade level. This would probably not be an appropriate expectation for students who were have trouble with this level of math.

- **Graphics fulfill important purpose and are not distracting to learners** — Pictures and animation are considered motivational to students, but this is not always true. For example, animated feedback may be charming the first ten times the students see it, but may achieve just the opposite effect after that. Also, some software attracts students' attention by flashing text or objects on the screen. This can be distracting when one is trying to focus on other screen text.

- **Criteria specific to software types** — The checklist also includes items that teachers should look for in each type of software function reflected in the software package.

Set 2: essential content characteristics: is content accurate, current, and appropriate?

- **No grammar, spelling, or punctuation errors on the screen** — Even math and science programs should reflect correct spelling, grammar, and word uses, since students learn more than just the *intended* skills from instructional materials. One early software release on punctuation skills misspelled the word "punctuation" three different ways in the program!

- **All content accurate and up to date** — Many people are surprised to find accuracy errors with software material; they seem to trust content presented on a computer, as if the computer would correct the text itself if it becomes out-of-date! Content inaccuracies have been observed in a number of packages. For example, one program referred to blood as a "red substance," which, of course, is not always true. Instructional materials in social studies should be carefully screened for inaccurate reflections of country names, which are changing rapidly. Examples should be free of slang or other content that dates material and makes it less than useful to current students.

- **No racial or gender stereotypes; not geared toward only one sex or to certain races** — Look for diversity in the names and examples used. Are they all for "Dick and Jane" and are they always in the suburbs? Also review examples for gender stereotypes. Are all doctors men? Are all homemakers women?

- **Social characteristics** — Does the software exhibit a sensitive treatment of moral and/or social issues? For example, do games and simulations avoid unnecessary violence?

- **Match to instructional needs** — Does software match district or state curriculum objectives teachers are required to teach?

Set 3: essential user interface characteristics: is it "user friendly" and easy to navigate?

- **User has appropriate control of movement within the program** — Depending on the purpose of the program, the students normally should be able to go from screen to screen and read each screen at their own desired rate. They should also have obvious exit options available at any time.

- **User can turn off sound, if desired** — Since software may be used in classrooms, the teacher should have the ability to make the software quiet so it will not disturb others.

- **Interface is intuitive** — Screens and usage are consistent, allowing students to easily use the software without extensive assistance.

Set 4: essential technical soundness characteristics: does it work correctly?

- **Program loads consistently, without error** — A common problem in early software, problems of this kind are now rarely seen.

- **Program does not break, no matter what the student enters** — Again, this was a more common problem in early software. Programs should be designed to expect any possible answer, not just the correct or most obvious ones. When unexpected answers are entered, programs should give an appropriate response to get the student back on track.

- **Program works on desired platform** — If one needs a Macintosh OS-based program, a program written exclusively for Windows is of little use (and vice versa). Also, the program should work on the version of the operating system in use by the school (e.g., Windows NT vs. Windows Server 2003).

- **Program does what the screen says it should do** — If the screen indicates the student should be able to exit or go to another part of the program, this capability should be allowed as stated.

- **Online links work correctly** — Many new software packages provide links to Internet websites for additional demonstrations or interactions with others.

Links should work as designated. If links are to non-working sites, the user should have the option to eliminate or correct them.

- **Videos and animations work correctly** — If a screen is to display a moving graphic object (e.g., video or animation), it should work as indicated. Sometimes, a graphic requires so much memory that it works too slowly to be practical for the classroom.

INTERACTIVE SUMMARY

The following is a summary of the main points covered in this chapter. To see additional examples and information on these points, go to this textbook's Companion Website at http://www.prenhall.com/roblyer and click on the Chapter 3 *Interactive Summary* module to visit each of the recommended websites.

1. **Types of instructional software** — Instructional software packages are computer programs designed specifically to deliver or support one or more kinds of learning activities. These programs can serve one or more of the following five functions:

   - **Drill and practice** — Students work example items, usually one at a time, and receive feedback on their correctness. See Transparent Software's *Before You Know It* series for some good examples of software products that include drill functions.

   - **Tutorial** — These provide an entire instructional sequence similar to a teacher's classroom instruction on a topic. See tutorial products available from the American Education Corporation to help students prepare for important state and national tests. Note that each software title is correlated to state and national curriculum standards.

   - **Simulation** — These are computerized models of real or imagined systems that are designed to teach how the system works. See examples of some of the most popular simulation software titles for business mathematics (e.g., *Hot Dog Stand* by Sunburst), social studies (e.g., *Decisions, Decisions 5.0* by Tom Snyder, a Scholastic Company, and the *SimCity* series by Maxis, Inc.), and science (PhysLink, Inc. and Chemistry Software.com).

   - **Instructional games** — These activities are designed to increase motivation by adding game rules and/or competition to learning activities. Probably the most famous instructional games are *Math Blaster*®, available from Education.com, and the *Carmen Sandiego*® series, available from riverdeep.com.

   - **Problem solving** — These programs serve one of three purposes: (1) foster component skills involved in solving problems, (2) teach or provide practice in general approaches to problem solving, or (3) teach or provide opportunities to practice solving various problems in specific content areas. See Riverdeep's *Thinkin' Things Collection* and *Zoombinis* series and Sunburst's *Factory Deluxe* for good examples of problem-solving software.

2. **Integrated learning systems** — These products offer computer-based instruction and other resources to support instruction, along with summary reports of student progress through the instruction; all are provided through networked or online sources. Now often referred to as "software solutions" or "technology solutions," the top software solutions or ILS companies are:

    • Compass Learning Systems. See assessment system features they offer to help teachers diagnose and remedy student deficits.

    • Pearson Digital Learning. *SuccessMaker Enterprise* uses more directed strategies, while *KnowledgeBox* takes a more constructivist approach.

    • PLATO Learning. They offer both assessment solutions and accountability solutions.

    • Renaissance Learning. They offer professional development options to help teachers use their products more effectively.

3. **Using instructional software to meet classroom needs** — Instructional software functions can meet each of the following classroom needs. Look at the company websites given above for examples of packages that can address each of these needs:

    • **Drill and practice** — Supplementing or replacing worksheets and homework exercises, preparation for tests

    • **Tutorial** — Self-paced reviews of instruction, alternative learning strategies, and instruction when teachers are unavailable

    • **Simulation** — In place of or as supplements to lab experiments, in place of or as supplements to role playing, in place of or as supplements to field trips, to introduce or clarify a new topic, to foster exploration and problem solving, and to encourage cooperation and group work

    • **Instructional game** — Use in place of worksheets and exercises, to teach cooperative group working skills, and as a reward

    • **Problem solving** — To teach component skills in problem-solving strategies, provide practice in solving problems, and to encourage group problem solving

4. **Planning lesson activities that integrate instructional software** — To see examples of lessons that can serve as models for how best to integrate instructional software, see the *Technology Integration Workshop* DVD that accompanies this text. (Search by software function.) Companies that market instructional software often provide lessons that illustrate how to integrate their products. For example, see Riverdeep's lesson projects.

5. **Evaluation of instructional software** — Software evaluation is reviewing software according to set criteria in order to determine its quality and appropriateness for a given instructional purpose. To accomplish this, teachers use a set of *essential criteria* that focus on instructional design and pedagogical approach, content, user interface, and technical soundness. They may also use *optional criteria* to help them decide between two or more packages that meet basic criteria. These focus on instructional design, interface/navigation, teacher use, presentation, technical, and publisher support. Software evaluation criteria and procedures vary but all have many criteria in common. See evaluation checklists offered by the following organizations and compare them with the ones offered in this chapter:

    • SREB's EvaluTech Program

    • The California Learning Resource Network

    • The SuperKids website

Online Activities

Visit this text's Companion Website at http://www.prenhall.com/roblyer to gain access to a variety of questions, activities, and exercises to help build your knowledge of this chapter's content.

Online Chapter 3 Self-Test

To review terms and concepts for this chapter, click on the *Self-Test* module for this chapter of the Companion Website.

Software Skill-Builder Tutorials

To access practical tutorial and skill-building activities and to build skills using popular software and hardware, click on the *Software Skill-Builder Tutorials* module for this chapter of the Companion Website.

Web-Enrichment Activities

To complete activities that connect to chapter content and provide web-based resources, click on the *Web-Enrichment Activities* module for this chapter of the Companion Website.

TECHNOLOGY INTEGRATION WORKSHOP

CLIPS FROM THE CLASSROOM: LEARNING WITH TECHNOLOGY

Go to the *Technology Integration Workshop* DVD located in the back of this text and click on *Clips from the Classroom*. View the video clips listed below that support this chapter's content:

- *Challenger Center Provides Problem-Based Learning*
- *Challenger Center Youth Leadership*
- Quizdom *System for Practice*
- *Presentation Software in Literature*
- Geometer's Sketchpad *for Inductive Reasoning*.

Now, visit this text's Companion Website at http://www.prenhall.com/roblyer to answer questions and complete activities that will guide you in analyzing each clip.

THE TIP MODEL IN ACTION

Read each of the following scenarios related to implementing the TIP Model, and go to the Companion Website to answer the questions that follow it based on your Chapter 3 reading and activities.

TIP Model Scenario #1   Ms. Andie uses a program called *Spelling Bee* to give her students practice before a spelling test or the language arts part of a standardized test. She knows the secret to her students doing well in spelling is getting them to spend time thinking about the words; she finds she can get them to spend more time with helpful practicing than she would with any paper-and-pencil exercise or other format. The software presents words via audio prompt and lets students enter correct spellings. They get points for every correct answer. If they play alone and attain a score they are shooting for, they win the spelling bee. They can also compete against each other in pairs.

1.1 What type of software function is Ms. Andie using? What did it offer that made it a good match for the problem?

1.2 If Ms. Andie wanted to have students practice in pairs to compete against each other, how would she have to set up the activity to make sure some students wouldn't become too frustrated by losing all the time?

1.3 Since the software gives audio prompts and feedback, what would Ms. Andie have to do if she wanted to use this effectively in a classroom of 30 students?

TIP Model Scenario #2   Mr. Sydney's students are not interested in learning about the U.S. Constitution. She wants to show them it is a document that affects their lives every day and in many situations they or people they know might encounter. Rather than just telling them about it, she found a software package that lets them practice applying it. Using the package, they role-play various people faced with creating articles of confederation that would let them deal effectively with issues such as threats to their borders, needs for currency, trade disputes, internal disagreements about key issues, and separate rights for states versus central power. As they work in groups on various problems, they come to understand why laws are necessary and how they affect our lives. As a final activity, each group presents an article of confederation and illustrates how it works in practice.

2.1 What software function is Mr. Sydney using? What did it offer that made it a good match for the problem?

2.2 What outcomes would you want to assess after this activity? How would you state these outcomes?

2.3 How would you measure students' progress on these outcomes?

TIP Model Scenario #3   In her Spanish I class, Ms. Sharon is having her students write an email newsletter describing in Spanish their school and events in their community to students in a Puerto Rico classroom. She finds that her students' Spanish vocabulary is very limited, and she wants to give them practice in using Spanish equivalents for many English words. She locates a software package that provides vocabulary practice by presenting words in English or Spanish to which they must supply equivalents in the opposite language. If they supply the correct word, the program pronounces both words. The Teacher's Manual gives a list of all the words.

3.1 What kind of software function does this software provide, and why does Ms. Sharon think the students need it?

3.2 Would it be best for students to use this package individually, in small groups, or as a whole class?

3.3 How would you assess whether this program was helping students learn enough vocabulary?

TIP Model Scenario #4 Mr. Carson finds that students in his honors algebra class can solve algebra equations, but they can't identify situations in everyday life that require them to set up and solve a simple equation. He finds a software package that has "virtual stores" in which students must solve various problems in order to "buy" items. They must use algebra equations to solve these problems. Mr. Carson has his students work in small groups to practice solving the problems and stating the strategies they used.

4.1 What kind of software function does this software provide, and why does Mr. Carson think the students will benefit from it?

4.2 What outcomes should Mr. Carson expect, and how should he state them?

4.3 What are the best ways to assess these outcomes?

TIP Model Scenario #5 Ms. Walker's science class is an academically diverse group, with some students learning concepts very quickly and others needing much more time to review and work on them. She has found a software series that provides a complete teaching sequence (instruction, practice items, testing) on each topic in the middle school physical sciences. Some students use it for review of topics they find particularly difficult; others use it to "catch up" when they have been absent. The students who learn quickly also use it to jump ahead and learn advanced topics on their own.

5.1 What kind of software function does this software provide and what problem does Ms. Walker have that it addresses?

5.2 Would one copy of the software meet Ms. Walker's needs? Why or why not?

5.3 How could Ms. Walker find out if most students enjoy using the software?

TIE INTO PRACTICE: TECHNOLOGY INTEGRATION EXAMPLES

The Technology Integration Example that opened this chapter (*Alien Rescue*) showed how a teacher might use an educational simulation package to give students highly motivational, hands-on experience with a scientific inquiry approach to problem solving. In the following activities, use the knowledge you have gained from Chapter 3 to do the following with this example:

1. Mr. Leroy created a rubric like the one shown on page 116 to assess students' presentations of new problems

and the methods they would use to solve them. **Create this rubric** by following the tutorial located on the *Hands-On with Technology* section of the DVD that accompanies this text.

2. Answer the following questions about the *Alien Rescue* lesson:

 • Phase 1 — How did the *Alien Rescue* software offer relative advantage in comparison with other ways of teaching scientific inquiry that Mr. Leroy had used in the past?

 • Phase 2 — Mr. Leroy designed a five-item survey to assess students' attitudes toward using this approach to learning science. What kind of items would you include on such a survey?

 • Phase 3 — What roles could you assign individuals in each working group of students to help focus their tasks and make their work more efficient?

 • Phase 4 — One of the tasks students completed to collect information was to design and send out space probes, which the Teacher's Manual said was a fairly complex activity. Why shouldn't Mr. Leroy create a directions sheet for them on how to do such a complex task?

 • Phase 5 — Mr. Leroy found that students' scores on the solar system test varied across the class. What could he do to make sure they were more uniformly successful on this kind of test?

3. What NETS for Students skills would students learn by doing the *Alien Rescue* project? (See front of book for a list of NETS for Students.)

TECHNOLOGY INTEGRATION LESSON PLANNING

The *Technology Integration Workshop* DVD includes a set of technology integration ideas and links to online lessons, arranged as a searchable database. The DVD comes packaged in the back of this textbook. Click on the *Hands-On with Technology* section of the DVD and complete the following exercise.

1. Locate lesson ideas — The DVD has several examples of lessons that use simulation, instructional game, and problem-solving software. Locate an example integration idea for using each of these software functions.

2. Evaluate the lessons — Use the *Evaluation Checklist for a Technology-Integrated Lesson* (located on the DVD and the Companion Website) to evaluate each of these lessons.

Category	Excellent Work	Very Good Work	Poor Work	No Credit
Problem and Solution Content	Reflected comprehensive knowledge of solar system; all facts and ideas were completely accurate; there was a good match of problem and solution.	Reflected fairly good knowledge of solar system; most facts and ideas were completely accurate; there was a good match of problem and solution.	Reflected some knowledge of solar system, but there were several factual inaccuracies; the solution was not the best match for the problem.	Reflected limited and/or inaccurate knowledge of solar system; there was little or no relationship between the problem and solution.
Clarity of Problem and Solution	Both problem and solution were clearly stated; other students could readily understand both.	Both problem and solution were fairly well stated, but needed some clarification.	Either the problem or the solution required extensive clarification.	Both the problem and the solution required extensive clarification.
Presentation Organization	Presentation was extremely well organized; content was divided into logical sections for presentation and transitions were smooth.	Presentation was usually well organized; content was divided into logical sections for presentation, but transitions were somewhat uneven and choppy.	Presentation was somewhat organized, but there were no transitions within the presentation.	Presentation was choppy, confusing, and difficult to follow.
Presentation Mechanics	Presentation was interesting and compelling; visual aids and/or multimedia were used and were well designed to support content.	Presentation was fairly interesting; some visual aids and/or multimedia were used and were well designed to support content.	Presentation was acceptable, but could have been more interesting and used visual aids and/or multimedia better.	Presentation was uninteresting; no visual aids and/or multimedia were used.
Cooperative Group Work	Project and presentation work was divided equally; each student had a clearly defined role in the work; it was clear that students worked well together.	Project and presentation work seemed to have been divided equally, but exact roles needed clarification; however, students seemed to work well together.	Project and presentation work was not divided equally; roles were unclear but students seemed to be working together.	Only one or two students did all the work of the project and presentation; there was little evidence of cooperative work.

Rubric to assess students' presentations of new problems and methods for solving them. (Create this product using the *Hands-On with Technology* tutorial on the DVD and Companion Website.)

3. Modify a lesson — Select one of the lesson ideas and adapt its strategies to meet a need in your own content area. You may choose to use the same software as the original or use a different software package and create a new lesson based on the strategy.

4. Add descriptors — Create descriptors for your new lesson like those found on the database (e.g., grade level, content and topic areas, technologies used, relative advantage, objectives, NETS standards).

5. Add the new lesson — Add your modified lesson with all its descriptors to the lesson idea database.

FOR YOUR TEACHING PORTFOLIO

For this chapter's contribution to your teaching portfolio, add the following products you created in the Technology Integration Workshop:

1. The rubric you created to assess the *Alien Rescue* presentations

2. The three evaluations you did using the *Evaluation Checklist for a Technology-Integrated Lesson*

3. The new lesson plan you developed, based on the one you found on the DVD.

CHAPTER 4

TEACHING WITH THE BASIC THREE SOFTWARE TOOLS: WORD PROCESSING, SPREADSHEET, AND DATABASE PROGRAMS

Hence, could a machine be invented which would instantaneously arrange on paper each idea as it occurs to us, without any exertion on our part, how extremely useful would it be considered.

Henry David Thoreau, as quoted by David Humphreys in
Computers in English and the Language Arts (1989)

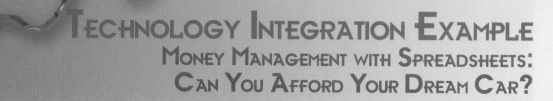

TECHNOLOGY INTEGRATION EXAMPLE
MONEY MANAGEMENT WITH SPREADSHEETS:
CAN YOU AFFORD YOUR DREAM CAR?

Based on: Berghaus, N. (1990). Teach spreadsheet proficiency with personal money management projects. *The Computing Teacher, 17*(7), 54–55.

Grade Level: Middle to high school • Content Area/Topic: Applied math skills • Length of time: One week

Phase 1: Determine relative advantage

Whenever Ms. Kiley teaches her Applied Mathematics Problem-Solving class for grades 9 through 12, she has teenagers of many ages and ability levels. She wants all of them to have experience applying math skills to real problems they will encounter in their daily lives. She tries to include projects that are interesting and relevant to all of them and that require a combination of research, mathematical problem solving, and production skills. One activity she found that meets all her criteria is called "Can You Afford Your Dream Car?" She selected this project because almost all of her students are beginning drivers and are very interested in car purchases. So that they can do calculations quickly and focus on the underlying concepts (e.g., the relationship among down payment, interest rate, and loan period), Ms. Kiley designed a spreadsheet template for students to use for the project. Each student does Internet research to locate the best price on a car he or she would like to buy, enters information into the spreadsheet template Ms. Kiley created, and answers various questions with problems about loan amounts and car payments.

Phase 2: Decide on objectives and assessments

To keep her students on track with what they are to accomplish, and make sure they learn what she has in mind for this project, Ms. Kiley created objectives and assessments to measure their research, problem-solving, and production outcomes. The outcomes, objectives, and assessments matched to them are:

- **Outcome:** Select a car to purchase and complete background research on it. **Objective:** Each student completes all required steps to select a car to "buy"; completes a list of required activities to research and locate comparison information about its price, loan, and features; and enters the information into a spreadsheet template. **Assessment:** A checklist with points for each required activity.

- **Outcome:** Do mathematical problem solving. **Objective:** Each student uses the spreadsheet to answer a series of questions about the amount of the car loan and payments at various interest rates and time periods. **Assessment:** Worksheet questions with points for each one; 80% is passing.

- **Outcome:** Do final report. **Objective:** Each student achieves a rubric score of at least 90% on a word-processed report that describes and illustrates the car, tells why it is a cost-effective purchase, and includes a spreadsheet (based on the template provided) showing how he or she will pay for it. **Assessment:** Rubric on report quality and accuracy.

Phase 3: Design integration strategies

Ms. Kiley wanted to make sure each student had personal hands-on experience with the research and production activities and was able to master each of the skills she outlined, so she decided to make this an individual activity. She designed the following activity sequence to carry out the project:

- **Day 1:** Introduce the project. Encourage students to talk about cars they have already purchased or are considering purchasing, and ask them to describe how they went about selecting one and, if they already bought it, how they decided on a loan amount, term, and payment size. Demonstrate the spreadsheet template and show them how the payments and total amount paid change automatically depending on the loan amount, interest, and period. Review the project checklists and rubrics and the timeframe for completing the work. Introduce the problems they are to work using their completed spreadsheets.

- **Day 2:** Take students to the computer lab and demonstrate some of the sites they may want to use to check out makes and models of cars. Also, demonstrate once again how to use the spreadsheet template. Have them do some calculations with the spreadsheet and answer any questions they have. Let them begin researching cars they want to buy.
- **Day 3:** In the computer lab, allow students to continue their research. Some students may have completed research on their home computers. These students can begin work on their final reports or complete the problem-solving exercise.
- **Day 4:** In the computer lab, allow students to continue their work on reports and exercises with the spreadsheet template.
- **Day 5:** Back in the classroom, let selected students present their "dream car purchase." Use the classroom computer workstation to show an online example of the car model and the dealer where they would buy it. Students who need more time can go to the computer lab.
- **Day 6:** Students turn in their projects and exercises.

Phase 4: Prepare the instructional environment

The first time Ms. Kiley taught this project, she had to create the spreadsheet template and handouts of the checklists and rubric for students to use. For subsequent times, she had to do the following:

- **Handouts:** Ms. Kiley made copies of the project requirements and grading criteria sheets (i.e., checklists and rubrics) to hand out to students. She also made sure these handouts were online at her classroom website as PDF files, so students could download additional copies if needed.
- **Software skills:** Although Ms. Kiley demonstrated and showed how to use the spreadsheet template, she checked with students individually as they worked in the lab to make sure they knew how to enter the required information in the cells and could copy and paste their completed worksheet into their report.
- **Computer scheduling:** Ms. Kiley made sure she could have her whole class in the computer lab for the 3 days she would need it, and that individual students could come to the lab for the two subsequent days to complete their research and reports.
- **Template copies:** Ms. Kiley made sure that a copy of the template was on the classroom website so that students could download it to their own disks.

Phase 5: Evaluate and revise

Each time she taught the project, Ms. Kiley reviewed the students' work and asked for their comments on how she could make the project even more meaningful. She quickly realized that students who did not have a home computer were at a disadvantage in completing the work in a timely way. Therefore, she made a special effort to help these students during their time in the lab and made sure they knew they could have additional lab time outside class or come by before or after school to use the classroom workstation. She found that, although students usually completed their spreadsheets correctly and could answer questions about them, their reports varied considerably in quality. She decided to consider other ways of having students present their work.

OBJECTIVES

After reading this chapter and completing the learning activities for it, you should be able to:

1. Use correct terminology to identify features and capabilities of word processing, spreadsheet, and database software tool programs.

2. Identify productivity applications for software tools that educators would find valuable to make their work more efficient and productive.

3. Describe specific kinds of teaching and learning tasks for both teachers and students that each kind of tool can support.

4. Develop instructional activities that integrate the functions and capabilities of the software tools.

KEY TERMS

- cells
- computer platforms
- data mining
- data warehouses
- databases
- disaggregation
- field
- files
- formulas
- integrated packages
- record
- search and replace
- software suites
- spreadsheets
- worksheets

For more information on Key Terms, go to the *Key Terms* module for this chapter of the Companion Website at http://www.prenhall.com/roblyer.

CW

Introduction to the Basic Three Software Tools

Why Use Software Tools?

In education and, indeed, in most other areas of our Information Society, three of the most widely used software support tools are word processing, spreadsheet, and database programs. (Other software tools that are often packaged with these "basic three" are graphics software, covered in Chapter 5 under "other tools," and presentation software, covered in Chapter 6 under multimedia applications.) As Thoreau envisioned, word processing and other software tools have become not only "extremely useful," but are an indispensable part of our daily work. Teachers choose them for the qualitites and benefits they bring to the classroom and the potential they offer not only to make more productive use of our time, but also to shape and guide the kinds of activities we are able to undertake. Depending on the capabilities of the tool and the needs of the situation, these programs can offer several benefits:

- **Improved productivity** — Getting organized, producing instructional materials, and accomplishing paperwork tasks all go much faster when software tools are used. Using a technology tool to do these tasks can free up valuable time that can be rechanneled toward working with students or designing learning activities.

- **Improved appearance** — Software tools help teachers and students produce polished-looking materials that resemble the work of professional designers. The quality of classroom products is limited only by the talents and skills of the teachers and students using the tools. Students appreciate receiving attractive-looking materials and find it rewarding and challenging to produce handsome products of their own.

- **Improved accuracy** — Software tools make it easier to keep precise, accurate records of events and student accomplishments. More accurate information can support better instructional decisions about curriculum and student activities.

- **More support for interaction** — Software tools have capabilities that promote interaction among students or allow input from several people at once. These qualities can encourage many creative, cooperative group-learning activities.

Introduction to the "Basic Three"

Since the early days of microcomputers, word processing, spreadsheet, and database programs have served as the most basic components in the teachers "technology toolkit." As Figure 4.1 shows, each of these performs a specific type of function and each helps support specific

Figure 4.1   An Overview of the "Basic Three" Software Tools

Software Tool	Software Function	Sample Products
Word Processing Example: *Microsoft Word*	Creates documents consisting of pages with text and graphics.	Student compositions, poetry, and reports; flyers; simple newsletters; letters
Spreadsheet Example: *Microsoft Excel*	Puts numerical information in row/column format; allows quick calculations and recalculations.	Budgets, checkbooks, gradebooks, illustrations of mathematics concepts
Database Example: *FileMaker Pro*	Organizes and stores collections of information; allows items to be easily and quickly retrieved	Data from surveys, inventories of materials, student information

Microsoft Word

Screen shot reprinted by permission from Microsoft Corporation.

http://www.microsoft.com

Microsoft Excel

Screen shot reprinted by permission from Microsoft Corporation.

http://www.microsoft.com

FileMaker Pro

Box shot reprinted with permission from FileMaker, Inc.

http://www.filemaker.com

productivity and teaching/learning activities. However, the three programs are usually designed to work together. For example, in the Technology Integration Example at the beginning of this chapter, a student completes a spreadsheet to demonstrate a mathematical concept such as loan terms, then inserts this spreadsheet into a word-processed report.

Overview of productivity uses. These three software products are often referred to as the "basic productivity tools," because they were the first such tools to be designed to save time on clerical types of tasks and, thus, make work proceed more efficiently. In schools, word processing is the most frequently used of the three for productivity purposes, since teachers and students use it across all subject areas whenever they need to do typed work such as a composition or report. Spreadsheet and database software tend to be used primarily to enhance teacher productivity, rather than student productivity.

Overview of instructional uses. A search of the Lesson Plan Database in the *Technology Integration Workshop* DVD located at the back of this text yields dozens of instructional ideas for using both word processing and spreadsheets to support instructional activities such as concept demonstrations and practice exercises. Word processing is used primarily to support English and foreign language exercises, such as learning vocabulary and punctuation. Spreadsheets are used most often for demonstrations in mathematics and business education areas, but also support instructional activities such as science experiments or social studies surveys. At one time, creating and searching databases was a popular strategy for teaching students organization, research, and study skills and for demonstrating how information is organized to serve various important functions in our society (e.g., census and tax records). With the emergence of Internet search engines such as Google, student creation of databases has given way to an emphasis on **data mining** techniques, which call for collecting data from all the information available and searching it to see relationships among the data elements.

Recent Development in Software Tools

Although software tools have been in existence for many years, they are constantly being updated with new features and capabilities. Most of the following recent developments have made these tools even more useful in the classroom:

- **PDA tools** — All of the basic software tools are now available on personal digital assistants (PDAs) or handheld computers. This portable format makes them easily accessible and flexible to use for both teachers and students. Since these basic software tools have been transferred to handheld format, the handhelds themselves have become more popular.

- **Web-enabled features** — All of the basic tools, like many tools described in other chapters, now allow insertion of "live" web page links in documents, and most allow documents to be saved in Hypertext Markup Language (HTML) or web page formats. This makes it even easier to connect documents to web page resources that embellish or add to the document's content. For example, students may include links in a project report to some of the resources they consulted during their research.

- **Better file-exchange compatibility** — In the early days of software tools, programs were often incompatible. That is, documents created in one program could not be opened in another program. Incompatibility was especially a problem between programs on Macintosh and Windows (PC) computers. This problem limited file sharing and hindered collaborative work, since people often had different **computer platforms** (types of computers) and tool programs. Today's software tools are designed to be much more compatible across programs and platforms, making it much easier for teachers and students to transfer documents and to work together on projects.

- **Software suites and integrated packages** — Because it is usually cheaper to buy several tools at one time than separately, software tools are increasingly used as parts of **software suites** or **integrated packages.** Keizer (1997) differentiates between integrated packages, which combine several functions such as word processing, spreadsheet, database, and graphics working under one program, and software suites, which are separate programs that companies place in the same package. For example, as Figure 4.2 shows, *AppleWorks* is an integrated package in which users can access several software tools from a central menu, while the most popular suite, *Microsoft Office,* also shown in Figure 4.2, has several separate applications that work well together. While any of these packages may be useful, depending on the needs of the classroom and the types of software included, the current trend is toward using *Microsoft Office,* since it includes Microsoft *Word* and Microsoft *PowerPoint,* two of the most popular applications.

Figure 4.2 A Comparison of Integrated Tools and Software Suites (*AppleWorks*® and *Microsoft Office*®)

Screen shot reprinted by permission of Apple Computer, Inc.

Screen shot reprinted by permission from Microsoft Corporation.

USING WORD PROCESSING SOFTWARE IN TEACHING AND LEARNING

Word Processing: Definition and Characteristics

Word processing programs allow people to produce typed documents on a computer screen. Although the lines between word processing and desktop publishing have become increasingly blurred, the programs still differ in the way they produce documents. Word processing programs essentially produce documents as a stream of text, whereas desktop publishing produces them as individual pages. Despite this difference, most word processing programs allow at least some desktop publishing capabilities, such as inserting text boxes and graphics at any location on a page. Word processing features are shown in Figure 4.3.

The Impact of Word Processing in Education

Why teachers use word processing. Perhaps no other technology resource has had as great an impact on education as word processing. Not only does word processing offer high versatility and flexibility, it also is "model-free" instructional software; that is, it reflects no particular instructional approach. A teacher can use it to support any kind of directed instruction or constructivist activity. Since its value as an aid to teaching and learning is universally acknowledged, word processing has become the most commonly used software in education. It offers many general relative advantages (unique benefits over and above other methods) to teachers and students:

- **Saves time** — Word processing helps teachers use preparation time more efficiently by letting them modify materials instead of creating new ones. Writers can also make corrections to word processing documents more quickly than they could achieve on a typewriter or by hand.

- **Enhances document appearance** — Materials from word processing software look more polished and professional than handwritten or typed materials. It is not surprising that students seem to like the improved appearance that word processing gives to their work (Harris, 1985).

- **Allows sharing of documents** — Word processing allows materials to be shared easily among writers. Teachers can exchange lesson plans, worksheets, or other materials on disk and modify them to fit their needs. Students can also share ideas and products among themselves.

Research on the impact of word processing. Research on the benefits of word processing in education yields contradictory findings. Results of studies of the effects of word processing on quality and quantity of writing are mixed (Bangert-Drowns, 1993). Three different reviews of research (Bangert-Drowns, 1993; Hawisher, 1989; Snyder, 1993) found that these differences in findings may reflect differences in researchers' choices of types of word processing systems, prior experience and writing ability of students, and types of writing instruction to evaluate. Generally, word processing seems to improve writing and attitudes toward writing only if it is used in the context of good writing instruction and if students have enough time to learn word processing procedures before the study begins.

When Goldberg, Russell, and Cook (2003) updated these findings with a meta-analysis of studies from 1992 to 2002, they focused not only on whether or not word processing had more impact than handwritten methods, but also on identifying when word processing could have the most impact on the quantity and quality of students' writing. Their meta-analysis showed a stronger relationship between computers and quality of writing than in previous such analyses. Students who use computers during writing instruction produce written work that is about 0.4 standard deviation better than students who develop writing skills on paper. Their analysis also suggested that

Figure 4.3   A Summary of Word Processing Features

Feature Categories/ General Benefits	Word Processing Features	Description
Basic features save time writing text and make changing text easier and more flexible.	Store documents for later use.	Documents saved to disk can be changed without reentering text.
	Store in many formats (e.g., RTF, PDF, HTML).	• Rich Text Format (RTF) removes all or most formatting commands so other word processors can read the file. • PDF format allows files to be read as formatted documents with Adobe *Acrobat Reader.* • HTML format allows documents to be placed on the Internet.
	Erase and insert text.	Allows easy insertion of additional letters, spaces, lines, paragraphs, or pages.
	Search and replace.	One command allows all occurrences of a word or phrase to be changed as specified.
	Move or copy text.	Allows cutting and pasting (deleting text and inserting it elsewhere) or copying and pasting (repeating text in several places).
	Allows word wraparound.	Automatically goes to next line at end of a line without pressing Enter or Return. (Also hyphenates words, as needed.)
Desktop publishing features make flyers, reports, newsletters, brochures, and student handouts more attractive and professional looking.	Alignment.	Centers or right- or left-justifies text.
	Change styles/appearance.	Allows a variety of fonts, type styles, font colors, margins, line spacing, tabs, and indentations in the same document.
	Insert automatic headers, footers, and pagination.	Automatically places text at the top (header) or bottom (footer) of each page in a document with or without page numbering (pagination).
	Insert graphics.	Inserts clip art or image files into documents and formats them; some programs allow image editing.
	Insert colors and shading.	Graphics can be filled with color or degrees of shading.
	Insert tables.	Organizes information into rows and columns without using tabs or indentations.
	Insert text boxes.	Allows text blocks to be inserted in any location in or around a document.
	Insert drawn figures.	Allows inserting shapes, callouts, and other figures to enhance documents.
Language features help teachers and students correct their work and do various language, spelling, and usage exercises.	Check and correct spelling.	Spell-checker feature compares words in a document to those stored in the program's dictionary files.
	Suggest words.	Thesaurus feature suggests synonyms for any word.
	Check grammar and usage.	Grammar checkers review documents for items such as sentence length, frequency of word use, and subject– verb agreement. Also marks phrases or sentences to be corrected.
Web features allow teachers and students to connect documents with Internet resources and create web page announcements, reports, and projects.	Insert "live" URLs.	Allows person reading the document to click on text and go automatically to a website. (*Note:* Web browser must be active.)
	Create web pages.	Acts as simple web page development software and creates HTML pages.
Support features make using the program easier and more flexible.	Use templates.	Users can easily adapt preformatted models of resumes, newsletters, and brochures to their own needs.
	Offer voice recognition.	Allows text to be received and entered via dictated words, rather than as typed entries.
	Merge text with data files.	• Automatically inserts words (e.g., names and addresses) into documents such as letters. • Lists of data can be stored within the word processing program or merged from a database.

Figure 4.4 Findings from Reviews of Word Processing in Education

	Hawisher (26 studies) (1989)	Snyder (57 studies) (1993)	Bangert-Drowns (32 studies) (1993)	Goldberg, Russell, and Cook (14 studies) (2003)
Better quality of writing	No conclusion	No conclusion	Positive results	Positive results
Greater quantity of writing	Positive results	Positive results	Positive results	Positive results
More surface (mechanical) revisions	No conclusion	Positive results	No conclusion	Not reviewed
More substantive (meaning) revisions	No conclusion	No improvement	No conclusion	Not reviewed
Fewer mechanical errors	Positive results	Positive results	Not reviewed	Not reviewed
Better attitude toward writing	Positive results	Positive results	No improvement	Not reviewed
Better attitude toward word processing	No conclusion	Positive results	Not reviewed	Not reviewed

when students write with computers, they "engage in the revising of their work throughout the writing process, more frequently share and receive feedback from their peers, and benefit from teacher input earlier in the writing process" (p. 19). Figure 4.4 summarizes some of the findings of all four research reviews.

Issues in using word processing. Educators seem to agree that although word processing is a valuable application, its use in education can be controversial:

- **When should students start word processing?** — Word processing software designed for young children is available, and schools can introduce word processing to students as young as 4 or 5 years old. Some educators feel that word processing will free students from the physical constraints of handwriting and free them to develop written expression skills, Others worry, however, that it will make students unwilling to spend time developing handwriting abilities and other activities requiring fine-motor skills.

- **Is it necessary to teach keyboarding skills?** — Discussion is ongoing about whether students need to learn keyboarding ("10-finger typing" on the computer) either prior to or in conjunction with word processing activities. Some educators feel that students will never become really productive on the computer until they learn 10-finger keyboarding. Others feel that the extensive time spent on keyboarding in-

struction and practice could be better spent on more important skills, and that students will pick up typing skills on their own.

- **What effects does word processing have on handwriting?** — While no researchers have conducted formal studies of the impact of frequent word processing use on handwriting legibility, computer users commonly complain that their handwriting isn't what it used to be, ostensibly because of infrequent opportunities to use their handwriting skills.

- **What impact does word processing have on assessment?** — Some organizations have students answer essay-type test questions with word processing, rather than by handwriting them. Many school districts also allow students to word process their writing tests. This practice introduces several issues. Roblyer (1997) reviewed research that found students' word-processed compositions tend to receive lower grades than handwritten ones. This surprising finding indicates that educational organizations that allow students to choose either handwriting or word processing must be careful to establish guidelines and special training to ensure that raters do not inadvertently discriminate against students who choose word processing.

Teachers and administrators are still deciding how best to deal with these issues. Despite these obstacles, education's dependence on word processing continues to grow.

ADAPTING FOR SPECIAL NEEDS

Young students and students with cognitive impairments are often confused by the complexity of standard productivity software packages such as *Microsoft Office*. One solution is a software product called *Max's Sandbox* (http://www.maxssandbox.com/). Designed for children ages 3 to 10, it provides a child-friendly interface and modified menus for Microsoft *Word, Excel,* and *PowerPoint*. It allows students to learn the basic operation of core productivity tools without being overwhelmed by all the options and advanced features. *Max's Sandbox* is a model learning scaffold that introduces young learners to essential concepts (e.g., save, print) so that they can later move easily into the full-featured version of *Microsoft Office.*

Contributed by Dave Edyburn

Figure 4.5 **Suggested Word Processing Items for a Teacher's File of Reusable Documents**

- Beginning of the year welcome letter
- Permission letters for field trips and other events
- Flyers and other announcements
- Request for fee payments letter
- Fund-raising letter
- List of class rules
- Posted flyer of class rules
- Letterhead stationeries
- Periodic student progress letters to parents
- Lesson plans and notes
- Student information sheets and handouts
- Newsletters
- Annual reports required by the school
- Frequently used worksheets and exercises

Word Processing in the Classroom: Productivity and Teaching Strategies

Productivity strategies. Word processing can help teachers prepare classroom materials they would otherwise have to type or write out by hand. These include handouts or other instructional materials, lesson plans and notes, reports, forms, letters to parents or students, flyers, and newsletters. Word processing saves preparation time, especially if a teacher uses the same documents every year. For example, a teacher may send the same letter to parents each year simply by changing the dates and adding new information. Teachers may want to keep files of templates or model documents that they can easily update and reuse. See Figure 4.5 for a suggested list of reusable word-processed documents teachers may want to have on hand.

Instructional integration strategies for word processing. Students can also use word processing for almost any written work, regardless of subject area, that they would otherwise write by hand. Research shows that word processing alone cannot improve the quality of student writing, but can help them make corrections more effi-

ciently; this can motivate them to write more and take more interest in improving their written work. Some current word processing integration strategies include the following (see a summary of these and the relative advantage of each in Figure 4.6):

- **Supporting the learning of writing processes** — Students can use word processing to write, edit, and illustrate stories; to produce reports in content areas; to keep notes and logs on classroom activities; and for any written assignments. (See Technology Integration Idea 4.1.)

- **Using a dynamic group product approach** — Teachers can assign group poems or letters to various students, adding and changing lines or producing elements of the whole document in a word processing program. (See the Technology Integration Idea *Poetry Made Easy Through Word Processing* on the DVD that accompanies this text.)

- **Assigning individual language, writing, and reading exercises** — Special word processing exercises allow individual students to work on-screen combining sentences, adding or correcting punctuation, or writing sentences for spelling words. Word processing may also make possible a variety of reading/language-related activities ranging from decoding to writing poetry and enjoying literature. Viau (1998) points out that adding colors to text can be the basis for activities to enhance critical thinking during writing instruction. (See

Figure 4.6   A Summary of Word Processing Integration Strategies and Benefits

Word Processing Integration Strategies	Benefits	Sample Lessons
Supporting the learning of writing processes	• Makes it easier to get started writing. • Makes it easier to revise and improve written drafts. • Allows students to illustrate their work to make their meaning more visual and increase their motivation to write.	**Technology Integration Idea 4.1:** Cartoon Commentaries on the Computer
Using a dynamic group process approach	• Makes it easier to share, exchange, and add onto drafts. • Makes it easier to work together on written products at a distance.	**See example on Technology Integration Workshop DVD (Hands-On with Technology):** Poetry Made Easy Through Word Processing
Assigning individual language, writing, and reading exercises	• Allows meaningful, hands-on practice in language use. • Makes identifying and correcting errors a more visual process.	**See example on DVD:** Creating Coherence Between Sentences **Technology Integration Idea 4.2:** Using Color in Composition
Encouraging writing through the curriculum	• Supports production of written work in any content area. • Has font and graphics features to represent science, math, and other concepts.	**See example on DVD:** Using Technology to Study Biospheres

Technology Integration Idea 4.2 and the example on the DVD titled *Creating Coherence Between Sentences*.)

• **Encouraging writing through the curriculum** — A recent trend in education is to encourage writing skills in courses and activities other than those designed to teach English and language arts. This practice of writing-through-the-curriculum is in keeping with the new emphasis on integrated, interdisciplinary, and thematic curricula. Word processing can encourage these integrated activities. Its font and graphics features allow students to represent concepts in mathematics, science, and other content areas. Word processors are also available in other languages to support foreign language learning. (See the Technology Integration Idea titled *Using Technology to Study Biospheres* on the DVD that accompanies this text. For additional lesson ideas on using word processing in

curriculum lessons, search the DVD database for the term "word processing.")

Teaching Word Processing Skills: Recommended Skills and Activities

Students just beginning to use word processing must have time to develop enough skills in using the software before teachers can begin to grade their word-processed products. Many online tutorials are available to teach various software packages. However, these may not always be accessible to students. Also, younger or less independent learners may not have the ability to use these self-instructional methods and may need teacher-led instruction.

For all of these reasons, teachers who would like to use word processing in classroom lessons may have to introduce their students to word processing and show them the features and uses of the software. Figure 4.7 shows a recom-

TECHNOLOGY INTEGRATION IDEA 4.1

USING WORD PROCESSING TO SUPPORT LEARNING OF WRITING PROCESSES

Title: Cartoon Commentaries on the Computer

Content Area/Topic: Writing persuasive essays

Grade Level: Middle school

NETS for Students: Standards 1, 3, 4

Description: This activity uses cartoons and comic strips to focus on two different skill areas that often present problems to middle school students and their teachers: writing persuasive essays or position papers and analyzing current affairs.

Instruction: Two computers are set up—one with drawing software and one with word processing software. The class is divided into small groups of three to four students each and the teacher distributes newspapers to the groups. The students go through the papers, selecting at least two comic strips and/or editorial cartoons. They "write the story" or idea of the comic using either a dialog, narrative, or essay form. Each group reports to the class on its analysis. The teacher asks the groups to add another paragraph to their write-ups to express their own opinions about the comic's purposes. To initiate their responses, the teacher asks questions such as these: Do you support the purpose and point of view of the person doing the cartoon? Why or why not? What mix of images and text does the person use to make his point? Is this mix effective? Again, these write-ups are shared with the class and used as the basis for discussions.

Assessment: Use rubrics to assess cartoon quality.

Source: Reissman, R. (1994). Computer cartoon commentaries. *The Computing Teacher, 21*(5), 23–25.

TECHNOLOGY INTEGRATION IDEA 4.2

USING WORD PROCESSING TO ASSIGN INDIVIDUAL LANGUAGE, WRITING, AND READING EXERCISES

Title: Using Color in Composition

Content Area/Topic: Examining the purpose of various types of text

Grade Level: Middle to high school

NETS for Students: Standards 1, 3, 4

Description: Students use the word processor's font color option to highlight various functions in compositions and advertisements in different colors. Examples: topic sentences, emotion-evoking content, factual content, and descriptive words and phrases.

Instruction: In compositions, they follow up these activities by analyzing how the text elements contribute to the paragraph meaning, and try to add text in a way that continues the purpose of the text. In advertisements, they analyze how the words and phrases work to shape the reader's perceptions.

Assessment: Use a rubric to assess the quality of the composition or ad.

Source: Viau, E. (1998). Color me a writer: Teaching students to think critically. *Learning and Leading with Technology, 25*(5), 17–20.

Figure 4.7 Tips on Teaching Word Processing
(Also see links to tutorials at http://www.internet4classrooms.com/on-line2.htm)

Suggested Steps	Tasks Under Each Step
Step 1—Prepare for teaching.	**Arrange for:** • A big screen or projection system • A disk for each student • Copying sample file(s) onto student disks • One computer per student • Alternative keyboards or other adaptive devices for students with disabilities. **Create or obtain:** • Handouts or wall posters on word processing features and common errors.
Step 2—Demonstrate the basics.	**Using a big screen or projection system, show how to:** • Load a disk into a computer disk drive (if needed) • Open a file from a disk • Move around in a document using the cursor and scroll bars • Add and delete text; undo changes • Name, save, and close document. **Point out common errors:** • Forgetting to move cursor before typing • Forgetting about automatic wraparound (pressing Enter or Return at end of lines) • "Losing" part of document on the screen by scrolling up or down • Forgetting to save all changes before closing a file.
Step 3—Assign individual practice.	**Give students a sample word processing file on disk and have them:** • Insert the disk and open the file • Do a list of changes to the file (e.g., inserting spaces, deleting lines, undoing changes) • Name, save, and close document.
Step 4—Demonstrate formatting features.	**Using big screen or projection system, show how to:** • Change fonts, styles, and alignment • Add clip art • Spell-check a document • Print a document • **Optional:** Search and replace procedures • **Optional:** Add bullets and numbering. **Point out common errors:** • Inserting too many spaces at top or bottom of document (by pressing Enter or Return) • Unexpected errors from Search and Replace feature (failing to predict results).
Step 5—Assign more individual practice.	**Have students open their sample word processing file from Step 3 and do the following:** • Change fonts, styles, and alignment • Add clip art • Spell-check a document • Print a document • **Optional:** Search and replace text • **Optional:** Add bullets and numbering.

Figure 4.7 (continued)

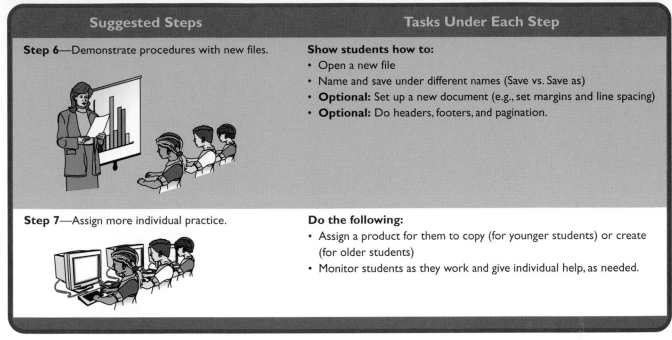

Suggested Steps	Tasks Under Each Step
Step 6—Demonstrate procedures with new files.	**Show students how to:** • Open a new file • Name and save under different names (Save vs. Save as) • **Optional:** Set up a new document (e.g., set margins and line spacing) • **Optional:** Do headers, footers, and pagination.
Step 7—Assign more individual practice.	**Do the following:** • Assign a product for them to copy (for younger students) or create (for older students) • Monitor students as they work and give individual help, as needed.

mended strategy teachers can use to introduce word processing to students in elementary and middle grades. Note that some features and steps are labeled as "optional." The teacher may choose to introduce these on an "as-needed" basis, or only with older, more experienced students.

USING SPREADSHEET SOFTWARE IN TEACHING AND LEARNING

Spreadsheets: Definition and Characteristics

Spreadsheets are programs designed to organize and manipulate numerical data. The term *spreadsheet* comes from the pre-computer word for an accountant's ledger: a book for keeping records of numerical information such as budgets and cash flow. Unlike the term *word processing,* which refers only to the computer software or program, the term *spreadsheet* can refer either to the program itself or to the product it produces. Spreadsheet products are sometimes also called **worksheets.** Information in a spreadsheet is stored in rows and columns. Each row–column position is called a **cell,** which may contain numerical values, words or character data, and **formulas** or calculation commands.

A spreadsheet helps users manage numbers in the same way that word processing helps manage words. Bozeman (1992) described spreadsheets as a way to "word process numbers" (p. 908). Spreadsheets were the earliest application software available for microcomputers. Some people credit them with starting the microcomputer revolution, since the availability of the first spreadsheet software,

Visicalc, motivated many people to buy a microcomputer. Spreadsheet features are shown in Figure 4.8.

The Impact of Spreadsheets in Education

Why teachers use spreadsheets. Spreadsheet programs are in widespread use in classrooms at all levels of education. Teachers use them primarily to keep budgets and gradebooks and to help teach mathematical topics. They offer teachers and students several kinds of unique benefits:

- **Saves time** — Spreadsheets save valuable time by allowing teachers and students to complete essential calculations quickly. They save time not only by making initial calculations faster and more accurate, but their automatic recalculation features also make it easy to update products such as grades and budgets. Entries also can be changed, added, or deleted easily, with formulas that automatically recalculate final grades.

- **Organizes displays of information** — Although spreadsheet programs are intended for numerical data, their capability to store information in columns makes them ideal tools for designing informational charts such as schedules and attendance lists that may contain few numbers and no calculations at all.

- **Supports asking "what if" questions** — Spreadsheets help people visualize the impact of changes in numbers. Since values are automatically recalculated when changes are made in a worksheet, a user can play with numbers and immediately see the result. This capability makes it feasible to pose "what if" questions and answer them quickly and easily.

Figure 4.8   A Summary of Spreadsheet Features

Feature Categories/ General Benefits	Spreadsheet Features	Description of Features
Basic features make it easier to display and manipulate budget, grade, or survey data; and do mathematics problem solving.	Line up information in rows and columns.	Row–column format makes numerical and other information easier to read and digest at a glance.
	Do basic calculations.	Use formulas in cells to do: • Basic arithmetic functions: adding, subtracting, multiplying, dividing • Weighted averages by combining these functions.
	Do complex calculations.	Use formulas in cells to do: • Mathematical functions such as logarithms and roots • Statistical functions such as sums and averages • Trigonometric functions such as sines and tangents • Logical functions such as Boolean comparisons • Financial functions such as periodic payments and rates • Special-purpose functions such as looking up and comparing data entries with other information (e.g., counting the number of grades above a certain number).
	Do automatic recalculation.	When a number in one cell changes (e.g., a grade) a spreadsheet formula automatically updates all calculations related to that number (e.g., an average grade).
	Copy cells.	Numbers, formulas, or other information in cells can be copied and pasted to any other cells.
	Sort data.	Data can be organized alphabetically or numerically.
	Search and replace.	One command allows all occurrences of a specified word, phrase, number, or formula to be changed.
Formatting features	Alignment.	Centers or right- or left-justifies cell entries.
	Change styles/appearance.	Allows: • A variety of fonts, sizes, font colors, and type styles in the same document • Cells and graphics to be filled with color or degrees of shading
	Insert automatic headers, footers, and pagination.	Allows text to be automatically placed at the top (header) or bottom (footer) of each page in a worksheet with or without page numbering (pagination).
Graphics/interactive features allow spreadsheet data to be shown in more visual formats.	Charting.	Creates charts and graphs automatically from spreadsheet data.
	Insert graphics or movies.	Clip art or other still or moving images can be pasted into cells to illustrate concepts or to change document appearance.
	Insert drawn figures.	Allows inserting shapes, callouts, and other figures to enhance worksheet appearance.
Web features allow teachers and students to connect documents with Internet resources and create web page announcements, reports, and projects.	Insert "live" URLs.	Allows person using the spreadsheet to click on text and go automatically to a website. (*Note:* Web browser must be active.)
	Save as web pages.	Allows worksheets to be displayed online.
Support features make using the program easier and more flexible.	Read and save to other formats.	Spreadsheets can: • Read and use other data files such as those produced by Statistical Packages for the Social Sciences (SPSS) software • Save documents in formats (e.g., tab-delimited) for use in SPSS or other programs.
	Use templates.	Users can easily adapt preformatted models of worksheets (e.g., budgets, checkbooks, and gradekeepers) to their own needs.

- **Increases motivation to work with mathematics** — Many teachers feel that spreadsheets make working with numbers more fun. Students sometimes perceive mathematical concepts as dry and boring; spreadsheets can make these concepts so graphic that students often express real delight with seeing how they work.

Research on the impact of spreadsheet use. Although spreadsheets are widely believed to help students visualize numerical concepts better than other, nondynamic tools, few studies have attempted to capture their comparative impact on achievement. Studies show, however, that spreadsheets can be useful tools for teaching concepts in many areas, including algebra problem solving (Sutherland, 1993), meteorology (Sumrall & Forslev, 1994), statistics (Black, 1999), and calculus (Hauger, 2000). The literature contains numerous testimonials by teachers who have used spreadsheets successfully in teaching topics ranging from mathematics to social studies.

Issues in using spreadsheets. One of the few disagreements about spreadsheets in education is whether to use them to keep grades or to rely instead on grade-keeping packages (gradebooks) designed especially for this purpose. (See a discussion of gradebooks in Chapter 5.) Spreadsheets usually offer more flexibility in designing formats and allowing special-purpose calculation functions, while gradebooks are simpler to use and require little setup other than entering students' names and assignment grades. Teachers appear to be about evenly divided on which is better; the choice comes down to personal preference.

Spreadsheets in the Classroom: Productivity and Teaching Strategies

Productivity strategies. Teachers can use spreadsheets to help them prepare classroom materials and complete calculations that they would otherwise have to do by hand or with a calculator. The most common uses of spreadsheets are for keeping club and classroom budgets, preparing performance checklists, and keeping gradebooks. An example spreadsheet a teacher might use for keeping grades is shown in Figure 4.9. They help with many activities and products in education, including those shown in Figure 4.10.

Instructional integration strategies for spreadsheets. The literature reflects an increasing variety of applications for spreadsheets. Although their teaching role focuses primarily on mathematics lessons, spreadsheets have also ef-

MAKING THE CASE FOR TECHNOLOGY INTEGRATION

Discuss these issues online with other students by selecting the *Making the Case* module for Chapter 4 of the Companion Website (http://www.prenhall.com/roblyer) or choose the *Message Board* module.

1. Word processing is a software program valued by many teachers, but it is criticized by some who feel that overreliance on it is ruining our handwriting and that increasing the quantity of what students write is not improving the quality of their writing. How would you respond to these critics?

2. The increasing use of databases in our society, combined with pervasive use of the Internet, is making it very easy to get access to personal information about anyone. However, teachers need specific information about students' learning problems in order to meet their needs. What implications arise from "data mining" regarding the safety and privacy of students in our schools? What do you think is the teacher's role in these privacy and security issues?

3. Spreadsheets, like calculators, can support rapid computations as students work on higher level problems. Some educators feel that using either kind of technology results in students with poor knowledge of underlying math principles. How would you respond to these criticisms?

fectively supported instruction in science, social studies, and even language arts. Lewis (2001) offers 40 different lessons to help teach various curriculum topics in grades K–8. Teachers can use spreadsheets in many ways to enhance learning. See a summary of these and the relative advantage of each in Figure 4.11.

- **Making possible visual teaching demonstrations** — Whenever concepts involving numbers and concrete representation can clarify the ideas, spreadsheets contribute to effective teaching demonstrations. Spreadsheets offer an efficient way of demonstrating numerical concepts such as multiplication and percentages and numerical applications such as the concept of electoral

Figure 4.9 An Example Spreadsheet for Keeping Grades

	A	B	C	D	E	F	G	H	I	J
1	Period 1: English									
2	Date: Fall, 2009									
3										
4	Name	Identifier	Assign #1	Assign #2	Assign #3	Vocab Quiz	Theme #1	Theme #2	Final Exam	Average
5										
6	Adams, Wanda	34812	100	97	70	80	85	92	95	88.43
7	Betts, Leelee	11900	67	70	82	86	70	85	85	77.86
8	Darnell, Quincy	29987	98	90	65	89	75	95	95	86.71
9	Johnson, Sid	10762	79	87	85	90	86	88	76	84.43
10	Moon, Chris	55950	90	95	92	98	90	96	95	93.71
11	Morrison, Will	97662	97	89	100	89	98	99	96	95.43
12	Sanchez, Valena	90011	76	79	80	87	95	98	97	87.43
13	Sondine, Joan	36599	89	89	100	87	90	91	89	90.71
14	Wertheimer, Arnold	11884	100	99	99	90	89	99	100	96.57
15	Yamamoto, Paul	63901	87	80	75	80	80	82	85	81.29
16										
17	Class Averages		88.30	87.50	84.80	87.60	85.80	92.50	91.30	Formulas

Figure 4.10 Suggested Productivity Uses for Spreadsheets

- Grade keeping to keep records and to prepare grade charts for posting
- Club and/or classroom budgets
- Computerized checkbooks for clubs or other organizations
- Performance assessment checklists

votes versus popular votes. A worksheet can make a picture out of abstract concepts and provide a graphic illustration of what the teacher is trying to communicate. (See Technology Integration Idea 4.3.)

- **Supporting student products** — Students can use spreadsheets to create neat timelines, charts, and graphs as well as products that require them to store and calculate numbers. (For an example, see Technology Integration Idea *Generating a Class Profile* on the DVD that accompanies this text.)

- **Supporting mathematical problem solving** — Spreadsheets take over the task of doing arithmetic functions so students can focus on higher level concepts (Black, 1999; Hauger, 2000; Ploger, Rooney, & Klingler, 1996). By answering "what if" questions in a highly graphic format, spreadsheets help teachers encourage logical thinking, develop organizational skills, and promote problem solving. (See Technology Integration Idea 4.4.)

- **Storing and analyzing data** — Whenever students must keep track of data from classroom experiments or online surveys, spreadsheets help organize these data and allow students to perform required descriptive statistical analyses. (See Technology Integration Idea 4.5.)

Figure 4.11   A Summary of Spreadsheet Integration Strategies and Benefits

Spreadsheet Integration Strategies	Benefits	Sample Lessons
Making possible visual teaching demonstrations	• Makes abstract concepts more concrete. • Makes it more efficient to demonstrate math concepts.	**Technology Integration Idea 4.3:** Spreadsheets and the Electoral Process
Supporting student products	• Saves time doing graphic displays of data. • Makes it easier to make changes, corrections.	**See example on DVD:** Learning Charting and Graphing with Spreadsheets
Supporting mathematical and "what if" problem solving	• Does lower level functions (e.g., arithmetic calculations) in high-level problems. • Makes solutions more visual and clear.	**Technology Integration Idea 4.4:** Solving Problems with Dimensions and Area **See example on DVD:** Tasty Problem-solving with Spreadsheets
Storing **and analyzing data**	• Makes it easier and more efficient to collect and store data. • Allows easy changes to formulas and items of data.	**Technology Integration Idea 4.5:** Analyzing Data from an Online Survey **See example on DVD:** Candy Is Dandy
Projecting grades	• Makes it easier to test and display a series of possible outcomes. • Encourages student responsibility and goal-setting behaviors.	

• **Projecting grades** — Students can be taught to use spreadsheets to keep track of their own grades. They can do their own "what if" questions to see what scores they need to make on their assignments to project desired class grades. This simple activity can play an important role in encouraging them to take responsibility for setting goals and achieving them.

For additional lesson ideas on using spreadsheets in curriculum lessons, see the DVD accompanying this text and search by "spreadsheet."

Teaching Spreadsheet Skills: Recommended Skills and Activities

Just as with word processing, students just beginning to use spreadsheets must have time to develop skills in using

TECHNOLOGY INTEGRATION IDEA 4.3

USING SPREADSHEETS FOR VISUAL TEACHING DEMONSTRATIONS

Title: Spreadsheets and the Electoral Process

Content Area/Topic: Civics

Grade Level: 5

NETS for Students: Standards 1, 3, 4, 5

Description: Teachers can use a spreadsheet to display data from a U.S. presidential election to show how popular votes and electoral votes differ and how it is possible for a person to win the popular vote and still lose the election.

Instruction: After the class holds a mock election and assigns electoral votes to each class in the school based on enrollment numbers, a spreadsheet is set up to match the list of classes and their popular and electoral votes. Data on election results are entered after the election is held and the spreadsheet is displayed on a large monitor so the whole class can see the results as they are entered. They are able to see that if very few of the popular votes in key areas are changed, the results of the election would be reversed. The class discusses these results as well as the possibility that a candidate could win the popular vote and lose the electoral vote.

Assessment: Answer questions on the electoral vote as part of an end-of-unit test.

Source: Goldberg, K. (1991). Bringing mathematics to the social studies classroom: Spreadsheets and the electoral process. *The Computing Teacher, 18*(1), 35–38.

TECHNOLOGY INTEGRATION IDEA 4.4

USING SPREADSHEETS TO TEACH PROBLEM SOLVING

Title: Solving Problems with Dimensions and Area

Content Area/Topic: Geometry/algebra

Grade Level: 4–12

NETS for Students: Standards 1, 3, 4, 5, 6

Description: Problems that engage students and teachers in mathematical problem solving are exciting because they encourage students to develop and test their own conjectures. Without technology, however, these explorations would be much more difficult, if not impossible.

Instruction: Present a problem such as the following: "Sabine will use her house as one side of a new fenced area she is making for her dog. If she has 96 meters of fencing, what are the dimensions of the largest rectangular pen she can make?" Use *Geometer's Sketchpad* to draw the figure with the known numbers, then help the students create an algebra equation for this problem. Lead them to see that a pen that uses 96 meters of fencing has to have a width of x and a length of $96 - 2x$, since the total fencing available is 96 meters and there are two sides with the same length and one of a different length. (The house serves as the fourth side.) Help them create a spreadsheet that calculates the possible dimensions, based on this information. The spreadsheet reveals that the maximum area is 1,152.

Assessment: After working in pairs to do several similar problems, students take a test with other problems.

(continued)

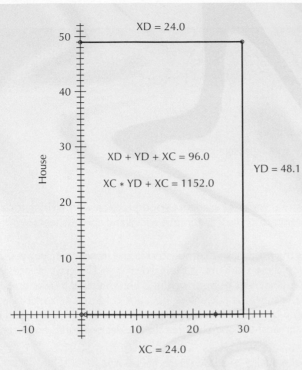

	A	B	C
1	width	length	area
2	1	94	94
3	2	92	184
4	3	90	270
5	4	88	352
6	5	86	430
7	6	84	504
8	7	82	574
9	8	80	640
10	9	78	702
11	10	76	760
12	11	74	814
13	12	72	864
14	13	70	910
15	14	68	952
16	15	66	990
17	16	64	1,024
18	17	62	1,054
19	18	60	1,080
20	19	58	1,102
21	20	56	1,120
22	21	54	1,134
23	22	52	1,144
24	23	50	1,150
25	24	48	1,152
26	25	46	1,150
27	26	44	1,144
28	27	42	1,134
29	28	40	1,120
30	29	38	1,102
31	30	36	1,080
32	31	34	1,054
33	32	32	1,024
34	33	30	990
35	34	28	952
36	35	26	910
37	36	24	864
38	37	22	814
39	38	20	760
40	39	18	702

Source: Both figures reprinted with permission from Brown, S., Galloway, C., Orrill, C., & Umberger, S. (2002). Lead your students in mathematical discovery. *Learning and Leading with Technology, 29*(5), 22–27, 64. Copyright © 2002 ISTE (International Society for Technology in Education), iste@iste.org, www.iste.org. All rights reserved.

TECHNOLOGY INTEGRATION IDEA 4.5

USING SPREADSHEETS TO STORE AND ANALYZE DATA

Title: Analyzing Data from an Online Survey

Content Area/Topic: Language arts–writing assignments

Grade Level: 3–12

NETS for Students: Standards 1, 3, 4, 5, 6

Description: Creating questions for a survey gives students good practice with writing for an intended audience. An online survey allows students to collect data more easily, and spreadsheets work to store data for easier analysis.

Instruction: The teacher introduces the project and demonstrates the Internet survey tool. The teacher can either decide on the survey topic or allow students to brainstorm one. The class creates a few of the items together as the teacher illustrates principles of item writing. Then the class breaks up into groups to write items in an assigned area. Once the survey is put online, data are collected automatically in a comma-delimited file. That is, items are separated by commas as they are stored. When the collection is complete, the teacher downloads the file into a spreadsheet and students do the desired totals and other formulas to analyze the data.

Assessment: Use a rubric to grade the quality of students' project work.

Source: Timmerman, A. (2003). Survey says.... *Learning and Leading with Technology, 31*(2), 10–13, 55.

the software before teachers can begin to grade their work. Some lessons require students to know only the most basic operations, as shown in Step 2 of Figure 4.12. Other activities require students to create their own spreadsheets and formulas, as shown in Step 4 of Figure 4.12. In the latter case, if students are not able to use the online tutorials that are available to teach spreadsheet software, teachers can use the strategies outlined in Figure 4.12. Even when teaching these advanced concepts, teachers may choose to introduce more complex functions and features on an as-needed basis, depending on the needs of the lesson.

USING DATABASE SOFTWARE IN TEACHING AND LEARNING

Databases: Definition and Characteristics

Databases are computer programs that allow users to store, organize, and manipulate information, including both text and numerical data. Database software can perform some calculations but its real power lies in allowing people to locate information through keyword searches. Unlike word processing software, which can be compared to a typewriter, or a spreadsheet, which can be compared to a calculator, a database program has no electronic counterpart. It is most often compared to a file cabinet or a Rolodex card file. Like these pre-computer devices, the purpose of a database is to store important information in

a way that makes it easy to locate later. This capability has become increasingly important as society's store of essential information grows in volume and complexity.

People often use the term *database* to refer both to the computer program and the product it creates; however, database products are also called **files.** Whereas a spreadsheet stores an item of data in a cell, a database stores one item of data in a location usually called a **field.** Although each field represents one item of information in a database, perhaps the more important unit of information is a **record,** which stores all items of information related to a particular database entry. For example, in a database of student records, each record corresponds to a student, and a record consists of several fields of information about the student such as name, address, age, and parents' names. In a database of information on a school's inventory of instructional resources, each record represents one resource and consists of several fields describing aspects such as title, publisher, date published, and location. A summary of database features is shown in Figure 4.13.

Database software packages vary considerably in the format and appearance of information. Figure 4.14 shows an example database file on genetic traits observed in students (Revenaugh, 1997). It is designed to help students see how human characteristics are based on heredity. In this database, each student has a record and each item about a student (e.g., age, eye color, and height) is a field.

Figure 4.12 Tips on Teaching Spreadsheets
(Also see links to tutorials at http://www.internet4classrooms.com/on-line2.htm)

Suggested Steps	Tasks Under Each Step
Step 1—Prepare for teaching.	**Arrange for:** • A big screen or projection system • A disk for each student • Copying sample file(s) onto student disks • One computer per student • Alternative keyboards or other adaptive devices for students with disabilities. **Create or obtain:** • Handouts or wall posters on spreadsheet features and common errors.
Step 2—Demonstrate the basics.	**Using a big screen or projection system, show how to:** • Open a spreadsheet file from a disk • Select a worksheet to work on in the file by clicking a tab at the bottom • Select any given cell location by row–column position. **Then demonstrate:** • Spreadsheet "magic": Show how it recalculates automatically when a number is changed. **Finally, show how to:** • Enter new information into a cell • Format given cells for appearance and as various kinds of numbers • Change column width • Copying information in a cell down the column or across a row. **Point out a common error:** • Forgetting to highlight cells to be formatted before selecting a format option.
Step 3—Assign individual practice.	**Give students a sample spreadsheet file on disk and have them:** • Insert the disk and open the file • Do a list of changes to the file (e.g., insert new data, copy down a column or across a row, format cells) • Name, save, and close the document.
Step 4—Demonstrate formatting features.	**Using a big screen or projection system, show how to:** • Create a formula to add a column • Copy a formula across the row to add other columns • **Optional:** Functions such as SUM and AVERAGE • **Optional:** Charting functions • **Optional:** Adding graphics and URLs. **Point out common errors with formulas:** • Forgetting to place the cursor in the cell where you want the formula • Pressing the Right Arrow key (instead of the Return or Enter key) to leave the cell while creating a formula (Show that this action adds something to the formula, rather than exiting the cell.) • Including the formula cell itself in the formula's calculation (i.e., circular reference error).
Step 5—Assign more individual practice.	**Have students open their sample spreadsheet file from Step 3 and do the following:** • Enter and format various new formulas • **Optional:** Create a chart based on the data • **Optional:** Add a graphic and/or a URL. Monitor students as they work and give individual help as needed.

Figure 4.13   A Summary of Database Features

Feature Categories/ General Benefits	Database Features	Description of Features
Basic features make it easier to store large amounts of data in an organized, easily accessible way; allow easy changes to information.	Store data.	Text, numerical, and graphic information in a database is organized by records (e.g., one student in a student information database) and fields (e.g., names, ages, and birth dates of all students).
	Do updates.	Items of information can be called up and easily edited (e.g., changing a student's address after a move or changing the name of a teacher assigned to a group of students).
	Sort data.	Data can be organized alphabetically or numerically by any desired field (e.g., by students' last names or by ages).
Search features make it easy to locate single items of information or all items that meet certain criteria.	Do queries.	Locates and lists all information that matches certain keywords or criteria; allows searches based on Boolean logic.
	Do reports.	Produces formatted summaries of information retrieved from a database (e.g., a teacher creates a report listing students whose scores made them eligible for tutoring on a state-mandated test and the report tells their name, address, and Social Security number).
Calculation features allow data to be analyzed and the results of the analysis displayed.	Do formulas.	Allows arithmetic calculations based on numerical information stored in fields (e.g., calculates the average age or grades of students in a certain group).
Web features allow teachers and students to connect documents with Internet resources and create web page announcements, reports, and projects.	Insert "live" URLs.	Allows person using the database to click on a URL and go automatically to a website. (*Note:* Web browser must be active.)
Other features make the program useful with other programs.	Merge with word-processed documents.	Database files can be used to insert fields automatically into letters and other documents (e.g., inserting student names to personalize letters to parents).

Figure 4.14   A Sample Database on Genetic Characteristics

Source: Microsoft Access from Productivity Tools in the Classroom. © 1997, Microsoft Corporation

The Impact of Databases in Education

Why teachers use databases. The uses of databases in education have changed in recent years, due to shifts in instructional focuses and data-keeping requirements. Current uses are described later in this chapter. Databases continue to offer educators the following benefits:

- **Reducing data redundancy** — In education, as in business and industry, many different organizations need access to the same kinds of information on the same people or resources. In pre-computer days, each school office and school district office often kept duplicate files on teachers and students. Nowadays, since databases can be accessed from multiple locations, an organization needs to keep only one actual copy of these kinds of information. This cuts down on both the expense and the physical space needed to store the information.

- **Saving time locating and/or updating information** — People need to locate information and keep it accurate—time is money. It takes time to find the information and keep it updated for everyone who needs it. Since a database stores information in a central computer instead of in several different file folders in various offices, users can find information more quickly and they can more easily make changes whenever updates are needed. For example, if a student's address or legal guardian changes, updating the information in a student information database is both quicker and easier than locating and changing it in many file folders.

- **Allowing comparisons of information through searches across files** — Electronic databases also offer an important capability of locating information that meets several criteria at once. For example, a teacher may want to locate all of the resources in video format at a certain grade level that focus on a certain topic. A database search would make locating these materials an easy task compared to a search of library shelves. For a large collection of information, this kind of search is possible only if information is stored in a database.

- **Helping to reveal relationships among data** — Databases have the potential to make concepts underlying data easier to spot. By asking questions and doing searches to answer them, students can see relationships among information elements that they might not otherwise be able to perceive. For example, students might create a database on U.S. presidents. By adding a field on which states entered the Union during each administration, they can ask questions such as the number of years each party was in power and how fast the country grew under each administration.

Research on the instructional uses of databases. Collis (1990) summarized six different studies on instructional uses of databases. She found that students can use databases to acquire useful skills in searching for and using information, but they need guidance to ask relevant questions and analyze results. If allowed to proceed on their own, students may regard a simple printed list of results as a sufficient measure of success. Studies by Maor (1991) in science and Ehman, Glenn, Johnson, and White (1992) in social studies yielded essentially the same results. Databases are most helpful when they are embedded in a structured problem-solving process and when the activity includes class and small-group discussion of search results.

In a review of technology in social studies, Berson (1996) reported that databases are one of the tools with demonstrated usefulness in teaching inquiry and problem-solving skills. Finally, Pugalee and Robinson (1998) also found that training in database use and search techniques can increase teachers' Internet skills and their skill in designing lessons and applications that use the Internet. This latter finding indicates that the quality of teachers' Internet use may hinge on their grasp of database concepts.

Issues in using databases. Databases are permanent and pervasive parts of life in the Information Age. They allow users to locate bits of important data in a landscape crowded with information; they support decisions with confirmed facts rather than assumptions; and they put the power of knowledge at our fingertips. Yet this power is not without its dangers, and knowing how to find information is not the same as knowing what one can or should do with it. The following are concerns about the use of databases in education:

- **Simplified access versus privacy** — Each of our names is listed, along with much of our personal information, on literally dozens of databases. This cataloging begins when we are born—even before we are named—when we appear on the hospital's patient database. Whenever we apply for credit cards, driver's licenses, or jobs, we enter still more databases. These information entities reside on computers that can communicate and exchange notes, so information in one database can be shared with many information systems. Education, like other systems in our society, has come to depend on ready access to these information sources. However, easy access to information about people long has been recognized as a threat to personal privacy. If information is easy to access, it may also be easy for unauthorized people to obtain and possibly misuse or for organizations to use it in ways that violate basic human rights. As educators use information from school and district databases, they are responsible for safeguarding this private information and protecting it from unauthorized access. This

The best kinds and uses of software tools such as word processing, spreadsheets, and databases depend on the content area and skills teachers need to address. The ten uses given here are among the most popular ones described in the literature.

1. **Sweet hypothesis testing** — Have students predict average numbers of M&Ms or Skittles of each color, then count various packages and build a spreadsheet to display and chart the numbers and calculate averages.

2. **Paragraph coherence** — Show students how good paragraphs are put together by using word processing software to scramble sentences in a paragraph and have students use the copy–cut–paste feature to put sentences in correct order.

3. **Process writing** — Have students use word processing software to do drafts of their compositions; have them email drafts and send them corrections and suggestions in a different color type.

4. **Colorful writing** — Students use the word processor's font color option to highlight and discuss various functions in compositions (e.g., topic sentences, emotion-evoking content, factual content, and descriptive words and phrases).

5. **Elections concepts** — Use spreadsheet software to demonstrate how many different ways a president could win the popular vote but lose the electoral vote.

6. **Pizza problem solving** — Students use a spreadsheet to calculate the most cost-effective pizza purchases to serve various numbers of people.

7. **Presidential comparisons** — Use database software to build a U.S. presidents database in order to compare characteristics such as an individual's background and experience before becoming president.

8. **Online surveys** — Show students how to do survey research by collecting data online and using a spreadsheet to receive and analyze it.

9. **Political cartoons** — Students use word processing and clip art to create political cartoons that illustrate various concepts and current events.

10. **Grave thoughts** — Have students collect birth–death date information from tombstones, enter it into a database, and query it to answer questions about life spans in various decades.

---

means making sure passwords remain secret and being sensitive to who is looking at screens or printouts containing personal student information.

- **Coping with information overload** — The recent calls for improved accountability in education have led to more data collection on student characteristics and achievement. However, the sheer amount of available information may make it difficult to locate and use parts of it. Before constructing student information databases, schools and school districts have to think carefully about how they want to use them. They also have to obtain or create database management systems that merge with their testing systems and that have tools to allow **disaggregation** or grouping of students by desired characteristics. These tools make it easier for teachers to identify groups of students that need special instruction and to evaluate the impact of certain kinds of instructional methods or materials.

Databases in the Classroom: Productivity and Teaching Strategies

Productivity strategies. Productivity uses of databases for teachers have not proven as popular as those with tools such as word processing. Most teachers need not create their own management system to keep inventories of classroom materials or records on student performance, relying instead on systems in the main office for such vital information. Teachers use prepared databases much more widely than ever before; however, they do not usually create them. Current uses of databases for productivity and record keeping include the following:

- **Inventorying and locating instructional resources** — Teachers can look up titles and descriptions of instructional resources in a database system to help them identify materials that meet certain instructional needs. If a school has a large collection of resources used by all of the teachers, the school's library/media center probably catalogs this collection on a database designed for this purpose.

- **Data mining for planning and reporting** — Student records information allows teachers to meet individual student needs in several ways. For example, a teacher might access information on student reading levels or learning problems in order to create appropriate instruction. Schools also use databases to create reports for accountability purposes. Locating information from databases in ways that reveal relationships among the data elements has come to be called *data mining*. This activity uses data to track achievement over time and to make appropriate plans for future instruction (Salpeter, 2004). Data mining involves pulling data together from several databases and placing it in **data warehouses** or central collection points for collected data. Educators then use data analysis tools, report writers, and decision support tools to analyze data and compile summaries.

- **Using information on students to respond to questions or perform required tasks** — Teachers often are asked to supply personal information on students or deal with situations relating to their personal needs, yet it is difficult to remember everything on dozens of students. For example, some students require special medication; the teacher is responsible for reminding them to take it. A teacher might need to decide quickly whether a particular adult is authorized to take a child from the school. The school may provide a database with these kinds of information so the teacher can look them up quickly.

- **Sending personalized letters to parents and others** — The capability to merge database information with a word processing document is convenient whenever the teacher wants to send personalized notes to parents or to the students themselves. The teacher has to create only one letter or note; the database program then takes care of the personalizing.

Instructional integration strategies for databases. When database software became available for microcomputers in the 1980s, instructional activities that made use of these tools quickly became popular. Thus, the literature reflects a variety of applications for databases. The heaviest uses seem to be in social studies, but effective applications have been designed for topics in content areas from language arts to science. Here are some ways teachers use databases to enhance learning (see a summary of these and the relative advantage of each in Figure 4.15):

- **Teaching research and study skills** — Skills in locating and organizing information to answer questions and learn new concepts have always been as fundamental as reading and writing skills. Students need good research and study skills not only for school assignments, but also to help them learn on their own outside school. As the volume of information in our society increases, the need to learn how to locate important information quickly also grows. Before computers, families strived to buy reference tools such as a good dictionary and a set of encyclopedias so that children could do research for their school reports and other assignments. Today, these and other sources are stored on electronic media and students need to know how to do computer searches of these references. (See Technology Integration Idea *A Database Journal for Mathematics* on the DVD that accompanies this text.) Many database activities are designed to introduce these kinds of searches along with information for a report or a group project.

- **Teaching organization skills** — Students need to understand concepts related to handling information. To solve problems, they must locate the right information and organize it in such a way that they can draw relationships between isolated elements. One way to teach these skills is to have students develop and use their own databases; many examples of this kind of activity have been reported. Even very young students can learn about organizing information by creating databases of information about themselves, including birth dates, heights, weights, eye colors, pets, and parents' names. They can then do simple searches of their databases to summarize information about the members of their class. These kinds of activities help students understand what information is and how to use it. In later grades, students can design and create databases related to areas of study. For example, a class might create a database of descriptive information on candidates running for office in their state or in a national election. (See Technology Integration Idea *Crating a Database Yearbook* on the DVD that accompanies this text.)

- **Understanding the power of information "pictures"** — Students need to be able to do their own data mining, by understanding the persuasive power of information organized into databases. Sometimes a database can generate an information "picture" or

Figure 4.15   A Summary of Database Integration Strategies and Benefits

Database Integration Strategies	Benefits	Sample Lessons
Teaching research and study skills	• Illustrates how many organizations in our society store data. • Helps students learn how to look for information in various sources. • Teaches study skills that will be useful across all content areas.	**See example on DVD:** A Database Journal for Mathematics
Teaching organization skills	• Teaches concepts related to handling information. • Shows where information in databases comes from and why it is useful.	**See example on DVD:** Creating a Database Yearbook
Understanding the power of information "pictures"	• Illustrates how data can be organized to reveal new ideas and concepts. • Shows the persuasive power of information organized in various ways. • Shows how to make decisions based on information summaries.	**See example on DVD:** Getting a Clearer Focus on History
Posing and testing hypotheses	• Demonstrates how to ask questions to support problem solving. • Shows how data can help support or refute a position.	**Technology Integration Idea 4.6:** A Nutrition Database **See additional example on DVD:** Investigating Graveyard Data with Spreadsheets
Searching for information during research	• Shows standard search procedures used in locating information during research.	**Technology Integration Idea 4.7:** Hunting for Celestial Bodies

relationships among bits of information that may not be visible in any other way. Although these pictures may or may not be completely accurate, many decisions are based on them. For example, the U.S. government uses information databases on those who have been convicted of past income tax offenses to generate descriptive profiles of people who may be likely to try to defraud the government in the future. Students can learn to use database information to generate these types of pictures. (See *Getting a Clearer Fo-*

cus on History example on the Technology Integration Workshop DVD that accompanies this text.)

• **Posing and testing hypotheses** — Many problem-solving activities involve asking questions and locating information to answer them. Therefore, using databases is an ideal way to teach and provide practice with this kind of problem solving. Students can either research prepared databases full of information related to a content area, or they may create their own databases, which is not as common nowa-

Technology Integration Idea 4.6

Using Databases to Pose and Test Hypotheses

Title: A Nutrition Database

Content Area/Topic: Science and Health

Grade Level: 5–12

NETS for Students: Standards 1, 3, 4, 5, 6

Description: This assignment helps students learn how to ask good, scientific questions and test possible answers to them by analyzing available data.

Instruction: The teacher shows students how to build a database of the nutritional elements of various foods. They can derive their data from another, larger nutrition database such as the one at the U.S. Department of Agriculture website (http://www.nal.usda.gov/fnic/foodcomp/Data/). Once the database is set up, the teacher demonstrates it and leads students to ask questions such as "Which food has the most protein?" The teacher shows them that, to do this, they must divide the Protein field by the Weight field and create a new field to hold the result. They do this as a whole class and examine the result. Then the teacher assigns small groups to create other questions to answer and procedures to answer them using the database. (See example below.)

Assessment: Grade students with a checklist of required activities with points assigned to each one.

Food Name	Weight	Common Measure	Fat	Calories	Protein	Calcium	Vitamin C	Protein Per Gram
egg	33.4	1 large egg	0.000	16.70	3.514	2.004	0.000	0.105209580838323
orange	131.0	1 orange	0.157	61.57	1.231	52.400	69.692	0.009396946564886
orange juice	248.0	1 cup	0.496	111.60	1.736	27.280	124.000	0.007
hamburger (fast food)	106.0	1 sandwich	9.773	272.42	12.317	126.140	2.226	0.116198113207547
fried chicken (fast food, white meat)	163.0	2 pieces	29.519	493.89	35.713	60.310	0.000	0.219096159509202
milk (whole)	244.0	1 cup	8.150	148.84	8.028	290.360	2.196	0.032901639344262
milk (2%)	244.0	1 cup	4.665	122.00	8.125	297.680	2.440	0.033299180327869
apple	138.0	1 apple	0.497	81.42	0.262	9.660	7.866	0.001898550724638
broccoli	88.0	1 cup	0.308	24.64	2.622	42.240	82.016	0.0297954545455
chocolate chip cookie	10.0	1 medium cookie	2.260	48.10	0.540	2.500	0.000	0.054
	0.0		0.000	0.00	0.000	0.000	0.000	

Protein Calculation : Select Query — Record: 1 of 10

Source: Figure reprinted with permission from Marcovitz, D. (2002). Q&A with *Microsoft Access. Learning and Leading with Technology, 30*(3), 14–19. Copyright © 2002 ISTE (International Society for Technology in Education), iste@iste.org, www.iste.org. All rights reserved.

days. Either way, these activities encourage them to look for information that will support or refute a position. In lower grades, the teacher may pose the question and assign students to search databases to answer it. Later, the activity may call for students to both pose and answer appropriate questions. For example, the teacher may ask students to address popular beliefs concerning artistic or gifted people. The students formulate questions, form debate teams, and design searches of databases on famous people to support their positions. (See Technology Integration Idea 4.6 and an additional example on the Technology Integration Workshop DVD titled *Investigating Graveyard Data with Spreadsheets.*)

- **Searching for information during research** — Much of the world's information is stored in databases, and these "information banks" are becoming more available to students and other nontechnical people for everyday use. As they develop their skills in locating and analyzing information during research, students need practice in using standard searching procedures to locate information in databases. (See Technology Integration Idea 4.7.)

Teaching Database Skills: Recommended Skills and Activities

Unlike word processing and spreadsheet tools, learning to use database features is a key focus of using the software.

USING ONLINE DATABASES TO SEARCH FOR INFORMATION DURING RESEARCH

Title: Hunting for Celestial Bodies

Content Area/Topic: Astronomy

Grade Level: 6 and up

NETS for Students: Standards 1, 3, 4, 5, 6

Description: Throughout the history of astronomy, ordinary people have discovered new comets and asteroids. Now databases of existing celestial bodies are available to help people determine if they have identified a previously unnamed object in the sky.

Instruction: Teachers can have their students choose an area of the night sky, download from the Internet two or more images taken on different evenings, and compare them to see if they have different objects in them. Then they can use a database such as *Starry Night* (a planetarium program available from Sienna Software) to see if the "new" objects are already identified. If they are not, students can contact astronomers to find out if they have discovered a new nova, asteroid, or comet.

Assessment: Grade students with a checklist of required activities with points assigned to each one.

Source: Erickson, D. (1999). Hunting for asteroids, comets, and novas. *Learning and Leading with Technology, 26*(6), 22–24.

It is only by seeing how databases work that students are able to understand their power and usefulness. If students are not able to use the online tutorials that are available to teach spreadsheet software, teachers can use the strategies outlined in Figure 4.16. Even when teaching these advanced concepts, teachers may choose to introduce more complex functions and features on an as-needed basis, depending on the needs of the lesson.

A SUMMARY OF SOFTWARE TOOL INTEGRATION STRATEGIES

Software tools are increasingly popular, in part because they address both productivity and instructional needs and in part because they can support either directed or constructivist learning activities. Their primary benefits to instruction are to reduce the labor involved in preparing student products and remove logistical barriers to learning. For a summary of all software tool uses discussed in this chapter matched to directed and constructivist integration strategies, see the matrix in Figure 4.17.

INTERACTIVE SUMMARY

The following is a summary of the main points covered in this chapter. To see additional examples and information on these points, go to this textbook's Companion Website at http://www.prenhall.com/roblyer and click on the Chapter 4 *Interactive Summary* module to visit each of the recommended websites:

Figure 4.16 Tips on Teaching Databases
(Also see links to tutorials at http://www.internet4classrooms.com/on-line2.htm)

Suggested Steps	Tasks Under Each Step
Step 1—Prepare for teaching.	**Arrange for:** • A big screen or projection system • A disk for each group of students with sample file(s) copied onto the disks OR access to an online database • One computer per student group • Alternative keyboards or other adaptive devices for students with disabilities. **Create or obtain:** • Handouts or wall posters on database features and how to use Boolean operations to complete searches.
Step 2—Demonstrate the basics.	**Using a big screen or projection system, show how to:** • Open a database file from disk or go to an online database • Show various views of the data (e.g., by records or by fields in one record). **Point out a common error:** • Confusing a database file with a spreadsheet file, because they look similar. **Then demonstrate:** • How data can be sorted by various fields • How to use keywords and criteria to locate items of information from a database that match them • **Optional:** Show how to structure Boolean searches to solve problems (e.g., create a diagram or picture that displays the expected results) • **Optional:** Point out common errors with Boolean searches (e.g., using AND and OR combinations without appropriate parentheses).
Step 3—Assign individual practice.	**Give student groups a sample database file on disk or online and have them:** • Do a series of searches to locate items of information and/or to answer a set of questions.
Step 4—Demonstrate database creation and use.	**Discuss with students how to:** • Think through how to create a database to meet a certain need • Decide on how to structure it according to records • Decide on fields to include. **Using a big screen or projection system, show how to:** • Add fields to create the database • Add records of information to the database • **Optional:** How to create a report after a search • **Optional:** How to do calculation functions.
Step 5—Assign more individual practice.	**Have students:** • Create their own database to meet a given need • Enter new data into the structure • Do searches to answer questions • **Optional:** Enter graphics and URLs • **Optional:** Create a report based on the data. Monitor students as they work and give individual help, as needed.

Figure 4.17 Software Tool Technology Integration Strategies for Directed, Constructivist, or Either Models

Integration Strategies for Basic Software Tools: Word Processing, Spreadsheets, and Databases	Directed Models — Remedy identified weaknesses or skill deficits	Promote skill fluency or automaticity	Provide efficient, self-paced instruction	Support self-paced review of concepts	Constructivist Models — Foster creative problem solving and metacognition	Build mental models, increase knowledge transfer	Foster group cooperation	Allow for multiple intelligences	Generate motivation to learn	Either Model — Optimize scarce personnel and material resources	Remove logistical hurdles to learning	Develop information literacy and visual literacy skills
Word Processing												
Supporting the learning of writing processes									×		×	
Using a dynamic group process approach							×		×		×	
Assigning individual language, writing, and reading exercises		×							×		×	
Encouraging writing through the curriculum									×		×	
Spreadsheets												
Making possible visual teaching demonstrations					×	×			×		×	
Supporting student products											×	
Supporting mathematical and "what if" problem solving					×	×					×	
Storing and analyzing data					×						×	
Projecting grades					×						×	
Databases												
Teaching research and study skills							×		×		×	×
Teaching organization skills					×	×					×	×
Understanding the power of information "pictures"					×	×						
Posing and testing hypotheses					×	×	×				×	
Searching for information during research											×	×

1. **Overview of the "Basic Three":** Three software tools that are considered basic educational resources are:

   - **Word processing** — Programs that allow people to produce typed documents on a computer screen. **Benefits of using them include** saving time, improving document appearance, and allowing easy exchange of work.

   - **Spreadsheets** — Programs designed to organize and manipulate numerical data. **Benefits of using them include** saving time, organizing displays of information, and increasing motivation to work with mathematics.

   - **Databases** — Programs that allow users to store, organize, and manipulate information, including both text and numerical data. **Benefits of using them include** reducing data redundancy (the number of places data must be stored), saving time locating and/or updating important information, allowing comparisons of information through searches across files, and revealing relationships among data.

   To see descriptions of features and capabilities of some of the most popular of these software tools, visit these sites:

   - **Integrated packages** — *Microsoft Works* and *Apple-Works*
   - **Software suites** — *Microsoft Office* (includes Microsoft *Word* for word processing, Microsoft *Excel* for spreadsheet, and Microsoft *Access* for database)
   - *FileMaker Pro* database software.

2. **Productivity applications for the three basic software tools:** These include:

   - **For word processing** — Creating handouts or other instructional materials, lesson plans and notes, reports, forms, letters to parents or students, flyers, and newsletters
   - **For spreadsheets** — Keeping club and classroom budgets, preparing performance checklists, and keeping gradebooks
   - **For databases** — Inventorying and locating instructional resources, data mining for planning and reporting, using information on students to respond to questions or perform required tasks, and sending personalized letters to parents and others.

3. **Teaching and learning tasks that each kind of tool can support:**

   - **For word processing** — Supporting the learning of writing processes; using a dynamic group process approach; assigning individual language, writing, and reading exercises; and encouraging writing through the curriculum

   - **For spreadsheets** — Making possible visual teaching demonstrations, supporting student products, supporting mathematical and "what if" problem solving, storing and analyzing data, and projecting grades
   - **For databases** — Teaching research and study skills, understanding the power of information "pictures," posing and testing hypotheses, and searching for information during research.

4. **Lesson activities for software tools:** For instructional activities that integrate the functions and capabilities of the software tools see the *Technology Integration Workshop* DVD that accompanies this text. For other lesson ideas on using these tools in curriculum lessons, visit the following websites:

   - **For word processing** — Visit the <u>Lesson Plans Website</u> and search by "word processing."
   - **For spreadsheets** — Visit the <u>Lesson Plans Website</u> and search by "spreadsheet," the <u>Technology Web Portal for Teachers,</u> or <u>Tammy's Technology Tips for Teachers.</u>
   - **For databases** — Visit the <u>Lesson Plans Website</u> and search by "database."

Online Activities

Visit this text's Companion Website at <u>http://www.prenhall.com/roblyer</u> to gain access to a variety of questions, activities, and exercises to help build your knowledge of this chapter's content.

Online Chapter 4 Self-Test

To review terms and concepts for this chapter, click on the *Self-Test* module for this chapter of the Companion Website.

Software Skill-Builder Tutorials

To access practical tutorial and skill-building activities and to build skills using popular software and hardware, click on the *Software Skill-Builder Tutorials* module for this chapter of the Companion Website.

Web-Enrichment Activities

To complete activities that connect to chapter content and provide web-based resources, click on the *Web-Enrichment Activities* module for this chapter of the Companion Website.

Technology Integration Workshop

Clips from the Classroom: Learning with Technology

Go to the *Technology Integration Workshop* DVD located in the back of this text and click on *Clips from the Classroom*. View the video clip listed below that supports this chapter's content:

- *Laptops for Data in Fifth Grade.*

Now, visit this text's Companion Website at http://www.prenhall.com/roblyer to answer questions and complete activities that will guide you in analyzing each clip.

The TIP Model in Action

Read each of the following scenarios related to implementing the TIP Model, and go to the Companion Website to answer the questions that follow each one based on your Chapter 4 reading activities.

TIP Model Scenario #1 Mr. Gilbert wanted to demonstrate various principles of probability to his junior high advanced math students and then let them test hypotheses on data sets to show the principles in action. However, the exercises he had them do required a series of calculations on a set of numbers. It took the students a long time to do these calculations with a calculator because they had to keep reentering the numbers and made a lot of entry errors. All the time spent on entering figures and correcting errors made it difficult for them to focus on the hypothesis testing.

1.1 What software tool would you recommend Mr. Gilbert use to address this problem?

1.2 What would be the relative advantage of using this software tool?

1.3 Would it be better to have the students work individually or in groups to do the exercises? How would you arrange the computer systems to carry out this strategy?

TIP Model Scenario #2 Mr. Hern has his class work in small groups to create a short story. As a whole class,

they discuss the plot and characters; then each group writes a part of the story. They exchange sections and critique each other's parts. Then they do a final version. After the draft is complete, they post the story on the school's web server along with stories posted from past classes.

2.1 What would be the relative advantages for Mr. Hern's students to use word processing for their drafts instead of doing typed or handwritten drafts?

2.2 What would be the relative advantages of posting the story on the Internet when it is completed?

2.3 What outcomes would Mr. Hern probably want to assess in addition to quality of writing in the final product? Suggest a way to carry out this assessment.

TIP Model Scenario #3 Ms. Sanchez is a high school AP composition teacher. She wants her students to do more spelling and grammar proofreading of their own written work and make required revisions on these items before turning papers in to her for grading. She feels word processing features will help them learn this habit, so she introduces the software to them in class. They have never used word processing before, but she feels AP students can learn word processing on their own. After a demonstration of word processing features on Monday, she tells them to go to the computer lab for the next two class periods, do a word-processed paper, and turn it in to her at the end of the class period Wednesday. When she grades the papers, she realizes they are far worse than usual. Not only are ideas not as well developed, spelling and grammar are worse.

3.1 What reasons related to Ms. Sanchez's teaching sequence might explain why word processing did not provide the help she expected?

3.2 Why do you think the ideas in the student papers were not as well developed as usual?

3.3 What are two things you suggest she do differently if she tries this again?

TIP Model Scenario #4 Mr. Borodin was trying to show his teenage students in the business education program how they could figure out quickly how much car they could buy with the money they had. He wanted to show them the relationship among the down payment, interest rate, and length of the loan and how this all affected monthly payments and the total they would spend on the car at the end of the loan period. However, he wanted them to be able to do the calculations quickly, so they could focus on the underlying math concepts.

4.1 What technology-based tool could Mr. Borodin use to help address this problem?

4.2 What would be the relative advantage of using this strategy?

4.3 Describe the steps you might use to carry out a simple lesson using this strategy.

TIP Model Scenario #5 Mr. David wants his students to compare the types of bills passed in each of several categories (e.g., technology, human rights) during the last five U.S. presidencies and then draw conclusions about the bills' impact in each administration. His students can get all the information on bills from legislative websites he knows. However, compiling the information would not be enough. He needs a way for them to compare features of bills in ways that will let students ask questions about them and discover relationships between them and the kind of impact they achieved (e.g., number of people affected).

5.1 What kind of software tool could Mr. David use to assist with organizing the information?

5.2 Would this kind of work be best done individually or in small groups? What might be a good way to organize this work in a classroom with a three-computer workstation?

5.3 In what ways might he assess students' work in such a project?

TIE INTO PRACTICE: TECHNOLOGY INTEGRATION EXAMPLES

The Technology Integration Example that opened this chapter (*Can You Afford Your Dream Car?*) showed how a teacher might use a spreadsheet to help students analyze all the variables to consider when making a large purchase. With the knowledge you have gained from Chapter 4, do the following with this example:

1. Ms. Kiley created a spreadsheet like the one shown here for students to use to calculate loan amount, term, and payment for a car purchase. **Create this spreadsheet** by following the tutorial located on the *Hands-On with Technology* section of the DVD that accompanies this text.

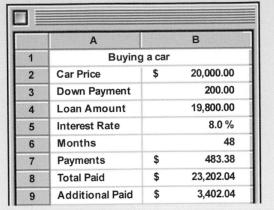

	A	B
1	Buying a car	
2	Car Price	$ 20,000.00
3	Down Payment	200.00
4	Loan Amount	19,800.00
5	Interest Rate	8.0 %
6	Months	48
7	Payments	$ 483.38
8	Total Paid	$ 23,202.04
9	Additional Paid	$ 3,402.04

Sample car buying spreadsheet. (Create this product using the hands-on, step-by-step tutorial located on the *Hands-On with Technology* section of the DVD and Companion Website.)

2. Answer the following questions about the *Dream Car* example:

- Phase 1: How did a spreadsheet project like this offer relative advantage in comparison with other ways of teaching students about money management?

- Phase 2: Ms. Kiley created a rubric to assess the quality and accuracy of the final report students did. What kinds of elements would you assess in such a rubric?

- Phase 3: Ms. Kiley chose to have students work individually on their spreadsheets. What might be some benefits of having students work in groups, rather than individually, on this project?

- Phase 4: Since Ms. Kiley demonstrated the use of the spreadsheet in the classroom, why did she take the trouble to check with each student individually as they worked in the lab to make sure they knew how to use it?

- Phase 5: What strategies might Ms. Kiley use to improve the quality of students' final reports? (*Hint:* Consider interdisciplinary projects with other teachers and having students use tools to facilitate writing their reports.)

3. What NETS for Students skills would students learn by doing the *Dream Car* project? (See the front of the book for a list of NETS for students.)

TECHNOLOGY INTEGRATION LESSON PLANNING

The *Technology Integration Workshop* DVD packaged with this text includes a set of technology integration ideas and links to online lessons, arranged as a searchable database. Click on the *Hands-On with Technology* section of the DVD and complete the following exercise.

1. Locate lesson ideas — The DVD has several examples of lessons that use word processing, spreadsheet, and database software. Locate an example integration idea for using each of these software functions.

2. Evaluate the lessons — Use the *Evaluation Checklist for a Technology-Integrated Lesson* (located on the DVD and the Companion Website) to evaluate each of these lessons.

3. Modify a lesson — Select one of the lesson ideas and adapt its strategies to meet a need in your own content area. You may choose to use the same software in the original or use a different software package and create a new lesson based on the strategy.

4. Add descriptors — Create descriptors for your new lesson like those found on the database (e.g., grade level, content and topic areas, technologies used, relative advantage, objectives, NETS standards).

5. Add the new lesson — Add your modified lesson with all its descriptors to the lesson idea database.

FOR YOUR TEACHING PORTFOLIO

For this chapter's contribution to your teaching portfolio, add the following products you created in the Technology Integration Workshop.

- The spreadsheet you created for the *Dream Car* project
- The three evaluations you did using the *Evaluation Checklist for a Technology-Integrated Lesson*
- The new lesson plan you developed, based on the one you found on the Technology Integration Workshop DVD.

CHAPTER 5

TEACHING WITH SOFTWARE TOOLS: BEYOND THE BASIC PROGRAMS

[T]he notion that computers are neutral and just another technological tool may seem quite a reasonable one....But ... think of the influence the automobile and television have had on our culture. The evidence is accumulating that computers are having a decided impact on the way our schools and society organize, communicate, and make decisions.

Joe Nathan, from *Micro-Myths* (1985)

TECHNOLOGY INTEGRATION EXAMPLE
A DESKTOP-PUBLISHED LITERARY ANTHOLOGY

Based on: Scharf, E., and Cramer, J. (2002). Desktop poetry project. *Learning and Leading with Technology, 29*(6), 28–31, 50–51.

Grade Level: Middle to high school • **Content Area/Topic: Language arts, poetry** • **Length of Time: Year-long project**

Phase 1: Determine relative advantage

Mr. Mortenson was the English teacher in charge of compiling the school's annual eighth-grade literary anthology. It was always a lot of work to prepare the copy for the printing company to format and typeset, and that meant Mr. Mortenson had to limit the number of entries in order to keep the size of the task manageable. However, he felt that it would motivate more students to do their best work if everyone knew at least one of their pieces would be included. An English teacher in another school told him how they prepared their own literary anthology using desktop publishing software called Adobe *PageMaker*. They were even able to add graphics and page numbering themselves. All the printing company had to do was print copies. Mr. Mortenson discussed the use of *PageMaker* with the English teachers in his school, and they were enthusiastic about it. They decided that all classes would prepare word-processed drafts of poetry and short stories throughout the first part of the year, and the teachers would upload their drafts to the school's network server so all students could see them. The computer applications teacher would prepare a desktop-published format for the pages, but all classes would use the format to finalize their own pages.

The teachers decided they would each tell students about the anthology at the beginning of the school year, then they would teach them the various literary forms in a directed way (e.g., showing examples, pointing out structure and devices, taking tests). Then for each form, each student would prepare a draft and work on refining it. In the spring, teachers would ask students to decide on what they considered their best work in each category, with the assurance that at least one item from each student would be published. Finally, each class would help prepare the desktop-published pages.

Phase 2: Decide on objectives and assessments

To make sure all students were clear on the expectations for their work, Mr. Mortenson worked with the other English teachers to create common objectives and assessment methods to measure students' knowledge of each literary form and to evaluate the quality of their written products. The outcomes, objectives, and assessments they decided on were:

- **Outcome:** Identify poetry forms. **Objective:** Each student had to identify at least two examples of each poetry form they studied. **Assessment:** A test consisting of a set of example poems for students to label.
- **Outcome:** Identify short story components and language devices. **Objective:** Each student had to identify structural components of any given short story (e.g., plot, characters, theme) and give at least one example of language devices it used (e.g., metaphor and simile). **Assessment:** A take-home test to read an assigned short story and complete a worksheet identifying the structural components and language devices.
- **Outcome:** Create a poem of each type. **Objective:** Each student writes a poem in the correct form for each genre. **Assessment:** Rubric on poem structure and creativity.
- **Outcome:** Create a short story. **Objective:** At least 90% of the students achieve a rubric score of 15/20 on a short story they create and revise based on teacher feedback. **Assessment:** Rubric on short story structure, required revisions, and creativity.
- **Outcome:** Create desktop-published pages. **Objective:** Students work in pairs to complete all assigned tasks required to format their anthology entries onto pre-designed page formats. **Assessment:** Checklist of required activities.

Phase 3: Design integration strategies

So that they could plan their classroom time, the teachers worked with Mr. Mortenson to design a timeline and sequence for completing the work on the anthology by late spring. They decided on the following:

- **September–February:** English classes introduce the concept of an anthology and show examples from another school; review the literary forms to be covered; take tests on structures; and have students do their word-processed drafts. Computer applications classes submit designs for anthology pages as a class project and vote on which to adopt.

- **March:** Students in all classes finish their revisions and decide on which work they want to appear in the anthology. The computer applications teacher shows English teachers how to paste students' word-processed drafts into the desktop-published pages.
- **April:** Teachers introduce the desktop-publishing software to the students in the computer lab and show them how to change fonts, styles, sizes, and colors to help them communicate meaning. Students also learn how to insert clip art and other graphics to illustrate their work. After completing small practice projects, students work in pairs in the lab to enter their poems and stories into the desktop-published pages. As they complete their pages, the teachers upload them to the school's server.
- **First 2 weeks in May:** Mr. Mortenson downloads the pages and compiles the anthology. He works with a committee consisting of students from the computer applications classes, the computer applications teacher, and one other English teacher.
- **Last 2 weeks in May:** The printing company completes the copies in time for teachers to distribute them during the final week of classes.

Mr. Mortenson and the computer applications teacher collaborated to prepare everything the teachers and students would need to do their work. They did the following:

- **Software copies:** Mr. Mortenson worked with the computer applications teacher to make sure the computer lab had copies of Adobe *PageMaker* on each computer. They obtained some wall charts of *PageMaker* "shortcuts" and hung the charts in the computer lab. Students used these as reminders of how to do common functions.
- **Example anthologies:** Mr. Mortenson obtained copies of past desktop-published anthologies for the students to review.
- **Software skills:** After the computer applications teacher gave a workshop to the teachers on how to use the *PageMaker* pages her classes had designed, Mr. Mortenson asked her to be available to answer teachers' questions about *PageMaker*. He also made sure teachers knew he was always available to discuss ideas for design items to include in the anthology.
- **Computer scheduling:** The computer applications teacher helped the teachers determine how much time their students would need to complete their work and assisted them with scheduling time in the computer lab.

At the end of the school year, Mr. Mortenson and the other teachers reviewed the work on the anthology and agreed it had been a success. Teachers, administrators, students, and parents were thrilled with the completed anthology, and English teachers reported that students were much more motivated than they had ever been in previous years. Rubric grades reflected generally good progress in writing skills. They all agreed that they could use more time in the computer lab with the desktop-publishing software. Although students had revised their work prior to entering the lab, the teachers found that even more revision work went on after students started seeing each other's work in the computer lab and became even more motivated to show off their best work. Teachers asked if they could get *PageMaker* software for their classroom workstations so that more revision work could go on there, and Mr. Mortenson and the computer applications teacher agreed to request it.

OBJECTIVES

After reading this chapter and completing the learning activities for it, you should be able to:

1. Use correct terminology to identify features and capabilities of several software tools.

2. Describe teaching and learning tasks for both teachers and students that each kind of tool can support.

3. Identify applications for software tools that educators would find valuable for making their work more efficient and productive.

4. Develop lesson activities that integrate the functions and capabilities of each of several software tools.

KEY TERMS

- calculator-based lab (CBL)
- charting/graphing tool
- clip art
- computer adaptive testing (CAT)
- computer-assisted design (CAD)
- computer-managed instruction (CMI) system
- concept mapping software
- desktop publishing
- electronic gradebook
- forms maker
- Geographic Information System (GIS)
- Global Positioning System (GPS)
- graphic document maker
- graphing calculator
- IEP generator

- image editing program
- microcomputer-based lab (MBL)
- Musical Instrument Digital Interface (MIDI) device
- morphing
- music editor
- music sequencer
- music synthesizer
- outlining tool
- Portable Document Format (PDF) file
- probeware

- puzzle generator
- sans serif typeface
- serif typeface
- statistical software package
- student information system (SIS)
- student response system
- test generator
- test item bank
- word atlas
- worksheet generator

 For more information on Key Terms, go to the *Key Terms* module for this chapter of the Companion Website at http://www.prenhall.com/roblyer.

INTRODUCTION TO OTHER SOFTWARE SUPPORT TOOLS

Why Use Software Support Tools?

Chapter 4 discussed three of the most widely used software support tools: word processing, spreadsheet, and database programs. These have come to be viewed as the "basic three." However, many other software tools are available to support teachers' and students' work. These tools vary greatly in their purposes, the kinds of benefits they offer, and their utility for teachers.

Each software tool described in this chapter has unique and powerful features, but each requires additional classroom resources and time to learn and to implement. Teachers should choose them for the qualities and benefits they bring to the classroom, rather than simply because they are available. Depending on the capabilities of a particular tool and the needs of the situation, a software support tool can offer the same kinds of benefits described for the basic tools in Chapter 4:

- Improved efficiency and productivity,
- Improved appearance,
- Better accuracy and timeliness of information, and
- More support for interaction and sharing.

The tools described in this chapter range in importance from nearly essential to nice to have, and in function from presenting instruction to supporting background tasks that make a classroom run smoothly. As Nathan (1985) emphasized, these tools, if used wisely and creatively, have the potential not only to support classroom activities, but also to transform the very nature of the way people learn and work.

Types of Software Support Tools

This chapter describes six general categories of software support tools. Figure 5.1 gives examples of software products under each of the following categories:

- **Materials generators** — Help teachers and students produce instructional materials.
- **Data collection and analysis tools** — Help teachers collect and organize information that indicates student progress.
- **Graphics tools** — Allow manipulation of images to illustrate documents and web pages.
- **Planning and organizing tools** — Help teachers and students conceptualize, organize, and communicate their ideas.
- **Research and reference tools** — Let students look up information in electronic versions of encyclopedias, atlases, and dictionaries.
- **Content-area tools** — Support teaching and learning activities in various content areas.

Software Support Tools Covered in Other Chapters: Multimedia, Web, and Video Tools

The purpose of this chapter is to provide a comprehensive overview of software tools used in education, but two categories of tools are addressed in other parts of this textbook. Authoring software and other software tools (e.g., presentation software such as *PowerPoint* and video development

Figure 5.1 Overview of Software Tool Categories

Tool Category	Software Tools	Purposes and Benefits
Materials generators	• Desktop publishing software • Test generators and test item banks • Worksheet and puzzle generators • IEP generators • Graphic document makers • PDF and forms makers	Allow creation and use of documents, tests, exercises, IEPs, certificates, PDFs, and forms.
Data collection and analysis tools	• Electronic gradebooks • Statistical packages • Student management systems • Online and computer-based testing systems • Student response systems	Collect data from students; track progress and support decision making; analyze data from experiments and research.
Graphics tools	• Draw/paint programs • Image editing software • Charting/graphing software • Clip art, animation, sound, and font collections	Illustrate documents and web pages, and create visual data summaries.
Planning and organizing tools	• Outlining and concept mapping software • Lesson planning software • Scheduling and time management tools	Help organize ideas for writing; help organize, plan, and schedule activities.
Research and reference tools	• Electronic encyclopedias • Electronic atlases and mapping tools • Electronic dictionaries and thesauruses	Help students research assigned topics.
Tools to support specific content areas	• CAD systems • MIDI tools: music editors and sequencers • Reading tools • MBLs/CBLs • GPS and GIS systems	Support tasks specific to content areas such as technology education, music, reading, science, math, geography, and social studies.

tools such as *iMovie* and *FinalCut Pro*) associated with developing multimedia and hypermedia products are described in Chapter 6. Software tools used with distance learning and the Internet, either to develop materials for use on the Internet or to allow people to use the Internet, are covered in Chapter 7.

Recent Developments in Software Support Tools

Although these tools have been in existence for many years, they are constantly being updated with new features and capabilities. Most of the following recent developments have made these tools even more useful in the classroom.

- **PDA tools** — As with the basic software tools, many other tools are now available on personal digital assistants (PDAs), or handheld computers. This portable format increases accessibility and flexibility of use for both teachers and students. Since these basic software tools were transferred to handheld format, the handhelds themselves have become even more popular.

- **Web-connectivity features** — All of the basic tools, like many tools described in other chapters, now allow "live" web page links to be inserted in documents, and most allow documents to be saved in HTML formats. This makes it even easier to connect documents to web page resources that embellish or add to the document's content. For example, students may include links in a project report to some of the resources they consulted during their research.

- **Software suites** — Increasingly, software tools are being packaged as software suites in order to combine their capabilities and make them easier to use together. One of the most popular of the software tool suites is desktop publishing software, which is being packaged with graphic software tools that work well with it and allow faster, more full-featured design of print or web pages. For example, Adobe's *Creative Suite* combines high-end desktop publishing software (*Adobe InDesign*) with *Adobe Photoshop* (image editor), *Adobe Illustrator* (drawing software), *Adobe GoLive* (web page editor), and *Adobe Acrobat* (portable document software).

USING MATERIALS GENERATORS

Materials generators include desktop publishing software, test generators and rubric generators, worksheet and puzzle generators, IEP generators, graphic document makers, and PDF and forms makers. A summary of these with sample products and classroom uses is shown in Figure 5.2.

Desktop Publishing Software

Definitions: Desktop publishing versus desktop publishing software. It is perhaps ironic that one of the most useful and widely used of the technology tools is one that communicates information in a traditional medium: the printed page. By allowing teachers and students to design elaborate printed products, however, desktop publishing tools give them the important advantage of complete control over a potentially powerful form of communication. This control over the form and appearance of the printed page is the defining quality of **desktop publishing,** a term coined in 1984 by Paul Brainerd, founder of the Aldus Corporation (Norvelle, 1992), to mean using a combination of software, microcomputers, and printers to allow individuals to be their own publishers.

It is possible to do desktop publishing with word processing software. Both it and true desktop publishing software allow users to mix text and graphics on each page. However, desktop publishing software offers more control over the design and production of a document. Teachers will find that they can use any available word processing software package to create most of the desktop publishing products they want to do (e.g., classroom brochures and newsletters). The more advanced layout features offered by desktop publishing software (e.g., elaborate layering of text and graphics elements) are needed only if the teacher is teaching students how to design and lay out large, complex documents such as newspapers and books.

From a technical standpoint, the primary difference between word processing software and desktop publishing tools is that the latter are designed to create documents as separate pages that are then linked together; the user clicks on icons for each page and only one page or facing pages display. Word processing "flows" pages in a continuous stream through a document; the user scrolls down to view pages in the document. Because desktop publishing software allows pages to be viewed as separate units, it provides more flexibility over the placement and formats of both text and graphics on individual pages. Word processing is designed to flow text from page to page as it is typed in. Text boxes can be done in word processing software, but they are harder to manage.

Making the most of desktop publishing software: Skills and resources. Like other technology tools, desktop publishing is most effective if the user knows something about the activity before applying the tool. Designing effective print communications is an entire field of expertise in itself with its own degree programs. Graduates frequently are in high demand in business and industry. As Knupfer and McIsaac (1989) observe, many aspects of page design can influence reading speed and comprehension. They describe four different categories of variables that have been

Figure 5.2 An Overview of Materials Generator Software Tools

Software Tools	Sample Products	Description/Sample Classroom Uses
Desktop publishing software Courtesy of Adobe. http://www.adobe.com	• Adobe: *InDesign,* and *PageMaker* http://www.adobe.com/ • Microsoft *Publisher* http://www.microsoft.com/ • *Quark Express* http://www.quark.com/	Students create their own letterhead, brochures, flyers/posters, newsletters, newspapers, and books.
Test generators and rubric generators Courtesy of FSCreations, Inc. http://www.examview.com	• *ExamView* http://www.examview.com/ • *Test Generator* http://www.testshop.com • *Test Creator* http://www.centronsoftware.com • *Easy Test Maker* http://www.easytestmaker.com/ • *Rubric Builder* http://landmark-project.com/classweb/ tools/rubric_builder.php • *RubiStar* http://rubistar.4teachers.org • *Rubric Generator* http://teach-nology.com/web_tools/ rubrics/general/	Teachers create test item banks and generate various versions of tests from them; they can administer tests online.
Worksheet and puzzle generators http://www.discoveryschool.com	• *Puzzlemaker* http://puzzlemaker.school. discovery.com/ • *Worksheet Generator* http://school.discovery.com/ teachingtools/worksheetgenerator/ • Centron *Crossword Puzzle Maker* http://www.centronsoftware.com/ • Teach-nology *Crossword Puzzle Maker* http://www.teach-nology.com/ web_ tools/crossword/	Teachers produce exercises and games for student skill practice.
IEP generators SchoolMAX™ i-Plan http://www.schoolmax.net	• *I-Plan* http://www.schoolmax.net/specialed.asp • *IEP Online* http://www.xperts.com/productsiep.htm	Teachers create individualized education programs (IEPs) for special education students.

(continued)

Figure 5.2 (continued)

Software Tools	Sample Products	Description/Sample Classroom Uses

Graphic document makers
 	
© 2005 Riverdeep Interactive Learning Limited, and its Licensors. All rights reserved.
http://www.riverdeep.com
	• *PrintShop Deluxe*
	  http://www.riverdeep.com
	• Teach-nology *Certificate Maker*
	  http://www.teach-nology.com/web_ tools/certificates/
	• *Smart Draw*
	  http://www.smartdraw.com
		Teachers and students create awards, recognitions, flyers, cards, and other decorated documents.

PDF and forms makers
 	
Courtesy of Adobe.
http://www.adobe.com
	• *Adobe Acrobat*
	  http://www.adobe.com
	• *PDF Maker Pilot*
	  http://www.colorpilot.com/pdfmaker.html
	• *Form Artist*
	  http://www.quask.com
		Teachers and students create PDF files to send formatted documents, and documents and web pages with forms that can be filled in on-screen.

researched: graphic design, instructional text design, instructional graphics, and computer screen design. Although the last category focuses on reading from a computer screen, Knupfer and McIsaac note that some of its features apply to both electronic and print-based research, including factors such as text density and uppercase versus lowercase type.

However, even with this in mind, teachers and students need not be professional designers to create useful desktop publishing products, and their skills will improve with practice. According to Parker (1989) and Rose (1988), desktop publishing products have greater impact and communicate more clearly if they reflect some fairly simple design criteria. Beginners may want to use the suggestions in the *Top Ten Rules for Effective Desktop Publishing* feature shown on page 159.

Example classroom applications. Desktop publishing software can be used for many of the same classroom activities and products as word processing software. Desktop publishing is the tool of choice, however, to produce elaborate, graphic-oriented documents (e.g., flyers and posters, brochures, newsletters and magazines, and books and booklets), and teachers can structure some highly motivating classroom projects around these products. Hermann (1988), McCarthy (1988), Newman (1988), Willinsky and Bradley (1990), and Reissman (2000) have reported instructional benefits for desktop publishing that include increases in children's self-esteem when they publish their own work, heightened interest in writing and

motivation to write for audiences outside the classroom, and improved learning through small group collaboration. Here is a list of common classroom applications and ideas for implementing them:

• **Practice in grammar, spelling, and communication** — The activity of creating a flyer or brochure can become an opportunity to learn about designing attractive and interesting communications and to apply language usage skills.

• **Methods of reporting research findings** — Popular examples of desktop publishing projects to report on students' research include creating travel brochures that report on student exploration during field trips, descriptions of the local region, and creative descriptions of organizations or activities. Sometimes this activity represents the culmination of a large project such as a series of science experiments or a social studies research unit; sometimes it simply is a way for every student to contribute writing for a class project. All of these projects are highly motivational to students, and they attract "good press" for the teacher and the school.

• **Opportunities for creative work** — Even very young students are thrilled to produce and display their own personal books, which sometimes represent work produced over the course of a school year. Sometimes the books show creative works resulting from a competition; frequently, examples of students' best work are

1. **Use a limited number of typefaces (fonts)** — Unusual typefaces can help direct the eye toward text, but too many different fonts on a page can be distracting, and some fancy fonts are difficult to read.

2. **Use different fonts for title and text** — To aid the reader, use a **serif typeface** (a font with small curves or "hands and feet" that extend from the ends of the letters) for text in the main body of the document. Use a **sans serif typeface,** a font without extensions, for titles and headlines.

3. **Use appropriate sizes for type** — Make type large enough to assist the reader (e.g., younger readers usually need large point sizes), but not too large to dominate the page.

4. **Avoid overuse of type styles** — Breaking up text with too many style changes interferes with reading. Avoid excessive underlining, boldfacing, and italics.

5. **Match text and background colors** — Use white or yellow type on a black block to add drama. Avoid color combinations that can be difficult to read (e.g., orange on green or red on blue).

6. **Use visual cues** — Attract reader attention to important information on the page by using frames or boxes around text; bullets or arrows to designate important points; shading of the part of the page behind the important text; different text styles (e.g., boldface or italic type); and captions for pictures, diagrams, and headings.

7. **Use white space well** — There is a saying in advertising that "white space sells." Don't be afraid to leave areas in a document with nothing in them at all to help focus attention on areas that do contain information.

8. **Create and use graphics carefully** — Use pictures and designs to focus attention and convey information, but remember that too many elaborate pictures or graphic designs can be distracting

9. **Avoid common text format errors** — Common desktop design pitfalls include using irregularly shaped text blocks and angled type, which are difficult to read (Parker, 1989).

10. **Avoid common text break errors** — Use desktop publishing software features to control for widows and orphans (leftover single words and phrases at the tops or bottoms of pages) and excessive hyphenation (Parker, 1989).

---

collected for a particular topic or time period. Students can sell their publications as a fund-raising activity, but this kind of project reaps other benefits for students of all abilities. Teachers report that getting published increases students' pride in their work and makes them want to spend more time on it (Reissman, 2000; Scharf & Cramer, 2002).

The Technology Integration Example at the beginning of this chapter (*A Desktop-Published Literary Anthology*) is one example of a powerful desktop publishing project. See Technology Integration Idea 5.1 for another good example.

Test Generators and Rubric Generators

Software tools help teachers with what many consider one of the most onerous and time-consuming instructional tasks: producing tests and other assessments. Test generators and rubric generators have become common software tools. Figure 5.2 lists where to locate many of these tools.

Test generators. Teachers use **test generators** to create and enter questions, and then have the program prepare the test. The teacher either may print the required number of copies on the printer or print only one copy and make the required copies on a copy machine. The features of test generators vary, but the following capabilities are common and offer several advantages, even over word processing programs:

- **Test creation and revision procedures** — Software produces tests in a standard layout; the teacher need not worry about arranging the spacing and format of the page. The software prompts teachers to create tests item by item in formats such as multiple choice, fill in the blank, true/false, matching, and—less often—short answer and essay. Changes, deletions, and updates to questions are also easy to accomplish, again without concern for page format.

- **Random generation of questions** — Test items are selected randomly from an item pool to create different versions. This is especially helpful when a teacher wants to prevent "wandering eye syndrome" as students take a test.

- **Selection of questions based on criteria** — Programs usually allow teachers to specify criteria for generating a test. For example, items can be requested in a specific content area, matched to certain objectives, or set up in a certain format such as short-answer items only.

- **Answer keys** — Most programs automatically provide an answer key at the time the test is generated. This is helpful with grading, especially if different versions of the test are used.

- **Test item banks** — Many test generators allow use of existing question pools, or **test item banks,** and some offer these banks for purchase in various content areas. Some programs also import question banks prepared on word processors.

Figure 5.3 shows an example test item created by test generator software. You can review a list of test generation

Figure 5.3 Sample Test Generator Item

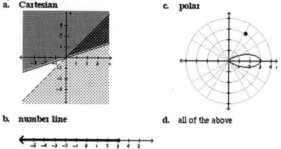

Source: Examples courtesy of FSCreations, Inc.

packages at http://www.educational-software-directory. net/teacher's/test-making.html.

Most test generators offer only on-paper versions of tests, but some allow students to take a test on-screen after it is prepared. These are discussed later in this chapter under Data Collection and Analysis Tools, since on-screen testing systems also collect and summarize data as they grade tests.

Online rubric generators. The popularity of rubrics has grown to such an extent that several Internet sites offer free rubric generators. The teacher follows a set of prompts, and the system creates a rubric that can be printed out or referred to online. See a list of rubric generation sites in Figure 5.2, and review an example rubric and tutorial on how to use a rubric generator in the end-of-chapter exercises for Chapter 3.

Worksheet and Puzzle Generators

Teachers also use software to produce worksheets, which are very similar in many ways to test generators. **Worksheet generators** help teachers produce exercises for practice rather than tests. Like the test generator, the worksheet generator software prompts the teacher to enter questions of various kinds, but it usually offers no options for completing exercises on-screen or grading them. In many cases, test generator software and worksheet generator software are similar enough to be used interchangeably and some packages are intended for both purposes. **Puzzle generators** automatically format and create crosswords, word search puzzles, and similar game-like activities. The teacher enters the content, and the software formats the puzzle. Refer to Figure 5.2 for popular worksheet and puzzle generation sites. Common uses of worksheet and puzzle generators include:

- Practice for lower level skills such as math facts,
- Cloze exercises (fill-in-the-blank comprehension checks), and
- Exercises to review words and definitions.

Individualized Education Program (IEP) Generators

Education is placing increasing emphasis on school and teacher accountability. With this emphasis comes an increase in paperwork on student progress. Teachers of students with special needs seem to have the most paperwork requirements of all. Federal legislation such as PL 94-142 and the Americans with Disabilities Act requires that schools prepare an individualized educational program, or IEP, for each special student. These IEPs serve as blueprints for each special student's instructional activities, and teachers must provide documentation that such a plan is on file and that it governs classroom activities. **IEP generator** software assists teachers in preparing IEPs (Lewis, 1993). Like test and worksheet generators, IEP generators provide on-screen prompts that remind users of the required components in the plan. When a teacher finishes entering all the necessary information, the program prints out the IEP in a standard format. Some IEP generation programs also accept data updates on each student's progress, thus helping teachers with required record keeping as well as IEP preparation.

MAKING THE CASE FOR TECHNOLOGY INTEGRATION

Discuss these issues online with other students by selecting the *Making the Case* module for Chapter 5 of the Companion Website (http://www.prenhall.com/roblyer) or choose the *Message Board* module.

1. Some educators object to the use of tools such as test generators and worksheet generators, saying that they encourage teachers to use technology to maintain current methods, rather than using technology in more innovative ways. What case can you make for keeping software tools like these in classrooms?

2. As mentioned in this chapter, the use of online and on-computer testing systems is becoming a popular, albeit controversial, practice (see http://www.fairtest.org/facts/computer.htm). What are the main points raised by critics of these systems? How would you address them?

3. Student information systems have become increasingly popular in recent years to help track student, class, and school progress and to help teachers with decision making. However, they have also proven to be a useful tool for communicating with parents. In what ways do they serve this purpose?

Graphic Document Makers

Graphic document makers are software tools that simplify the activity of making highly graphic materials such as awards certificates and greeting cards. They offer sets of clip art and predesigned templates to which teachers and students can add their own content. For example, teachers have found certificates to be a useful kind of recognition. Certificates congratulate students for accomplishments, and the students can take them home and share them with parents and friends. Most certificate makers include templates for various kinds of achievements. The teacher selects one appropriate for the kind of recognition desired (completing an activity or first-place winner) and enters the personal information for each student. Also, students frequently find it motivating to use these packages to design their own certificates, cards, and flyers. The most popular of these document makers is *Printshop* (Riverdeep). This and similar software tools are listed in Figure 5.2.

Figure 5.4 Overview of Data Collection and Analysis Tools

Software Tools	Sample Products	Description/Sample Classroom Uses
Electronic gradebooks Courtesy of Cal Ed Software http://www.classactiongradebook.com	• *Class Action Gradebook* http://www.classactiongradebook.com • *GradeQuick* http://www.jacksoncorp.com/ • *Gradekeeper* http://www.gradekeeper.com/ • *Easy Grade Pro* http://easygradepro.com/	Teachers keep track of and calculate student grades.
Statistical packages Courtesy of SPSS Inc. http://www.spss.com	• SPSS Inc. http://www.spss.com/ • *XLStat* http://www.xlstat.com • *FlexPro* http://www.flexpro-usa.com/ • NCSS Stat System http://www.ncss.com/ • Stata Statistical Software http://www.stata.com/	Teachers and students use statistical procedures to analyze data from experiments and research projects.
Student information systems http://www.apple.com	• *PowerSchool* http://www.apple.com/education/powerschool/ • *Pinnacle* http://www.excelsiorsoftware.com • *SASIxp* and *InteGrade*® Pro http://www.pearsondigital.com/ • *Pro/Star* http://www.prostarbyhightouchinc.com/ • *eSIS* http://www.aalsolutions.com	Teachers, administrators, and parents keep track of student and class progress on required curriculum objectives; teachers give online tests and use data to support decision making.
Computer-based testing systems SimpleQuiz and the SimpleQuiz logo © 2006 Robert Peake. http://simplequiz.peakepro.com/	• *Simple Quiz Online Testing System* http://simplequiz.peakepro.com/ • *LaserGrade* http://www.lasergrade.com/ • *Computer Test* http://www.softcities.com/ • *ExamBuilder* http://www.exambuilder.com/	Teachers have students take tests on a computer screen; software grades tests and compiles data.
Student response systems Reproduced with permission of H-ITT, LLC. http://www.h-itt.com/	• *Hyper Interactive Teaching Technology* http://www.h-itt.com • *Classroom Performance System* http://www.einstruction.com • *Qwizdom Interactive Learning System* http://www.qwizdom.com • Turning Point http://turningtechnologies.com	All students answer a question at the same time, and the system summarizes/displays results immediately; teachers use systems to engage students and check comprehension.

PDF and Forms Makers

Acrobat **Portable Document Format (PDF) file** software was created by the Adobe company to permit viewing and sending of documents as images. With free *Acrobat Reader* software, documents can be viewed with all of the formatting and design elements (e.g., margins, graphics) of the original document without requiring the viewer to have access to the desktop publishing or word processing software used to create the original. PDF software is often used in conjunction with **forms makers** such as *PDF Pilot,* a software tool that creates documents and web pages with forms that can be filled in on-screen. Teachers find forms makers useful because they make it easier for them to create forms to collect information from students, parents, or faculty or to implement surveys as part of research projects. Formatting even the simplest form can be time consuming on a word processor. These software tools structure the process and make the design simple to accomplish. As teachers create these forms, they can store them as templates for later use, perhaps with revisions. There are many other non-PDF forms maker tools, but *PDF Pilot* is so simple to use and meshes so well with the already-popular *Acrobat* software that it is quickly becoming an indispensable forms software tool for teachers and others.

USING DATA COLLECTION AND ANALYSIS TOOLS

Data collection and analysis tools include electronic gradebooks, statistical packages, student information systems, online and computer-based testing systems, and student response systems. A summary of these with sample products and classroom uses is shown in Figure 5.4.

Electronic Gradebooks

Although some teachers prefer to keep their grades on flexible spreadsheet software, many prefer to use special software designed exclusively for this purpose. An **electronic gradebook** (electronic grade-keeping) program allows a teacher to enter student names, test/assignment names, data from tests, and weighting information for specific test scores. The program then analyzes the data and prints reports based on this information. Some gradebooks even offer limited-purpose word processing capabilities to enter notes about tests. The software automatically generates averages and weighted averages for each student and averages across all students on a given test. Gradebooks require less teacher setup time than spreadsheets, but also allow less flexibility on format options. See a sample gradebook screen in Figure 5.5, and review the list of gradebook packages at: http://www.educational-software-directory.net/teacher's/gradebook.html.

Figure 5.5 **Sample Screens from the *Class Action Gradebook* Package**

Source: Courtesy of Cal Ed Software.

Statistical Packages

As Gay (1993) once joked, many teachers believe that the field of statistics should be renamed sadistics. Yet teachers may find several uses for statistical analyses. If they choose to do action research in their classrooms, as this text encourages, teachers must collect and analyze data on student performance. Depending on the type of research, several typical analyses yield helpful information, including descriptive statistics (e.g., means and standard deviations) and inferential statistics (e.g., *t*-tests and analyses of variance). **Statistical software packages** can also help with qualitative data collection and analysis and analysis of student performance on tests. Finally, teachers may have to teach beginning statistics to their own students in, for example, a business education course.

Statistical software packages perform the calculations involved in any of these kinds of procedures. Naturally, a teacher must have considerable knowledge of the proper applications of various statistical procedures; the software merely handles the arithmetic. But this alone can save considerable time. Popular statistical software tools are listed in Figure 5.4.

Student Information Systems

Student information systems (SIS) are networked software systems that help educators keep track of student,

Figure 5.6 Sample Screen Created with *PowerSchool* Student Management System

Source: Courtesy of Apple Computer, Inc.

class, and school data (e.g., attendance, test scores) to maintain records and support decision making. Schools purchase various operations they want the system to keep track of. Depending on what they choose, the system may do any or all of the following:

- Track and report on attendance.
- Maintain records on student demographic data (e.g., birth date, address).
- Schedule students.
- Track and report on test scores and achievement by objective.
- Allow parents to have online access to student grades and attendance information.
- Notify parents about problems with grades or attendance.

In the 1970s, these systems were known by the general term **computer-managed instruction (CMI) systems.** At that time, there was a burgeoning interest in mastery learning in which teachers specified a sequence of objectives for students to learn and prescribed instruction to help the students master each objective. The teacher had to keep track of each student's performance on each objective—a mammoth record-keeping task. CMI systems, such as the Teaching Information Processing System (TIPS) and the Program for Learning in Accordance with Needs (PLAN), ran on large, mainframe computers and were designed to support teachers in these efforts.

Today's educators also must be concerned about monitoring student progress, but the concern now is in com-

plying with accountability requirements such as those specified by the No Child Left Behind Act. Also, these systems can make it easier for teachers to keep parents notified about student progress. Systems such as Apple's *PowerSchool* and Excelsior Software's *Pinnacle Plus* system allow online access to students' grade reports. Figure 5.6 shows sample SIS screens.

Some SIS are components of integrated learning systems (ILSs). Integration with ILSs allows instruction to be tailored to each student's needs and collects data as students go through the instruction. Reports show the teacher what students have accomplished and point out areas where they may still need assistance and off-computer work.

Computer-Based Testing Systems

Also known as computer-assisted testing, computer-based testing systems allow students to take tests onscreen or put test answers on optically scanned "bubble sheets" and provide reports on performance data afterward. Some current testing systems overlap with the function of true test generators (see earlier description under Materials Generators), which are designed to produce tests from data banks. Some of the major standardized tests such as the SAT and GRE are now given on computerized testing systems and offer benefits such as immediate knowledge of results. The capabilities of computerized testing systems let educators go beyond the limits of multiple-choice tests and make possible alternative assessments. These systems also simplify test scheduling, because everyone need not take tests at the same time.

With testing systems, tests can also be shorter, since the software assesses each person's ability level with fewer questions. The software continuously analyzes perform-

Figure 5.7 Student Response Systems Allow All Students to Respond at the Same Time

Source: Reproduced with permission of H-ITT, LLC.

ance and presents more or less difficult questions based on the student's performance, a capability known as **computer adaptive testing (CAT)** (Strommen, 1994). CAT is being used more and more frequently for testing in professional courses like those in nursing education. However, computer-based testing is often controversial. Some people feel that computer-based testing is not equivalent to other kinds of testing and that it actually discriminates against some students. (See comparisons of paper-and-pencil versus computer-based testing at http://www.fairtest.org/.)

Student Response Systems

Unique among data collection resources, **student response systems** (also called *personal response systems* or *classroom response systems*) are a combination of handheld hardware and software that permit each student in the classroom to answer a question simultaneously (see Figure 5.7) and permit the teacher to see and display a summary of results immediately. Johnson and McLeod (2004–2005) describe 11 such systems, as well as a variety of instructional uses for them. These uses range from vocabulary games to comprehension checks during a classroom presentation and are an easy way to engage all students at once.

USING GRAPHICS TOOLS

Graphics tools include draw/paint programs; image editing tools; charting/graphing tools; and clip art, photo, animation, sound, video, and font collections. A summary of these with sample products and classroom uses is shown in Figure 5.8.

Draw/Paint Programs

Drawing and painting software tools help teachers and students create their own graphics to insert in documents or web pages. In simpler draw/paint programs such as *Kid Pix,* users select the graphics components (e.g., colors, shapes, lines) from menus and toolbars, making the programs so easy to use that anyone can sit down and create an image in a matter of minutes. Students may use these programs to illustrate their work or help convey information in reports. One example product from *Kid Pix* software is shown in Figure 5.9 (p. 167), and Technology Integration Idea 5.2 (p. 167) illustrates how draw/paint programs could be useful in a science lesson. Catchings and MacGregor (1998) are among those who believe that draw/paint programs allow many students to develop their visual–verbal literacy and creativity. O'Bannon, Krolak, Harkelroad, and Dick (1999) show how students can practice this creativity by designing banners and images for school web pages. Other draw/paint programs, such as *Adobe Illustrator* and *Macromedia Freehand,* allow more complex drawings and require more knowledge of art and graphic techniques. These are usually used in high school level courses in communications and technology education.

Image Editing Tools

To modify photographic images, **image editing programs** are the technology software tool of choice. These tools usually are used to enhance and format photos that are then imported into desktop publishing systems or web page products. Image editing programs are known for their

Figure 5.8 Overview of Graphics Tools

Software Tools	Sample Products	Description/Sample Classroom Uses

Draw/paint programs
 	
© 2005 Riverdeep Interactive Learning Limited, and its Licensors. All rights reserved.
http://www.riverdeep.com
	• *Adobe Illustrator*
	  http://www.adobe.com
	• *Macromedia Freehand*
	  http://www.macromedia.com
	• *Kid Pix*
	  http://www.riverdeep.com
		Students create their own drawings and illustrations to show on-screen or to print.

Image editing tools
 	
Courtesy of Adobe.
http://www.adobe.com
	• *Adobe Photoshop*
	  http://www.adobe.com
	• *Picture It!* and *Digital Image*
	  http://www.microsoft.com
		Teachers and students create, modify, and combine images (e.g., clip art, photos, drawings) to illustrate documents, web pages.

Charting/graphing tools
 	
Courtesy of Tom Snyder Productions.
http://www.tomsnyder.com
	• Tom Snyder's *Graph Master* and *The Graph Club 2.0*
	  http://www.teachtsp.com/
	• *Advanced Grapher*
	  http://www.serpik.com/
	• *NetCharts Reporting Suite*
	  http://www.visualmining.com
		Students create charts and graphs to illustrate and study data summaries.

Clip art, animation, sound, video, and font collections
 	
Courtesy of Bonnell Technology Pty Ltd, Australia.
http://www.flamingtext.com
	• *Graphics for Teachers*
	  http://www.teachingheart.net/graphicl.html
	• Microsoft's *Clip Art and Media Collection*
	  http://office.microsoft.com/clipart
	• *FlamingText*
	  http://www.flamingtext.com/
	• *Animation Factory*
	  http://www.teachingheart.net/graphicl.html
	• SmartDraw's *Clip Art Collection*
	  http://www.smartdraw.com/resources/collections/clipart/
		Teachers and students insert these into documents and media they create.

sophistication and wide-ranging capabilities. Many of these packages, such as *Adobe Photoshop,* require considerable time to learn. Technology Integration Idea 5.3 (p. 168) shows how these programs could be used in a science lesson.

Charting/Graphing Tools

Charting/graphing tools automatically draw and print desired charts or graphs from data entered by users. The skills involved in reading, interpreting, and producing graphs and charts are useful both to students in school and adults in the workplace. However, people with limited artistic ability usually find it difficult to draw charts and graphics freehand. Fortunately, charting and graphing software takes the mechanical drudgery out of producing these useful "data pictures." If students do not have to labor over rulers and pencils as they try to plot coordinates and set points, they can concentrate on the more important aspects of the graphics: the meaning of the data and what they represent. This kind of

Figure 5.9 Sample *Kid Pix* Screens

TECHNOLOGY INTEGRATION IDEA 5.2

USING DRAW/PAINT GRAPHICS TOOLS TO ILLUSTRATE SCIENCE CONCEPTS

Title: Weaving Art Throughout the Curriculum

Content Area/Topic: Science–nature

Grade Level: 4

NETS for Students: Standards 1, 3, 4, 6

Description: Students use the *Kid Pix* drawing program to create compositions that demonstrate patterns and structures in nature.

Instruction: The teacher demonstrates some example products from artists who use geometric patterns as the basis of a collection of paintings and drawings. Then she asks the students to think about collections of their own and bring in anything they have collected that has to do with nature (e.g., rock, seashells). Students design their own nature sculptures based on these collections. They use digital cameras to take pictures of their works, then use *Kid Pix* to add special effects to the images to create a final product to share with the class.

Assessment: A rubric is used to assess the creativity and concepts demonstrated by the final product.

Source: Lach, C., Little, E., & Nazzaro, D. (2003). From all sides now: Weaving technology and multiple intelligences into science and art. *Learning and Leading with Technology, 30*(6), 32–35, 59.

activity supports students in their efforts at visualizing mathematical concepts and engaging in inquiry tasks.

Graphing activities in science, social studies, and geography also profit from applications of these kinds of software tools. Moersch (1995) lists and gives example instructional applications for nine kinds of software produced graphs: bar, pie, stacked bar, *X/Y,* scatter, box, stem and leaf, best fit, and normal curve. Figure 5.10 shows how graphing software supports learning in various con-

tent areas. Also, see Technology Integration Idea 5.4 (p. 169) for an example lesson with graphing software.

Clip Art, Photo, Animation, Sound, Video, and Font Collections

Clip art packages were originally collections of still pictures drawn by artists and graphics designers and placed in a book or on a disk for use by others. Nowadays, the clip art idea has expanded to include drawings, cartoons, photos, and

TECHNOLOGY INTEGRATION IDEA 5.3

USING IMAGE EDITING SOFTWARE

Title: Bringing the Planets Closer to Home

Content Area/Topic: Math (measurement) and astronomy

Grade Level: 5–12

NETS for Students: Standards 1, 3, 4, 5, 6

Description: This activity is designed to make the connection between science and mathematics more hands-on and meaningful for students by having them analyze real data in the form of images.

Instruction: Students begin by downloading NASA photos from the Internet (e.g., images of the solar system at http://spaceart.com/solar) and converting them to an uncompressed TIF format using an image editing program such as *Adobe PhotoShop*. Their task is to learn how to measure the images. First, they use the software to calibrate the images (determine the scale) by comparing the size of the image to a known measurement such as the diameter of Mars. Then they multiply the measured distance by the scale to determine the size of other features they have downloaded. In this way, the students can measure and compare features that change, such as the Martian and Earth polar ice caps. These measurements can be the basis of many projects to study space phenomena.

Assessment: Use a checklist to assess correct completion of required tasks.

Source: Slater, T., & Beaudrie, B. (2000). Far out measurements: Bringing the planets closer to home using image-processing techniques. *Learning and Leading with Technology, 27*(5), 36–41.

Figure 5.10 **Sample** *Graph Club 2.0* **Screens**

Students can see the same data represented differently side by side.

Source: Graph Club 2.0: Tom Snyder Productions.

Standards-aligned activities are an interactive and fun way for students to master graphing skills.

animations. When teachers prepare presentations with desktop publishing or presentation tools, they used these instead of drawing their own original images or taking their own photos. Most word processing, desktop publishing, image editing, and draw/paint programs can import these items from a disk or website. Font collections are also available to expand the font options that come with a computer or software.

These collections offer invaluable resources to help both teachers and students illustrate and decorate their written products. Teachers find that such pictures help make flyers, books, and even letters and notices look more polished and professional. Some teachers feel that students are more motivated to write their own stories and reports when they can also illustrate them.

TECHNOLOGY INTEGRATION IDEA 5.4

ILLUSTRATING MATH CONCEPTS WITH CHARTING/GRAPHING TOOLS

Title: A Project with Teeth

Content Area/Topic: Math concepts—data collection and analysis

Grade Level: K–3

NETS for Students: Standards 1, 3, 4, 5, 6

Description: Teachers use email to connect their K–3 students with "keypals" around the world in order to exchange information on how many teeth children lose during the year. This activity is used as a springboard for learning geography (locations of the keypals), literature and culture (tooth fairy traditions and other stories from their regions), art (creating pictures or murals illustrating tooth fairy traditions), creative writing (email messages to participants, poems and rhymes on teeth), and mathematics (graphing data on lost teeth).

Instruction: After they have at least 3 months of data on lost teeth, students learn how to use a graphing program to compile the data and prepare line or bar graphs. Each student or small group may choose a part of the data to graph; then they compose a letter explaining the results to their keypals. As a cumulative or final whole-class activity, students may use a calculator to add up all the teeth data for each month from all the schools and then enter all the data into one common spreadsheet. Results may be shared among the participants through email.

Assessment: Use a rubric to assess small-group work and demonstration of graphing concept knowledge.

Source: Boehm, D. (1997). I lost my tooth! *Learning and Leading with Technology, 24*(7), 17–19.

For teachers and students who want to develop their own websites or multimedia presentations, collections of sound effects and video clips (e.g., MPEG files) are also becoming common. A system may need special hardware such as sound cards or synthesizers, as well as software such as *Quicktime,* in order to incorporate these elements.

USING PLANNING AND ORGANIZING TOOLS

Planning and organizing tools include outlining and concept mapping software, lesson planning software, and scheduling/time management tools. A summary of these with sample products and classroom uses is shown in Figure 5.11.

Outlining Tools and Concept Mapping Software

Several kinds of technology tools are available to help students learn writing skills or to assist accomplished writers in setting their thoughts in order prior to writing. **Outlining tools** are designed to prompt writers as they develop outlines to structure documents they plan to write. For example, the software may automatically indent and/or supply the appropriate number or letter for each line in the outline. Outliners are offered either within word processing packages or as separate software packages for use before word processing.

Other writing aids include software designed to get students started on writing reports or stories: a story starter. This kind of program provides a first line and invites students to supply subsequent lines. Other tools give students topic ideas and supply information about each topic they can use in a writing assignment. Sometimes a software package combines outlining tools and other writing aids.

Concept mapping software tools are designed to help people think through and explore ideas or topics by developing concept maps. *Inspiration* is one of the most popular of these tools (see Figure 5.12), and *Kidspiration* is a version of this software designed for younger users. Concept maps are visual outlines of ideas that can offer useful alternatives to the strictly verbal representations provided by content outlines. Dabbagh (2001), Anderson-Inman and Zeitz (1993), and Kahn (1997b) discuss the learning theory behind using these powerful instructional tools and give good examples of classroom applications. (See Technology Integration Idea 5.5.) Also, see "Fifty Uses for *Inspiration*

Figure 5.11 Overview of Planning and Organizing Tools

Software Tools	Sample Products	Description/Sample Classroom Uses
Outlining and concept mapping software **inspiration** Inspiration® is a registered trademark of Inspiration Software®, Inc. Used with permission. http://www.inspiration.com	• *Inspiration* http://www.inspiration.com • *VisiMap* http://www.projectkickstart.com • *StoryWeaver* http://www.storymind.com/	Help students organize their ideas in outline or concept map form to prepare for writing; help create story structures.
Lesson planners **Lesson Plans 4 Teachers** Courtesy of The Educator's Network Inc. http://www.lessonplans4 teachers.com	• *Lesson Planner for Windows* http://www.sites4teachers.com • Centron's *Lesson Power* http://www.centronsoftware.com/lesson%20power.html • *Master Planit* http://www.codework.com	Help teachers prepare and document lesson plans.
Scheduling and time management tools Courtesy of Hands High Software, Inc. http://www.handshigh.com	• *ThoughtManager* for Teachers http://www.handshigh.com • *Reel Logix* http://www.thecalendarplanner.com/	Help teachers organize their time and plan activities.

Figure 5.12 Sample *Inspiration* Screen

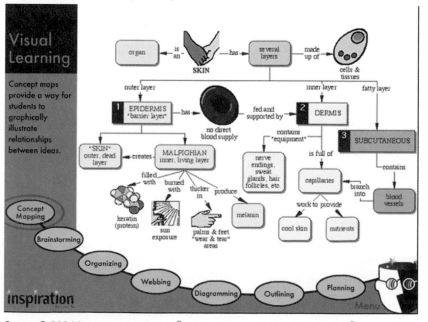

Source: © 2004 Inspiration Software®, Inc. Diagram created in *Inspiration*® by Inspiration Software®, Inc. Used with permission.

TECHNOLOGY INTEGRATION IDEA 5.5

SUPPORTING WRITING PROCESSES WITH CONCEPT MAPPING

Title: Authors in Residence and Online Mentors

Content Area/Topic: Writing process skills

Grade Level: Elementary

NETS for Students: Standards 1, 3, 4

Description: Students use word processing to write drafts of their stories and email them to their online writing mentor.

Instruction: Students first use *Kidspiration* software to create a graphic organizer for their written work. After they complete a word-processed first draft, they email the files to their mentors and receive comments, suggestions for improvements, and encouragement. For example, one mentor suggested that one young writer expand her story by playing a "what if" game. She asked what the characters in the story might do in response to the events she had already written. Then she could describe these responses in order to embellish her story. Students and mentors bond through this process, and students are more motivated to revise their writing. Word processing software makes revisions easier and faster, which further encourages students to improve their work.

Assessment: Use rubrics to assess final drafts.

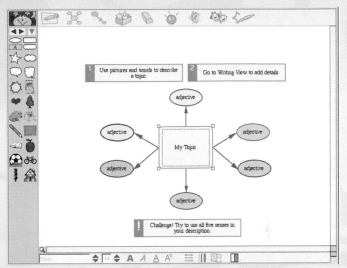

Source: © 2004 Inspiration Software®, Inc. Diagram created in *Kidspiration®* by Inspiration Software® Inc. Used with permission. (http://www.inspiration.com)

Source: Hagins, C., Auston, J., Timmons, T., Weeg, P. (2004). Authors "in residence" make writing fun: Online mentors help fourth graders compose original stories. *Learning and Leading with Technology, 31*(6), 36–39.

---

and *Kidspiration*" at http://www.uwstout.edu/soe/profdev/conceptmap/50uses.html.

Lesson Planning Software

Most teachers do not rely heavily on written lesson plans to guide their teaching activities. However, many occasions demand some form of documentation to show what teachers are teaching and how they are teaching it. Tools that help teachers develop and document their descriptions of lessons are sometimes called *lesson makers* or *lesson planners*. Most of these programs simply provide on-screen prompts for specific lesson components such as objectives, materials, and activity descriptions. They also print out lessons in standard formats, similar to the way test generators format printouts of tests. Review http://www.lessonplans4teachers.com for a list of lesson planning software, and see Figure 5.13 for a sample screen from *Lesson Planner for Windows*.

Figure 5.13 **Sample Screen from *Lesson Planner for Windows***

Source: Courtesy of The Educator's Network.

Figure 5.14   Overview of Research and Reference Tools

Software Tools	Sample Products	Description/Sample Classroom Uses
Electronic encyclopedias Courtesy of High Beam Research, LLC. http://www.encyclopedia.com	• *Encarta* http://encarta.msn.com • *Encyclopedia.com* http://www.encyclopedia.com/ • *Britannica* http://www.britannica.com/ • *Grolier Online* http://auth.grolier.com	Help students research any topics.
Electronic atlases and mapping tools Image provided by www.WorldAtlas.com. http://www.graphicmaps.com	• WorldAtlas.com http://www.graphicmaps.com • U.S. Atlas http://www.nationalatlas.gov/ • *Political World Atlas* http://www.siteatlas.com/Atlas/PolAtlas/polatlas.htm • *Atlas of the Universe* http://www.anzwers.org/free/universe	Help students learn local, national, world, and extraterrestrial geography.
Electronic dictionaries and thesauruses Courtesy of Jupiter Media. http://www.webopedia.com	• Technology words: *Webopedia* http://www.webopedia.com/ • Any words: *Merriam-Webster* http://www.m-w.com/dictionary.htm • Any words: *Dictionary.com* http://dictionary.reference.com • Thesaurus: *Thesaurus.com* http://thesaurus.reference.com/	Give definitions and synonyms.

Scheduling and Time Management Tools

Several kinds of tools have been designed to help teachers organize their time and plan their activities. Schedule makers help formulate plans for daily, weekly, or monthly sequences of appointments and events. Calendar makers are similar planning tools that actually print graphic calendars of chosen months or years with the planned events printed under each day. Other time management tools are available to help remind users of events and responsibilities. The teacher enters activities and the dates on which they will occur. Then, when he or she turns on the computer each day, the software displays on the screen a list of things to do. Some integrated packages combine all of these tools. Time management tools are an especially popular application on handheld computers, since people can update their calendars wherever they are.

USING RESEARCH AND REFERENCE TOOLS

Research and reference tools include electronic versions of the following tools: encyclopedias, atlases and mapping tools, and dictionaries and thesauruses. A summary of these with sample products and classroom uses is shown in Figure 5.14.

Electronic Encyclopedias

For many years, American families kept sets of encyclopedias to support their children's education. Young people used these books for research on school projects, and parents used them to take advantage of "teachable moments" when their children required more than quick answers. Now most major encyclopedias come on CD-ROM or websites with some kind of database structure. (See an ex-

Figure 5.15   Sample Screen from WorldandISchool.com Encyclopedia

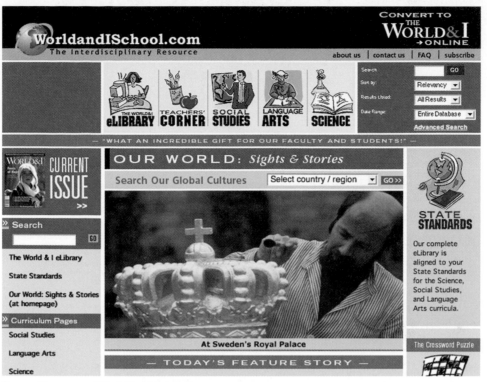

Source: Courtesy of The World & I Online.

ample online encyclopedia in Figure 5.15.) These electronic encyclopedias have several advantages over books. Users can search to locate one specific item or all references on a given topic. They usually offer multimedia formats that include sound and/or film clips as well as hypertext links to related information on any topic. Because electronic encyclopedias are considered a form of multimedia, Chapter 6 presents more information on and examples of these applications.

Electronic Atlases and Mapping Tools

Like encyclopedias, atlases are popular educational reference tools for families as well as schools. They summarize geographic and demographic information ranging from population statistics to national products. CD-ROM versions of these atlases are especially helpful since they are so interactive. Students can see information on a specific country or city or gather information on all countries or cities that meet certain criteria. Some atlases even play national songs on request! See a sample online atlas in Figure 5.16. Mapping sites such as *MapQuest* also help teach geographic concepts by showing distance between points.

Electronic Dictionaries (Word Atlases)

Sometimes called **word atlases,** electronic dictionaries and thesauruses give pronunciations, definitions, and example uses for each word entry. They also offer many search and multimedia features similar to those of encyclopedias and atlases. Many electronic dictionaries can play an audio clip of the pronunciation of any desired word, a capability of special help to young users and others who cannot read diacritical marks.

USING TOOLS TO SUPPORT SPECIFIC CONTENT AREAS

Content-area tools include CAD systems; music tools such as music editors, sequencers, and MIDI tools; reading tools; microcomputer-based labs, graphing calculators, and calculator-based labs; and Geographic Information Systems and the Global Positioning System. A summary of these with sample products and classroom uses is shown in Figure 5.17.

CAD and 3-D Modeling/Animation Systems

A **computer-assisted design (CAD)** system is a special kind of graphics production tool that allows users to prepare sophisticated, precise drawings of objects such as houses and

Figure 5.16 Sample Screen from the WorldAtlas.com Site

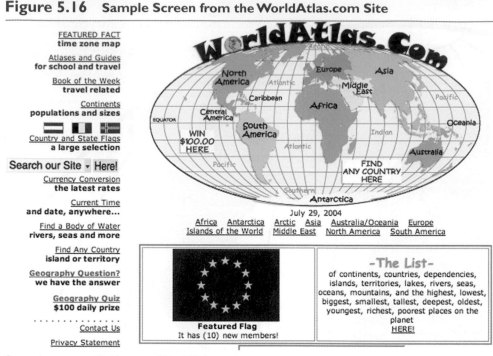

Source: Image provided by www.WorldAtlas.com.

cars. Like presentation tools, CAD systems began to appear in classrooms after their introduction in business and industry. This kind of software is usually employed in vocational-technical classrooms to teach architecture and engineering skills. However, some teachers use CAD software to teach drawing concepts in art and related topics. (See Figure 5.18 for a sample of CAD software.) More advanced graphics students may use 3-D modeling and animation software systems to do fancy visual effects such as **morphing.** This term is short for *metamorphosing* and refers to an animation technique in which one image gradually turns into another.

Music Editors, Sequencers, and MIDI Tools

Music editor software provides blank musical bars on which the user enters the musical key, time, and individual notes that constitute a piece of sheet music. This software is designed to help people develop musical compositions on-screen, usually in conjunction with hardware such as a **Musical Instrument Digital Interface (MIDI) device,** a standard adopted by the electronic music industry for controlling devices that play music, for example, **music synthesizers.** Music editors allow a user to either hear the music after it is written or create music on the keyboard and automatically produce a written score.

Music sequencers are software packages that support the creation of music scores with several parts. Steinhaus (1986–1987) explained that music editors offer powerful assistance in the processes of precomposing, composing, revising, and even performing. Forest (1993) offers examples of these activities in a school setting as well as a list of

good music-related software and media. Ohler's (1998) thorough review of MIDI technology and its current applications for teaching music reminds us that technology tools can help students "flex the musical muscle that [Howard] Gardner reminds us has always been there" (p. 10). (See Chapter 13, Technology in Music and Art Instruction, for more classroom uses of these tools.)

Reading Tools

Both reading teachers and teachers of other topics occasionally need to determine the approximate reading level of specific documents. A teacher may want to select a story or book for use in a lesson or to confirm that works are correctly labeled as appropriate for certain grade levels. Several methods are available for calculating the reading level of a written work; all of them are time consuming and tedious to do by hand. Readability analysis software automates calculations of word count, average word length, number of sentences, or other measures of reading difficulty.

Another software tool related to reading instruction, Cloze software, provides passages with words missing in a given pattern, for example, every fifth word or every tenth word. Students read the sentences and try to fill in the words. Cloze passages have been found to be good measures of reading comprehension. Some teachers also like to use them as exercises to improve reading comprehension.

Many books for children as well as adults are available in interactive CD-ROM versions called *interactive storybooks* or *electronic books* (Truett, 1993). Some of these allow children to hear narrations in English or Spanish.

Figure 5.17 **Overview of Content-Area Specific Tools**

Software Tools	Sample Products	Description/Sample Classroom Uses
CAD systems AutoCAD Autodesk and AutoCAD are registered trademarks of Autodesk, Inc. Certain images used with permission of Autodesk, Inc. © 2004. All rights reserved. http://usa.autodesk.com	• *AutoCAD* http://usa.autodesk.com • *Alibre Design* http://www.alibre.com	Students create visual models of houses and other structures as they study design concepts.
Music editors, sequencers, and MIDI tools GarageBand http://www.apple.com	• Korg MIDI products http://www.korg.com/ • Yamaha MIDI products http://www.nationalatlas.gov/ • *Apple GarageBand* http://www.apple.com • *Emagic's MicroLogic Sequencer* http://www.emagic.de • *MIDI Maestro* http://www.tomdownload.com	Students create and revise their own musical pieces.
Reading tools Accelerated Reader Courtesy of Renaissance Learning Inc. http://www.renlearn.com/ar/default.htm	• Readability calculation software http://www.readabilityformulas.com • Renaissance Learning's *Accelerated Reader* http://www.renlearn.com/ar/default.htm	Support reading instruction.
Microcomputer-based labs, graphing calculators, and calculator-based labs Vernier Courtesy of Vernier Software & Technology http://www.vernier.com/	• TI graphing calculators http://education.ti.com/educationportal/ • Vernier LabPro Packages http://www.vernier.com/	Students collect and analyze data from experiments.
Geographic Information Systems and Global Positioning Systems Adventure GPS Courtesy of Adventure GPS Products Inc. http://www.gps4fun.com/	• GPS Products for Education http://www.gps4fun.com/ • ARCView GIS http://www.esri.com/software/arcview • GIS products for U.S. Census data http://www.census.gov/geo/www/maps/	Students study geographical and social studies information and concepts.

Figure 5.18   Sample *AutoCAD* Screen

Others, like the *Living Books* series (*Just Grandma and Me*), let children explore the screen, activating animations and sounds when they click in various locations. These books are designed to provide an interesting, interactive way to read and increase reading fluency.

A product called *Accelerated Reader* or *AR* (Lopez, 2000; Poock, 1998), designed to track students' reading skills, has become increasingly popular. The purpose of the *AR* system is to motivate students to increase the amount of reading they do for enjoyment. It keeps track of the number of books they read and tests them on comprehension. Teachers can get individual or aggregate data on books read at each readability level. This gives them a better idea of how students are progressing in their reading abilities, and whether they are spending enough time reading at desired levels. Though they caution that further study is needed to draw reliable conclusions, Topping and Paul (1999) found that schools using *AR* for longer periods of time show higher rates of reading, which may correlate with higher tested reading levels.

Microcomputer-Based Labs (Probeware)

A technology tool that has proven particularly useful in math and science classrooms is the **microcomputer-based lab (MBL),** sometimes referred to as **probeware.** MBL packages consist of software accompanied by special hardware sensors designed to measure light, temperature, voltage, and/or speed. The sensors are connected to the microcomputer, and the software processes the data collected by the probes. Bitter, Camuse, and Durbin (1993) said that microcomputer probeware actually can replace several items of lab equipment such as oscilloscopes and voltmeters because MBLs outperform this traditional equipment. Ladelson (1994) points out that probeware achieves a dual purpose of gathering empirical data and revealing the relationship between science and math. Stan-

ADAPTING FOR SPECIAL NEEDS

To support students who are struggling with reading and writing, teachers can use websites that provide text-to-speech so readers can listen to what they type. Examples are *StarChild* (http://starchild.gsfc.nasa.gov/docs/StarChild/StarChild.html) and Harcourt *Multimedia Math Glossary* (http://www.harcourtschool.com/glossary/math2/index_temp.html). If students have difficulty reading text, they can copy and paste it into a specialized program that will read it to them. This strategy is especially helpful when reading on the Internet (e.g., see *ReadingBar2* at http://www.readplease.com/) or when typing papers in a word processor to proofread (hear) what they have written (e.g., see Don Johnston's *Write: OutLoud* at http://www.donjohnston.com).

Contributed by Dave Edyburn

ton (1992) describes a variety of MBLs, covering their capabilities and prices along with grade levels and science subjects they can help teach. Walsh (2001) refers to these devices as stand-alone microprocessor-based data acquisition devices or SAMDADS. He reviews 13 different data-gathering devices and describes their uses in various

TECHNOLOGY INTEGRATION IDEA 5.6

STUDYING SLOPE WITH MBLs/PROBEWARE

Title: Using Probeware to Integrate Math and Science

Content Area/Topic: Concept of slope

Grade Level: High school

NETS for Students: Standards 1, 3, 6

Description: Students use the line equation in software that is intended for calibrating the probes in MBL probeware to explore mathematical concepts underlying the general linear equation $y = mx + b$ (where m = slope and b = the y intercept). This process establishes a relationship between the input to the computer from the probe and the value that the measurement represents.

Instruction: For example, if the MBL is measuring voltage, the probe is calibrated by connecting it to an AA battery previously confirmed by a multimeter to output 1.5 volts. The computer registers 215 counts for 1.5 volts. The beginning point of 0 counts and the ending point of 215 defines a line. This line is used to calibrate the probe. After the probe is calibrated, an equation is developed for the line (0, 0 and 215, 1.5). Students sketch the graph of the line defined by these points using either paper or graphing software. They predict values for counts given specific voltages using their graph by locating the value on the x axis and finding the corresponding y value for counts. They use the general linear equation $y = mx + b$ to discuss the slope of the line as the rise (vertical distance between the two points) divided by the run (horizontal distance between the points). The teacher has the students calculate the slope for their lines. They enter the value for the slope into the general linear equation and do the final equation for the example calibration. Once the equation has been determined, students calculate counts for specific voltages. When the probe is ready to be used, students bring in samples to be tested.

Assessment: Use a checklist to assess completion/accuracy of required processes.

Source: Ladelson, L. (1994). Calibrating probeware: Making a line. *The Computing Teacher, 21*(6), 46–47.

---

classroom experiments in mathematics and science. (See Technology Integration Idea 5.6.)

Graphing Calculators and Calculator-Based Labs

For many years, calculators have played a widespread—and often controversial—role in mathematics education. Even more capable, software-programmed devices called **graphing calculators** have emerged (see Figure 5.19) and are becoming an indispensable tool in both mathematics and higher level science curriculum. Albrecht and Firedrake (1997) describe uses in physics instruction for these devices in conjunction with the Internet and what they call "data-grabbing devices" (probeware, MBLs, or CBLs). Borenstein (1997) reviews uses of graphing calculators to make possible various experiments and concept demonstrations in algebra. Plymate (1998) and Manouchehri and Pagnucco (1999–2000) describe the use of graphing calculators to explore linear properties of real-world data sets and make

Figure 5.19   A Graphing Calculator

USING CBLs TO STUDY ELLIPSES

Title: Graphing the Ellipse

Content Area/Topic: Math—geometry

Grade Level: 10–12

NETS for Students: Standards 1, 3, 6

Description: In this activity, the students use a Texas Instruments (TI) graphing calculator to add interest to the study of ellipses.

Instruction: The teacher begins by demonstrating occurrences of ellipses in the real world: orbits of planets and comets, arches of stone bridges (semi-ellipses), elliptical gears, various artworks. Then they are challenged to use the calculators to create their own ellipses. As they add points to construct their ellipses, the teacher discusses mathematical properties needed to build them. After they understand these properties, they can use the TI software to define a macro to create the actual figures so they will be able to focus more time on exploring proofs and on investigation and problem-solving activities with the calculators.

Assessment: Use a checklist to assess completion of required steps.

Source: Davis, J., & Hofstetter, E. (1998). A graphing investigation of the ellipse. *Learning and Leading with Technology*, 26(2), 32–36.

---

concepts like slope more visual and understandable. (See Technology Integration Idea 5.7.) When probes or sensors are connected to a graphing calculator as opposed to a computer (as described in the previous section on MBLs), they also are called **calculator-based labs (CBLs).**

Geographic Information Systems and Global Positioning Systems

Both of these powerful tools are useful in teaching in geography, as described in Chapter 12. A **Geographic Information System (GIS)** is a computer system that is able to store in a database a variety of information about geographic locations. After it has stored all data that describe a given location, the GIS can then display the data in map form. According to Parmenter and Burns (2001), the three primary uses of GISs are (1) to record and maintain large amounts of geographic information, (2) to produce up-to-date, customized maps, and (3) to allow analysis and comparison of information on different locations. A **Global Positioning System (GPS)** is a worldwide radionavigation system made possible by a bank of 24 satellites and their ground stations. Using

Figure 5.20   Global Positioning System (GPS)

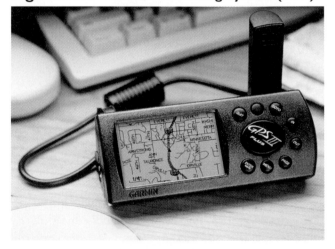

satellites as reference points, a GPS unit can calculate positions of anything on earth accurate to a matter of feet or inches. A GPS receiver connected to mapping software is what most people think of as a GPS. These small devices can be useful in a car, home, or even a portable laptop. (See an example GPS device in Figure 5.20.)

INTERACTIVE SUMMARY

The following is a summary of the main points covered in this chapter. To see additional examples and information on these points, go to this textbook's Companion Website at http://www.prenhall.com/roblyer and click on the Chapter 5 *Interactive Summary* module to visit each of the recommended websites.

1. **Benefits of software tools are the same as those described for Chapter 4 tools:** Benefits include improved efficiency and productivity, improved appearance, better accuracy and timeliness of information, and more support for interaction and sharing.

2. **Recent developments in software tools:** These include increased use of PDAs, more web connectivity features, and more collections of tools available in software suites.

3. **Materials generators:** Tools that help teachers and students produce instructional materials. They include desktop publishing software, test generators and rubric generators, worksheet and puzzle generators, IEP generators, graphic document makers, and PDF and forms makers.

4. **Data collection and analysis tools:** Tools that help teachers collect and organize information that indicates student progress. They include electronic gradebooks, statistical packages, student information systems, online and computer-based testing systems, and student response systems.

5. **Graphics tools:** Tools that allow manipulation of images to illustrate documents and web pages. They include draw/paint programs; image editing tools; charting/graphing tools; and clip art, photo, animation, sound, video, and font collections.

6. **Planning and organizing tools:** Tools that help teachers and students conceptualize, organize, and communicate their ideas. They include outlining and concept mapping software, lesson planning software, and scheduling/time management tools.

7. **Research and reference tools:** Tools that let students look up information in electronic versions of encyclopedias, atlases, and dictionaries. They include electronic versions of the following tools: encyclopedias, atlases and mapping tools, and dictionaries and thesauruses.

8. **Content-area tools:** Tools that support teaching and learning activities in various content areas. They include CAD systems, music tools such as music editors and sequencers, reading tools, microcomputer-based labs, graphing calculators and calculator-based labs, and Geographic Information Systems and Global Positioning Systems.

Online Activities

Visit this text's Companion Website at http://www.prenhall.com/roblyer to gain access to a variety of questions, activities, and exercises and to help build your knowledge of this chapter's content.

Online Chapter 5 Self-Test

To review terms and concepts for this chapter, click on the *Self-Test* module for this chapter of the Companion Website.

Software Skill-Builder Tutorials

To access practical tutorial and skill-building activities and to build skills using popular software and hardware, click on the *Software Skill-Builder Tutorials* module for this chapter of the Companion Website.

Web-Enrichment Activities

To complete activities that connect to chapter content and provide web-based resources, click on the *Web-Enrichment Activities* module for this chapter of the Companion Website.

TECHNOLOGY INTEGRATION WORKSHOP

CW

CLIPS FROM THE CLASSROOM: LEARNING WITH TECHNOLOGY

 Go to the *Technology Integration Workshop* DVD located in the back of this text and click on *Clips from the Classroom*. View the video clips listed below that support this chapter's content:

- *Website and* Photoshop *in Photography*
- *Graphing Calculators in Trigonometry*
- *Composition Software and MIDI in Music*
- *Tablet Computers in World History*.

CW Now, visit this text's Companion Website at http://www.prenhall.com/roblyer to answer questions and complete activities that will guide you in analyzing each clip.

THE TIP MODEL IN ACTION

Read each of the following scenarios related to implementing the TIP Model, and go to the Companion Website to answer the questions that follow it based on your Chapter 5 reading activities.

TIP Model Scenario #1 Ms. Chinita was teaching her students higher level study skills. She wanted to show them how they could outline a complicated article by drawing a diagram to illustrate the ideas in it and how they relate to each other. She found this visual display worked very well for her, and she wanted her students to learn it, too. However, she found the approach didn't work very well because students who were just learning this technique tended to make a lot of mistakes drawing the boxes and connecting lines, and then they didn't want to do the work of erasing and revising them.

1.1 What software tool would you recommend Ms. Chinita use to address this problem?

1.2 What would be the relative advantage of using this software tool?

1.3 Would this kind of activity be best done on an individual basis, in pairs, or in groups? Explain why.

TIP Model Scenario #2 Whenever Mr. Jackson had his students do a research project for his social studies class, he would send them to the library/media center to look up the information in reference books. Because several students usually wanted to use the same text, a lot of time was wasted; it was difficult to keep students focused on the information gathering. Mr. Jackson had heard about a software tool that several students could use easily at the same time. It had pictures and videos, as well as text descriptions, so students got more out of the information they did find.

2.1 What software tool does Mr. Jackson have in mind to address this problem?

2.2 What would be the relative advantage of using this software tool?

2.3 How would it be possible for a class of 30 students to use this tool at the same time?

TIP Model Scenario #3 Ms. Hortense's Consumer Math classes have more than 40 students each. She likes to give them weekly quizzes to make sure everyone is keeping up on the skills and to spot students who may need additional help. However, the class is so large and students sit so close together, she also feels she needs several different versions of each test to prevent "sharing answers." She has heard about a software tool that she can use to create a pool of items. It also lets her generate different versions of the same test from the items.

3.1 What software tool would you recommend Ms. Hortense use to address this problem?

3.2 What would be the relative advantage of using this software tool?

3.3 What tool could she use to make these tests easier to score?

TIP Model Scenario #4 Mr. Charles wants to make his middle school classes hands-on, with students doing experiments by collecting and analyzing their own data. However, taking accurate readings of variables such as temperature is very difficult for his students to do. Also, the students find the repetitious recording and calculating very boring, and it is difficult to keep them focused on the experiment. He has heard about a software tool that can collect temperature readings quickly and feed the data automatically into a computer for analysis. He thinks that using this tool will be much more motivating to his students than doing all the operations by hand.

4.1 What software tool would you recommend Mr. Charles use to address this problem?

4.2 What would be the relative advantage of using this tool?

4.3 If Mr. Charles has 36 students in a class and only five such tools, how could he arrange the tool so that all students could learn to use it?

TIP Model Scenario #5 Ms. Keishan, a high school Current Issues teacher, has learned about GIS tools and knows that they are becoming as essential to studying geography and local issues as word processing is to learning to write. She wants her students to learn about these tools in a meaningful project that will let them see their real-life applications. She has learned that the science class does an environmental studies project every fall at a local river in which they collect water samples and do tests to analyze sources of degradation and contaminants. Then they try to determine the sources of these withdrawals and contaminants. She asks the science teacher if they could work together on a project that provides GIS information to help students with these water analyses.

5.1 What instructional problems did Ms. Keishan see that she wanted to address in the new project?

5.2 In what ways could a GIS system help this project?

5.3 How might GPS tools also be useful with such a project?

TIE INTO PRACTICE: TECHNOLOGY INTEGRATION EXAMPLES

The Technology Integration Example that opened this chapter (*A Desktop-Published Literary Anthology*) showed how a teacher might use desktop publishing software to help produce the annual literary anthology of student work. With the knowledge you have gained from Chapter 5, do the following with this example:

1. Mr. Mortenson created a page format for the anthology like the one shown here.

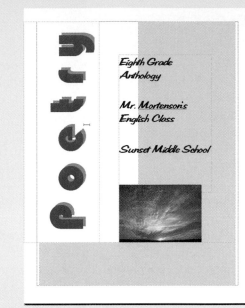

First Page of a Desktop-Published Anthology Format. (Create this product using the *Hands-On with Technology* section of the DVD.)

2. Answer the following questions about the *Anthology* example:

• Phase 1 — How did using desktop publishing for the anthology offer relative advantage in comparison with the way the teachers had done it before?

• Phase 2 — Mr. Mortenson created a rubric to assess the students' work on short story structure, required revisions, and creativity. How would you structure the levels of performance for the "creativity" element?

• Phase 3 — How might Mr. Mortenson involve the art classes in the preparation of this anthology? What software tools might they use that would work well with the desktop publishing software?

• Phase 4 — Online tutorials on software tools may be used to help train teachers and/or students in various desktop publishing software tools. Where might you direct Mr. Mortenson and the computer applications teacher to locate such tutorials?

• Phase 5 — If the principal said no funds were available to purchase the desktop publishing software the teachers wanted, how might the teachers raise the money they need?

3. What NETS for Students skills would students learn by working on the *Anthology* project? (See the front of the book for a list of NETS for Students.)

Technology Integration Lesson Planning

The *Technology Integration Workshop* DVD includes a set of technology integration ideas and links to online lessons, arranged as a searchable database. The DVD comes packaged in the back of this textbook. Click on the *Hands-On with Technology* section of the Technology Integration Workshop DVD and complete the following exercises.

1. **Locate lesson ideas** — The DVD has several examples of lessons that use desktop publishing, draw/paint and image editing software, charting/graphing tools, concept mapping software, and MBLs/CBLs. Locate an example integration idea for using each of these software tools.

2. **Evaluate the lessons** — Use the *Evaluation Checklist for a Technology-Integrated Lesson* (located on the DVD and the Companion Website) to evaluate each of these lessons.

3. **Modify a lesson** — Select one of the lesson ideas and adapt its strategies to meet a need in your own content area. You may choose to use the same software in the original or use a different software package.

4. **Add descriptors** — Create descriptors for your new lesson like those found on the database (e.g., grade level, content and topic areas, technologies used, relative advantage, objectives, NETS standards).

5. **Add the new lesson** — Add your modified lesson with all its descriptors to the lesson idea database.

For Your Teaching Portfolio

For this chapter's contribution to your teaching portfolio, add the following products you created in the Technology Integration Workshop:

- The desktop-published pages you created for the *Anthology* project

- The evaluations you did using the *Evaluation Checklist for a Technology-Integrated Lesson*

- The new lesson plan you developed, based on the one you found on the Technology Integration Workshop DVD.

CHAPTER 6

TEACHING WITH MULTIMEDIA AND HYPERMEDIA TOOLS

Multimedia learning is not something new.
It is woven into the fabric of our childhood....

Tom Boyle, in *Design for Multimedia Learning* (1997)

TECHNOLOGY INTEGRATION EXAMPLE
INTERACTIVE MULTIMEDIA STORYBOOKS

Based on: Frederickson, S. (2002). Interactive multimedia storybooks. *Learning and Leading with Technology, 25*(1), 6–10.

Grade Level: 7–8 and 1–2 (working together) • **Content Area/Topic: Language arts, literature** • **Length of Time: Nine weeks**

Phase 1: Determine relative advantage

Ms. Dubey was the Language Arts Department Chair for her small, rural K–8 school. While watching first- and second-grade students using interactive storybooks on CD-ROM, she was struck by how absorbed they were in the use of language, as well as in the content of the stories. She realized that they seemed to be learning a great deal about story elements and structure, as well as enjoying the reading activity. As she reflected on the difficulties that the seventh- and eighth-grade teachers were having in capturing their students' interest in reading and language, she had an idea for a project that could benefit both the elementary and middle school students. She decided to ask the grade 7–8 teachers if they would like to have their students create interactive storybooks for the grade 1–2 students. She knew the school had several copies of **HyperStudio®**, a popular multimedia software, and the technology coordinator had been looking for curriculum projects in which this software might be useful. When Ms. Dubey approached the teachers about this idea, they were excited about it, and the technology coordinator promised to help support their work. They decided that the grade 1–2 students would create storylines for the grade 7–8 students to turn into interactive books. That would give each group a meaningful role in the project.

Phase 2: Decide on objectives and assessments

The teachers worked together to decide on what they wanted students to achieve as a result of this project. In addition to *HyperStudio* skills and completed products, they also wanted to make sure grade 7–8 students were learning about story structure and components. They stated project objectives for each grade level and created assessment methods to measure each skill. The outcomes, objectives, and assessments they decided on were as follows:

- **Grade 1–2 Outcome:** Create story lines. **Objective:** Working with the teacher as a whole class, students verbally outline stories to be turned into interactive storybooks. **Assessment:** Rubric to assess on-task behaviors, communications skills, and creativity.

- **Grade 7–8 Outcome:** Demonstrate basic *HyperStudio* design skills. **Objective:** Each student completes all steps to create three frames in a *HyperStudio* **stack** (a sequence of *HyperStudio* frames) to demonstrate the following skills: creating new frames, entering text, entering graphics, creating buttons, and linking frames. **Assessment:** Checklist of required frames and elements and *HyperStudio* skills.

- **Grade 7–8 Outcome:** Design an interactive multimedia story. **Objective:** Students work in groups to prepare an interactive story structure based on the grade 1–2 students' story line, place it on **storyboards** (planning blueprints from which the multimedia product will be designed), create the *HyperStudio* stack, and revise it based on feedback. Each group achieves at least 20 of 25 points on the rubric. **Assessment:** Rubric on story structure, completion of *HyperStudio* tasks, completion of required revisions, and creativity.

- **Grade 7–8 Outcome:** Work effectively in small groups. **Objective:** All students demonstrate effective group work behaviors by scoring at least 90% on a group work rubric. **Assessment:** Rubric to assess group behaviors.

- **Grade 7–8 Outcome:** Identify story components on a test. **Objective:** Each student demonstrates grasp of story structure and components (e.g., plot, sequence, characters) by identifying all of them in at least one completed story. **Assessment:** Checklist of correctly identified story elements.

Phase 3: Design integration strategies

The teachers knew that this project would take some coordination among classes, as well as substantial planning and outlining work before students would be able to begin their story production work. They decided on the following timeline for the project:

- **Week 1: Story outlining:** Grade 1–2 classes work with their teachers to create outlines of stories. After the teacher introduces one of their favorite stories, she asks them to brainstorm ideas for a new story. The students dictate the stories as the teachers write them down. Then they read them together and revise them as they like. Each class prepares two stories in this way.

- **Weeks 2–4: Multimedia skill building:** The technology coordinator works with the grades 7–8 teachers and their classes to help them learn the *HyperStudio* skills they will need for this project. Together they do small projects (e.g., an interactive map of their school) to build the required technical skills. At the same time, the teacher begins assigning individual students areas of expertise, so there will be "experts" working on each part of the final product. Some students are assigned to produce graphics to illustrate the story, some become experts on animations, some on buttons, some on sounds, and some on text.

- **Week 5: Storyboarding:** The grades 7–8 students begin their work by interviewing the grade 1–2 students to see what they have in mind for the stories. Working together as a whole class, they identify the story elements on one story. Then each small group identifies elements in an additional story. After they review the structure in this way, the grade 7–8 teachers help their students make the story outlines into frames for the storybook. They design frames on 4-in. by 6-in. cards, which serve as their storyboards. They place the storyboards in the order in which they will go in the interactive book, and place "buttons" on the cards to show where the decision points will be.

- **Weeks 6–8:** The grade 7–8 students work in teams to create interactive stories based on their storyboard blueprints. The technology coordinator again provides help as students work with the *HyperStudio* program to develop their products.

- **Week 9: Assessment and presentation:** After drafts are completed, each team reviews the work of another team. Each team makes revisions on its product, as needed. Finally, the grade 7–8 students present their work to the grade 1–2 students, who go through the stories and give their feedback.

To make sure they had all of the resources they would need for the project, the teachers did the following:

- **Lab scheduling:** Ms. Dubey and the teachers knew that much of the work would need to be done in the computer lab, so Ms. Dubey confirmed lab time for the classes.

- **Software copies:** The technology coordinator knew that the computer lab had only one "five-pack" (five copies) of *HyperStudio* software. However, because he had sufficient notice, he was able to obtain a lab-pack, or 30 additional copies on one site license. This allowed him to place one legal copy on each lab computer, as well as two copies for each grade 7–8 class computer.

- **Handouts:** The technology coordinator obtained wall posters and handouts that summarized the *HyperStudio* features and how to do each one. He also placed copies of these on the school website, so anyone could download additional copies later.

- **Other equipment:** So that students would be able to create images for use in *HyperStudio* stacks, the technology coordinator made sure the optical scanner was working in the lab and gave each class the use of a digital camera.

As Ms. Dubey and the teachers looked at the rubric results and interviewed the students, they knew the project had been a success. For the most part, students had worked well together in small groups, and the resulting products were of high quality. There were some problems coordinating group work, due to student absences, but the products all were completed on time. Results of the story component identification task indicated that grade 7–8 students had a good grasp of the structure and parts of their stories. The grade 1–2 students clearly were thrilled with the results. The teachers decided to repeat the project the following year, this time focusing on producing and comparing various genres of stories.

OBJECTIVES

After reading this chapter and completing the learning activities for it, you should be able to:

1. Define multimedia and hypermedia from historic and current perspectives.

2. Evaluate the quality and capabilities of a commercial multimedia/hypermedia product.

3. Describe resources and skills required for multimedia/hypermedia authoring.

4. Use an authoring system to develop a product that meets visual, navigational, and instructional criteria.

5. Design lesson activities appropriate for each kind of hypermedia product.

KEY TERMS

- Audio Video Interleave (AVI) format
- avatars
- electronic slide shows
- Extensible Mark-up Language (XML)
- full immersion systems
- haptic interfaces
- head-mounted display (HMD)
- hypermedia
- *HyperStudio*
- Moving Picture Experts Group (MPEG) format
- multimedia
- *QuickTime* movies
- *QuickTime VR Authoring Studio*
- stack
- storyboard
- video editing software
- virtual reality (VR)
- Virtual Reality Modeling Language (VRML)

 For more information on Key Terms, go to the *Key Terms* module for this chapter of the Companion Website at http://www.prenhall.com/roblyer.

INTRODUCTION TO MULTIMEDIA AND HYPERMEDIA

We live in a multimedia world, surrounded by complex images, movement, and sound. So perhaps it is not surprising that part of our human evolution has focused on making our technology reflect the color and clamor of our surroundings. In educational technology, multimedia has been a steadily growing presence for some time. Computer-based multimedia learning stations have been used since 1966, and noncomputer multimedia methods have been around even longer. This chapter looks at current classroom uses of electronic multimedia and its companion concept, hypermedia.

Multimedia and Hypermedia: How Do They Differ?

Like other educational technology concepts, definitions for multimedia and hypermedia defy consensus (Moore, Myers, & Burton, 1994; Tolhurst, 1995); people find the two concepts either too close to distinguish between or too slippery to get words around. Tolhurst quoted one source

as saying, "By its very nature, [multimedia] is invertebrate. You poke it and it slithers away" (p. 21). Definitions used in this chapter come to us from two paths that were separate initially but have converged over time.

Multimedia simply means "multiple media" or "a combination of media." The media can be still pictures, sound, motion video, animation, and/or text items combined in a product whose purpose is to communicate information in multiple ways.

Hypermedia refers to "linked media" or "interactive media" that have their roots in a concept developed by Vannevar Bush (1986) in his landmark article "As We May Think." In 1945, Bush proposed a "memex" machine that would let people quickly access items of information whose meanings were connected but which were stored in different places. In the 1960s, Ted Nelson coined the term *hypertext* to describe a proposed database system called Xanadu based on Bush's idea (Boyle, 1997). In this system, items of information from all over the world were to be logically connected with hypertext links. For example, one could select "apple" and get information on all related concepts such as trees, fruit—even the Garden of Eden. The technology at that time was inadequate to produce Xanadu, but the idea was the forerunner of today's hypermedia systems in which information stored in various media are connected (often via the Internet), thus the term *hypermedia*.

In current technologies such as Internet browsers (see Chapter 7) and authoring systems, most multimedia products also are hypermedia systems. That is, media elements are either linked with buttons to click on or menus from which to select or are part of an immersive environment. Clicking on or selecting one item sends the user to other, related items. This chapter gives many examples of hypermedia products; all also are multimedia. The combination of media such as video and audio with text makes them multimedia; the ability to get from one media/information element to another makes them hypermedia. Because most of these tools nowadays are actually linked media, subsequent discussion in this chapter will refer to them as *hypermedia* unless the term *multimedia* is more appropriate, as in the case of digitized video products.

Types of Hypermedia Systems

Hypermedia systems come in a variety of hardware, software, and media configurations and, until recently, were usually classified according to their primary storage equipment: interactive videodiscs (IVDs), CD-ROMs (compact disc–read-only memory), digital versatile discs (DVDs), and other technologies. However, dramatic changes in the capabilities of presentation software and Internet multimedia formats, as well as the decline in use of videodisc systems, have changed the focus of this classification system from delivery medium to the purpose and the type of capability the products offer.

This chapter focuses on the following five kinds of hypermedia formats: commercial hypermedia, presentation software, video systems, hypermedia authoring software, and virtual reality systems. The first represents products developed by companies and sold to educators and other consumers; the other four are authoring systems that educators and others can use to develop their own products.

- **Commercial hypermedia software packages** — These are prepackaged products developed by software publishing companies that offer a variety of media, including animation, video, audio, and links to the Internet. The trend is for most software packages to include all of these features.

- **Authoring tools: Presentation software** — This authoring software used to be linear and primarily a combination of text, still pictures, and limited audio and animation. But it has grown in capability and now offers branching capabilities and the ability to include many of the same features as published products (e.g., embedded audio and video clips).

ADAPTING FOR SPECIAL NEEDS

Hypermedia environments have often posed barriers for student learners who are deaf and those who have difficulty using a mouse to control the computer. As a result, access to multimedia and hypermedia has been an area of concern for the disability community, which has challenged designers to use tools that create accessible lessons and activities. One innovative tool for creating accessible multimedia is *IntelliPics Studio* (http://www.intellitools.com). Comparable to other multimedia author tools in its ease of use; ability to manipulate text, graphics, and media; and multiple platform availability, *IntelliPics Studio* includes features that provide speech output, single-switch scanning, and access via a standard keyboard, an IntelliKeys alternative keyboard, a mouse, or a touch screen. *IntelliPics Studio* is an essential multimedia design tool for teachers and students committed to developing accessible hypermedia products that can be used by everyone.

Contributed by Dave Edyburn

- **Authoring tools: Video production and editing systems** — Digitized videos used to be difficult to produce and edit and were used primarily to capture short video clips for use in hypermedia authoring products. New video editing systems have changed this. Now anyone, even nontechnical consumers, can produce professional-looking movies with a variety of special effects like fading and titles.

- **Authoring tools: Hypermedia authoring systems** — These systems, too, have come a long way since the first versions. They are increasingly capable, allowing users to include many of the features they see in professional products with substantially greater ease.

- **Authoring tools: Virtual reality (VR) systems** — VR systems are designed to immerse users in virtual environments that simulate real ones. VR comes in several formats, some of which are in common use in education.

Hypermedia systems published as web page documents also represent a powerful technology of the future. Hypermedia systems used in distance communications and online learning are described in Chapters 7 and 8.

Current and Future Impact of Hypermedia on Education

The current widespread educational uses of hypermedia systems augur an even heavier reliance on these products in classrooms of the future. Educators recognize and use these systems when they see the powerful capabilities they offer to enhance classroom learning:

- **Increased motivation** — Hypermedia programs offer such varied options that most people seem to enjoy using them. Students who usually struggle to complete a project or term paper often will tackle a hypermedia project enthusiastically. Many educators believe the most important characteristic of hypermedia is its ability to encourage students to be proactive learners.

- **Flexible learning modes** — Hypermedia programs can draw on such diverse tools that they truly offer something for students who excel in any of what Gardner calls "intelligences" (see Chapter 3). For example, a student who may not be good at written expression but has visual aptitude can document learning with sound or pictures.

- **Development of creative and critical thinking skills** — The tremendous access to hypertext and hypermedia tools opens up a multitude of creative avenues for both students and teachers. Creation of hypermedia products constantly requires the learner to make decisions and evaluate progress. This forces students to apply higher order thinking skills. Turner and Dipinto (1992) say that the hypermedia environment encourages students to think in terms of metaphors, to be introspective, and to give free rein to their imaginations.

- **Improved writing and process skills** — Turner and Dipinto (1992) also find that exposure to hypermedia authoring tools helps give students a new and different perspective on how to organize and present information and a new insight into writing. Instead of viewing their writing as one long stream of text, students now see it as chunks of information to be linked.

Our society's heavy reliance on hypertext and hypermedia to communicate information seems likely to expand in the future. The ever-accelerating number of Internet sites is evidence that linking data with hypertext and hypermedia is an effective way to present and add value to large bodies of information. Numerous hypermedia documents have been published on the Internet in the hope of attracting viewers, readers, and listeners.

Hypermedia tools also may permit sophisticated evaluations of learning. In the process of using hypermedia, people are said to "leave a track" (Simonson & Thompson, 1994), which may help teachers analyze how students approach learning tasks. Future hypermedia systems might apply pattern-recognition techniques from the field of artificial intelligence to help schools assess student mastery of higher order cognitive skills. Bagui (1998) says multimedia "may have unique capabilities to facilitate learning because of the parallels between multimedia and the natural way people learn" (p. 4), that is, through visual information and imagery.

Research on the Impact of Multimedia and Hypermedia Systems

Roblyer (1999) found that hypermedia's benefits seem to center on its ability to offer students multiple channels through which to process information. Reviews of research by Mayer (1997) from studies of hypermedia use offered support for this position. He found that students who received explanations in both visual and verbal format (as opposed to students who received verbal presentations only) tended to generate more creative solutions on problem-solving transfer tests. He found that effects were strongest for students with high spatial ability and low prior knowledge. Subsequent studies (Mayer & Moreno, 1998; Moreno & Mayer, 2002) also found that learners showed greater comprehension and retention of learned materials when pictures were accompanied by spoken words, rather than written words. Mayer and Moreno observed that this "split attention" effect was consistent with a model of working memory that had separate visual and auditory channels.

Swan and Meskill (1996) examined how effectively current hypermedia products support the teaching and acquisition of critical thinking skills in reading and language. They reviewed hypermedia products in terms of how well they made possible response-based approaches to teaching and learning literature, that is, instructional activities that "place student-generated questions at the center of learning . . . (and encourage) a problem-finding as well as a problem-solving approach to critical thinking" (p. 168). They evaluated 45 hypermedia literature programs using criteria in three areas: technical items, response-based concerns, and classroom issues. The majority of the 45 products used a CD-ROM format, but 10 used a combination of CD-ROM and videodisc, and 4 used computer software. They found that most products were technically sound and linked well with classroom topics, but few were designed to promote the response-based methods that promote critical thinking. "Programs designed for elementary students ... equated literature education with reading instruction; programs designed for high school ... generally adopted a traditional text-centered approach" (p. 187). These findings indicate that teachers who want to use multimedia/hypermedia products specifically to promote higher level skills must select products judiciously and warily.

In another review of the impact of hypermedia on learner comprehension and learner control, Dillon and Gabbard (1998) echo the caution voiced by Swan and Meskill (1996). They conclude that:

- Hypermedia's primary advantage is allowing rapid searches through lengthy or multiple information resources. For other purposes, nonhypermedia resources seem equally useful.

- Increased learner control is more useful to higher ability students; lower ability students experience the greatest difficulty with hypermedia.

- Learner style helps determine whether or not certain hypermedia features are effective in various learning situations. Passive learners may profit more from the cueing offered by hypermedia, whereas more capable learners who are more willing to explore may be more capable of exploiting other hypermedia features.

Research on the Design and Use of Multimedia and Hypermedia Systems

Stemler (1997) reviewed findings on various multimedia/hypermedia characteristics that could have an impact on the potential effectiveness of these systems: screen design, learner control and navigation, use of feedback, student interactivity, and video and audio elements. Her findings are too extensive to give adequate treatment here, but educators who are committed to high-quality multimedia development should review the full text of her article.

- **Instructional design** — Stemler recommends that developers analyze each element in a multimedia product to determine which of Gagné's nine Events of Instruction (see Chapter 2) it aims to achieve and how well it achieves it (p. 342).

- **Screen design** — Well-designed screens focus learners' attention, develop and maintain interest, promote processing of information, promote engagement between learner and content, help students find and organize information, and support easy navigation through lessons (p. 343).

- **Interaction and feedback** — Keep feedback on the same screen with the question and student response and provide immediate feedback. Verify correct an-

swers and give hints and another try for incorrect answers. Tailor feedback to the response and provide encouraging feedback, but do not make it more entertaining for students to provide wrong answers rather than correct ones. If possible, let students print out the feedback (p. 345).

- **Navigation** — Support navigation with orientation cues, clearly defined procedures, clearly labeled back-and-forth buttons, and help segments (pp. 346–347).

- **Learner control** — In general, give older and more capable students more control over the sequence; younger, less experienced students should have less control (p. 348).

MAKING THE CASE FOR TECHNOLOGY INTEGRATION

Discuss these issues online with other students by selecting the *Making the Case* module for Chapter 6 of the Companion Website (http://www.prenhall.com/roblyer) or choose the *Message Board* module.

CW

1. In his essay in *Wired* magazine ("*PowerPoint* Is Evil: Power Corrupts. *PowerPoint* Corrupts Absolutely"), Edward Tufte (2003) opines, "Alas, slideware often reduces the analytical quality of presentations. In particular, the popular *PowerPoint* templates (ready-made designs) usually weaken verbal and spatial reasoning, and almost always corrupt statistical analysis. . . . Particularly disturbing is the adoption of the *PowerPoint* cognitive style in our schools. Rather than learning to write a report using sentences, children are being taught how to formulate client pitches and infomercials." What do you think causes poor classroom use of *PowerPoint*? What would you recommend teachers do to make sure students are using it effectively?

2. Sherry Turkle (2004) says, "Information technology is identity technology. Embedding it in a culture that supports democracy, freedom of expression, tolerance, diversity, and complexity of opinion is one of the decade's greatest challenges (p. B28)." What role could multimedia instructional materials and student multimedia projects play in bringing about this culture? How can teachers' use of multimedia support the development of such a culture?

- **Color** — Use color sparingly and employ it primarily for cueing and highlighting certain elements to bring them to the learner's attention. Use a consistent color scheme throughout to promote ease of use (pp. 350–351).
- **Graphics** — Use graphics as well as text to present information to serve students who prefer one kind of presentation over the other. Use graphics sparingly for other purposes (to entertain or amuse) (p. 351).
- **Animation** — Use animation sparingly and only to present dynamic processes or to highlight key information (p. 352).
- **Audio** — Use audio for short presentations of program content, but do not let it compete with video presentation. Do not require long readings on each screen. Separate material into chunks on each of several screens (p. 353).
- **Video** — Use video sequences for broader, abstract material (that with emotional impact) and for advance organizers rather than for presenting detailed information (p. 354).

An ongoing series of studies by Mayer focuses on design and usage characteristics for educational multimedia that can optimize impact on student achievement (e.g., Mayer, Fennell, & Farmer, 2004; Mayer & Moreno, 2003). These include methods of reducing *cognitive load* (the required cognitive processing of materials exceeds the learners available cognitive capacity) during multimedia learning, and personalizing multimedia presentations to help students process material more actively.

Recent Developments in Hypermedia Systems

Three trends in hypermedia system use in education are evident:

- **The "vanishing videodisc"** — It is one of the more unfortunate developments in educational technology that videodisc technology has all but disappeared from the technology landscape, taking with it the rich array of classroom resources that were developed for this easy-to-use format. Some of the materials have been transferred to the Internet or to DVD; many others have been lost.
- **Convergence of offline (disc) and online (Internet) development** — Much of hypermedia either has embedded Internet links, or has been uploaded to the Internet after development. Because of this growing hypermedia migration to online formats, many educators view hypermedia and web pages as synonymous.

- **Increasing ease of use** — Hypermedia development used to be a fairly technical enterprise. However, thanks to user-friendly authoring systems (e.g., *HyperStudio* for author hypermedia, *Quicktime VR Authoring Studio* for author virtual environments) and photography and graphics software tools, the development of all forms of hypermedia from presentation software to video production has become accessible to nontechnical teachers and students.

COMMERCIAL HYPERMEDIA SOFTWARE PACKAGES

Background on Commercial Hypermedia Software Packages

As noted in Chapter 3, instructional software is becoming increasingly more like hypermedia in nature. Software tools discussed in Chapters 4 and 5 also reflect this trend. The increased storage capability and availability of CD and DVD media has made it easier to store complex programs with motion graphics, movies, audio, and links to the Internet. Several types of commercial hypermedia products are now available, including instructional software (e.g., tutorials, drills, simulations), interactive books and ebooks, reference materials, and collections of development materials. These are discussed here and summarized in Figure 6.1.

Instructional Software

As described in Chapter 3, instructional software packages, once primarily text-based materials, now often have hypermedia features. Hypermedia features have increased the capability and value of these programs. For example:

- **Tutorials** — Descriptions and explanations can be more visual and can be spoken to the student, as well as written.
- **Drill and practice** — Practice items can be posed in audio or video, as well as text, and feedback for correct and incorrect answers can also be in these modes.
- **Simulations** — Because multimedia presentations can include movement and sound, simulations can be even more realistic. (See http://www.thinkport.org/Technology/simulations.tp for example online multimedia simulations.)
- **Instructional games** — Motion and sound can make presentations more attractive and can further enhance the motivational qualities of games.
- **Problem solving** — Problems may not be stated in video format, thus clarifying the problems to be solved and demonstrating visually the relationship among items of information needed to solve them.

Figure 6.1   **Summary of Commercial Multimedia Products**

Type of Multimedia Product	Sample Sources of Materials	Description
Instructional software Courtesy of A.D.A.M. Inc. http://www.adam.com	• **MCH Multimedia Developers of Interactive Software** http://mchmultimedia.com/ • **Tutorial Finder** http://www.tutorialfind.com • **DK Multimedia at educate-me.net** http://www.educate-me.net/ • *A.D.A.M.: The Inside Story* http://education.adam.com • **Riverdeep** http://www.riverdeep.com	• Tutorials • Drills • Simulations • Instructional games • Problem solving
Interactive books and ebooks Courtesy of Scholastic, Inc. http://teacher.scholastic.com/clifford1/	• **Clifford Interactive Storybooks** http://teacher.scholastic.com/clifford1/ • **Interactive storybooks from Computer Games Station** http://www.computer-games-station.com/ • **Interactive storybooks from Sepharus** http://www.sepharus.com/	• Interactive storybooks
Courtesy of eBooks N' Bytes. http://www.free-ebooks.net/	• **Listing of books online** http://digital.library.upenn.edu/books/ • **Free downloadable ebooks** http://www.free-ebooks.net/	• Ebooks
Reference materials Courtesy of High Beam Research, LLC. http://www.encyclopedia.com	• **Encarta** http://encarta.msn.com • **Encyclopedia.com** http://www.encyclopedia.com/ • **Encyclopedia Britannica** http://www.britannica.com/ • **Grolier Online** http://auth.grolier.com	• Encyclopedias
The Old Farmer's Almanac® and Design Mark® are the exclusive property of Yankee Publishing Inc. and used with permission. http://www.almanac.com	• **The Old Farmer's Almanac** http://www.almanac.com/ • **World Almanac for Kids** http://www.worldalmanacforkids.com/ • **Nation by Nation Almanac** http://www.nationbynation.com/	• Almanacs
	• **World Atlas** http://www.graphicmaps.com/aatlas/world.htm • **World Map** http://www.worldatlas2000.com/	• Atlases

(continued)

Figure 6.1 (continued)

Type of Multimedia Product	Sample Sources of Materials	Description
	• **USA Today** http://usatoday.com • **New York Times** http://www.nytimes.com	• Newspapers and newsletters
Collections of development resources Courtesy of Bonnell Technology Pty Ltd. http://www.flamingtext.com/	• **Graphics for Teachers** http://www.teachingheart.net/graphicl.html • **Microsoft's Clip Art and Media Collection** http://office.microsoft.com/clipart • **Flaming Text** http://www.flamingtext.com/ • **Animation Factory** http://www.teachingheart.net/graphicl.html • **SmartDraw's Clip Art Collection** http://www.smartdraw.com/resources/collections/clipart/	• Clip art • Audio clips • Video clips • Animations

Interactive Books and ebooks

Two kinds of interactive books are currently available: interactive storybooks and interactive texts. The first type target primarily younger students, while the second are most often used by older students and adult learners (e.g., inservice teachers).

On-screen stories have become extremely popular with primary teachers and students (Glasgow, 1996, 1996–1997, 1997; Kahn, 1997a). On the audio tracks, narrators read pages as the words are highlighted on screen. If a student needs to hear a word again, just clicking on it with the mouse pointer activates the audio. Some electronic storybooks have a straightforward approach, allowing students to read them at their own pace. Other books are structured to be more interactive and open ended, some allowing students to choose the story path and ending where they want each time the story is read. A study by Doty, Popplewell, and Byers (2001) found that students' ability to answer comprehension questions was higher when they read stories in an electronic storybook format than when they read a traditional book format.

ebooks have become a valuable resource for students and teachers alike, since they offer more flexibility than print texts. Many of the classics are free downloads, since they are no longer copyrighted. (See Figure 6.1 for notes on ebook download sites.)

Reference Materials

Many reference materials are available on CD and DVD at very reasonable costs. To add still more value, these resources are accompanied by search engine software that makes searching for information both easy and efficient.

Some materials have Internet links to still more material. Below are just a few of the categories and example titles.

- **Encyclopedias** — Most of the major encyclopedias are no longer published exclusively in book format; they are available on CD and DVD. Some, like Microsoft's *Encarta,* were designed solely for the electronic format and are available only on disc or the Internet. However, others, such as the *World Book Encyclopedia,* now have a version on disc after many years in book format.

- **Almanacs** — Popular information collections such as *The Time Almanac* are increasingly shifting to electronic format. Most are on the Internet.

Students use commerical multimedia products as reference materials.

Figure 6.2 Commercial Multimedia Product with a Combination of Functions: A.D.A.M. Interactive Anatomy 4.0

- **Atlases** — Map utilities such as the *Picture Atlas of the World* allow teachers and students to do a variety of interactive activities such as determining distances and routes from one location to another. Others, like the *World Factbook* (http://www.cia.gov/cia/publications/factbook/), summarize many kinds of geographical information.

- **Newspapers and newsletters** — Most newspapers have searchable online sites and many, including the *New York Times,* have special educational programs for students. These can be indispensable sources of news and other current events information, as well as great lesson ideas and support materials.

- **Proceedings and other conference materials** — Major education conferences, like the National Educational Computing Conference (NECC), distribute to each registrant proceedings, presenter handouts, vendor samples, and shareware on a CD-ROM.

Some new commercial multimedia products combine instructional software functions with a set of reference materials to create a multifaceted product that can meet a variety of educational needs. One example of this combination approach is the *A.D.A.M. Interactive Anatomy* software shown in Figure 6.2. It combines into one package simulations of dissections, animated body images, and a set of reference images and notes on anatomy.

Collections of Development Resources

Many collections of resources used to develop multimedia are now shipped on CD-ROM. These include collections of clip art, sound effects, photographs, video clips, fonts,

and document templates. These are discussed in Chapter 5 in the Using Graphics Tools section (see p. 165).

Evaluating Commercial Hypermedia Products

Because so many hypermedia products are on the market, teachers must become savvy consumers of these materials. Gibbs, Graves, and Bernas (2000) used Delphi surveys of a panel of instructional technology experts to derive criteria to use to evaluate software. Perhaps not surprisingly, the list of criteria emphasizes the instructional and pedagogical aspects of the products rather than their hypermedia characteristics. The result is a list similar to that found in Chapter 4 for instructional software. The *Multimedia Software Evaluation Checklist* may be found in checklist format on the Technology Integration Workshop DVD that accompanies this text and on the Companion Website (http://www.prenhall.com/ roblyer) (see Figure 6.3). Criteria include the following:

- **Instructional planning and support** — The product or documentation that comes with the product specifies the target audience and the prerequisite skills required to use the product successfully.

- **Instructional design** — The objectives are clearly specified and instructional activities are well designed to accomplish them. Examples, practice exercises, and feedback are relevant and useful.

- **Content** — Facts, data, and depictions of events are current and accurate. Information is presented in a truthful way and is not misleading or biased.

- **Interface design and navigation** — Product is easy to use and directions are clear and understandable. Screen elements (titles, text areas, buttons, or links) are clear and easy to use.

- **Feedback and interactivity** — User input is an integral part of the product. Users receive helpful feedback in response to input.

Integration Strategies for Commercial Hypermedia Products

Because products in this category vary so widely, instructional uses for them are also varied and rich. Integration strategies for instructional software are discussed in detail in Chapter 3, and strategies for software tools are described in Chapters 4 and 5. Technology Integration Idea 6.1 illustrates ways in which interactive storybook resources can be used in classrooms. Technology Integration Idea 6.2 shows how an electronic encyclopedia and *PowerPoint* presentation (discussed in the next section) can provide important support for a student project.

Figure 6.3 Criteria for Evaluating Commercial Multimedia Software Products

_____ **Instructional planning.** Target audience and prerequisite skills are specified.
Comments:

_____ **Support.** Computer hardware and software requirements are specified.
Comments:

_____ **Instructional adequacy.** Instructional objectives are clearly stated. Practice activities are provided that actively involve the learner. Instructional activities needed to complete learning tasks are made explicit.
Comments:

_____ **Information content.** Information is current and accurately represents the topic. Examples, practice exercises, and feedback are meaningful and relevant.
Comments:

_____ **Information reliability.** Information is accurate, i.e., presented in a truthful, valid way.
Comments:

_____ **Clear, concise, and unbiased language.** Courseware content is presented clearly. (Text, pictorial, graphical, auditory, and video information all are presented clearly.)
Comments:

_____ **Interface design and navigation.** Courseware screen elements (titles, text areas, navigation buttons, etc.) are easy to understand. Directions are understandable.
Comments:

_____ **Feedback and interactivity.** If tests are present, they are matched to objectives. Feedback is appropriate to content, learning tasks, learner response, and learning environment.
Comments:

_____ **Evidence of effectiveness.** During student uses of courseware, there was evidence of learning/performance gains. The courseware supplies information to teachers and students on how it measures student learning.
Comments:

INTRODUCTION TO MULTIMEDIA AND HYPERMEDIA AUTHORING

Background on Multimedia and Hypermedia Authoring Systems

One of the most amazing things about how multimedia and hypermedia systems have evolved is that people with fairly nontechnical skill levels now can develop their own complex, professional-looking hypermedia products. Perhaps most importantly for schools, hypermedia authoring may play a major role in preparing students for the information-intensive and visually oriented world of the future. In tomorrow's digital world, powerful personal computers and ubiquitous electronic networking will allow people to incorporate a variety of media into their communications. Indeed, hypermedia publishing may eventually supersede paper publishing in importance and impact. Four kinds of

TECHNOLOGY INTEGRATION IDEA 6.1

INTERACTIVE STORYBOOKS

Title: CD-ROM Storybooks Enhance Reading Centers

Content Area/Topic: Language arts/reading

Grade Level: K–4

NETS for Students: Standards 1, 3, 4

Description: Interactive books play some of the same roles that parents and teachers do for children who cannot yet read well. By reading aloud to young students and asking questions about the content, interactive books provide help and support to build students' developing literacy skills.

Instruction: Teachers often begin by reading aloud a story from a print book to the whole class, talking about it and explaining items, as needed. They place the interactive version of the story at a classroom reading center, making sure that the learning station has headphones plugged into the computer so students will not disturb the class as they listen to the story. Each student has a turn at the reading center. The teacher asks each student to listen to the story all the way through first before doing the fun branching activities. They give students 3-in. by 5-in. cards and ask them to copy down any words they see and hear that are new vocabulary for them. In their writing journals (or for nonwriting students, during sharing time), students describe their favorite part of the story.

Source: Kahn, J. (1997a). Scaffolding in the classroom: Using CD-ROM storybooks at a computer reading center. *Learning and Leading with Technology, 25*(2), 17–19.

TECHNOLOGY INTEGRATION IDEA 6.2

ELECTRONIC ENCYCLOPEDIAS AND PRESENTATION SOFTWARE

Title: Selling a Space Mission

Content Area/Topic: History/science

Grade Level: Middle school

NETS for Students: Standards 1, 3, 4, 5

Description: This activity asks students to design, write, edit, and publish a brochure and prepare a *PowerPoint* presentation to "sell" a space research project.

Instruction: Students pair up into space mission planning teams. Each team conceptualizes a mission that would accomplish both scientific and social goals that the public could enthusiastically support, with the right encouragement. Then students "sell" their space mission. The teacher uses the Microsoft *Encarta* encyclopedia or another such resource, along with an overhead projection device or large monitor, to take a journey through the history of space exploration, from the *Sputnik* days of the 1960s through the *Apollo* moon mission, the *Challenger* disaster, and to the recent remote-robot exploration of Mars. When students design their brochures, they can paste in pictures from the encyclopedia to illustrate their slides.

Assessment: Rubrics are used to assess group work and the quality of the final projects.

Source: Based on a lesson from *Microsoft Productivity in the Classroom.* Copyright 1997 by the Microsoft Corporation.

Figure 6.4 Summary of Hypermedia Authoring Resources

Types of Resources	Items of Each Type	Instructional Roles in Multimedia Products
Audio	• **CD audio**—Digitized music, speech, or sound effects captured from audio CD or video DVD • **Recorded sounds**—Voice recordings • **Prerecorded sounds**—From collections of sound effects offered in multimedia software or from CD-ROM collections.	• Background music for presentations • Illustrations of musical types • Portions of famous speeches • Readings of poetry • Directions to students • Sound effects to add interest or humor or to signal transitions
Video	• **Digitized videos**—Imported from DVD or VCR using video digitizer, or camcorder and edited with movie software (e.g., Apple's *iMovie*) • **Collections of prerecorded video clips**—Available on CD-ROM or DVD	• Demonstrations of procedures (e.g., labs, sport movements) • Recorded lectures • Illustrative examples of topics being discussed • Video decision-making simulations • Video problem-solving situations
Photograph	• **Scanned photos**—Digitized from print photographs using scanners • **Captured from video sources**—Freeze-frames from DVD or VCR • **Digital camera images**—Downloaded from camera to computer • **Commercial collections**—From CD-ROM	• Historical events, documents, or famous people • Geographical locations or objects in outer space • Illustrative tools (e.g., machines or art implements)
Graphic images	• **Created or imported**—Using draw/paint software, from clip art collections, or scanned images from drawings or hard copy images • **Animations**—From CD-ROM collections or created using animation tools	• Illustrative cartoons (e.g., political) • Attention-getting cues
Text *WordArt*	• **Entered by author**—Typed into product or added as a graphic item (e.g., Microsoft *WordArt*) • **Imported**—From word processing files	• Signs or titles • Summaries of written procedures or explanations • Definitions

multimedia/hypermedia authoring tools for use by both teachers and students are described in this chapter. These are listed here and their uses and sample products are given later in various figures as the following types are discussed:

• Presentation software,

• Video production and editing systems,

• Hypermedia authoring software, and

• Virtual reality systems and other immersion tools.

Although these systems vary in capability and authoring procedures, all allow people to summarize and display information and knowledge using a combination of text, video, animation, music, graphics, and sound effects. The various skills and resources that students and teachers will need in order to use any of these four categories of authoring tools are described here. In addition, integration strategies common to all of these authoring formats are discussed.

Multimedia and Hypermedia Authoring Resources

Over time, multimedia/hypermedia programs have become increasingly more powerful and user friendly, and features and capabilities are being added with every new version released. Authors now can draw on a wide variety of resources to put a full range of sound and motion in their multimedia/hypermedia products. The newest feature available in hypermedia authoring is the ability to insert Internet links into products. Users can click on these links and go immediately from the software screen to an Internet site. Hypermedia resources include audio, video, photographs, graphic images, and text. Figure 6.4 summarizes sources of multimedia/hypermedia authoring materials under each of these categories.

Audio resources. Hypermedia authoring programs offer users a number of ways to incorporate audio clips. These include audio from CD, recording sounds, and prerecorded sounds.

Video resources. Motion video clips can add a whole new dimension to a program and provide authors with many new communication possibilities. As with audio, authors have several options for incorporating video displays into a product, including digitized and prerecorded videos.

Photos. As in other settings, in hypermedia a picture is worth a thousand words. Photographs provide a powerful resource for authors in all subject areas. Photos can be scanned, captured from video, taken with digital cameras, or imported from a CD-ROM.

Graphic images. Graphic elements, drawings, and animations offer other tools for authors to communicate their ideas. Often an illustration will demonstrate a point that is difficult to get across with words. This aspect of hypermedia authoring is particularly appealing to artistically inclined users. Images can be created by authors, imported from clip art collections, scanned from hard copy, or imported from CD-ROM. In addition, animations can be created with animation software.

Text. Despite the attention paid to other components of hypermedia, text remains one of the most powerful ways to communicate ideas. Text can be generated as a multimedia project develops or can be imported from word-processed files.

Hardware Requirements for Hypermedia Authoring

Although hypermedia authoring can be accomplished with a fairly minimal computer system, more complex products require additional hardware and software capabilities. Depending on the complexity of the product,

Figure 6.5 Hypermedia Authoring Hardware Resources

Source: Courtesy of Apple Computer, Inc.

some or all of the following hardware resources (some of which are shown in Figure 6.5) are needed:

- **Computer with keyboard and monitor** — Hypermedia development can be done on any platform as long as the system has a hard drive and sufficient random-access memory (RAM). The minimum requirements to utilize programs such as *HyperStudio* or *Macromedia Director* are much more affordable for the average classroom than they used to be.

- **Digital cameras** — These let users take digital photographs and store them as digital files. The images can then be incorporated into hypermedia projects. Students of all ages enjoy using their own digital photographs in projects.

- **Scanners** — If no digital camera is available, scanners can be used to digitize photos so they can be saved to a disk. Scanners also can capture still images from magazines or books.

- **Video digitizers** — Video digitizers, also known as digitizing boards, are devices that can capture full-motion video from video cameras, VCRs, videodisc players, or live TV. The device that provides the video must be connected to the computer via a cable. Once video segments are transferred, they are stored as digitized computer files and can be edited using software such as Adobe *Premier*. Both teachers and students should recognize copyright restrictions when digitizing and editing video.

- **Camcorders and other video input** — Video cameras or camcorders, VCRs, videodiscs, or CD-ROMs are possible sources for motion video sequences to include in a production.

- **Microphones** — To incorporate sound, an audio source such as a microphone is needed. Most computer systems sold in recent years have built-in audio cards.
- **Audio speakers** — To monitor quality and simply to hear the audio parts of a program, speakers are mandatory for hypermedia development. Many newer computers are shipped with either external or internal speakers.

Hypermedia Authoring Procedures

Whether teachers are developing their own skills or those of their students, the hypermedia authoring process involves two distinct phases. Initially, authors need to learn the mechanics of the programs and develop their understanding of the concept of hypermedia. No one can develop a quality product without first being reasonably comfortable with the tools. However, at the next level, hypermedia authors must develop insights on the complexities of the various media and knowledge of visual and navigation design. This is a long-term process that will emerge through a great deal of experience. A number of strategies can aid the classroom teacher in helping students use their time efficiently and focus on developing quality products. Consider the following steps, summarized in Figure 6.6, students should take when engaging in hypermedia development.

1. **Review others' products** — An effective way of developing authoring skills for beginners is to look at what others have done. It is also helpful to examine some effective uses of commercial media; Ken Burns's series on the Civil War, for example, demonstrates the power of images and sound when melded together in the context of a story.

2. **Do research first** — Most hypermedia development projects require research to locate materials and data, analyze the findings, and summarize them in a format for use in the hypermedia product. It is important to allow adequate time for this research phase because it is the heart of the learning activity.

3. **Storyboard** — Storyboarding helps students make better use of their time. On index cards or sticky notes, students can lay out what they want on each individual frame. But planning is the most difficult thing for students; they want to get right to the "fun stuff." Most students prefer to develop only on the computer. Teachers must insist that on-paper planning be done first. It may help to explain that professional media creators practice storyboarding and that

Figure 6.6 **Sequence of Development Steps for Multimedia Resources**

even famous movie directors such as Alfred Hitchcock and Steven Spielberg storyboarded entire movies before doing a single camera shot because it saves time in the long run.

4. **Develop individual frames and segments** — In the case of hypermedia products with authoring software (e.g., *HyperStudio*), students should develop each frame, including text fields, before adding links or graphics (e.g., clip art, photos, animations, movies, and other media). For video productions, students should shoot video footage in segments.

5. **Add links and/or scripts** — For software-authored products, links or "buttons" should be added last. Most such authoring software allows the creator to see most or all of the frames at one time. This and the card or sticky-note storyboards help students keep links organized among cards. For both software and video products, now is the stage for adding transitions between frames or segments and additional audio to the final product.

6. **Test and revise the product** — After it is drafted, students should test their products, preferably with the help of others who have not been involved in its development. The aim is to revise their products and meet criteria outlined in a later section of this chapter, Evaluating Student-Developed Hypermedia. Rembelinsky (1997–1998) offers a development sequence designed specifically for creating multimedia summaries of project-based research. She recommends students do steps in each of the following general headings: written summary, historical background, creative narrative, scanned images, video, and self-evaluation.

Authoring Skills to Develop over Time

The beauty of hypermedia authoring is that students can create products with skills that range from basic to extraordinarily complex and sophisticated. Teachers have a growing number of tutorials at their disposal to help students learn the basics of authoring software packages. (See the *Internet4Classrooms* site for links to many of these tutorials: http://www.internet4classrooms.com/on-line2.htm.) Students can begin with these and teachers can help them move on to advanced techniques in several areas, as discussed next.

Media literacy. Given the complexities and proliferation of different media, an understanding of media basics will become a fundamental skill for the Information Age. Because most people will have tremendous capabilities to adapt and alter existing media in the near future, a critically important part of instruction in hypermedia authoring will focus on how to be critical and ethical producers and consumers of media (Roblyer, 1998).

Using music and art. Visual arts and music play major roles in the effectiveness of hypermedia products. As students gain more knowledge in the theory and aesthetics of music and art, they will use these resources more productively in the authoring process.

Print design principles. Many principles of desktop publishing also apply to hypermedia designs. When students first see the array of graphics and sound options available, they typically overindulge and use so many colors, graphics, and sounds that content is overshadowed. Some of the design principles that can help guide more judicious use of these options are described later in the section on Evaluating Student-Developed Hypermedia.

Video design principles. For video projects, students learn over time the best ways to illustrate concepts using motion and camera effects. They also learn how to intersperse print and animated titles with their projects.

Creativity and novel thinking. When assessing student projects, look for and encourage creative uses of the potential of hypermedia. Too many student projects resemble glorified paper-based projects; they do not take advantage of the true power of this medium. Classroom activities that encourage creative and critical thinking in all subject areas help develop skills and a mind-set that naturally enhances the authoring process.

Considering the audience. Whenever possible, teachers should try to give students an opportunity to display their projects. Students will be much more motivated if they believe their work is valued. Research on writing has shown that students will invest more effort in the writing process when they know others will read their writing. Turner and Dipinto (1992) and others have observed that this sense of audience carries over to hypermedia authoring. However, teachers sometimes find that components of a student project make sense only to the author. Younger students in particular should be reminded constantly that they need to think of their projects from the user's point of view. Encourage them to test their projects on other students, family, or friends.

Evaluating Student-Developed Hypermedia

When students create their own multimedia/hypermedia products, Dipinto and Turner (1995) suggest that student self-assessment of hypermedia projects may be the most important component of the assessment process. They say that it may enable students to construct a microworld where assessment becomes a feedback mechanism, leading to further exploration and collaboration (p. 11). Several authors have developed criteria and rubrics for assessing the quality of students' hypermedia products. Litchfield (1995), Brunner (1996), Clark (1996), and Royer and Royer (2002) describe

Figure 6.7 Checklist for Assessing Multimedia Products

Content

_____ All information is the most current, up-to-date available.

_____ All information is factually accurate.

_____ Content is free from typos and misspellings, and from punctuation and grammatical errors.

_____ No ethnic, slang, or rude names are used; content is presented in a professional way.

_____ No questionable vocabulary, slang terms, or curse words are used.

_____ Content sources (including sources of graphics) are properly referenced.

Instructional Design

_____ Instructional objectives are clear; the instructional purpose is aligned with school curriculum, rather than being for entertainment.

_____ All necessary information is provided in the product to make concepts clear; users will be able to understand what is being presented from the information provided.

_____ If tests or other assessments are provided, they are matched directly to objectives.

_____ To add interest and motivation for users, information is presented in an innovative and creative way.

Organization and Navigation

_____ Screens are designed for easy navigation; it is clear how to get to and from various parts of the product.

_____ To aid navigation and use, the product has a consistent look and feel throughout.

_____ Buttons and links all work as indicated.

Appearance

_____ Use of varying fonts and type sizes is controlled, so as not to interfere with readability.

_____ Type is large enough to read when projected.

_____ Color contrasts with background for easy reading.

_____ Bold or plain style is used for main text; no shadow and outline if text is more than a few words. Fancy fonts and type styles are readable.

_____ Only brief main ideas are listed in a single frame, rather than paragraphs of text.

Graphics, Videos, and Sound

_____ Graphics, videos, and sound are included as appropriate to help communicate information on the topic; they are not included just for show.

_____ No obscene or rude graphics or visuals are included.

_____ Use of graphics (e.g., animations, screen changes) is controlled and does not distract from reading.

_____ Pictures and sounds associated with buttons and links are appropriate to the purpose and content of the frames.

Source: Based on concepts from Brunner, C. (1996). Judging student multimedia. _Electronic Learning, 15_(6), 14–15; Clark, J. (1996). Bells and whistles ... but where are the references: Setting standards for hypermedia projects. _Learning and Leading with Technology, 23_(5), 22–24; and Litchfield, B. (1995). Helping your students plan computer projects. _The Computing Teacher, 22_(7), 37–43.

qualities to look for in effective products. These are summarized in the _Checklist for Assessing Multimedia_ products, which can be found on the DVD accompanying this text or on the Companion Website (http://www.prenhall.com/roblyer) (also see Figure 6.7). Also see a _Rubric for Evaluating Video Projects_ at the University of Wisconsin website (http://www.uwstout.edu/soe/profdev/videorubric.html) and Royer and Royer's _Multimedia Project Rubric_ in their 2002 article. Teachers may use these instruments to grade student projects, as well as to encourage students to self-assess their work.

Multimedia Authoring Tools Type 1: Presentation Software

Introduction to Presentation Software

Presentation software tools help users create on-screen descriptions, demonstrations, and summaries of information. An example of a technology that migrated from business and industry to education, these tools were first adopted by business executives and salespeople who used them to give reports at meetings and presentations to clients. Their capabilities to demonstrate, illustrate, and clarify information became evident and presentation tools began to make their way into K–12 and university classrooms.

Presentation tools began exclusively as **electronic slide shows,** or sequences of frames shown in a linear way. They have evolved into multimedia authoring tools that allow users to incorporate motion sequences from CD-ROM and other video media into their presentations. Originally designed to display in a linear sequence, they now offer branching by allowing authors to include clickable buttons or "hot spots" to jump to any location in the presentation. Presentation software also allows authors to include graphics of all kinds, audio and video clips, and Internet links. For large classes and other groups, presentation software products usually are used in conjunction with computer projection systems. These may be devices such as LCD panels that fit on top of overhead projectors or systems that operate as stand-alone devices. All of these

TOP TEN TIPS FOR EFFECTIVE POWERPOINT PRESENTATIONS

All of the following are qualities that can greatly enhance readability and/or communication of content during a *PowerPoint*-type presentation.

1. **Large enough type** — Use at least a 32-point font; use larger type if the audience is large and a long distance away from the presenter.

2. **Contrast text and background** — The audience cannot see text too similar in hue to the background. Use text with high contrast to background (e.g., dark blue on white, black on yellow).

3. **Minimize text on each frame** — Use text to focus attention on main points, not present large amounts of information. Summarize ideas in brief phrases.

4. **Too many different items on one frame** — Frame designs should be simple, clear, and free of distractions. Too many items on one frame can interfere with reading, especially if some items are in motion.

5. **Avoid too many fancy fonts** — Many fonts are unreadable when projected on a screen. Use a plain *sans serif* (straight lines with no "hands and feet") font for titles, a plain *serif* font for other text.

6. **Avoid gratuitous graphics** — Graphics interfere with communication when used solely for decoration. Use them to help communicate the content.

7. **Avoid gratuitous sounds** — Sounds interfere with communication when used solely for effect. They should always help communicate the content.

8. **Use graphics, not just text** — Well-chosen graphics can help communicate messages. Text alone does not make best use of the capabilities of presentation software.

9. **Present in a dark room** — Frames can fade away if the room is too bright. Cover windows and turn off lights during a presentation.

10. **Avoid reading text aloud** — Do not read what the audience can read for themselves. Use text to guide main points of discussion.

---

devices enlarge the image produced by the software by projecting it from a computer screen onto a wall screen.

As the most popular of these tools, *PowerPoint* presentations have attracted much criticism in recent years for their tendency to be linear and overly simplistic (Tufte, 2003). However, the effectiveness of a presentation tool depends largely on the communications skills of the presenter. While presentation software makes it possible for students and teachers to communicate in the "grammar of multimedia," new users make some common "grammatical mistakes." Ten of the most common errors made by users of presentation software and how to avoid them are described in the *Top Ten* feature above.

Integration Strategies for Presentation Software

Because it is readily available and relatively easy to use, *PowerPoint* software is often the multimedia tool of choice for classroom use. A variety of integration strategies have emerged for these versatile tools. Some of these are described here and summarized in Figure 6.8. Technology Integration Idea 6.3 illustrates how students can do group-based *PowerPoint* presentations to enhance their understanding of content.

- **Support for lectures or presentations of content** — By far the most popular use of these tools is for supporting classroom presentations. Teachers use them to focus student attention and guide note-taking.

- **Practice screens** — Many teachers set up presentations of spelling or vocabulary words or objects to identify (e.g., lab equipment, famous names or places) to run automatically in the classroom, knowing that students' eyes are drawn to the moving slides.

- **Assessment screens** — When teachers need students to identify pictures of items (e.g., lab equipment, famous people), *PowerPoint* screens can enable visual assessment strategies.

- **Brief tutorials** — Teachers can create *PowerPoint* reviews of simple concepts (e.g., grammar rules) or "how-to" procedures (e.g., a lab procedure) so that students can review these on their own to make up work or to prepare for tests.
- **Book reports** — Instead of presenting book reports verbally or as written summaries, it is becoming increasingly common for students to report on their reading through *PowerPoint* slideshows. Teachers often design a standard format or template, and students fill in the required information and add their own illustrations.
- **Student-created presentations** — As Technology Integration Ideas 6.2 and 6.3 illustrate, the most power-

Figure 6.8 Presentation Software Authoring Software Tools

Types of Tools	Types of Products	Instructional Uses
Presentation software Box shot reprinted by permission from Microsoft Corporation.	• **Microsoft *PowerPoint*** http://www.microsoft.com • **Upresent** http://www.codeblazer.com/ • **OpenOffice.org** (free productivity software) http://www.openoffice.org/	• Support for lectures or presentations of content • Practice screens (e.g., spelling words, new vocabulary) • Assessment screens (e.g., identification of objects) • Brief tutorials • Book reports • Student-created presentations

TECHNOLOGY INTEGRATION IDEA 6.3

PRESENTATION SOFTWARE PROJECTS

Title: *PowerPoint* Projects Enhance Learning About Biomes

Content Area/Topic: Science/ecology

Grade Level: 9–10

NETS for Students: Standards 1, 3, 4, 5, 6

Description: The aim of having students' create *PowerPoint* presentations to document and present their findings is to make their learning experience more meaningful and engaged. To accomplish this, teachers assign projects that call for creation of multiple solutions, inquiry, and decision making around a theme or "big idea." One example of such a project is the Biome Inquiry project.

Instruction: The teacher tells students the "big idea" for the project: "Organisms live in a selected biome because they are adapted to the conditions there." He begins by discussing essential background questions: What is a biome? What are characteristics of various biomes? How are organisms adapted to conditions in each one? What species in each are threatened and why? The assigned task for the *PowerPoint* presentation is to simulate the work of members of the National Academy of Science, who have been asked to appear before the United Nations (UN) and present a plan to reduce human impact on one of the world's biomes. Students are assigned to select a biome to research, answer key questions on it (e.g., What is the significance of this biome?), and present information on it as though making a presentation to the UN. Students are placed in small groups with assigned roles and work together to do the research and create the presentation.

Assessment: Student presentations are assessed using a rubric created especially for this project (see article).

Source: Royer, R., & Royer, J. (2002). Developing understanding with multimedia. Learning and Leading with Technology, 29(7), 40–45.

ful strategy for presentation multimedia is for students to create individual or small-group presentations to document and display the results of their research and/or to practice making persuasive presentations.

PowerPoint-type presentations have become so popular that assessment instruments matched to them have been designed. See the University of Wisconsin rubric for evaluating students' *PowerPoint* presentations at http://www.uwstout.edu/soe/profdev/pptrubric.html.

MULTIMEDIA AUTHORING TOOLS TYPE 2: VIDEO PRODUCTION AND EDITING SYSTEMS

Introduction to Video Production and Editing Systems

Once the exclusive domain of Hollywood, video production is now a growing presence in school activities. **Video editing software** is to motion images what word processing is to text. The next decade likely will see an explosion in video editing and production to rival the rapid increase in word processing of documents. As Howard (2001) observed, video software can be very time consuming for anyone who wants to do high-quality videos, and especially so for novice users. However, schools across the country are beginning to use these systems to produce school news programs and to develop digitized video for use in authoring hypermedia products (Hoffenburg & Handler, 2001).

Video can be brought into a computer from a source such as a camcorder and changed into digital format [**Audio Video Interleave (AVI) format** or **Moving Picture Experts Group (MPEG) format**], or it may be transferred in digital form from a digital camera. Once digital video is stored on a computer, the resulting digitized video clips can be inserted in a multimedia package or uploaded to the Internet. Video clips stored in this way

are often called **QuickTime® movies,** since Apple Computer provides free player software that is frequently used to view them. Video editing software allows these movies to be edited and combined with special effects such as titles, screen fades, and voice-over audio. Movie production and editing packages are listed in Figure 6.9, along with sample integration strategies.

When Apple Computer included a free copy of its video production software *iMovie* with some of its computer systems, it heralded the beginning of widespread interest in video editing among educators and other consumers. An example of an *iMovie* video editing software screen is shown in Figure 6.10. At the bottom of the figure are two tracks, audio and video. By sliding markers on these tracks, students can cut, copy, and/or paste sections of a video and/or combine them with special effects such as fades or background music.

Integration Strategies for Video Production and Editing Systems

Students and teachers are using computer-based video production and editing systems for a variety of purposes ranging from presenting the daily school news to teaching professional-grade video production skills. Some of these strategies are described here and summarized in Figure 6.7. Technology Integration Idea 6.4 illustrates one of these uses.

- **Demonstrations of procedures** — For frequently repeated activities, for example, procedures for science experiments, teachers can film themselves or others completing the steps. These short clips allow demonstrations that are the same each time and can be repeated as many times as desired. For example, Jacobsen, Moore, and Brown (2002) describe a CD-ROM of 600 movie clips that illustrate chemistry laboratory techniques and procedures.

Figure 6.9 **Video Software Authoring Software Tools**

Types of Tools	Types of Products	Instructional Uses
Video production and editing software Courtesy of Apple Computer, Inc.	• **FinalCut Pro** http://www.apple.com • **Apple's iMovie** http://www.apple.com • **Avid Xpress Pro** http://www.avid.com • **Adobe Premier Pro** http://www.adobe.com • **Pinnacle Studio** http://www.pinnaclesys.com	• Demonstrations of procedures (e.g., science experiments) • Student-created presentations • Video lectures • Video portfolios • Video decision-making/problem-solving simulations • Documenting of school activities (e.g., yearbooks) • Visual literacy demonstrations • Teaching of video production

Figure 6.10 *iMovie Editing Screen*

05:00

Clip 04

Clips Photos Audio Titles Trans Effects iDVD

Source: Courtesy of Apple Computer. Photo courtesy of Bill Wienke.

TECHNOLOGY INTEGRATION IDEA 6.4

VIDEO PROJECTS

Title: A Monarch Butterfly Movie Project

Content Area/Topic: Science/biology

Grade Level: Elementary

NETS for Students: Standards 1, 3, 4, 5

Description: This project helps students gain more insight into the process of metamorphosis than they could by viewing it via traditional methods. They collect Monarch butterfly eggs and create a digital movie of the stages as the eggs grow to become butterflies.

Instruction: Students begin by visiting several Internet sites to learn more about Monarch butterflies. Then they collect the eggs and set up the environment in which the cocoons will grow. The teacher helps them position the camera to film the development of the butterfly as it goes through the four stages of metamorphosis. After they capture the process, the teacher shows them a speeded up version, and they discuss what they are seeing using correct scientific terms. They write up their findings and place them and the movie on a web page to share with other classes.

Assessment: Teachers use a rubric to evaluate students' group work and involvement in the learning activities.

Sources: Stuhlmann, J. (1997). Butterflies: Using multimedia to capture a unique science project. *Learning and Leading with Technology, 25*(3), 22–27; and Hoffenburg, H., & Handler, M. (2001). Digital video goes to school. *Learning and Leading with Technology, 29*(2), 10–15.

- **Student-created presentations** — Although students can produce a video as a way of documenting their research findings, as they do with *PowerPoint* presentations, they often create videos that illustrate real-life examples of concepts they have learned (e.g., showing how algebra applies to everyday situations) or document conditions they want to bring to light (e.g., social issues in their community).

- **Video lectures** — Teachers can take video of themselves or other experts explaining key concepts. These come in handy if students miss the original presentation or want to review material in a visual way. It is also a means of making a classroom presentation of consistently high quality each time students see it.

- **Video portfolios** — Student portfolios have become more common for assessment purposes, and video systems have assumed a central role in portfolio development. Many teachers also are required to develop portfolios to document their teaching methods in preparation for promotion or additional certification.

- **Video decision-making/problem-solving simulations** — This strategy was made popular with the *Adventures of Jasper Woodbury* videodiscs. Videos are used to depict problem scenarios that require math skills, and students can review information in the videos as they create solutions to the problems.

- **Documenting of school activities** — Many middle and secondary schools use video cameras and video editing software to produce a daily news show or morning announcements. These productions "star" the students themselves, and students also do the camera and editing work. News shows offer valuable opportunities to help students develop their on-camera presentation skills, as well as their technical production skills. When schools do video yearbooks, students take video of events and merge them into a collage of the year's events (Kwajewski, 1997a).

- **Visual literacy instruction** — Now that video is playing a greater role in our society, visual literacy is a requirement. By analyzing information in video format, students learn how people can use visual images to communicate biases and make persuasive arguments in advertisements and news stories.

- **Teaching of video production** — Technology education labs usually feature video production as one of the required learning stations. Students in these labs usually do the school's news shows and morning announcements.

MULTIMEDIA AUTHORING TOOLS TYPE 3: HYPERMEDIA SOFTWARE

Introduction to Hypermedia Software Tools

In the late 1980s, early hypermedia authoring programs included *HyperCard* for Macintosh, *LinkWay* for MS-DOS machines, and *TutorTech* for Apple II computers. These programs represented a major jump forward in technology, but because authors had to make major time commitments to learn and use the software, their use was limited. Things began to change when Roger Wagner's *HyperStudio* was released. This program used the same basic "card and stack" metaphor as *HyperCard* but eliminated much of the need for extensive scripting or for programming commands. In recent years, other programs have become available that emulate *HyperStudio*'s easy-to-use format (see Figure 6.11).

Integration Strategies for Hypermedia Authoring Software

Multimedia and hypermedia development projects are taking the place of many traditional activities to accomplish the same purposes. Some common classroom applications of multimedia and hypermedia are described here and summarized in Figure 6.9. See the *HyperStudio* website for a collection of illustrative curriculum lessons and products (http://www.hyperstudio.com/showcase/index.html). Technology Integration Idea 6.5 illustrates one such lesson.

- **Brief tutorials** — Both teachers and students can create multimedia instructional sequences that step the user through the components of a subject. Figure 6.12 shows two cards from a *HyperStudio* tutorial on the instruments in an orchestra. In this product, the user may click on an instrument to hear it play and to read more about it.

Figure 6.11 **Hypermedia Authoring Software Tools**

Types of Tools	Types of Products	Instructional Uses
Hypermedia authoring software *macromedia* **AUTHORWARE 7** Courtesy of Macromedia.	• *HyperStudio* http://www.hyperstudio.com/ • *Authorware* http://www.macromedia.com	• Brief tutorials • Student-created presentations • Interactive storybooks

TECHNOLOGY INTEGRATION IDEA 6.5

HYPERMEDIA AUTHORING

Title: Quilting Our History

Content Area/Topic: U.S. history and multimedia design

Grade Level: High school

NETS for Students: Standards 1, 3, 4, 5

Description: Students develop high-end multimedia design skills as they create a CD-ROM "quilt" that describes local history.

Instruction: This schoolwide project requires a great deal of planning and collaboration among teachers in several content areas, but the basic goal is to document the history of the local area and the families whose personal histories were intertwined with the history of the region. After all of the content-area teachers have worked together to decide on the project design and how it should be carried out, students form teams to accomplish the production tasks: researching information about the history of the local region and the families, geometric design of quilted squares to represent various families, gathering video documentation, and multimedia design. This project used high-end multimedia software (*Macromedia Director*) along with *Adobe PhotoShop* and 3D and audio packages. The technology education classes carried out the actual multimedia design and production tasks.

Assessment: Rubrics can be used to evaluate the quality of students' participation and final products.

Source: van Buren, C., & Aufdenspring, D. (1998). Quilting our history: An integrated schoolwide project. *Learning and Leading with Technology, 26*(2), 22–27.

• **Student-created presentations** — Scholten and Whitmer (1996), Bennett and Diener (1997), and Stuhlmann (1997) point out that hypermedia presentations not only let students present their findings attractively and with impact, but the act of producing and sharing what they have learned also helps students learn even more about the topics and enhance their research, study, and communication skills.

• **Interactive storybooks** — Frederickson (1997) describes a use that builds on the book report purpose. Students document existing stories or write their own so they can be read interactively by others. Those reading these hypermedia stories can click on various places on the screen to hear or see parts of a story. This format also lets students go beyond one basic sequence and create their own branches and endings to stories. Wilkerson (2001) described how teacher-created interactive books can help support mathematics instruction.

MULTIMEDIA AUTHORING TOOLS TYPE 4: VIRTUAL REALITY AND OTHER IMMERSION TOOLS

Introduction to Virtual Reality and Other Immersion Tools

Once only dreamed of in science fiction, some types of **virtual reality (VR)** are now seen frequently in classrooms. Through various visual and tactile devices, VR can represent real or imaginary worlds in which the user interacts through multiple senses: a true multimedia environment. Although the first VR systems, created for the military and aerospace industry, required sophisticated computers with advanced computer graphics, other types of VR have been developed that require less sophisticated capabilities.

The potential of VR systems to make cyberspace seem real has been talked about since William Gibson's 1984

Figure 6.12 **Sample Screens from Multimedia Tutorial**

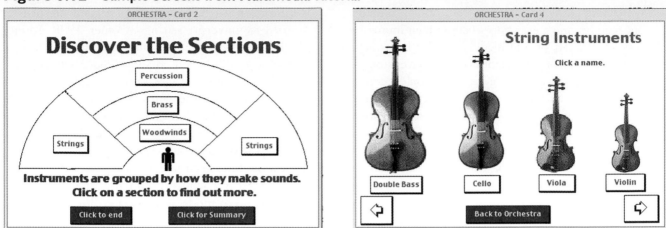

Source: Screen images from *The Sections of the Orchestra* courtesy of Jolaine Sims.

novel *Neuromancer,* in which people used **avatars**, or graphic icons, to represent themselves in virtual environments. However, that potential has been tapped more for video games than for education. Four types of VR are described here, two of which are often used in K–12 classrooms. Educational uses of the other two types are usually limited to university research settings.

- **Full immersion systems** — Though not often used in education, this is what people usually envision when they think of VR. In **full immersion systems,** the user places a headset (e.g., goggles or a helmet) over the eyes. Known as a **head-mounted display (HMD),** this headset is the channel through which the wearer "sees" the computer-generated environment (see Figure 6.13). Other configurations use a large curved projection screen to immerse the user in the environment. In both, views of the "real" world are replaced with those of the virtual one. The senses create an illusion of actually being in the environment the system displays. Other devices for full immersion sys-

Figure 6.13 **Head-Mounted VR Display**

Source: Courtesy of Georgia Tech Communications.

tems include sound and tactile or **haptic interfaces.** Sound usually is presented to the user through stereo headphones that may or may not be built into the HMD. The user wears a glove or brace-like device that provides tactile feedback when the user "grasps" an object in the virtual world.

- **Web-based VR** — This kind of VR is made possible by **Virtual Reality Modeling Language (VRML)** and **Extensible Mark-up Language (XML).** Just as Hypertext Mark-up Language (HTML) describes what a web page will look like in a browser (see Chapter 7), VRML and XML describe the geometry and behavior of the virtual world or scene. VRML files can be viewed in either *Netscape Communicator* or *Internet Explorer* browsers with the necessary plug-in. Creating worlds in VRML also requires building a 3-D model of the environment, as with the traditional VR models described above. This can be accomplished with modeling software, which can then output the VRML code, or students can code the world directly as they would a web page with HTML. Although not as realistic as full immersion VR, VRML costs less to implement. However, the technical requirements for creating VRML products have caused education uses to remain limited.

- **3-D models** — These are made possible with sophisticated software that creates three-dimensional replicas of objects or locations. The products are then viewed on a flat screen computer (as opposed to an immersive environment). Some 3-D models are transferred to VRML and viewed via web browsers, as described above. Steed (2001) describes several educational uses of these models and gives examples of 3-D software.

- *QuickTime* **VR (QTVR)** — Made possible by *QuickTime VR Authoring Studio* from Apple Computer, this type of VR is easy to access using the standard *QuickTime* player available free from Apple Computer, but requires much less effort to create than immersion systems, VRML, or 3-D models. In QTVR, a teacher can take a series of photographs at 360 degrees around a pivotal point. For example, a classroom could record by setting up the camera in the middle of the room on a tripod. A series of 16 photos would be taken at 22.5-degree intervals. The photos are then input into *QuickTime VR Authoring Studio,* which "stitches" them together into a seamless panoramic view of the room. In addition, because QTVR uses actual photographs to create the panorama, it provides a more realistic representation than the computer-generated systems. This seems to be the most common use of VR in K–12 classrooms.

Integration Strategies for Virtual Reality and Other Immersion Tools

Though not as common as other forms of hypermedia, VR is gaining interest for some instructional needs. Some common classroom applications of VR resources are described here and summarized in Figure 6.14.

- **Imaging for virtual field trips** — Perhaps the most common VR application is *QuickTime* VR panoramas created and used for virtual field trips. Stevenson (2001) describes a variety of virtual field trips that use *Quicktime* VR movies to give tours of locations around the world. She also provides related links on how to create a field trip.

- **3-D models to illustrate how systems work** — Although still limited to more technical topics in mathematics and science, 3-D modeling is seeing increasing use in education as a way to help students visualize mathematics and science concepts. Example models are described to study characteristics of the solar system (Bakas & Mikropoulos, 2003; Barab, Hay, & Barnett, 2000) and processes of photosynthesis (Mikropoulos, Katsikis, & Nikolou, 2003).

- **Immersion learning environments for practice and exploration** — Full immersion systems are usually limited to university settings (Comer, 1999; Young, 2000), but they have seen fairly extensive use in special education as a way to allow students to practice skills in a realistic, but safe, setting. Goldstein (2002) describes one such use with software designed to help students with attention deficit disorders and/or mobility and visual problems. Mohnsen (2003) also described VR systems that would be useful for physical education, but are currently too expensive to be practical. Becker and Schuetz (2003) describe one VRML-based lesson to model groundwater flow for geology students. Orman (2003) described a virtual environment for training performing musicians to prepare for the pressures of live performance, which she feels has great promise for this purpose.

INTERACTIVE SUMMARY

The following is a summary of the main points covered in this chapter. To see additional examples and information on these points, go to this textbook's Companion Website at http://www.prenhall.com/roblycr and click on the Chapter 6 *Interactive Summary* module to visit each of the recommended websites.

1. **Definitions of multimedia and hypermedia:** Although *multimedia* means "multiple media," and *hypermedia* means "linked media," the terms have come to be used interchangeably. The hypermedia concept is based on the ideas of <u>Vannevar Bush</u> in his landmark article "<u>As We May Think.</u>"

2. **Current and future impact of multimedia/hypermedia:** Multimedia products, already seeing substantial use in education, are predicted to have even greater impact in the future, since they mirror the increased emphasis on visual media in the modern world. Educational contributions are being seen in

Figure 6.14 **VR and Immersion Authoring Software Tools**

Types of Tools	Types of Products	Instructional Uses

Virtual reality and other immersion tools
 	
Courtesy of Apple Computer, Inc.
	• *Virtual Reality Toolbox*
	  http://www.mathworks.com
	• *QuickTime VR Authoring Studio*
	  http://apple.com
	• *3DS Max*
	  http://www4.discreet.com
		• Imaging for virtual field trips
		• 3-D models to illustrate how systems work
		• Immersion learning environments for exploration and practice

four areas: increased motivation, more flexible learning modes, development of creative and critical thinking skills, and improved writing and process skills.

3. **Research on multimedia/hypermedia:** Research finds that multimedia's benefits center on its ability to offer students multiple channels through which to process information. Several studies also have offered recommendations on designing and using multimedia products for instructional purposes.

4. **Four types of multimedia/hypermedia resources in education:** Types of multimedia/hypermedia resources include commercial multimedia/hypermedia software packages and three kinds of multimedia/hypermedia authoring tools: presentation software (e.g., Microsoft's *PowerPoint*), video production and editing systems (e.g., Apple's *iMovie*), and virtual reality (VR) systems (e.g., Apple's *QuickTime VR Authoring Studio*).

5. **Commercial multimedia/hypermedia resources:** These include instructional software (e.g., tutorials, drills, simulations), interactive books and ebooks, reference materials, and collections of development materials. Educators use criteria under the following headings when selecting these materials: instructional planning and support, instructional design, content, interface design and navigation, and feedback and interactivity.

6. **Authoring resources, procedures, and skills:** When teachers or students create their own multimedia/hypermedia materials, they need a variety of digital resources (e.g., audio, video, photos, graphics, and text) and hardware (e.g., computers, scanners, digital cameras, camcorders, microphones, audio speakers) at their disposal, as well as a set of authoring skills, which they can develop over time.

7. **General authoring procedures:** These include reviewing others' work, doing background research, storyboarding, creating individual frames or segments, adding links and scripts, and testing and revising.

8. **Authoring with presentation software:** Integration strategies for *PowerPoint*-type presentations include support for lectures or presentations of content, practice screens (e.g., spelling words, new vocabulary), assessment screens (e.g., identification of objects), brief tutorials, book reports, and student-created presentations. Rubrics help assess presentations.

9. **Authoring with video production and editing software:** Integration strategies include demonstrations of

procedures (e.g., science experiments), student-created presentations, video lectures, video portfolios, video decision-making/problem-solving simulations, documenting school activities (e.g., yearbooks), visual literacy demonstrations, and teaching video production. Rubrics are available to assess video products.

10. **Authoring with hypermedia authoring software:** Integration strategies include brief tutorials, student-created presentations, and interactive storybooks. Rubrics and checklists are available to assess hypermedia projects. (See checklist on the DVD accompanying this text.)

11. **Authoring with virtual reality and other immersion resources:** These tools include full immersion environments, web-based VRML, 3-D software, and *QuickTime* VR. Integration strategies include imaging for virtual field trips, 3-D models to illustrate how systems work, and immersive learning environments for exploration.

Online Activities

Visit this text's Companion Website at http://www.prenhall.com/roblyer to gain access to a variety of questions, activities, and exercises to help build your knowledge of this chapter's content.

Online Chapter 6 Self-Test

To review terms and concepts for this chapter, click on the *Self-Test* module for this chapter of the Companion Website.

Software Skill-Builder Tutorials

To access practical tutorial and skill-building activities and to build skills using popular software and hardware, click on the *Software Skill-Builder Tutorials* module for this chapter of the Companion Website.

Web-Enrichment Activities

To complete activities that connect to chapter content and provide web-based resources, click on the *Web-Enrichment Activities* module for this chapter of the Companion Website.

TECHNOLOGY INTEGRATION WORKSHOP

CLIPS FROM THE CLASSROOM: LEARNING WITH TECHNOLOGY

Go to the *Technology Integration Workshop* DVD located in the back of this text and click on *Clips from the Classroom*. View the video clips listed below that support this chapter's content:

- *Benefits of Tablet Computers*
- *Tablet Computers in Fourth-Grade Science*
- *Tablet Computers in First-Grade Mathematics*
- PowerPoint *Guides and Prompts Teaching*
- *Presentation Software in Literature.*

Now, visit this text's Companion Website at http://www.prenhall.com/roblyer to answer questions and complete activities that will guide you in analyzing each clip.

THE TIP MODEL IN ACTION

Read each of the following scenarios related to implementing the TIP Model, and go to the Companion Website to answer the questions that follow it based on your Chapter 6 reading activities.

TIP Model Scenario #1 Mr. Joaquin is looking for a more motivating alternative to traditional written book reports. His fifth-grade students do not especially like reading books or writing book reports. Mr. Joaquin was talking to a colleague who uses *HyperStudio* multimedia software to make doing book reports more appealing to students.

1.1 Describe how you think using *HyperStudio* multimedia software would make it more likely Mr. Joaquin's students would enjoy doing book reports.

1.2 What would be the relative advantage of using this software tool?

1.3 Would it be better to have the students work individually or in groups to do the exercises? How would you arrange the computer systems to carry out this strategy?

TIP Model Scenario #2 Mr. Clint and Ms. Snyder, two junior high school social studies teachers, plan a school-wide project to document the history of the local area by focusing on the families whose personal histories are intertwined with the history of the region. They plan to have students interview many individual family members and research local sources of historical information. Then they want the students to organize all of the information into a book about the history of the local region.

2.1 What multimedia tools could the teachers use to enhance and support this project?

2.2 What would be the relative advantage of using such multimedia tools?

2.3 This kind of project would require a lot of work to research and organize information and to produce the final product. Suggest some ways this work could be divided up and accomplished among classes to model for students how to organize work tasks in a large, complex project.

TIP Model Scenario #3 Mr. Eliott is a fourth-grade teacher and has several students in his class who speak English as a second language. He works on increasing the comprehension skills for each of his students and encourages them to read books and stories to practice their skills. His students who speak English as their second language have trouble reading independently, and Mr. Eliott does not have the time to read to each of them individually. He would like a way they can have books read aloud to them in an enjoyable way and also answer comprehension questions about what they have heard and read.

3.1 What kind of multimedia tool could help Mr. Eliott address this problem?

3.2 What would be the relative advantages of using this tool with his students who speak English as a second language?

3.3 How would it be possible for these students to use this tool in class but not disturb or distract other students?

TIP Model Scenario #4 Ms. Warnick is a high school curriculum coordinator who wants the students to prepare an electronic portfolio they can take with them to display the quality of their work and what they have accomplished throughout their courses. She would like this to include film footage of them giving class presentations, as well as digital samples of their work. The completed portfolio for graduating seniors would be placed on a CD they could take with them.

4.1 What multimedia tool would you recommend Ms. Warnick use to address this problem?

4.2 What would be the relative advantage of using this tool?

4.3 If she wanted teachers to assist with this activity, what would she have to make sure was done before the portfolio concept was introduced to students?

TIP Model Scenario #5 Ms. Bradley's eighth-grade language arts students have a spelling test every Friday, and spelling counts for 10% of their overall semester grade. There is no time during the regular class period during the week to allow students to practice, and it is obvious from their grades that many students do not study the words outside class. Ms. Bradley thought of a way to use Microsoft *PowerPoint* software to make sure

her students see all the spelling words and hear them pronounced every time they come in the classroom and every time they leave.

5.1 How do you think Ms. Bradley uses *PowerPoint* software to address this problem?

5.2 What would be the relative advantage of using *PowerPoint* software for this purpose?

5.3 Which of *PowerPoint*'s multimedia benefits is Ms. Bradley using for this activity?

TIE INTO PRACTICE: TECHNOLOGY INTEGRATION EXAMPLES

The Technology Integration Example that opened this chapter (*Interactive Multimedia Storybooks*) showed how a teacher might use hypermedia authoring software to help produce the annual literary anthology of student work. With the knowledge you have gained from Chapter 6, do the following with this example:

1. Ms. Dubey's students created an interactive storybook like the *HyperStudio* one shown here.

2. Answer the following questions about the *Interactive Storybook* example:

HyperStudio Interactive Storybook Example (Create this product using the *Hands-On with Technology* tutorial section of the DVD.)

- Phase 1 — How would having the high school students work on an interactive storybook for younger students offer relative advantage for language development in comparison with other reading-related activities the teachers could do?

- Phase 2 — One of the desired outcomes of this project was effective cooperative group work skills. Look at the Kathy Schrock website (http:// school.discovery.com/schrockguide/assess.html) to locate two different rubrics to help assess this kind of outcome.

- Phase 3 — Why does the technology coordinator have the students do small projects (e.g., an interactive map of their school) before getting started on the interactive storybooks? Why is storyboarding such an important part of the hypermedia development sequence?

- Phase 4 — If no money were available to purchase a lab-pack of *HyperStudio* copies, could the technology coordinator make temporary copies to be used just for this project, then destroy them afterward?

- Phase 5 — Can you think of strategies Ms. Dubey might use to coordinate group work on the project and cope with student absences?

3. What NETS for Students skills would students learn by working on the *Interactive Storybook* project? (See the front of the book for a list of NETS for students.)

TECHNOLOGY INTEGRATION LESSON PLANNING

The *Technology Integration Workshop* DVD includes a set of technology integration ideas and links to online lessons, arranged as a searchable database. The DVD comes packaged in the back of this textbook. Click on the *Hands-On with Technology* section of the DVD and complete the following exercises.

1. **Locate lesson ideas** — The DVD has several examples of lessons that use *HyperStudio,* video development, 3-D modeling, and virtual field trips with *QuickTime* movies. Locate an example integration idea for using each of these software tools.

2. **Evaluate the lessons** — Use the *Evaluation Checklist for a Technology-Integrated Lesson* (located on the DVD and the Companion Website) to evaluate each of these lessons.

3. **Modify a lesson** — Select one of the lesson ideas and adapt its strategies to meet a need in your own content area. You may choose to use the same multimedia software in the original or a different one.

4. **Add descriptors** — Create descriptors for your new lesson like those found on the database (e.g., grade level, content and topic areas, technologies used, relative advantage, objectives, NETS standards).

5. **Add the new lesson** — Add your modified lesson with all its descriptors to the lesson idea database.

FOR YOUR TEACHING PORTFOLIO

For this chapter's contribution to your teaching portfolio, add the following products you created in the Technology Integration Workshop:

- The *HyperStudio* product you created for the *Interactive Storybook* project

- The evaluations you did using the *Evaluation Checklist for a Technology-Integrated Lesson*

- The new lesson plan you developed, based on the one you found on the DVD.

PART 3

LINKING TO LEARN: TOOLS AND STRATEGIES

Chapter 7   **Introducing the Internet and Other Distance Learning Tools**

Chapter 8   **Integrating the Internet into the Curriculum**

Thanks to microcomputers, the last 25 years have seen an explosion of computer technology-related activity in schools and classrooms. But the emergence of a graphically oriented Internet in 1994 suddenly and dramatically shifted the spotlight from stand-alone microcomputers to the importance of linking with others: other people, other cultures, other points of view. The chapters in this section focus on the resources and strategies that link students and teachers with each other and with the world outside the classroom.

PART 3

REQUIRED BACKGROUND FOR TEACHERS

In Part 3, two chapters help teachers build the skills they will need to take advantage of the potential of distance learning resources.

Chapter 7 · Introducing the Internet and Other Distance Learning Tools

Although most people think of distance learning as the Internet, other distance delivery systems are also in common use. This chapter reviews web-based and other tools and methods to link learners with each other and with needed resources at distant sites. It also describes and gives practice in skills and techniques needed to implement distance learning strategies.

Chapter 8 · Integrating the Internet into the Curriculum

This chapter focuses on uses of the Internet that address current educational needs. It describes the unique capabilities of web-based tools and gives examples and practice in applying them in various instructional situations. Finally, it focuses on how to design effective web-based lessons and the websites to support them.

CHAPTER 7

INTRODUCING THE INTERNET AND OTHER DISTANCE LEARNING TOOLS

It is obvious that both teaching and learning…will be influenced in varying
ways by "the death of distance."

Michael Moore, in an editorial for the *American Journal of Distance Education*, 1995

But the Net, I guarantee you, really is fire. I think it's more important than the
invention of moveable type.

Brad Ferren, as quoted by David Remnick in "Future Perfect," *The New Yorker* (October 1997)

TECHNOLOGY INTEGRATION EXAMPLE
A RESEARCH PAPER WEBSITE

Based on: "So You Have to do a Research Project?" at http://www.ri.net/schools/East_Greenwich/research.html.

Grade Level: High school • Content Area/Topic: Research, study skills • Length of Time: Nine weeks

Phase 1: Determine relative advantage

Ms. Almon was the library media specialist at Werebest High School. One of her tasks was to help all teachers and students use the library resources effectively for students' research paper assignments. Over the years, she had compiled a substantial collection of handouts, lists of sources, and assessment materials, which she copied, placed in notebooks, and updated periodically. However, she and the teachers agreed it was difficult to get students to use these notebooks. The students' study skills and organizational strategies left a lot to be desired, and each teacher seemed to have a different approach to teaching these important skills. As she and the teachers talked about this situation, they agreed that it would be better to have these materials in a website, so that students could access them wherever they were, they could be easily updated, and the approach for doing research would be consistent across all classes. They decided to work together to create a Research Paper Resource Website. They also decided they would use this site and a set of video tutorials to structure a series of teaching activities that would help students complete research paper assignments.

Phase 2: Decide on objectives and assessments

Ms. Almon and the teachers decided they would structure their assessments around the "Big Six" information literacy skills (see http://www.big6.com/), as well as the quality of content in the students' research papers. To make sure all teachers would structure students' learning in the same way, they agreed on objectives for each of these skill areas and created assessment methods to measure each. They also decided to measure student attitudes toward research and writing. The outcomes, objectives, and assessments they decided on were:

- **Big Six Information Skills #1–#3:** Defining, searching for, and acquiring information. **Objective:** Students will identify a topic for a research paper, use the project website to identify published sources of information related to the topic, and locate the information items. **Assessment:** Checklist of required tasks and products from information searches.
- **Big Six Information skills #4–#6:** Analyze, synthesize, and evaluate information. **Objective:** Students will

write summary analyses of the information in each item they locate, write a synthesis across all information, and prepare an outline of points they will emphasize in their research papers. **Assessment:** Checklist of required tasks and products from information analyses.
- **Final paper:** Write a research paper. **Objective:** Students will achieve a rubric score of at least 15 of 20 possible points on an assigned research paper. **Assessment:** Rubric on research paper content, structure, mechanics, and creativity.
- **Attitudes toward writing: Objective:** The students will demonstrate a good attitude toward the writing approach used in the project by reporting a rating of at least 45 of 50 possible points on an attitude survey. **Assessment:** Likert scale attitude survey.

Phase 3: Design integration strategies

Ms. Almon and the teachers worked together to determine what they would place on the resource website and how students would use it. They decided the site would be most useful if it served to provide links to helpful sites and a structure to help students work through the process of doing their searches and writing their papers. They also decided they should create short video tutorials on key points in the process such as how to select a research paper topic and how to use a graphic organizer to create a visual outline. The website and the tutorials would also help make the teaching process more consistent across teachers. They decided to recommend the following time frame for the research paper project:

- **Week 1: Introducing the project and identifying a topic:** All teachers introduce the research paper project by displaying the website to the whole class using a large monitor or projection system. They review the steps, discuss the process (displaying some of the links at each step), show the first video tutorial, and help students select their research paper topics.
- **Weeks 2–3: Helping students obtain information:** The teachers show students how to use website links to search for information related to their topic. One of the activities is deciding which type of resource to use. For

resources that can best be found in the library, Ms. Almon arranges to show students how to access these resources in the library media center, using a video tutorial as an overview. Students use the website resources at the classroom workstation and in the computer center, depending on what else the teacher is doing in the classroom during this time.

- **Weeks 4–6: Helping students analyze and synthesize information:** The teachers help students review their information and make decisions on how to structure their paper and what to include in it. They show videos on doing graphic organizers and let students practice using these techniques.
- **Weeks 7–8: Writing the papers:** During this time, students complete most of the writing on their papers at home or in the library media center after school. Some teachers allocate some class time for students to work in class and to review and give feedback on their word-processed drafts.
- **Week 9: Presentations:** Students present their papers using the strategy selected by their teacher. Some prepare *PowerPoint* presentations to accompany their oral presentations; others create a video or a web page with links to other resources.

Phase 4: Prepare the instructional environment

The main preparation task for the project was creating the website and video tutorials and deciding what to include in each. However, Ms. Almon had to coordinate the students' trips to the library media center. Preparation tasks included:

- **Creation of website content:** Ms. Almon and the teachers decided on the sections of content to include. Then each of them searched for the best links to include, made a Bookmark/Favorites file of the sites they found, and wrote the content for that section. Ms. Almon compiled the materials into a website and uploaded the site to the school server.
- **Video development:** The teachers also decided on four topics that would support the teaching of research paper strategies and could be presented well via video. Ms. Almon worked with the district media department to create the four brief video tutorials on how to select a research paper topic, how to create a graphic organizer, how to use the library media center resources, and strategies for presenting a research paper. These were placed on the school computers and on a DVD and copies were given to each teacher.
- **Handout:** To make sure students understood the assignment and had access to all resources, Ms. Almon created a handout that all teachers could give their students. She also posted this handout on the website so

students could **download** it (transfer it from the Internet to their computer) whenever they wished.
- **Library media center and computer lab scheduling:** Before students began work on the projects, the teachers scheduled time for their students in the lab and in the library media center.

Phase 5: Evaluate and revise

After all students had completed their research papers, the teachers met to review the data they had collected. Students did very well on the first set of information skills, but less well on the second set. Student attitudes toward the writing process were generally high; about 75% of students rated it 20 points or more. Comments volunteered by students on the surveys indicated they would like more in-class time to revise their products and more individual assistance with the revision process. Rubric scores on research papers were also generally good, with noticeable improvement on structure and content. Scores were lowest on mechanics. The teachers decided to create a set of writing exercises so that students would have more concentrated practice on the analysis and synthesis skills before doing their own written summaries. They also decided to target one or two mechanics skills for special practice with word-processed exercises. All the teachers agreed that the website and video tutorials had been critical focal points to make instruction across classes more consistent and easy to follow.

From http://www.ri.net/schools/East_Greenwich/research.html
Source: Courtesy of Cole Junior High, East Greenwich, RI.

OBJECTIVES

After reading this chapter and completing the learning activities for it, you should be able to:

1. Define distance learning.

2. Describe two different ways of classifying distance learning delivery systems.

3. Describe four kinds of distance learning activities.

4. Describe how each of the following kinds of current major issues in distance learning helps shape its impact and future directions: Digital Divide, child development and socialization, impact on school reform, and virtual schooling.

5. Describe strategies teachers can use to address each of the following potential pitfalls related to Internet use: accessing inappropriate materials, threats to safety and privacy, viruses and hacking, and copyright and plagiarism problems.

6. Describe findings from research on distance learning that can help shape practice and enhance impact.

7. Use each of the following: URLs, site navigation strategies, Bookmarks or Favorites, and search engines.

8. Evaluate website content for quality and usefulness.

9. Troubleshoot basic problems with Internet use.

10. Describe the purpose of each of the following Internet resources and identify how it would meet a specific communications need: email, listservs, bulletin boards, blogs, chatrooms, instant messaging (IM), videoconferencing, and MUDs/MOOs/avatar spaces.

11. Identify materials and effective procedures needed to design and evaluate online courses.

Key Terms

- ARPAnet
- asynchronous
- avatar spaces
- blog
- Bookmarks file
- bulletin board (BB)
- chatroom
- cookies
- course management system
- crackers
- distance learning
- domain designator
- download
- electronic whiteboard
- emoticons
- Favorites file
- filtering software
- firewall software
- hackers
- hits
- HyperText Transfer Protocol (HTTP)
- instant messaging (IM)
- intensifiers
- intranet
- learning communities
- links/hot links
- listserv (list)
- *Mosaic*
- MUDs/MOOs
- netiquette
- spam
- synchronous
- uniform resource locators (URLs)
- videoconferencing
- web browser
- World Wide Web (WWW)

 For more information on Key Terms, go to the *Key Terms* module for this chapter of the Companion Website at http://www.prenhall.com/roblyer.

Background on Distance Education

Distance Education: Placing the Internet in Context

Technology has changed no aspect of society more quickly and dramatically than its communications capabilities. Children today regard revolutionary technologies such as fax machines, cellular phones, and the Internet as normal, everyday parts of the electronic landscape in which they live. Even in the rapid environment of technological evolution, these remarkable changes in communications have come about with incredible speed; some resources have developed from possible to pervasive in only a few years. These changes are by no means completed or even slowing down. The primary reason for this breathtaking revolution in communications is society's recognition of the importance of ready access to people and resources. If knowledge is power, as Francis Bacon said, then communication is freedom—freedom for people to reach information they need in order to acquire knowledge that can empower them. This heady freedom permeates the atmosphere of an Information Society.

Rapid developments in communication technologies have brought about what Moore (1995), quoting an issue of *The Economist,* called "the death of distance," which happens "when the cost of communications comes down to next to nothing, as seems likely in the first decade of the next century" (p. 1). But the death of distance seems to have given new life to education. Distance learning (DL) has not only changed how quickly educators and students can exchange and access information, it has altered the educational equation in fundamental ways. Thanks to distance technologies such as broadcast systems and the Internet, learning has escaped the physical boundaries of the classroom and the school, and students and teachers have become part of a virtual classroom they share with counterparts around the world. Our society is just beginning to understand and take advantage of the potential of this new classroom.

The Internet burst on the scene in our society and in education a relatively short time ago, but quickly set fire to the interest and imagination of even the least technical teachers, students, and parents. Now most computer-based distance learning applications involve some Internet resource or activity, and many rely exclusively on Internet materials. As the example at the beginning of this chapter shows, distance learning is not just the delivery of whole courses. DL also refers to the use of the Internet and other resources to play key roles in all kinds of classroom communications. Because the Internet figures so prominently in many distance learning activities, this chapter focuses primarily on this rapidly growing and evolving force in education.

Defining Distance Learning

The United States Distance Learning Association (USDLA at http://www.usdla.org/) defines **distance learning** as follows:

> *The acquisition of knowledge and skills through mediated information and instruction, encompassing all technologies and other forms of learning at a distance.*

This definition leaves open the door to more constructivist views of learning, including the possibility that, though learning is taking place, there may not be an instructor at all, and no formal or organized instruction may be offered. The USDLA definition says simply that learning may take place where learners are connected with information resources, with each other, with instructors, or with any combinations of these resources.

Distance Learning Delivery Systems

Although the Internet was the catalyst for an unprecedented interest in distance learning, it is by no means

MAKING THE CASE FOR TECHNOLOGY INTEGRATION

Discuss these issues online with other students by selecting the *Making the Case* module for Chapter 7 of the Companion Website (http://www.prenhall.com/roblyer) or choose the *Message Board* module.

1. Durden (2001) says that "...no existing form of distance learning can similarly affirm students as individuals and also force them to acknowledge the ideas of others....Disenfranchised students, as much as their affluent and advantaged peers, deserve a chance at a residential, liberal education—not an unproven alternative." What evidence can you cite to contradict Durden's belief that distance learning cannot help students acknowledge each others' ideas? How would you respond to Durden's criticisms of distance learning as an unproven alternative to face-to-face education?

2. The following is a quote from the report *Fool's Gold: A Critical Look at Computers and Childhood* by the Alliance for Childhood: "Those who place their faith in technology to solve the problems of education should look more deeply into the needs of children. The renewal of education requires personal attention to students from good teachers and active parents, strongly supported by their communities. It requires commitment to developmentally appropriate education and attention to the full range of children's real low-tech needs—physical, emotional, and social, as well as cognitive" (Cordes & Miller, 2000, p. 4). In light of the increasing importance of the Internet as an information resource and an instrument for students' research, how would you respond to this statement?

the only delivery system for distance learning. Indeed, distance learning can be done without any electronic assistance at all. Distance learning has been done by correspondence study via postal mail (a.k.a. snail mail) since the 19th century. Changes in our technological capabilities have brought about gradual changes to our methods of delivering instruction at a distance. The first major change to correspondence courses came when presentations were placed on videotape and mailed

Figure 7.1   Classification System for Distance Learning Delivery

	Types of Interaction	Delivery Methods
Most abstract, least realistic	One-way, print-based	Correspondence courses via postal mail and/or fax
	Tape or broadcast audio mailed or downloaded to students	Prerecorded audio or video
	One-way, synchronous audio from instructor to students	Broadcast radio
	Two-way, synchronous audio between students and instructor	Audioconferencing: telephone systems
	Taped or broadcast video mailed or downloaded to students (no synchronous interaction with instructor)	Broadcast television: microwave or satellite link
Most realistic, least abstract	Text and multimedia interactions	Web-based course management systems
	Live video from instructor to students (with synchronous audio interaction)	Teleconferencing
	Two-way, synchronous video between instructor and students	Videoconferencing

along with print materials. Later, improvements in the quality and availability of broadcast technologies made it possible to send audio and video information, either live or taped.

Distance delivery systems can be classified in any of several ways. Simonson, Smaldino, Albright, and Zvacek (2000) suggested a classification scheme based on Dale's cone of experience, a system designed by Edgar Dale to categorize media according to their degree of realism. Dale said media range from concrete (e.g., hands-on or multisensory experience) to abstract (verbal symbols such as text descriptions), and that younger or less experienced students require more concrete experiences before they can understand abstract ones. Thus, distance delivery systems can be classified according to the degree to which they approximate reality. However, this classification system also may be overlaid with the methods and technologies used to deliver them.

Sometimes several of the technologies shown in Figure 7.1 are used in combination to achieve the desired level of realism. Currently, two of the most popular arrangements for distance learning are video courses or *telecourses* and web-based courses. Telecourses are still more common in higher education than they are in K–12 levels, but some K–12 curriculum materials are delivered in this way (e.g., integrated science units broadcast from the University of Alabama to schools). **Videoconferencing** (live video and

audio communications) via the Internet also is becoming increasingly popular in K–12 classrooms (McCullen, 2001).

Types of Distance Learning Activities

Once a rarity in education, distance activities have become a mainstream alternative to and supplement for face-to-face learning. As Figure 7.1 indicates, some distance activities are carried out via broadcast and stored video (e.g., lectures on DVDs), but the Internet has become the primary medium for most distance learning. Although most educators think of distance learning only as courses, there are actually four types of activities that fall under this rubric: student research, online classroom materials, web-based lessons, and virtual courses and programs. A summary of the instructional benefits of these activities is given in the *Top Ten* feature on the next page.

Student research. Students use the Internet to search for materials and information to support their research and production work. Although search engines have become easier and more productive to use for this purpose, students still need help applying what Ms. Almon in the opening example referred to as the "Big Six" skills (see http://www.big6.com). These skills are an important foundation to ensure students make best use of this form of distance learning.

The following characteristics of distance resources have the ability to enhance teaching and learning activities in unique ways.

1. **Fast access to information** — Students use the Internet to locate information quickly for classroom research and development projects and educational opportunities.

2. **Access to experts not available locally** — Internet projects let students tap the expertise of experts at a distance.

3. **Fast communication to groups** — Internet pages, email, and listservs help teachers and students send updates and stay in touch with each other and with parents and community members.

4. **Communication resources to support collaboration** — Email, bulletin boards/conferences, blogs, chats, web pages, and other resources make it easier for students and teachers to work together and share products, whether they are in the same physical location or at a distance.

5. **Access to learning materials** — Teachers download prepared handouts, tests, images, and other materials to use with students; students can use online self-instructional tutorials to surge ahead on a topic.

6. **Access to courses and lessons not locally available** — Teachers and students can take courses on topics for which teachers are not available at their sites.

7. **Access to education for homebound students** — Students who are homebound due to illness, disability, or discipline can take courses and complete degree programs online.

8. **Learning communities support collaboration** — Teachers and students support and encourage each other and share ideas and materials to advance learning.

9. **Lesson ideas from multiple sources** — Teachers can locate teaching ideas on any topic from a variety of Internet sites set up for this purpose.

10. **Increased interaction among students and between students and teachers** — Many educators and students feel that the communication options available in distance courses make it possible for them to interact more than is possible in face-to-face environments.

Online classroom materials. In this type of distance learning, teachers use online materials to help teach themselves and/or their students a topic or skill. The example at the beginning of this chapter is illustrative of this approach. Online tutorials such as those available at the Internet4Classrooms website (http://www. internet4classrooms.com/on-line2.htm) are the most common example of this type.

Web-based lessons. In this type of learning, teachers use website resources to structure a curriculum lesson. Judy Harris (1998b) lists 18 different kinds of these lessons, which she calls *activity structures.* This type of distance learning will be covered in more depth in Chapter 8.

Virtual courses and programs. Distance courses were popular in higher education long before they caught on at K–12 levels. Since 1996, virtual courses and diploma pro-

grams have sprung up around the United States and other countries (Clark, 2001; Loupe, 2001; Roblyer & Marshall, 2002–2003; Zucker & Kozma, 2003).

Current Issues in Distance Learning

When communications became more global and accessible, many in education hoped it would mean better access to high-quality education for all students, regardless of location and economic status. These hopes have not been universally realized, and unexpected problems have occurred, including the widening of the Digital Divide, socialization issues, and impact on educational reform.

Digital Divide issues. As discussed in Chapter 1, greater dependence on the Internet has served to widen still further the Digital Divide. Recent studies show that while more students are using the Internet and other distance resources,

Many distance learning classes are taught via interactive video systems.

children from underserved populations (e.g., low-income and some minority students) still have far less access at home and school than other students (Corporation for Public Broadcasting, 2003). If this gap persists, it augurs future problems in providing equitable access to the resources distance learning offers.

Development and socialization issues. Spending too much time on computers has been cited as harmful to children's development of relationships and social skills. The American Academy of Pediatricians, recognizing these potentially harmful effects of overexposure to mass media (including the Internet), calls for limiting children's use of media to 1 to 2 hours per day (McNabb, 2001). In light of increasing dependence on virtual courses at high school levels, this advice will be difficult to heed.

Positive and negative impact on education reform. Many educators predict that distance learning will reform teaching methods and increase access to quality education. Advocates have been optimistic that the distance learning movement would alter traditional, teacher-centered methods and bring about richer, more constructivist ones. However, recent reports at higher education levels dispute this belief (Zemsky & Massey, 2004), finding that distance resources are usually used to support traditional approaches. Virtual K–12 schools are a growing phenomenon, but their impact on educational reform is often hampered by issues such as high dropout rates and funding disputes. Virtual schooling has also become a political issue, since some educators and parents fear that virtual schools could become the primary vehicle to allow federal and state funding for private and home-schooled students (Roblyer, 2004).

Virtual schooling issues. Although an increasingly popular strategy, K–12 virtual courses and programs present the following ongoing challenges:

- **Curriculum alignment** — To award credit, virtual school curriculum standards have to be aligned to state and local standards where the students reside. This is especially difficult when students from a given virtual school come from more than one state.

- **Teacher certification** — To ensure they are qualified, online teachers must receive certification from a state agency. Schools either must identify one agency or accept teachers from several different certifying agencies.

- **Accreditation** — Course credit can be granted either by the virtual school or the school district. Accrediting agencies have emerged to certify online schools, but it is sometimes difficult to tell if the agency itself is reliable.

- **Funding** — Lawsuits have arisen over whether or not virtual schools should be authorized to use public funds. Some people believe that virtual schools are an attempt to implement home schooling at public expense.

- **Possible negative consequences** — There is an ongoing dialog on the possible negative effects of virtual schooling on students' socialization. Also, the dropout rate is usually higher for online courses, and it has become clear that not all students can succeed in online environments (Roblyer & Marshall, 2002–2003). Successful online students seem to need more than the usual degree of organization and self-motivation, as well as better than average computer skills.

ADAPTING FOR SPECIAL NEEDS

Given the importance of the Internet in K–12 education, it is essential that students with disabilities have access to the web. Standard web browsers can be problematic for some types of computer users, for example, individuals who are blind or have poor vision, and individuals who are unable to use a mouse for screen navigation.

One example of an alternative web browser that is sensitive to physical and sensory disabilities is *Opera* (http://www.opera.com). Valuable features of this browser include single-key navigation, which makes it possible to browse the web using only the keyboard, and visual presentation control to zoom in and enlarge the content and change the font and colors. The research and development involved in this product have contributed to making the web more accessible for individuals with disabilities as well as those in the nonhandicapped population who might need simpler interfaces for searching the web via palm devices and cell phones. This software may be downloaded free for Windows, Macintosh, Linux, and the Smartphone/PDA.

Contributed by Dave Edyburn

Current Research in Distance Learning

Although fueled by the popularity of the Internet, the current wellspring of support for distance learning seems unlikely be just a passing fad. Years of research have confirmed the effectiveness of some forms of distance learning, and studies on other strategies are on the increase. This section captures some current research that indicates how distance learning is helping shape the future of teaching and learning. In the past, the most popular kind of research compared a distance learning method with a traditional one. However, several other kinds of questions also are proving useful in shaping the impact of distance learning. Findings on these topics are described here and summarized in Figure 7.2 on page 224.

Effectiveness of distance learning compared with face-to-face (FTF) learning. Some distance learning methods are among the most well studied in education. For example, course delivery via instructional television has long been considered equivalent to FTF instruction in its impact on achievement and on attitudes of students (Russell, 1992). A more recent review (Russell, 1997) comparing distance education with traditional classroom instruction also found no overall difference, although there was significant variation. In addition, **asynchronous** courses, where information and messages are left for the receiver to read later, tended to show greater gains than **synchronous** ones, where communications are sent and received immediately (Bernard et al., 2004). There is also no doubt that distance students tend to drop out at higher rates than students in FTF courses (Oblender, 2002; Zucker & Kozma, 2003).

More recently, Machtmes and Asher's (2000) meta-analysis of video-based distance courses, or telecourses, found that courses with two-way interaction between instructor and students were more effective than traditional courses. Peterson and Bond (2004) found no differences in achievement between preservice teachers' learning of instructional planning in online and FTF courses. In the latter study, data also suggested a FTF advantage for lower performing students, but the authors said further research on this area was needed to explore this finding. When Zucker and Kozma (2003) compared virtual high school courses with face-to-face ones, they found comparable frequency of interaction with teachers, but lower interaction among students and a slightly higher dropout rate in virtual courses. While they did not report achievement comparisons, Zucker and Kozma did note special challenges for virtual courses in presenting and solving visual problems (e.g., designing a structure) and in teacher inspection of hands-on work. They said that, while virtual courses could be successful with these activities, they would require substantially more planning than face-to-face ones.

Course characteristics that affect success. Some studies focus on course factors that correlate directly to dropout rates in distance learning courses (Bernard & Amundsen, 1989; Gibson & Graf, 1992). However, many researchers agree with Wilkes and Burnham (1991) that course success should be measured by more than just endurance and achievement, since "highly motivated learners may be willing to endure almost (anything) to achieve a passing grade" (p. 43). Therefore, the majority of studies in this area focus on attitude surveys of students who complete distance learning courses. Researchers agree that the handful of factors described here are the major contributors to course satisfaction (Biner, 1993; Bolliger & Martindale,

Figure 7.2 Summary of Research Findings and Major Reports on Distance Learning

Research Topic	Research Questions	Findings
Effectiveness and impact	• Are distance courses as effective as FTF courses?	• No significant overall differences in achievement between distance and FTF courses. • Asynchronous courses reflect higher achievement than synchronous ones. • Dropout rate usually higher in distance courses. • Harder to teach topics that have visual problems and solutions in distance courses.
Course quality	• What are the characteristics of effective distance courses?	The most successful courses have: • High interaction • Instructor and other support throughout the course • Fewer technical problems and good technical support when problems occur.
Effective distance learners	• What are the characteristics of students who are effective distance learners?	• Mixed evidence on whether single cognitive factors (e.g., self-efficacy) predict success. • Combination of achievement beliefs, responsibility, self-organization ability, and technology skill/access appears to predict student success.
Effective distance instructors	• What are the characteristics of effective distance instructors?	Effective distance instructors have good: • Course planning and organizational skills specific to distance environments • Verbal and nonverbal presentation skills specific to distance learning situations • Ability to involve and coordinate student activities among several sites • Communication and classroom organizational skills.
Cost effectiveness	• What cost factors enter into preparing and implementing distance education programs? How do we determine cost effectiveness?	• Costs factors include technology, transmission, maintenance, infrastructure, production, support, and personnel. • Distance education becomes more cost effective when resources are used more efficiently and with more courses.

2004; Cheng, Lehman, & Armstrong, 1991; and Hardy & Boaz, 1997):

- **High interaction** — Though some studies find that the convenience distance learning offers means more to students than teacher interaction (Klesius, Homan, & Thompson, 1997), the single greatest determinant of satisfaction across studies is the amount of interaction between instructor and students (Fulford & Zhang,

1993; Furst-Bowie, 1997; Roblyer & Wiencke, 2003, 2004; Smith, 1996; Thompson, 1990; Westbrook, 1997; Zirken & Sumler, 1995). McHenry and Bozik (1997) found that lack of "classroom community" among distance learners can decrease interaction and affect course satisfaction. But, as is typical of distance learning and traditional classes alike, smaller class size can determine student perception of interactivity and, therefore, satisfaction with distance learning instruction. Riddle (1990) suggests that meeting students face to face for the first class meeting helps establish a rapport that can lead to better interaction throughout the course. Roblyer and Ekhaml (2000) created an interaction rubric to help define what interaction means in practical terms and to help instructors reflect on how they can make their courses more interactive. Roblyer and Wiencke (2003, 2004) offer an updated version.

- **Support during course** — Many studies show that students value and profit from instructor and other support during their course experiences, from registration through course activities and evaluation (Gibson & Graf, 1992; Hardy & Boaz, 1997; Zucker & Kozma, 2003). McHenry and Bozik (1997) find that lack of library resources and slow transfer of paperwork are among the support problems that affect course satisfaction.

- **Low technical problems** — Consistent evidence exists that technical problems can doom the best planned course (Cheng, Lehman, & Armstrong, 1991; Thomerson & Smith, 1996; Zucker & Kozma, 2003). Successful courses are those that minimize technical problems.

Characteristics of successful distance learners. Some researchers have tried to identify certain student capabilities or other factors that could predict whether or not a student might drop out, be less satisfied with, or do less than others in an online activity. Hypothesized characteristics include self-motivation and ability to structure one's own learning (Gibson & Graf, 1992; Hardy & Boaz, 1997), previous experience with technology (Richards & Ridley, 1997), good attitude toward course subject matter (Coussement, 1995), and locus of control (Dille & Mezack, 1991). Studies disagree on whether single cognitive factors can predict success. Wang and Newlin (2000) and Osborn (2001) found that higher internal locus of control and spending more time online can predict whether or not students will be successful in online learning environments. Also, Lim (2001) found that students' computer self-efficacy (i.e., belief in their ability to use computers effectively) could predict their degree of satisfaction in online courses. However, DeTure (2004) found that self-efficacy and cognitive style were poor predictors of higher grades. Roblyer and Marshall (2002–2003) found that a set of four characteristics working in combination (achievement beliefs, responsibility, self-organization ability, and technology skill/access) offered a better prediction of whether or not virtual high school students will succeed in online courses.

Characteristics of effective distance learning instructors. Cyrs (1997) emphasizes that distance learning in-

structors need different skills than instructors for traditional courses. His review of research reveals several areas of unique competence, all of which require experience with distance learning environments:

- Course planning and organization that capitalize on distance learning strengths and minimize constraints
- Verbal and nonverbal presentation skills specific to distance learning situations
- Collaborative work with others to produce effective courses
- Ability to use questioning strategies
- Ability to involve and coordinate student activities among several sites.

Moskal, Martin, and Foshee (1997) refer to these skills in general as instructional design skills specific to distance learning. In their review of studies in this area, Roblyer and McKenzie (2000) found that many of the same factors that make for a successful online instructor are the same as those for any successful instructor: good communication and classroom organization skills.

Research on cost effectiveness of distance learning. The University of Idaho's Engineering Outreach home page (http://www.uidaho.edu/eo) posted a list taken from Threlkeld and Brzoska (1994) on several categories of cost factors involved with offering a distance learning course:

- **Technology** — Hardware and software
- **Transmission** — Ongoing expenses of leasing transmission access (e.g., T1 lines, satellite)
- **Maintenance** — Repairing and updating equipment
- **Infrastructure** — Foundational network and telecommunications infrastructure located at originating and receiving sites
- **Production** — Technical and personnel support to develop/adapt teaching materials
- **Support** — Expenses needed to keep the system working successfully, for example, administrative costs, registration, advising/counseling, local support costs, facilities, and overhead costs
- **Personnel** — Instructors and support staff.

Although studies show that the initial costs of starting distance learning programs are high, research also suggests that as course management strategies become more efficient and used over more courses, program costs should decrease (Ludlow, 1994).

Introducing the Internet

A Brief History of the Internet in Education

The Internet has made such a difference in our society that it is difficult to remember when we did not depend on it for communications, instruction, and even entertainment. There is so much to learn about the uses of the Internet in education that many educators find it difficult to know where to begin. Yet today's educational uses of the Internet bear little resemblance to its original purpose. The U.S. Department of Defense (DOD) developed the first version of the Internet during the 1970s to allow quick communication among researchers working on DOD projects in about 30 locations. The DOD also saw it as a way to continue communications among these important defense sites in the event of a worldwide catastrophe such as a nuclear attack. Because these projects were funded by the DOD's Advanced Research Projects Agency (ARPA), the network was originally called **ARPAnet.**

In the 1980s, just as desktop computers were becoming common, the National Science Foundation funded a high-speed connection among university centers based on the ARPAnet structure. By connecting their individual networks, universities could communicate and exchange information in the same way the DOD's projects had. However, these new connections had an additional, unexpected benefit. A person accessing a university network from home or school could also get access to any site connected to that network. This connection began to be called a gateway to all networks, and what we now call the Internet was born.

Networks connect computers to allow users to share resources and exchange information easily. The Internet or the Net, as it is commonly known, has been called the ultimate network or "the mother of all networks" because it is a network of networks. It is a way for people in network sites all over the world to communicate with each other as though they were on the same local-area network. The name *Internet* means literally "between or among networks." Though most people think of the Internet as synonymous with the **World Wide Web (WWW),** the latter really is a subset of the Internet system. The WWW is an Internet service that links sites around the world through hypertext documents. We use a program called a **web browser** to bring up one of these hypertext or web page documents, and one can click on text or graphics linked from it to other pages in other locations. In this way, one "travels" around the Internet from site to site. (See the Navigating the Net section later.)

The very first web browser was **Mosaic,** introduced in 1993. It was its highly graphic nature that caused an explosion of Internet use by the following year. The most common current web browsers are *Netscape Communicator* and *Internet Explorer,* although others (e.g., *Mozilla,* a *Netscape* derivative, and Apple's *Safari*) are also used.

Current Pitfalls in Internet Use

As it has become a society-wide tool, the Internet also has spawned its share of society-wide debates and problems. In many ways, it is a reflection of the best and worst qualities of our society. Problems with equity and human behavior (and misbehavior) have already begun to emerge. Five kinds of potential problem areas are discussed here along with strategies that educators can use to make the Internet a safer, more worry-free place for teaching and learning.

Potential pitfall #1: Accessing sites with inappropriate materials. Like a big-city bookstore, the Internet has materials that parents and teachers may not want students to see, either because they are inappropriate for an age level or because they contain information or images considered objectionable. Yet the Internet is designed to make information easily obtainable, and, unfortunately, such materials can be accessed all too easily by accident. For example, only the **domain designator**—the three letters at the end of a URL that identify the type of site—differentiate the web site for our nation's Executive Branch (http://www.whitehouse.gov/) from one with X-rated images and materials. Because it is so easy to access these sites without meaning to, classroom or lab Internet-usage rules do not safeguard against this problem.

The Children's Internet Protection Act, signed into law December 21, 2000, is designed to ensure that libraries receiving federal e-rate funds take measures to keep children away from Internet materials that could be harmful to them (McNabb, 2001). Most schools have found that the best way to prevent access to sites with inappropriate materials is to install **firewall** and/or **filtering software** on individual computers or on the school or district network that connects them to the Internet. See Figure 7.3 for definitions of firewall and filtering software and information on strategies to prevent inappropriate access.

Potential pitfall #2: Safety and privacy issues for students. Because they lack the experience that helps alert them to dangerous situations, young people are at special risk on the Internet in three different ways:

- **Online predators** — Some people get on the Internet to seek out and take advantage of vulnerable young people. Young people tend to believe what they hear and read. Therefore, in a **chatroom** (online location where people may drop in and exchange messages) they may not consider the possibility that a

Figure 7.3 **Strategies to Prevent Inappropriate Internet Access**

Go to **Get Net Wise** to explore these and other strategies: http://kids.getnetwise.org/

Strategy #1: Filtering software—Limits access to sites on the basis of keywords, a list of off-limit sites, or a combination of these:

Courtesy of LookSmart Ltd.

- *Cyber Patrol* (http://www.cyberpatrol.com)
- *Cyber Sitter* (http://www.cybersitter.com)
- *Cybersnoop* (http://www.pearlsw.com)
- *Net Nanny* (http://www.netnanny.com)
- *SurfWatch* (http://www1.surfcontrol.com)
- *WatchDog* (http://www.sarna.net/watchdog.com)
- *X-Stop* (http://www.xstop.com)

Strategy #2: Firewall software—Protects a computer from attempts by others to gain unauthorized access to it and also prevents access to certain sites:

- *Norton Internet Security* (http://www.symantec.com)
- *Spyware Doctor* (http://www.pctools.com)

Courtesy of Symantec Corporation.

12-year-old named "Mary" may actually be a 50-year-old man. A survey reported by Mitchell, Finkelhor, and Wolak (2001), found that one out of five youths between the ages of 10 and 17 who use the Internet regularly are exposed to unwanted sexual solicitations. Students should be told never to provide their complete names, addresses, or telephone numbers to any stranger they "meet" on the Internet, and they should report to teachers any people who try to get them to do so.

- **Sales pitches aimed at children** — This is a problem similar to that posed by television commercials. Many Internet sites have colorful, compelling images that encourage people to buy. Young people may make purchase commitments they cannot fulfill.
- **Privacy issues** — As Ross and Bailey (1996) note, "Student privacy in public education is a credo enforced by the Family Rights and Privacy Act" (p. 51).

In their web products, teachers should be careful not to identify students with last names, addresses, and other personal information. Another privacy issue surrounds the use of **cookies,** or small text files placed on a hard drive by a web server contacted on the Internet. The purpose of cookies is to provide the server with information that can help personalize web activity to your needs. But cookies also may track behavior on the Internet in ways that violate privacy. See Figure 7.4 for a summary of strategies to address privacy and safety issues.

Potential pitfall #3: Fraud on the Internet. Teachers may find that the fastest, easiest way to order computer products and/or teaching materials is to go to a company's website and order them online. However, most areas of the Internet are not secure. That is, what you do on the Internet can be monitored by others. Some people use this monitoring capability to look for a credit card number or other information they can use fraudulently. As online consumers, teachers must be sure to purchase products only from well-known, reputable sites that offer a secure server. Secure servers have special programs to prevent outside monitoring of transactions. The URL for a secure server usually begins with "https" instead of the usual "http."

Potential pitfall #4: Computer viruses and hacking. Viruses are programs written for malicious purposes. They come in several varieties and are named according to the way they work, for example, worms, logic bombs, and Trojan horses. Two ways to get viruses on your computer from the Internet are through email attachments and downloaded files.

- **Email attachments with viruses** — An increasingly popular way to send files and programs to friends or colleagues is to attach them to email messages. However, if a computer contains a virus that is programmed to attach itself to files, the virus can inadvertently be sent along with the file. When the person receiving the attachment opens it, the virus transfers to his or her computer.
- **Downloaded files and programs with viruses** — As with email attachments, viruses can attach themselves to files and programs and be received along with the item being downloaded.

See Figure 7.5 for strategies to address these virus problems.

An additional problem is attacks by **hackers** (a.k.a. **crackers**) or those who seek to gain unauthorized access to computer systems for the purpose of stealing and corrupting

Figure 7.4   Strategies to Increase Privacy and Safety on the Internet

SafeKids.Com

Go to **the SafeKids site** to explore these and other strategies:
http://www.safekids.com/child_safety.htm/
Created by site founder Lawrence J. Magid.

Strategy #1: Teach the rules—Review the following *Kids' Rules for Online Safety* with students. Think of some ways you could teach these online rules to students. For example, have students create a multimedia presentation of the rules or role-play how they would react if they encountered one of these problems:

1. I will not give out personal information such as my address, telephone number, parents' work address/telephone number, or the name and location of my school without my parents' permission.

2. I will tell my parents right away if I come across any information that makes me feel uncomfortable.

3. I will never agree to get together with someone I "meet" online without first checking with my parents. If my parents agree to the meeting, I will be sure that it is in a public place and bring my mother or father along.

4. I will never send a person my picture or anything else without first checking with my parents.

5. I will not respond to any messages that are mean or in any way make me feel uncomfortable. It is not my fault if I get a message like that. If I do I will tell my parents right away so that they can contact the service provider.

6. I will talk with my parents so that we can set up rules for going online. We will decide on the time of day that I can be online, the length of time I can be online, and appropriate areas for me to visit. I will not access other areas or break these rules without their permission.

7. I will not give out my Internet password to anyone (even my best friends) other than my parents.

8. I will be a good online citizen and not do anything that hurts other people or is against the law.

Strategy #2: Manage cookies—Do the following:

• Set your browser to prevent or limit cookies.

• Use a "cookie manager" program to control the information given to cookies (see list of cookie managers at http://www.spychecker.com/software/cookiemanager.html).

Cookie Pal
http://www.kburra.com/epal.html

---

data. However, many schools are finding that firewalls, software designed to protect users from harmful sites, also can have the undesirable side effect of preventing students and teachers from accessing some harmless, useful sites. Occasionally, firewalls also can prevent those outside a network from reaching users of the network. School systems find firewalls to be an essential, but problematic, component of being part of the web community.

Potential pitfall #5: Copyright and plagiarism issues. The Internet is such a rich and easy-to-access source of documents, images, and other resources, it sometimes is easy to forget that many of these resources are copyrighted and protected by U.S. copyright laws. Also, the growing wealth of written products available on the Internet makes it all too easy for students to locate material and cite it without crediting the author or even to turn in whole papers as their own. See Figure 7.6 for strategies to address these concerns.

Using Uniform Resource Locators (URLs)

Our use of the Internet depends on common procedures or Internet protocols that allow computers to communicate with each other, despite differences in programs or operating systems. One important protocol is how we list website addresses. Every home in the United States has an address so people can find it and make deliveries of mail and other items. Each place you "visit" on the Internet also has an address, and for much the same reasons. However, the Internet is less tolerant of mistakes in an address than is the U.S. Post Office! Each address must be entered exactly, with every punctuation mark in place, or it will not work.

Figure 7.5 Strategies to Prevent Computer Viruses

Strategy #1: Keep virus protection software up to date—Maintain, use, and frequently update your virus protection software.

Strategy #2: Download only from reputable sites—Avoid shareware programs, a frequent source of attached viruses.

Strategy #3: Never open email attachments from unknown senders.

Strategy #4: Never open email attachments until you confirm their intent—Some viruses are programmed to send emails and attachments automatically through someone's email program and infect the computers of the recipients. If you weren't expecting a file from the person, do not open until confirming they sent it.

Figure 7.6 Strategies to Address Copyright and Plagiarism Problems

Strategy #1: Teach the rules—Teach students what plagiarism is, why it is wrong, what is permitted, and what is not.

- **If the site clearly is copyrighted,** request permission from owners.
- **If the site has no copyright statement,** reference the site by its URL and owner name.

Strategy #2: Use sites to check for and prevent plagiarism.

- **Plagiarism prevention website:** (http://www.turnitin.com)
- **MyDropBox.com website** (http://www.mydropbox.com/)

Courtesy of iParadigms, LLC.
http://www./turnitin.com

Internet addresses are called **uniform resource locators,** or **URLs.** Look at the example URL shown in a browser window in Figure 7.7. The line where the URL is entered is called the address line.

Note that *net* is often used instead of *org* for many schools and other organizations. There are many more designators, and more are being added all the time as the need arises. The U.S. nonprofit organization that sets up domain names is the Internet Corporation for Assigned Names and Numbers (ICANN). You can learn more about ICANN at http://www.icann.org.

Optional parts of a URL. If an organization is a large one, it may have more than one server; or it may split up a large computer into sections. Then the domain name will have more parts. For example, the University of Maryland University College **(umuc)** has a server called **tychousa1** used for its distance courses:

    http://tychousa1.umuc.edu

Optional parts called *suffixes* can come after a domain designator. Suffixes show locations on the server that are set aside for specific purposes. For example, the UMUC Academic Calendar is shown at a certain location on the UMUC server indicated by the suffix after the slash (shown here as the underlined part):

    http://www.umuc.edu/calendar

Three URL uses. Three things to learn about URLs are how to locate them, read them, and "fix" errors in them.

- **Locating URLs** — If you want to visit a site, but you don't know its URL, one way to find it is to make an educated guess. For example, let's say you want to find the website for the National Council of Social Studies. Since you know it will have an "org" designator and organizations usually use their initials in URLs, a good guess would be http://www.ncss.org. See if you can "guess" the URL for the organizations in Figure 7.8.

- **Reading URLs** — If someone gives you a URL, very often you can tell what and where it is by reading its parts. Look at an example:

    http://www.noaa.gov

If you knew that the URL someone gave you was one on weather, you might guess this is for the National Oceanic and Atmospheric Administration (NOAA), a government agency that offers students and teachers a

Figure 7.7 URL in a Browser Window

Address line for URL

Three required parts of every URL (although it can have more optional ones):

http:// / www.nasa.gov

①   **②** **③**

① Each web page address begins with **http://**, which stands for **HyperText Transfer Protocol (HTTP)**.
The "http://" shows it is an Internet address.
(Most, but not all, addresses contain **www**, which stands for **World Wide Web**.)

② The next part of the address here is **nasa,** the name of the computer or *server* to which you connect. Every server on the Internet has an assigned label called the *domain name*.
nasa shows that this computer belongs to the National Aeronautics and Space Administration, a government agency with a wealth of resources on its website.

③ Finally, another required part of the domain name, called a *domain designator,* tells what kind of group owns the server. Some example domain designators are:

org = organization   **com** = business
gov = government agency   **edu** = university
k12._.us = public schools   **net** = network
mil = military agency   **aus** = Australia

Figure 7.8 Locating URLs Exercise

Answer these questions online at the Companion Website. Select Chapter 7 Exercises. (http://www.prenhall.com/roblyer)

Guess a URL for each of the following. Then go on the Internet and type in the URLs to see if you are correct.

1. **National Council of Teachers of Mathematics**
Correct answer: _____

2. **The Music Educators National Conference**
Correct answer: _____

wealth of up-to-date information on the weather. Try to read the URLs shown in Figure 7.9.

- **Fixing errors in URLs** — Someone may give you a URL with an error in it (or you may write it down in-

correctly). There are five common errors you can look for and correct. Read about them and get practice in spotting them in the exercise in Figure 7.10.

Navigating the Net

You can move around from web page to web page on the Internet by using three different options: clicking on links, using Forward and Back buttons, and using the Go Menu. Read about these methods, then try them out in Figures 7.11, 7.12, and 7.13.

Method #1: Navigating with links. You can "travel" on the Internet by using your mouse to click **links** (also known as **hot links** or *hot spots*), text or images that have been programmed into the web page to send your browser to another location on the Internet, either within the site or to another site, when you click on them. These programmed links can be either text or images, as shown in Figure 7.11.

How do you know when images are links? When you pass a mouse pointer over the image (without clicking)

Figure 7.9 Reading URLs Exercise

Answer these questions online at the
Companion Website. Select Chapter 7 Exercises.
(http://www.prenhall.com/roblyer)

Can you read the URL for each of the following?
Type in the URL, and go to the site to see if you are right.

1. For students with vision problems: **http://www.afb.org**
   Whose site is this? _____

2. For a department in the federal government:
   http://www.ed.gov
   Whose site is this? _____

Figure 7.10 Fixing URLs Exercise

Five Types of Errors in URLs

- **Error #1: Omitting one of the parts**—The most common omission is the "http://" (or the "www" if it needs it).
- **Error #2: Wrong domain designator**—For example, people often substitute "com" for "org."
- **Error #3: Punctuation errors**—People often confuse forward slashes (/) and back slashes (\), and hyphens (-) with underlines (_). Also, there are no spaces in a URL. Spaces are designated with an underscore (_).
- **Error #4: Punctuation omitted**—If you leave out a "dot" or a slash, the URL will not work.
- **Error #5: Misspellings**—Most misspellings in URLs occur in suffixes.

Answer these questions online at the
Companion Website. Select Chapter 7 Exercises.
(http://www.prenhall.com/roblyer)

Can you spot the errors in each of the following URLs?
Correct each, then enter it in a browser to check.

1. The Eisenhower National Clearinghouse, a site with lesson plans and other resources for teachers: What's the error? **http//enc.org** _____

2. The American School Health Association: What's the error? **http://www.ashaweborg** _____

and the pointer turns into a "browser hand" such as the one at the bottom of the NASA Educator Astronaut Program image in Figure 7.11, you know it is a link. Any part of a web page can be programmed to be a link.

Method #2: Navigating with buttons. Forward and backward buttons are available on your browser menu bars. See the NASA web page example in Figure 7.12. As this figure shows, you can use the Back button to return to a page you were just on (in this example, back to the NASA home page from the "For Educators" page). If you want to return to the "For Educators" page, you can use the Forward button. You can travel back and forth in this way, just as if you were traveling back and forth visiting houses on the same road.

Method #3: Navigating with the Go Menu. While the Forward and Back buttons let you go in a straight line, back and forth to pages you have been, the Go Menu lets you "jump around" randomly to web pages you have visited. Look at the example in Figure 7.13 for an example Go Menu. You can click on the *Go Menu* and scroll down to select and visit any of the pages listed there. Try out your own Go Menu by doing the activity in Figure 7.14.

Using Bookmarks or Favorites

You may visit so many sites on the Internet that you can quickly lose track of where you found a valuable site on a certain topic. You could write all of them down, but a quicker way is to let a feature in your browser help you create a list. This list is called a **Bookmarks file** (in *Netscape Communicator*) or a **Favorites file** (in *Internet Explorer*).

Figure 7.11 Navigating with Links Example

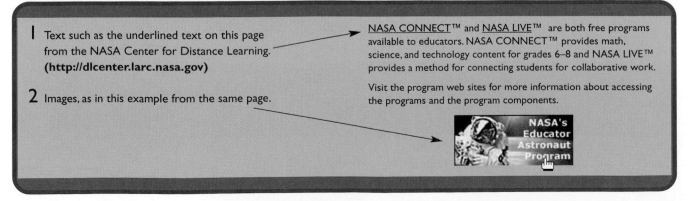

1. Text such as the underlined text on this page from the NASA Center for Distance Learning. **(http://dlcenter.larc.nasa.gov)**

2. Images, as in this example from the same page.

NASA CONNECT™ and NASA LIVE™ are both free programs available to educators. NASA CONNECT™ provides math, science, and technology content for grades 6–8 and NASA LIVE™ provides a method for connecting students for collaborative work.

Visit the program web sites for more information about accessing the programs and the program components.

NASA's Educator Astronaut Program

Figure 7.12   Navigating with Forward and Back Buttons

Browser Menu Bar

Back button

Forward button

Forward and Back buttons let you go *one step at a time* on a linear path through a chain of web pages you have visited. For example, if you go to the NASA web page and click the "For Educators" link shown here, you can click on the **Back button** to take you back to the NASA home page.

Figure 7.13   Sample Go Menu

We clicked on these links:

- NASA home page (Home)
- The Multimedia tab (Multimedia—Highlights)
- NASA Images (Image of the Day Gallery)

Figure 7.14   Exercise in Creating and Using a Go Menu

Create your own Go Menu listing and try it out. Go to a URL such as **http://www.si.edu** (the website for the Smithsonian Institution).

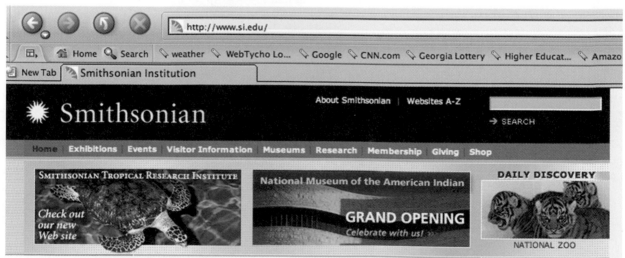

Click on some of the underlined text and/or image links on this page. After each visit, look at the **Go Menu** and see how it has changed. Now pull down the **Go Menu** and select one of the pages listed there to travel to it.

Adding a Bookmark or Favorite. Making a Bookmark or Favorite is very simple. Just travel to the site and when it is on the screen, go to the Bookmarks or Favorites Menu at the top of the browser frame and select "Bookmark This Page" in *Netscape Communicator* or "Add Page to Favorites" in *Internet Explorer*. (The names of these options may vary, depending on the version of the browser.) A Bookmark or Favorite title for that site appears at the bottom of the Bookmark or Favorites list. (See Figure 7.15 for examples in two different browsers.)

Organizing a Bookmarks or Favorites file. Harris (1998a) says that "well-prepared bookmarks files are great resources for teachers and should be shared with others who have similar interests." But what is a "well-prepared bookmarks file"? For a Bookmark collection to be most useful to you and others, it should be organized into sections, much like a library or any collection of materials. After you create Bookmarks, you can organize them into categories of related items. For example, let's say you are a middle school language arts teacher and you want to make a file of Bookmarks or Favorites for a set of English and reading sites you have found. Figure 7.16 shows a Bookmark/Favorites file for this content area. (Also see the tutorial on creating and organizing Bookmarks/Favorites files in the end-of-chapter exercises.)

Starting Up Search Engines

Before the Internet, it was difficult to locate specific resources or items of information. Now there is so much information that companies have developed special searching programs to help us locate things. These searching programs are called *search engines*. Some popular search engines and how to use them are described here.

Types of search engines. According to SearchEngineWatch, a site with information on all available search engines, there are many kinds of search engines. For various types of sites (e.g., filtered ones for kids, multimedia search engines), check out SearchEngineWatch at http://www.searchenginewatch.com. Two commonly cited types of search engines are:

- **Type #1: Major search engines** — The most popular ones cited by SearchEngineWatch are:
  - **Google**   http://www.google.com
  - **Yahoo!**   http://www.yahoo.com
  - **AskJeeves**   http://www.ask.com

Figure 7.15 Add Bookmarks (in *Netscape*) and Add Favorites (in *Internet Explorer*)

Source: Netscape and the "N" logo are registered trademarks of Netscape Communications Corporation. Netscape content © 2005 Netscape Communications Corporation. Used with permission.

Source: Courtesy of Microsoft Corporation.

Figure 7.16 A Sample Bookmarks or Favorites File

Source: Netscape and the "N" logo are registered trademarks of Netscape Communications Corporation. Netscape content © 2005 Netscape Communications Corporation. Used with permission.

Figure 7.17 Yahoo Subject Index

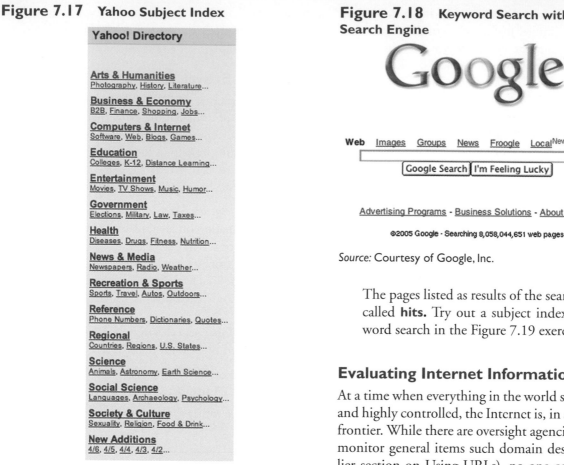

Source: Reproduced with permission of Yahoo! Inc.© 2004 by Yahoo! Inc.YAHOO! and the YAHOO! logo are trademarks of Yahoo! Inc.

- **Type #2: Metacrawlers** — These programs use more than one search engine at the same time to locate things. The top five cited by SearchEngine Watch are:
  - **Dog Pile**   http://www.dogpile.com
  - **Vivisimo**   http://vivisimo.com/
  - **HotBot**   http://www.hotbot.com
  - **Kartoo**   http://www.kartoo.com
  - **Mamma**   http://www.mamma.com

Two search strategies. Search engines can be used in two ways:

- **Subject index searches** — The search engine site provides a list of topics you can click on. See an example in Figure 7.17.
- **Keyword searches** — Type in a combination of words that could be found in the URLs of sites or documents you want. See Figure 7.18 for a sample site that allows keyword searches. In all of these sites, just type in the search word or phrase, and the search engine displays a list of websites with the word or phrase.

Figure 7.18 Keyword Search with the Google Search Engine

Source: Courtesy of Google, Inc.

The pages listed as results of the search are sometimes called **hits.** Try out a subject index search and keyword search in the Figure 7.19 exercise.

Evaluating Internet Information

At a time when everything in the world seems so high tech and highly controlled, the Internet is, in some ways, a wild frontier. While there are oversight agencies that set up and monitor general items such domain designators (see earlier section on Using URLs), no one controls who posts web pages or the quality of their content.

Three kinds of problems arise from this lack of control. One of these, the hazards of offensive or dangerous subject matter or illegal activities, has already been discussed (see earlier section on Current Issues in Distance Learning). The other two problems are less perilous but still have serious implications for teachers and students. Web pages can be less than useful for reasons related to content and design.

Content. The Internet's vast information storehouse, unfortunately, contains some information that is incomplete, inaccurate, and/or out of date. It even has some sites that are works of complete fiction presenting themselves as fact. Students frequently accept as authoritative any information they find on the Internet. However, young people must learn that blind acceptance of any information (on the Internet or elsewhere!) is a risky practice. An essential skill for the Information Age is being able to evaluate information critically and look for indications that content is accurate and reliable. Figure 7.20 shows a checklist of criteria to use when evaluating website content. Try applying these in the exercises in Figure 7.21.

Design. We have learned a great deal in recent years about what makes a website functional and easy to use. However, some sites are so poorly designed that people may find it difficult or impossible to locate and/or read the informa-

Figure 7.19 Search Engine Strategies

Example #1: Using subject index searches

Problem: You want to know about distance learning programs in K–12 schools. Using "distance learning" keywords would yield many higher education sites. Instead, do the following subject search:

- Go to the Yahoo! search engine site: http://www.yahoo.com. (All the underlined text titles you see on Yahoo!'s main page actually are hot links of categories you can click on to locate Internet websites under that heading.)
- Click on the "Education" link. The search engine sends you to yet another listing.
- Click on the "K–12" link. It sends you to yet another listing.
- Click on "Distance learning."
- Review the list of links on distance programs in K–12 schools. Each link is a web page.

Example #2: Using keywords

Problem: You want to know about literacy criticism on the novel *Showboat* by Edna Ferber. A keyword search with the phrase "Edna Ferber's Showboat" yields hundreds of hits on the music and the movie. However, you want to know ONLY about the book. Try the following:

- Go to the Google search engine site: http://www.google.com.
- Click the Advanced Search button on the right.
- Fill in the terms *Showboat* and *Edna Ferber*, separated by commas, as shown below in the **with all of the words** box.
- Fill in the terms *musical, theater,* and *movie,* separated by commas, as shown below, in the **without the words** box.
- Review the list of results.

Courtesy of Google, Inc.

tion they have to offer. (Design criteria are discussed along with web page/website design procedures in Chapter 8.)

Basic Internet Troubleshooting

Like most technologies, the Internet presents its share of "head scratchers." The majority of these errors and problems can be corrected easily; others require more complicated "fixes" or adjustments. Two of the most common difficulties for Internet users are discussed here.

Problem type #1: Site connection failures. After you enter the URL, the site won't come up on the screen. This is the most common problem people encounter, and it may occur because of URL syntax errors, problems with the local or domain server, bad links, or fire-

wall issues. The error message for each problem indicates the cause.

- **URL syntax errors** — As mentioned earlier, each dot and letter in a URL has to be correct, or the site will not load. The most common error message for this problem is: ". . . unable to locate the server. Please check the server name and try again." If this message appears, check the URL syntax and make sure you have not done any of the following:
  - Confused the letter "l" with the number "1"
  - Confused the letter "O" with the number "0"
  - Confused the hyphen "-" with the underscore "_"
  - Confused forward slash "/" with backward slash "\" in the "http://" or in suffixes

Figure 7.20   Criteria for Evaluating Website Content

WWW CYBERGUIDE RATINGS FOR CONTENT EVALUATION

Site Title: _____ Subject: _____

URL: _____ Audience: _____

Purpose for exploring this site: _____

Notes on possible uses of this site and URLs for useful linked sites: _____

_____

_____

To determine the worth of the website you are considering, evaluate its content according to the criteria described below. Circle Y for Yes, N for No, NA for Not Applicable.

1. First look			
A. User is able to quickly determine the basic content of the site.	Y	N	NA
B. User is able to determine the intended audience of the site.	Y	N	NA
2. Information Providers			
A. The author(s) of the material on the site is clearly identified.	Y	N	NA
B. Information about the author(s) is available.	Y	N	NA
C. According to the info given, author(s) appears qualified to present information on this topic.	Y	N	NA
D. The sponsor of the site is clearly identified.	Y	N	NA
E. A contact person or address is available so the user can ask questions or verify information.	Y	N	NA
3. Information Currency			
A. Latest revision date is provided. Date last revised_____	Y	N	NA
B. Latest revision date is appropriate to material.	Y	N	NA
C. Content is updated frequently.	Y	N	NA
D. Links to other sites are current and working properly.	Y	N	NA
4. Information Quality			
A. The purpose of this site is clear: business/commercial— entertainment — informational — news—personal page—persuasion	Y	N	NA
B. The content achieves this intended purpose effectively.	Y	N	NA
C. The content appears to be complete (no "under construction" signs, for example) .	Y	N	NA
D. The content of this site is well organized.	Y	N	NA
E. The information in this site is easy to understand.	Y	N	NA
F. This site offers sufficient information related to my needs/purposes.	Y	N	NA
G. The content is free of bias, or the bias can be easily detected.	Y	N	NA
H. This site provides interactivity that increases its value.	Y	N	NA
I. The information appears to be accurate based on user's previous knowledge of subject.	Y	N	NA
J. The information is consistent with similar information in other sources.	Y	N	NA
K. Grammar and spelling are correct.	Y	N	NA
5. Further Information			
A. There are links to other sites that are related to my needs/purposes.	Y	N	NA
B. The content of linked sites is worthwhile and appropriate to my needs/purposes.	Y	N	NA
Totals			

Based on the total of Yes and No answers and your overall observations, rate the content of this site as:

__ Very useful for my information needs __ Worth bookmarking for future reference __ Not worth coming back to

Comments:

©Karen McLachlan, 7/31/2002   East Knox High School   Howard, Ohio   mclachlan_k@treca.org

Source: Reprinted courtesy of Karen B. McLachlan; research to complete MLIS degree, Kent State University, July 31, 2002.

Figure 7.21   Website Reliability Exercise

> To understand how important it is to confirm website information, do the following two exercises:
>
> **Exercise 1:** Look at the following site and use Figure 7.20 criteria to evaluate content accuracy:
>
> **http://descy.50megs.com/New Hartford/ newhtfd.html**
>
> (HINT: There is no such place as New Hartford, MN!)
>
> **Exercise 2:** Get into groups. Each group locates a website with information they know to be unreliable. Exchange websites and use Figure 7.20 criteria to evaluate the site. Challenge each group to identify why the website content should not be used.

- Omitted a required punctuation mark
- Misspelled a part of the URL
- Used the wrong domain designator (e.g., *edu* instead of *org*).

Many URL errors occur in suffixes that follow the domain designator. Try omitting all suffixes beyond the slash and going directly to the main part of the URL. The main page may show the links you want, or the site may have a built-in search engine you can use.

- **Local or domain server down** — If you have checked the URL syntax and are positive it is correct, it may be that the server that hosts the website is not working temporarily. It may have a technical problem or simply may be down for regular maintenance. In this case, you may get an error message like the one shown previously. Wait a day or two and try it again.

- **Server traffic** — A rarer cause of connection failures is that the server handling Internet traffic for the network or for users in the geographic region is not working properly. Error messages say: "Failure to resolve domain error. Try this site again later" or "Page has no content."

- **Bad or dead links** — If a URL repeatedly fails to connect and you are sure the syntax is correct, the site may have been taken off the Internet. This is a *bad* or *dead link.* If this is the case, you may get the same error message given previously or the site may provide a message that says: "bad link."

- **Firewalls** — Sometimes a site will not connect because a network's firewall blocks it. If you think your network's firewall is blocking your access to a site in error, contact your network administrator and request that this be adjusted.

Problem type #2: Feature on the site will not work. If an Internet site indicates that it has a special feature such as an animation, movie, or sound but it will not work for you, there are three possible causes:

- **Plug-in required** — It may be that your computer does not have the special program or plug-in required in order to play the movie or sound. Usually, if a special plug-in is needed, the site will have a link where you can go to download the plug-in and install it on your computer (see Chapter 8).

- **Compatibility errors** — The Internet works because there are agreements in place about how to make various machines and programs "talk" to each other. However, sometimes differences exist between operating systems or versions of software that make them incompatible. Some sites can be seen only with *Netscape;* some only with *Internet Explorer.* The web page usually indicates if it requires a specific browser.

- **Java and other program errors** — Internet web pages usually are written in a combination of three programming languages: HyperText Markup Language (HTML), Java, and less often, Perl. HTML is the basic language that sets up and formats a page, Java is used for special features like counters or chatrooms, and Perl is used to write *CGI scripts,* which are used when the site wants people to enter information into the web page (e.g., a survey). If you get a Javascript error message, make sure Java is enabled (select *Preferences* under the *Edit Menu*) and/or download a newer version of Java. If you have an enabled, up-to-date version but still get a Javascript error message, there really may be an error in the Java or Perl language of the program or script. In this case, the only thing you can do is to contact the site and alert them to the error.

COMMUNICATING ON THE INTERNET

Increasingly, the Internet has become a primary form of communication for teachers and students, replacing traditional channels such as sending letters and making telephone calls. Described here and summarized in Figure 7.22 are a variety of written and visual Internet resources that make this communication possible and support many instructional strategies.

Email

Electronic mail (email) is the most common way to exchange personal, written messages between individuals or small groups. Email may be sent via a program (e.g., Microsoft's *Outlook Express*) or through capability built into an Internet browser. This versatile medium supports a variety of classroom activities. Researchers have found

Figure 7.22 Resources for Communicating on the Internet

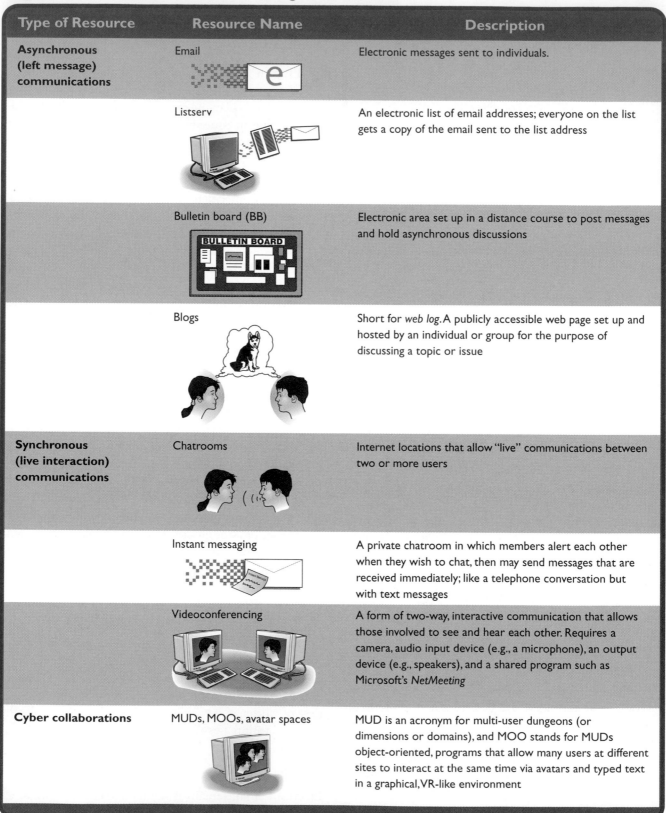

Type of Resource	Resource Name	Description
Asynchronous (left message) communications	Email	Electronic messages sent to individuals.
	Listserv	An electronic list of email addresses; everyone on the list gets a copy of the email sent to the list address
	Bulletin board (BB)	Electronic area set up in a distance course to post messages and hold asynchronous discussions
	Blogs	Short for *web log*. A publicly accessible web page set up and hosted by an individual or group for the purpose of discussing a topic or issue
Synchronous (live interaction) communications	Chatrooms	Internet locations that allow "live" communications between two or more users
	Instant messaging	A private chatroom in which members alert each other when they wish to chat, then may send messages that are received immediately; like a telephone conversation but with text messages
	Videoconferencing	A form of two-way, interactive communication that allows those involved to see and hear each other. Requires a camera, audio input device (e.g., a microphone), an output device (e.g., speakers), and a shared program such as Microsoft's *NetMeeting*
Cyber collaborations	MUDs, MOOs, avatar spaces	MUD is an acronym for multi-user dungeons (or dimensions or domains), and MOO stands for MUDs object-oriented, programs that allow many users at different sites to interact at the same time via avatars and typed text in a graphical, VR-like environment

DISTANCE LEARNING VIA EMAIL COMMUNICATIONS

Courtesy of ePals Classroom Exchange, Inc.

Title: Learning with Keypals

Content Area/Topic: All content areas

Grade Level: All grades

NETS for Students: Standards 1, 3, 4, 5, 6

Description: The exchanging of messages with students at distant sites, "keypals," has long been recognized as a way to motivate students to use language. The activities described here show that keypal exchanges also can help students learn a variety of topics ranging from Spanish to multicultural education.

Instruction: The teacher begins by contacting a site such as the ePals Classroom Exchange (http://www.epals.com) or Teaching.com (http://www.iecc.org/), organizations designed to host projects that encourage email collaborations. Some example activities on the ePals website are as follows:

- *Space day* — In partnership with Space Day(SM), an initiative of the Space Day Foundation, fourth- to eighth-grade students collaborate on real challenges encountered by people living and working in space.
- *Healthy wetlands* — High school students work together to make the connection between clean, safe drinking water and the wetlands located in their own community. Teachers and students use research manuals to guide them through the water cycle, watersheds, wetland types, and other topics. They visit a wetland to record their observations and meet with guests and experts in environmental science.
- *The way we are* — Students work together to break down commonly held stereotypes about people in other regions of the world. After exchanging information and becoming familiar with an individual, a culture, and a community, student partners reexamine their beliefs about that culture and community.
- *EPals Book Club* — Students from around the world talk about and post comments, writings, surveys, and reviews on their favorite books and authors.

Sources: Baugh, I., and Baugh, J. (1997). Global classrooms: E-mail learning communities. *Learning and Leading with Technology, 25*(3), 38–41; and The ePals Classroom Exchange website, http://www.epals.com.

---

that email not only has great potential to improve communications among students, teachers, and parents (Boulware & Tao, 2002), but it can also improve students' writing. For example, Berkson and Britsch (1997) found that having students email others gave more immediate purpose for their writing, motivated them to write more frequently and produce longer passages, and gave them greater confidence in their writing. See some examples hosted by the ePals Classroom Exchange in Technology Integration Idea 7.1.

The etiquette guidelines that govern behavior when communicating on the Internet have become known as **netiquette.** Netiquette covers not only rules of behavior during discussions, but also guidelines that reflect the unique electronic nature of the medium. Netiquette usually is enforced by fellow users who are quick to point out infractions of netiquette rules. The summary of email rules in Figure 7.23 is based on published sources such as Shea's (2004) online book *Netiquette* at http://www.albion.com/netiquette/book/index.html.

Listservs, Bulletin Boards, and Blogs

Three kinds of communication take the form of asynchronous messages rather than synchronous exchanges: listservs, bulletin boards, and blogs.

Listservs. **Listservs** or **lists** are discussion groups that feature ongoing emailed "conversations" among groups who belong to an organization or share common interests. When an email message is addressed to a listserv mailing list, it is automatically duplicated and sent to everyone on the list. Replies to a listserv also go to everyone on the list.

Bulletin boards. Like listservs, **bulletin boards (BBs)** are electronic message centers but are used for posting messages of interest to group members who visit the BB, rather than for emailed notices that all members receive at once. Bulletin board members must go to the BB location to review and leave messages. Bulletin board communications are sometimes known as "threaded discussions."

Figure 7.23 Netiquette: Rules of Behavior on the Internet

- **Identify yourself:**
  —Begin messages with a salutation and end them with your name.
  —Use a signature (a footer with your identifying information) at the end of a message

- **Include a subject line.** Give a descriptive phrase in the subject line of the message header that tells the topic of the message (not just "Hi, there!")
- **Avoid sarcasm.** People who don't know you may misinterpret its meaning.
- **Respect others' privacy.** Do not quote or forward personal email without the original author's permission.
- **Acknowledge and return messages promptly.**
- **Copy with caution.** Don't copy everyone you know on each message.
- **No spam (a.k.a. junk mail).** Don't contribute to worthless information on the Internet by sending or responding to mass postings of chain letters, rumors, etc.
- **Be concise.** Keep messages concise—about one screen, as a rule of thumb.
- **Use appropriate language:**
  —Avoid coarse, rough, or rude language.
  —Observe good grammar and spelling.
- **Use appropriate emoticons (emotion icons) to help convey meaning.** Use "smiley's" or punctuation such as :-) to convey emotions. See website list of emoticons at http://netlingo.com/smiley.cfm and http://www.robelle.com/smugbook/smiley.html.
- **Use appropriate intensifiers to help convey meaning.**
  —Avoid "flaming" (online "screaming") or sentences typed in all caps.
  —Use asterisks surrounding words to indicate italics used for emphasis (*at last*).
  —Use words in brackets such as (grin) to show a state of mind.
  —Use common acronyms (e.g., LOL for "laugh out loud").

(2004) find that blogs have revived journaling as a way to encourage students to write more.

Chatrooms, Instant Messaging, and Videoconferencing

Three kinds of synchronous (real-time) communications are chatrooms, instant messaging (IM), and videoconferencing.

Chatrooms. **Chatrooms** are Internet locations that allow "live" communications between two or more users. As users in a chatroom type in their comments, everyone in the "room" sees what they type. See Technology Integration Idea 7.2 for a sample teaching strategy that chatrooms can support.

Users of chatrooms sometimes use avatars or moving 3-D figures that represent people in virtual environments. Avatars may or may not actually look like the person they represent. These uses are more common in higher education than in K–12 environments.

Instant messaging. One of the newest types of Internet communications is **instant messaging (IM),** a service that allows users to use private chatrooms in which members alert each other when they wish to chat, then may send messages that are received immediately, like a telephone conversation but with text messages. The IM system alerts a person when someone wishes to chat with him or her. IMs are usually live, but also may be left as messages to be read later. The person notified can then initiate a chat session. IM communications make frequent use of abbreviations (see http://www.webopedia.com/quick_ref/textmessageabbreviations.asp for a list of common ones). Students are natural IMers, and schools are just beginning to find ways to make instructional use of this versatile communication tool.

Videoconferencing. This form of two-way interactive communication allows those involved to see and hear each other. Each person must have a camera, an audio input device such as a microphone, and an output device such as speakers, and each participant must be using a program such as Microsoft's *NetMeeting.* It is also helpful to have a high-speed connection so the video will move smoothly. Those who want to videoconference may also subscribe to a free hosting service such as *Yahoo! Messenger* or *AOL Messenger.* Videoconferencing is used more in higher education than in K–12 schools, but it promises to become more common as high-speed connections in schools become more common.

Cyber Collaborations: MUDs and MOOs, and Avatar Spaces

Odasz (1999–2000) recommends two resources to support online collaboration, usually for older and more sophisticated learners: multiuser dungeons (or dimensions

Blogs. Short for *web log,* a **blog** is a web page that serves as a publicly accessible location for discussing a topic or issue. Each is usually set up and maintained by an individual. They began as personal journals, but their use rapidly expanded to a public discussion forum in which anyone can give opinions on the topic. Kajder, Bull, and Van Noy

DISTANCE LEARNING VIA INTERACTIVE CHATS

Title: Ripley's Freaky Fridays: An Interactive Chat Activity

Content Area/Topic: Science

Grade Level: All grades

NETS for Students: Standards 1, 3, 4, 5, 6

Description: Each week, the site moderators introduce a new science topic for discussion that is facilitated by a Teacher's Guide distributed to participating classrooms. The Teacher's Guide includes a short excerpt from *Ripley's Believe It or Not!,* discussion topics designed to engage students, and Ripley Riddles to test knowledge of the topics. To discuss the topics, teachers and students join a 1-hour, moderated chat each week hosted by the ePALS Classroom Companion website.

Source: Ripley's Freaky Fridays Website, http://ripleysfreakyfridays.com/

or domains) or **MUDs,** and a MUDs object-oriented **(MOOs),** a MUD whose code is available and is, therefore, free. These whimsical-sounding resources are programs that allow many users at different sites to interact at the same time. The environment is graphical but, unlike virtual reality, interaction is through typed text or, less often, voice. Odasz says that sample applications include "interactive fiction" or having students role-play characters from literature. An example MUD may be seen at http://angalon.tamu.edu/.

The future of the Internet will be increasingly visual, and one feature contributing to this is the use of **avatar spaces** or MUD locations where users can interact through their graphic representations. (Also see avatars described earlier under chatrooms.) The widespread use of avatars on the Internet was proposed in Neal Stephenson's 1992 science fiction novel *Snow Crash.* These figures can be made to look much like the person they represent or may be complete fantasy figures, selected by a user to project a certain aura or point of view. The uses of avatar spaces in education are limited but have great potential for fostering visual literacy, motivating students to develop writing and other communication skills, and helping teach skills that involve visual design.

OFFERING COURSES AND PROGRAMS WITH DISTANCE TECHNOLOGIES

As described earlier in this chapter (see section on Types of Distance Learning Activities), web-based courses and degree programs, although problematic (see earlier discussion of virtual schools), are becoming increasingly common in K–12 education. More and more teachers are participating in the design and delivery of these activities.

Described here are tools and information they will find useful in their new roles as course designers and online instructors.

Web Course Development and Support Tools

Developing and hosting web courses require an array of online and offline tools. Distance courses are made possible by a **course management system** (an online collection of web course design and delivery tools). Other helpful tools used in the design and delivery of web-based courses include site capturing software, intranets, and whiteboards (a.k.a. smartboards).

- **Course management systems** — Since around 1997, course management systems have become the most common means of designing and delivering web-based courses. A school or district usually buys a license for a system such as WebCT or Blackboard (see Figure 7.24), and their personnel use the system's features (e.g., graphics, conferences, chatrooms, email, links to PDFs and web pages) to design and deliver courses that are hosted by their servers. The course management system also includes gradekeeping and student tracking features such as an electronic portfolio for each student.

- **Site capturing software** — On a high-traffic day, the Internet can be as slow as a highway traffic jam. Slow-moving screens can play havoc with teachers and students trying to carry out learning activities. An alternative is to use a product such as Blue Squirrel's *Web Whacker* software (http://www.bluesquirrel.com), which downloads pages or sites to a computer's hard

Figure 7.24 Two Common Course Management Systems

Source: Courtesy of WebCT Inc.

Source: Courtesy of Blackboard Inc.

Figure 7.25 Sample Electronic Whiteboard

Source: © SMART Technologies Inc. Used with permission.

drive where they later can be run through a browser without benefit of an Internet connection. The popularity of this software created the term *site whacking*.

- **Intranets** — Another way to speed up access to the Internet is through an internal network called an **intranet.** This network, like the Internet, is based on comunications protocols, but belongs only to an organization and can be accessed only by the organization's members. An intranet's websites look and act just like any other websites, but the network has a firewall that will not allow unauthorized access. A school might maintain its own intranet of selected sites for use in courses, while allowing access to the larger Internet for other sites. More information about creating and maintaining intranets is available from online magazines such as *Intranet Journal* (http://www. intranetjournal.com).

- **Electronic whiteboards (or smartboards)** — **Electronic whiteboards** are display screens connected to a computer that multiple users can write or

draw on. Whiteboard is the generic name and Smartboard is the trade name of SMART Technologies, Inc. (http://www.smarttech.com/). Whiteboards are often used along with videoconferencing and course management systems because they make it possible for everyone to see illustrations and demonstrations of concepts and products as they are being drawn and revised. See Figure 7.25 for an example.

Characteristics of Effective Distance Courses and Programs

Effective online courses have been offered in every content area from math to music and from physics to physical education. A review of these courses yields the following four common, essential characteristics: effective course structure and design, engaging learning activities, interactive learning communities, and effective assessment strategies.

Well designed and structured to support learning. Just as with any course, effective online courses must be well planned and systematically designed to take advantage of the unique capabilities and constraints of the learning environment. Alley and Jansek (2001) list 10 characteristics of a high-quality online learning environment:

1. Knowledge is constructed, not transmitted.
2. Students can take full responsibility for their own learning.
3. Students are motivated to want to learn.
4. The course provides "mental white space" for reflection.
5. Learning activities appropriately match student learning styles.
6. Experiential, active learning augments the website environment.
7. Solitary and interpersonal learning activities are interspersed.
8. Inaccurate prior learning is identified and corrected.
9. "Spiral learning" provides for revisiting and expanding prior lessons.
10. The master teacher is able to guide the overall learning process.

Engaging, collaborative activities. Although some students prefer courses to be individual, tutorial-like ones where they work at their own pace through a sequence of tasks, the most enjoyable courses seem to be those in which students are highly engaged in discussion and collaboration. Many online courses encourage this kind of engagement through the bulletin boards or conferences provided by course management systems. Klemm (1998) described eight ways of achieving more student engagement through online conferences:

1. **Require participation**—Participation in each conference should be a required, graded activity rather than an optional one.
2. **Form learning teams**—If handled properly, collaborative activities can encourage a "team spirit" toward learning.
3. **Make activity interesting**—Consider student backgrounds, experiences, interests, and concerns.
4. **Don't settle for opinions**—Student contributions should be based on their readings and research.
5. **Structure the activity**—Have a specific set of tasks and a definite beginning and end to each.
6. **Require a deliverable**—The activity should revolve around a product to develop and turn in.

7. **Know what you are aiming for**—Set up expectations for adequate participation and communicate them clearly to students. Instructors should provide consistent, ongoing critiques and feedback to encourage involvement.
8. **Use peer grading**—Ask students to rate each other on their contributions to the conference. (The most controversial of Klemm's recommendations, not all experts agree this is feasible.)

An interactive learning community. Teachers and students agree that online courses are more motivating if they simulate the community one finds in a good face-to-face course. Solloway and Harris (1999) say that so-called **learning communities** (groups of people who "meet" via email or web pages to support each other's learning) in web-based courses are the result of careful planning and strong support by the instructor and a support team. However, it is apparent that learning communities require more than just well-designed instruction. They also involve strategic, ongoing efforts by the instructor to encourage student-to-student interaction, as well as student-to-instructor interaction, and to have students get to know each other as learners and as people. They are communities in the truest, most culture-based sense of the word.

Effective assessment strategies for online courses and programs. While alternative assessments are popular in online lessons, many online learning course systems also offer traditional assessment options. WebCT, for example, has a test module so instructors can develop objective tests, have students take them online, grade them automatically, and summarize test results across the class. Other systems such as UMUC's Web Tycho have an assignments area in which students can post files of compositions and other electronic products.

Assessing the Quality of Distance Courses

Two rubrics on the DVD that accompanies this text lay out the elements that teachers and students can use to assess the overall quality and usefulness of a distance learning course. The *Rubric for Online Instruction* designed and hosted online by the California State University–Chico, focuses on the characteristics shown in Figure 7.26 and allows courses to be assessed prior to delivering or taking them.

The other rubric (*Rubric for Assessing Interactive Qualities of Distance Courses*), developed by the author of this textbook, is useful as a post-course evaluation instrument. It focuses on the following characteristics:

Figure 7.26   Rubric for Online Instruction

Learner Support & Resource	Online Organization & Design
Course contains extensive information about being an online learner and links to campus resources. It also provides a variety of course-specific resources, contact information..More	Course is well-organized and easy to navigate. Students can clearly understand all components and structure of the course. The syllabus identifies..More

Instructional Design & Delivery	Assessment & Evaluation of Student Learning
Course offers ample opportunities for interaction and communication student to student, student to instructor and student to content. Goals are clearly defined and aligned..More	Course has multiple timely and appropriate activities to assess student readiness for course content and mode of delivery. Learning objectives, instruct..More

Innovative Teaching with Technology	Faculty Use of Student Feedback
Course uses a variety of technology tools to appropriately facilitate communication and learning. New teaching methods are applied and innovative enhance..More	Instructor offers multiple opportunities for students to give feedback on course content. Instructor offers multiple opportunities for students to give feedback on..More

Source: Reproduced with permission of Academic Technologies and the Center for Excellence in Learning and Teaching, California State University, Chico; http://www.csuchico.edu/celt/roi.

- Social/rapport-building designs for interaction
- Instructional designs for interaction
- Interactivity of instructional resources
- Evidence of learner engagement
- Evidence of instructor engagement.

INTERACTIVE SUMMARY

The following is a summary of the main points covered in this chapter. To see additional examples and information on these points, go to this textbook's Companion Website at http://www.prenhall.com/roblyer and click on the Chapter 7 *Interactive Summary* module to visit each of the recommended websites.

1. **Background on distance learning:**
   - **Distance learning is defined by the** United States Distance Learning Association (USDLA) as "The acquisition of knowledge and skills through mediated information and instruction, encompassing all technologies and other forms of learning at a distance."
   - **Distance learning delivery systems may be classified as most abstract to most realistic,** according to types of interaction (one-way, print-based to two-way video) and delivery methods (from correspondence courses to videoconferencing).
   - **Types of distance activities include** student research, online materials, web-based lessons, virtual courses and programs.
   - **Current distance learning issues include** the widening Digital Divide, concerns about children's devel-

opment and socialization, impact on school reform, and virtual schooling issues.
   - **Types of Internet pitfalls include** accessing inappropriate materials, threats to safety and privacy, Internet fraud, viruses and hacking, and copyright and plagiarism problems.
   - **Findings from current research on distance learning include** distance learning and face-to-face learning can yield equivalent results; successful distance courses are those that have high interaction, good support, and low technical problems; successful learners are those who have achievement beliefs, responsibility, self-organization ability, and technology skill/access; successful instructors are those who have good communication and classroom organization skills; and distance learning programs are more cost effective when used with more courses.
   - **Internet concepts** — Students and teachers who use the Internet should know how to use URLs, site navigation strategies, Bookmarks or Favorites, and search engines.
   - **Internet strategies** — Students and teachers should also know how to evaluate website content and do basic Internet troubleshooting.

2. **Communicating on the Internet** — Online communication resources include email, listservs, bulletin boards, blogs, chatrooms, instant messaging, videoconferencing, and MUDs/MOOs/avatar spaces.

3. **Distance courses and programs** — To design and use distance courses and programs, teachers and students use web course development and support tools such as course management systems (e.g., WebCT

and <u>Blackboard</u>), <u>site capturing software</u>, <u>intranets</u>, and <u>whiteboards</u>.

4. **Effective course design requires** structure designed to support learning, engaging, collaborative activities, supportive online learning community, and good assessment strategies.

5. **Distance course quality may be assessed** during design by the <u>Rubric for Online Instruction</u> and after a course through the <u>Rubric for Assessing Interactive Qualities of Distance Courses</u>.

Online Activities

Visit this text's Companion Website at <u>http://www.prenhall.com/roblyer</u> to gain access to a variety of questions, activities, and exercises and to help build your knowledge of this chapter's content.

Online Chapter 7 Self-Test

To review terms and concepts for this chapter, click on the *Self-Test* module for this chapter of the Companion Website.

Software Skill-Builder Tutorials

To access practical tutorial and skill-building activities and to build skills using popular software and hardware, click on the *Software Skill-Builder Tutorials* module for this chapter of the Companion Website.

Web-Enrichment Activities

To complete activities that connect to chapter content and provide web-based resources, click on the *Web-Enrichment Activities* module for this chapter of the Companion Website.

TECHNOLOGY INTEGRATION WORKSHOP

CLIPS FROM THE CLASSROOM: LEARNING WITH TECHNOLOGY

Go to the *Technology Integration Workshop* DVD located in the back of this text and click on *Clips from the Classroom*. View the video clips listed below that support this chapter's content:

- *Online and Face-to-Face High School*
- *Virtual School Advantages*
- *Learning Online*
- *Virtual School Teacher Skills*
- *Virtual English Course*
- *Virtual Geometry Course*
- *Virtual School Philosophy.*

Now, visit this text's Companion Website at http://www.prenhall.com/roblyer to answer questions and complete activities that will guide you in analyzing each clip.

THE TIP MODEL IN ACTION

Read each of the following scenarios related to implementing the TIP Model, and go to the Companion Website to answer the questions that follow it based on your Chapter 7 reading activities.

TIP Model Scenario #1 Ms. Eltona was very pleased when her school placed a three-computer workstation in each classroom so that students could do Internet research for classroom assignments. However, she finds that when students have a research paper to do for her class, they do a quick keyword search, locate a number of web pages on the topic, copy down what each page says, and put it in their research papers. She tells other teachers that she thinks using the Internet makes her students' papers worse instead of better because it makes it too easy to find information that may or may not be reliable.

1.1 What skills do Ms. Eltona's students need to learn so that they are able to realize better benefits from their Internet use?

1.2 How could Ms. Eltona help teach these skills as part of her research paper assignments?

1.3 What criteria should she include in her research paper rubric in order to make sure students are using appropriately the information they locate from Internet searches?

TIP Model Scenario #2 Mr. Omrey is a high school business education teacher and is teaching a unit on software tools. He finds that nearly all of his senior students come into his class knowing something about word processing and spreadsheets; a few even know databases. Since they are at so many different levels of knowledge, he would like a way to individualize their instruction, allowing students to start with what they know and build more skills on each tool. Yet he has no funds for tutorial workbooks or software.

2.1 What distance learning tools available on the Internet may be useful to address Mr. Omrey's needs?

2.2 If he used such tools, what strategies and materials could Mr. Omrey use to track his students' skill development?

2.3 If Mr. Omrey has 15 computers in his classroom and 25 students, how might he give his students equitable access to the distance resources?

TIP Model Scenario #3 Ms. Pomeroy has heard that students tend to want to write better and observe more spelling, grammar, and usage rules when they write for distance audiences. She would like to have her students exchange messages with students in other English-speaking countries.

3.1 How could Ms. Pomeroy identify students in other countries for her students to correspond with via email?

3.2 Since Ms. Pomeroy would like to make sure students behave courteously during their email exchanges, she would like to create a classroom poster of the "Top Ten Rules" to observe when emailing. What could she use as the basis for these rules? What ten items would you suggest she place on the poster?

3.3 What elements should be included in a rubric to assess students' email messages?

TIP Model Scenario #4 Mr. Sloan is a high school principal in a small, rural community. Several parents have complained to him because the school does not offer advanced placement courses in several areas (e.g., physics, foreign languages). He knows his district cannot afford to hire teachers for these subjects. He has heard about virtual courses in these topics offered by a consortium in another state, and he thinks this would be a good idea for his district. He tells the superintendent that since the more advanced students would be the ones taking these courses, they should do well in them.

4.1 If the district could make these courses available to the students, what would be the relative advantage of offering them via distance learning?

4.2 What does past research show about Mr. Sloan's assumption that more advanced students would do well in virtual courses?

4.3 Assuming these courses could be made available to students in his school, what strategies could Mr. Sloan implement to support the students' access to and use of them?

TIP Model Scenario #5 Ms. Courtney's students are working in groups to do their research projects. However, each group wants to bookmark many websites for their projects, and the list of Bookmarks is so long, students cannot locate theirs anymore; it takes too long to find them.

5.1 If you were Ms. Courtney, what browser resource could you recommend students use to address this logistical problem?

5.2 What would be the relative advantage of using this resource, as compared to writing them all down or placing them in a word-processed file?

5.3 How could you add this to the list of things you assess for their projects?

TIE INTO PRACTICE: TECHNOLOGY INTEGRATION EXAMPLES

The Technology Integration Example that opened this chapter *(A Research Paper Website)* showed how a teacher might collect web resources on doing research and create a website to support students' research projects. With the knowledge you have gained from Chapter 7, do the following with this example:

1. To organize the online resources they found to act as links from their research project website, Ms. Almon and the teachers would need to create a Bookmark/Favorites folder like the one shown here. **Create this Bookmark/Favorites folder** by following the hands-on tutorial located on the *Hands-On with Technology* section of the DVD that accompanies this text.

2. Answer the following questions about the *Research Paper Website* example:

   • Phase 1 — What are relative advantages to students and to Ms. Almon and the teachers of having the research paper website? Of the video tutorials?

   • Phase 2 — One of the outcomes from this project is a Likert scale measuring student attitudes toward the writing approach used in the project. Prepare a Likert scale with items that address these attitudes.

Sample Bookmarks File (Create this product using the *Hands-On with Technology* tutorial section of the DVD.)

(See Chapter 2 for an explanation and example of Likert scales.)

- Phase 3 — Would it be a good idea to have students work individually, in pairs, or in small groups on the learning tasks outlined for Phase 3? Explain.

- Phase 4 — To create a handout that would stay in the format in which it was created in word processing when downloaded from the website, in what format would Ms. Almon have to save it after she created it? (*Hint:* See the discussion of materials generators software tools in Chapter 5.) How could she send this file to someone who did not have access to the Internet?

- Phase 5 — What might Ms. Almon and the teachers do to improve student performance on the second set of research skills?

3. What NETS for Students skills would students learn by working on the *Research Paper Website* project? (See the front of the book for a list of NETS for students.)

TECHNOLOGY INTEGRATION LESSON PLANNING

The *Technology Integration Workshop* DVD includes a set of technology integration ideas and links to online lessons, arranged as a searchable database. The DVD comes packaged in the back of this textbook. Click on the *Hands-On with Technology* section of the DVD and complete the following exercises.

1. **Locate lesson ideas** — The DVD has several examples of lessons that use email and student resource websites. Locate an example integration idea for using each of these resources.

2. **Evaluate the lessons** — Use the *Evaluation Checklist for a Technology-Integrated Lesson* (located on the DVD and the Companion Website) to evaluate each of these lessons.

3. **Modify a lesson** — Select one of the lesson ideas and adapt its strategies to meet a need in your own content area. You may choose to use the same multimedia software in the original or a different one.

4. **Add descriptors** — Create descriptors for your new lesson like those found on the database (e.g., grade level, content and topic areas, technologies used, relative advantage, objectives, NETS standards).

5. **Add the new lesson** — Add your modified lesson with all its descriptors to the lesson idea database.

FOR YOUR TEACHING PORTFOLIO

For this chapter's contribution to your teaching portfolio, add the following products you created in the Technology Integration Workshop:

- The Bookmark/Favorites file and the Likert scale you created for the research paper project.

- The evaluations you did using the *Evaluation Checklist for a Technology-Integrated Lesson*

- The new lesson plan you developed, based on the one you found on the DVD.

CHAPTER 8

INTEGRATING THE INTERNET INTO THE CURRICULUM

The Internet has had a profound impact on the social, economic, and political life of America . . . we have seen enormous changes in the way we conduct research, make purchases, learn about the world, live our lives.

Jeffrey Cole, in *The Chronicle of Higher Education* (April 2004)

Based on: The American Presidency Field Trip at http://www.field-guides.com/ss/prez/

Grade Level: Middle School • Content Area/Topic: American history, presidents • Length of Time: One week

Phase 1: Determine relative advantage

Mr. Cole was looking for a way to get his 10th-grade students more excited about American history. It was always difficult to motivate them to spend much time studying history topics. He found that they were sometimes intrigued when he talked about the lives of U.S. presidents, but they seemed to lose interest when he gave them reading assignments or assigned research projects on the backgrounds of presidents. A social studies teacher at the junior high school had told him that she had great success with **webquests** (curriculum projects in which students explore websites to find and analyze information on a topic). She found that webquests helped her students become more actively engaged in learning; they often were so caught up in the activities, they actually did more work than the project called for. Mr. Cole decided to create an American presidents webquest. It would require students to look for examples of the roles and limitations of presidential power, and it would have links to sites where students could go to find the information. For a culminating activity that would help prepare them for the exam, he would have the class participate in an online Presidents Jeopardy game that would be a link from the website. It would be a motivating way to review the history and contributions of various presidents.

Phase 2: Decide on objectives and assessments

Mr. Cole wanted his students to feel more motivated to study American history, but he also wanted to make sure the students were able to use appropriate search strategies to explore websites and that they learned information that would be on the exam. To make sure they achieved all of these goals, he wrote down the following outcomes and objectives and designed assessments matched to each one:

- **Outcome:** Skills in locating required information. **Objective:** Students will achieve a 90% rubric score to show they can employ efficient methods to use online sources, locate required information about American presidents, and work cooperatively to complete a series of questions related to presidential powers. **Assessment:** Rubric covering completion of required tasks, search

strategies, locating required information, and cooperative group work.

- **Outcome:** Improved attitudes about learning American history. **Objective:** Students will demonstrate increased motivation to learn about American history by making at least 25% higher scores on an attitude survey after the instruction than before. **Assessment:** Likert scale attitude instrument.

- **Outcome:** Knowledge about presidential powers throughout history. **Objective:** Students will demonstrate they understand a president's constitutional powers and limitations by scoring at least 85% on an exam in which they are asked to identify which constitutional power or limitation of power is reflected in various events in U.S. history. **Assessment:** Short-answer exam on presidential powers.

Phase 3: Design integration strategies

Mr. Cole felt it would best capture students' attention if he introduced the project by presenting two actual events—one from the immediate past president's administration and one from the 1800s—and showed how they represented the same constitutional authority. Then he would show them how to use the webquest to find similar examples of this authority and give them a worksheet to help guide their search strategies. He planned the following 5-day timeline for the project:

- **Day 1**: Introduce the project and website; give attitude survey. Give pre-instruction attitude survey. Using the classroom computer with an electronic whiteboard, show websites with the two historical examples and lead classroom discussion about what these events demonstrate about presidential powers.

- **Days 2–3**: Assign webquest. Demonstrate use of search strategies handout. Students work in groups of two or three in the computer lab to complete the webquest. With any remaining time, play online Presidents Jeopardy game to review the presidents and the significant events from their administrations that demonstrate the constitutional powers/limitations concepts.

- **Day 4**: Play Presidents Jeopardy. As a whole-class review, students play the Presidents Jeopardy game in groups of two or three. Award extra points on exam for Jeopardy winners.

- **Day 5**: Give exam and get feedback. Give the exam and post-instruction attitude survey. Collect the papers and spend the last 15 minutes of class reviewing the exam answers.

Phase 4: Prepare the instructional environment

With help from the school's technology education teacher, Mr. Cole prepared the website for the president's webquest and Presidents Jeopardy game. Preparation tasks included the following:

- **Creation of website content:** Mr. Cole located the resource websites to include in the webquest and designed the examples to use for demonstration and to pose as webquest problems. He uploaded it to the school server.

- **Research handout:** Mr. Cole created a handout summarizing recommended search strategies and providing a checklist of steps for students to complete for each search problem. He would use these completed sheets, together with his observations and the students' answers, to complete their grading rubric for this work.

- **Presidents Jeopardy game:** Mr. Cole compiled a set of questions about the presidents and events in their administration. The technology education teacher showed him how to create an online gameboard with these questions and upload it to the school server. It would be accessed as a link from his webquest site.

- **Computer lab scheduling**: Mr. Cole scheduled time for his students to use the lab to complete their webquests. He also allowed them to do some of the work at home, if they liked.

Phase 5: Evaluate and revise

After students had completed their webquests and exams, Mr. Cole reviewed the data from the activities. As he had hoped, he found attitudes toward studying history much improved after the project. Many students made unsolicited comments such as "Why can't we learn everything this way?" and "I love webquests!" The rubrics on search activities revealed considerable variation in search strategies and information located. He realized that he would need more demonstrations, examples, and practice of these strategies to help students learn more efficient, productive ways of looking for information. Exam scores were much improved over what he had seen in the past. Students told him that both the

webquest and the Presidents Jeopardy game helped a lot. It was evident that students who had home computers did better on the game than students who only had access at school. He decided to research ways he could give all students more Internet access at school.

OBJECTIVES

After reading this chapter and completing the learning activities for it, you should be able to:

1. Apply criteria to determine if a web-based activity could enhance learning for a given topic or skill.

2. Describe types of web-based learning activities and match them with appropriate integration strategies.

3. Create web-based learning activities that meet the criteria for effective lessons.

4. Match web-based authoring and development tools with products they are designed to create.

5. Demonstrate how to download images, programs, and plug-ins for use in web page development and use.

6. Give examples of functions that websites serve in web-based projects and learning activities.

7. Identify resources and procedures for developing web pages and websites.

8. Follow effective procedures to design and create web-based products.

9. Select and apply instruments to assess the quality of web-based lessons and products.

KEY TERMS

- anchors
- BMP (format)
- Common Gateway Interface (CGI)
- download
- electronic field trip
- electronic mentors
- electronic publishing
- EPS (format)
- File Transfer Protocol (FTP)
- frames
- GIF (format)
- HTML
- image formats
- Java

- Java applets
- JPEG (format)
- PERL
- PICT (format)
- plug-ins
- Portable Document Format (PDF)
- problem-based learning (PBL)

- site map
- social action projects
- storyboard
- streamed video and audio
- TIF (format)
- VRML
- webquest

For more information on Key Terms, go to the *Key Terms* module for this chapter of the Companion Website at http://www.prenhall.com/roblyer.

BACKGROUND ON WEB-BASED LEARNING ACTIVITIES

Web-based activities have great potential to enhance learning, but they are time consuming to develop and implement and difficult to design in ways that have substantial, positive impact on students' learning (Coulter, Feldman, & Konold, 2000; Fabos & Young, 1999; Harris, 2000). Coulter et al. point out that "The Internet is no silver bullet for improving education" (p. 43). They encourage teachers considering web-based activities to ask several questions before deciding to do an online project. They are, in effect, asking teachers to document the relative advantage of online activities in comparison with other strategies they might use to accomplish the same purposes. The following questions are based on those outlined by Coulter et al. (2000) and can form the basis of an integration plan for doing web-based activities:

1. **What is the curriculum-related purpose of the activity?** Using the Internet should not be thought of as an end in itself. The activity should accomplish some objective or purpose in required school curriculum.

2. **Does the Internet enhance the activity?** The rule of thumb is that if the activity could be done without the Internet, it probably should be!

3. **How will students use online resources (as opposed to just locating them)?** The object of the activity should be for students to do something with what they locate on the Internet. Once they locate information, they should be asked to determine its meaning, compile and synthesize various sources, or critique its usefulness.

4. **Do students have the necessary information analysis/information synthesis skills or am I including these in the instruction?** To make sure the project doesn't become an "information locating" exercise, it should call for additional, higher level tasks *after* the students find the information. However, teachers must be sure their students have the prerequisite skills to do these higher level tasks.

5. **Do I have the necessary time and support for the activity?** Harris points out that two problems are frequently cited in the failure of online activities. First, online projects can take longer than other learning strategies, and teachers do not allow sufficient time. Harris recommends doubling the original time estimate. Second, any number of technical problems can and do occur during an online project. Teachers must make sure they have technical support to resolve these problems in an efficient way so as not to slow down the momentum of the project.

Types and Examples of Web-Based Lessons and Projects

Some of the most exciting distance learning applications call for students to use technology as a means of collaboration so they can address significant problems or issues or to communicate with people in other cultures throughout the world. Judi Harris (1998) refers to these as "telecollaborations" and describes three general application categories:

1. **Interpersonal exchanges** — Students communicating via technology with other students or with teachers/experts

1. In a 1998 debate in *Time* magazine, powerful representatives of two sides squared off. The following quotes are in response to the question "Should schools be connected to the Internet?"

   Vice President Al Gore: "Access to the basic tools of the information society is no longer a luxury for our children. It is a necessity.... We must give our children ... the chance to succeed in the information age, and that means giving them access to the tools that are shaping the world in which they live" (Tumulty & Dickerson, 1998, p. 54).

   David Gelernter (victim of the Unibomber): "First learn reading, writing, history, and arithmetic. Then play Frisbee, go fishing, or surf the Internet. Lessons first, fun second.... If children are turned loose to surf, then Internet in the schools won't be a minor educational improvement, it will be a major disaster" (Tumulty & Dickerson, 1998, p. 55).

   Using information in this chapter combined with other readings, which of these positions is more plausible? How would you respond to each of these statements?

2. Speaking of distance courses via the Internet, Hartley and Bendixen (2001) warn that, "... most would agree that learning on the web is troublesome for the less motivated student. If web learning is dependent on motivation and motivation is correlated with socioeconomic status, we may be contributing to an expansion of the digital divide" (p. 25). What ways would you suggest to counteract the effects they refer to and to ensure that better access means more equitable access to learning opportunities?

2. **Information collection and analysis** — Using information collections that provide data and information on request

3. **Problem solving** — Student-oriented and cooperative problem-solving projects.

Harris lists strategies she calls *activity structures* that fall under these three categories. Lessons based on a given activity structure all follow the same basic design, even though their content and objectives may vary. Detailed descriptions of these activity structures may be found in Harris's book. Some forms these models can take are described here, and examples of each are given in Figure 8.1.

Electronic penpals or "keypals." Teachers link up each student with a partner or penpal in a distant location to whom the student writes letters or diary-type entries. As discussed in Chapter 7, a good resource for locating classroom keypals is http://www.epals.com.

Electronic mentoring. Dyrli (1994) referred to subject matter experts who volunteer to work closely with students online as **electronic mentors** (p. 34). Guidance may be one-to-one links between students and expert resources or may take the form of chats, discussion groups (e.g., in blogs), or learning communities. (See Technology Integration Idea 4.2 in Chapter 4.)

Electronic (or virtual) field trips. An **electronic field trip** in its simplest form fills classroom screens with visual images of a place considered to offer some educational value and to which students would not routinely be able to travel. As Tuthill and Klemm (2002) note, real field trips enhance learning but are seldom used due to logistical problems. They describe premade electronic field trips as ways to circumvent these problems and bring real-world situations into the classroom. These activities explore unique locations around the world, and, by involving learners at those sites, share the experience with other learners at remote locations.

Electronic publishing. When students submit their written or artistic products to a website, it is called **electronic publishing.** This allows their work to be shared with other students and visitors to the site.

Group product development. Teachers have developed many variations of online group development of products. For example, students may use email to solicit and offer feedback on an evolving literary project, sometimes involving advice from professional authors. Or students may work independently toward an agreed-on goal, each student or group adding a portion of the final product. This is sometimes called *chain writing.*

Problem-based learning. Sage (2000) described **problem-based learning (PBL)** as "learning organized around the investigation and resolution of an authentic, ill-structured problem" (p. 10). This kind of problem solving can take many forms, four of which are described here:

- **Collaborative problem solving** — This model involves several students or student groups working together to solve a problem. These kinds of lessons

Figure 8.1   Types and Examples of Web-based Lessons and Projects

Type of Web-based Activity	Sample Sites	Description

Electronic pen pals (keypals)
 	
ePALS
CLASSROOM EXCHANGE™
Courtesy of ePals.com.
http://www.epals.com
	• **ePals**
	  http://www.epals.com
	• **International E-Mail Classroom Connections (IECC)**
	  http://www.iecc.org/
		Links students at a distance to exchange information.

Electronic mentoring
 	
NASA Quest
http://quest.arc.nasa.gov/
	• **International Telementor Program**
	  http://www.telementor.org/
	• **Chats with NASA Personnel**
	  http://quest.arc.nasa.gov/sso/chats/
		Links students with experts to answer questions and support learning.

Electronic (virtual) field trips
 	
TRAMLINE
Courtesy of Tramline.
http://www.tramline.com
	• **Tramline Virtual Field Trips**
	  http://www.tramline.com
	• **National Health Museum**
	  http://www.accessexcellence.org/RC/virtual.html
		Visit sites to view people, places, and resources not locally available.

Electronic publishing
 	
CHILDREN'S EXPRESS
Courtesy of Children's Express.
http://www.childrens-express.org/
	• **Children's Express**
	  http://www.childrens-express.org/
	• **Midlink Magazine**
	  http://www.cs.ucf.edu/~MidLink/
		Share written and artistic products on websites.

Group product development Collaborative Projects Courtesy of Stevens Institute of Technology's Center for Innovation in Engineering and Science Education (CIESE). http://www.stevens.edu/ciese/collabprojs.html	• **CIESE Online Classroom Projects** http://www.edu/currichome.html	Work on written or artistic products with students at different sites.

(continued)

were dubbed *webquests* by Bernie Dodge and Tom March at San Diego University and became a model for teachers across the country to use in creating their own lessons. All of these lessons give students a scenario and a task to do in response to it; usually they have a problem to solve or a project to complete.

• **Parallel problem solving** — In this strategy, students in a number of different locations can work on similar problems. They solve the problem independently and then compare their methods and results or build a database or other product with information gathered during the activity.

Figure 8.1 (continued)

Type of Web-based Activity	Sample Sites	Description
Problem-based learning http://www.globe.gov	• **The GLOBE Program** http://www.globe.gov • **Pathfinder Science projects** http://kancrn.org/ • **International Schools CyberFair** http://www.gsn.org/gsh/cf/index.html • **MIDI Music Relay** http://www.kidlink.org/KIDPROJ/Midi/ • **Project Mars Millennium** http://www.projectpioneer.com/mars	Explore topics, obtain and analyze data, or participate in simulated problem solving with other students.
Social action projects Image courtesy of The Earth Day Groceries Project. http://www.earthdaybags.org	• **IEARN Network** http://www.iearn.org/ • **Cranes for Peace Project** http://www.cranesforpeace.org/ • **I Have a Dream Project** http://www.kidlink.org/dream/ • **Earth Day Groceries** http://www.earthdaybags.org	Discuss and create solutions for social or environmental problems with other students.

- **Data analysis** — These activities give students access to data from real phenomena such as weather or solar activity. Using these data, students are able to answer questions and solve problems posed for them.

- **Simulated activities** — These are the web equivalent of simulation software. For example, Hartley (2000) describes sites with a variety of virtual "labs" in which students can learn chemistry, physics, and math principles.

Social action projects. In **social action projects,** students are responsible for learning about and addressing important global social, economic, political, or environmental conditions. For example, students collaborating on a peace project write congressional representatives to voice concerns and present their viewpoints. The emphasis in this kind of project is collaboration to offer solutions to an issue of practical community (global or local) concern.

Integration Strategies for Web-Based Activities

These types of projects help address a variety of classroom needs, and it is this match of activity types with needs that defines and shapes integration strategies. Web-based projects are so rich in resources and learning possibilities that each one can usually be used with more than one of the integration strategies discussed next. These strategies are summarized in Figure 8.2, along with the types of activities that can be used to address them and example lesson ideas. Also see Figure 8.3 for good sources of web-based lesson plans, activities, and collaborative projects.

Support for student research. Students frequently use websites and web-based video resources and videoconferencing to gain insights into topics they are studying and to locate information for research papers and presentations. This work may be individual or group-based. (See Technology Integration Idea 8.1.)

Motivation for writing. As discussed in Chapter 7 under the email section, strategies that have students writing for distance audiences help motivate them to write more and to do their best writing. (See Technology Integration Idea 8.2.)

Practice for information literacy skills. Locating and using information on Internet sources has become a key part of classroom learning. It is important that students have opportunities to learn how to use web resources more efficiently and effectively. (See Technology Integration Idea 8.3.)

Visual learning problems and solutions. Many sites provide access to data, images, animations, and videos that help students understand complex problems and guide

Figure 8.2 Summary of Web-based Integration Strategies

Integration Strategy	Types of Web-Based Activities	Sample Technology Integration Idea
Support for student research	• Individual and cooperative research projects • Electronic mentoring	**Technology Integration Idea 8.1:** Connecting Science Students with NASA Resources
Motivation for writing	• Keypals • Electronic publishing	**Technology Integration Idea 8.2:** New Millennium Newspapers
Practice for information literacy skills	• Individual and cooperative research projects	**Technology Integration Idea 8.3:** The American Dream
Visual learning problems and solutions	• Individual and cooperative research projects • Problem-based learning	**Technology Integration Idea 8.4:** Bringing the Planets Closer to Home
Development of collaboration skills	• Individual and cooperative research projects • Electronic publishing • Group development of products • Problem-based learning • Social action projects	**Technology Integration Idea 8.5:** Working Together to Build Worlds
Multicultural experiences	• Electronic (virtual) field trips • Social action projects	**Technology Integration Idea 8.6:** Connecting with the Past—A Native American Memory Box Project

them in creating their own solutions. (See Technology Integration Idea 8.4.)

Development of collaboration skills. Web-based projects provide rich opportunities for students to learn how to work together to solve problems. Many web-based projects call for students to produce a product, such as a brochure, web page, or multimedia presentation. McGrath (2004) describes ways to help make these collaborative projects most productive. (See Technology Integration Idea 8.5.)

Multicultural experiences. Many web-based projects focus on broadening students' perspectives on their own and other cultures and providing insights into how their culture relates to others in the world. (See Technology Integration Idea 8.6.)

Figure 8.3 Sites with Collections of Web-Based Lessons and Projects

Here is a wealth of award-winning web-based lessons and activities. Many of these sites are described in detail on the Technology Integration Workshop DVD, *Hands-On with Technology* section.

Also see clickable links to all these sites on the Companion Website (http://www.prenhall.com/roblyer).

Source	Description	Content Areas
Annenburg Foundation http://www.learner.org/exhibits/	"Exhibits" or web-based explorations of concepts or themes depicted in the Annenberg video resources	All content areas—mostly science, geography, and history
Camp Silos http://www.campsilos.org/	Interactive lessons	Farming and prairie life
Center for Improved Engineering and Science Education (CIESE) http://www.stevens.edu/currichome.html	Collaborative projects that use real-time data available from the Internet	Science and mathematics
Co-Nect teleprojects http://exchange.co-nect.net/Teleprojects	Interactive data collection projects	All content areas
Consumer Jungle http://www.consumerjungle.org/students/s_default.htm	Interactive lessons from the Young Adult Consumer Education Trust	Consumer skills
Cyberbee Web Projects http://www.cyberbee.com/projects.html	Two ongoing international projects	Geography, history
Educational Media and Technology Curriculum Resources http://www.itdc.k12.ca.us/curriculum/	Webquests and lesson plans	All content areas
Exploring the Environment Modules and Activities http://www.cotf.ete/modules/modules.html	Scenario-based problem-solving activities and projects	Science, ecology, and geography
Exploratorium: The Museum of Science, Art, and Human Perception http://www.exploratorium.edu/educate/index.html	How-to descriptions of classroom projects	Science
Eyes on Art Lessons http://www.kn.pacbell.com/wired/art2/index.html	How-to lessons and activities	Art
The Franklin Institute Online http://www.fi.edu/fellows	Lesson plans and classroom activities	Science
The Global Schoolhouse http://www.globalschoolnet.org/GSH/	Clearinghouse for more than 2,000 online collaborative projects, organized by topic, grade, and project date	All content areas
Knowledge Network Explorer http://www.kn.pacbell.com/wired	Online curriculum, webquests, and other materials	All content areas
Microsoft lesson plans database http://www.microsoft.com/Education/LessonPlans.aspx	Searchable database of case studies, how-to articles, tutorials, virtual classroom tours	All content areas
National Geographic lessons and resource sites http://www.nationalgeographic.com/features/	More than 100 website "explorations" of various topics	Science, geography, history
National Geophysical Data Center http://www.ngdc.noaa.gov/education/education.html	Collections of resources on various topics	Science and geography
Teacher's Desk Lesson Plans http://www.teachersdesk.com/lessons/lessons.htm	Classroom lesson and projects	All content areas
Tramline's Virtual Field Trips http://www.tramline.com	Structures and guided teacher-designed "field trips" through a series of websites and dozens of topics	All content areas

TECHNOLOGY INTEGRATION IDEA 8.1

SUPPORT FOR STUDENT RESEARCH

Title: Connecting Science Students with NASA Resources

Content Area/Topic: Earth science

Grade Levels: All grades

NETS for Students: Standards 1, 3, 4, 5, 6

Description: The Earth According to WORF (World Observation Research Facility) is an interdisciplinary project that takes advantage of some of the resources available from NASA to support education. Using imagery from WORF, students learn to analyze visual data and gather information from websites and NASA experts to support their own research questions.

Instruction: The project begins by having students learn to analyze photographic detail. Then they obtain WORF images from four earth locations, analyze them, and document their findings. Each student develops five questions he or she would like to ask in a videoconference with NASA experts. Each class involved in the project forwards its best 10 questions, which the experts address in the videoconference.

Assessment: Students take pre- and post-tests on earth science and image analysis concepts.

Sources: Peterson, R., Starr, B., & Anderson, S. (2003). Real NASA inspiration in virtual space. *Learning and Leading with Technology, 31*(1), 14–19.

TECHNOLOGY INTEGRATION IDEA 8.2

MOTIVATION FOR WRITING

Title: New Millenium Newspapers

Content Area/Topic: English, writing

Grade Levels: 5–9

NETS for Students: Standards 3, 4, 5

Description: This activity has students creating newspaper-type stories with predictions about the future. These Special Edition newspapers are published in a "web newspaper."

Instruction: Some motivating activities to get students writing include creating a sample entertainment newspaper section circa 2010, or writing time capsule predictions about various areas of society in the future, for example, education, fashion, the environment, health, sports, and science.

Assessment: Teacher-developed rubric over newspaper story (writing quality, accuracy of information, creativity)

Source: Reissman, R. (1999). Predicting the future: Students create content for new millennium newspapers. *Learning and Leading with Technology, 27*(2), 18–21.

TECHNOLOGY INTEGRATION IDEA 8.3

PRACTICE FOR INFORMATION LITERACY SKILLS

Title: The American Dream

Content Area/Topic: Social studies

Grade Levels: 4–10

NETS for Students: Standards 1, 3, 4

Description: In this webquest activity, students are asked to investigate and answer questions about the American dream. This activity makes use of the "American Memory Collection" at http://memory.loc.gov.

Instruction: Teachers begin by discussing the concept of the American dream. Then students write about their own visions of what the dream means to them personally and for the country. The teacher introduces the American Memory Collection and reviews research techniques for using it. Students assume roles within small groups to create a product that documents their vision for the American dream.

Assessment: Teacher-developed rubric on their use of research techniques and their final product documenting their vision.

Source: Donlan, L. (1999). Come dream with us: America dreams. *Learning and Leading with Technology, 24*(5), 26–28.

TECHNOLOGY INTEGRATION IDEA 8.4

VISUAL LEARNING PROBLEMS AND SOLUTIONS

Title: Bringing the Planets Closer to Home

Content Area/Topic: Science and mathematics: Astronomy, measurement

Grade Levels: 5–8

NETS for Students: Standards 1, 3, 4, 5, 6

Description: This activity is designed to make the connection between science and mathematics more hands-on and meaningful for students by having them analyze real data in the form of images.

Instruction: They begin by downloading NASA photos from the Internet (e.g., images of the Solar System at http://spaceart.com/solar) and converting them to an uncompressed TIF format using an image processing program such as Adobe *PhotoShop*. Their task is learning how to measure the images. First, they use the software to calibrate the images (determine the scale) by comparing the size of the image to a known measure such as the diameter of Mars. Then they multiply the measured distance by the scale to determine the size of other features they have downloaded. In this way, the students can measure and compare features that change, such as the Martian and Earth polar ice caps. These measurements can be the basis of many projects to study space phenomena.

Assessment: Teacher-developed exercise to assess students' ability to measure and determine the scale of various images.

Source: Slater, T., & Beaudrie, B. (2000). Far out measurements: Bringing the planets closer to home using image processing techniques. *Learning and Leading with Technology, 27*(5), 36–41.

TECHNOLOGY INTEGRATION IDEA 8.5

COLLABORATIVE SKILLS DEVELOPMENT

Title: Working Together to Build Worlds

Content Area/Topic: Astronomy, geology, biology, meteorology

Grade Levels: 9–12

NETS for Students: Standards 1, 3, 4, 5, 6

Description: This project has students working in groups to build their own worlds by learning about and applying concepts from each of 10 areas: astronomy (design a solar system), geology (make maps), meteorology (define topography and weather), microbiology (create cellular life forms), marine biology (define sea plants), marine zoology (define sea creatures), marine ecology (design ocean ecosystems), botany (define land plants), zoology (define land animals), and land ecology (design land ecosystems).

Instruction: The teacher helps students brainstorm about what kind of planet they want. Then they use the project website to work through the 10 units on the concepts related to building various parts of their world. Finally, students do a web page or *PowerPoint* presentation to display their world.

Assessment: Teacher-created rubrics on group work and quality of science concepts reflected in the final product presentation.

Source: Viau, E. (2004). Building a world. *Learning and Leading with Technology, 31*(5), 18–21.

TECHNOLOGY INTEGRATION IDEA 8.6

MULTICULTURAL EXPERIENCES

Title: Connecting with the Past—A Native American Memory Box Project

Content Area/Topic: History, multicultural education

Grade Level: Middle school

NETS for Students: Standards 1, 3, 4, 5, 6

Description: Artists across cultures and throughout time have sought to incorporate the multifaceted connections between past and present in their artworks. George Catlin visited more than 140 Native American tribes and painted in excess of 325 portraits and 200 scenes of American Indian life. This site presents and interprets Catlin's artworks from the Smithsonian American Art Museum's permanent collection. Catlin viewed his subjects as a "vanishing race" and sought to preserve their images for future generations. In this activity, students create their own memory box, linking the past and the present and, in doing so, examine Catlin's ideas and motives.

Instruction: Acquaint students with artworks that have dealt with issues of memory and the connection of the past and present. Use resources on the *Artifacts and Memory—For Students* page of the Campfire Stories website to guide the activity. Discuss the ways in which these artworks make an effort to connect elements of past and present cultures. Students then create their own memory box using objects that hold personal significance. On completion of the project, have students present their boxes to other class members for constructive feedback on the project.

Assessment: Use a checklist to assess completion of tasks.

Source: Campfire Stories with George Catlin, http://catlinclassroom.si.edu.

Figure 8.4 **Website Support Functions**

Function	Description	Sample Site
1. Project overview, announcement, and application	Describes existing projects and offers signup location.	**Westward Ho!** http://www.cyberbee.com/wwho/
2. Tutorial instruction	Offers instruction and information on topics.	**Cool Cosmos** http://www.coolcosmos.ipac.caltech.edu/
3. Information summaries and exchanges	Allows information to be added to a collection that will be shared with others.	**KIDLINK Multicultural calendar** http://www.kidlink.org/KIDPROJ/MCC/
4. Communication and support	Provides virtual meeting places to support students' communications and resources to support project work.	**Math Forum** http://mathforum.org/
5. Displays of past and current student work	Shows examples of students' work in web publications centers.	**Kid Plus** http://www.kidplus.org
6. Project development centers	Invites the creation of new distance learning projects.	**Global SchoolNet Foundation** http://www.gsh.org

Figure 8.5 **Example of Project Overview, Announcement, and Application Website Function**

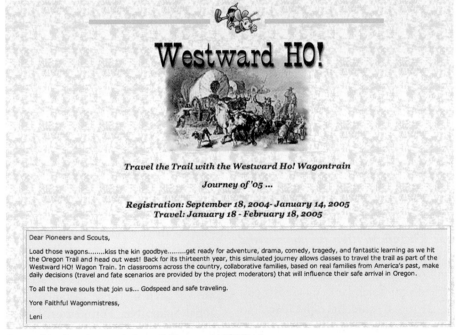

Source: Used with permission of Westward HO! Project.

Website Support for Web-Based Learning Activities

Harris (1998) pointed out that websites can perform several different functions to support distance learning activities. The following discussion of website support functions is based on Harris's description. Note that a single website can serve one or more of these functions. (See Figure 8.4 for a summary of these functions and example sites that fulfill them.)

Website function type #1: Project overview, announcement, and application. Sites can introduce the goals and purposes of existing projects and invite people to participate. For example, the Westward Ho! website gives an overview of available projects and gives participants a place to sign up, as shown in Figure 8.5.

Website function type #2: Tutorial instruction. A website can serve to deliver actual instruction and information

Figure 8.6 Example of Tutorial Instruction Website Function

Source: Courtesy of NASA/JPL–Caltech.

on a topic or project. For example, CalTech's Cool Cosmos website, shown in Figure 8.6, has web tutorials about topics such as multiple-wavelength astronomy, as well as resources such as a multiple-wavelength gallery that shows celestial objects observed in different wavelengths.

Website function type #3: Information summaries and exchanges. Students can use websites to add information to a collection that will be shared with others. For example, KIDLINK's Multicultural Calendar database is a collection of descriptions written by students of holidays and festivals around the world. Students use the site to enter summaries and can search the resulting database by month, holiday, country, and author. See an example in Figure 8.7.

Website function type #4: Communication and support. Websites can serve as a virtual meeting place to support students' communications as they work together at distant locations. These websites can be even more helpful if they build in streaming video or videoconferencing. They may also offer links to resources to support project activities and make gathering information for project work more efficient. See an example in Figure 8.8.

Website function type #5: Displays of past and current student work. Students can use sites as web publication centers in which students show examples of their poems, stories, pictures, and multimedia products. Some sites also show ongoing descriptions of past, current, and planned project activities. See an example in Figure 8.9.

Website function type #6: Project development centers. Finally, websites sometimes are set up for the specific purpose of inviting new distance learning projects. The Global SchoolNet Foundation has hundreds of existing projects and invites teachers around the world to register new ones. See an example in Figure 8.10.

Assessing the Quality of Web-Based Lessons

Hundreds of web-based activities are available for teachers to use in their classrooms or join online; some work better than others. How can teachers evaluate the quality of given activities and select those that will work best for their students? One useful assessment instrument is the *WebQuest Rubric.* Although webquests represent just one of many possible types of web-based lessons, the elements

Figure 8.7   Example of Information Summary and Exchange Website Function

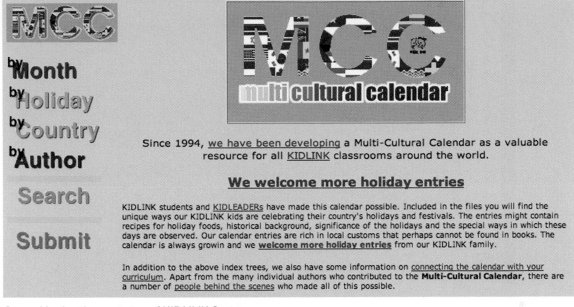

Figure 8.8   Example of Communication and Support Website Function

Figure 8.9 Example of Student Work Website Function

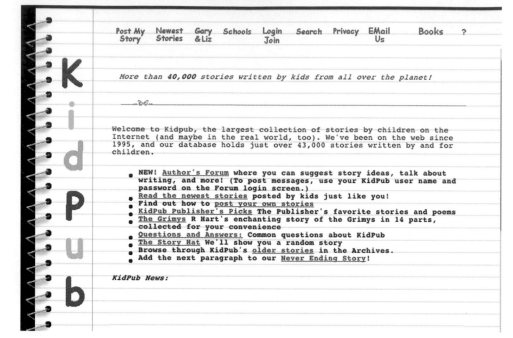

Figure 8.10 Example of Project Development Center Website Function

of this rubric actually apply to most of them. This rubric is shown in Figure 8.11 and is also on the Companion Website (http://www.prenhall.com/roblyer) and the DVD that accompanies this text.

RESOURCES FOR WEB PAGE AND WEBSITE DEVELOPMENT

Developing personal, professional, school, and project web pages and websites has become an excellent way for both teachers and students to learn the power of the In-

ternet, to participate in cooperative projects, and to display the project results. This section describes the resources needed to develop a web product and outlines procedures required to create effective web page products.

Web Page and Website Authoring Tools

Only a few years ago, web pages could not be developed without program authoring languages and scripting tools. Now, thanks to web page development software, it is possible to develop whole sites without writing a line of code or

TOP TEN STRATEGIES FOR INTEGRATING THE INTERNET INTO THE CURRICULUM

The following 10 powerful web-based lessons and projects have proven successful in classrooms around the country.

1. **Writing with Writers** `http://teacher.scholastic.com/writewit` — In this series of writing projects, students work with authors, editors, and illustrators to develop their skills in various genres, then publish their work online to share with other young writers at this Scholastic-sponsored website.

2. **Hello Dolly! A Webquest on Cloning** `http://www.pusd.info/projects/dolly/main.htm` — Because governments around the world are currently debating the potential impact of cloning on society, this website asks students to propose how to legislate cloning. They use resources at the site to learn about the issues, create a proposal, and present their findings during a "Cloning Summit."

3. **Electronic Postcards from Around the World** `http://www.genevaschools.org/austinbg/class/gray/internet/electronic` — In this project, students exchange postcards from their sites with classrooms in distant locations. They are told what to include in their postcard, how to create one, and how to protect their privacy as they post their work for all to see.

4. **WeatherScope: An Investigative Study of Weather and Climate** `http://www.k12science.org/curriculum/weatherproj2/en` — Schools pretend that they have been selected by a world famous meteorological institution to conduct an investigation and report on local and world weather and climate. To complete the assignment, they are shown how to create weather instruments and how to access the Internet to locate real-time weather information from around the world.

5. **Journey North** `http://www.learner.org/jnorth` — Students study wildlife migration and seasonal change by sharing their own field observations with classmates across North America. They track the coming of spring through the migration patterns of birds and mammals such as monarch butterflies, bald eagles, robins, hummingbirds, whooping cranes, the budding of plants, changing sunlight, and other natural events.

6. **Unsung Heroes: An ePals project** `http://www.epals.com/projects/unsung_heroes` — ePals invites classes around the world to exchange information about students, teachers, and others in their communities whose positive actions are making a difference in the quality of life of those around them. Students exchange email and contribute to the ePals Unsung Heroes discussion board.

7. **The North American Quilt: A Living Geography Project** `http://www.onlineclass.com/NAQ/NAQhome.html` — North American students research weekly geography questions and contribute their findings to a "quilt of information" on the website. Geography topics covered include natural land features, ecosystems, weather, wildlife, land use (agriculture, cities, undeveloped land), immigration and population histories, and North American folk and home-grown art. Expert guests answer student questions via email.

8. **Voices from the Past: An Oral History Webquest** `http://oldsegundo.com/webquests/voices_from_past/student-home.htm` — In this webquest, students learn about and follow oral history processes to contact and interview a World War II veteran or person alive during the World War II era. They then use the information to write a script for an historical documentary to be submitted to Old Segundo Productions to consider for documentary production.

9. **Global Grocery List Project** `http://www.landmark-project.com/ggl/index.html` — In this ongoing email project, students visit their local grocery stores and record the prices of items on the grocery list and share their prices with classes all over the world. The result is a growing table of current, peer-collected data that can be used in math, social studies, science, and health classes.

10. **The National Math Trail** `http://www.nationalmathtrail.org` — To illustrate that "math is all around you," this project challenges K–12 teachers and teams of students to observe their surroundings and create math problems about what they see and what they would like to figure out. The site provides examples of math trail projects and other resources, and students can submit their class's math trails to the site for posting.

To visit these web links online, go to this text's Companion Website at http://www.prenhall.com/roblyer

Figure 8.11 Rubric for Evaluating Webquests

The webquest format can be applied to a variety of teaching situations. If you take advantage of all the possibilities inherent in the format, your students will have a rich and powerful experience. This rubric will help you pinpoint the ways in which your webquest isn't doing everything it could do. If a page seems to fall between categories, feel free to score it with in-between points.

	Beginning	Developing	Accomplished	Score
Overall Aesthetics (This refers to the webquest page itself, not the external resources linked to it.)				
Overall Visual Appeal	0 points There are few or no graphic elements. No variation in layout or typography. OR Color is garish and/or typographic variations are overused and legibility suffers. Background interferes with the readability.	2 points Graphic elements sometimes, but not always, contribute to the understanding of concepts, ideas, and relationships. There is some variation in type size, color, and layout.	4 points Appropriate and thematic graphic elements are used to make visual connections that contribute to the understanding of concepts, ideas, and relationships. Differences in type size and/or color are used well and consistently. See Fine Points Checklist.	
Navigation and Flow	0 points Getting through the lesson is confusing and unconventional. Pages can't be found easily and/or the way back isn't clear.	2 points There are a few places where the learner can get lost and not know where to go next.	4 points Navigation is seamless. It is always clear to the learner what all the pieces are and how to get to them.	
Mechanical Aspects	0 points There are more than 5 broken links, misplaced or missing images, badly sized tables, misspellings, and/or grammatical errors.	1 point There are a few broken links, misplaced or missing images, badly sized tables, misspellings, and/or grammatical errors.	2 points No mechanical problems noted. See Fine Points Checklist.	
Introduction				
Motivational Effectiveness of Introduction	0 points The introduction is purely factual, with no appeal to relevance or social importance. OR The scenario posed is transparently bogus and doesn't respect the media literacy of today's learners.	1 point The introduction relates somewhat to the learner's interests and/or describes a compelling question or problem.	2 points The introduction draws the reader into the lesson by relating to the learner's interests or goals and/or engagingly describing a compelling question or problem.	
Cognitive Effectiveness of the Introduction	0 points The introduction doesn't prepare the reader for what is to come, or build on what the learner already knows.	1 point The introduction makes some reference to learner's prior knowledge and previews to some extent what the lesson is about.	2 points The introduction builds on the learner's prior knowledge and effectively prepares the learner by foreshadowing what the lesson is about.	
Task (The task is the end result of student efforts . . . not the steps involved in getting there.)				
Connection of Task to Standards	0 points The task is not related to standards.	2 points The task is referenced to standards but is not clearly connected to what students must know and be able to do to achieve proficiency of those standards.	4 points The task is referenced to standards and is clearly connected to what students must know and be able to do to achieve proficiency of those standards.	
Cognitive Level of the Task	0 points Task requires simply comprehending or retelling of information found on web pages and answering factual questions.	3 points Task is doable but is limited in its significance to students' lives. The task requires analysis of information and/or putting together information from several sources.	6 points Task is doable and engaging, and elicits thinking that goes beyond rote comprehension. The task requires synthesis of multiple sources of information, and/or taking a position, and/or going beyond the data given and making a generalization or creative product. See WebQuest Taskonomy.	

(continued)

Figure 8.11 (continued)

	Beginning	Developing	Accomplished	Score
Process (The process is the step-by-step description of how students will accomplish the task.)				
Clarity of Process	0 points Process is not clearly stated. Students would not know exactly what they were supposed to do just from reading this.	2 points Some directions are given, but there is missing information. Students might be confused.	4 points Every step is clearly stated. Most students would know exactly where they are at each step of the process and know what to do next.	
Scaffolding of Process	0 points The process lacks strategies and organizational tools needed for students to gain the knowledge needed to complete the task. Activities are of little significance to one another and/or to the accomplishment of the task.	3 points Strategies and organizational tools embedded in the process are insufficient to ensure that all students will gain the knowledge needed to complete the task. Some of the activities do not relate specifically to the accomplishment of the task.	6 points The process provides students coming in at different entry levels with strategies and organizational tools to access and gain the knowledge needed to complete the task. Activities are clearly related and designed to take the students from basic knowledge to higher level thinking. Checks for understanding are built in to assess whether students are getting it. See: • Process Guides • A Taxonomy of Information Patterns • Language Arts Standards and Technology • WebQuest Enhancement Tools • Reception, Transformation and Production Scaffolds	
Richness of Process	0 points Few steps, no separate roles assigned.	1 point Some separate tasks or roles assigned. More complex activities required.	2 points Different roles are assigned to help students understand different perspectives and/or share responsibility in accomplishing the task.	
Resources (Note: you should evaluate all resources linked to the page, even if they are in sections other than the Process block. Also note that books, video, and other off-line resources can and should be used where appropriate.)				
Relevance and Quantity of Resources	0 points Resources provided are not sufficient for students to accomplish the task. OR There are too many resources for learners to look at in a reasonable time.	2 points There is some connection between the resources and the information needed for students to accomplish the task. Some resources don't add anything new.	4 points There is a clear and meaningful connection between all the resources and the information needed for students to accomplish the task. Every resource carries its weight.	
Quality of Resources	0 points Links are mundane. They lead to information that could be found in a classroom encyclopedia.	2 points Some links carry information not ordinarily found in a classroom.	4 points Links make excellent use of the Web's timeliness and colorfulness. Varied resources provide enough meaningful information for students to think deeply.	
Evaluation				
Clarity of Evaluation Criteria	0 points Criteria for success are not described.	3 points Criteria for success are at least partially described.	6 points Criteria for success are clearly stated in the form of a rubric. Criteria include qualitative as well as quantitative descriptors. The evaluation instrument clearly measures what students must know and be able to do to accomplish the task. See Creating a Rubric.	
Total Score				/50

Source: Original WebQuest rubric by Bernie Dodge. This is Version 1.03. Modified by Laura Bellofatto, Nick Bohl, Mike Casey, Marsha Krill, and Bernie Dodge and last updated on June 19, 2001; http://webquest.sdsu.edu/webquestrubric.html. Reprinted with permission.

Figure 8.12 Sample Web Page with Partial HTML Source Code

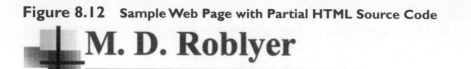

M. D. Roblyer

University of Maryland University College
Graduate School of Management and Technology

Contact: mroblyer@polaris.umuc.edu

Education   **Experience**   **Publications**   **Courses Taught**   **Papers**   **Awards, Funded Projects, and Other**

```
<html>
<head>
  <meta http-equiv="Content-Type"
content="text/html; charset=iso-8859-1">
  <meta name="GENERATOR"
content="Mozilla/4.78 (Macintosh; U; PPC) [Netscape]">
  <title>MDRpage.htm</title>
</head>
<body alink="#0000ff" bgcolor="#ffffff" link="#0000ff" text="#000000"
vlink="#551a8b">
 
<table cellpadding="0" cellspacing="0" width="50%">
  <tbody>
    <tr>
      <td width="10%"><img src="primarycolors.jpg" align="texttop"
border="0" height="69" width="85"> </td>
      <td valign="CENTER" width="100%"><b><font color="#1822cd"><font
size="+4">M. D. Roblyer</font></font></b>
      <hr noshade="noshade" size="5" width="100%"></td>
    </tr>
  </tbody>
</table>
<br>
    <br>
<blockquote>
  <blockquote> <font color="#1822cd"><font size="+2">University of
Maryland University College</font></font> <br>
      <font color="#1822cd"><font size="+2">Graduate School of Management
and Technology</font></font>
```

script. However, even if one uses a web development tool such as Microsoft *FrontPage* or Macromedia *Dreamweaver* that generates code automatically, it is good to know enough about each of the major program authoring languages to make minor adjustments to developed pages or to troubleshoot problems as they occur. Program authoring tools include: Hypertext Markup Language (HTML), Java, Virtual Reality Modeling Language (VRML), and Practical Extraction and Report Language (PERL). Also described here are web page and website software tools that allow developers to create web products without programming.

HTML. **HTML** is the Internet standard for how web pages are formatted and displayed. An example of HTML and the beginning of the page it generates is shown in Figure 8.12. (Note that the example displays only the beginning of the complete code.) Beginners can find a variety of HTML tutorials, tips, and tools on the Internet. Although HTML is the language microcomputer users will hear about most, other languages are also used, such as Standard Generalized Markup Language (SGML), a

system for organizing and tagging document elements (Seamon, 1999), and dynamic HTML (DHTML), which allows the same URL to display a different page depending on conditions such as time of day or the previous pages read (Bull, Bull, & Lewis, 1998).

Java. Originally called OAK, **Java** is a high-level programming language developed by Sun Microsystems. An object-oriented language similar to C++, it was originally developed for more general use but has become popular because of its ability to allow users to create interactive graphic and animation activities on web pages. Many predeveloped Java applications called **Java applets** are available for downloading from a web server (see http://java.sun.com/applets) and can be run on any computer that has a Java-compatible web browser. As Bull, Bull, and Bull (2000) note, Java applets make possible web page features such as animations and special effects, graphics and buttons, interactive displays, and web data collection forms. Applets also make chat rooms possible. The example applet in Figure 8.13 shows a counter that keeps track of the number of times the page is accessed.

ADAPTING FOR SPECIAL NEEDS

The Internet has important instructional applications for all students. Students with disabilities can particularly benefit from web resources that expand the palette of available information resources. For example, students who cannot read the textbook may be directed to websites where the reading/interest level can be adjusted (Windows on the Universe, http://www.windows.ucar.edu). Tools such as TrackStar (http://trackstar.hprtec.org) offer a useful alternative to report writing for many students as they gather and organize web links into a web page known as a *track,* which is subsequently published on the web. A variety of tools are available to assist teachers in designing instructional lessons and units that integrate the Internet into the curriculum. Two useful starting points are:

- Cheryl Wissick's Web Toolboxes, http://www.ed.sc.edu/caw/toolbox.html, and

- Teach-nology, http://www.teach-nology.com/themes/.

Contributed by Dave Edyburn

VRML. Although not in common use by most developers, **VRML** develops and displays 3-D objects on web pages. These objects give the illusion of being "real" much more than videos or animations and can be used to create virtual worlds. VRML has great potential for making web pages very interactive and lifelike (Skipton, 1997). Skipton notes that most VRML packages let developers create basic shapes (primitives) such as cubes, spheres, and cylinders and include polygon-based modeling tools for creating more complex objects. Some offer further modeling features—free-form or cutouts—that enable users to extrude or cut out shapes to create more complicated models. Skipton adds that, in combination with other programs, VRML can create "a multi-user avatar space" like that in the science fiction novel *Snow Crash* (Stephenson, 1993).

Figure 8.13   Example of a Java Applet

Source: Used with permission of Chami.com.

PERL and other programming languages. Developers can use **PERL** or another programming language (e.g., Java, C++, Visual Basic) to write **Common Gateway Interface (CGI)** programs that create *dynamic documents.* That is, web page users can insert their comments or answers into active web pages as they run on a server. Many web pages contain forms that use a CGI program to process the form's data once submitted. All information entered at these sites is gathered and processed by a CGI server, which prepares a summary of the information using a database software such as *FileMaker Pro* (FileMaker, Inc.). Repp (1999) described some uses of CGI scripts for education. These include sites for handing in student assignments, dynamic calendars that can be updated regularly, and online surveys and other research instruments for gathering and storing data. Figure 8.14 shows a CGI script to gather information across students.

Web development software. Web development tools generate HTML, CGI scripts, and other code so that users can develop web page and website products without having to know programming languages. Web development tools range from simple programs for development of single web pages (e.g., Netscape *Composer*) to complex, full-featured packages (e.g., Macromedia's *Dreamweaver Fireworks Studio*) that allow development of multiple-page websites with sophisticated multimedia components. Figure 8.15 summarizes these web authoring tools, the web products they make possible, and the web development tools we usually use to do the code creation for us.

Downloading Images, Programs, and Plug-ins

Several of the resources that are useful in both developing and using web pages can be **downloaded**—that is, transferred from a website to your computer—free from company sites. Some of these are images, programs (e.g., updated versions of browsers), and *plug-ins* or "player" programs that allow you to play audio and video clips in web pages.

Figure 8.14 Example CGI Application for Collecting Data from Students

Add a Checklist question

This is a "Checklist" question. Respondents can check more than one response. Each response will be stored in the Survey Center.

Here is an example:

What is your favorite subject in school?

Name: | Enter your name here |

Email: | Enter your email address here |

☐ English
☐ Science
☐ Social Studies
☐ Math
[Submit]

Source: Used with permission of Tom Snyder Productions.

Figure 8.15 Summary of Web Page and Website Development Tools and Products

Program authoring tools
(used by programmers, technical personnel)

HTML, VRML, PERL, JAVA, other authoring languages

Web development tools
(used by most teachers and students)

Netscape *Composer*, Microsoft *FrontPage*, Macromedia *Dreamweaver*, Macromedia *Flash*

Created Web Products

Web documents, 3-D environments, animated applets, CGI scripts for data gathering

Downloading images. The Internet has been around in text format since 1969. However, it became the society-wide phenomenon we know today only when the first web browser, *Mosaic,* made it possible for the Internet to appear on computer screens as images. Why do images make such a difference? There may be two reasons. First, pictures are an "information shortcut." The old adage that "a picture is worth a thousand words" means that people grasp many concepts more quickly when they are presented as images rather than as text. Second, people seem able to remember a great deal of information visually.

But it is possible to take advantage of the visual tapestry of the Internet in ways other than receiving information. You can use your browser to "capture" or download any image you see from any web page and store it on your computer. Once you download an image, you can use it in your own web pages. Try downloading an image in the exercise given in Figure 8.16. Downloading an image from the Internet is easy, but remember that many images you find on web pages are copyrighted. Their legal use is determined by copyright law and by the owner of the website. If you are not sure if you can use an image legally, contact the website owner to request permission.

Figure 8.16   Downloading Images Exercise

Problem: Let's say you want to have students use word processing to make an illustrated booklet of the three branches of the U.S. government. You might go to sites for each of these branches and capture images for them to use in their booklets. Do the following:

- Go to the White House website for kids located at http://www.whitehouse.gov/kids/timeline/.

- Click (on a PC, right-click) on the image of the 1777 flag you see here, but instead of letting up the mouse after you click, hold it down until a menu like one of the following appears: ————————

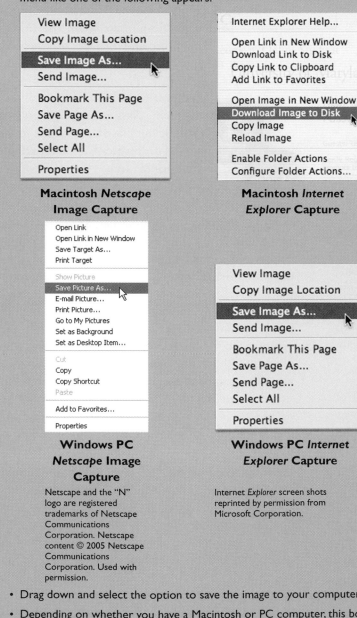

- Drag down and select the option to save the image to your computer.

- Depending on whether you have a Macintosh or PC computer, this box will look something like the following. The file name is the one under which it was stored when it was put on the web page: **timeline1_r2_c1.gif**:

  Save As: timeline1_r2_c1.gif

- Change this name to something you may find easier to remember and save it. For example:

  Save As: flag.gif

After you save an image on your computer, you can insert it in documents or other web pages. However, you may need to change the image format from the original file format. Several **image formats,** or ways of storing images, have been developed over the years to serve various purposes: either a certain computer or operating system required it, or certain formats deal better with differences among image types (e.g., photos rather than drawn images or clip art). You can tell the format of an image by its suffix. The most common formats follow:

- **BMP** — Stands for "bitmapped." Originally developed for use on Disk Operating System (DOS) and Windows-compatible computers.
- **EPS** — Stands for "Encapsulated PostScript." Allows transfer of artwork between any software packages that use PostScript printing files.
- **PDF** — Stands for "Portable Document Format." Stores document pages as images.
- **PICT** — Short for "Picture" format. Originally developed for use on Macintosh computers.
- **TIF** — Stands for "Tagged Image File." A flexible format used to exchange files among various software applications and computers.
- **GIF** — Stands for "Graphics Interchange Format." Used for drawn images, illustrations, clip art, or animations.
- **JPEG** — Stands for "Joint Photographic Experts Group," and the filename extension is jpg. Used for photographs.

Images downloaded from web pages will be in either GIF or JPEG format. If you want to use images to do your own web pages, they must be in one of these two formats. If you want to change an image to one of these formats, you will need to bring it into an image manipulation program (e.g., Adobe *PhotoShop*) and save it in either GIF or JPEG format.

Downloading programs and plug-ins. Web browsers made the Internet visual, but subsequent developments gave it sound and motion. Special programs called **plug-ins** have been created to allow people to see and hear the multimedia features that make the Internet increasingly lifelike. Although plug-ins tend to change and update rapidly, the Internet has a built-in way of allowing people to take full advantage of the Internet's multimedia features and to keep up with advancements required for their use. Instead of buying the programs on disk or CD, Internet users can download many of them directly from the company site. Five of the most commonly downloaded programs and plug-ins are described here and summarized in Figure 8.17.

- **Updated browser versions** — Most new computers come with a browser program stored on the hard drive. However, browsers update frequently, constantly adding new features and capabilities. It is necessary to use an up-to-date version in order to see newer Internet features. You can download newer versions of browsers from the Netscape and Microsoft websites.
- **PDF reader** — This program lets you see Portable Document Format files. These are pages stored as images so they may be printed out with a page appearance identical to the original document. A PDF format is particularly important when the original text contains both print and images, or when one wants to see the appearance of the original document. For example, one might photograph and store the pages of the Declaration of Independence so history students could see them. Although the program to create PDF files must be purchased, the Adobe *Reader* viewer plug-in required to see already-stored PDF files is available free from Adobe, Inc.
- **Streaming video and audio player plug-ins** — An exciting Internet capability is being able to see action or hear sounds live on the Internet. **Streamed video and audio** is so called because it sends or "streams" images and sounds a little at a time so one need not download the files completely before using the contents. This is especially useful for large videos that take a long time to download. Video quality is dependent on the quality and speed of the line connecting the computer to the Internet. Knee, Musgrove, and Musgrove (2000) describe methods of producing streamed video for classroom use. Once these files are seen and stored on a computer, they also may be seen and/or heard later. *Real Player* is one commonly used example. (For more information on streaming video, see http://www.streamingvideos.com.)
- **Movie player plug-in** — Videos that have been digitized and stored as movie files may be viewed through a plug-in. Programs such as Apple's *QuickTime* are used to create these movies, which usually are shot with a camcorder and stored in a Moving Picture Experts Group (MPEG) or MP3 format. To see them, one needs a *QuickTime* or MPEG player plug-in. Although originally designed as a movie player, more recent versions of *QuickTime* can also be used with streaming video and audio.
- **Animation plug-in** — Special programs that create animated content (e.g., sliding menus, games, movies) for the web also come with their own players. One such commonly used program and player is Macromedia's *Flash*.

Figure 8.17   Popular Programs to Download for Web Page Development and Use

Type of Program	Program Name	Download Source
Browsers	• *Netscape Communicator*® Netscape and the "N" logo are registered trademarks of Netscape Communications Corporation. Netscape content © 2005 Netscape Communications Corporation. Used with permission. • *Internet Explorer*® Screen shot reprinted by permission from Microsoft Corporation	• **Netscape** http://www.netscape.com • **Microsoft** http://www.microsoft.com/downloads
PDF reader	*Adobe Reader*® Get Adobe Reader Courtesy of Adobe, Inc.	• **Adobe** http://www.adobe.com/products/ acrobat/readstep2.html
Streaming video and audio players	*RealPlayer* (audio/video) real	• **RealNetworks** http://www.real.com/
Movie players	*QuickTime*® movie player QuickTime Courtesy of Apple Computers.	• **Apple Computer** http://www.apple.com/
Animation player	*Flash*® animations player macromedia Courtesy of Macromedia Inc.	• **Macromedia** http://macromedia.com

File Transfer Options: Email Attachments and FTP Programs

When teachers and students engage in distance collaborations, they often need to exchange files of their work. Two ways to transfer large written documents, graphic files, and programs from one computer to another include email attachments and **File Transfer Protocol (FTP).**

Sending files as email attachments. One easy way to send files is merely to attach them to email messages. Browsers and email programs have built-in options for selecting files to send as attachments. Usually, it's as easy as selecting the attachment option from a menu while preparing an email message. The receiver must have the appropriate software to view these files. Files are some-times sent in compressed (stuffed) format and the user must decompress (unstuff) them with a utility program such as *Stuffit Expander* (Allume Systems). Although transferring files is rapidly getting easier, a few technical issues remain concerning the compatibility of files prepared in one program and sent to another. Compatibility problems often can be overcome by sending files as PDF documents (described earlier in this chapter). Adler (2000) described some ways PDFs are useful to teachers.

Sending files via File Transfer Protocol (FTP). A common procedure for uploading files to servers on the Internet, FTP requires software (e.g., *WS_FTP, CuteFTP*) and a server set up to receive files. (Most computer systems also have built-in FTP capabilities, but they must be compatible

Figure 8.18   Sample FTP Window in *WS_FTP* Software

Source: Reprinted with permission from Ipswitch, Inc.

with the server to which they are being sent.) After teachers and students create web pages, they usually use FTP software to send the files to the school or district server. FTP software both allows them to send files and view, move, or delete files that they have already sent. Figure 8.18 shows a sample FTP program window with files that have been up-loaded from a computer hard drive to a server.

Most schools or districts that have their own server also have their own FTP software and procedures they want teachers to follow for uploading new files. However, if they use another site (e.g., one made available to them by an Internet service provider or ISP), they have to contact the web administrator of that server for the usernames and passwords required to send files via FTP.

PROCEDURES FOR DEVELOPING AND EVALUATING WEB PAGES AND WEBSITES

Required Development Resources

Teachers and students can use two different strategies to create their own web pages and websites:

- Creating pages from scratch and linking them, or
- Downloading or "grabbing" existing pages and modifying them for your own use.

To implement either of these strategies, you will need three different resources:

1. **Web development software** — Although you can create pages by programming them in HTML code,

Teachers and students use design and content criteria to evaluate website quality.

teachers will find that using web page development software is preferable; it is easier and faster, and it requires much less technical skill. As with most tool software, web page development software packages vary considerably as to features and prices. Packages such as Microsoft *FrontPage* and Macromedia *Dreamweaver* are full featured and must be purchased. Netscape *Composer* is a free built-in web page development software component of Netscape *Communicator*. As described in the previous section, it can be downloaded free from the Netscape website.

2. **FTP software** — After developing the pages for your site, you must transfer or upload them to a server. To do this, you need FTP software, as discussed in the

Figure 8.19 Recommended Eight-Step Website Development Sequence

preceding section. If your website will be housed on your school or district server, technical personnel there may provide an FTP package or they may want to upload your pages for you. If your site will be on another server, contact the web administrator to determine required procedures.

3. **Server to house the website** — Your website must have a "home," that is, a computer or server on which it resides. Most teachers choose to have their website on their school or district server. In this case, you may want to determine the procedures that have been established in your school or district for obtaining required permissions and for uploading pages to the server.

Caveats When Creating Web Page Information

Before you begin developing pages, consider these items:

- **Limit sharing of personal information** — Because so many people will have access to your website, you

may wish to limit personal information such as pictures and telephone numbers. For example, most educational websites include only first names and email addresses, rather than full names and street addresses.

- **Limit photos and large graphics** — These take a long time to load and can be frustrating to users (e.g., parents) who wish to see the information on your site.

- **Address web page criteria** — Use the same criteria for your own page that you wish to see in other sites. Review criteria for effective web pages later in this chapter. You may want to review educational sites you like and follow their structure.

Recommended Web Page Development Sequence

The following eight steps are recommended as a development sequence. Figure 8.19 summarizes these steps. Also see a tutorial on how to develop a web page for a webquest in the Technology Integration Workshop at the end of this chapter.

Step 1: Plan and storyboard. Planning and design are the most difficult and important—and most frequently neglected—first steps in developing a website. Though most people want to get to the fun of development, planning is critical to a well-designed website. Create **storyboards** (i.e., make a rough sketch of each page) for the site by using cognitive mapping software such as *Inspiration* or 3-in. by 5-in. sticky notes placed on large pieces of poster board to represent the web pages.

Step 2: Develop pages with text. The next step is to create blank web pages and insert text elements such as titles, paragraphs of description, and any text labels that will later serve as links. There are three kinds of page structures: basic, basic with **anchors** (locations on the page to link to), and **frames.** Frames are sections on a web page; the contents of each frame are actually different web pages. Frames are useful for showing different kinds of information side by side on the same page, but not all browsers support them. Designers of frame-based pages usually also give viewers a no-frames option.

Step 3: Insert images and media. Pictures, animations, photos, and movies come next. Images and animations must be in GIF or JPEG format; movies and sounds must be in MPEG format. If movies or audio are to be streamed, the page should inform the user and provide a way to obtain the plug-in needed to see or hear the item.

Step 4: Insert links and frames. After all pages are designed, insert links or "hot spots" from text and images to other pages in the site and locations on the Internet.

Step 5: Insert interactive elements. If desired, make the web page "interactive" by inserting Java applets, interactive forms, and mail-to commands to gather comments from users who visit your site.

Step 6: Test in a browser. Many development programs have a built-in preview system, but it is essential to test the site with an actual browser to observe how it will work when it is published on the web.

Step 7: Publish (upload) the site. For others to see created web pages, developers must place them on a server. This is called *publishing the site.* If the user can sit down at the keyboard of the computer acting as the server, the files may be moved over from a disk to the hard drive. For servers that are not nearby, the user may upload the pages to the server as FTP files.

Step 8: Gather evaluation comments, revise, and maintain the site. The best websites are those that are updated regularly based on user comments and the continuing insights of the developers. This may be done through interactive forms built into the page (see step 5) or simply through inviting emailed comments.

Criteria for Evaluating Web Pages and Website Design

Chapter 7 included a description of criteria and procedures for evaluating website content (see Figure 7.20). Another way to evaluate a web page is by its design. As teachers and students do their own web page products, they can use the following characteristics to judge design quality:

- **Good structure and organization** — The first page of the site indicates clearly how to get to its various parts. Some sites do this with an option bar that appears at the top, bottom, or side of every page in the site. Option bars allow you to easily move around the site. See an example option bar from the U.S. DOE at: http://www.ed.gov/ in Figure 8.20.

- **Clear text and/or graphic links** — Branches are organized so that you can get back to the main page in no more than three clicks. One device for large sites provides a link to a **site map** or an at-a-glance guide to the contents. Figure 8.21 provides an example of a site map for the National Oceanic and Atmospheric Administration web site (http://www.noaa.org).

- **Good visual design** — Pages are designed for good readability. A limited number of colors and fonts are used; fonts are easy to read, and colors are selected for contrast with the background. Graphics do not distract from reading the content. You can tell from looking at an icon what information you will get when you click it.

- **Easy navigation** — Pages load quickly. It's easy to get around in the site. Links are provided so you can get back to the main page from any part of the site. The most important information is given at the top of the page. All links work as they should. Larger sites have their own built-in search engine. Figure 8.22 is an example of the search engine at the U.S. House of Representatives website (http://thomas.loc.gov).

A checklist of criteria based on the items described in this chapter is shown in Figure 8.23 (p. 278). This checklist is also on the DVD that accompanies this book and can be completed and saved on your computer. This can be used to evaluate your own and others' website designs.

Figure 8.20 Sample Option Bar to Aid Website Navigation

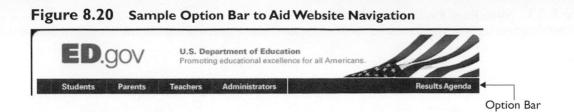

Option Bar

Figure 8.21 Sample Site Map

Site Map

| Tue October 26 2004 | Home | Contacts | Media | Disclaimer | Search | People Locator |

Site Index

Home Page Menu ▼

Pull-down Menu Text

Air Quality
Aviation
Charts
Climate
Coasts
Contacts
Disclaimer
Diving
Drought
Fire Weather
Fisheries
Floods
Hurricanes
Jobs
Lightning
Meet the Administrator
Navigation
Ocean
NOAA Leadership
Past Weather
Privacy Policy
Question of the Month
Research
Satellites
Search this site
Site Map
Solar and Space

Charting and Navigation

- Aeronautical Charts (Federal Aviation Administration)
- Coastal Aerial Photography
- Coastal Survey Maps
- Environmental Sensitivity Index Maps
- Estuarine Bathymetry
- Geodetic Control Points
- Historical Maps and Charts
- Hydrographic Survey Outlines
- Nautical Charts
- Map Finder
- Other Products and Services
- Promote Safe Navigation
- Surveying and Mapping
- Surveying and Mapping Links
- Tide and Tidal Current Tables
- Topography
- Water Level Observation Network

Climate

- Climate Data - Degree days, precipitation, winds, temperatures
- Climate Diagnostics Center
- Climate Monitoring and Diagnostics Lab
- Climate Prediction Products
- Climate Prediction Center
- Climate Visualization

Figure 8.22 Sample Site Search Engine

Congress Now: House Floor This Week | House Floor Now | Senate Schedule: Majority Minority

Search Bill Text 108th Congress (2003-2004):

Bill Number [   ]   Word/Phrase [   ]   Search   Clear

Figure 8.23 **Web Page Evaluation Checklist**

1. Content

_____ All information is accurate. The "last time updated" date is given.

_____ Information is complete but not excessive or redundant.

_____ Information is well organized and clearly labeled.

_____ Information is interesting, informative, and worthwhile.

_____ Information is not redundant to other sources; there is a reason to put it on the web.

_____ All text has correct spelling, grammar, and punctuation.

_____ Level of content and vocabulary are appropriate for intended audience.

_____ Content is free from stereotyping, coarse or vulgar language, or matter that could be offensive to typical users.

_____ Author(s) of the page are clearly identified.

_____ The page gives an email address or other way to contact authors.

2. Visual and Audio Design

_____ The site has a consistent, common look and feel across pages.

_____ Graphics, animations, videos, and sounds make an important contribution.

_____ Pages have only one or two fonts.

_____ Each page uses limited numbers of colors, especially for text.

_____ Colors have been selected to be compatible with the _Netscape_ 216-color palette.

_____ Type colors/styles and text-to-background contrast were selected for readability.

_____ Each graphic is designed to fit 640 × 480 pixel screens (allowing for scroll bars/toolbars).

_____ Each page is limited to 2–3 screens; the most important information is at the top.

_____ The pages are simply and attractively designed and make a user want to read them.

3. Navigation

_____ Pages load quickly.

_____ Pages have simple, consistent navigation scheme for quick, easy navigation.

_____ The first page shows clearly how the site is organized and how to get to all items.

_____ Text and icon links are easy to identify. Graphics and sounds are clearly identified.

_____ Icons have been well chosen to represent the information they link to.

_____ Each supporting page has a link back to the home page.

4. Miscellaneous (for larger sites and pages)

_____ Requests for private information are secured.

_____ Page information is kept short enough that it can be printed quickly.

_____ Users can choose to load alternate versions of pages (e.g., text only, smaller images).

_____ The site has its own search engine for locating things within the pages.

_____ Branching is organized so all content is three clicks or fewer from the home page.

Use the following tips to make your sites and pages easier to design and use:

_____ Organize the site on paper ahead of time before inputting it into the computer.

_____ To speed loading, limit graphics to no more than 50K and reuse images whenever possible.

_____ Use GIFs for line art or graphics with limited colors and sharp edges; use JPEGs for photos with many colors and smooth gradients. Avoid PICT and other formats that must be converted by users.

_____ Test out your page in a real browser.

_____ Use a GIF spacer (1×1 transparent GIF) to space paragraphs, indents, or alignments on pages.

Criteria for Evaluating Student Web Products

As students begin to create their own web page products, it is helpful to give them criteria in the form of rubrics that describe the quality they are aiming for in each of several aspects. Many such web page rubrics are available. Two of the best are shown in Figures 8.24 and 8.25 and are included on the DVD that accompanies this book (_Web Page Rubric for Younger Learners_ and _Web Page Rubric for Older Learners_). Figure 8.24 shows a rubric designed especially for young learners, and Figure 8.25 shows one for older students.

Figure 8.24 Rubric for Assessing Young Learners' Web Pages

Excellent	Very Good	Fair	Unacceptable
_____ directions followed	_____ directions followed	_____ directions mostly followed	_____ directions not followed
_____ visually pleasing	_____ visually pleasing	_____ visually distracting	_____ visually confusing
_____ excellent organization of information	_____ mostly clear writing	_____ writing occasionally unclear	_____ writing unclear
_____ information grammatically sound (French and English)	_____ few grammatical and/or spelling mistakes	_____ many grammatical errors and/or misspellings	_____ many grammatical errors and/or misspellings
_____ all words are correctly spelled	_____ font shows accent marks	_____ font does not display accents	_____ font does not display accents
_____ font shows accent marks	_____ links and anchors work	_____ not all links and anchors work	_____ links and anchors do not work
_____ links and anchors work	_____ special effects usually enhance, not detract		_____ special effects distract
_____ special effects enhance, not detract			

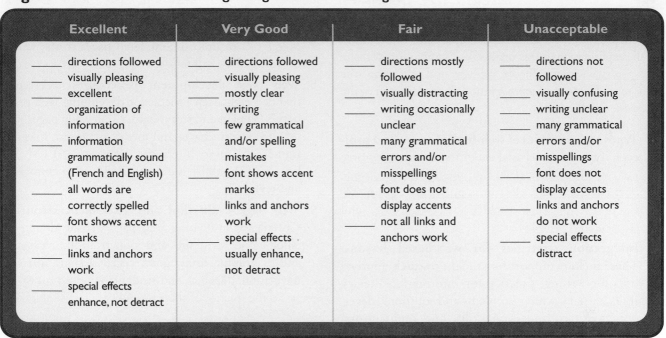

Criteria	Standards				
	Level 1	Level 2	Level 3	Level 4	Level 5
Development Process	Handwritten proposal sheet submitted to teacher	Text for page entered into simple word processor or HTML-creation program (BBEdit, PageMill, Claris HomePage, FrontPage)	Draft page is printed out from within Netscape; text on page partially achieves proposal	Evidence of revision of page in web browser (Netscape, Explorer); substantially achieves (or explains changes to) proposal	Critical reflection of development process is submitted in writing (individually)
Network Skill	Student has problems bring up their Web Page within a web browser (Netscape, Explorer)	Text is in a program other than the word processor; Images not saved in .gif or .jpg format; One or more files in wrong location or have wrong file name	All .html files in simple word-processor of HTML-creation program; All images .gif or .jpg; All file names and group numbers correct	Running word-processor or HTML-creation program and web browser (Netscape or Explorer) simultaneously; efficient use of Internet access programs	Efficient revision: testing changes by switching between word-processor or HTML-creation program and web browser (Netscape or Explorer)
Thinking Process	Disconnected and unrelated thoughts; vague ideas	Concrete description and evaluation; no analysis of causes, no meaning	Description, analysis, meaning, evaluation; identifies problems and solution	Integrates multiple sources of information to assess issue; balances personal and external	Identifies and examines root causes as well as immediate issue; persuasive and convicted
Writing Process	Difficult to understand, tangents, spelling and other errors	Many errors but consistent line of thought	Easy to understand; perfect spelling; one or two grammar, syntax, or semantic problems	Same as Level 3 but no errors	Clear, concise, well written
HTML Skill	No HTML formatting tags; Text is not broken into paragraphs	Text is broken in paragraphs; Headings are used; no other tags	Paragraphs; headings; title ; and the following tags as appropriate: preformatted text ; styles ; centered text ; horiz. rule	Same as Level 3 plus: images > and links	Same as Level 4 plus at least two lists, images as Links, "Return to..." links, colored text/background, background image
Layout	Layout has no structure or organization	Text broken into paragraphs and/or sections	Headings label sections and create hierarchy; some consistency	Hierarchy closely follows meaning; Headings and styles are consistent within pages; Text, images, and links flow together	Consistent format extends page-to-page; design is intentional; attention to different browsers and monitor size
Navigation	One Page	One Page with TITLE, Heading	2 pages (or one page with links to other resources)	3 pages with clear order, labeling and navigation between pages; all links work	Title Page with other pages branching off, and at least four pages total; Navigation path is clear and logical, all links work
Images	No images	Images are unrelated to page/text/proposal; most images were recycled from other pages on the Internet; Images too big/small in size or resolution; Images poorly cropped or have color problems	Images have strong relation to text; some Images are student produced; Images have proper size, resolution, colors, and cropping	Same as Level 3 plus images are from 3 or more sources (scan, CD-ROM, QuickCam, ZapShot, video tape, net, SuperPaint, PhotoShop, LogoMotion, etc.)	Same as Level 4 with either: more advanced Photoshop, PhotoDeluxe or Illustrator work

Figure 8.25 Rubric for Evaluation of Older Learners' Web Pages

The following is a summary of the main points covered in this chapter. To see additional examples and information on these points, go to this textbook's Companion Website at http://www.prenhall.com/roblyer and click on the Chapter 8 *Interactive Summary* module to visit each of the recommended websites.

1. **Types and examples of web-based lessons and projects:** Types of web-based activities include electronic pen pals (keypals), electronic mentoring, electronic (virtual) field trips, electronic publishing, group development projects, problem-based learning, and social action projects.

2. **Integration strategies for web-based lessons:** These include support for student research, motivation for writing, practice for information literacy skills, visual learning problems and solutions, development of collaboration skills, and multicultural experiences.

3. **Web site functions to support web-based learning activities:** These include project overview, announcement, and application; tutorial instruction; information summaries and exchanges; communication and support; displays of past and current student work; and project development centers.

4. **Assessment of web-based lessons:** The quality of web-based lessons such as webquests may be assessed with a webquest rubric developed by webquest originator Bernie Dodge.

5. **Web page and website software tools:** Programmers and other technical experts use tools such as HTML, VRML, PERL, and other programming/authoring tools to develop web pages and websites. Teachers and students are among those who use web development tools such as Netscape *Composer*, Microsoft *FrontPage*, Macromedia *Dreamweaver*, and Macromedia *Flash*, which produce the same web products but require less technical expertise.

6. **Downloading images, programs, and plug-ins:** Resources that may be downloaded for web page development and use include browser versions, PDF readers, and players for movies and other web media.

7. **File transfer options:** When developing web products, teachers and students use email attachments to send files to each other, and FTP programs (e.g., WS_FTP) to upload completed pages to the servers on which they will reside.

8. **Web page development procedures:** A recommended eight-step process for developing web products is (1) plan and storyboard, (2) develop pages with text, (3) insert images and media, (4) insert links and frames, (5) insert interactive elements, (6) test in a browser, (7) publish the site, and (8) gather comments and revise.

9. **Web page evaluation and assessment resources:** Criteria for evaluating web page/website design include good structure and organization, clear text and/or graphic links, good visual design, and easy navigation. Teachers and students may use rubrics to assess the quality of their products.

Online Activities

Visit this text's Companion Website at http://www.prenhall.com/roblyer to gain access to a variety of questions, activities, and exercises to help build your knowledge of this chapter's content.

Online Chapter 8 Self-Test

To review terms and concepts for this chapter, click on the *Self-Test* module for this chapter of the Companion Website.

Software Skill-Builder Tutorials

To access practical tutorial and skill-building activities and to build skills using popular software and hardware, click on the *Software Skill-Builder Tutorials* module for this chapter of the Companion Website.

Web-Enrichment Activities

To complete activities that connect to chapter content and provide web-based resources, click on the *Web-Enrichment Activities* module for this chapter of the Companion Website.

TECHNOLOGY INTEGRATION WORKSHOP

CLIPS FROM THE CLASSROOM: LEARNING WITH TECHNOLOGY

Go to the *Technology Integration Workshop* DVD located in the back of this text and click on *Clips from the Classroom*. View the video clips listed below that support this chapter's content:

- *Scholarly Writings Online Engage Students*
- *EZ Geometry Website Supports Student Work*
- *Website and* Photoshop *Software in Photography.*

Now, visit this text's Companion Website at http://www.prenhall.com/roblyer to answer questions and complete activities that will guide you in analyzing each clip.

THE TIP MODEL IN ACTION

Read each of the following scenarios related to implementing the TIP Model, and go to the Companion Website to answer the questions that follow each based on your Chapter 8 reading activities.

TIP Model Scenario #1 Each year, Mr. Gill has his fifth-grade students identify an issue of current popular concern, for example, local pollution problems, homeless or migrant people, and quality of education for students with English as a second language. Mr. Gill has them use the Internet to research what other communities and groups are saying and doing about the problem. Then the students develop a position statement with a proposed solution and post it on the school's Internet site. They request that feedback on their site be emailed to the teacher.

    1.1 What relative advantage does Mr. Gill see for using the Internet for this project as opposed to other resources?

    1.2 According to the textbook, what is the name for this kind of problem-based learning?

    1.3 Why do they have people email feedback to the teacher rather than the students?

TIP Model Scenario #2 Mr. LeDoux is trying to get his English students to think about possible careers in jour-nalism or other areas that require writing. He has his students contact one or more of the people he knows in these areas who have agreed to be interviewed online. They answer students' questions about how they entered the field, what they do on a daily basis, and what they do and don't like about their work. When they complete the interview, students write a summary and present it to the class.

    2.1 What relative advantage does Mr. LeDoux see for using the Internet for this project as opposed to other resources?

    2.2 According to the textbook, what is the name for this kind of online activity?

    2.3 Why doesn't Mr. LeDoux let the students research and find their own people to be their online information sources?

TIP Model Scenario #3 Each year, Dr. Prida has her ninth-grade students do a project in which they interview ninth graders at other schools and create a newsletter documenting their current shared views and concerns and stories they feel are noteworthy. The newsletter is posted on the school's web page. When the newsletter is done, Dr. Prida contacts the teachers of the cooperating ninth-grade classrooms and gives them the URL for the newsletter. The teachers ask their students to create and email Dr. Prida "Letters to the Editor" giving their comments and opinions about the newsletter stories.

    3.1 What relative advantages does Dr. Prida see for using the Internet for this project as opposed to other resources?

    3.2 What relative advantages do the other teachers see for having their students use the Internet and email as opposed to other resources?

    3.3 What outcomes might Dr. Prida assess for this project and how would she assess them?

TIP Model Scenario #4 To introduce his unit on the Constitution, Mr. Lorrie has his students do a web-based scavenger hunt. He gives them a list of questions about presidents and a list of websites with annotations about the kinds of information they supply about various historical figures. He also has them document the search method they used to locate each of their answers. Then he asks them to write a brief description of other noteworthy facts/data they found in the course of the hunt. He awards several kinds of "prizes" for the hunt: most correct answers at end of allotted time, most efficient/organized search techniques, and best "other information" found.

4.1 What relative advantages does Mr. Lorrie see for using the Internet for this project as opposed to other resources?

4.2 Why do you think Mr. Lorrie recognizes three different aspects about the hunt?

4.3 Do you think Mr. Lorrie should have his students work individually, in pairs, or in small groups to do this kind of activity? Explain why.

TIP Model Scenario #5 Each semester two science teachers in two different schools give their students an ecological problem to solve related to conditions in their local area. After each class has collected data from online sources provided by the teachers, the students each have to analyze the data, figure out the cause of the problem, and create a proposed solution. They use the project website to display their collected data and solutions. Local scientists and interested citizens are asked to judge the solutions and write an analysis of the feasibility of each. Then the students discuss their solutions and how they might improve them, based on the judges' input.

5.1 What relative advantages do the teachers see for using the Internet for this project as opposed to other resources?

5.2 According to the textbook, what is the name for this kind of problem-based learning?

5.3 Why would the teachers have judges assess the answers, rather than evaluating the solutions themselves?

TIE INTO PRACTICE: TECHNOLOGY INTEGRATION EXAMPLES

The Technology Integration Example that opened this chapter (*American Presidency Webquest*) showed how a teacher might create a web-based lesson to teach students concepts about the administrative branch of our government. With the knowledge you have gained from Chapter 8, do the following with this example:

1. Mr. Cole created a website like the one shown on page 283. **Create this sample webquest** by following the *Hands-On with Technology* tutorial section of the DVD.

2. Answer the following questions about the *American Presidency Webquest* example:

   • Phase 1: What relative advantage did Mr. Cole hope the webquest would have for learning about history? How would the Presidents Jeopardy exercise be a better strategy than the usual way of reviewing for the exam?

   • Phase 2: One of the desired outcomes Mr. Cole hoped his students would achieve was employing efficient methods to locate and use online sources, which he planned to assess with a rubric. Create a rubric that he might use to assess completion of required tasks, knowledge of search strategies, ability to locate required information, and quality of cooperative group work.

   • Phase 3: Mr. Cole has students working in groups of two or three to complete the webquest. What are the advantages and disadvantages of having students work in groups on an activity like this, instead of working individually?

   • Phase 4: One of the strategies Mr. Cole plans to use as part of his website is the Presidents Jeopardy game. Explain strategies you would use to implement this game so it would proceed smoothly and involve all of the students.

   • Phase 5: In evaluating the results of the webquest activity, Mr. Cole found that students who had home computers did better on the game than students who only had access at school. In what ways might he improve access to the Internet so that all students would do better?

3. What NETS for Students skills would students learn by working on the *American Presidency Webquest?* (See front of book for a list of NETS for students.)

TECHNOLOGY INTEGRATION LESSON PLANNING

The *Technology Integration Workshop* DVD includes a set of technology integration ideas and links to online lessons, arranged as a searchable database. The DVD comes packaged in the back of this textbook. Click on the *Hands-On with Technology* section of the DVD and complete the following exercises.

1. **Locate lesson ideas** — The DVD has several examples of lessons that use the integration strategies de-

Sample webquest created in Netscape *Composer*. (Create this product using the *Hands-On with Technology* section of the DVD.)

scribed in this chapter: support for student research, motivation for writing, practice for information literacy skills, visual learning problems and solutions, development of collaboration skills, and multicultural experiences. Locate an example integration idea for each of these strategies.

2. **Evaluate the lessons** — Use the *Evaluation Checklist for a Technology-Integrated Lesson* (located on the DVD and the Companion Website) to evaluate each of these lessons.

3. **Modify a lesson** — Select one of the lesson ideas and adapt its strategies to meet a need in your own content

area. You may choose to use the same approach in the original or adapt it to meet your needs.

4. **Add descriptors** — Create descriptors for your new lesson like those found on the database (e.g., grade level, content and topic areas, technologies used, relative advantage, objectives, NETS standards).

5. **Add the new lesson** — Add your modified lesson with all its descriptors to the lesson idea database.

FOR YOUR TEACHING PORTFOLIO

For this chapter's contribution to your teaching portfolio, add the following products you created in the Technology Integration Workshop:

- The webquest product you created for the *American Presidency Webquest* project

- The evaluations you did using the *Evaluation Checklist for a Technology-Integrated Lesson*

- The new lesson plan you developed, based on the one you found on the DVD.

PART 4

INTEGRATING TECHNOLOGY ACROSS THE CURRICULUM

Parts 1 through 3 have introduced the full range of educational technology resources and provided examples and practice with integration strategies for each one. The chapters in Part 4 describe how these resources and strategies are being used in each of six content areas and in special education.

PART 4

REQUIRED BACKGROUND FOR TEACHERS

In an effort to model subject-area integration, disciplines are addressed by chapter as described here.

Chapter ⑨ Technology in English and Language Arts Instruction

Language arts in this chapter includes the communications skills (reading, listening, speaking), addressed primarily in the elementary grades, as well as English topics (writing and literature), which are the focus at secondary levels.

Chapter ⑩ Technology in English Language Learning and Foreign Language Instruction

This chapter focuses both on the learning of foreign languages, as well as English language learning (ELL) for non-native speakers.

Chapter ⑪ Technology in Mathematics and Science Instruction

Science and mathematics topics are considered closely related, and curricula for them are often intertwined. This chapter looks at how technology applications help integrate the teaching of these topics and how they address the special curriculum needs of each.

Chapter ⑫ Technology in Social Studies Instruction

Technology applications covered in this chapter include those for history, social studies, civics, and geography. Social sciences may be one of the subject areas most influenced by recent technological advances.

Chapter ⑬ Technology in Music and Art Instruction

This chapter focuses on technology applications for the topics in arts instruction to which the majority of K–12 students are exposed: music (appreciation, theory, and performance) and art (drawing, painting, and image production).

Chapter ⑭ Technology in Physical Education and Health Education

The closely related subjects of physical education and health are generally not allocated the status of the more "academic" subject areas. However, the quality of the teaching of these subjects may play a major role in the future success of our students. Instructional technology provides a number of resources that may maximize the effectiveness of the limited time that typically is given to these subjects.

Chapter ⑮ Technology in Special Education

Chapter 15 is the only chapter identified by population rather than by topic. Technology applications for students with special needs are addressed in Part 4 because the curriculum for them has many unique characteristics. Needs of special students addressed in this chapter include those for learners with mental disabilities and behavioral/emotional disorders as well as those with physical disabilities (e.g., hearing impairments, visual impairments, wheelchair-bound), and gifted and talented students.

CHAPTER 9

TECHNOLOGY IN ENGLISH AND LANGUAGE ARTS INSTRUCTION

M. D. ROBLYER
UNIVERSITY OF MARYLAND UNIVERSITY COLLEGE

REBECCA ANDERSON
UNIVERSITY OF MEMPHIS

The Internet and other forms of information and communication technology (ICT) such as word processors, Web editors, presentation software, and e-mail are regularly redefining the nature of literacy. To become fully literate in today's world, students must become proficient in the new literacies of ICT.

Position statement of the International Reading Association (2001, p. 2)

TECHNOLOGY INTEGRATION EXAMPLE
CLASSROOM REVOLUTIONS

Based on: Skarecki, E., & Insinnia, E. (1999). Revolutions in the classroom. *Learning and Leading with Technology, 26*(7), 22–27.

Grade Levels: 8–10 • Content Area/Topic: English literature and information literacy skills • Length of Time: Two weeks

Phase 1: Determine relative advantage

As Ms. Skerritt searched the Internet for materials to help teach her literature unit, she was amazed at the rich array of images and background information on Dickens' *A Tale of Two Cities* and the history surrounding the period it depicted. It was always a struggle to get her students interested in books and events from so long ago, but as she looked over the Internet resources, she realized they could make all the difference. Not only would students be able to locate more information much more quickly than they would in the library, the compelling images and vivid personal accounts could help make the story come alive. It also offered fertile ground for exploring various approaches to literary criticism. She realized how important it was becoming that students learn to use the Internet to locate relevant and reliable information and select items that illustrated their ideas about what they were reading in class. She decided to build the unit around using Internet resources for researching and analyzing information on Dickens' famous book. She would have students work in groups, using laptops checked out from the media center, to research various events and themes in *A Tale of Two Cities*. In the process, she would teach them how to locate and select useful resources on the Internet.

Phase 2: Decide on objectives and assessments

Ms. Skerritt knew that the goals for this unit would focus on both literary analysis and developing good Internet skills to support the analysis. She decided that the following outcomes, objectives, and assessments captured what she felt was important for students to learn:

- **Outcome:** Skills in locating reliable information. **Objective:** Students will apply criteria accurately to determine if given Internet sites are reliable. **Assessment:** A checklist of criteria to select reliable sites.
- **Outcome:** Literary critique skills. **Objective:** Students will demonstrate abilities to critique events and themes in *A Tale of Two Cities* by researching and preparing a *PowerPoint* presentation of findings on a selected theme. **Assessment:** Rubric to assess *PowerPoint* presentation.
- **Outcome:** Knowledge about events in history and in the novel. **Objective:** Students will demonstrate they have learned and remembered key events and characters from the novel and the historical period by answering correctly at least 90% of a set of short-answer questions. **Assessment:** Short-answer exam on events/characters.

Phase 3: Design intergration strategies

Ms. Skerritt felt that exploring Internet sites could be done in conjunction with reviewing the novel. That way, students could develop their Internet skills as they discussed the story and the historical events on which it was based. Then they would research and present a theme from the book. She planned the following 2-week timeline for the project:

- **Days 1–4: Reviewing the novel using the Internet:** After introducing the project, Ms. Skerritt begins a review of the book using Internet sites. She shows students the set of sites she wants them to use, assigns students to groups, and gives each group a different question to answer for each of three sections of the book. To emphasize the point that not all websites are useful, Ms. Skerritt shows them a site that is not reliable and has them go through the checklist to see why it is not. For every site they use, they have to apply criteria to show why it is reliable.
- **Day 5: Reviewing major themes:** After students complete their reviews, they hold a class discussion on the answers they found and brainstorm the main themes of the book. Ms. Skerritt assigns each group a theme for which they will locate information and report. She gives the groups a handout on items to include in their research and presentation.
- **Days 6–8: Researching themes and creating *PowerPoint* presentations:** The groups complete their research and develop their *PowerPoint* presentations. They select images and information from the sites to illustrate their points and the events in the book.
- **Days 9–10: Giving *PowerPoint* presentations and final test:** Each group gives its presentation and the

class discusses it. Finally, Ms. Skerritt gives them a test covering the main events and characters in the book.

Phase 4: Prepare the instructional environment

As she prepared for this project, Ms. Skerritt's tasks included:

- **Creation of Bookmark/Favorites file:** As Ms. Skerritt located the sites she wanted students to use, she bookmarked them. She uploaded the Bookmark file to the school's network and transferred it to the computer lab so her students could access it there.

- **Research handout:** She created a handout of the checklist for judging website reliability and placed it on the school's website for easy viewing and downloading.

- **Hardware checkout:** The school had a wireless network so that teachers and students could use computers in any classroom. Ms. Skerritt arranged to check out a set of laptops from the library-media center so that her students could do their research in her classroom. She also arranged for a projection system on days she would demonstrate Internet use and example sites and at times when students would need them to display their *PowerPoint* presentations at the end of the project.

- **Adaptations:** One of Ms. Skerritt's students had cerebral palsy and could not use the keyboard. Ms. Skerritt arranged for an adaptive keyboard and software to allow the girl to use the computer without typing.

- **Development of assessments:** Finally, Ms. Skerritt created the rubrics and tests she needed for the unit.

Phase 5: Evaluate and revise

After students had completed the unit, Ms. Skerritt talked to the students about how they liked the unit, and she reviewed their products and test results. It was obvious they loved this approach to learning about literature. The most common comment she heard was "I never knew a 'classic' could be so exciting." The websites seem to make the events in the book more real and interesting to them. Ms. Skerritt was especially pleased with the results of the test on the novel and the history surrounding it. The only students who had difficulty were two students who were absent for a large portion of the project work. She decided to create a website that described the project and led students through it so that they could do work from home or on their own, if they needed to. Finally, she found that students seemed to have a good grasp of judging web page reliability. However, several had difficulty locating relevant information from the sites she assigned. She

Woodberry Forest School's Site on the French Revolution

Source: Adapted from the Woodberry Forest School Web page (http://www.woodberry.org). Painting is *Mort de Louis Capet 16th Nom, le 21 Janvier 1793* by Giraudon, from Art Resource, NY.

realized she needed to include more instruction on locating and analyzing information from websites.

OBJECTIVES

After reading this chapter and completing the learning activities for it, you should be able to:

1. Identify and discuss current issues related to the integration of technology into English and language arts.

2. Describe effective ways in which technology can be integrated into English and language arts instruction.

3. Design and implement instructional activities that model effective ways to integrate technology into English and language arts instruction.

KEY TERMS

- concept mapping software
- decoding
- electronic outliners
- QWERTY keyboard
- talking word processor
- webbing software

For more information on Key Terms, go to the *Key Terms* module for this chapter of the Companion Website at http://www.prenhall.com/roblyer.

INTRODUCTION

The "language arts" are those language-based processes by which we think, learn, and communicate. (See NCTE and IRA Standards for the English/Language Arts in Figure 9.1.) In the elementary grades, the language arts curriculum focuses primarily on developing the fundamental skills of reading, writing, listening, and speaking. In the later grades, language arts instruction is usually in courses that focus on literature, composition, and formal communication (either in a student's native language or a foreign one). Because literacy skills and processes are fundamental to success in most other disciplines, language arts instruction is often stressed in content-area courses (e.g., the social studies, sciences, and mathematics.) This latter is often referred to as "reading and writing in the content area," or is addressed as study skills and strategies. In this chapter we provide an overview of how technology can be used to enhance language arts instruction in all of the above ways.

ISSUES AND PROBLEMS IN ENGLISH AND LANGUAGE ARTS INSTRUCTION

Reading, writing, and critically analyzing written texts are considered fundamental skills for a literate person. However, teachers of English and language arts encounter many issues when teaching these skills and integrating technology into the curriculum. Specifically, we as teachers need to understand the importance of expanding the definition of literacy, exploring new instructional practices, making decisions on keyboarding instruction, creating social learning environments, working with diverse learners, motivating students, and teachers' growth as literacy professionals, all of which are discussed in the following subsections.

Figure 9.1   NCTE/IRA Standards for English/Language Arts

The standards for English/Language Arts were copublished by the National Council for Teachers of English (NCTE) and the International Reading Association (IRA) in 1996. Listed below are summaries of the 12 standards, taken from the NCTE website (http://www.ncte.org/standards).

1. Students read a wide range of print and nonprint texts to build an understanding of texts, of themselves, and of the cultures of the United States and the world; to acquire new information; to respond to the needs and demands of society and the workplace; and for personal fulfillment. Among these texts are fiction and nonfiction, classic and contemporary works.

2. Students read a wide range of literature from many periods in many genres to build an understanding of the many dimensions (e.g., philosophical, ethical, aesthetic) of human experience.

3. Students apply a wide range of strategies to comprehend, interpret, evaluate, and appreciate texts. They draw on their prior experience, their interactions with other readers and writers, their knowledge of word meaning and of other texts, their word identification strategies, and their understanding of textual features (e.g., sound–letter correspondence, sentence structure, context, graphics).

4. Students adjust their use of spoken, written, and visual language (e.g., conventions, style, vocabulary) to communicate effectively with a variety of audiences and for different purposes.

5. Students employ a wide range of strategies as they write and use different writing process elements appropriately to communicate with different audiences for a variety of purposes.

6. Students apply knowledge of language structure, language conventions (e.g., spelling and punctuation), media techniques, figurative language, and genre to create, critique, and discuss print and nonprint texts.

7. Students conduct research on issues and interests by generating ideas and questions, and by posing problems. They gather, evaluate, and synthesize data from a variety of sources (e.g, print and nonprint texts, artifacts, people) to communicate their discoveries in ways that suit their purpose and audience.

8. Students use a variety of technological and information resources (e.g., libraries, databases, computer networks, video) to gather and synthesize information and to create and communicate knowledge.

9. Students develop an understanding of and respect for diversity in language use, patterns, and dialects across cultures, ethnic groups, geographic regions, and social roles.

10. Students whose first language is not English make use of their first language to develop competency in the English language arts and to develop understanding of content across the curriculum.

11. Students participate as knowledgeable, reflective, creative, and critical members of a variety of literacy communities.

12. Students use spoken, written, and visual language to accomplish their own purposes (e.g., for learning, enjoyment, persuasion, and the exchange of information).

Expanding the Definition of Literacy

Students graduating from high school today use traditional hard copies of reading and writing materials, but they also use highly sophisticated electronic forms of literacy. The way they were taught and the way they learn have changed significantly during their school lives. These students are entering an era when they will spend the majority of their literacy time engaged in electronic forms of communication. Our charge as teachers is to recognize that traditional definitions of literacy are no longer sufficient and to shift our conception to new literacies (Kinzer, 2003). As new technologies emerge, the nature, expansion, and definition of literacy change (Coiro, 2003; Karchmer, 2001a; Leu & Kinzer, 2000; Reinking, McKenna, Labbo, & Kieffer, 1998). According to Leu (2002a), "the new literacies include the skills, strategies, and insights needed to successfully exploit the rapidly changing information and communication technologies (ICT) that continuously emerge in our world" (p. 313). Leu (2002a) points out that as new technologies emerge, so does the need for new literacies; therefore, it is critical that students *learn how to learn* new technologies of literacy. This view is also supported by the International Reading Association (IRA) in their literacy and technology position statement, which reads (2001): "Traditional definitions of reading, writing, and viewing, and traditional definitions of best practice instruction—derived from a long tradition of book and other print media—will be insufficient" (p. 2).

Exploring New Instructional Practices

There is a direct correlation between the emergence of new literacies and the need for new instructional practices. Teachers are expected to provide new forms of literacy instruction so that students know how to locate, critically evaluate, use, and communicate through technology resources. For instance, students need instruction on how to find appropriate electronic information sources to be incorporated into their research products and presentations, as well as how to access and use information stored in a variety of sources (e.g., still and moving images, text, sound, and print). This perspective is supported in Standard 8 of the National Council of Teachers of English (NCTE) and IRA *Standards for the English Language Arts* (1996), which specifically emphasizes how important it is for students to use technology in their learning: "Students use a variety of technological and informational resources (e.g., libraries, databases, computer networks, video) to gather and synthesize information and to create and communicate knowledge" (p. 39).

Students also need knowledge about the hardware (e.g., computers, televisions, VCRs, scanners, camcorders, digital cameras) and how to use these devices to create and present multimedia products. Providing instruction in this area can support the integration of technology across curricular areas and can give students opportunities to integrate information into meaningful learning experiences, projects, and presentations (Toomey & Ketterer, 1995).

In addition, there is a growing need for teachers to instruct students to comprehend language in the context of visual images since images play an increasing role in communication. These images are often in technology-based formats ranging from digital pictures to streaming video. Students need instruction in processing the information and separating out bias and inaccuracies (intentional and otherwise). For example, image manipulation software allows us to alter images in ways that completely change how a person or event is depicted. Students must be taught to be aware of and search for these changes and the alterations in ideas and concepts that they communicate. Clearly the new literacies require a high level of critical sophistication from our students, and it is only through instruction that they will develop these skills. These expectations can add pressure to an already full curriculum, in terms of both time and material resources.

Fortunately, a growing body of literature illustrates ways to implement new instructional practices. For instance, Myers and Beach (2001) provide examples of how hypermedia fosters critical literacy; Labbo, Eakle, and Montero (2002) discuss how to use digital photographs and software in a language experience approach; Labbo, Sprague , Montero, and Font (2000) suggest ways to connect computer centers to themes, literature, and kindergartners; Leu (2002b) tells how to integrate the Internet using an Internet workshop framework; and Labbo et al. (2003) share teacher wisdom in stories about using technology for literacy instruction.

Making Decisions About Keyboarding Instruction

The most common way to write using a computer requires input through a regular **QWERTY keyboard,** so named because of the first six letters in the first line of a typewriter keyboard. There is an ongoing discussion of whether we should teach keyboarding instruction as a prerequisite to the use of computers for writing. Those in favor argue that students will learn bad habits if they use the keyboard without proper training, that these bad habits might become permanent, and that failure to learn proper fingering will inhibit fluent and speedy keyboarding. Those against requiring keyboarding instruction as a prerequisite argue that too much student time and computer resources are spent on getting kids trained to type quickly, that students need only basic keyboard familiarization, and that keyboarding instruction will likely be a waste of time unless students have real-world applications in which to use the computer. Both arguments are legitimate and most teachers have resolved the issue, at least temporarily, by favoring keyboarding instruction if it is available and needed, but not preventing students from using the computer if they do not yet have good keyboarding skills.

Teachers disagree about the need for keyboard instruction.

Creating Social Learning Environments

New forms of literacy are much more contingent on social interactions with others than traditional literacies (Leu, 2002a). According to the *Standards for the English Language Arts* (NCTE/IRA, 1996), teachers should begin "giving students the enjoyment and pride of sometimes being their teachers' teachers" (p. 40). One teacher (Bryan, 2000) emphasizes that technology has consented for students to become experts, helping to redefine the student–teacher relationship. These examples illustrate the power of people working together and are grounded in the social constructivist theory (Vygotsky, 1962) that states learning occurs through interactions with others.

Another reason that new literacies demand a more social environment is because teaching and learning are no longer confined to a traditional classroom context. Thanks to the Internet we have a worldwide classroom. Networked technologies for literacy enable us to communicate with people around the world. We transmit and receive information in different formats and from different people. These interactions provide a tremendous multicultural benefit to our classrooms that has never existed before.

Working with Diverse Learners

Our schools have more diverse student populations today than ever before. This cultural and linguistic diversity creates classrooms that are richer, yet more complex. Although we value and celebrate the opportunity to interact with students of different nationalities, races, and ethnicities, this creates new challenges and opportunities for English and language arts teachers (Matthews, 2000; Mora, 2000/2001). This is especially true when working with ESL and ELL students (see Chapter 10). It is also true when working with struggling readers. Often when students experience literacy problems at a young age, they continue to have reading difficulties throughout their schooling. Students who typically experience this problem include children who begin school without a solid literacy foundation, learn English as a second language, live in literacy-impoverished homes, have attention deficit/hyperactivity disorder, or do not receive appropriate instruction in school. Because many students need additional instruction in literacy, appropriate use of technology (e.g., books on CD, tapes, online, and software) can support their growth. Fortunately, numerous Internet resources are available to assist teachers with struggling readers (Johnson, 2002).

Motivating Students

The more students read, the better developed their language and writing skills become. However, we as teachers find it an ongoing challenge to motivate students to read—either for study or pleasure. Indeed, students rarely choose reading as

For Literature

Students with reading difficulties often struggle in English classes with literature assignments. Their lack of fluency often interferes with comprehension and the task may take longer for them than for students who read at grade level. Several strategies are described for making the literature curriculum accessible for struggling students.

Electronic texts (etexts) contain the full text of a book. A wide variety of electronic texts are available, particularly books that have had the copyright expire (e.g., many of the classics) and can be simply downloaded to your computer. Here are a few good websites for locating these etexts:

- Infomotions (http://www.infomotions.com)
- Bibliomania (http://www.bibliomania.com/)
- Electronic Text Center (http://etext.lib.virginia.edu/)
- Project Gutenberg (http://promo.net/pg/)
- The Plays of William Shakespeare (http://www.theplays.org).

Once the etext is on your computer, it is possible to manipulate the text in several ways to make it more accessible for students. First, the font and text size can be enlarged for students with low vision. Second, the etext can be copied and pasted into talking word processors (e.g., Don Johnston's *Co:Writer*, http://www.donjohnston.com) or text-to-speech programs (e.g., *ReadPlease*, http://www.readplease.com) so that the student can listen to the text as the computer reads it. Finally, for students whose first language is not English, etext can be copied and pasted into a language translation tool (e.g., *Babel Fish*, http://world.altavista.com/) to obtain a translation that can be used to assist them in understanding the text.

Another strategy for supporting students who struggle to understand key concepts in literature is to use study aids that provide advanced organizers for their reading, for example, summaries of plots and character descriptions. A number of websites feature complete resource collections for the most popular books taught in school:

- SparkNotes (http://www.sparknotes.com)
- NovelGuide (http://www.novelguide.com)
- Free Book Notes (http://www.freebooknotes.com)
- Pink Monkey (http://www.pinkmonkey.com)

For Writing

Some students struggle with the physical process of handwriting, which interferes with their development of written expression skills. An alternative is dictation. USB handheld digital dictation devices can be purchased at any office supply store ($50 to $150) that allow the user to dictate information into the handheld device and then upload the file to the computer. Currently, the information will still need to be transcribed. However, a second resource may complete the process. iDictate (http://www.iDictate.com) is a transcription service. Users may submit information by dictating it over the telephone and it will be transcribed and returned via email in 20 minutes to 24 hours at a cost of a penny per word—very affordable! Because supports like this are built into the adult world, it is probably appropriate to begin teaching students how to access and use such tools so they can evaluate their personal usefulness.

Contributed by Dave Edyburn

a free-time activity. Fortunately, one of the supporting findings from the research is that both students and teachers are highly motivated and interested in the new literacies (Leu, 2002a). Teachers are turning to the interactive and visual qualities of software and websites to increase this motivation. Also, computer-based tracking systems such as *Accelerated Reader* (Lopez, 2000; Poock, 1998) are designed especially to increase the amount of reading students do for enjoyment.

Teachers also find it an ongoing challenge to motivate students to express themselves in writing. Students especially resist the labor involved in revising research papers and compositions. In addition to word processing, which has been in use for many years, a variety of technology tools and strategies have emerged to spur students' desire to write, to improve the quality of their written products (e.g., email projects, blogs), and to provide authentic publication sources. According to the *English Language Arts Standards* (NCTE/IRA, 1996), technology not only enhances students' motivation to write but also encourages them to assume greater responsibility for their learning.

Teachers' Growth as Literacy Professionals

The position statement published by the International Reading Association (2001) clearly states what literacy teachers need to know about integrating technology into the curriculum. According to the IRA, students have the right to:

- Teachers who are skilled in the effective use of technology for teaching and learning,
- A literacy curriculum that integrates the new literacies of technology into instructional programs,
- Instruction that develops the critical literacies essential to effective information use,
- Assessment practices in literacy that include reading and writing with technology tools,
- Opportunities to learn safe and responsible use of information and communication technologies, and
- Equal access to technology.

Obviously, these visions will not be fully reached unless teachers receive continued and systematic professional development. Unfortunately, at this point in time, this is not happening. Even though the U.S. Department of Education recommends that 30% of a school district's technology budget be spent on professional development, currently only 6% is being appropriated for this endeavor (IRA, 2001). Thus, the burden falls on teachers' shoulders to take responsibility to learn how to integrate ICT effectively into the curriculum. Teachers are expanding their own professional growth through school/university partnership projects (Bauer & Anderson, 2001; Maring, Boxie, & Wiseman,

2000) and "cybermentoring" (Boxie & Maring, 2001), use of online resources for professional development (Johnson & Zufall, 2004), and increased access to professional organizations such as IRI and NCTE (see *Reading Online*, IRA's Online Journal of Literacy Education, (http://www.readingonline.org; and RTEACHER, the electronic mailing list for *The Reading Teacher*, http://www.reading.org/publications/rt/rt_listserv.html).

TECHNOLOGY INTEGRATION STRATEGIES FOR ENGLISH AND LANGUAGE ARTS INSTRUCTION

Perhaps the most creative and prolific array of strategies and applications for enhancing teaching with technology is to be found in the English and language arts. New ways to use technologies to support students' learning are emerging constantly. One reason for this burgeoning interest may be the sheer diversity of skills and concepts to be learned in these areas. Another is surely that needs for teaching these skills and concepts find a good match in the capabilities technology has to offer.

This section focuses on integration strategies that support the following three English and language arts areas: language skills development, literacy development, and the process writing approach. Strategies and resources under these three headings are summarized in Figure 9.2. Also see the accompanying *Top Ten* feature for additional strategies.

Language Skills Development

Though technology uses in English and language arts clearly emphasize motivation and support for reading fluency and writing production, many programs are also in use to instruct or give practice in individual reading and writing skills. These programs address primarily lower level thinking skills that generally involve rote drill-and-practice activities. Clearly there is a time and place for these in the classroom, although higher order, problem-solving skills should be emphasized. Here we describe some important strategies for supporting language skills development.

Teaching decoding skills. We generally teach skills in **decoding** or "sounding out" words in the early primary grades, and according to a limited amount of research, students who have access to digitized speech support increase their decoding abilities (Reitsma, 1988). Several websites offer interactive sites with speech support. Bertelsen, Kauffman, Howard, and Cochran (2003) methodically examined phonics websites and identified four as the most useful for children. First, *GameGOO: Learning That Sticks* (http://

Figure 9.2   Summary of Technology Integration Strategies for English and Language Arts

Technology Integration Strategies	Benefits	Sample Resources and Activities
Language skills development: decoding/phonics, comprehension, vocabulary Courtesy of Educational Insights/KEH Communications. http://www.educationalinsights.com/	• Gives motivational, individual instruction and/or practice in individual reading and writing skills. • Supplies private, individual feedback to scaffold students' learning.	• Reading instructional systems • Electronic dictionaries and thesauruses • Electronic devices • Talking word processors
Literacy development eBN Educational Bloggers Network Courtesy of EBN. http://www.ebn.weblogger.com/	• Helps match books to students' own interests. • Presents reading assignments in ways that students find compelling; helps track reading. • Engages students in reading by helping them visualize the people and places in books. • Supports the reflection and frequent modification called for in process writing.	• Networked literacy projects • Interactive storybooks (electronic or talking books) • Tracking systems • Digital storytelling activities • Online reading materials • Writing in blogs • Script writing in video projects • Threaded discussions in distance tools **Also see Technology Integration Idea 9.1:** Reading and Writing Ideas with Blogs
Process approach to writing Paradigm Online Writing Assistant www.powa.org Courtesy of Paradigm. http://my.powa.org	• Supports students as they produce and revise text; frees them to focus on generating and sharing ideas. • Supports all stages of the writing process: planning, drafting, revising and editing, and publishing.	• Word processing • Planning for writing: electronic outliners, concept mapping software, Internet resource sites • Drafting, revising, editing: projected images of word-processed drafts, spell checkers, grammar checkers • Publishing: desktop-published brochures, newspapers, and booklets; electronic slide shows; and web pages **Also see Technology Integration Idea 9.2:** Using Handhelds for Literacy Instruction

www.cogcon.com/gamegoo/gooeyhome.html) is an interactive site for prekindergarten through grade 3 based on state standards for language arts. Most activities use phonic elements such as letter recognition, letter–sound correspondence, and spelling. It is especially appropriate for students with special needs because it links to the Earobics Literacy site, which provides voice output. Second, *Between the Lions* (http://pbskids.org/lions/) includes videos, books, and interactive games from PBS's award-winning children's program.

This website offers information on phonics skills and word activities and also provides visual and auditory assistance for students who have learning difficulties. Third, *Chateau Meddybemps: Fun with Letters* (http://www.meddybemps.com/letterary/index.html) was named by the International Reading Association as the third best site on the web for helping children learn phonics. In addition to activities that reinforce letter recognition and formation, it includes a writer's workshop area with pages for creating stories. The

TOP TEN STRATEGIES FOR TECHNOLOGY IN ENGLISH/LANGUAGE ARTS

Take advantage of these 10 powerful strategies for using technology to enhance the teaching of reading, writing, and language skills.

1. **Electronic publishing projects to encourage student writing** — Students spend more time writing when they know their work will be displayed on a website or in a print product that others will see.

2. **Electronic penpal (keypal) activities to encourage student writing** — Students are more likely to want to write and take more care with spelling and language conventions when they have an authentic audience.

3. **Internet resources to engage students in literature** — Internet sites offer examples, background, and analysis to enrich students' study of literary works and help make literature more real and relevant to them.

4. **Internet resources to motivate student reading** — Many websites offer electronic books to match students' varying interests and reading levels.

5. **Concept mapping software to help students plan their writing** — Concept mapping software (e.g., *Inspiration*) helps students create visual outlines to plan what they want to write about.

6. **Talking books to engage students in reading** — Interactive storybooks or electronic books scaffold students' initial reading skills and draw them into reading activities.

7. **Spelling and grammar checkers to help students edit their work** — Students learn better grammar, usage, and spelling by seeing correct examples as they word process their work.

8. **Threaded discussions to motivate student writing** — These draw students into writing by giving them a supportive, nonjudgmental environment for expressing their ideas.

9. **Blogs to motivate student writing** — Students practice written expression as they engage in dialogue with others about topics of mutual interest.

10. **Tracking systems to motivate student reading** — Systems such as *Accelerated Reader* give students opportunities for reading at their own levels and rewards them for improved comprehension.

---

final identified site, *Words and Pictures* (http://www.bbc.co.uk/education/wordsandpictures/phonics) aligns the United Kingdom's national curriculum standards with teaching words through interactive games and activities.

Developing other reading skills. A variety of other technology resources support teachers as they work to increase students' fluency with phonics, comprehension, and vocabulary skills:

- **Software-based and online systems** — The editors of *Technology and Learning* (2003) recommend several software-based and online systems for providing instruction in phonics, decoding, comprehension, and vocabulary skills to young learners. These systems generally promise individualized, interactive exercises to promote students' literacy development. These include *The Imagination Station* (istation.com), *Balanced Literacy* (Intelli-tools), *Lexia Early Reading* (Lexia Learning), *OpenBook to Literacy* (OpenBook Learning), FOCIS Reading and Language (PLATO), STAR Early Literacy (Renaissance Learning), *Destination Reading* (Riverdeep), *Early Reading Program* (Lightspan), Orchard Language Arts K–3 (Siboney), and *The Literacy Center* (LeapFrog SchoolHouse). Figure 9.3 shows an example frame from Intellitools' *Balanced Literacy* program.

- **Reference resources** — Electronic dictionaries and thesauruses, discussed in Chapter 5, provide support to students as they learn vocabulary and spelling skills. These handy resources are integrated into most word processing software, but more complete, full-featured ones are also available as separate software packages.

- **Electronic devices** — These include battery-operated devices such as Educational Insights' GeoSafari Phonics Pad, which has a collection of phonics

Figure 9.3 Frame and Logo from Intellitools' *Balanced Literacy* Program

pig popping popcorn
p p p

Source: Used with permission of Intellitools, Inc.

games for preK–2 grades. Rankin-Erickson, Wood, and Beukelman (2003) describe a computer for first graders that comes equipped with a **talking word processor**, a software package that reads typed words aloud. This type of processor helps them "read" words they did not know, thus supporting their vocabulary acquisition. Intellitools' *IntelliTalk* is one example of this versatile resource. Other products, such as Alphasmart's (http://www2.alphasmart.com/) *Dana,* are specifically targeted to young learners to encourage more writing without the expense of desktop or laptop computers.

Creating everyday teacher activities. Through his work with teachers across Georgia, Tennessee, and Kentucky, Grant (see, e.g., Grant, 2002; Hill, Reeves, Grant, Wang, & Hans, in press; http://www.the-atec.org) notes how teachers can quickly develop "Everyday Activities with Everyday Applications" using word processors, spreadsheets, and electronic presentations to support small phonics, vocabulary, and other literacy lessons. For example, with whole-class instruction, the teacher can use a word processor with large point sizes to have students demonstrate correct verb tenses, correct conjugations, and plurals. The large point size allows the teacher to see student responses at a distance while monitoring the class. For on-screen reading, the teacher can use the commenting feature to add supplemental instruction to unknown words or difficult passages, such as adding definitions. Spreadsheets likewise can be used as a method to keep up with vocabulary words, definitions, and sentence usages. Finally, electronic presentations can be used by teachers or students to develop flash cards for phonics and vocabulary, including foreign languages, or early childhood teachers could use the slide sorting feature to mix up the order of a story and have students re-sequence it.

Literacy Development

When teachers look for ways to motivate and support students' literacy development, they usually try to tap into students' own interests, present books in ways that students find compelling, and engage them in "book talks"

about authors and stories to help them visualize the people and places in books. Teachers develop telecollaborative inquiry projects that are meaningful and authentic and promote higher levels of engagement. The following examples are among those designed by teachers to accomplish these purposes:

- **Networked literacy projects** — Activities like the one in the chapter opener example use Internet sites to engage students in reading books. Also, Helt (2003) describes the use of online literature circles and pairing students with online mentors to discuss literature as ways to spur students' interest in reading. Classroom teachers may also use story starters, having each student write one sentence, paragraph, line, or stanza and then email it to the next student who then adds to it.

- **Activities with interactive storybooks (electronic books) and talking books** — As described in Chapter 5, these tools are regular literature books that have been placed into electronic format, usually on CD, DVD, or Internet sites. They are interactive for several reasons. First, they often allow stories and/or language elements (e.g., specific words or phrases) to be read aloud to students. Second, they can let students vary the sequence in which they read parts of stories. Finally, they can be formatted to allow students to choose alternate paths or endings. Doty, Popplewell, and Byers (2001) found that these interactive qualities can result in greater comprehension for students than reading in a static format. Johnson (2003) describes Project LITT (Literacy Instruction Through Technology), which focuses on the use of electronic versions of books (talking storybooks) to improve the reading skills of students with learning disabilities. Its website (http://edweb.sdsu.edu/SPED/ProjectLitt/LITT) profiles more than 200 talking storybook programs they recommend for this purpose.

- **Uses of tracking system** — *Accelerated Reader,* a popular system from Renaissance Learning, is among the most studied tools in educational technology (Lopez, 2000; Poock, 1998). Most teachers use the system to diagnose students' reading levels, provide books and stories for students to read, and track their comprehension by administering questions on each item they read. Studies have shown it to be successful in motivating students to read and, in many cases, in raising comprehension levels faster than unguided reading activities.

- **Digital storytelling** — Kajder and Swenson (2004) find that good readers create "a mental movie of images evoked by the story" (p. 18). To support this process, they had students produce a series of digital images to visually communicate meaning and provide a narration for the video. They find that this activity helps make the reading process more visual to them and, therefore, easier to understand. Electronic presentation software that includes narration capabilities is another method for students to practice oral presentations, which may also provide additional practice for struggling readers as well.

- **Connections to online reading materials to engage students** — Finally, an often-used strategy that teachers use is to locate books, stories, and Internet sites that match up with students' interests and reading levels. Schmar-Dobler (2003) cautions us to remember that students first need modeling and instruction on how to read on the Internet. This cannot be overemphasized: Morkes and Nielson (1997) assert that Internet users typically do not read on-screen in the same way we read books or magazines. Instead, text is scanned, with Internet users looking for bulleted or highlighted points. Do not be discouraged, however; the Internet offers a wealth of resources for connecting students and literacy. For example, the International Children's Digital Library (http://www.icdlbooks.org/) has more than 500 free online books from which students may select.

Naturally teachers use these resources in numerous ways. Karchmer (2000) shares how one teacher used children's literature to support interdisciplinary instruction. Forbes (2004) talks about web-based bookmarking as an important strategy for creating a list of favorite Bookmarks and storing them on the web. This process provides structure and content for elementary students and those with special needs by saving time and providing them access to appropriate web materials.

- **Writing in blogs** — One strategy that is currently increasing in popularity is having students respond to blogs (web logs). Introduced in Chapter 7, blogs are web pages that serve as publicly accessible locations for discussing topics or issues. Students can use these either as personal journals or as public discussion forums for trading opinions and interactions (Oravec, 2002) They can create their own blog by using a blog website (http://www.blogger.com/) or can join a blog initiated by others. Kajder and Bull (2003) find that blog characteristics such as immediate feedback and active participation are very motivational to struggling students. See Technology Integration Idea 9.1 for a list of activities they recommend for motivating student writing.

- **Motivating writing with video projects** — Just as Kajder and Swenson (2004) found that creating a nar-

TECHNOLOGY INTEGRATION IDEA 9.1

MOTIVATING STUDENT WRITING

Title: Reading and Writing Ideas with Blogs

Content Area/Topic: English, writing

Grade Levels: All grades

NETS for Students: Standards 3, 5, 6

Description: Blogs are becoming an increasingly popular way to help students engage with text and provide opportunities for an authentic writing experience.

Instruction: Ten instructional activities that make use of blogs include (1) character journals (challenging students to write a fictional character); (2) character roundtable (several students write to each other as they role-play fictional characters); (3) open minds (drawing an outline of an empty head and "filling it" in the blog space with what the character might be thinking); (4) think-aloud postings (students post reflections and analyses of assigned readings; (5) literature circle group responses (sharing and reflecting on reports of reading assignments); (6) nutshelling (posting "most meaningful" lines from literature and using them as prompts for reflective writing); (7) devil's advocate writing (online debates to explore positions on topics for later writing); (8) exploding sentences (adding descriptive detail to posted sentences); (9) photoblogs (using blogs that incorporate images to annotate and write captions for pictures); and (10) storyblogs (class-constructed stories and essays).

Source: Kajder, S., & Bull, G. (2003). Scaffolding for struggling students: Reading and writing with blogs. *Learning and Leading with Technology, 31*(2), 31–35.

rated video parallels the reading process, Scot and Harding (2004) say that "the process of creating a digital video parallels the writing process" (p. 27). Script writing for their videos becomes an excellent way to get students engaged in written communications. The simplicity and intuitiveness of such video production tools as Apple's *iMovie* allows students to focus on the writing content without having to confront a significant software learning curve.

- **Threaded discussions at a distance** — Finally, many teachers find that having students participate in discussion boards instigates both reading and writing. Especially if the topic is one in which they are already interested, students want to share their thoughts. Course management systems provide discussion boards that teachers can set up for this purpose. Viani (2004) describes the Southern Oregon Write Site, a multipurpose website set up at his school's site (http://www.soesd.k12.or.us) to allow students to engage in discussions about writing, as well as see samples of other students' writing and post some of their own.

The Process Approach to Writing

In reviewing two decades of research on writing skills, Bruning and Horn (2000) found that teaching writing requires special attention to motivational aspects, including fostering engagement using authentic writing tasks and providing a supportive context for writing. The mid-1980s saw a new approach to writing instruction that focused on writing as a process, as opposed to using writing as a tool for learning, such as note taking or journal writing. With the introduction of word processing software, students gained access to electronic tools to support this new approach, allowing the reflection and frequent modification called for in process writing. As discussed in Chapter 4, writing in a word processing environment supports students as they produce and revise text, thus freeing them to focus on generating and sharing ideas. Inherent in the process approach is the need to give and receive feedback from others; thus, writing groups are a necessity.

Fortunately, numerous online resources are available to help teachers conduct process writing (Johnson, 2002). For instance, after working with classroom teachers for the past 5 years to integrate technology into the curriculum, Linda Labbo (2004) provided guidelines for implementing what she coined the *Author's Computer Chair*. The *Author's Computer Chair* encourages students to discuss the computer-related process of meaning making during all stages of the process. Described next are an array of other technology resources that have emerged to support all stages of the writing process.

Prewriting. Getting started is often one of the most difficult aspects of writing, and young writers find it particularly onerous. During the prewriting stage teachers communicate to students the format, audience, topic, purpose, and assessment for the writing assignment. It is critical that teachers model the type of writing expected. For instance, when writing poetry, students find it motivational to see samples from other students or to view unusual or experimental forms of poetry for which word processors can facilitate development: dada, sound poems, optophonetic poems, oulipo, snowballing, iceograms, iterative poetry, and transformations. Internet sites offer rich sources of these examples (e.g., the American Poetry site at http://www.americanpoems.com). During this stage students also need to organize their thoughts graphically. For instance, if students are writing a fictional story, they need to brainstorm ideas for the story line, setting, and major characters; refine and organize those ideas; and generate a plan for presenting each story element in an intriguing manner. If the assignment is to write a report, then students need to gather information on the topic from a variety of sources; synthesize and arrange this information into categories or subtopics; and generate a plan for presenting the information in a logical way. All types of prewriting activities can be facilitated by using information organizing software such as electronic outlining and concept mapping programs.

- **Electronic outlining** — These are now integrated into almost all major word processing programs and are easily accessible as planning tools. **Electronic outliners** automatically generate headings and subheadings from typed information. The advantages to using them are new headings/subheadings can be easily inserted anywhere in the outline, headings/subheadings can be shifted around quickly to reflect a student's thinking and planning, and the prefixes serving as organizational clues are automatically changed to reflect the outline's revised organization.

- **Concept mapping software** — Also known as **webbing software, concept mapping software** is popular as a prewriting planning tool. It allows students to produce an outline as a visual map (see Figure 9.4). The most popular concept mapping programs are *Kidspiration* for grades K–3, and *Inspiration* for grades 4 and above (Inspiration Software, Inc.), products that have electronic tools for both outlining and diagramming. The diagramming side of the program can be used to create a variety of graphic displays, all of which are useful for students who like to think and plan using visual representations of their ideas. For example, students can easily brainstorm a cluster map of ideas for a story and then rearrange or

Figure 9.4 *Inspiration* Concept Map for *To Kill a Mockingbird*

Source: © 2005 Inspiration Software®, Inc. Diagram created in Inspiration® by Inspiration Software, Inc. Used with permission.

expand on the ideas for later development. Students can also use the program to generate a hierarchical map of key concepts to be explored for a research paper, and link those concepts with labels that demonstrate their conceptual relationship. *Inspiration* now has a personal digital assistant (PDA) version to assist students in the trend toward mobile learning.

New strategies to support the prewriting planning process are emerging as new technologies develop. Baumbach, Christopher, Fasimpaur, and Oliver (2004) describe one such strategy: using handhelds as "personal literacy assistants" to aid students with brainstorming, research, and organizing tasks prior to writing. (See Technology Integration Idea 9.2.)

Drafting. Drafting is the stage of the writing process when students put ideas and information into words, sentences, and paragraphs. When drafting, the student is engaging in the act of composing text, a creative act leading to words and sentences that might later be revised or refined. The term *drafting* for this stage implies an impermanence to the product (i.e., a draft) and therefore reflects the notion that students will continue to plan, rethink, and reorganize their ideas, even while producing text. Depending on the availability of equipment, students can draft directly on the computer using a word processing

program or type in their handwritten draft when they reach some level of completion. Electronic note card templates may also assist students in research, as well as the transition from research to drafting.

Revising and editing. Revising is the stage during which students make changes in the paper's content or structure that reflect decisions about how to improve its overall quality. To revise well, students have to move from composing text to analyzing it, looking for what needs to be added, deleted, or rearranged. One of the best ways for teachers to assist in this process is to project a student's typed draft onto a screen, then model the thinking and decision making that goes into analyzing and revising the text. If projected from a computer, changes can be made to the text as the students watch. Students consistently report that the writing process is easier when completed on a computer, and teachers report more and better writing when students use computers (Hill et al., in press; Lowther, Ross, & Morrison, 2003; Russell & Plati, 2000). After teachers' model, students revise each other's papers using word processing capabilities such as highlighting in various colors. This allows students to visually identify the thesis sentence and supporting sentences and transition sentences within a passage.

Editing, as opposed to revising, is the process of refining a paper so that it adheres to standard conventions for

TECHNOLOGY INTEGRATION IDEA 9.2

PLANNING FOR WRITING

Title: Using Handhelds for Literacy Instruction

Content Area/Topic: English, writing

Grade Levels: K–5

NETS for Students: Standards 3, 5, 6

Description: Handheld computers can be a powerful means of engaging students in reading, writing, listening, and speaking activities to support writing assignments. In this activity, each participating class uses handhelds to gather information to write "autobugraphies" or short stories written from a bug's point of view.

Instruction: The teacher begins by explaining to students what an "autobugraphy" is. To help them select a bug they want to learn more about, they brainstorm as many bugs as they can think of for each letter of the alphabet. Then each student selects a bug. The teacher helps students see that some bugs can be grouped together by mapping the relationships among them and displaying the map on a projector. Students collect information from a variety of sources and place all of their findings on their handhelds. To help them organize their writing, the teacher places a completion worksheet on the handheld word processor, for example, "I am a ... I live in ... I eat ..." and students fill in information on their bug. When students have enough information, they use the handhelds to write their stories and share them by "beaming" them to one another.

Assessments: Checklist of required tasks and a rubric covering technology skills and language usage.

Source: Baumbach, D., Christopher, T., Fasimpaur, K., and Oliver, K. (2004). Personal literacy assistants: Using handhelds for literacy instruction. *Learning and Leading with Technology, 32*(2), 16–21.

---

spelling, syntax, punctuation, and style. Editing is a far more superficial task than revising, but no less important. All word processing programs have features that support the editing process. These include spell checkers and grammar checkers, as well as electronic search capabilities to verify consistent word usage, tone, and tense. Once again the teacher can model the editing process followed by students editing each other's papers.

Publishing. Reports, newspaper articles, brochures, slide shows, and web pages are all publishing formats available to students for sharing their written work with peers, teachers, and the larger community. (See Technology Integration Idea 9.3 and the chapter-opening example in Chapter 5.) As mentioned earlier in this chapter, publishing writing on the Internet provides students with a wider audience and purpose for their writing (Karchmer, 2001), which increases both students' motivation for writing (Turner & Paris, 1995) and for doing their best work. Teachers can use two types of publishing approaches:

- **Traditional (paper) publishing** — Students produce paper products such as reports, books, newspaper articles, and brochures. Desktop publishing programs are designed to facilitate the production of professional looking printed products. In the past, there were significant differences between word processing software and the programs used for desktop publishing. As word processing programs have become increasingly sophisticated, however, these distinctions have little significance for most teachers and students. Now, both types of software include features that support layout, design, and high-end graphic manipulation.

- **Electronic publishing** — Students can also share their writing in electronic forms such as websites, electronic books, multimedia slide shows, and news broadcasts. Many Internet websites have been set up specifically to allow students to publish their work. For example, the Generations Can Connect website (http://generations-canconnect.ic.gc.ca) gives students around the world a place to publish their writing about people they have interviewed in their local communities. Viani (2003–2004) describes how to set up a site especially for sharing students' written work in online electronic portfolios, which serve both instructional and assessment purposes. Email and website projects are also a way to connect student writers with distant audiences (Lemkuhl, 2002). Electronic penpal (keypal) projects are growing in popularity and provide creative and

PUBLISHING STUDENT WRITING

Title: New Millenium Newspapers

Content Area/Topic: Writing news stories

Grade Levels: 5–9

NETS for Students: Standards 3, 4, 5

Description: This activity has students creating newspaper-type stories with predictions about the future; these Special Edition newspapers are published in a "web newspaper." Some motivating activities to get students writing include creating a sample entertainment newspaper section circa 2010 or writing time capsule predictions about various areas of society in the future, for example, education, fashion, the environment, health, sports, and science.

Source: Reissman, R. (1999). Predicting the future: Students create content for new millinnium newspapers. *Learning and Leading with Technology, 27*(2), 18–21.

---

authentic opportunites for communication. One handy reference is ePALS Classroom Exchange (http://www.epals.com), which connects 4.6 million students and educators in 191 countries. Another electronic publishing example is to have two or more classrooms work together on a common project, such as a travel brochure or collection of sayings, stories, or poems. See Technology Integration 9.3 for an example.

INTERACTIVE SUMMARY

The following is a summary of the main points covered in this chapter. To see additional examples and information on these points, go to this textbook's Companion Website at http://www.prenhall.com/roblyer and click on the Chapter 9 *Interactive Summary* module to visit each of the recommended websites.

1. **Issues in English and language arts instruction:** These include:
   - Expanding the definition of literacy
   - Exploring new instructional practices
   - Making decisions on keyboarding instruction
   - Creating social learning environments
   - Working with diverse learners
   - Motivating students
   - Teachers' growth as literacy professionals (see the English/Language Arts standards)

2. **Integration strategies for English and language arts:** Strategies for integrating technology into this area include three general areas:

- Language skills development (see the Intellitools and Educational Insights websites for examples)
- Literacy development (see Renaissance Learning's Accelerated Reader as an example)
- The process writing approach (see Inspiration Software's concept map software for outlining).

Online Activities

Visit this text's Companion Website at http://www.prenhall.com/roblyer to gain access to a variety of questions, activities, and exercises to help build your knowledge of this chapter's content.

Online Chapter 9 Self-Test

To review terms and concepts for this chapter, click on the Self-Test module for this chapter of the Companion Website.

Software Skill-Builder Tutorials

To access practical tutorial and skill-building activities and to build skills using popular software and hardware, click on the Software Skill-Builder Tutorials module for this chapter of the Companion Website.

Web-Enrichment Activities

To complete activities that connect to chapter content and provide web-based resources, click on the Web-Enrichment Activities module for this chapter of the Companion Website.

TECHNOLOGY INTEGRATION WORKSHOP

CLIPS FROM THE CLASSROOM: LEARNING WITH TECHNOLOGY

Go to the *Technology Integration Workshop* DVD located in the back of this text and click on *Clips from the Classroom*. View the video clips listed below that support this chapter's content:

- *Presentation Software in Literature*
- SmartBoards *for Students with Hearing Impairments*

Now, visit this text's Companion Website at http://www.prenhall.com/roblyer to answer questions and complete activities that will guide you in analyzing each clip.

THE TIP MODEL IN ACTION

Read each of the following scenarios related to implementing the TIP Model, and go to the Companion Website to answer the questions that follow it based on your Chapter 9 reading activities.

TIP Model Scenario #1   Ms. Mirabel has great difficulty getting her students to prepare an outline to plan what they will write for a composition assignment. She has taught them how to do outlines, but they seem unwilling or unable to do them. They have a great deal of trouble organizing information for writing, and she thinks it might be better for them to create a diagram that shows in pictures how concepts are related. She has heard about a software tool that can help them do this activity easier and faster.

1.1 What technology resource would help Ms. Mirabel address this problem?

1.2 What would be the relative advantage of using this resource as opposed to others?

1.3 Would it be better to have the students work individually or in groups to do the activity? Explain why.

TIP Model Scenario #2   Mr. Gerard has his class work in small groups to create a short story. As a whole class, they discuss the plot and characters; then each group writes a part of the story. They exchange sections and critique each other's parts. Then they do a final version. After the draft is complete, they post the story on the school's web server along with stories posted from past classes.

2.1 What would be the relative advantages for Mr. Gerard's students to use word processing for their drafts instead of doing typed or handwritten drafts?

2.2 What would be the relative advantages of posting the story on the Internet when it is completed?

2.3 What outcomes would Mr. Gerard probably want to assess in addition to the quality of the writing in the final product? Suggest a way to carry out this assessment.

TIP Model Scenario #3   Mr. Norton has noticed that his students write as little as possible and writing tests show they are badly in need of more practice in this area. He thinks if he can get them to keep weekly journals, it might give them the practice they need to begin improving their written expression.

3.1 What technology resource might provide a motivational environment for students to keep weekly journals?

3.2 If Mr. Norton has only three computers in the room, what are some ways he could manage student access to the resource?

3.3 What kind of assessment might be appropriate for an activity like this?

TIP Model Scenario #4   Several of Ms. Watts' second-grade students speak English as a second language and have great difficulties with English vocabulary. She wants to give them a fun, motivational way to practice using new vocabulary. Her principal says that he has about $150 to buy some resources to help, if she can identify something that would work well.

4.1 What kind of technology resource might be within the budget she has and could help Ms. Watts' students get the motivating practice they need?

4.2 If Ms. Watts has five students who need help, what would be an effective way to have students get access to these resources in a way that would not disturb other class members?

4.3 How could Ms. Watts determine if there had been improvement in her students' vocabulary skills?

TIP Model Scenario #5 Ms. Vignioti's 10th-grade students think poetry is irrelevant and boring. When she asks them to read poems in books and study their forms, they either refuse or do as little as possible. She has heard about an Internet project in which students see poems other students have written, write poems of their own, post them on a shared website, and write critiques of others' work. She wonders if this might get her students more interested in learning about poetry.

5.1 What might be the relative advantage of using a website project like this?

5.2 How might Ms. Vignioti begin such a project in a way that would capture students' interest?

5.3 How might Ms. Vignioti determine the impact of such a project on students' motivation and knowledge of poetry forms?

TIE INTO PRACTICE: TECHNOLOGY INTEGRATION EXAMPLES

The Technology Integration Example that opened this chapter (*Classroom Revolutions*) showed how a teacher might have students use Internet sites to research a novel and report their findings in a *PowerPoint* presentation. Having students use this presentation strategy can be helpful in many kinds of literature projects ranging from book reports to critical analysis projects. With the knowledge you have gained from Chapter 9, do the following to explore this strategy:

1. Young students can create a *PowerPoint* book report like the example shown below. **Create this sample presentation** by following the *Hands-On with Technology* tutorial on the DVD that accompanies this text.

2. Answer the following questions about the *Classroom Revolutions* example:
   - Phase 1 — What kinds of relative advantage did Ms. Skerritt feel that Internet use would bring to her students' study of the novel *A Tale of Two Cities*? Why did she choose a *PowerPoint* presentation as the way students would display their findings?
   - Phase 2 — One of the desired outcomes Ms. Skerritt identified for her students to achieve was to

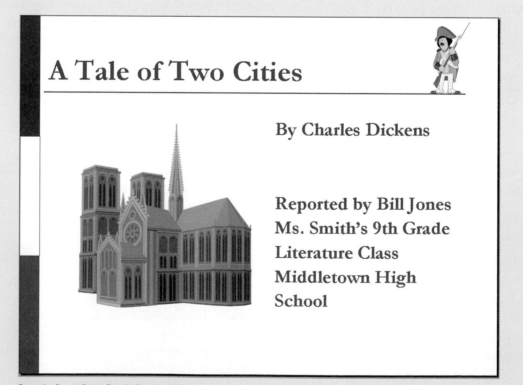

Sample *PowerPoint* Book Report Presentation. (Create this product using the *Hands-On with Technology* tutorial section on the DVD.)

create a *PowerPoint* presentation on their research findings. Create a rubric that she might use to assess this presentation. (*Hint:* Look at Kathy Schrock's Guide for Educators at http://school.discovery.com/schrockguide/assess.html to locate an existing rubric you can modify.)

- Phase 3 — On days 9 and 10 of the timeline, Ms. Skerritt has students giving their *PowerPoint* presentations. What could she do to make this serve as a review for the test, as well as a display of the students' research?

- Phase 4 — Ms. Skerritt uploaded her Bookmark file to the school's network and transferred it to the computer lab so that her students could use it. How might she organize this file so that each group would have a separate set of Internet sites?

- Phase 5 — In evaluating the outcomes of the activity, Ms. Skerritt found that her students needed more instruction on locating and analyzing information from websites. However, only some of her students lacked these skills. How could she provide this instruction to students who needed it without taking up class time?

3. What NETS for Students skills would students learn by working on the *Classroom Revolutions* project? (See the front of the book for a list of NETS for Students.)

TECHNOLOGY INTEGRATION LESSON PLANNING

The *Technology Integration Workshop* DVD includes a set of technology integration ideas and links to online lessons, arranged as a searchable database. The DVD comes packaged in the back of this textbook. Click on the *Hands-On with Technology* section of the DVD and complete the following exercises.

1. Locate lesson ideas — The DVD has several examples of lessons that use the integration strategies described in this chapter: generating interest in and support for reading and writing, providing support for learning to write, and computer-supported language skills learning (decoding, comprehension, and vocabulary development). Locate an example integration idea for each of these strategies.

2. Evaluate the lessons — Use the *Evaluation Checklist for a Technology-Integrated Lesson* (located on the DVD and the Companion Website) to evaluate each of these lessons.

3. Modify a lesson — Select one of the lesson ideas and adapt its strategies to meet a need in your own content area. You may choose to use the same approach in the original or adapt it to meet your needs.

4. Add descriptors — Create descriptors for your new lesson like those found on the database (e.g., grade level, content and topic areas, technologies used, relative advantage, objectives, NETS standards).

5. Add the new lesson — Add your modified lesson with all its descriptors to the lesson idea database.

FOR YOUR TEACHING PORTFOLIO

For this chapter's contribution to your teaching portfolio, add the following products you created in the Technology Integration Workshop:

- The sample *PowerPoint* book report you created

- The evaluations you did using the *Evaluation Checklist for a Technology-Integrated Lesson*

- The new lesson plan you developed, based on the one you found on the DVD.

CHAPTER 10

TECHNOLOGY IN ENGLISH LANGUAGE LEARNING AND FOREIGN LANGUAGE INSTRUCTION

ADRIENNE L. HERRELL
FLORIDA STATE UNIVERSITY, PANAMA CITY

M. D. ROBLYER
UNIVERSITY OF MARYLAND UNIVERSITY COLLEGE

MICHAEL JORDAN
CALIFORNIA STATE UNIVERSITY, FRESNO

English learners need a variety of language experiences. They need to hear language, write language, speak language and read language. Computers can play an integral part in providing English learners with valuable language experiences as they are acquiring a new language.

Ybarra and Green (2003)

TECHNOLOGY INTEGRATION EXAMPLE
A DISCUSSION BOARD EN FRANÇAIS

Based on: DeLuca, A., & Hoffman, B. (2003). Vamos a darles algo a discutir (let's give 'em something to talk about). *Learning and Leading with Technology, 30*(5), 36–41.

Grade Levels: 9–12 • Content Area/Topic: French, art • Length of Time: One semester

Phase 1: Determine relative advantage

The French teachers at Sabine High School all agreed that their students needed more practice writing in French. They had tried various kinds of writing assignments, but students always seemed to do the minimum required and their fluency in writing the language remained low. The teachers agreed that students would be more motivated if assignments were in a more authentic environment and allowed students to see and respond to each other's work, thus generating more awareness of the quality of their written communication. While visiting another school, one of the teachers saw a project for Spanish language students that seemed to fulfill all of these requirements. The teachers at that school held a Spanish art identification contest using an online discussion board. They would post images of Spanish artworks, and students had to identify and discuss the artwork en Espanol. Students who were first to do the required written descriptions for a given artwork earned points, and the students who accumulated the most points won recognition and prizes. The Spanish teachers said that the strategy worked well for students just learning English, as well. Also, it helped immerse students in some of the background culture of countries whose languages the students were learning. Because their school had a Blackboard® online course management system that all teachers and students could use via the Internet from any location, the French teachers decided to implement the project using discussion forums on that system.

Phase 2: Decide on objectives and assessments

The French teachers wanted to make sure the expectations for the activity were clear to students and teachers alike, so they agreed on the following objectives and assessment methods to measure students' performance:

- **Outcome:** Participation in online forums. **Objective:** All students must access each of the forums and post all of the required descriptions. **Assessment:** A checklist of items students were required to post about each artwork, with points for each posting and extra points for being first/second to identify and describe the artwork.

- **Outcome:** Amount and quality of writing. **Objective:** All students will demonstrate improved writing in French by achieving a 90% rubric score. **Assessment:** A rubric to assess the quality and quantity of students' writing in French.

- **Outcome:** Knowledge of French art. **Objective:** Each student must score at least 80% on a short-answer test of French art and culture. **Assessment:** A pre- and post-test consisting of questions on French art and culture represented in the forums.

Phase 3: Design integration strategies

The teachers knew that it would take some time to review students' French language skills, prepare content and procedures for the forums, and get students used to using them. They decided to take the first part of the year to prepare for the project and implement it after the winter holiday break. They designed the following sequence of activities to prepare for and carry out the project:

- **August–December:** Assess students' language skills and target vocabulary, grammar, and usage weaknesses for each student to address. Use interactive software and special projects (e.g., preparing a French menu, giving directions en Français) to give individual practice in usage and vocabulary. Prepare artwork graphics to place on the forums and do administrative tasks to use online forums (see Phase 4 for details).

- **January:** Introduce the Blackboard environment and the art identification tasks. Assign the first forum as a practice to iron out any logistical problems. Go over the items students are required to post about each artwork and review assessment strategies. Point out to the students that they can see each other's postings and can challenge each other on their written grammar, spelling, and usage in their French communications.

- **February–April:** Introduce one online forum for credit each month. Assess each and review the answers on the forum at the end of the month.

- **May:** Review points won, do student recognitions, and award prizes.

Phase 4: Prepare the instructional environment

The teachers knew that setting up the project would be more work the first time they did it, so they divided the following tasks among themselves to lessen the load on each of them:

- **Setting up forums:** They obtained the required information about how to create discussion forums and set up one forum for each month. Each student had to have a unique sign-on, so they made a list of students, created usernames and passwords for them, and entered them into the system.

- **Preparing content for assignments:** They selected a set of paintings and sculptures for each forum, making sure they represented various French-speaking countries and cultures they had studied. For each forum, they wrote a set of questions to be answered about the artworks.

- **Preparing assessments and handouts:** They created the checklists and rubrics they would use to assess student progress. They also prepared a handout describing the project and giving the URLs for accessing the system.

- **Ensuring student access:** They had already confirmed that most students had Internet access at home. However, to make sure everyone had adequate time and access whenever they wanted (so they all had equal chance to be first with the correct answers), the teachers designated times in their classrooms and in the language lab when students could get online.

Phase 5: Evaluate and revise

Teachers observed that students posted increasingly faster in each forum and most wrote more sentences each time. They also confirmed that there were more challenges to students' written language with each successive forum. The post-test on students' art and cultural knowledge reflected substantial improvement over the pre-test results. When the teachers interviewed the students, it was apparent all were enthusiastic about the project, with a few exceptions. Some students had no Internet access at home or had to share access with family members. They felt it was unfair that others had more opportunities than they to look up and post answers. The teachers decided to designate more time in each forum for lab work so that all students would have the access they needed. Students also suggested that the competition be by class instead of across classes, giving more students opportunities for winning awards. The teachers decided that the project had worked so well that they would expand it to include musical works by French composers next time.

OBJECTIVES

After reading this chapter and completing the learning activities for it, you should be able to:

1. Identify current issues in English language learning (ELL) and foreign language learning that may impact the selection and use of technology.

2. Describe key strategies for integrating technology into ELL and foreign language curricula.

3. Identify example software and web resources required to carry out each integration strategy.

4. Create instructional activities for ELL and foreign language instruction that model successful integration strategies.

KEY TERMS

- American Council for the Teaching of Foreign Languages (ACTFL)
- basic interpersonal communication (BIC)
- cognitive academic language proficiency (CALP)
- English as a second language (ESL)
- English language development (ELD)
- Teachers of English for Speakers of Other Languages (TESOL)

For more information on Key Terms, go to the *Key Terms* module for this chapter of the Companion Website at http://www.prenhall.com/roblyer.

ISSUES AND PROBLEMS IN ELL AND FOREIGN LANGUAGE INSTRUCTION

Although both involve foreign languages, the issues that shape the ELL educational environment are very different from those for foreign language learning. Both are discussed in this section along with how technology responds to and helps address the requirements in each of these areas.

Challenges Presented by Diversity

As the U.S. population becomes more diverse and a growing minority population enters school in overwhelming numbers, teachers face a continuing challenge to teach English to students of other language backgrounds while meeting academic standards mandated by the state and local school districts. Teachers often feel ill equipped to teach students who do not have a command of the English language.

In addition, many states have begun to reduce or discontinue bilingual classroom settings, in which students are taught in their native language. Instead, they are placed into English immersion classes in which instruction is done entirely in English, and there are great variations in support offered to those just acquiring the language. Many **English as a second language (ESL)** students are not literate in their first language, which compounds the problem. These students must be taught to read, so in English immersion classes, they are learning to speak and read English at the same time. Teachers often have students in their classrooms with many different home languages.

Federal mandates for ESL instruction require that students be grouped by language level and have their individual needs addressed. For example, in a single classroom the teacher may have to address the needs of students at four different levels of English development. Some schools have addressed this challenge by using a "deploying" or pullout strategy, which means that all students of a certain **English language development (ELD)** level are sent from their home class into another class where instruction is geared to their specific level of performance.

Technology resources can help meet the needs of students at varying levels of English development, supporting their acquisition of both oral and written skills. Oral and written language practice programs can give individuals simulated authentic practice while the teacher is working with students at other levels of development. With the new multimedia programs that include actual spoken models, ESL students can use the computer to help them practice their oral English language production. Grammar check programs allow students to receive instant feedback on their use of vocabulary and verb tenses as they practice their written English.

Because so many teachers do not speak the home languages of their students, the use of programs to help students translate unknown English words or provide scaffolding in the students' home language is valuable for the student and teacher alike. Many of the new programs allow the teacher to use a vocabulary list specific to future lessons to help prepare students to be more successful in participating in English immersion classrooms.

ADAPTING FOR SPECIAL NEEDS

Machine translation tools, when used appropriately, can be a valuable learning and productivity aid. For students learning a second language, language translation tools are helpful for exploring new words and phrases. For students whose first language is not English, language tools are often helpful for converting information in order to help them make sense of the topic when they do not know specific English words. Among the most common free language translation tools on the web are these:

- Babel Fish (http://world.altavista.com)
- Free Translator (http://www.free-translator.com)
- Free Translation (http://www.freetranslation.com)
- World Lingo (http://www.worldlingo.com)

In addition, the Google search engine site provides an array of language tools (http://www.google.com/language_tools?hl=en) that can be used for translating text or web pages, and it offers options for presenting the Google interface in a native language or accessing a native language Google search engine.

Language Learning Versus Language Acquisition in Foreign Language Programs

Students in the United States traditionally have a low success rate in foreign language learning. Many of the students in high schools across the nation take a foreign language for several years but do not master either the speaking or reading of the language at any acceptable level. In his research, Stephen Krashen (1982) has differentiated among (1) the learning of a language; (2) the study of the vocabulary, grammar, syntax, and rules and the acquisition of a language; and (3) being able to speak and write the language fluently. Several noted linguists concur that the acquisition of a second language requires practice in verbal and written interactions in meaningful contexts (Cummins, 1986; Krashen, 1982; Swain, 1993.)

In addition, Cummins (1986) helps us understand language acquisition by defining the level and complexity of the language that is acquired. **Basic interpersonal communication (BIC)** or social language is acquired mainly through verbal interactions in social settings. **Cognitive academic language proficiency (CALP)** is the more complex language that students must understand before they can benefit in a meaningful way from reading or engaging in academic discussions in the language. These differentiations explain why students can often engage in simple, social conversations in a language but cannot understand more complex written and oral communications. Technology can provide the support necessary to facilitate the acquisition of a foreign language in many of the same ways as it can support English acquisition in students learning and acquiring English.

Standards from TESOL and ACTFL

Teachers of English for Speakers of Other Languages (TESOL), the national organization for foreign language teachers, has established national standards for English language learners. These standards address the different purposes of language: social and academic. The standards also address the importance of using the appropriate register (vocabulary and formality of speech) in differing situations, as well as the need for English learners to adopt self-monitoring strategies for improving their own oral and written production. The standards are presented by grade level: preK–3, grades 4–8, and grades 9–12. They also include sample progress indicators for the different grade levels and classroom vignettes demonstrating ways of addressing the standards in the classroom.

Standards for foreign language acquisition were developed jointly by a number of professional organizations and are also available at the **American Council for the Teaching of Foreign Languages (ACTFL)** website. Although these standards are written with English learners in mind, the same ideas apply to the acquisition of a foreign language by English speakers. While the foreign language standards look very similar to the ESL standards in the area of communication, the foreign language standards also address four additional areas: cultures, connections, comparisons, and communities. These standards also include sample progress indicators at grades 4, 8, and 12 as well as sample learning scenarios with reflection on the practices presented.

- **TESOL standards** (http://www.tesol.org/)
- **ACTFL foreign language standards** (http://www.actfl.org/)

Many online resources and computer programs support students learning English, French, German, or any other language. To use these resources effectively, the teacher must be familiar with the purposes and approaches of the programs and sites and, most importantly, must match resources carefully to instructional needs. The most important thing a teacher can do in choosing technological supports for students is to be observant, recognize the individual needs of each student, and choose technology resources to meet the needs and language development levels of the individuals. The good news is that most of the technology resources have easy ways to identify the levels of the activities. Many of the sites and programs can be adapted for specific needs as well as very specific vocabulary.

TECHNOLOGY INTEGRATION STRATEGIES FOR ELL AND FOREIGN LANGUAGE INSTRUCTION

A variety of technology-based strategies are available to support both ELL and foreign language learners. These strategies include support for authentic oral and written practice, language subskill practice, presentations, text production, virtual field trip immersion experiences, virtual collaborations, and productivity and lesson design support for teachers. Many teaching resources are also available to help teachers prepare lessons. See a summary of these strategies and resources to support them in Figure 10.1. Also see the *Top Ten* feature on page 314 for additional strategies.

Support for Authentic Oral and Written Practice

Resources to support strategies for oral and written practice include the following:

- **Multimedia software and interactive storybooks —** These are designed to support language acquisition and vocabulary development and have several strengths. First, these programs allow teachers to individualize instruction for the students' differing language levels. Second, they give students an opportunity to interact in English authentically in a less stressful environment. Interactive books are a good example of using technology in this manner. These books appear on the screen and the student can set the program to read the book aloud as the student follows along. This gives the reader the chance to see the word and the illustrations, and to hear the words pronounced. The reader can opt to read the story unaided, touching a word with a stylus when a

Figure 10.1 Summary of Technology Integration Strategies for ELL and Foreign Language Instruction

Technology Integration Strategies	Benefits	Sample Resources and Activities
Support for authentic oral and written practice LEAPFROG SCHOOLHOUSE, the LeapFrog SchoolHouse logo, and *LANGUAGE FIRST!* are trademarks or registered trademarks of LeapFrog Enterprises, Inc. © LeapFrog Enterprises, Inc. All Rights Reserved. http://www.leapfrogschoolhouse.com	• Helps individualize instruction for students' differing language levels. • Helps students internalize word meanings and give additional practice in using the new words. • Gives practice in following oral English direction and reading and responding in written English. • Builds listening competence.	• *Language First!* and other interactive resources from LeapFrog SchoolHouse http://www.leapfrogschoolhouse.com • Clifford interactive books from Scholastic http://teacher.scholastic.com • Other interactive storybooks at BAB Books http://www.sundhagen.com/babbooks • Randall's Cyber Listening Lab http://www.esl-lab.com/ • Internet Picture Dictionaries http://www.Enchantedlearning.com/Dictionary.html
Support for practice in language subskills **Transparent** *Language* Courtesy of Transparent Language, Inc. http://www.transparent.com/	• Provides intense practice in specific language skills and vocabulary sets. • Corrects common errors being made by the students. • Incorporates vocabulary currently being studied in class.	• Practice programs: Rosetta Stone Software (http://www.rosettastone.com) and Transparent Software (http://www.transparent.com) • Idioms and slang http://www.stuff.co.uk/phrasal.htm
Presentation aids http://www.2learn.ca	• Helps reduce students' stress and focus their presentations. • Teaches valuable skills in making effective presentations. • Makes classroom presentations more understandable and interesting.	• See presentation aids available from the Telus Learning Connection http://www.2learn.ca • Digital cameras and scanners
Support for text production *translation.net* Courtesy of Translation.net and ESL.net. http://www.translation.net	• Supports authentic use of language in creating journals, descriptions of experiences, oral reports, and research projects. • Supports correct usage with grammar checks, correct spelling (spell checks), and reminders to employ good style.	• Foreign language word processing and other tools at Translation.net http://www.translation.net • Internet Picture Dictionaries http://www.pdictionary.com **Also see Technology Integration Idea 10.1:** Word Processing in Early Foreign Language Learning
Virtual field trips for modified language immersion experience the field trips ➤ Let's Go! Take a Virtual Field Trip Now Courtesy of TramLine. http://www.tramline.com	• Offers expanded opportunities for language acquisition. • Allows students to "visit" locations and have experiences that wouldn't be available to them otherwise.	• Tramline field trips http://www.tramline.com • The Virtual Geography Department at the University of Wisconsin http://www.uwsp.edu/geo/projects/virtdept/vft.html **Also see Technology Integration Idea 10.2:** Cyber Traveling in the Loire Valley

(continued)

Figure 10.1   (continued)

Technology Integration Strategies	Benefits	Sample Resources and Activities

Virtual collaborations
 	
Courtesy of Global SchoolNet. Copyright GlobalSchoolNet.org.
http://www.globalschoolnet.org
	• Helps motivate students to use new language skills.
	• Helps students learn more about the diversity of their own country than they would from textbooks.
		See online collaborative projects to join at
		• The Global SchoolHouse
		  http://www.globalschoolnet.org
		• IEARN
		  http://www.iearn.org/projects/

Productivity and lesson design support for teachers
 	
http://www.esl.net
	• Saves teacher time in locating and preparing lesson ideas and materials.	• ESL.net
		  http://www.esl.net
		• The Intercultural Development Research Association
		  http://www.idra.org
		• The EST Internet Group
		  http://www.esl-group.com/tres.html
		• Telus Learning Connection
		  http://www.2learn.ca
		• Translations sites
		  http://babelfish.altavista.com
		• Ohio University site:
		  http://www.ohiou.edu/esl/english/vocabulary.html
		• Integrating ESL into the curriculum
		  http://www.teach-nology.com/tutorials/teaching/esl/

prompt is needed. Many of these programs have additional learning games attached, using the vocabulary and illustrations from the storybook. LeapFrog SchoolHouse has a variety of these books available.

LeapFrog also has programs available in French and Spanish, and one product gives support in five languages, including Lao and Hmong. LeapFrog SchoolHouse's *Language First!*™ program is suitable for grades K–5 and provides 36 theme-based interactive books written at four language development levels. Scholastic has a number of titles available in interactive storybooks including the Clifford books. Many of these interactive book programs emphasize crucial vocabulary games to help the student internalize the word meanings and give additional practice in using the new words encountered in the storybooks. See components of LeapFrog SchoolHouse's *Language First!* program in Figure 10.2; links to these and other interactive storybook resources are listed in Figure 10.1.

• **Learning games on handheld computers** — LeapFrog also has learning games appropriate for older language learners. Their iQuest handheld computer is designed to give middle and high school students practice in math, science, and social studies using content from the most common textbooks across the country. Because the acquisition of a new language must be supported by oral and written practice with monitoring and correction in order to be effective (Swain, 1993), it is important that students' work with interactive programming be carefully monitored. The students should always be given the opportunity to present their work orally to the teacher (and receive feedback and congratulations).

• **Language labs** — These have long been a mainstay in ESL and foreign language instruction. In the 1960s and 1970s these labs consisted of audiotapes that the students listened to and imitated. Since we have learned much about the importance of communication, authentic practice, monitoring, and feedback, language labs look very different these days. Students now have headphones so they can hear themselves and "self-monitor" their oral production (see Figure 10.3). The new

Take advantage of these 10 powerful strategies for using technology to enhance the teaching of both English and foreign languages.

1. **Images downloaded from the Internet help illustrate language concepts** — Illustrations serve as "visual scaffolding" to help students just learning to use English.

2. **Interactive storybooks support language acquisition** — Students can strengthen their language skills by hearing the language read to them.

3. **Interactive software and handheld devices provide language skills practice** — Students use these resources to get individual, private feedback as they practice their vocabulary and usage skills.

4. **Presentation aids help scaffold students' language use** — Visual formats of presentation software and videos help students learn how to use a language effectively for communication.

5. **Websites offer exercises for students to practice subskills** — Online exercises are easy to access and provide intense practice in specific language skills and vocabulary sets.

6. **Virtual collaborations provide authentic practice** — Students who work with native speakers of other languages gain both valuable practice and multicultural insights.

7. **Virtual field trips provide simulated immersion experiences** — Students see people and places in locations they could not "visit" otherwise.

8. **Foreign language word processing supports writing in other languages** — Students are able to check spelling and grammar as they practice writing in other languages.

9. **Language labs support language acquisition** — Students get personal instruction with monitoring, feedback, and authentic verbal interaction.

10. **Listening lab exercises provide language skills practice** — Short listening exercises help students sharpen their listening comprehension skills.

Figure 10.2 **LeapFrog SchoolHouse's *Language First!* Program**

Placement Guide to assess student language level

Skills Matrix

Language Posters

Teaching Strategies Cards

Interactive books, 4 levels in each theme

Teacher's Manual– 1 for each theme

LeapPad® Personal Learning Tool

language labs provide students with a tape recorder, video monitor, and/or a computer in each individual station, and activities are much more interactive. Many of the more advanced language lab activities require only individual tape recorders and blank tapes. Such activities as recorded dialog journals, in which the students speak about an assigned topic or a topic of their choice, give the teacher an opportunity for monitoring, feedback, and authentic verbal interaction. Listening instruction can be built into the lab setting by having the students listen to oral instructions while building a project such as a paper airplane, Lego construction, or origami figure.

Additional resources for building listening competence can be found at Randall's Cyber Listening Lab. This site provides short (1- to 3-minute) and long (5- to 10-minute) listening exercises with *RealAudio,* a downloadable player available from http://www.real.com/.

- **Radio broadcasts** — For more advanced students National Public Radio offers live radio broadcasts on the Internet at http://www.npr.org. They offer both news and drama from which teachers can create motivational activities to give the learner practice in oral and written language.

Support for Practice in Language Subskills

Technology can be very useful in providing intense practice in specific language skills and vocabulary sets. Many websites are available that provide in-depth practice in areas that often give students great difficulty. Examples are English Zone (http://www.english-zone.com), ESP Bears, (http://www.eslbears.homestead.com), and Tower of English (http://www.towerofenglish.com).

One value in these types of websites is that the exercises provide models of activities that can be used by teachers to create similar activities to correct common errors being made by the students or to incorporate vocabulary currently being studied in class. This approach helps the teacher meet the individual needs of the students in the class as well as the federal mandate for differentiated instruction. Whenever possible, teachers should have students read exercises aloud after completing them.

Several companies offer software that students can use to practice language skills and vocabulary. Two well-known providers of these materials are Rosetta Stone and Transparent Software.

Presentation Aids

Presentations to groups can be stressful even for those who know the language well. Imagine having to give a presentation in a language other than your own! When students are asked to give oral presentations, they use *PowerPoint* software or homemade videos to assist them. In addition to supporting the concepts being presented, the students who use visuals learn some valuable skills in

Figure 10.3   Students Practice New Skills in a Foreign Language in a Language Lab

Figure 10.4 A Resource Website for Teacher Presentation Tools

Source: Courtesy of 2Learn.ca Education Society, TELUS Learning Connection.

making effective presentations. Visuals also help reduce students' stress and focus their presentations.

The Telus Learning Connection sponsors a website that gives both teacher and student the support needed to make and use technology in presentations (see Figure 10.4). Under the *Educators Resources for Teaching and Learning* section, click *Teacher Tools* to find many ideas and supports for presentations. Under the *Presentation Tools* option you will find reflections on why presentations with visuals are effective both as teaching and learning tools. The *Outcomes* section shows the effect of using these approaches, both on teaching and learning. The *How to* section is jam-packed with information on how to create and use *PowerPoint, Kid Pix, HyperStudio,* and other software.

In addition to the websites and programs available for creating good oral presentations, digital cameras and scanners can also help create visuals to make the presentations more understandable and interesting. Scanned or digital

pictures can easily be made into color transparencies or *PowerPoint* slides that are very effective for supporting student learning. Many teachers of English learners have found it vital to create a file of overhead pictures to use in scaffolding instruction. The slides can be alphabetized, grouped by topic, or organized in any way that makes them accessible. The Internet serves as a valuable resource for photographs and other images to add to presentations. Images can be downloaded from the Internet and then used to make overhead transparencies, or even added to printed text. These illustrations serve as "visual scaffolding," a valuable addition to lessons for English learners (Herrell & Jordan, 2003).

Support for Text Production

It is important throughout the process of acquiring a language, no matter which language, that students have multiple opportunities to listen, speak, read, and write using the language. Word processing programs are available in many

TECHNOLOGY INTEGRATION IDEA 10.1

SUPPORT FOR TEXT PRODUCTION

Title: Word Processing in Early Foreign Language Learning

Content Area/Topic: ELL writing, foreign language learning

Grade Levels: 7–8

NETS for Students: Standards 3, 4

Description: Beginning language students need the practice of writing simple compositions in the language they are studying. Yet students who have limited vocabulary and grammar mastery frequently find it difficult and tedious to accomplish this. Word processing lets them make corrections more quickly, and combining their writing with graphics makes the activity more exciting and helps them convey complex thoughts they are not yet able to express.

Instruction: One such activity is student autobiographies: a self-portrait in writing. In an assignment presented to them in Spanish, ask them to incorporate items such as name, age, birthday, family members, grandparents and their nationalities, friends, activities they like to do on weekends, religion, favorite TV programs, foods they like to eat, favorite sports, places they have visited, remarks about their school, and languages they speak.

Assessment: Rubric to assess self-portrait.

Source: Lewis, P. (1997). Using productivity software for beginning language learning. *Learning and Leading with Technology, 24*(8), 14–17.

---

languages: French, Spanish, Russian—even Chinese. In addition to the authentic use of language in creating journals, descriptions of experiences, oral reports, and research projects, word processing programs support correct usage with grammar checks, correct spelling (spell-checks), and reminders to employ good style (e.g., use active, rather than passive voice). (See Technology Integration Idea 10.1 for a sample classroom strategy.) Spell-checks and grammar checks are not foolproof, however. Students should always be encouraged to read their writing aloud and to listen for clues that corrections or refinements should be made.

A valuable addition to the writing process is the writing group, in which the author reads his or her piece aloud to a small group and they provide feedback and questions if something is not clear to them. This provides opportunities for oral English practice and listening practice and also gives the author some ideas for revisions. The beauty of the use of word processors is that the student-author can then revise easily without rewriting by hand. The finished, printed copy of the text is also very motivational to the writer. It is also highly readable, without penmanship issues.

The presentation programs discussed in the previous section are an interesting addition to the production of text. Using these same programs allows the author to add illustration and charts to the text to make it even more interesting.

Virtual Field Trips for Modified Language Immersion Experience

Field trips provide a wealth of opportunities for language acquisition but are being greatly limited by funding. A good use of technology is the "virtual field trip," in which the teacher takes the field trip, videotaping the trip and recording running commentary. For English learners the narrator would focus on vocabulary and making sure that there was a good match between what was being viewed and what was being said. This also provides opportunities for students to go places "virtually" that would be impossible otherwise. As a matter of fact, many of the world's outstanding art museums have "virtual tours" that can be viewed online. A directory of more than 300 virtual free sites may be found at http://www.virtualfreesites.com/museums.html. This site includes tours of museums, exhibits, and points of interest around the world. Some examples include:

- Ocean field trips (http://www.field-trips.org/sci/oceank-12)

- Virtual dissections (http://www.accessexcellence.org/RC/virtual.html)

- A library of the best virtual field trips (http://www.vickiblackwell.com/vft.html).

Making the Case for Technology Integration

1. Are virtual trips to foreign countries and virtual conversations with citizens of those countries as good as actually going there? If not, what are the differences between them and what could teachers do (or not do) to make up for them?

2. Online projects can link students of different backgrounds and allow them to learn more about people of other cultures without meeting them in person. Learning about people in this way presents both unique benefits and problems. Can you think of some of each? What are some ways to implement online strategies that maximize the benefits and minimize the problems? (*Example:* Language differences can lead to misunderstandings.)

Also see Technology Integration Idea 10.2 for a strategy based on the virtual tour concept.

As with any field trip, students should be prepared ahead of time for their experience, building background knowledge, vocabulary, and expectations. The "virtual field trip" should then be followed with activities that encourage students to use their experience and practice their oral and written language.

Virtual Collaborations

Many teachers have found student collaboration via email very effective in motivating students to use new language skills (Ybarra & Green, 2003). Using email and the Internet to work with students of other cultures provides students with authentic writing and research experiences. These collaborations often start because two teachers establish email connections and begin an exchange of email messages between their students. See sites such as the Global SchoolHouse for help on establishing contacts with distant students (see links in Figure 10.1).

Productivity and Lesson Design Support for Teachers

The Internet holds a wealth of resources to help teachers of English and foreign languages prepare for and carry out lessons. Some of these are listed in Figure 10.1. Projects

---

Technology Integration Idea 10.2

Virtual Field Trips for Modified Language Immersion Experiences

Title: Cyber Traveling in the Loire Valley

Content Area/Topic: French

Grade Levels: 5–6

NETS for Students: Standards 3, 4, 5

Description: In this activity, students practice their French language skills by taking a virtual trip to the Loire Valley region of France and writing in French about their findings.

Instruction: They are asked to prepare a written report on a chateau of their choice, writing (en Français) facts about it such as when it was built, who built it, architectural style, its history, its location, and when you can visit it. Students use the French version of *AppleWorks* to prepare their reports. When they are done writing, they create web pages to publish and share their work.

Assessment: Rubric to assess web page information.

Source: Chenuau, J. (2000). Cyber traveling through the Loire Valley. *Learning and Leading with Technology, 28*(2), 22–27.

and programs in ESL and foreign language instruction are evaluated and discussed at ESL.net. The Intercultural Development Research Association offers a number of teaching resources and professional development opportunities. Many ESL teacher resources and free downloads are available at the ESL Internet Group site. The Telus Learning Connection website also provides a format for teachers to network and share ideas and concerns.

The Internet also serves as a resource in finding translations for use in planning lessons. Many times a teacher needs a word in the student's native language in order to build on prior knowledge and make lessons more comprehensible. Two good sites for translations are Babylon and BabelFish.

- Support for text production. See especially tools at Translation.net (http://www.translation.net).
- Virtual field trips for modified language immersion experience. See Tramline field trips (http://www.tramline.com).
- Virtual collaborations. See collaborative projects to join at the Global SchoolHouse (http://www.globalschoolnet.org) and IEARN (http://www. iearn.org/projects/).
- Productivity and lesson design support for teachers. See especially ESL.net (http://www.esl.net) and translation sites such as Babel Fish (http://babelfish.altavista.com).

Interactive Summary

The following is a summary of the main points covered in this chapter. To see additional examples and information on these points, go to this textbook's Companion Website at http://www.prenhall.com/roblyer and click on the Chapter 10 Interactive Summary module to visit each of the recommended websites.

1. **Issues in ELL and foreign language instruction:** These include:
   - Challenges presented by diversity
   - Language learning versus language acquisition in foreign language programs
   - Required standards from TESOL and ACTFL.
2. **Integration strategies for ELL and foreign language instruction:** Strategies for integrating technology into this area cover three general topics:
   - Support for authentic oral and written practice. See especially products from Leapfrog (http://www.leapfrog.com).
   - Support for practice in language subskills. See especially products from Rosetta Stone Software (http://www.rosettastone.com/) and Transparent Software (http://www.transparent.com/).
   - Presentation aids. See especially resources from the Telus Learning Connection (http://www.2learn.ca).

Online Activities

Visit this text's Companion Website at http://www.prenhall.com/roblyer to gain access to a variety of questions, activities, and exercises to help build your knowledge of this chapter's content.

Online Chapter 10 Self-Test

To review terms and concepts for this chapter, click on the Self-Test module for this chapter of the Companion Website.

Software Skill-Builder Tutorials

To access practical tutorial and skill-building activities and to build skills using popular software and hardware, click on the Software Skill-Builder Tutorials module for this chapter of the Companion Website.

Web-Enrichment Activities

To complete activities that connect to chapter content and provide web-based resources, click on the Web-EnrichmentActivities module for this chapter of the Companion Website.

TECHNOLOGY INTEGRATION WORKSHOP

CLIPS FROM THE CLASSROOM: LEARNING WITH TECHNOLOGY

Go to the *Technology Integration Workshop* DVD located in the back of this text and click on *Clips from the Classroom.* View the video clips listed below that support this chapter's content:

- *Tablet Computers in Spanish*
- *Communication System for Foreign Language.*

Now, visit this text's Companion Website at http://www.prenhall.com/roblyer to answer questions and complete activities that will guide you in analyzing each clip.

THE TIP MODEL IN ACTION

Read each of the following scenarios related to implementing the TIP Model, and go to the Companion Website to answer the questions that follow it based on your Chapter 10 reading activities.

TIP Model Scenario #1   Ms. Griggs is helping her AP Spanish students prepare for the exam. She knows that there will be a lot of vocabulary on the exam many of the students may not have encountered, so she decides to offer them the opportunity to practice vocabulary using a Spanish drill-and-practice program she has available. However, she has only one copy.

1.1 How would you recommend Ms. Griggs have her students use this one copy of the software?

1.2 What would be the relative advantage of using this software?

1.3 What data could Ms. Griggs gather to get some indication the program was helping her students be better prepared for the exam?

TIP Model Scenario #2   Mr. Caesar would like to motivate his students to spend more time on their German translations. They will do practice exercises he creates for them only under duress. He hears about a website that will link individual students to a keypal in a German school so they can communicate in both German and English.

2.1 What would be the relative advantages for Mr. Caesar to use this strategy with his students?

2.2 How would you advise Mr. Caesar to structure this project to make it most meaningful for both students in this country and in Germany?

2.3 Would you advise Mr. Caesar to encourage students to communicate with the German students from their home computers if they have them? Why or why not?

TIP Model Scenario #3   Ms. Sartori wants the students in her AP Spanish class to have an immersion experience, where they go to a Spanish-speaking country and interact with native speakers. However, the school is in a small, rural community and has no funds for this kind of activity. Ms. Sartori has read that virtual collaborations can be a good replacement for immersion experiences, but she does not know how to get started finding school partners for such a project.

3.1 How would you advise Ms. Sartori to locate school partners for a virtual collaboration?

3.2 What would be the relative advantage of such a project?

3.3 What kind of assessment might be appropriate for an activity like this?

TIP Model Scenario #4   Several of Mr. Junita's students are new to the school and speak little English. They seem very hesitant to try out their English skills; Mr. Junita thinks they are afraid of being laughed at by the other children. Mr. Junita requests some special funds to obtain some iQuest handheld computers for these students so they can practice using English words and phrases at school and at home.

4.1 What would be the relative advantages of using these handheld computers for practicing English?

4.2 How would you instruct these students to use the handhelds in order to obtain the maximum benefit from them (i.e., not just to "play with them")?

4.3 How would you assess the benefits to the students using these devices?

TIP Model Scenario #5 The students in Ms. Liu's Chinese class need practice writing in Chinese. She has noticed that when she assigns word-processed work in Chinese, the students tend to make a lot of spelling and grammar errors. She would like for them to be able to self-correct their work more before they turn it in. She feels that this would be a good way to help them learn the language and to practice good writing production skills.

5.1 What resource might Ms. Liu obtain to help her students self-correct their Chinese writing?

5.2 What would be the best way to have students use this resource: individually, pairs, small groups? Why?

5.3 What would Ms. Liu have to do before she assigned students to use this resource for a graded assignment?

TIE INTO PRACTICE: TECHNOLOGY INTEGRATION EXAMPLES

The Technology Integration Example that opened this chapter (*A Discussion Board en Français*) showed how a teacher might have students use various technology resources to enhance French language learning. One strategy has them doing a French menu in order to practice their language use skills in an authentic task. With the knowledge you have gained from Chapter 10, do the following to explore how the rest of the activities in this lesson would work:

1. Foreign language students might create a menu like the example shown below to practice their skills. **Create this sample presentation** by following the hands-on tutorial located on the *Hands-On with Technology* section of the DVD that accompanies this text.

Sample French Menu in Microsoft *Word*. (Create this product using the *Hands-On with Technology* tutorial section on the DVD.)

2. Answer the following questions about the *Discussion Board en Français* example:

- Phase 1 — The teachers felt that students needed an authentic way to practice their French language skills. What makes an activity "authentic," and what kinds of relative advantage does an authentic approach have?

- Phase 2 — One of the desired outcomes the teachers want to accomplish with this project is better writing in French. To assess this, they will use a rubric to assess the quality and quantity of students' writing in French. How will they have to handle this assessment if they want to measure *improved* writing ability?

- Phase 3 — In May, at the end of the project, teachers will recognize students and give awards on correct identifications. What would be a way to use technology to do these recognitions?

- Phase 4 — One thing that always seems to happen with student usernames and passwords is that they forget them. How should the teachers handle this efficiently?

- Phase 5 — In evaluating the outcomes of the activity, the teachers found that students wrote more each time. What would they need to do to determine if quality of writing improved? Which criterion should they have set to gauge "improvement"?

3. What NETS for Students skills would students learn by working on the *Discussion Board en Français* project? (See the front of the book for a list of NETS for Students.)

TECHNOLOGY INTEGRATION LESSON PLANNING

The *Technology Integration Workshop* DVD includes a set of technology integration ideas and links to online lessons, arranged as a searchable database. The DVD comes packaged in the back of this textbook. Click on the *Hands-On with Technology* section of the DVD and complete the following exercises.

1. Locate lesson ideas — The DVD has several examples of lessons that use the integration strategies described in this chapter: support for authentic oral and written practice, support for practice in language subskills, presentation aids, support for text production, virtual field trips for modified language immersion experience, virtual collaborations, and productivity and lesson design support for teachers. Locate an example integration idea for several of these strategies.

2. Evaluate the lessons — Use the *Evaluation Checklist for a Technology-Integrated Lesson* (located on the DVD and the Companion Website) to evaluate each of these lessons.

3. Modify a lesson — Select one of the lesson ideas and adapt its strategies to meet a need in your own content area. You may choose to use the same approach in the original or adapt it to meet your needs.

4. Add descriptors — Create descriptors for your new lesson like those found on the database (e.g., grade level, content and topic areas, technologies used, relative advantage, objectives, NETS standards).

5. Add the new lesson — Add your modified lesson with all its descriptors to the lesson idea database.

FOR YOUR TEACHING PORTFOLIO

For this chapter's contribution to your teaching portfolio, add the following products you created in the Technology Integration Workshop:

- The sample French menu you created in *Microsoft Word*

- The evaluations you did using the *Evaluation Checklist for a Technology-Integrated Lesson*

- The new lesson plan you developed, based on the one you found on the DVD.

CHAPTER 11

TECHNOLOGY IN MATHEMATICS AND SCIENCE INSTRUCTION

ED DICKEY
UNIVERSITY OF SOUTH CAROLINA

M. D. ROBLYER
UNIVERSITY OF MARYLAND UNIVERSITY COLLEGE

MICHAEL ODELL
UNIVERSITY OF IDAHO

The terms and circumstances of human existence can be expected to change radically during the next human life span. Science, mathematics, and technology will be at the center of that change—causing it, shaping it, responding to it. Therefore, they will be essential to the education of today's children for tomorrow's world.

Benchmarks for Scientific Literacy (American Association for the Advancement of Science, 1993)

Based on: Caniglia, J. (1997). The heat is on! Using the calculator-based laboratory to integrate math, science, and technology. *Learning and Leading with Technology, 25*(1), 22–27.

Grade Levels: Middle to high school • Content Area/Topic: Physics, graphing, and measurement • Length of Time: Three weeks

Phase 1: Determine relative advantage

Ms. Belt and Mr. Alter, the physics and mathematics teachers, respectively, at Pinnacle High School, were excited about the new **calculator-based laboratories (CBLs)** that had just arrived. As they learned about how CBLs can "grab" temperature data and display it in graphs and spreadsheets, they realized that activities with CBLs provide a natural link between science and mathematics studies. Having students use CBLs would be an ideal way to give them hands-on insights into the relationship between these two important skill areas. They also agreed that CBL activities would address an ongoing challenge of making abstract science and math concepts more concrete and visual. Having students collect and analyze their own data, they felt, would give them authentic, hands-on application of these concepts. They decided that a unit on heating and cooling experiments would be a good first activity. Students could take temperature measurements with the CBL probes, then use mathematical procedures to graph and analyze the resulting data.

Phase 2: Decide on objectives and assessments

The teachers decided they would assess student progress in each of four areas: CBL performance tasks, carrying out scientific experiments, investigating physics principles, and using mathematics to analyze and display data. They decided on the following outcomes and objectives they hoped students would achieve, and outlined assessment methods to measure students' performance on them:

- **Outcome 1:** CBL procedures. **Objective:** Each student will score at least 85% on a performance test designed to measure competence with CBL procedures. **Assessment:** A checklist with points assigned for successful completion of each task.

- **Outcome 2:** Completing and reporting on scientific experiments, with teacher assistance. **Objective:** All students demonstrate they can work in groups to carry out the steps in an assigned experiment and write summaries of their findings by achieving a rubric score of at least 85% on their work. **Assessment:** A checklist with points assigned to each step done correctly; a rubric to assess quality of written summaries.

- **Outcome 3:** Interpreting data from experiments. **Objective:** All students will demonstrate the ability to review and interpret data derived from experiments by correctly answering at least 8 of 10 questions requiring data interpretation. **Assessment:** A mid-unit test with each student reviewing example charts and answering questions on how to interpret the data.

- **Outcome 4:** Completing and reporting on scientific experiments, without teacher assistance. **Objective:** All students demonstrate they can replicate and interpret data from a CBL experiment by working in pairs to complete the required tasks without assistance. **Assessment:** A checklist with points assigned to each step done correctly; a rubric to assess quality of written summaries.

Phase 3: Design integration strategies

The teachers decided to team-teach the unit to draw together even more the links between the two content areas. Working together, they designed the following sequence of activities:

- **Week 1:** Introduce unit activities and CBLs and provide hands-on practice. Introduce the unit with a *Consumer Reports*-type scenario. Makers of camp stoves each claim their product heats water faster than the competitors' stoves. The various stoves used three different fuels: white gas, kerosene, and butane. The students have to establish which manufacturer is correct and write up their findings for the *CR* magazine. Demonstrate how students can use the CBL to grab data and how it displays temperatures in graph form. Hold a discussion about interpreting CBL data. Students carry out the introductory experiment in three large groups. Using camp stoves borrowed from a local sporting goods store, students use the CBLs to heat water to boiling. They go through the step-by-step procedures for hands-on experiments, write up their findings, and present them to the whole class. Hold a whole-class discussion to interpret results and write up a summary for *CR*.

- **Week 2:** Carry out heating/cooling experiments and present findings. As Ms. Belt helps small groups prepare materials for the next set of experiments, Mr. Alter has students do individual performance checks on CBL procedures and provides additional instruction, as needed. Each small group is assigned a heating/cooling experiment, for example, which cup holds heat longest: styrofoam, paper, or ceramic? Which color container holds heat longest: white, black, or metallic? Each group completes its assigned experiment, answers the question, writes up findings, and presents them to the class by inserting spreadsheet and graphed data into a *PowerPoint* presentation.

- **Week 3:** Do mathematical analyses and presentations; take final tests. Each group works with the data to explore linear, quadratic, and exponential functions of graphed data. Finally, students work in pairs to do their replication experiment and answer questions on the meaning of the graphs.

entific experiments; they asked Ms. Belt to give them information on careers in science and mathematics. The teachers concluded that this kind of multidisciplinary unit worked very well. They decided to plan other CBL experiments to be carried out on a long-term basis and at locations outside the classroom.

| Phase 4: | **Prepare the instructional environment** |

The teachers get a local sporting goods store to loan them three different camp stoves for the first experiment/demonstration. They tested each of the CBLs and calibrated them, as needed. They designed and copied each of the performance measures and made copies of lab sheets they needed during the experiments.

| Phase 5: | **Evaluate and revise** |

At the end of the unit, the teachers reviewed the students' products and discussed how the unit had worked. Mr. Alter and Ms. Belt were happy with the overall performance of the class. They were impressed at how engaged students had become in using the CBLs to gather and analyze data. Perhaps most encouraging, two female students seemed especially excited by the work they had done on the sci-

OBJECTIVES

After reading this chapter and completing the learning activities for it, you should be able to:

1. Identify some of the current issues in mathematics and science instruction that may impact the selection and use of technology.

2. Describe key strategies for integrating technology into mathematics and science curricula.

3. Identify example software and web resources required to carry out each integration strategy.

4. Create instructional activities for mathematics and science instruction that model successful integration strategies.

KEY TERMS

- calculator-based laboratories (CBLs)
- interactive or dynamic geometry software
- scientific inquiry
- virtual manipulatives

For more information on Key Terms, go to the *Key Terms* module for this chapter of the Companion Website at http://www.prenhall.com/roblyer.

INTRODUCTION

Science and technology have a unique relationship. Technology supports science and science makes new technology possible. Both will play a critical role in our students' future. Thus, it is not surprising that efforts to reform teaching and learning in these two areas have been at the center of the national standards movement. U.S. elementary students perform well compared to students in other nations, but that performance diminishes as our students progress through school (Beaton et al., 1997–1998). Technology provides many opportunities to build students' conceptual knowledge of mathematics and science, as well as to connect their learning to problems found in our world. This chapter highlights current issues and problems in mathematics and science education and describes strategies for integrating technology into teaching and learning processes for these areas.

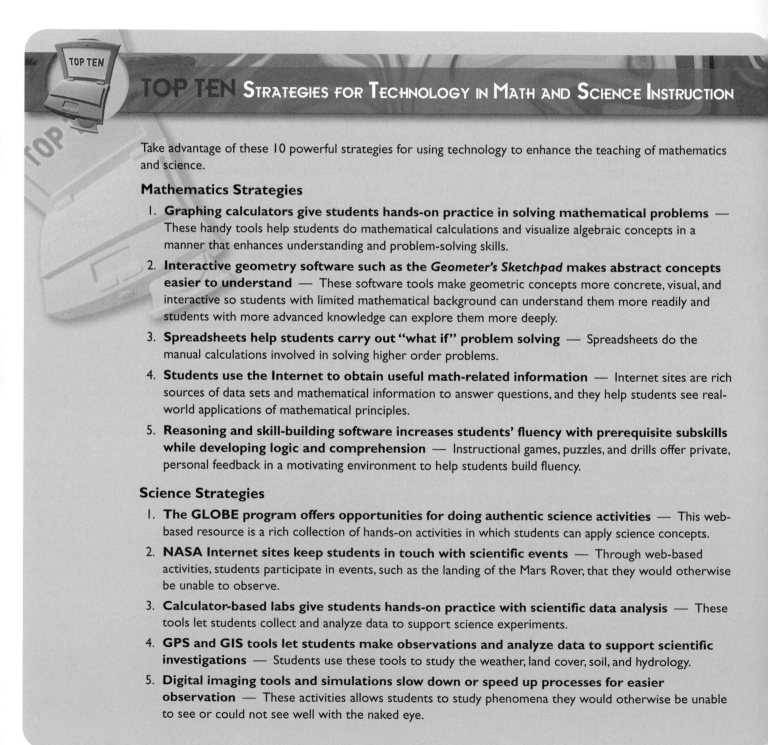

TOP TEN STRATEGIES FOR TECHNOLOGY IN MATH AND SCIENCE INSTRUCTION

Take advantage of these 10 powerful strategies for using technology to enhance the teaching of mathematics and science.

Mathematics Strategies

1. **Graphing calculators give students hands-on practice in solving mathematical problems** — These handy tools help students do mathematical calculations and visualize algebraic concepts in a manner that enhances understanding and problem-solving skills.

2. **Interactive geometry software such as the *Geometer's Sketchpad* makes abstract concepts easier to understand** — These software tools make geometric concepts more concrete, visual, and interactive so students with limited mathematical background can understand them more readily and students with more advanced knowledge can explore them more deeply.

3. **Spreadsheets help students carry out "what if" problem solving** — Spreadsheets do the manual calculations involved in solving higher order problems.

4. **Students use the Internet to obtain useful math-related information** — Internet sites are rich sources of data sets and mathematical information to answer questions, and they help students see real-world applications of mathematical principles.

5. **Reasoning and skill-building software increases students' fluency with prerequisite subskills while developing logic and comprehension** — Instructional games, puzzles, and drills offer private, personal feedback in a motivating environment to help students build fluency.

Science Strategies

1. **The GLOBE program offers opportunities for doing authentic science activities** — This web-based resource is a rich collection of hands-on activities in which students can apply science concepts.

2. **NASA Internet sites keep students in touch with scientific events** — Through web-based activities, students participate in events, such as the landing of the Mars Rover, that they would otherwise be unable to observe.

3. **Calculator-based labs give students hands-on practice with scientific data analysis** — These tools let students collect and analyze data to support science experiments.

4. **GPS and GIS tools let students make observations and analyze data to support scientific investigations** — Students use these tools to study the weather, land cover, soil, and hydrology.

5. **Digital imaging tools and simulations slow down or speed up processes for easier observation** — These activities allows students to study phenomena they would otherwise be unable to see or could not see well with the naked eye.

ISSUES AND PROBLEMS IN MATHEMATICS INSTRUCTION

Accountability for Standards in Mathematics

The *Principles and Standards for School Mathematics,* released in 2000 by the National Council of Teachers of Mathematics (NCTM), serves as a primary resource and guide for all who make decisions that affect the mathematics education of students in pre-kindergarten through grade 12. Through this document, mathematics educators describe a vision of mathematics teaching and learning. Achieving this vision requires "solid mathematics curriculum, competent and knowledgeable teachers who can integrate instruction with assessment, education policies that enhance and support learning, classrooms with ready access to technology, and a commitment to both equity and excellence" (NCTM, 2000, p. 3). The *Principles and Standards* document calls for a common foundation of mathematics to be learned by all students. Six principles address crucial issues fundamental to all school mathematics programs:

- Equity
- Curriculum
- Teaching
- Learning
- Assessment
- Technology.

In the technology principle, NCTM stresses that "technology is essential in teaching and learning mathematics" and "it influences the mathematics that is taught and enhances students' learning" (NCTM, 2000, p. 24). "In the mathematics classroom envisioned in *Principles and Standards,* every student has access to technology to facilitate his or her mathematics learning under the guidance of a skillful teacher" (NCTM, 2000, p. 25).

There are 10 mathematics standards for pre-kindergarten through grade 12:

Content Standards
- Number and Operations
- Algebra
- Geometry
- Measurement
- Data Analysis and Probability.

Process Standards
- Problem Solving
- Reasoning and Proof
- Communication
- Connections
- Representations.

Through these principles and standards, NCTM provides guidance on how to prepare students for a society that requires mathematical knowledge for filling crucial economic, political, and scientific roles in a highly technological workplace.

Challenges in Implementing the *Principles and Standards for School Mathematics*

Helping teachers change their teaching styles to meet the vision described in the NCTM standards is not an easy task. The standards seek a fundamental shift in the way most teachers work (Burrill, 1997). Technology can serve as a catalyst to move teachers toward an instructional style that is more student centered, active, and relevant to the world we now live in. Technology also provides learners with the opportunity to visualize and make more concrete the generally abstract world of mathematics.

Research points to three implications for the selection and use of technology related to mathematics education. First, teachers should consider an appropriate combination of off- and on-computer activities. Second, they should consider technology as a mathematical tool rather than as a pedagogical tool. Third, they should view technology as a tool for developing student thinking. One way to accomplish these goals is to use computer software and applications that can be extended for long periods of time across topics to engage students in meaningful problems and projects, rather than provide a variety of applications with no internal coherence (Clements, 1998).

In "Great Expectations: Leveraging America's Investment in Educational Technology," researchers at the Benton Foundation concluded that after more than two decades of research on the benefits of technology, mounting evidence exists to document the positive influence of technology on student achievement in mathematics (Benton Foundation Communications Policy Program, 2002). The researchers concluded that mathematics software, particularly programs that promote experimentation and problem solving, enables students to embrace key mathematical concepts that are otherwise difficult to grasp. This research-based evidence has also been described more metaphorically by mathematics teacher Dan Kennedy (1995) in his article "Climbing the Tree of Mathematics" in which he articulates how technology provides his students with a means of achieving mathematical understanding previously unknown. Both through systematic research and common wisdom derived by accomplished teachers, ample evidence exists to

For Mathematics

Students with disabilities and students who are at risk often fail to achieve high levels of competency in math due to problems with completing accurate calculations. This may involve procedural knowledge about what steps to complete in what sequence, as well as lack of fluency in manipulating numbers during a calculation. An obvious (albeit controversial) solution is to teach them how to use a calculator. A vast number of online calculators are available:

- Calculator: http://www.calculator.com/
- Online Converters: http://onlineconverters.com/
- Martindale's Calculators On-line Center: http://www.martindalecenter.com/ Calculators.html.

A different tactic is to combine an online calculation tool with instructional support. WebMath (http://www.webmath.com) provides how-to help and calculating support for students struggling with all levels of math by providing step-by-step guidance on how to complete a specific problem.

For Science

Students with disabilities often struggle in science due to an inability to manipulate the science lab equipment or because they are unable to read the textbook. Recent technology advances can address both concerns.

The Intel Play QX3 Computer Microscope (http://www.intelplay.com) is a powerful microscope that attaches to the computer so that students can view the images on the microscope slide via the computer or a projection system. For students unable to access the lenses of a microscope, this tool provides an opportunity for students and teachers to point to a specific part of the image to ensure that all students are observing the same phenomena.

BrainPop (http://www.brainpop.com) provides instruction in a multimedia format that is very helpful for students who are unable to read the textbook. Students select science from a menu of curriculum areas and see a vast array of science instructional topics. After selecting a particular topic, for example, electricity, BrainPop offers streaming video, lab activities, and resources to engage students in the topic and provide fundamental information and skills.

Contributed by Dave Edyburn

---

support strategies for integrating technology into the teaching and learning of mathematics to increase student understanding and achievement.

TECHNOLOGY INTEGRATION STRATEGIES FOR MATHEMATICS INSTRUCTION

Technology resources have made possible a variety of teaching and learning strategies to help address the *Principles and Standards for School Mathematics*. These include using virtual manipulatives, fostering mathematical problem solving, allowing representation of mathematical principles, implementing data-driven curriculum, supporting math-related communications, and motivating skill building and practice. Figure 11.1 summarizes these strategies and gives examples of some of the technology resources that make them possible.

Using Virtual Manipulatives

Computer software can play an important role in the way students perceive mathematics. At the elementary level, teachers can display models for numbers and operations on the computer screen so that students can derive and construct their own meaning for mathematical concepts. At higher levels, they can use software models to make abstract concepts more concrete. Both of these strategies are called **virtual manipulatives** because students use them

Figure 11.1   Summary of Technology Integration Strategies for Mathematics

Technology Integration Strategies	Benefits	Sample Resources and Activities
Using virtual manipulatives Copyright 1999–2005 Utah State University. All rights reserved. Reproduced with permission. http://matti.usu.edu/nlvm/nav/vlibrary.html	• Supports hands-on activities for learning mathematics. • Offers flexible environments for exploring complex concepts. • Provides a concrete representation of abstract concepts.	• **National Library of Virtual Manipulatives for Interactive Mathematics at Utah State University** http://matti.usu.edu/nlvm/index.html • **National Library of Virtual Manipulatives at the Shodor Foundation website** http://www.shodor.org • **Manipula Math with Java** http://www.ies.co.jp/math/java/index.html • **Mathematics, Science, and Technology Education at UIUC** http://www.mste.uiuc.edu/java/default.php
Fostering mathematical problem solving Reproduced with permission. © 2006 Texas Instruments. http://education.ti.com/us/product/tech/datacollection/features/features.html	• Helps students gather data to use in problem solving. • Provides rich, motivating problem-solving environments. • Gives students opportunities to apply mathematical knowledge and skills in meaningful contexts.	• CBLs • Software (e.g., Riverdeep's *Zoombinis, Thinkin' Things*) • Programming languages **Also see Technology Integration Idea 11.1:** What If? Problem Solving with Spreadsheets
Allowing representation of mathematical principles KaleidoMania, Key Curriculum Press, 1150 65th Street, Emeryville, CA 94608; 1-800-995-MATH, www.keypress.com. http://www.keypress.com/catalog/products/software/Prod_KaleidoMania.html	• Makes abstract mathematical concepts more visual and easier to understand. • Gives students environments in which to make discoveries and conjectures related to geometry concepts and objects.	• Graphing calculators • Software (e.g., *Geometers Sketchpad, KaleidoMania*) • Spreadsheets **Also see Technology Integration Idea 11.2:** Studying Graphs and Functions
Implementing data-driven curriculum Fathom, Key Curriculum Press, 1150 65th Street, Emeryville, CA 94608; 1-800-995-MATH, www.keypress.com. http://www.keypress.com/catalog/products/software/Prod_Fathom.html	• Provides easy access to many data sets. • Provides real statistics to support investigations that are timely and relevant. • Supports development of student knowledge and skill related to data analysis. • Allows for exploration and presentation of data in a graphical form.	• Software (e.g., *Fathom, Tabletop, Tabletop Jr.*) • U.S. Census http://www.census.gov/ • Spreadsheets • Statistical software (e.g., StatCrunch, http://www.statcrunch.com/) **Also see Technology Integration Idea 11.3:** Measuring Up

(continued)

Figure 11.1 (continued)

Technology Integration Strategies	Benefits	Sample Resources and Activities
Supporting math-related communications 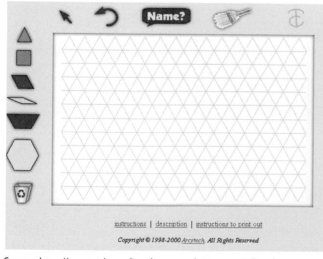 	• Allows easy contacts with experts. • Promotes social interaction and discourse about mathematics. • Allows teachers to reach other teachers for the exchange of ideas.	• Math Forum—Dr. Math http://mathforum.org/dr.math/ • Math Forum—Problem of the Week http://mathforum.org/pow/ • Math Forum—Public Discussions http://mathforum.org/discussions/ • ON-Math, the Online Journal of School Mathematics http://www.nctm.org/onmath **Also see Technology Integration Idea 11.4:** Taking Shape—Linking Geometry and Technology
Motivating skill building and practice PLATO L E A R N I N G 	• Provides motivating practice in foundation skills needed for higher order learning. • Provides guided instruction within a structured learning environment. • Delivers instruction when teacher may not be available.	• **Boxer Math** http://www.boxermath.com • **PLATO Learning** http://www.plato.com • **Waterford Early Science and Math** http://www.pearsondigital.com

Figure 11.2 Sample Virtual Manipulatives

to do simulated activities they used to do with real objects (Moyer, Bolyard, & Spikell, 2002). These simulated activities offer more flexibility than actual objects in the way teachers can use them to illustrate concepts.

Mankus (2000) describes and provides several examples of how online interactive manipulatives can be used to develop understanding. Utah State University maintains a library of virtual manipulatives for all grade levels that are tied to each of the standards' content strands. Figure 11.2

is an example of a virtual manipulative. For other examples, see the websites listed in Figure 11.1.

Fostering Mathematical Problem Solving

NCTM defines problem solving as ". . . engaging in a task for which the solution method is not known in advance. In order to find a solution, students must draw on their knowledge, and through this process, they will often develop new mathematical understandings. Solving problems is not only a goal of learning mathematics but also a major means of doing so" (NCTM, 2000). Regardless of how many mathematical facts, skills, or procedures students learn, the true value of mathematics is realized only when students can apply their knowledge to solve problems. Technology, by its definition, is a tool for solving problems. To prepare mathematically powerful citizens for the future, learning to solve problems using mathematics and appropriate technological tools is essential to education at all levels.

As students acquire number sense, they can begin to make generalizations that lead them to concepts in algebra. Technology tools provide students with a variety of means for exploring the critical concept of functions. Through graphing calculators and computer algebra systems, students can graph functions accurately, explore mathematical models of real-life phenomena, and explore symbolic representations and patterns. Calculator-based labs (a.k.a. probeware) provide a means to link either calculators or computers to scientific data–gathering instruments such as thermometers

MAKING THE CASE FOR TECHNOLOGY INTEGRATION

CW Discuss these issues online with other students by selecting the *Making the Case* module for Chapter 11 of the Companion Website (http://www.prenhall.com/roblyer) or choose the *Message Board* module.

1. The Mathematical Sciences Education Board offers a view on reforming mathematics instruction: "The national call for the reform in mathematics teaching and learning can seem overwhelming, because it requires a complete redesign of the content of school mathematics and the way it is taught. The basis for reform is the widespread belief that the United States must restructure the mathematics curriculum.... Simply producing new texts and retraining teachers will not be sufficient to address the major changes being recommended."

   How might various technologies and technology-based methods be able to shape and support a restructured mathematics curriculum?

2. Cavanagh's (2004) article "NCLB Could Alter Science Teaching" presents contrasting beliefs about effective science instruction:

Quote #1: "Advocates of discovery learning say direct instruction can easily regress into lecture-style teaching, heavy on rote recitation of scientific facts and memorization. 'It's cheaper, faster, and not as effective,' contended Wayne Carley, the executive director of the National Association of Biology Teachers, in Reston, Va. 'If you want kids to memorize a bunch of facts, it's a great way to learn … (however) science is not just a set of facts, but a process for discovering more facts.'" (p. 12).

Quote #2: "Directors of the Baltimore Curriculum Project, a nonprofit program that works with three schools serving both elementary and middle school students in that city, have been using direct instruction for the past six years in subjects from reading and language arts to mathematics. Leaders of the project, which largely serves students from low-income families and has seen an improvement in test scores among its participants in recent years, plan to use direct instruction in science over the next few years…" (p. 12).

Why do these groups have such different beliefs about effective science instruction? How might technology be able to merge these seemingly disparate methodologies?

Figure 11.3 Data Gathering and Analysis Devices: (a) Graphing Calculator, (b) CBL, and (c) ImagiProbe Sensor Interface System with PalmOne Handheld Computer

(a)

(b)   (c)

Sources: (a, b) Reprinted with permission. © 2006 Texas Instruments; http://education.ti.com. (c) Reprinted with permission of Pasco Scientific; http://www.imagiworks.com.

or pH meters, which allows students to gather data and then analyze it. Probes are also available for Palm-powered handheld devices (http://www.imagiworks.com). A selection of these data-gathering devices is shown in Figure 11.3.

As Technology Integration Idea 11.1 shows, spreadsheets can be a powerful means of supporting problem-solving exercises. Computer programming can help develop problem-solving abilities by allowing students to analyze and de-compose a problem and use systematic trial and error to find solutions. A modern (and free) language such as *Python* (Van Rossum, 2001) can provide students with a means of learning to write computer code for the purpose of solving problems.

Mathematical problem solving does not have to resemble work. To many learners, young and old, it can actually be a form of recreation. Software resources have been developed to create problem-solving environments that require the exercise of mathematical ideas in a context that resembles a game or puzzle. Riverdeep's *Zoombinis Logical Journey* for young learners is made up of numerous puzzles in a colorful and engaging environment that allow students to use logic, data

FOSTERING MATHEMATICAL PROBLEM SOLVING

Title: What If? Problem Solving with Spreadsheets

Content Area/Topic: Algebra

Grade Levels: 6–9

NETS for Students: Standards 3, 5, 6

Description: Students tend to solve math word problems by using an intuitive "guess and check" strategy. Spreadsheets are a natural tool to support this strategy because they allow students to find patterns, guess and check, and set up tables. Spreadsheet-based strategies are illustrated for several different kinds of algebra word problems, including "How many coins of each kind in a given total?" and "What is the temperature when Celsius and degrees Fahrenheit are equal?"

Source: Feicht, L. (2000). Guess and check: A viable problem solving strategy. *Learning and Leading with Technology,* 27(5), 50–54.

Figure 11.4 *Thinkin' Things* and *Zoombinis* **Problem-Solving Software**

Source: Courtesy of Riverdeep Interactive Learning Limited and its Licensors. All rights reserved. http://www.riverdeep.com.

analysis, algebra, and graphing concepts as if they were playing a game. Similarly, software like the Riverdeep *Thinkin' Things* series integrates mathematics and science into an entertaining problem-solving environment. (See Figure 11.4.) Different titles in the series focus on young (preK–3), elementary (grades 2–5), and middle (grades 3–8) learners.

Allowing Representation of Mathematical Principles

Mathematics is an abstract subject. Our understanding of mathematical ideas and concepts is closely tied to how we represent the abstractions of mathematics. To some, the concept of "five" is literally five objects (apples, pennies, etc.); to others, it is the numeral 5; to the ancient Romans it was represented by the numeral V. Technology has greatly enriched the way the abstractions of mathematics can be represented, and today students must learn mathematics using several

representations: symbolic (with numerals, variables, equations, etc.), verbal (with words such as "What percent increase is needed to reach $32,000?"), graphical (using two- or three-dimensional graphs), or numerical (using tables of numbers or spreadsheets). For each of these representations, technology resources have been developed to allow learners to explore mathematics within that representation and to explore the interaction among representations.

Research has shown that the use of graphing calculators can improve students' understanding of functions and graphs as well as the interconnections among the symbolic, graphical, and numerical representations of problems (Dunham & Dick, 1994). Without technology, it is difficult, if not impossible, to have students move from the symbolic realm of $f(x) = x^2 - 3$ to the equivalent graphical rendering shown in Figure 11.5a to the numerical representation in Figure 11.5b that resembles a spreadsheet.

In addition to calculators, many computer-based programs such as *Green Globs* (Sunburst), *Derive* (TI), and *TI Interactive* provide learning environments across three different mathematical realms. **Interactive or dynamic geometry software** provides students with an environment in which to make discoveries and conjectures related to geometry concepts and objects. Here abstract ideas can be played out on a computer screen, making concepts more real and providing a doorway into mathematical reasoning and proof. As Renne (2000) illustrates, Internet resources also can help students make connections between abstract geometry and real objects in the world around them. (See Technology Integration Idea 11.2.)

Instead of memorizing geometric facts or concepts, students can explore and arrive at conclusions on their

TECHNOLOGY INTEGRATION IDEA 11.2

ALLOWING REPRESENTATION OF MATH PRINCIPLES

Title: Studying Graphs and Functions

Content Area/Topic: Algebra graphs and functions

Grade Levels: 7–11

NETS for Students: Standards 3, 5, 6

Description: In this activity, students use spreadsheets and graphing calculators to graph the pattern in a scenario that describes a morning run taken by a boy named Julio. After each student presents a spreadsheet-generated graph of Julio's run, small groups work together to decide which graph is the best representation of the data in the scenario. This leads to a class investigation on two topics: the best fit function for the data and the families of curves and the effects of parameters on the behavior of the defined function. They use graphing calculators to do these investigations, discussing questions such as "Can a linear function, a quadratic function, a third-degree polynominal, or an equation in exponential form describe the data adequately and accurately?" The activity can be extended by doing the same investigation of other scenarios.

Source: Manoucherhri, A., & Pagnucco, L. (1999–2000). Julio's run: Studying graphs and functions. *Learning and Leading with Technology, 27*(4), 42–45.

Figure 11.5 **(a) Graphical Representation and (b) Table or Numerical Representation of Mathematics Principle** $f(x) = x^2 - 3$

(a)

(b)

Source: Courtesy of Ed Dickey.

own. For instance, using a program like the *Geometer's Sketchpad* (Key Curriculum), students can construct and measure the interior angles of a polygon (see Figure 11.6) and determine the formula that relates the measure of the angle to the number of sides.

Software capable of depicting solid or three-dimensional objects on a screen provides learners with a way to visualize objects that are difficult to imagine. Understanding the nature and properties of transformations and symmetry has become increasingly important and can be found in nearly all state mathematics standards. Again, software packages can facilitate learning and instruct students in this area. Websites are available that teach symmetry (Dorsey et al., 2001) and software such as *KaleidoMania!* (Key Curriculum), shown in Figure 11.7, goes further into the process of using symmetry and geometric transformations to create artistic objects.

Figure 11.6 **Example of a *Geometer's Sketchpad* Activity**

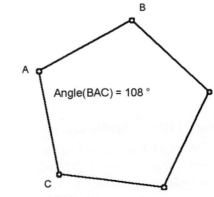

Source: Courtesy of Ed Dickey.

Figure 11.7 **Illustrating Transformations and Symmetry with *KaleidoMania!***

Source: Courtesy of Key Curriculum Press, 1150 65th Street, Emeryville, CA 94608; 1-800-995-MATH, www.keypress.com.

Figure 11.8 *Fathom:* **An Example Data Source for Mathematical Problem Solving**

Source: Courtesy of Key Curriculum Press, 1150 65th Street, Emeryville, CA 94608; 1-800-995-MATH, www.keypress.com.

Figure 11.9 **Spreadsheet for Solving "What If" Problems**

\multicolumn{8}{c	}{What's in the Bag?}
NAME	RED	YELLOW	GREEN	ORANGE	BROWN	BLUE	TOTAL
Tisha	8	13	7	9	15	1	53
Suzie	7	17	5	7	16	3	55
Ming	11	19	3	7	12	4	56
Juan	9	11	8	5	17	7	57
Tod	12	10	8	4	17	4	55
SAMPLE SIZE	5						
CLASS TOTALS	52	70	31	32	77	19	276
MEAN	9.4	14	6.2	6.4	15.4	3.8	55.2
MEDIAN	9	13	7	7	16	4	55
MODE	NONE	NONE	8	7	17	4	55
PERCENTS	18.8%	25.4%	11.2%	11.6%	27.9%	6.9%	

Source: Used by permission from Drier, H. (2001, January 4). Collecting and numerically analyzing M&M's data. Available online: http://curry.edschool.virginia.edu/teacherlink/math/activities/excel/M&Mnumerical/home.htm.

Implementing Data-Driven Curriculum

U.S. students scored well in the area of data analysis on the Third International Mathematics Science Study (Beaton et al., 1997–1998). The importance of statistical inference and probability has already had an impact in U.S. schools. Technology provides an ideal means of developing student knowledge and skill related to data analysis. *Fathom* (Key Curriculum), an example of which is shown in Figure 11.8, is a comprehensive package designed for schools to analyze and represent statistical data in a wide range of forms.

Data resources from the Internet also provide students with realistic statistics and the opportunity to conduct investigations that are timely and relevant. Examples 5.4 and 5.5 from the NCTM *Principles and Standards for School Mathematics* website illustrate how data collection and representation might occur (NCTM, 2001). Dixon and Falba (1997) also describe activities for producing graphs using Internet data.

Computer spreadsheets also provide environments in which children can explore number concepts, operations, and patterns with data they obtain from various sources. (See Technology Integration Idea 11.3.) Students can work with the basic operations, explore "what if" type problems, and build a foundation for algebraic thinking. Activities such as planning a fund-raising activity (Zisow, 2001) or analyzing M&M's data (Drier, 2001) provide teachers with an important software tool to help build students' number sense. (See Figure 11.9.)

Supporting Math-Related Communications

The Internet offers students the opportunity to communicate with each other or even with experts in different fields. Expressing ideas in written form is essential; therefore, students must convert their mathematical thinking

Using calculators in small-group settings also promotes social interaction and discourse.

TECHNOLOGY INTEGRATION IDEA 11.3

IMPLEMENTING DATA-DRIVEN CURRICULUM

Title: Measuring Up

Content Area/Topic: Measurement: ratios and proportions

Grade Levels: 7–10

NETS for Students: Standards 3, 5, 6

Description: Students create a spreadsheet to calculate ratios and proportions, using the measurements of students in the class as a database. They begin by taking measurements of each student in the class and entering these data into a spreadsheet. They use their own data and compare it to Leonardo da Vinci's calculations based on his 1492 drawing "The Proportions of the Human Figure" to predict "the perfect numbers." After they compare their results, they discuss their conclusions about da Vinci's hypothesized "perfect proportions."

	A	B	C	D	E	F	G
1				Body Proportions Spreadsheet			
2							
3	Student	Sex	Total Height	Height to Belly Button	Arm Span	Ratio of Belly Button Height to Total Height	Ratio of Arm Span to Total Height
4	Suzy Q.	F	64	38.25	63.5	=D4/C4	=E4/C4
5	Martha P.	F	70	42.75	72	=D5/C5	=E5/C5
6	John B.	M	72	48	72	=D6/C6	=E6/C6
7	Sam S.	M	60	35.5	63	=D7/C7	=E7/C7
8							
9	Class Average		=AVERAGE(C4..C7)	=AVERAGE(D4..D7)	=AVERAGE(E4..E7)	=AVERAGE(F4..F7)	=AVERAGE(G4..G7)
10	Male Average		=AVERAGE(C6..C7)	=AVERAGE(D6..D7)	=AVERAGE(E6..E7)	=AVERAGE(F6..F7)	=AVERAGE(G6..G7)
11	Female Average		=AVERAGE(C4..C5)	=AVERAGE(D4..D5)	=AVERAGE(E4..E5)	=AVERAGE(F4..F5)	=AVERAGE(G4..G5)

Source: Morgan, B., & Jernigan, J. (1998–1999). A technology update: Leonardo da Vinci and the search for the perfect body. *Learning and Leading with Technology, 26*(4), 22–25.

into words. Projects such as the Math Forum's different *Problems of the Week* (http://mathforum.org/pow/) allow teachers to pose problems that their students must solve and then communicate the solution. (See Figure 11.10.) *Ask Dr. Math* (also from the Math Forum at http://mathforum.org/dr.math/) provides contacts with experts who can answer questions.

As Technology Integration Idea 11.4 shows, student-created websites can be a valuable form of communication for student projects. Using computers and calculators in small-group settings also promotes social interaction and discourse. Teachers often find that grouping students in pairs greatly enhances learning, augmenting communication from teacher-to-student or computer-to-student to a richer student-to-student-to-computer type of communication.

Figure 11.10   Math Forum Problems of the Week

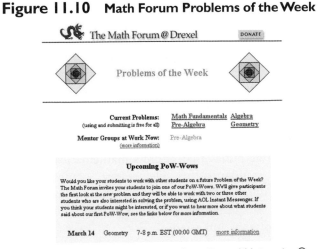

Source: Reproduced with permission from Drexel University,© 2006 by the Math Forum @ Drexel. All rights reserved.

TECHNOLOGY INTEGRATION IDEA 11.4

SUPPORTING MATH-RELATED COMMUNICATIONS

Title: Taking Shape—Linking Geometry and Technology

Content Area/Topic: Geometry

Grade Levels: 3–5

NETS for Students: Standards 3, 4, 5, 6

Description: Teachers often help students understand geometry concepts by having them make lists and draw items with various shapes in the world around them, for example, basketball hoops for circles and monkey bars for rectangles. This activity expands on that strategy. Students bring in pictures of objects with various geometrical shapes and scan them into files to create a *Geometry in the World* virtual book. By reviewing all of the pictures as a whole class, they create categories to account for all of the pictures: cones, angles, horizontals and verticals, multiple shapes, and circles. Each category becomes a chapter for the book. Students work in small groups to do a web page for their chapter. They end with a class presentation of the whole site and a discussion of the geometry concepts they learned.

Source: Renne, C. (2000). Taking shape: Linking geometry and technology. *Learning and Leading with Technology, 27*(7), 58–62.

Motivating Skill Building and Practice

Although the current emphasis is on learning higher order mathematics skills, students often need more resources to support practice of basic skills. These skills provide an important foundation on which they can build more advanced skills. Some technology resources that can support this practice include the following:

- *Boxer Math* (http://www.boxermath.com/) provides interactive and dynamic software addressing fundamental mathematics (grades K–3) as well as high school level concepts in algebra, geometry, trigonometry, and other areas.

- The Plato Learning Company (http://www.plato.com) has been developing tutorial and skill-building software for more than 40 years, making it one of the longest standing companies in the computer industry. Courseware is available at all levels, from early childhood to adult, and across numerous content areas. Its mathematics titles address fundamental skills as well as problem solving and explorations.

- Waterford *Early Math and Science* software (http://www.pearsondigital.com) includes daily instructional activities that address mathematics and science standards for elementary grades. These curriculum materials foster exploration and inquiry while providing a foundation in basic skills, problem solving, and science.

Figure 11.11 (p. 337) lists some useful websites for mathematics instruction.

ISSUES AND PROBLEMS IN SCIENCE INSTRUCTION

Several needs and problems specific to the teaching of science topics help shape the uses of technology in this area. These issues include meeting science standards, a "narrowing pipeline" of scientific talent, the increasing need for scientific literacy, difficulties in teaching K–8 science, and a new emphasis on teaching scientific inquiry.

Accountability for Standards in Science

In 1989 the American Association for the Advancement of Science published *Science for All Americans.* This document set out recommendations for what all students should know and be able to do in science, mathematics, and technology by the time they graduate from high school. In 1993, *Benchmarks for Science Literacy* was published. This document translated the science literacy goals in *Science for All Americans* into learning goals or benchmarks for students in grades K–12. The *National Science Education Standards* (NSES) were released in 1995 by the National Research Council. These standards define the content that all students should know and be able to do and provide guidelines for assessing student learning in science. The NSES provide guidance for science teaching strategies, science teacher professional development, and support necessary to deliver high-quality science education. The NSES also describe the policies to bring coordination, consistency, and coherence to science education programs. Many of the state standards documents have drawn their content from the *Benchmarks* and/or the *National Science Education Standards.*

Figure 11.11 Recommended Websites for Mathematics Instruction

- **National Council of Teachers of Mathematics** (http://www.nctm.org)—Home page of the professional organization that developed the first curriculum standards. Offers a wide range of resources including journals, conferences, newsletters, and products, as well as an electronic version of the *Principles and Standards* document (http://standards.nctm.org).

- **Math Forum** (http://mathforum.org/)—Resources for students, teachers, and anyone interested in mathematics education. Among the best: Ask Dr. Math (to answer questions), Problems of the Week (challenges at all levels and math subjects), and Discussion Groups (virtual communities interested in math).

- **Texas Instruments Resources for Educators** (http://education.ti.com/educationportal/)—As one would expect, this site includes numerous resources for using calculators and computers in the classroom. It also includes ideas for parents to help their children develop an interest in and comfort with mathematics.

- **MathWorld** (http://mathworld.wolfram.com/)—Billed as the "web's most extensive mathematics resource," MathWorld is a comprehensive, interactive encyclopedia of mathematics. Definitions, diagrams, and explanations of mathematics ideas, concepts, and terms are all explained in detail and with illustrations.

- **History of Mathematics** (http://www-groups.dcs.st-and.ac.uk:80/~history/)—Biographies, historical topics, even "famous curves" can be found at this comprehensive collection, illustrating how mathematics has developed as a human endeavor.

- **PBS Mathline** (http://www.pbs.org/teachersource/math.htm)—High-quality lessons, activities, and professional development for teachers addressing mathematics concepts and connections.

The Narrowing Pipeline of Scientific Talent

There is growing concern about America's ability to compete in science, mathematics, and technology in the future. With the declining number of students—especially females and minorities pursuing studies in math, science, and engineering fields—America faces a growing crisis in leadership for much-needed science/technology/mathematics/engineering initiatives. This trend could have serious consequences for the long-term economic and national security outlook of our country. (See *Fueling the Pipeline: Attracting and Educating Math and Science Students* [EMC Corporation, 2003].)

Increasing Need for Scientific Literacy

As the science benchmarks and standards reflect, there is a need for all citizens to be scientifically literate in order to make informed decisions that affect our country's future. More than ever before, America's economic and environmental progress depends on the character and quality of the science education that the nation's schools provide.

Difficulties Teaching K–8 Science

In a study conducted by the Educational Testing Service, Gitomer, Latham, and Ziomek (1999) compared SAT scores for teacher candidates passing the Praxis II exam with the average score for all college graduates. The researchers concluded that elementary education candidates have much lower math and verbal scores than other college graduates. Part of this problem may stem from the minimal content preparation in mathematics and science. As a result, teaching science for understanding becomes difficult due to the lack of a deep understanding of the discipline on the part of the teacher. One way to assist teachers in science is through increased professional development. The Eisenhower National Clearinghouse offers a guide to improving professional development in the areas of math, science, and technology. The site, entitled "By Your Own Design," is at http://www.enc.org/professional/guide/?ls=ho.

New Emphasis on and Controversies About Scientific Inquiry

As many educators place increasing emphasis on hands-on science skills, as opposed to rote learning of concepts, technology can play a special role in improving classroom practice in teaching **scientific inquiry,** or the processes of approaching problems scientifically. Describing this trend, Rubin (undated) says, "When learning with technology focuses on doing inquiry-based learning, the following approaches are commonly adopted in classrooms:

- Technology is viewed as a tool, much like a pencil or pen, but considerably more powerful.

- Use of the technology is primarily taught in the context of solving problems.

- Students help one another with the mechanics of the technology; in fact, in many classrooms, students are the local experts on technological details.

- Talk about and around technology is as important as the technology itself, just as talk about how one finds and uses information is as important as the information itself.

- Technology is used to augment communication by expanding audience (e.g., over networks and by producing hard copy) and expressive options (e.g., mixing graphs and words)."

This new emphasis is not without controversy. Cavanagh (2004) reports on a new study by the Carnegie

Figure 11.12   Summary of Technology Integration Strategies for Science

Technology Integration Strategies	Benefits	Sample Resources and Activities
Supporting authentic science experiences © Exploratorium. Reprinted by permission. http://www.exploratorium.edu	• Provides resources needed for doing each phase of authentic science activities. • Some Internet projects provide environments that support all phases of an authentic science project.	• **The GLOBE Project** http://www.globe.gov • **NASA** http://www.nasa.gov • **Jason Project** http://www.jason.org/ • **Archimedes Laboratory** http://www.archimedes-lab.org/index_optical.html
Supporting scientific inquiry skills Moon Phases Courtesy of Christopher Dolan, Astronomy Department, University of Wisconsin. http://www.astro.wisc.edu	• Helps students locate and obtain information to support inquiry. • Makes data collection and analysis easier and more manageable. • Makes it easier to visualize and understand phenomena. • Supports communicating results of inquiry.	• **GIS Population Data** http://www.esri.com • **Journey North project** http://www.learner.org/jnorth/ • **RedRover Goes to Mars** http://planetary.org/rrgtm/ **Also see Technology Integration Idea 11.5:** Measuring with Precision versus Accuracy
Supporting science concept learning Courtesy of NOVA, University of Idaho, IMITS. http://nova.ed.uidaho.edu/library/inet_technology/java_applets.asp	• Allows simulating and modeling of scientific processes. • Provides opportunities to engage in problem-solving activities.	• **Web-based Chemistry Simulations** http://cse.edc.org/products/simulations/default.asp • **University of Idaho Visuals** http://nova.ed.uidaho.edu/library/inet_technology/java_applets.asp • **Drinking Water project** http://www.peacecorps.gov/wws/research/water/index.html **Also see Technology Integration Idea 11.6:** Digital Imaging on the (Butter)fly
Accessing science information and tools Exploring the Environment © 1997–2005 Wheeling Jesuit University/Classroom of the Future. All rights reserved. Used with permission. http://www.cotf.edu/ete/modules/modules.html	• Allows access to unique tools and collections of information. • Expands opportunities for learning.	• Information on space at NASA http://spacelink.nasa.gov • Information on weather at NOAA http://www.noaa.gov • NIH http://www.nih.gov • Information for science teachers at the Eisenhower National Clearinghouse http://www.enc.org • Exploring the Environment Curriculum http://www.cotf.edu/ete • National Academy Press http://www.nap.edu **Also see Technology Integration Idea 11.7:** Collecting Science in a Net

Mellon University and the University of Pittsburgh which found that students taught through direct instruction (rather than inquiry or discovery learning methods) were more likely on average to become "experts" in designing scientific experiments—an important step in the development of scientific-reasoning skills. Also, Cavanagh noted that "The students who showed expertise in designing those experiments through direct instruction performed just as well as those who developed similar expertise through discovery paths on a separate test of their broader scientific judgment—countering some previous claims that direct instruction produces weaknesses in that area" (p. 1). As a result of such studies, the National Science Teachers Association (NSTA) recommends a combination of direct and inquiry methods.

TECHNOLOGY INTEGRATION STRATEGIES FOR SCIENCE INSTRUCTION

Technology resources support many kinds of teaching and learning strategies to help address science standards. These strategies include supporting authentic science experiences, supporting scientific inquiry skills, supporting science concept learning, and accessing science information and tools. Figure 11.12 summarizes these strategies and gives examples of some of the technology resources that make them possible.

Supporting Authentic Science Experiences

Authentic science in the classroom is when students "do science" as a scientist would, not simply hear it discussed or see a demonstration. Authentic science is also referred to as *scientific inquiry*, the process of asking questions and investigating those questions by making hypotheses, collecting data, analyzing the data, and communicating the results, which are then peer reviewed. Scientists use a variety of technologies to create authentic science experiences. The GLOBE program is an excellent example of utilizing technologies to do authentic science. GLOBE is an environmental science program that utilizes remote sensing and ground-based observations to study the local environment. The program makes use of a number of technologies to conduct local investigations. Teachers and students can investigate the weather, land cover, soil, and hydrology. Students utilize Global Positioning Systems (GPS), Geographic Information Systems (GIS), and information technologies to collect and analyze data. Figure 11.13 is an example activity from the GLOBE program.

In this example, students take ground observations using traditional and state-of-the-art technology. They use temperature data-loggers, a GPS unit, and traditional technologies such as a weather shelter and a U-tube thermometer. Then they record their data in a notebook and enter the data into a database at the GLOBE site. They manipulate data with online graphing and visualization tools. The data can also be displayed in a graphical form,

Figure 11.13 Atmosphere Investigation in the GLOBE Environment

Source: From the GLOBE website (http://www.globe.gov).

allowing students to look for patterns over time. To complete the process, students write up their results and post them to the GLOBE Student Research website. In the write-up, students report on their research questions, discuss their procedures, communicate the results using graphs and charts, and make conclusions. Once posted on the website, the report is peer-reviewed by GLOBE participants. Additional information on this powerful learning environment can be found at http://www.globe.gov.

Supporting Scientific Inquiry Skills

The preceding section describes one example of authentic science using a combination of technologies. Teachers do not always have time to complete long-term investigations that encompass the entire scientific process. However, technology can be used to teach specific elements of the scientific inquiry process, as discussed next.

Locating information to investigate scientific issues and questions. The Internet has become an indispensable tool for investigating important scientific questions. Science teachers and students have access to a number of exciting resources for teaching and learning science. For many of the science areas, teachers and students can access information from good sources such as NASA (http://www.nasa.gov) or museums such as the Exploratorium (http://www.exploratorium.org).

The National Science Foundation (NSF) has funded the creation of digital libraries for science. The Digital Library for Earth Science Education (DLESE) is a wonderful resource for teachers and students. The DLESE is a community of educators, students, and scientists working to improve the teaching of and learning about the Earth system at all levels. DLESE provides access to a number of collections of educational and scientific resources. Digital libraries provide a starting point for the investigation of scientific questions.

TECHNOLOGY INTEGRATION IDEA 11.5

Collecting data. Data collection and archiving are important parts of the scientific inquiry process. Science bases its conclusions on data. A number of tools are available for data collection and archiving. The calculator or computer-based laboratory (CBL) is an ideal tool for middle school through high school science. CBL sensors collect data and the data can be downloaded into a computer or calculator, and then manipulated in a spreadsheet. By archiving data in a spreadsheet, the data can be used at another time or compiled for long-term investigations. Technology Integration Idea 11.5 provides an example of how probes can be used to gather data for an inquiry activity.

Visualizing data and phenomena. A number of visualization tools exist that allow students to see representations of data and phenomena that may be difficult to see directly. Computer simulations differ from illustrations and pictures in that students can manipulate elements in them. These include tools that help students visualize macroscopic phenomena, such as the phases of the moon, that are difficult to understand because they cannot be seen directly.

Visualization tools can also be used to examine microscopic or other phenomena that would otherwise be difficult or impossible to observe, for example, molecular structure or growth of plants or animals. Technology Integration Idea 11.6 illustrates how digital imaging can help students study butterfly metamorphosis.

Some tools make it possible to rotate and examine structures from multiple viewpoints to help students understand

them (see, e.g., http://www.reciprocalnet.org). Visualizations can be used in a variety of teaching situations. They can be used by teachers as a tool for lecture, a demonstration, or as a way to invite students to describe what they see, leading students to explain concepts for themselves. Visualizations can also be used as a remedial tool for tutorials. Visualizations are used in the workplace as well. Meteorologists regularly show computer-generated visualizations on television to help explain weather phenomena. City planners use GIS to plot population growth (see, e.g., http://www.esri.com).

Analyzing data. Analyzing data can be done with a number of existing programs that come standard on computers. Spreadsheets allow data to be entered and analyzed using simple statistics or algorithms supplied by the students. In the GLOBE program, *MultiSpec* software provides students with the ability to identify land cover types on a LandSat image. GIS software allows students to analyze factors in an image by removing or adding attributes and looking for connections among attributes.

Communicating results. Once data are analyzed, scientists write up the results and submit them for publication using standard productivity software (e.g., word processing). Scientists collaborate on scientific problems, and the Internet facilitates the communication process. In addition to graphs and visualizations, scientists use images from digital cameras and other digital instruments to record data and compare and contrast over time. This is especially useful in land cover investigations and in astronomy.

SUPPORTING SCIENTIFIC INQUIRY SKILLS

Title: Digital Imaging on the (Butter)fly

Content Area/Topic: Biology

Grade Levels: 9–12

NETS for Students: Standards 3, 5, 6

Description: This lesson shows how digital imaging can support scientific inquiry by letting students do observations better than they could with the naked eye. To better understand the process of metamorphosis, the teacher shows students how to set up a digital camera to take time-lapse images. They focus the camera on the caterpillar as it is about to emerge and take the video. By speeding up the completed footage, students can see and discuss each phase of the process.

Source: Bowen, A., & Bell, R. (2004). Winging it: Using digital imaging to investigate butterfly metamorphosis. *Learning and Leading with Technology, 31*(6), 24–27.

Figure 11.14 **Colors Simulator Created by IMITS at the University of Idaho**

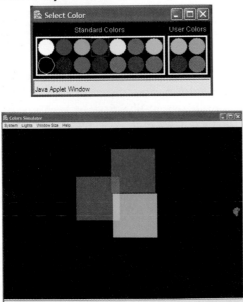

Source: Reprinted with permission from NOVA, University of Idaho, IMITS.

Figure 11.15 **Chemical Mixing Simulations**

Source: Images © Murray Roberston 1999–2004. Reproduced by permission of The Royal Society of Chemistry.

The Internet also provides a medium for communication among scientists. Data can be e-mailed to researchers around the globe. Classroom teachers can also have scientists interact in their classroom by participating in webcasts. NASA regularly has webcasts in which schools can participate.

Supporting Science Concept Learning

Technology-based strategies that simulate and model scientific processes can help students develop the foundation knowledge and skills they need to engage in inquiry. Students often have difficulty understanding complex scientific concepts, especially when such concepts are only presented and explained in text as nonmoving static images. Simulations and animations can make these concepts clearer by showing how they work in action. These include animations where students can see and sometimes manipulate applets to learn a scientific concept. For example, mixing colored light is an elementary science activity that is often confusing to students. Utilizing the "color mixer" simulation tool shown in Figure 11.14, learners can use the RGB screen as a mechanism to clarify these abstract concepts.

Other simulations, like the one shown in Figure 11.15, allow students to mix chemicals and simulate the results, saving dollars and providing a safe environment for chemistry

TECHNOLOGY INTEGRATION IDEA 11.7

ACCESSING SCIENCE INFORMATION AND TOOLS

Title: Collecting Science in a Net

Content Area/Topic: Earth science

Grade Levels: 2–12

NETS for Students: Standards 3, 4, 5, 6

Description: This activity focuses on gathering data to investigate greenhouse gases in the atmosphere and global warming. Students use two Internet sites to obtain data on global temperatures and atmospheric concentrations of carbon dioxide and use the data to answer questions about these topics. Students plot monthly average carbon dioxide concentrations for a given year and observe patterns in increases and decreases. Then they graph the temperature data for a year and compare these data with the carbon dioxide data. They discuss possible links between the biosphere and atmosphere. Finally, they use the Internet to gather other information on global warming and discuss the current trends.

Source: Slattery, W., Hundley, S., Finegan-Stoll, C., & Becker, M. (1998). Collecting science in a net. *Learning and Leading with Technology, 26*(1), 25–30.

Figure 11.16 The Mars Rover Online

Source: Reprinted with permission from The Planetary Society (http://planetary.org/rrgtm/Rrsites.php).

and physical science study. Virtual dissections also allow students to examine anatomy without coming into contact with preservation chemicals. In physics, students can use simulations to conduct historical experiments.

Accessing Science Information and Tools

The Internet has opened up a world of opportunities for learning beyond the classroom. For example, students can control a Rover like the ones on Mars (see Figure 11.16) or operate a telescope or a camera from the space shuttle.

It is also an unlimited source of data for classroom experiments and investigations. (See Technology Integration Idea 11.7).

The Internet also is an invaluable resource for up-to-date science information. Science knowledge changes faster than most school libraries can keep up. Books are out of date the minute they are published. If you want the latest information on space, you can access NASA; the weather, NOAA; medicine, the NIH. Most of these sites provide content targeted for teachers and students. A number of curriculum projects are also available online to teachers and students. NASA's classroom of the future provides a free Exploring the Environment curriculum (http://www.cotf.edu/ete) that integrates science and social studies to examine current issues.

Teachers can also use the Internet for assistance with content knowledge and for professional development opportunities that may not be available locally. They can also exchange ideas and teaching strategies with other teachers. The Eisenhower National Clearinghouse (ENC) provides a comprehensive website to connect teachers with resources and training. The ENC provides a number of online publications containing the latest research on teaching and learning science. Teachers can also utilize the National Academy Press website (http://www.nap.edu) to examine the most current publications in science and science education available online for free. Figure 11.17 lists additional useful websites for science instruction.

Figure 11.17 Recommended Websites for Science Instruction

- **The National Science Teachers Association** (http://www.nsta.org)—This is the professional organization for science educators. See science education standards at http://www.nsta.org/standards.
- **The Eisenhower National Clearinghouse (ENC)** (http://www.enc.org)—This science organization provides many teaching resources and training opportunities.
- **NASA websites** (http://www.nasa.gov, http://dlcenter.larc.nasa.gov/, and http://edspace.nasa.gov/index.html)—These websites offer a wealth of space-related information, free teaching resources, and educational opportunities for kids and teachers.

INTERACTIVE SUMMARY

The following is a summary of the main points covered in this chapter. To see additional examples and information on these points, go to this textbook's Companion Website at http://www.prenhall.com/roblyer and click on the Chapter 11 *Interactive Summary* module to visit each of the recommended websites.

1. **Issues in mathematics instruction:** These include:
   - Accountability for Standards in Mathematics
   - Challenges in implementing the Principles and Standards for School Mathematics.

2. **Integration strategies for mathematics instruction:** Six strategies are described for integrating technology into this area:
   - Using virtual manipulatives (see examples)
   - Fostering mathematical problem solving (see Riverdeep products)
   - Allowing representation of mathematical principles (Geometer's Sketchpad)
   - Implementing data-driven curriculum (see *Fathom* example)
   - Supporting math-related communications
   - Motivating skill building and practice (see Dr. Math website)

3. **Issues in science instruction:** These include:
   - Accountability for standards in science
   - The narrowing pipeline of scientific talent
   - Increasing need for scientific literacy
   - Difficulties teaching K–8 science
   - New emphasis on and controversies about scientific inquiry.

4. **Integration strategies for science instruction:** Four strategies are described for integrating technology into this area:
   - Supporting authentic science experiences (see the GLOBE project)
   - Supporting scientific inquiry skills (see the Exploratorium)
   - Supporting science concept learning (see example simulations)
   - Accessing science information and tools.

Online Activities

Visit this text's Companion Website at http://www.prenhall.com/roblyer to gain access to a variety of questions, activities, and exercises to help build your knowledge of this chapter's content.

Online Chapter 11 Self-Test

To review terms and concepts for this chapter, click on the Self-Test module for this chapter of the Companion Website.

Software Skill-Builder Tutorials

To access practical tutorial and skill-building activities and to build skills using popular software and hardware, click on the Software Skill-Builder Tutorials module for this chapter of the Companion Website.

Web-Enrichment Activities

To complete activities that connect to chapter content and provide web-based resources, click on the Web-Enrichment Activities module for this chapter of the Companion Website.

TECHNOLOGY INTEGRATION WORKSHOP

CLIPS FROM THE CLASSROOM: LEARNING WITH TECHNOLOGY

Go to the *Technology Integration Workshop* DVD located in the back of this text and click on *Clips from the Classroom.* View the video clips listed below that support this chapter's content:

- *Laptops for Data in 5th Grade*
- Quizdom *System for Practice*
- *Challenger Center Provides Problem-Based Learning*
- Geometer's Sketchpad *for Inductive Reasoning*
- *Tablet Computers in Fourth-Grade Science*
- *Tablet Computers in First-Grade Mathematics*
- *E-Z Geometry Website Supports Student Work*
- *Graphing Calculators in Trigonometry.*

Now, visit this text's Companion Website at http://www.prenhall.com/roblyer to answer questions and complete activities that will guide you in analyzing each clip.

THE TIP MODEL IN ACTION

Read each of the following scenarios related to implementing the TIP Model, and go to the Companion Website to answer the questions that follow it based on your Chapter 11 reading and activities.

TIP Model Scenario #1 Ms. Waldrup, the AP mathematics teacher, wanted to have her students do simple correlations with two data sets to demonstrate the mathematical principles involved. However, it took students too long to do these calculations by hand and there were too many data entry errors using a calculator.

1.1 What technology-based strategy could Ms. Waldrup use to address this problem?

1.2 What would be the relative advantage of using this strategy?

1.3 Would it be better to carry out this strategy as a whole class or with students working individually or in groups? Explain how you would do it.

TIP Model Scenario #2 Mr. Brino was trying to show his teenage students in the business education program how they could figure out quickly how much car they could buy with the money they had. He wanted to show them the relationship among the down payment, interest rate, and length of the loan and how this all affected monthly payments and the total they would spend on the car at the end of the loan period. However, he wanted them to be able to do the calculations quickly, so they could focus on the underlying math concepts.

2.1 What technology-based strategy could Mr. Brino use to address this problem?

2.2 What would be the relative advantage of using this strategy?

2.3 Describe the steps you might use to carry out a simple lesson using this strategy.

TIP Model Scenario #3 Dr. Ahmed wanted his students to take readings at a local stream to do an experiment on acid and alkaline substances in water. He wanted to use the handheld probeware devices when they went on the field trip. With these devices, they could collect the data, bring the readings back in a data file, and download the file to the computer for analysis. However, he had 27 students and only 15 handhelds.

3.1 What grouping strategy could Dr. Ahmed use to make the available devices work well with this many students?

3.2 How you would advise Dr. Ahmed about his students carrying out the strategy?

3.3 What would be the relative advantage of using this strategy as opposed to manual methods of collecting the readings?

TIP Model Scenario #4 Ms. Lyndia was the school counselor in charge of helping students prepare for the test her school district had developed to select those students eligible for the special math/science magnet program, which offered all expenses paid to those who were selected. She knew a lot about the kinds of items that would be on the test, and she knew some of the students needed to practice some of the skills.

4.1 What technology-based strategy would you recommend Ms. Lyndia use to address this problem?

4.2 What would be the relative advantage of using this strategy, as opposed to a paper-and-pencil format?

4.3 Should students practice individually, in pairs, or in small groups? Explain.

TIP Model Scenario #5   Mr. Cardillo's ninth-grade students had a lot of problems understanding geometry concepts. They seemed to understand them better when he drew the figures and angles for them as he explained the concepts, but this was not feasible for every problem. It took too long, and he couldn't draw well enough to show everything clearly.

5.1 What technology-based strategy would you recommend Mr. Cardillo use to address this problem?

5.2 What would be the relative advantage of using this strategy?

5.3 If Mr. Cardillo has 32 students in his class and only one computer, what would you recommend he do to carry out this strategy most effectively?

TIE into Practice: Technology Integration Examples

The Technology Integration Example that opened this chapter (*Hot and Cold Data*) showed how a teacher might have students use CBLs and spreadsheet activities to carry out experiments. As each group completes its assigned experiment, it presents the results to the class by displaying the graphed data in a *PowerPoint* presentation. With the knowledge you have gained from Chapter 11, do the following to explore this strategy:

1. Create a spreadsheet graph like the example shown here. **Create this example graph** by clicking on the *Hands-On with Technology* tutorial section on the DVD that accompanies this text.

2. Answer the following questions about the *Hot and Cold Data* example:

   - Phase 1 — What kinds of relative advantage did the teachers feel the use of CBLs would bring to the learning activity? How would using spreadsheets help?

   - Phase 2 — Outcomes 2 and 4 are very similar statements. Why are they stated as separate outcomes? How would the assessment for them differ? How would it be similar?

Example Graph Created to Insert in *PowerPoint*. (Create this product using the *Hands-On with Technology* tutorial section of the DVD.)

- Phase 3 — Students may not be familiar with *Consumer Reports* and its approach to comparing products. If the teachers did not have access to the magazines themselves, what could they do to help students understand this approach?

- Phase 4 — What could the teachers do with the performance measures and lab sheets to make them more accessible to students both inside and outside class?

- Phase 5 — In evaluating the outcomes of the activity, the teachers found that all students showed competence with CBL procedures and were able to carry out the experiments with teacher assistance. However, some students still had difficulty with the final outcome. How might they change the implementation to help students better achieve this outcome?

3. What NETS for Students skills would students learn by working on the *Hot and Cold Data* project? (See the front of the book for a list of NETS for Students.)

TECHNOLOGY INTEGRATION LESSON PLANNING

The *Technology Integration Workshop* DVD includes a set of technology integration ideas and links to online lessons, arranged as a searchable database. The DVD comes packaged in the back of this textbook. Click on the *Hands-On with Technology* section of the DVD and complete the following exercises.

1. Locate lesson ideas — The DVD has several examples of lessons that use the mathematics and science integration strategies described in this chapter. Locate an example integration idea for at least two of these strategies for each content area.

2. Evaluate the lessons — Use the *Evaluation Checklist for a Technology-Integrated Lesson* (located on the DVD and the Companion Website) to evaluate each of these lessons.

3. Modify a lesson — Select one of the lesson ideas and adapt its strategies to meet a need in your own content area. You may choose to use the same approach in the original or adapt it to meet your needs.

4. Add descriptors — Create descriptors for your new lesson like those found on the database (e.g., grade level, content and topic areas, technologies used, relative advantage, objectives, NETS standards).

5. Add the new lesson — Add your modified lesson with all its descriptors to the lesson idea database.

FOR YOUR TEACHING PORTFOLIO

For this chapter's contribution to your teaching portfolio, add the following products you created in the Technology Integration Workshop:

- The sample graph and *PowerPoint* frame you created
- The evaluations you did using the *Evaluation Checklist for a Technology-Integrated Lesson*
- The new lesson plan you developed, based on the one you found on the DVD.

CHAPTER 12

TECHNOLOGY IN SOCIAL STUDIES INSTRUCTION

MICHAEL J. BERSON
UNIVERSITY OF SOUTH FLORIDA

M. D. ROBLYER
UNIVERSITY OF MARYLAND UNIVERSITY COLLEGE

We shall not cease from exploration
And the end of all our exploring
Will be to arrive where we started
And know the place for the first time.

T. S. Eliot

TECHNOLOGY INTEGRATION EXAMPLE
STUDYING OUR PAST, MAPPING OUR FUTURE

Based on: Parmenter, B., & Burns, M. (2001). GIS in the classroom: Challenges, opportunities, and alternatives. *Learning and Leading with Technology, 28*(7), 10–17.

Grade Levels: 7–8 • **Content Area/Topic: Geography, civics, and history** • **Length of Time: Six weeks**

Phase 1: Determine relative advantage

Mr. McVee taught the state and local studies classes for his school's eighth-grade students. He had always felt that one of his most important tasks as a social studies teacher at this level was to help his students see that people shape the history and growth of an area, and that the students themselves could have a major role in shaping the future of areas in which they live. He knew this was important preparation and background for the civics and history courses they would take in high school. However, he also knew how difficult it was to get students to grasp complex, abstract concepts like the relationship between past history, current conditions, and future developments. He decided that this concept would become more meaningful to students if they gathered information from local citizens about the history of their local area and used their findings to hypothesize plans for the area's future.

As he brainstormed activities, he looked for resources that could make historical and geographical concepts more real and compelling to students and would emphasize their ability to shape their future. In a recent district workshop, he had learned that the Environmental Systems Research Institute (ESRI) (http://www.esri.com) provides a free **Geographic Information System (GIS)** viewer on its website through which students can see actual maps overlaid with census data. GISs are software systems that house database collections of graphic and text information about the surface of the earth and also provide tools for viewing, manipulating, and analyzing these data. He read about a project where students created "life maps" of people and places on GIS maps of the area during different periods of time (Audet & Ludwig, 2000). He had also experimented with the simulation software that gave students an active role in decision making about social issues. He decided to integrate these and other resources into a 6-week unit around three major activities: identifying events that shaped the history and growth of the area, creating life maps of people from the history of the local area, and developing a "growth scenario" for the future.

Phase 2: Decide on objectives and assessments

Mr. McVee decided that each activity in the unit should result in a graded, small-group product. The products would be timelines showing local events and population growth; life maps of people, places, and events in the local area; and a map presentation of their growth scenario for the future. The following outcomes, objectives, and assessments would help identify and measure students' achievement on these products:

- **Outcome:** Timelines and population growth. **Objective:** Each group will complete all tasks to produce a timeline of the major phases of development in the local area, with events and population figures noted for each time period. **Assessment:** Ratings checklist of required components and characteristics.

- **Outcome:** Life maps. **Objective:** Each group will complete all tasks to produce a life map of a well-known figure from each time period in the area's history. **Assessment:** Ratings checklist of required components and characteristics.

- **Outcome:** Future growth plans. **Objective:** Each group will achieve at least 90% on a rubric covering their plan for future growth of the area, which they create based on their analysis of past and current events and growth. **Assessment:** Rubric to cover quality of research, required components, and cooperative group work.

Phase 3: Design integration strategies

Mr. McVee decided he would use the following sequence to accomplish the goals of the unit:

- **Week 1: Introduce the unit:** Introduce the unit to the class as *Our Area: Past, Present, and Future.* Show actual photos of the same local area at different periods of time. Compare the photos and discuss what kinds of things changed and why. Tell them about the products they will create during their study of the evolution of their area. Ask students to "volunteer" parents, grandparents, or great grandparents who would come to school so the class could interview them and gather information about events that shaped the local area. Have the class brainstorm questions to ask during interviews with their "senior authorities." Demonstrate the Tom Snyder *TimeLiner* software. Form small groups and assign each small group a time period. Give each some background history materials on the time periods, and have them experiment with creating timelines of events that occurred in the United States and the world during their particular time period.

- **Week 2: Gather information and create timelines:** Have student groups interview the local expert(s) for their assigned time period. Have them visit websites that give general information about the time period. After compiling their notes on answers to the questions, have each group use the *TimeLiner* software to create a timeline of events during their time period. From local newspaper records, library records, and local "historians," they obtain pictures to illustrate world, national, and local events. Each group presents its timeline and describes how the people and events they learned about helped shape the local area.

- **Weeks 3–4: Create life maps**: Demonstrate ESRI's GIS viewer. Show students how they can get census data on their local area from the U.S. Census Bureau site and use the ESRI *ArcExplorer* viewer to see maps of census data for their area. Form small working groups and have each group experiment with displaying a different kind of data on the same area. They also answer questions such as "Why are congressional districts drawn as they are?" and "Have they changed over time?" Have them present their displays to the whole class. Discuss how the "life map" will look and how to go about creating it. Group members import the GIS map they produced earlier into a graphics package and create a "life map" of the person they interviewed, showing places and events the person discussed and the boundaries of the town at that time. They present their maps to the class.

- **Weeks 5–6: Create future scenarios with GIS data**: Introduce this phase in the unit by having student groups use the Tom Snyder *Decisions, Decisions: Town Government* software to explore citizens' roles in governing the local community. Lead a discussion comparing each of their findings. Then tell students to imagine they are part of a citizen's action committee assigned the task of planning a growth scenario for their community for the next decade. Have each group look at a different area of growth (e.g., housing, transportation, recreational areas, services such as waste disposal and water). As a whole class, they download historical census data from the U.S. Census Bureau website, put it in a spreadsheet, and use it to project population statistics for the area during the next 10 years. In small groups, they discuss the implications of this population growth for their area of concern. Using the maps they created for their life maps, they show what would need to be planned for development to keep up with the area's growth. Mr. McVee helps them

print their maps on transparency sheets. Using an overhead projector, they overlay the maps and "negotiate" to resolve any conflicts they see (e.g., new housing versus a larger city park). As a whole class, they merge the maps into one to reflect on the plan for the future. They end the unit by reflecting on their decisions and the implications they would have for the area.

Phase 4: Prepare the instructional environment

In the weeks before the project began, Mr. McVee had to organize several kinds of resources. First, with the help of students, he had to obtain historical photos and data on the community. Then he had to identify the resource people who could be used as authorities on each decade from 1950 through 2000 and set up interview times. To have his students see and discuss the U.S. Census Bureau website and GIS maps as a whole class, Mr. McVee needed to schedule the use of a large-screen projection system and obtain permission to print transparencies on the computer lab's laser printer. He also had to locate and set up websites on the historical periods for the students to view. Finally, he had to make sure the two software packages worked on his classroom computers.

Phase 5: Evaluate and revise

Mr. McVee tried out the lesson and administered the following self-assessment to review how it worked for him:

- Did students' products reflect growth in their thinking about people's roles in shaping their future?
- Did the students become engaged in each of the tasks?
- Did each of the software and web resources and small groups work as smoothly as expected?
- Did most students score well on the checklists and rubric?

Also, he interviewed students about their perceptions of the unit. As expected, they were most positive about the interviews of local people and the hands-on work with the website. They were less enthusiastic about having to work in small groups. After considering students' work on all the outcomes, Mr. McVee decided the unit was a success. He resolved to contact the state GIS office for more local data for various time periods that students could use in their work. He also decided to look for strategies to make his students feel more positive about working in groups.

ArcExplorer
GIS Data Viewer

Source: Reprinted with permission of ESRI. Copyright © 2004 ESRI. All rights reserved.

OBJECTIVES

After reading this chapter and completing the learning activities for it, you should be able to:

1. Identify current issues in social studies instruction that may impact the selection and use of technology.

2. Describe key strategies for integrating technology into social studies curricula.

3. Create instructional activities for social studies instruction that model successful integration strategies.

For more information on Key Terms, go to the *Key Terms* module for this chapter of the Companion Website at http://www.prenhall.com/roblyer.

KEY TERMS

- digital storytelling
- geocaching
- Geographic Information System (GIS)
- Global Positioning System (GPS)
- social studies

INTRODUCTION

Since the Industrial Revolution, science and technology have shaped the world in fundamental ways. In the 1990s, computer technologies and the emergence of the Internet have accelerated this influence. Better, faster, worldwide communications have made the world at once smaller and more complex. Life was simpler—and less informed—when people did not know so much about themselves and others so quickly. Now, with so much new information at hand, we have much to discover about our world and its people. But it is through this exploration that we make our world more like the place we want it to be.

The National Council for the Social Studies (NCSS) has adopted the following formal definition for the **social studies:**

> Social studies is the integrated study of the social sciences and humanities to promote civic competence. Within the school program, social studies provides coordinated, systemic study drawing upon such disciplines as anthropology, archaeology, economics, geography, history, law, philosophy, political science, psychology, religion, and sociology, as well as appropriate content from the humanities, mathematics, and the natural sciences. The primary purpose of social studies is to help young people develop the ability to make informed and reasoned decisions for the public good as citizens of a culturally diverse, democratic society in an interdependent world. (NCSS, 1994, p. 3)

As an area that focuses on the interconnections of people and the earth, social studies education has been af-

fected by the impact of technology perhaps more than any other content area. Not only is there more to learn about the world than ever before, the information is changing constantly and dramatically. Fortunately, the same technologies that created this more complex world also can help teach about it.

ISSUES AND PROBLEMS IN SOCIAL STUDIES INSTRUCTION

Methods of Addressing Social Studies Instruction Standards

The national social studies standards were released by the NCSS in 1994. These standards address overall curriculum design and comprehensive student performance expectations. However, standards also exist for civics, economics, geography, government, and history, which provide more specific content detail for these disciplines.

The NCSS hopes that curriculum designers will use the NCSS social studies standards for creating the overall framework and then fill in the detail using the discipline standards. The 10 themes that form the framework of the social studies standards, along with a brief description of each, are presented next (NCSS, 1994; http://www.ncss.org/standards). At the elementary and middle school levels, school systems usually address social studies curriculum by teaching a variety of topics from these strands. In high school, social studies tends to become divided into more specific areas such as history and civics. Thus, when referring to a course, the term *social studies* is more commonly used to describe K–8 classes.

- **Theme 1: Culture** — The study of culture prepares students to answer questions such as these: What are the common characteristics of different cultures? How do belief systems, such as religion or political ideals, influence other parts of the culture? This theme typically appears in units and courses dealing with geography, history, sociology, and anthropology as well as multicultural topics across the curriculum.

- **Theme 2: Time, continuity, and change** — Humans seek to understand their historical roots and to locate themselves in time. Knowing how to read and reconstruct the past allows one to develop a historical perspective and to answer questions such as these: Who am I? What happened in the past? How am I connected to those in the past? How has the world changed and how might it change in the future? Why does our personal sense of relatedness to the past change? This theme typically appears in courses in history and others that draw on historical knowledge and habits.

- **Theme 3: People, places, and environments** — The study of people, places, and human–environment interactions assists students as they create their spatial views and geographic perspectives of the world beyond their personal locations. Students need the knowledge, skills, and understanding to answer questions such as these: Where are things located? Why are they located where they are? What do we mean by "region"? How do landforms change? What implications do these changes have for people? This theme typically appears in units and courses dealing with area studies and geography.

- **Theme 4: Individual development and identity** — Personal identity is shaped by culture, groups, and institutional influences. Students should consider such questions as these: How do people learn? Why do people behave as they do? What influences how people learn, perceive, and grow? How do people meet their basic needs in a variety of contexts? How do individuals develop from youth to adulthood? This theme typically appears in units and courses dealing with psychology and anthropology.

- **Theme 5: Individuals, groups, and institutions** — Institutions such as schools, churches, families, government agencies, and the courts play an integral role in our lives. It is important that students learn how institutions are formed, what controls and influences them, how they influence individuals and culture, and how they are maintained or changed. Students may address questions such as these: What is the role of institutions in this or other societies? How am I influenced by institutions? How do institutions change? What is my role in institutional change? This theme typically appears in units and courses dealing with sociology, anthropology, psychology, political science, and history.

- **Theme 6: Power, authority, and governance** — Understanding the historical development of power, authority, and governance and their evolving functions in contemporary U.S. society and other parts of the world is essential for developing civic competence. In exploring this theme, students confront questions such as these: What is power? What forms does it take? Who holds it? How is it gained, used, and justified? What is legitimate authority? How are governments created, structured, maintained, and changed? How can individual rights be protected within the context of majority rule? This theme typically appears in units and courses dealing with government, politics, political science, history, and law.

- **Theme 7: Production, distribution, and consumption** — Because people have wants that often exceed available resources, a variety of ways have evolved to answer these questions: What is to be produced? How is production organized? How are goods and services distributed? What is the most effective allocation of factors of production such as land, labor, capital, and management? This theme typically appears in units and courses dealing with economic concepts and issues.

- **Theme 8: Science, technology, and society** — Modern life would be impossible without technology and the science that supports it. But technology raises many questions: Is new technology always better than old? What can we learn from the past about how new technologies result in broader social change, some of which is unanticipated? How can we cope with the ever-increasing pace of change? How can we preserve our fundamental values and beliefs in the midst of technological change? This theme draws on the natural and physical sciences, social studies, and the humanities and appears in a variety of social studies courses, including history, geography, economics, civics, and government.

- **Theme 9: Global connections** — The realities of global interdependence require an understanding of the increasingly important and diverse global connections among world societies and the frequent tension between national interests and global priorities. Students need to be able to address such international issues as health care, the environment, human rights, economic competition and interdependence, age-old ethnic hostilities, and political and military alliances. This theme typically appears in units or courses dealing with geography, culture, and economics, but may also draw on the natural and physical sciences and the humanities.

The study of current events is an important strand in social studies. Although teachers increasingly use video tools to engage students, print materials continue to be an important resource for learning about current events. One innovative tool for engaging students in news media stories is creating a personalized newspaper. Using technology known as selective dissemination of information (SDI), users create a set of filters that allow topics of interest to be presented. One of the most popular personalized newspaper services is known as Crayon (http://crayon.net). Personalized news services can also be found in some web hosting systems (http://my.yahoo.com) that even allow the presentation of selected daily comics. The value to students is that they take responsibility for deciding what types of stories they want to monitor, which typically helps to engage them in reading. This can also be an excellent way to prepare students for writing following a period of monitoring the news. For students with difficulty reading, web-based plug-ins like the ReadingBar (http://www.readplease.com) can be installed in the web browser. Students click on individual words or whole sections of text and have them read to them.

For students with mild or moderate cognitive impairments, specially designed resources are available to provide current events information at an appropriate level. News-2-You (http://www.news-2-you.com) is a subscription-based service that prepares an 8-page current events reader each week that is downloaded in PDF format and copied for distribution to the students. These specially written resources feature high-interest, low-vocabulary stories with each word accompanied by a rebus image.

Contributed by Dave Edyburn

- **Theme 10: Civic ideals and practices** — An understanding of civic ideals and practices of citizenship is critical to full participation in society and is a central purpose of the social studies. Students confront questions such as these: What is civic participation and how can we be involved? How has the meaning of citizenship evolved? What is the balance between rights and responsibilities? What is the role of the citizen in the community and the nation and as a member of the world community? This theme typically appears in units or courses dealing with history, political science, and cultural anthropology and fields such as global studies, law-related education, and the humanities.

Dilemmas in Teaching Social Studies Effectively

Despite their obvious value and relevance to future citizens, social studies themes and topics are not usually among those included in statewide assessments. Many states limit their graduation tests to language arts (e.g., reading and writing) and mathematics. Since many teachers tend to focus instruction primarily on tested topics, social studies areas are often placed on the back burner (Flannery, 2004). Consequently, school resources such as technology materials tend to be directed toward other content areas.

The sheer amount of material to review in many social studies topics is also a concern. A good example is a world history course, which often covers the period from the dawn of civilization to the present day. The amount of content, coupled with the de-emphasis on social studies topics, creates an ongoing challenge to schools to teach social studies in a meaningful way.

Adding to this challenge is the changing role of technology itself. At first, teachers looked at technology resources as a collection of tools to help teach specific content and skills. However, as teachers began to see technology making profound changes in social, civic, and economic functioning, they saw value in more constructivist uses (Berson & Balyta, 2004). Unfortunately, using technology in constructivist ways, while potentially powerful, is also more time consuming than directed uses, which further adds to the dilemma of how to teach social studies in an effective way.

Finally, there is the issue of costs for high-quality resources. For example, to equip 30 computers with the *TimeLiner* software costs about $900. Social studies teachers have to make the case that the expense of these resources is worth it due to increased achievement or other benefits.

The "History Wars" and Other Debates on the Content and Focus of Social Studies

Social studies has attracted more debate and criticism than perhaps any other content area, and much of this discussion centers around the appropriate role of history

TOP TEN Strategies for Technology in Social Studies Instruction

Take advantage of these 10 powerful strategies for using technology to enhance the teaching of social studies topics.

1. **Do webquests to learn the history behind political issues** — Students do Internet research to learn that current issues have historical roots in past events and debates.

2. **Send students on a geocaching treasure hunt with GPS devices** — These motivating activities get students to spend more time studying geographical information and techniques.

3. **Use Tom Snyder's *TimeLiner* software to help teach history** — The software makes the sequence of historical events more visual and real to students.

4. **"Live through" history with *Muzzy Lane's* simulated immersion experience** — Students play the role of decision maker in historical situations in order to see the relevance of these events in their daily lives and develop better problem-solving skills.

5. **Virtual field trips help students learn about other cultures** — The wealth of information and images available about other cultures enriches students' study of other lands and ways of life.

6. **Tom Snyder's *Decisions, Decisions* software helps students understand the U.S. Constitution** — Simulations put students in the role of writing the Constitution that will determine how our country is governed.

7. **Students learn economic principles with stock market simulation games** — The complexities of the stock market become easier to understand when students play the role of stockbroker, investing "their own" money and seeing the return over time.

8. **Teach local and other history with electronic storytelling** — Images and audio make the stories of lives, events, or eras come alive for students and play a key role in preparing oral histories.

9. **Use software such as Tom Snyder's *Neighborhood Map Machine* to teach map concepts** — This kind of hands-on software takes the manual labor out of drawing maps and helps students build essential skills in making and using maps.

10. **Use digital cameras to explore community-based history and current issues** — Digital photography allows students to capture images from their vantage point, participate in the construction of knowledge, and learn how diverse perspectives can be shaped.

---

in the curriculum (Evans, 2004). Schools have struggled to give proper emphasis to all of the social studies topics. However, some critics feel strongly that schools should focus more squarely on teaching history and civics, rather than taking a broader approach to covering a number of social studies topics. In recent years, leaders in the field of social studies have made the case that students should be aware of the broad array of influences that shaped our country's history. Critics of this approach feel that the content of history courses has become diluted, focusing too much on topics that they consider outside the mainstream, traditional historical themes and important events that shaped the United States. These critics feel that teachers who are not well prepared in the latter approach are ill equipped to teach history effectively. Two reports from the Fordham Foundation summarize these criticisms:

- *Back to Basics: Reclaiming Social Studies* (http://www.edexcellence.net/foundation/global/page.cfm?id=56)
- *Where Did Social Studies Go Wrong?* (http://www.edexcellence.net/foundation/publication/publication.cfm?id=317).

A response to the reports from the NCSS can be found at http://www.socialstudies.org/media/releases/fordham/.

Perils of the Information Explosion

The ready availability of information on the Internet has created several concerns for social studies education. First,

Figure 12.2 Resources and Social Studies Themes: Simulated Problem-Solving Environments

Sample Simulated Problem-Solving Environments	Social Studies Themes
Muzzy Lane's *Making History* http://www.muzzylane.com/home/home.htm	Theme 2: Time, continuity, and change Theme 6: Power, authority, and governance
Riverdeep's *The Oregon Trail* http://www.riverdeep.com	Theme 2: Time, continuity, and change Theme 7: Production, distribution, and consumption
Tom Snyder's *Decisions, Decisions 5.0* http://www.tomsnyder.com	Theme 6: Power, authority, and governance Theme 10: Civic ideals and practices
StocksQuest: A Global Stock Market game http://investsmart.coe.uga.edu/10326/test/cgi-bin/main.cgi?c=1	Theme 7: Production, distribution, and consumption
The International Communication and Negotiation Simulations (ICONS) http://www.icons.umd.edu/	Theme 9: Global connections
Who Killed William Robinson? http://web.uvic.ca/history-robinson/indexmsn.html	Theme 1: Culture Theme 4: Individual development and identity

Figure 12.3 Resources and Social Studies Themes: Graphic Representation Products

Sample Graphic Representation Products	Social Studies Themes
Tom Snyder's *Neighborhood MapMachine 2.0* http://www.tomsnyder.com	Theme 3: People, places, and environments
Tom Snyder's *TimeLiner 5.0* http://www.tomsnyder.com	Theme 2: Time, continuity, and change
Tom Snyder's *The Graph Club* and *GraphMaster* http://www.tomsnyder.com	All themes

studies in their daily lives, they also develop better problem-solving skills. Some popular examples of simulated problem-solving environments that address various social studies themes are listed in Figure 12.2.

Graphic Representations

Students often have problems visualizing abstract concepts such as timelines and maps. Teachers can use various technologies to represent these concepts graphically, which can let even novices understand and apply them. Products such as graphing software and spreadsheets (e.g., Microsoft's *Excel*) put data into a concrete form for easier analysis and representation of concepts and allow geographic concepts to be depicted visually. Graphic representation products (see Figure 12.3) such as timeline generators allow students to understand time sequences and track change over time.

Virtual Trips

Virtual trips are "visits" students make to Internet sites to see places they could not easily go to in real life or that can help them get more out of trips they are able to take. Virtual trips do not have the interactive qualities of the simulated environments described earlier, but they have some of the same instructional benefits. Visiting these foreign locations gives students a richer, more comprehensive perspective on the world around them and makes the world a living part of their classroom. For students who may travel little, the wealth of images and information from virtual trips helps them see and understand the variety of cultures, sights, and events outside their own communities. To best explain methods of using virtual trips in the middle school classroom, Beal and Mason (1999) have described four different objectives of virtual field trips such as those listed in Figure 12.4:

Discuss these issues online with other students by selecting the *Making the Case* module for Chapter 12 of the Companion Website (http://www.prenhall.com/roblyer) or choose the *Message Board* module.

1. Harp's 1996 article "The History Wars" described the conflict that resulted when some historians proposed altering the "traditional" treatments of American and world history to include emphasis on multicultural influences. He said, "While some are still fighting hard for a set, traditional curriculum—with standards to match—technology has opened the history classroom door to a dizzying array of data, artifacts, and perspectives. Helping teachers to make sense of it all is more than half the battle."

    What role has technology played in causing "the history wars"? What needs to be done to help teachers make sense of it all?

2. The National Council for the Social Studies said, "Powerful social studies teaching is integrative across time and space, connecting with past experiences and looking ahead to the future. It helps students appreciate how aspects of the social world function, not only in their local community but also in the past and in other cultures" (1994, p. 33).

    What are some ways in which technology can enable teaching strategies with these characteristics?

1. To help students synthesize what they learned on a class field trip.
2. To prepare students for an upcoming class field trip.
3. To provide students with information about areas they are unable to visit as a class.
4. To provide students with information about areas their teacher visited.

Student Telecollaborations

Email and Internet-based projects offer a way for students in distant locations to work together to share perspectives and gain insights that would not be possible if they

Collaborative projects promote communication and reflection, as well as providing information to support research.

Figure 12.4   Resources and Social Studies Themes: Virtual Field Trips

Sample Sites to Support Virtual Trips	Social Studies Themes
Bodie, California, a gold mining boomtown in the 1800s http://www.bodie.net/	Theme 3: People, places, and environments
Virtual Tour of Israel http://www.tourism.gov.il/tourism/virtual%20tour/map_index2.html	Theme 2: Time, continuity, and change
Colonial House, a tour of life in the Colonial Era http://www.pbs.org/wnet/colonialhouse/history/index.html	Theme 2: Time, continuity, and change
Paris Yellow Pages with photos http://photos.pagesjaunes.fr/	Theme 1: Culture Theme 4: Individual development and identity

TECHNOLOGY INTEGRATION IDEA 12.1

STUDENT TELECOLLABORATIONS

Title: Student Webquest on Anne Frank

Content Area/Topic: History

Grade Levels: 7–9

NETS for Students: Standards 3, 4, 5

Description: After a beginning discussion about the Holocaust, students are asked to imagine they have been hired to create a documentary for a major news network about Anne Frank and the children of the Holocaust. They are assigned to small groups to work on various sources of information, for example, literature about the children, art produced by children about the Holocaust, and information from interviews of people who knew Anne Frank. The teacher gives the students a variety of websites to visit and specific questions to answer and items of information to obtain. After each group obtains its information, they work on combining it to develop a multimedia documentary.

Source: Yoder, M. (1999). The student Web Quest. *Learning and Leading with Technology, 26*(7), 6–9, 52–53.

Figure 12.5 **Resources and Social Studies Themes: Student Telecollaborations**

Sample Sites to Support Student Telecollaborations	Social Studies Themes
Virtual Architecture: Designing and Directing Curriculum-Based Telecomputing http://virtual-architecture.wm.edu	All themes
The Global School House—Global SchoolNet http://www.gsn.org	All themes
International Education and Resource Network (iEARN) http://www.iearn.org	All themes

worked by themselves. Such projects are often called *telecollaborations*. As students collaborate to study a topic or create a product, these projects promote communication, encourage reflection, and provide a wealth of information to support students' research. The sites listed in Figure 12.5 are good sources for telecollaborative projects. Technology Integration Idea 12.1 provides an example of this strategy.

Digital Storytelling

Digital storytelling is the process of using images and audio to tell the stories of lives, events, or eras. With this technique, students use personal narrative to explore community-based history, politics, economics, and geography. These projects offer students the opportunity to make their own lives a part of their scholarly research.

The use of digital images in the social studies can accomplish many purposes (Berson, 2004; Berson & Berson, 2003):

1. Assist students in comparing and contrasting the past and the present.
2. Sensitize students to diverse perspectives and biases.
3. Provide visual cues that reinforce geographic concepts.
4. Represent abstract and concrete social studies concepts (e.g., democracy, liberty, needs and wants).
5. Foster skills in analysis and critical thinking.
6. Facilitate greater connections to the community.
7. Personalize associations with the study of geography, history, economics, government, and other related disciplines.

Figure 12.6   Resources and Social Studies Themes: Digital Storytelling

Sample Products to Support Digital Storytelling	Social Studies Themes
Digital Diaries: Pioneer History Project http://www.adobe.com/education/curriculum/exchange/winnebago.html	Theme 2: Time, continuity, and change
PBS Civil War http://www.pbs.org/civilwar/	Theme 2: Time, continuity, and change
National Archives and Records Administration http://www.archives.gov/	Theme 2: Time, continuity, and change
Digital Resource Centers (DRC) http://www.teacherlink.org/content/social/digresources/	Theme 2: Time, continuity, and change Theme 3: People, places, and environments
The Oral History Society Home Page http://www.oralhistory.org.uk/	Theme 2: Time, continuity, and change Theme 3: People, places, and environments

Figure 12.7   Resources and Social Studies Themes: Digital Information Critiques

Sample Products to Support Digital Information Critiques	Social Studies Themes
Jeff Share's *The Camera Always Lies: Breaking the Myth of Objectivity* http://www.medialit.org/reading_room/article639.html	Theme 8: Science, technology, and society
Media Construction of War: A Critical Reading of History (Project Look Sharp) http://www.ithaca.edu/looksharp/	Theme 8: Science, technology, and society
DeKorne and Chin's *Photo Forgery: Getting to the Heart of a Photojournalist's Code of Ethics* http://www.nytimes.com/learning/teachers/lessons/20040311thursday.html?searchpv=learning_lessons	Theme 8: Science, technology, and society
Don't Buy It http://pbskids.org/dontbuyit/	Theme 8: Science, technology, and society

One type of digital storytelling requires students to create their own images with camcorders or digital cameras. By sending students into their world with a digital camera in hand, teachers provide opportunities for them to bring their lives into the classroom, creating a rich, authentic authoring space. Writing and arranging pictures as artifacts within a digital space allow students to explore events from multiple perspectives. As an extension or adaptation, students might create digital movies about an event, place, or individual, using the camera to capture scenes and artifacts that would be woven together to tell a particular story. Figure 12.6 lists websites that support digital storytelling.

Students can also collect audio available on websites and by interviewing resource people in their communities. These can be in the form of oral histories or music that helps tell the history of a period or place.

Digital Information Critiques

History is replete with examples of using manipulated images to control people's impressions and opinions. Part of developing skills as citizens in a digital age is to learn how to critically evaluate digital information. Students have to learn how to analyze images and tell fact from fiction. Social studies activities provide a context for simultaneously exploring the social impact of images while developing media literacy skills (Van Hover, Swann, & Berson, 2004). (See Figure 12.7.)

Electronic Research

As students study areas such as politics, economics, and current events, information is likely to change quickly and frequently. Internet sources give students and

TECHNOLOGY INTEGRATION IDEA 12.2

ELECTRONIC RESEARCH

Title: Invention Events

Content Area/Topic: Technology education, history

Grade Levels: 5–8

NETS for Students: Standards 3, 5

Description: Students select an invention of interest to them. They peruse a series of websites to gather information and background on their inventions. After they complete their research, students enter the inventions and the information about them into a database. Fields include items such as invention name, category, date of patent or invention, inventor, and significant effect of invention. After discussion about the inventions selected and researched by the class members, students each create timelines to place their inventions historically. They show events surrounding the introduction of their inventions.

Source: Barrett, J. (2001). Indispensable inventions. *Learning and Leading with Technology, 29*(1), 22–26.

Figure 12.8   **Resources and Social Studies Themes: Electronic Research**

Sample Sites to Support Electronic Research	Social Studies Themes
Democratic and Republican Party websites http://www.democrats.org/ http://www.rnc.org	Theme 6: Power, authority, and governance Theme 10: Civic ideals and practices
U.S. Congress http://thomas.loc.gov	Theme 6: Power, authority, and governance Theme 10: Civic ideals and practices
U.S. Information Agency http://civnet.org	Theme 10: Civic ideals and practices
The White House http://www.whitehouse.gov	Theme 6: Power, authority, and governance Theme 10: Civic ideals and practices
Census in Schools http://www.census.gov/dmd/www/teachers.html http://www.census.gov/main/www/cen2000.html	Theme 1: Culture Theme 10: Civic ideals and practices
Ellis Island Records http://www.ellisisland.org/?google_ad5 http://www.ellisislandimmigrants.org/	Theme 1: Culture Theme 2: Time, continuity, and change
Multiculturalpedia http://www.netlaputa.ne.jp/~tokyo3/e/	Theme 1: Culture

teachers up-to-date information they could not obtain easily from any other sources. Also, access to information summaries and examples of data "pictures" on the Internet help students learn to analyze information in both graphic and text forms. Since we are relying more and more on Internet sources for reliable, up-to-date information, students must learn where they can look for various kinds of data and facts they need to complete research in school and, later, at work. Technology Integration Idea 12.2 provides an example of this strategy and Figure 12.8 lists sample products that support electronic research.

GIS AND GPS LESSONS

Title: Disaster Preparedness with GIS and GPS Tools

Content Area/Topic: Social studies, civics

Grade Levels: All grade levels

NETS for Students: Standards 4, 5, 6

Description: In this project-based learning activity, students use GPS and GIS tools to help plan how they and their community will respond in the event of a natural or human-made disaster. Students must have access to GIS data on the geography of their local areas. They begin by using their GPS receivers to find the school's latitude/longitude location. They can also locate their streets and houses to get practice with the tools. The teacher divides the class into groups and assigns them information to gather about their school (e.g., capacity of the building, number of classrooms, large rooms such as gymnasiums). They also collect information to determine whether or not their school or other local sites would be good shelters in the event of emergencies (e.g., availability of food storage, medical supplies, electrical generators). They use GIS imagery to analyze what areas are in danger from certain kinds of disasters (e.g., floods) and decide where the people in these areas might go for shelter.

Source: Gauthier, S. (2004). GIS helps prepare students for emergencies. *Learning and Leading with Technology, 32*(3), 22–25.

Figure 12.9 A GIS Example

Source: The ESRI globe logo, www.gis.com, and the GIS map layers are the intellectual property of ESRI and are used here with permission. TM and copyright © 2004 ESRI. All rights reserved.

GIS and GPS Lessons

Since Geographic Information Systems (GISs) house a wealth of information about the surface of the earth and provide tools for viewing, manipulating, and analyzing the information, the result is a highly graphic way of looking at numerical information, such as population information overlaid on an area map. Look at Figure 12.9 from the GIS.com website for an example. The technology integration example at the beginning of this chapter shows how powerful these tools can be to al-

low exploration of the relationship between people and their environment. This technology is becoming a very popular way to help students visualize data distributed over geographical areas.

Another tool that lets students look at geography from many different perspectives is a **Global Positioning System (GPS).** Lary (2004) describes a popular GPS activity in the classroom called **geocaching.** She calls it a "high-tech, worldwide treasure hunt ... where a person hides a cache for others to find" (p. 15). Students look at a database of caches at the geocaching website (http://www.geocaching.com), decide on a cache to hunt for, and use GPSs to help them locate it. Figure 12.10 lists some good sources of other GIS and GPS lessons. Gauthier (2004) also describes a science and social studies project that uses GIS and GPS together and may be done at any grade level. See Technology Integration Idea 12.3, which is based on Gauthier's description.

Practice of Factual Information

A more traditional, but still useful, integration strategy is having students use drill-and-practice, instructional game software, or pay-to-view Internet sites (e.g., Princeton Review's AP/SAT tutorials) to help them learn and remember important facts, such as states and capitals or dates of famous events. For example, Riverdeep's *Classroom Jeopardy*

Figure 12.10 Resources and Social Studies Themes: GIS and GPS Lessons

Sample Sites to Support GIS and GPS Lessons	Social Studies Themes
Mapping Our World: GIS Lessons for Educators http://gis.esri.com/esripress/display/index.cfm?fuseaction=display&websiteID=29	Theme 3: People, places, and environments
GIS in the Classroom: Using Geographic Information Systems in Social Studies and Environmental Science http://www.heinemann.com/shared/products/E00479.asp	Theme 3: People, places, and environments
Math lessons with GPS http://www.teacherlink.org/content/math/activities/gps.html	Theme 3: People, places, and environments
Science/geography lessons with GIS and GPS http://education.ssc.nasa.gov/fad/	Theme 3: People, places, and environments

Figure 12.11 Resources and Social Studies Themes: Practice of Factual Information

Sample Products to Support Practice of Factual Information	Social Studies Themes
States Web Games http://www.sheppardsoftware.com/web_games.htm	Theme 3: People, places, and environments
Riverdeep's *Classroom Jeopardy: Middle School Social Studies/History Games* http://www.riverdeep.com	All themes

game (see Figure 12.11) provides a unique and highly motivational approach to this kind of practice by placing it in the context of a quiz show game in which the whole class can participate.

INTERACTIVE SUMMARY

The following is a summary of the main points covered in this chapter. To see additional examples and information on these points, go to this textbook's Companion Website at http://www.prenhall.com/roblyer and click on the Chapter 12 *Interactive Summary* module to visit each of the recommended websites.

1. **Issues in social studies instruction:** These include:
   - Methods of addressing social studies standards
   - Dilemmas in teaching social studies effectively
   - The "history wars" and other debates on the content and focus of social studies (read the reports at *Back to Basics: Reclaiming Social Studies* and *Where Did Social Studies Go Wrong?*, and a response to the reports from the NCSS.
   - Perils of the information explosion.

2. **Integration strategies for social studies instruction:** Nine strategies are described for integrating technology into this area:
   - Simulated immersion experiences (see Muzzy Lane simulation)
   - Graphic representations (see Tom Snyder's Timeliner software)
   - Virtual trips (see the Bodie, California, site)
   - Student telecollaborations (see the Global School House—Global SchoolNet and International Education and Resource Network sites)
   - Digital storytelling (see the Oral History Society Home Page)
   - Digital information critiques (see PBS's Don't Buy It website)
   - Electronic research
   - GIS and GPS lessons (see the ESRI website)
   - Practice of factual information.

Online Activities

Visit this text's Companion Website at http://www.prenhall.com/roblyer to gain access to a variety of questions, activities, and exercises and to help build your knowledge of this chapter's content.

Online Chapter 12 Self-Test

To review terms and concepts for this chapter, click on the *Self-Test* module for this chapter of the Companion Website.

Software Skill-Builder Tutorials

To access practical tutorial and skill-building activities and to build skills using popular software and hardware, click on the *Software Skill-Builder Tutorials* module for this chapter of the Companion Website.

Web-Enrichment Activities

To complete activities that connect to chapter content and provide web-based resources, click on the *Web-Enrichment Activities* module for this chapter of the Companion Website.

TECHNOLOGY INTEGRATION WORKSHOP

CLIPS FROM THE CLASSROOM: LEARNING WITH TECHNOLOGY

Go to the *Technology Integration Workshop* DVD located in the back of this text and click on *Clips from the Classroom*. View the video clips listed below that support this chapter's content:

- *Tablet Computers in World History*
- *Technology Improves Teaching Skills*
- *Student Achievement Increases*
- *Technology Manages Flow of Activities*
- *Assessment Examples Illustrated*
- PowerPoint *Guides and Prompts Teaching*
- *Parent Pleased with Son's Opportunities*
- *Scholarly Writings Online Engage Students.*

Now, visit this text's Companion Website at http://www.prenhall.com/roblyer to answer questions and complete activities that will guide you in analyzing each clip.

THE TIP MODEL IN ACTION

Read each of the following scenarios related to implementing the TIP Model, and go to the Companion Website to answer the questions that follow it based on your Chapter 12 reading activities.

TIP Model Scenario #1 Mr. Daley wanted to show his sociology students how they could test hypotheses about correlations among social factors such as population centers and crime statistics. He had heard of a technology tool that would allow students to do this with maps, so they could see at a glance if their hypotheses were correct.

1.1 What technology-based strategy could Mr. Daley use to address this need?

1.2 What would be the relative advantage of using this strategy?

1.3 What would you suggest Mr. Daley have his students produce to show the results of their work? How might he assess this product?

TIP Model Scenario #2 Dr. France's students were going to be studying the Early American period in our country's history in the spring semester, and she wanted to make the class more engaging than it had been in the past. She wished she could have her students visit places like Williamsburg, Philadelphia, and Monticello, but they did not live near any of these sites.

2.1 What technology-based strategy could Dr. France use to address this problem?

2.2 What would be the relative advantage of using this strategy?

2.3 What could Dr. France's students produce to show what they had learned? How might she assess their products?

TIP Model Scenario #3 Ms. Rodrigues's social studies students were about to study the U.S. Constitution. She not only wanted to show them what was included in our Constitution, but she also wanted them to see all the factors that must be considered when any new country creates a charter to guide its development and reflect its national principles. She had heard about software that allowed students to do this in a role-playing way.

3.1 What technology-based tool could Ms. Rodrigues use to address this need?

3.2 What would be the relative advantage of using this strategy instead of holding a class discussion on this topic?

3.3 Should students work individually, in pairs, in small groups, or as a whole class on this activity? Explain.

TIP Model Scenario #4 Ms. Fernanda wanted to have her students study their local area, so she arranged to have them work via email with a class of students in another state. They exchanged background information about each other's locations and asked questions about weather conditions, favorite spots to visit, and other items of interest to both. Finally, they each worked on a travel brochure that included a local map and summarized the information they had gathered. They ended the project by emailing each other a copy of the brochure.

4.1 What problems did Ms. Fernanda address with this technology-based strategy?

4.2 What would be the relative advantage of using this strategy, as opposed to having students do a brochure without contacting other students?

4.3 What outcomes should be assessed in such a project, and how might they be assessed?

TIP Model Scenario #5 Dr. Levar's students were studying how the stock market both reflects our country's economy and helps shape it. He asked them to track five stocks over the course of 2 months and chart their progress. At the same time, they tracked events in the country and the world that might affect stock market performance for the stocks they picked. They ended the project by describing the events that corresponded with major dips and peaks and how they thought these events affected the stocks.

5.1 What problems is Dr. Levar addressing with this technology-based strategy?

5.2 If he had the students work in small groups on this activity, explain how this strategy might best be carried out in the classroom.

5.3 What would be a good way for Dr. Levar to have students present their findings? Explain why this presentation strategy would be effective.

TIE INTO PRACTICE: TECHNOLOGY INTEGRATION EXAMPLES

The Technology Integration Example that opened this chapter (*Studying Our Past, Mapping Our Future*) showed how teachers might use a variety of technology tools to study the history of their local area. Since each group has to visit assigned websites, the teacher may want to consider using an online management system such as *TrackStar* to organize these sites and give students quick access to them. With the knowledge you have ganed from Chapter 12, do the following to explore this strategy:

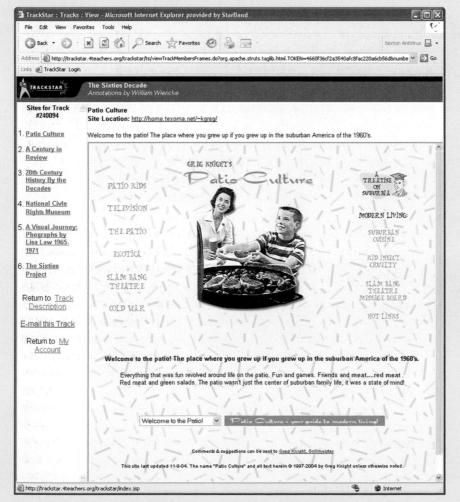

Example from the *TrackStar* Website at http://trackstar.4teachers.org. (Create this product using the *Hands-On with Technology* tutorial section of the DVD.)

1. Using the *TrackStar* website, organize the project like the example shown on page 365. **Create this tracking system** by following the tutorial located on the *Hands-On with Technology* section of the DVD that accompanies this text.

2. Answer the following questions about the *Studying Our Past, Mapping Our Future* example:

   • Phase 1 — What were the kinds of relative advantage that Mr. McVee felt this project would have for his students' study of their local area? What would use of GIS add to this study?

   • Phase 2 — Mr. McVee also has to grade his students with percentage grades that will add to their class average. If his rubric has a total of 35 points, how will he translate a rubric score into a percentage grade?

   • Phase 3 — What technology resources could be helpful as student groups interview the local expert(s) for their assigned time period?

   • Phase 4 — One important task to prepare for the unit was obtaining historical photos and data on the community. Where might he obtain these?

   • Phase 5 — One of the end-of-project questions Mr. Mc Vee asked was if most students "scored well" on the checklists and rubric. What would he have to do at the beginning of the project in order to ascertain this?

3. What NETS for Students skills would students learn by working on the *Studying Our Past, Mapping Our Future* project? (See the front of the book for a list of NETS for Students.)

Technology Integration Lesson Planning

The *Technology Integration Workshop* DVD includes a set of technology integration ideas and links to online lessons, arranged as a searchable database. The DVD comes packaged in the back of this textbook. Click on the *Hands-On with Technology* section of the DVD and complete the following exercises.

1. Locate lesson ideas — The DVD has several examples of lessons that use the social studies integration strategies described in this chapter. Locate an example integration idea for at least one of these strategies for the content area.

2. Evaluate the lessons — Use the *Evaluation Checklist for a Technology-Integrated Lesson* (located on the DVD and the Companion Website) to evaluate each of these lessons.

3. Modify a lesson — Select one of the lesson ideas and adapt its strategies to meet a need in your own content area. You may choose to use the same approach in the original or adapt it to meet your needs.

4. Add descriptors — Create descriptors for your new lesson like those found on the database (e.g., grade level, content and topic areas, technologies used, relative advantage, objectives, NETS standards).

5. Add the new lesson — Add your modified lesson with all its descriptors to the lesson plan database.

For Your Teaching Portfolio

For this chapter's contribution to your teaching portfolio, add the following products you created in the Technology Integration Workshop:

• PDFs of pages you created using the tutorial on the *TrackStar* system

• The evaluations you did using the *Evaluation Checklist for a Technology-Integrated Lesson*

• The new lesson plan you developed, based on the one you found on the DVD.

CHAPTER 13

TECHNOLOGY IN MUSIC AND ART INSTRUCTION

DANIEL NEWSOM
BERKLEE COLLEGE OF MUSIC

M. D. ROBLYER
UNIVERSITY OF MARYLAND UNIVERSITY COLLEGE

BARBARA HOUGHTON
NORTHERN KENTUCKY UNIVERSITY

...students must learn how to manipulate the language of the new technology.... This language—sound, animation, music, drama, video, graphics, text, and voice—is also the language of the arts.

R. Robinson and C. Roland, from *Technology and Arts Education* (1994, p. 11)

TECHNOLOGY INTEGRATION EXAMPLE
THE FINE ART OF ELECTRONIC PORTFOLIOS

Based on: Duxbury, D. (2000). Make sweet music with electronic portfolios. *Learning and Leading with Technology, 28*(3), 28–31, 41.

Grade Levels: Middle to high school• Content Area/Topic: Music and art composition, technology • Length of Time: Ongoing

Phase 1: Determine relative advantage

The music, arts, and technology resource teachers at Eureka High School were discussing the new block scheduling plans in which music, art, and technology credits would share one of the four 90-minute units students would attend each day. The teachers realized that a logical thread among these three curricula would be to have students develop a web-based portfolio of their music, art, and poetry. They felt this would meet several needs. First, it would be a way of working with each student at individual levels of musical and artistic expertise. This was important because students in their classes would range from beginners at musical composition or art skills to advanced musicians or artists who were active in choir, band, orchestra, and/or art studios. Second, it had always been difficult to find an audience for student work; the teachers knew that having others view their work was motivating and provided helpful feedback to students at all levels. A web-based format would make it easier to share the students' works. Third, it would be easy to create projects that linked skills across the disciplines, for example, having students use a **Musical Instrument Digital Interface (MIDI)** keyboard and music editor to prepare a musical composition that expresses the feeling or mood of a painting. (MIDI refers to a standard that has been adopted by the electronic music industry for controlling devices, such as synthesizers and sound cards.) Finally, the teachers realized that an electronic portfolio could serve as a valuable, ongoing assessment tool for students' art, music, technology, and language development, and would help students develop skills in using technology to present their work and to communicate and share information with others.

Phase 2: Decide on objectives and assessments

The teachers decided they each would use a component of the portfolio as the basis of student assessment each grading period. The art and music teachers would assign each student individual benchmarks to achieve in their composition and skill development, and the technology teacher would use the website the students produced to assess their production skills. Students' grades would be a combination of the three assessments,

with each content area weighted according to which one was being emphasized during the grading period. They decided on the following outcomes, objectives, and assessment strategies:

- **Outcome:** Progress in art. **Objective:** Students will meet their assigned benchmark for progress in art skills. **Assessment:** Rubric to assess portfolio component.
- **Outcome:** Progress in music. **Objective:** Students will meet their assigned benchmark for progress in music skills. **Assessment:** Rubric to assess portfolio component.
- **Outcome:** Progress in language expression. **Objective:** Students will meet their assigned benchmark for development in written expression. **Assessment:** Rubric to assess portfolio component.
- **Outcome:** Technology skills. **Objective:** Students will demonstrate competence in each required web page development skill by completing assigned tasks. **Assessment:** Web production checklist.

Phase 3: Design integration strategies

The teachers decided they would follow the same sequence of activities for each grading period:

- **Review skill levels and set benchmarks**: The art and music teachers meet with each student, review accomplishments to date, and set benchmarks for individual skill development. Some students with lower skill levels are placed in small groups so teachers can spend more time working with them.
- **Review portfolio requirements**: The technology teacher meets with each student, reviews the portfolio, and sets tasks to add to the technical and aesthetic presentations.
- **Decide on projects**: A different project is set for each grading period. For example, for the first project, the teachers decide to have students use their MIDI keyboards and notation software to write a musical composition based on the music of a period they have been studying in their history classes. Then the students use

image manipulation software to create a collage of colors and images that come to mind as they listen to the music composition they or their fellow students have created. The technology teacher helps them add their sound and graphics creations to their portfolios.

- **Determine group presentations**: Each teacher identifies whole-group presentations that need to be done. For example, the music teacher demonstrates techniques with the MIDI keyboard and music notation software. The art teacher designs a presentation on how to use layering techniques in *Adobe Photoshop* to create a graphic collage. The technology teacher develops demonstrations of video and audio editing techniques. After a group presentation, the teachers work with each student as needed to complete the required products.

- **Arrange reviews and final presentations**: The teachers arrange for various experts in other locations to do online reviews of the students' creations and give them feedback. Students will revise their products as time permits and as they feel appropriate. The teachers arrange for an "Evening at Eureka" show to be given at the end of the grading period, with computers set up in a lab to display each student's work. Parents and friends are to be invited via the school website and via desktop-published invitations created by the art students.

Phase 4: Prepare the instructional environment

The technology teacher creates a "main page" for the student portfolios, with links to each student's work. He also creates a link from the school's main page to the portfolio section. The music teacher has a MIDI keyboard classroom, but there aren't enough keyboards for each student to have one for a whole period. The teachers arrange the schedule so that half the class attends band or orchestra practice, works in the art studio, or works on their individual portfolios in the computer lab, while the other half works on composition.

Phase 5: Evaluate and revise

At the end of each grading period, the teachers review the students' portfolios, assess progress, and discuss ways to make the work go more smoothly. Some of the questions they asked were:

- Did most students meet the individual benchmarks set for them?
- Are students actively engaged in the project work?
- Do the group demonstrations provide adequate initial instruction before students begin individual work?
- Were the classrooms and lab times organized for efficient work?

The teachers are gratified to see that most students seem motivated by the idea of using a multimedia web format to display their work and are making good progress on their benchmarks. However, it is apparent that many students need more individual instruction than the demonstrations can provide. The teachers decide to begin videotaping a series of short demos so that students can view them individually or in small groups, as needed, after the initial presentation. They agree that the scheduling proves a continuing challenge. They decide to request that additional MIDI keyboards and software be obtained to support this work. Also, English and history teachers have approached them about coordinating the portfolio work with students' writing and research projects. The teachers agree to work together to merge these skill areas into students' portfolio assessments.

Photograph courtesy of SoundTree.

OBJECTIVES

After reading this chapter and completing the learning activities for it, you should be able to:

1. Identify some of the current issues in music and art education that may impact the selection and use of technology.

2. Describe key strategies for integrating technology into music and art curricula.

3. Create instructional activities for music and art instruction that model successful integration strategies.

KEY TERMS

- computerized kilns
- morphing
- Music Educators National Conference (MENC)
- Musical Instrument Digital Interface (MIDI)
- music literacy
- notation software
- Orff instruments
- sequencers
- tweening

For more information on Key Terms, go to the *Key Terms* module for this chapter of the Companion Website at http://www.prenhall.com/roblyer.

INTRODUCTION: THE ARTS IN THE INFORMATION AGE

Many arts educators have resisted pressure to use computers and other instructional technologies, complaining of the contradiction inherent in blending impersonal machines with traditionally humanistic endeavors. In reality, however, technology has always played a part in the arts. Over the centuries, technology has provided tools, materials, and processes that aided artists' creative expression. In more recent times, the phonograph in music and the camera in visual arts have changed people's definitions of art. The integration of computers and other forms of electronic technology represents the next logical step in the evolution of the arts.

Many educators and members of the community question the need for instructional technology in the arts curriculum. Even some proponents of technology applications in other disciplines balk at investments in technology for the arts. Robinson and Roland (1994) offer four reasons to link the goals of a school arts program with rapidly developing instructional technologies:

1. **Expanded modes of expression** — By integrating new technologies into the arts curriculum, instructors expose students to new and exciting modes of artistic expression. All media have a place in the curriculum if they enable students to achieve desired instructional outcomes. New technologies warrant special atten-

tion because they constitute entirely new genres that may alter paradigms about art.

2. **Literacies for an Information Age** — The new technological culture requires today's students to develop a whole new set of literacies that go far beyond computer literacy. Arts instruction provides many unique opportunities for students to hone analytical skills to critically evaluate the flood of messages that fill a technologically saturated environment. The communicative language of the new technologies—sound, animation, music, drama, video, graphics, text, and voice—is also the language of the arts. Thus, arts teachers are particularly well positioned to help students develop skills as both critical producers and critical consumers of electronic media.

3. **Creative approaches to modern problems** — In the workplace of tomorrow, workers often will have to generate creative solutions to problems. An arts program that develops students' potentials for innovation in the areas of music, animation, graphics, multimedia, desktop publishing, and other emerging technologies will enable those students to compete in tomorrow's global business environment.

4. **Arts as aesthetic balance** — The arts counterbalance the massive infusion of technological change that society is experiencing. Technology can be seductive, and people need to keep in mind unique human abilities. Citizens of tomorrow's world will need coping skills

that enable them to keep their aesthetic sensibilities in the face of breathtaking technological advances. Arts education will help develop and maintain these skills.

Another version of this view, which calls for an understanding of "appropriate technologies," is described as follows in the national *Standards for Arts Education* (Music Educators National Conference [MENC], 1994):

> For the arts, technology thus offers means to accomplish artistic, scholarly, production, and performance goals. But the mere availability of technology cannot ensure a specific artistic result: the pencil in a student's hand ensures neither drawing competency nor a competent drawing. Nor, by itself, will exchanging the pencil for an airbrush or a computer graphics program create a change in the student.

ISSUES AND PROBLEMS IN MUSIC INSTRUCTION

Redefining Music Literacy

In music education, the term **music literacy** usually means an ability to read standard music notation. But the computer enables—if not encourages—experimentation with alternative ways to represent music. The earliest sequencers, even those with notation capability, have always included a "graphic" or "matrix" editor, a window in which the user could edit music by dragging, deleting, or expanding small rectangles on a grid. Composer Morton Subotnick authored *Making Music,* a software package that allows children to draw lines that are then rendered into melodies with a similar contour. More recently, Tod Machover of the MIT Media Lab has developed numerous projects for children and adults such as *Hyperscore* that require no formal training or music literacy. (See Figure 13.1 for examples of both.)

Today, the desktop music production software industry (e.g., Apple, Emagic, Cakewalk, Propellerheads, Cubase) is helping to accelerate a trend away from reliance on printed sheets and toward a sound artifact. This means that many students discouraged by a requirement to learn notation-based theory can now participate in the school music program as both composers and performers with little, if any, ability to read music.

Training Teachers to Meet Music Standards

Until states begin requiring teacher candidates to demonstrate proficiency with technology, teacher preparation programs will have a difficult time making a case for including required technology courses in their curricula. Teacher preparation programs, already overloaded with content, would be reluctant to displace a more traditional course with one whose skills remain in the "optional" category with respect to licensure.

However, in its publication, *The School Music Program: A New Vision,* the music professional organization **Music Educators National Conference (MENC)** said: "The K–12 music curriculum that was established by the 1930s has evolved only gradually since that time.... [T]he curricula that were acceptable in the past will be inadequate to prepare students for the 21st century" (1994, p. 3). The pamphlet goes on to designate technology as one of seven areas where the new music curriculum is fundamentally different from the traditional curriculum. Figure 13.2 lists music technology and education standards.

The Intersection of Popular Music, Technology, and Music Instruction

In 2004, the MENC published a collection of essays addressing the issue of popular music. *Bridging the Gap: Popular Music and Music Education* made very little mention

Figure 13.1 **(a)** *Making Music* **and (b)** *Making More Music* **by Morton Subotnick and (c)** *Hyperscore*

(a)　　　　　(b)　　　　　(c)

Source: (a, b) Reprinted courtesy of Viva Media LLC, New York. © 2004; http://www.creatingmusic.com. (c) Courtesy of Tod Machover, http://www.media.mit.edu/hyperins/topics.

Figure 13.2 Standards in Music Technology and Music Education

Areas of Competency in Music Technology (http://www.ti-me.org/standards/section2.html)	MENC Standards (http://www.menc.org/publication/books/standards.htm)
1. Electronic musical instruments (keyboards, controllers, synthesizers, samplers, sound reinforcement equipment) 2. Music production: data types (MIDI, digital audio); processes (sequencing, looping, signal processing, sound design) 3. Music notation software 4. Technology-assisted learning (instructional software, accompaniment/practice tools, Internet-based learning) 5. Multimedia: authoring (web pages, presentations, digital video); digital image capturing (scanning, still/video camera); Internet; electronic portfolios 6. Productivity tools, classroom and lab management: productivity tools (word processing, spreadsheet, database); computer systems (CPU, I/O devices, storage devices/media); lab management systems; networks	1. Singing, alone and with others, a varied repertoire of music. 2. Performing on instruments, alone and with others, a varied repertoire of music. 3. Improvising melodies, variations, and accompaniments. 4. Composing and arranging music within specified guidelines. 5. Reading and notating music. 6. Listening to, analyzing, and describing music. 7. Evaluating music and music performances. 8. Understanding relationships among music, the other arts, and disciplines outside the arts. 9. Understanding music in relation to history and culture.

of popular music's heavy reliance on technology for both production (composition) and live performance. Any music teacher seeking to start and sustain a program component dedicated to rock, hip hop, or other pop genres must have (or have access to) extensive knowledge of desktop music production and live sound reinforcement—not to mention a credible familiarity with pop music's complex web of music, culture, and traditions.

The Music Director as Small Business Administrator

A typical secondary school music program involves hundreds of students, rooms full of instruments and other equipment, wardrobes of uniforms and choral robes, libraries of sheet music, methods books and other print resources, and large budgets: The music director usually oversees the largest inventory of physical assets outside the athletic department. The music director is responsible for tracking students' academic progress and other duties common to all classroom teachers. In addition, the music teacher must be his or her own director of development, constantly on the lookout for continuing or increased funding. All of these issues make knowledge of information management software a high priority—if not a stated requirement—for the efficient operation of a successful music program.

TECHNOLOGY INTEGRATION STRATEGIES FOR MUSIC INSTRUCTION

In addition to general-purpose software (e.g., word processing, spreadsheet, web authoring), two broad categories of computer-based tools serve the needs of music teachers: *in-structional software* or programs developed primarily for teaching music skills, and *music production software,* which allows professional composition, recording, and performance. Muro (1994), Rudolph (2004), and Mauricio (2000) say that the most effective technology for music classrooms is not necessarily the computer. The first step in the process of integrating music technology may well be the purchase of an electronic keyboard or synthesizer. For financial reasons, many schools that have to choose between a *computer* or *keyboard* lab choose the latter. Strategies that make use of all these resources include support for music composition and production, music performance, self-paced learning and practice, teaching music history, and interdisciplinary strategies. These are summarized in Figure 13.3 and discussed next.

Support for Music Composition and Production

For the purposes of this chapter, music production and music composition mean the same thing. The two essential tools in this process are **sequencers** and **notation software,** and each can contribute substantially to teaching both production and performance. Sequencers allow the user to record, edit, and play back digital audio and MIDI data. Notation programs generally have fewer recording and playback options, but offer more flexibility in score and page setup, part extraction, text formatting, and other print-related issues. In other words, a sequencer facilitates music making in the *aural* domain, while notation facilitates music making in the *visual* domain.

Sequencers and notation software allow students to compose music in both traditional and nontraditional ways.

A MIDI synthesizer arranged to support music production and composition.

CW Discuss these issues online with other students by selecting the *Making the Case* module for Chapter 13 of the Companion Website (http:// www.prenhall.com/roblyer) or choose the *Message Board* module.

1. Consider the following quote from *The Electronic Word: Democracy, Technology, and the Arts* by Richard Lanham (1995): "Many areas of endeavor in America pressured by technological change have already had to decide what business they were really in, and those making the narrow choice have usually not fared well. The railroads had to decide whether they were in the transportation business or the railroad business; they chose the latter and gradual extinction. Newspapers had to decide whether they were in the information business or only the newspaper business; most who chose the newspaper business are no longer in it. A fascinating instance of this choice is now taking place in the piano industry. Steinway used to own the market, and it has decided to stay in the piano business. Yamaha decided it was in the keyboard business—acoustic and electronic—and has, with Roland, Korg, and other manufacturers, redefined the instrument. Time has yet to tell who will win, financially or musically" (p. 64).

   Following Lanham's examples of the newspaper, railroad, and musical instrument industries, what "businesses" were music educators in before the advent of the "electronic word," and has this development forced a similar reassessment? Do you see the "business" of teaching music facing redefinition with the emergence, proliferation, and dominance of computerized technologies?

2. In her discussion of issues and problems in arts education, Janis Boyd (undated) cites the following quote: "Excellence and innovation are critical to our collective future in generating the industries we require to enhance the nation's economic and social well-being. Creativity and innovation drive not only the cultural industries, but also developments in science, technology, industrial and management practices, all major contributors to our continuing socioeconomic growth."

   How does this intersection between technology and art education help make the case for including technology in art education?

With either tool, they can enter music with the mouse, play it with a MIDI-equipped keyboard or other input device (e.g., guitar or wind controller), or import it by opening standard MIDI files created by others (e.g., their fellow students, their teachers, or files found on the Internet). Designed *primarily* for desktop music production, the sequencer typically offers more options for creating a *sonic* artifact: more sophisticated mixing and sound design features. Notation software is designed *primarily* to facilitate the production of music as a *visual* artifact, music on paper or on screen that can then be performed by a live musician. Note, however, that almost all sequencers now offer at least a basic notation component, while notation software programs are giving the user more and more playback options.

Music production software includes sequencing (MIDI and digital audio), digital audio editing (often a component of a sequencing program), and music notation. Although these programs offer teachers maximum flexibility in designing curriculum, they require more involvement from the teacher in creating curricula, directing instruction, assessment, training, and technological maintenance.

Sequencers are available in both hardware and software form. The hardware sequencer is usually found as an integrated component of a synthesizer workstation—a synthesizer with the ability to record multiple tracks of MIDI information. Software sequencers run as an application on a computer and therefore require a more complete MIDI workstation (computer, MIDI controller, sound module, and a MIDI interface), but are exponentially more powerful with increased processing speed, storage capacity, and a bigger screen on which to display data.

TOP TEN STRATEGIES FOR TECHNOLOGY IN MUSIC AND ART INSTRUCTION

Take advantage of these 10 powerful strategies for using technology to enhance the teaching of music and art.

Music Strategies

1. **Students use software like Apple's *GarageBand* as a personal recording studio** — Students have the flexibility and resources they need to support their own creative musical explorations.

2. **Teachers use an electronic keyboard lab to develop students' skills in keyboarding, theory, and harmony** — Networked systems allow the teacher to monitor individual students as they build their skills.

3. **Software such as *Practica Musica* serves as a tutorial in music fundamentals** — Interactive software gives students hands-on practice in music theory and ear training.

4. ***Music Ace's "Doodle Pad"* teaches young students about parts for different instruments** — The software makes it easy for young learners to "write" music with parts for different instruments.

5. **Students build a website to help teach music history** — The wealth of images and information on the Internet gives students the material they need to research composers, compositions, and periods of musical history and share their findings on the web.

Art Strategies

1. **Students take virtual field trips to art museums** — Through virtual tours available at many sites, students can "visit" museums and see great works of art to serve as illustrations of artists' work and models for their own work.

2. **Students create electronic portfolios to illustrate their creative products** — *PowerPoint* presentations, videos, electronic books, and websites offer versatile venues for students to document and share their work.

3. **Illustrate artworks/techniques with digital slide shows** — Teachers can store large collections in very little space and show parts of collections to illustrate techniques and products of various artists.

4. **Teacher-created websites give short tutorials on art concepts** — The Internet offers an easy, motivating way to let students develop background knowledge of art concepts on their own.

5. **Students create an illustrated desktop-published brochure or newsletter** — This activity is a great way for students to practice writing, as well as visual design skills.

Most sequencing programs simulate the functions of the physical recording studio. Music is recorded on tracks and assigned to channels for playback and editing. Software plug-ins are digital equivalents of outboard (hardware) signal modifiers such as echo chambers and compressors and, depending on the processing power of the computer being used, provide the composer with a desktop recording studio equipped with virtually unlimited mixing options. Many sequencers offer the ability to record sound directly on the computer's hard drive with the use of a microphone. Live, simultaneous multichannel recording is possible with an external digital audio interface. After recording, digital audio data, as represented by a wave shape, can be manipulated (edited) with the ease and precision of text in a word processor.

With very few exceptions, all sequencers support both step- and real-time recording of MIDI data. Once MIDI notes are entered, they can be edited like any other data on the computer: cut, copied, and pasted. All performance parameters of MIDI data can be controlled by the user independently of one another, including pitch, tempo, volume, and dynamics.

Some programs designed for young children have sequencing components that enable composition. The "Doodle Pad" component of *Music Ace,* for example, allows the user to drag different shaped happy faces (repre-

Figure 13.3 Summary of Technology Integration Strategies for Music

Technology Integration Strategies	Benefits	Sample Resources and Activities
Support for music composition and production Courtesy of Apple Computers. http://www.apple.com	• Offers a range of mixing and sound design options to support composition for students of any age. • Supports both traditional and nontraditional composition. • Offers teachers maximum flexibility in designing music curriculum.	• Apple/Emagic Logic http://www.apple.com/logic/ • Apple *GarageBand* http://www.apple.com/ilife/garageband/ • Reason (Propellerhead) Software http://www.propellerheads.se/ **See also Technology Integration Idea 13.1:** Play the Recorder on the Computer
Support for performance Courtesy of Notation Software, Inc. http://www.notation.com/	• Expedites preparation for performance (e.g., rearranging music for alternate instrumentations, re-creating lost or missing parts from the score, transposing parts, and simplifying difficult passages). • Helps teachers with theory lessons, quizzes, and other handouts to aid student performance.	• *Sibelius* notation software http://www.sibelius.com • *Finale* and *Print Music* software http://www.finalemusic.com/ • *MidiNotate* http://www.notation.com/
Support for self-paced learning and practice Courtesy of Ars Nova. http://www.ars-nova.com/	• Offers individual, personal help with needed skills, ear training, or music theory.	• *Practica Musica* http://www.ars-nova.com/
Support for teaching music history Courtesy of Vulcan Productions, Inc. http://www.pbs.org/theblues/	• Internet sites provide easy-to-access background information on composers and musical periods/compositions. • Website generation offers a venue for students to share their research.	• Classic Motown timeline http://classic.motown.com/timeline/ • See also pbs.org for other interactive and educational timelines and music history resources.
Support for interdisciplinary strategies Courtesy of Wildridge Education. http://www.wildridge.com/	• Builds on natural relationships between music and other topics (e.g., physics). • Helps promote musical literacy while teaching related concepts.	*Math & Music* http://www.wildridge.com/

TECHNOLOGY INTEGRATION IDEA 13.1

TECHNOLOGY IN MUSIC INSTRUCTION

Title: Play the Recorder on the Computer

Content Area/Topic: Music composition

Grade Levels: K–5

NETS for Students: Standards 4, 5, 6

Description: Studying the recorder is often used as a way of teaching and reinforcing music composition concepts to students at all levels. In this lesson, students use *Recorder Teacher* software to learn how to play the recorder. The teacher demonstrates the fingering for various notes by showing the software tutorial. As students try playing notes, the program plays them to let students check that they are playing them correctly. Tonguing and blowing concepts also are demonstrated. As students begin to write their own musical compositions, the computer plays them. Finally, students test their skills in two different ways: fingering or note reading. *Recorder Teacher* and other similar programs are available at http://www.theshops.co.uk/childsplay.

Source: Dillon, R. (1998). In the key of "see and hear": How students can learn to play the recorder by playing musical computers. *Learning and Leading with Technology, 26*(2), 15–17.

senting notes of different rhythmic values) onto a staff. In addition, the user can assign each note to one of several different sounds (e.g., piano, violin) as represented by a different color. With proper direction, however, elementary school students can be taught the basic operations of even the most sophisticated professional software. By middle school many students possess the instrumental technique and/or the computer skills necessary to take advantage of more complicated processes such as digital audio editing and adding musical expression to their MIDI data (Ohler, 1998). (See Technology Integration Idea 13.1.)

Projects that begin at a computer workstation in a lab can be used in other situations throughout the music program. Students can create notation files that are then used to facilitate performance in the rehearsal room or at a concert. Students who are especially proficient on an instrument (including voice) can create a sequenced instrumental "bed" to accompany a live performance or group or individual rehearsal.

Desktop music systems (e.g., the MIDI sequencer) have prompted new definitions of musicianship that recognize intuition and innate musical creativity as well as traditional conservatory-track modes of preparation. As suggested earlier, students with little or no "formal" musical training or (piano) keyboard skills can create and edit compositions using a sequencing program with step entry capability. Students can also perform analyses on music

using preexisting MIDI files and/or digital audio imported from a CD. Once the pieces have been imported into a sequencer, students can explore all aspects of musical form, harmony, orchestration, and other parameters. Sequencers and audio editing software offer the student the ability not only to *listen* to prerecorded music but also to *manipulate* it. Students can demonstrate their understanding of musical form by literally separating a piece of recorded music into its structural components. In this way, expositions, recapitulations, second choruses, guitar solos, all become discrete audio events, which can in turn be rearranged—resequenced—into new formal configurations. Apple's *GarageBand* has become popular among young people for mixing and playing their own music. (See the example in Figure 13.4.)

Students with performance skills can record MIDI data over their favorite audio recordings using different kinds of MIDI controllers. More advanced analysis projects, such as those that might take place in an advanced placement music theory class, can now be undertaken using music software as a presentation tool. Consequently, the general music class can accomplish a great deal more than simply providing those students who are supposed to be unmusical or at least untrained with a passive listening experience.

While the preceding scenarios lend themselves best to a lab environment with multiple computers, even a single computer can provide valuable support for a general mu-

Support for Music Performance

Notation software offers all of the power and flexibility of word processing applied to sheet music. In a school music program, it expedites all the tasks related to ensuring that each student has something to play: rearranging music for alternate instrumentations, recreating lost or missing parts from the score, transposing parts, and simplifying difficult passages. When printed, notation documents are legible and have a professional look, eliminating the confusion that often results from handwritten parts. And, as is the case with all computer-generated data, existing documents can be corrected and/or revised without having to reenter the music from scratch. Notation files are small by comparison to digital audio, video, and graphics files, so entire libraries (hundreds of scores, parts, and handouts) can be stored in an insignificant amount of disk space.

Using notation software, teachers can create theory lessons, quizzes, and other handouts that combine notation with text and other graphics. Screen captures of short passages can be made in the notation document and then inserted into a word processing document. Advanced notation programs also allow for maximum flexibility in generating more unusual or irregular layouts.

To clarify the different roles of the sequencer and the notation program in the teaching of performance, it is helpful to consider the hypothetical scenario of an ensemble class. To support sectional or individual practice, the teacher would enter the score of a piece into a sequencer. Once the music had been entered, the student or teacher can choose which parts need to be heard. In this way, a clarinet section could rehearse to a sequence consisting of the entire ensemble minus the clarinets. The second clarinet player could practice sectional passages by selecting only the clarinet parts for playback, but muting the second clarinet part. Meanwhile the notation program would be used to create those parts. These techniques have been demonstrated effectively by Rudolph and Peters (1996).

Meanwhile, the piano lab has given way to the electronic keyboard lab, where students can develop keyboard skills as well as learn theory and harmony (Mark, 1996). Keyboard labs can now be networked with devices that allow the teacher to communicate with individual students or groups of students by means of a microphone and headphones.

Support for Self-Paced Learning and Practice

Most CD-ROM-based programs can accommodate both self-paced learning or an activity more closely directed and monitored by the teacher. *Practica Musica,* for example, can be used as a tutorial in music fundamentals with little or no

sic curriculum. Rudolph and Peters (1996) have demonstrated how a computer running sequencing software can support music instruction with **Orff instruments.** These are instruments for children developed by K. Maendler under the direction of composer Carl Orff. Modeled after a wooden African instrument, they were specially designed to provide a successful and fun first experience with making music.

Figure 13.4 Frame from Apple Computer's *GarageBand*

Source: Reprinted by permission of Apple Computer.

Figure 13.5 *Practica Musica* Music Theory and Ear Training Software

Source: Courtesy of Emagic, Inc.

input from the teacher. (See Figure 13.5.) It can also serve as a drill program when a student needs help with a particular topic relating to ear training or music theory. Teachers need to consider multiple integration strategies when evaluating and using instructional software. While interactivity and multimedia make instructional software a *potentially* more powerful teaching aid than an inert textbook, these programs cannot replace the teacher's careful supervision. In the end, the responsibility for effective teaching—with or without technology—rests with the teacher.

Almost all music instructional software packages either have a designated drill component or can be utilized as such. They are probably the easiest programs to install and learn. Many have the capability of maintaining the records of multiple students on the same computer. Companies generally provide online demos of these programs, so teachers can sample them before they buy.

Support for Teaching Music History

Of the nine national standards for music education the only one that refers specifically to music history is the last one: "Understanding music in relation to history and culture." General music teachers have long sought to foster a deeper understanding of the musical work (especially for the musically nonliterate) by situating it in its historical context. This is an excellent way to introduce younger students to the practice of research, while offering older students unlimited opportunities for independent projects. The Internet is rapidly becoming the most powerful research tool available to students and teachers at all levels of education. Students and teachers can access card catalogs, electronic books, online journals, archived and current newspaper articles, audio and MIDI files, video clips, databases of thousands of out-of-print books, and discussion groups on every topic imaginable. Productive educational use of the Internet is limited only by the user and, to some extent, the connection speed and processing power of the computer.

Building a website is in many ways the perfect culminating activity for a general music class. Students can do much of the planning in groups—even offline, if computer access is limited. Within each group, students can assign areas of the site according to individual strengths and literacies: A student who can't read music may be proficient with a web page authoring tool; some students can search the Internet for relevant graphics while others look for text or sound. Videos and now DVDs continue to be a source of valuable historical reference material. Many documentaries formerly available on videotape are now available on DVD, which offers the user random access to the entire film. Any of these media can be captured on a computer's hard drive and incorporated into a student- or teacher-authored web page or software presentation. Finished projects can be viewed locally on a single computer, burned to a CD for multiple computers, posted on a school intranet, or uploaded to an Internet site so that parents or other students around the world can see it, link to it, and perhaps even contribute their own material.

Finally, a compelling general music class has the potential to be a highly effective recruiting tool. Students who initially feel out of place in their school's music program may find an exciting and challenging alternative role for themselves after taking a general music class. Often, it is access to music technology that attracts these students.

Figure 13.6   Recommended Websites for Music Instruction

- The Music Educators National Conference (http://www.menc.org/)
- Technology Institute for Music Educators (http://www.ti-me.org/index.html)
- Resource center for designing and equipping music/computer labs in schools (http://www.soundtree.com/welcome.asp)
- Sibelius Educational Suite (http://www.sibelius.com/education/)
- Free sheet music in PDF format (http://www.free-scores.com/cd-sheet/piano.php)
- Library of Congress recordings (http://www.loc.gov/rr/record/)
- The Media Machine-Making Music with the Macintoshes (http://www.mashine.com/)

Support for Interdisciplinary Strategies

Beyond the opportunities for interdisciplinary study that will inevitably present themselves in a general music class, student-produced music and research can enhance a variety of other aspects of school life. Multimedia-based research projects in the humanities can easily include music that underscores a presentation or that is the object of study itself. A sequencer can facilitate the work of student composers who want to supply music for dance projects or video footage of athletic events. The close relationship between music and physics calls for projects that examine the science of sound.

Figure 13.6 lists some valuable music education websites.

ISSUES AND PROBLEMS IN ART INSTRUCTION

Funding for Art Instruction

As a result of lean economic times and the ever-increasing emphasis on accountability in mathematics and reading as reflected in the No Child Left Behind Act, funding for art education is at an all-time low. Teachers must increasingly find ways to stretch available funds to teach art. In light of this reality, funding for technology in art is especially difficult; updating technology resources and buying electronic supplies present continuing problems. For example, production of graphics is a popular art activity, but the need to buy expensive ink for printers and specialized paper supplies taxes budgets. Teachers are forced to take measures such as password-protecting printers and putting software print controls in place to limit the number of pages a student may print for free.

Ethical Issues with Using Images

Since it is becoming easy to use images from the Internet and other sources, it is increasingly important to teach students that they must cite sources and request permission to use them. When students are doing research or creating artwork on the computers for websites or graphic design or other art projects, it is important to instruct them about issues of appropriation and repurposing of images and how this use intersects with plagiarism. There are precedents for using other artists' images for inclusion in one's own work but without altering the image considerably, problems could arise. Discussions should take place about issues of copyright. Perhaps a short assignment could be done to have students look at what the issues are and how they feel about copying someone else's work whether written or as artwork.

Accessing Images Used in Art Instruction

If schools put filters onto computers to protect students from unsavory materials (i.e., pornography), many great works of art will also be filtered out unless the filter is carefully constructed. All care should be made to allow for these artworks to be visible and accessible to students. The works of lesser known, more contemporary artists can sometimes skirt the line between what is generally considered to be art and what is not. In photography, the nude figure has been a long-used subject. Some of the great artists have used the nude as metaphor for beauty, nature, and life. Limiting access by allowing only the names of the most famous artists to pass through a filter will not solve the problem. Strategies must be designed for allowing complete access to images of artworks for students to use. If all else fails, teachers must make sure the library in the school has a good collection of art and art history books. Also, many museums are making available images from their collections on CD for purchase.

The Challenge of Meeting Standards in Arts Instruction

Despite the dearth of funding for the arts and arts education, a group of professional organizations joined with the Consortium of National Arts Education Associations to promote a vision of K–12 arts education as described in the National Standards for Arts Education (http://www.ed.gov/pubs/ArtsStandards.html). The standards ask that students know and be able to do the following by the time they have completed secondary school:

- Be able to communicate at a basic level in the four arts disciplines—dance, music, theatre, and the visual arts. This includes knowledge and skills in the use of the basic vocabularies, materials, tools, techniques, and intellectual methods of each arts discipline.

- Be able to communicate proficiently in at least one art form, including the ability to define and solve artistic problems with insight, reason, and technical proficiency.

- Be able to develop and present basic analyses of works of art from structural, historical, and cultural perspectives, and from combinations of those perspectives. This includes the ability to understand and evaluate work in the various arts disciplines.

- Have an informed acquaintance with exemplary works of art from a variety of cultures and historical periods, and a basic understanding of historical development in the arts disciplines, across the arts as a whole, and within cultures.

- Be able to relate various types of arts knowledge and skills within and across the arts disciplines. This includes mixing and matching competencies and understandings in art making, history and culture, and analysis in any arts-related project.

Schools are challenged to find ways of meeting these standards in an educational climate in which arts are clearly not a priority.

TECHNOLOGY INTEGRATION STRATEGIES FOR ART INSTRUCTION

As with music instruction, technology resources in art instruction support a variety of classroom strategies, from simple demonstrations of materials to student production techniques. Strategies include accessing art examples for classroom use, using teaching examples and materials, producing and manipulating digitized images, supporting graphic design and 3-D modeling, supporting desktop publishing with graphics, virtual field trips to art museums, creating movies as an art form, using computerized kilns, and sharing students' creative and research works. These are summarized in Figure 13.7.

Accessing Art Examples for Classroom Use

Internet sites and DVD collections are rich sources of artworks that students can use as illustrations of artists' work and as models for their own work. Teachers can generate a set of sites to bookmark for regular use in classes. They can also get students involved in these searches. For example, they might give an assignment that asks students to find sources for paintings that use still life as subject matter or that use the technique of chiaroscuro or that are 15th-century Florentine. When the students are actively

Figure 13.7 Summary of Technology Integration Strategies for Art

Technology Integration Strategies	Benefits	Sample Resources and Activities
Accessing art examples for classroom use Courtesy of Masters of Photography. http://www.masters-of-photography.com	• Internet and CD collections provide ready access to works of art to use as samples, illustrations, and models.	• *Masters of Photography* CD http://www.masters-of-photography.com • World Wide Arts resources art history section http://www.ar.com/artists • KinderArt's Multicultural Art resources http://www.kinderart.com/multic
Using teaching examples and materials Courtesy of Barbara Houghton. http://www.nku.edu/~houghton/docent	• Multimedia slide lectures are easier to use than slides and allow quick, random access to examples, illustrations. • Teacher-created websites can provide easy-to-access exercises in color theory, design theory, and photography techniques.	• *PowerPoint, HyperStudio, Apple's Keynote* • Teacher-created websites, e.g., http://www.nku.edu/~houghton/docent
Producing and manipulating digitized images Courtesy of Barbara Houghton. http://www.nku.edu/~houghton	• Offers an easy, flexible system for creating images. • Lets novice artists create high-quality products. • Lets novice artists scan found objects to use in compositions.	• Camcorders, VCRs, digital cameras, scanners • Digitizing software, e.g., *FotoFinish* http://www.fotofinish.com • Paint programs, e.g., Riverdeep's *KidPix*, Adobe's *Photoshop Elements*
Supporting graphic design and 3-D modeling Courtesy of Morpheus Software LLC. http://www.morpheussoftware.net/	• Makes possible graphic techniques that can be done only on the computer with this software. • Offers many opportunities for artistic expression. • Demonstrates how easily images can be altered, thus fostering visual literacy skills.	• Image manipulation software, e.g., *Adobe PhotoShop* http://www.adobe.com • Morphing software, e.g., *Morpheus* http://www.morpheussoftware.net/ • 3-D modeling software, e.g., *Ulead COOL 3D* http://www.ulead.com **Also see Technology Integration Idea 13.2:** Visualize It in 3-D
Supporting desktop publishing with graphics Courtesy of Adobe Systems, Inc. http://www.adobe.com	• Lets students illustrate their brochures, newsletters, and other documents with high-quality graphics.	• *Adobe PhotoShop* http://www.adobe.com

(continued)

Figure 13.7 (continued)

Technology Integration Strategies	Benefits	Sample Resources and Activities
Virtual field trips to art museums online tours NATIONAL GALLERY OF ART http://www.nga.gov/	• Allows students to see models and examples of artworks not locally available. • Makes possible multicultural "field trips" to gather examples of art and music around the world.	• Virtual Tour of the Louvre Museum, Paris http://www.louvre.fr/anglais/visite/vis_f.htm • Art Institute of Chicago http://www.artic.edu/ • Museum of Modern Art http://www.moma.org • Metropolitan Museum of Art http://www.metmuseum.org/ • Smithsonian museums http://www.si.edu/ • National Gallery of Art http://www.nga.gov/
Creating movies as an art form QuickTime http://www.apple.com	• Students can produce their own creative works for research, reports, assignments, and entertainment.	• Apple Computer offers *iMovie* and *GarageBand* http://www.apple.com • ArcSoft's *VideoImpression* http://www.arcsoft.com/ • Microsoft's *Movie Maker* http://microsoft.com
Using computerized kilns Courtesy of Cress Manufacturing Company. http://www.cressmfg.com	• Automatic monitoring frees student and teacher time during production of ceramic works. • Allows for more precise control of processes and repeatable results. • Easy preset programs with multizone controls and advanced capabilities. • Takes care of monitoring for non-school hours.	• Cress kilns http://www.ceramicssf.com • Bailey kilns http://www.baileypottery.com
Sharing students' creative and research works Courtesy of Barbara Houghton http://www.nku.edu/~houghton	• Allows students many different ways of documenting work and easily sharing it with others.	• *PowerPoint* presentations • Videos • Electronic books • Websites

looking and sharing, more learning will take place. Other example activities include:

• Have students use the library to find specific works of art and then challenge them to locate on the Internet other examples of the artist's work or work from the same period.

• To teach about the work of contemporary artists, have students look at galleries and exhibitions online to see the new work.

Figure 13.8 Sample Teacher-Created Website for Art Instruction

Source: Courtesy of Barbara Houghton; http://www.nku.edu/~houghton/docent/.

- For instructional reinforcement, use DVD collections on art techniques.
- Create a digital library to use for slide shows and presentations. Assign students who are traveling during the school year or during the summer to visit galleries and museums and bring back pamphlets, postcards, or examples of artwork they see. Scan the examples to create images for the classroom digital library.
- Obtain and use resources such as the *Masters of Photography* CD (http://www.masters-of-photography.com).

Using Teaching Examples and Materials

Computers can be used by faculty in art to create *PowerPoint* slide lectures (Gleeson, 1997) and bring in images either by scanning or photographing with digital cameras. Also faculty who are web savvy can create interactive websites to help students learn color theory, design theory, and photography techniques. Figure 13.8 provides an example of an art teaching site.

Producing and Manipulating Digitized Images

The most common type of hardware resource in art instruction is image digitizing equipment. Graphic scanners are computer peripherals that transfer print materials into digital images on a computer. A scanner can transfer images, photographs, line drawing, or text into graphics files in a cost-effective and efficient manner. An artist can also capture an image from a video source (camcorder or VCR) using digitizing software. Finally, a digital camera records images directly to disk. This equipment provides the user with an extremely flexible system for developing digital images. Students can then use computer software to manipulate digital images. This is a good example of using technology to foster creativity. Indeed, the ability to digitize still images and video has opened up a whole new genre of art.

A wide variety of software is available to teachers and students who are interested in producing computer art. Simple paint programs are available for very young students; in fact, teachers often use these types of programs when first introducing students to the computer. Integrated software and hypermedia authoring programs always include fairly sophisticated draw or paint tools, which provide good intermediate tools for the developing computer artist. High-level programs suitable to the advanced artist would be used primarily at the high school level. One way a student might use paint or draw software would be to design the layout for a hypermedia project. By using these tools, a student who does not possess a great deal of artistic ability can produce a very attractive design. Using technology in this fashion models the strategy of integration to remedy an identified weakness.

Supporting Graphic Design and 3-D Modeling

Art educators can choose among a number of software options to let students explore graphic design. A range of animation programs is available, from simple cell-type animation to more advanced programs that offer features like **tweening** or **morphing.** The latter enable the user to change one frame to the next by moving through as many as 64 intermediate positions in between. These graphic techniques can be done only with computer software. Other programs are specifically geared toward cartoon production and allow artists to add music and sound. Today's more powerful programs speed up the process by providing two-dimensional animation.

An art studio would not be complete without an image manipulation program like *Adobe Photoshop,* which enables students to edit clip art or digitized photos. High-end programs provide hundreds of options and special effects for altering images. Morphing software enables the user to transform images smoothly from one shape to another. This technique offers tremendous potential for artistic expression and, by demonstrating how easily images can be altered, helps foster the development of visual literacy skills.

Finally, as Quesada (1998) and Steed (2001) describe, students can use 3-D, modeling, and animation software to communicate ideas visually through computer-generated models, animation, and imagery. One such activity is in an interdisciplinary assignment called "Pocket Lint Project." Students use whatever they can pull out of their purses or pockets as the basis for developing a character. They use 3-D and animation software to create a model for their characters and use geometry to "convey a sense of emotion" (Quesada, 1998, p. 54). Other good curriculum uses are described in Technology Integration Idea 13.2.

TECHNOLOGY INTEGRATION IDEA 13.2

TECHNOLOGY IN ART INSTRUCTION

Title: Visualize It in 3-D

Content Area/Topic: Art, astronomy

Grade Levels: 7–12

NETS for Students: Standards 4, 5, 6

Description: Many concepts in school learning are symbolic, rather than concrete, and students spend a great deal of time learning what the symbols mean. A good way to make many symbolic concepts more understandable is by making them more visual through 3-D models. One such concept in which a 3-D model is useful is for depicting a solar eclipse. After students discuss what a solar eclipse is and view a video or photos of it in class, they create a 3-D model of the sun and moon. Then they use animation effects to demonstrate how the eclipse takes place, and store the animation as a *QuickTime* movie. Models created by various groups are presented for comparison and discussion. Other activities in which learning can be enhanced through 3-D models include cell structures and air flow patterns in science, volume problems in math, choreography in the performing arts, and virtual sculptures in art.

Source: Steed, M. (2001). 3-D visualization: Using 3-D software to represent curricular concepts. *Learning and Leading with Technology, 29*(3), 14–20.

Supporting Desktop Publishing with Graphics

Many schools look to their own graphics arts programs to create brochures and newsletters as part of student learning activities. Because students get such good experience creating and producing these publications, the activities can be considered a kind of internship to prepare for actual jobs as graphic artists for newspapers or other companies.

Virtual Field Trips to Art Museums

Many museums around the world have sites that allow a virtual tour through the museum. Although clearly this is not the same as viewing the works in person, these sites do offer a way for students to explore and expand their knowledge base. Some sites make their server available for students to post their own creations and learn how to create art using a certain medium like paper maché, batik, or origami. These sites also can be the basis for multicultural "field trips" to gather examples of art and music around the world (Quesada, 1998). It is important to remember when using the Internet for arts instruction that the images are reproductions; students will need to be made aware of the idea of scale and constantly be reminded that they need to keep in mind the limitations of digital imagery. Figure 13.9 is list of recommended art museums.

Creating Movies as an Art Form

Students can now make short digital movies with software that often comes with the computer. For example, Macintoshes come with *iMovie,* which students can use to produce their own creative works using images from drawing, painting, photography, digital video, and sound for reports, assignments, and entertainment. These inexpensive little movies can be shared across platforms by saving them in *QuickTime* format. Doing video projects used to be expensive and difficult but, with the new video editing software, it is affordable and relatively easy for students to use. Videotape from old analog sources can be fed through newer digital video cameras and digitized for use in these movies.

Using Computerized Kilns

Art teachers who work in fired pottery media can use computerized electric kilns to save student time and assure better quality products. **Computerized kilns** automatically set required temperature, monitor length of time, and begin the process of cooling down and shutting off. Without the computer, teachers and students must keep a careful eye on the kiln to check the temperature by using cone indicators viewed through a peephole in the door of the kiln. The process of firing a kiln can take days, depend-

Figure 13.9   Recommended Websites for Art Enrichment Virtual Field Trips

- Virtual Tour of the Louvre Museum, Paris (http://www.louvre.fr/anglais/visite/vis_f.htm)
- Art Institute of Chicago (http://www.artic.edu/)
- Museum of Modern Art (http://www.moma.org)
- Metropolitan Museum of Art (http://www.metmuseum.org/)
- Smithsonian Museums (http://www.si.edu/)
- National Gallery of Art (http://www.nga.gov/)
- Whitney Museum of American Art (http://www.whitney.org/)
- Andy Warhol Museum (http://www.warhol.org/warhol/)
- Art Museum Image Consortium (http://www.amico.org/)
- Tour of Florence Cathedral (http://www.nku.edu/~houghton/duomoweb)
- Photography Exhibition of the work of Douglas Prince (http://www.nku.edu/~photo/prince/index.html)
- Great Artists: DaVinci to Picasso (http://www.theartgallery.com.au/ArtEducation/greatartists/)
- Fine Art History Quick Reference (http://www.theartgallery.com.au/ArtEducation/greatartists/)
- Masters of Photography (http://www.masters-of-photography.com/)
- Photography of Henri Cartier-Bresson from NPR (http://www.npr.org/display_pages/features/feature_1318621.html)
- International Sculpture Center (http://www.sculpture.org/)
- Architect Frank Lloyd Wright Foundation (http://www.franklloydwright.org/)
- Architect Zaha Hadid (http://www.zaha-hadid.com/)
- Great Buildings Online (http://www.GreatBuildings.com/gbc.html)
- Non-Western art listings at Penn State Library (http://www.libraries.psu.edu/artshumanities/art/nonwestern.html)
- Non-Western art links (http://www.bc.edu/bc_org/avp/cas/fnart/links/non_western.html)
- Non-Western art links on *The Educator*, online magazine for the professional in education (http://www.the-educator.co.uk/mainsite/links/art/nonwes.htm)
- Science, Art and Technology course from Art Institute of Chicago for science teachers (http://www.artic.edu/aic/students/sciarttech/)

ing on the type and size of the kiln and its load, so this represents a considerable time savings.

Sharing Students' Creative and Research Works

Through electronic publishing, videos, and presentation software, students can share their art creations with others. Portfolios have long been a way for art students to demonstrate their achievements and abilities, and electronic portfolios are a natural extension of this strategy. Students can create *PowerPoint* presentations, videos, electronic books, and websites to show their research and creative work. Artists' books can be created and printed using desktop publishing and color inkjet printers. See an example of "how to" at http://www.nku.edu/~photo/295/makebook.html and the result in Figure 13.10.

Figure 13.10   An Artist's Online Book

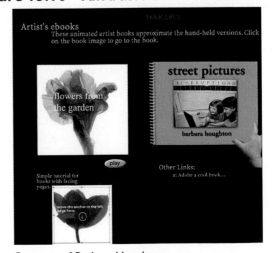

Source: Courtesy of Barbara Houghton.

INTERACTIVE SUMMARY

The following is a summary of the main points covered in this chapter. To see additional examples and information on these points, go to this textbook's Companion Website at http://www.prenhall.com/roblyer and click on the Chapter 13 *Interactive Summary* module to visit each of the recommended websites.

1. **A rationale for teaching arts in the Information Age:** Four parts of the justification for including art and music in school curriculum are expanded modes of expression, literacies for an Information Age, creative approaches to modern problems, and arts as aesthetic balance.

2. **Issues in music instruction:** These include:
   - Redefining music literacy
   - Training teachers to meet music standards (see music standards and music technology standards)
   - The intersection of popular music, technology, and music education
   - The music director as small business administrator.

3. **Integration strategies for music education:** Five strategies are described for integrating technology into this area:
   - Support for music composition and production (see *Apple's GarageBand*)
   - Support for music performance (see Sibelius' notation software)
   - Support for self-paced learning and practice (see *Practica Musica*)
   - Support for teaching music history (see example at Classic Motown timeline)
   - Support for interdisciplinary strategies (see math and music strategies).

4. **Issues in art instruction:** These include:
   - Funding for art education
   - Ethical issues with using images
   - Accessing images used in art education
   - The challenge of meeting standards in arts education.

5. **Integration strategies for art instruction:** Eight strategies are described for integrating technology into this area:
   - Accessing art examples for classroom use (see the *Masters of Photography CD*)
   - Using teaching examples and materials
   - Producing and manipulating digitized images
   - Supporting graphic design and 3-D modeling (see *Adobe PhotoShop*)
   - Supporting desktop publishing with graphics
   - Virtual field trips to art museums (see tours available from the Louvre website)
   - Creating movies as an art form
   - Using computerized kilns (see Cress kilns)
   - Sharing students' creative and research works.

Online Activities

Visit this text's Companion Website at http://www.prenhall.com/roblyer to gain access to a variety of questions, activities, and exercises to help build your knowledge of this chapter's content.

Online Chapter 13 Self-Test

To review terms and concepts for this chapter, click on the *Self-Test* module for this chapter of the Companion Website.

Software Skill-Builder Tutorials

To access practical tutorial and skill-building activities and to build skills using popular software and hardware, click on the *Software Skill-Builder Tutorials* module for this chapter of the Companion Website.

Web-Enrichment Activities

To complete activities that connect to chapter content and provide web-based resources, click on the *Web-Enrichment Activities* module for this chapter of the Companion Website.

TECHNOLOGY INTEGRATION WORKSHOP

CLIPS FROM THE CLASSROOM: LEARNING WITH TECHNOLOGY

Go to the *Technology Integration Workshop* DVD located in the back of this text and click on *Clips from the Classroom*. View the video clips listed below that support this chapter's content:

- *Website and* Photoshop *in Photography*
- *Composition Software and MIDI in Music.*

Now, visit this text's Companion Website at http://www.prenhall.com/roblyer to answer questions and complete activities that will guide you in analyzing each clip.

THE TIP MODEL IN ACTION

Read each of the following scenarios related to implementing the TIP Model, and go to the Companion Website to answer the questions that follow it based on your Chapter 13 reading activities.

TIP Model Scenario #1 Mr. Orson, a music performance teacher, has been talking to his friend and colleague Mr. Niesson, who is a music teacher in Dublin, Ireland. Mr. Orson and Mr. Niesson would like to have their students work together on creating new musical pieces based on a series of Irish folk tunes that Mr. Niesson has collected in the rural areas near the city. Mr. Niesson would send recordings of the tunes, and the students would play them and work on variations based on them. However, the teachers and students need a way to make both the music production tasks and communicating their products faster and easier.

1.1 What technology-based strategies could the teachers use to address these needs?

1.2 What would be the relative advantages of using these strategies?

1.3 What would be a good way to display their products, once they were created?

TIP Model Scenario #2 Mr. Daniel, the school's music teacher, is doing an interdisciplinary project with Ms. Merrill, the history teacher. They plan to have Ms. Mer-

rill's students research backgrounds of the musical composers of the Romantic period, listen to some of their works, and locate information on events of the times that helped shape their perspectives and, consequently, the music they created.

2.1 What technology-based strategy could the teachers use to carry out such a project?

2.2 What would be the relative advantage of using this strategy?

2.3 If they wanted to have Ms. Merrill's students work in small groups, how would they implement this in the class?

TIP Model Scenario #3 Students in Dr. Hadley's music appreciation class were preparing for their end-of-semester recitals. There were a variety of musical pieces, and Dr. Hadley would be accompanying each student during the recital. He wanted students to be able to practice individually with accompaniment, but he did not have time to accompany each of them as they practiced.

3.1 What technology-based tool could Dr. Hadley use to address this need?

3.2 What would be the relative advantage of using this strategy instead of allowing them to practice without accompaniment?

3.3 If Dr. Hadley has 30 music students and only eight music stations, what strategy could he use to allow each student to practice individually?

TIP Model Scenario #4 Mr. Lucien wanted to teach his art students some visual literacy skills he had been reading about. He had heard that these skills were becoming increasingly important for students as consumers of news information and potential buyers of products. He wanted to show them how easy it was to create fictional images that looked real or to alter real images to create false impressions.

4.1 What technology-based strategy could Mr. Lucien use to address this need?

4.2 Why could this skill probably not be taught in a nontechnology way?

4.3 How could Mr. Lucien arrange this activity so students could work on it in groups?

Ms. Samda was an art resource teacher in a small, rural school district. She wanted her students to have opportunities to look at and appreciate various works of art and learn something about the artists. However, they were far from any art museum, and there was no money for field trips even if there were one close by.

5.1 What technology-based strategy could Ms. Samda use to address this need?

5.2 What planning would Ms. Samda have to do before she introduced this activity to students?

5.3 What could she do to help structure this activity to keep students on task?

TIE INTO PRACTICE: TECHNOLOGY INTEGRATION EXAMPLES

The Technology Integration Example that opened this chapter *(The Fine Art of Electronic Portfolios)* showed how teachers might conduct an interdisciplinary unit combining music, art, and technology. One activity students are asked to create to demonstrate their skills is to use image manipulation software to create a collage of colors and images that come to mind as they listen to the music composition they or their fellow students have created. With the knowledge you have gained from Chapter 13, do the following to explore this strategy:

1. Using Adobe *Photoshop* software, create a graphic collage like the example shown below. **Create this ex-ample collage** by following the tutorial located on the *Hands-On with Technology* section of the DVD that accompanies this text.

2. Answer the following questions about *The Fine Art of Electronic Portfolios* example:
   - Phase 1 — What kinds of relative advantage did the teachers feel the intersection of arts and technology offered for student portfolios?
   - Phase 2 — The teachers will measure each student's progress in meeting assigned benchmarks in their composition and skill development. How will they set these benchmarks?
   - Phase 3 — What is the purpose of having the "Evening at Eureka" show at the end of the grading period? What could teachers do to ensure that this event will have the most positive instructional impact on students that it can have?
   - Phase 4 — There are a lot of activities going on at the same time for these students. What could the teachers create or use to keep track of what each student is doing and what level they are on at a given time?
   - Phase 5 — One of the end-of-project questions the teachers asked was if students were actively engaged in the project work. How might they ascertain this?

3. What NETS for Students skills would students learn by working on *The Fine Art of Electronic Portfolios* project? (See the front of the book for a list of NETS for the students.)

Example of a Graphic Collage. (Create this product using the *Hands-on with Technology* tutorial section of the DVD.)

Technology Integration Lesson Planning

The *Technology Integration Workshop* DVD includes a set of technology integration ideas and links to online lessons, arranged as a searchable database. The DVD comes packaged in the back of this textbook. Click on the *Hands-On with Technology* section of the DVD and complete the following exercises.

1. Locate lesson ideas — The DVD has several examples of lessons that use the art and music integration strategies described in this chapter. Locate an example integration idea for at least one of these strategies for each content area.

2. Evaluate the lessons — Use the *Evaluation Checklist for a Technology-Integrated Lesson* (located on the DVD and the Companion Website) to evaluate each of these lessons.

3. Modify a lesson — Select one of the lesson ideas and adapt its strategies to meet a need in your own content area. You may choose to use the same approach in the original or adapt it to meet your needs.

4. Add descriptors — Create descriptors for your new lesson like those found on the database (e.g., grade level, content and topic areas, technologies used, relative advantage, objectives, NETS standards).

5. Add the new lesson — Add your modified lesson with all its descriptors to the lesson plan database.

For Your Teaching Portfolio

For this chapter's contribution to your teaching portfolio, add the following products you created in the Technology Integration Workshop:

- The sample Adobe *Photoshop* collage you created using the tutorial
- The evaluations you did using the *Evaluation Checklist for a Technology-Integrated Lesson*
- The new lesson plan you developed, based on the one you found on the DVD.

CHAPTER 14

TECHNOLOGY IN PHYSICAL EDUCATION AND HEALTH EDUCATION

BONNIE MOHNSEN
BONNIE'S FITWARE

M. D. ROBLYER
UNIVERSITY OF MARYLAND UNIVERSITY COLLEGE

Schools could do more than perhaps any other single institution in society to help young people, and the adults they will become, to live healthier, longer, more satisfying, and more productive lives.

Carnegie Council on Adolescent Development

TECHNOLOGY INTEGRATION EXAMPLE
PERSONAL FITNESS PLANS YOU CAN LIVE WITH

Based on: Manteno (Illinois) Community Unit No. 5 School District Webquest at http://www.manteno.k12.il.us/lweedon/webquest.htm

Grade Level: 9–12 • Content Area/Topic: Biology, health, physical education, and technology • Length of Time: Three weeks

Phase 1: Determine relative advantage

Mr. Martinez, a high school physical education/health teacher, is concerned that not all students are choosing to take health or physical education courses and that there is a national trend toward low exercise levels and poor eating habits among teenagers. He talks to the biology teacher and the technology education (TE) teachers about a project the three of them could do on eating habits and exercise that would meet requirements for courses in physical education/health, biology, and technology. They agree the project would have more impact for current and future students if it could be presented as videos. That way, it could be more easily presented to many students, would be in a visually compelling format, and could serve as a resource for future classes.

    The teachers decide to write descriptions of various "example teenagers" and have their students work in pairs and small groups to design health and fitness plans appropriate for each example. The plans students develop will relate to human growth and development concepts they are covering in biology, and the video design will address skills required in the technology education class. Mr. Martinez shows several simulations that the teachers agree will help make concepts about the need for fitness more visual and compelling to students. He will demonstrate heart monitors, devices that track the heart rate of the person wearing them, to show students how diet and exercise affect heart rate and other physical characteristics. Then he will show students how to document and track this information on a spreadsheet.

Phase 2: Decide on objectives and assessments

The teachers decide on three outcomes and assessments:

- **Outcome:** Video production/group work. **Objective:** Students will demonstrate video production skills and group work skills by achieving at least an 85% rubric score on videos they produce. **Assessment:** Rubric to evaluate videos and cooperative work skills.

- **Outcome:** Knowledge of human anatomy/physiology, nutrition, and body system functions. **Objective:** All students will demonstrate knowledge of human anatomy/physiology, nutrition, and body systems by correctly responding to at least 90% of questions about these systems.

Assessment: List of questions requesting example images and written descriptions as responses.

- **Outcome:** Feasible lifestyle plans. **Objective:** Students will achieve a rubric score of at least 85% on plans they produce with specific and appropriate recommendations for lifestyle changes, exercises, and eating habits. **Assessment:** Rubric adapted from one at the Manteno website.

Phase 3: Design integration strategies

The three teachers agree on the following sequence of instruction and activities:

- **Week 1: Assign the project and collect information**—Describe and discuss in each class the requirements for the project and the learning activities that will take place. **Biology class:** Assign readings and hold class discussions of body systems. To review concepts, use assignment sheets with *A.D.A.M.: The Inside Story* (A.D.A.M.), *InnerBody Works* (Tom Snyder Communications), and *Muscle Flash* (Bonnie's Fitware). **PE/Health class:** Show video *Personal Fitness: Looking Good/Feeling Good* (Kendall-Hunt). Review concepts about diet and exercise. Analyze the impact of diet with simulations such as *Pyramid Challenge* and *DINE Healthy* (DINE Systems), and analyze fitness performance and prepare fitness plans using *Health-Related Fitness* (Bonnie's Fitware). **Technology class:** The teacher works with the whole class to design the video structure and assigns each group to work on a video depicting each teenager.

- **Week 2: Prepare information and materials**— **Biology class:** The teacher assists as students finish working on their simulation assignments and as they take notes and gather materials to answer the biology questions. **PE/Health class:** Students begin their word-processed descriptions of appropriate fitness plans for their "example teenagers." **Technology class:** The small groups work on video production techniques and learning the video editing software.

- **Week 3: Prepare and display video products**— **Technology class:** The small groups storyboard their videos and prepare scripts based on information from the word-processed descriptions. They complete work

Pre-Fitness Report

Mohammed	Pre Score	Minimum	Met/ Not Met	Suggested Change	Goal
Curl Ups	12	18	Not Met	2-5	13
Flexed Arm Hang	1	8	Not Met	1-4	2
Mile Run	7.30	10	Met	30-60 sec	7.28
Pacer	1	41	Not Met	4-6	2
Walk Test	122	35	Met	1-2	130
Trunk Lift	12	9	Met	0-1	12
Sit/Reach	12 12	12	Met Met	0-1	12 12
Shoulder	1 1	1	Met Met	T	2 2
BMI	33.79	17.5-26.0	Not Met	reduce	27.8
Skinfolds	19	17-32	Met	maintain	17

Period **5** Age **17** Grade **7**

Comments:

Met minimum standards on 6 test items

Health-Related Fitness Tutorial/Portfolio
Source: Courtesy of Bonnie's Fitware, Inc.

on their videos and edit them as needed. Students present their videos in each class, and teachers use their checklists and rubrics to assess the work.

Phase 4: Prepare the instructional environment

The teachers check out the software and videos from the Media Center and gather the assignment sheets to be used with them. Each teacher prepares copies of the rubrics and checklists. The TE teacher agrees to put these on the website, so students can look at them online. The biology teacher decides to have students do most computer simulations at the computer lab, so she schedules times for it. Mr. Martinez coordinates which students can work in pairs or small groups and prepares materials to communicate this information to the students.

Phase 5: Evaluate and revise

After they completed the unit, the three teachers reviewed the videos, looked at summary data from the checklists and rubrics, and discussed how the activities progressed. They agreed that the project worked well and determined how they might share class time in the future to make the work easier to coordinate. They agreed that, although students loved the body and nutrition simulations, they were time consuming. They decided to limit the number done inside class time, and allow students to do more on their own time for extra credit. They also found that some groups took more time with script writing than originally planned, so their videos took more than a week to complete; this would need to be built into the plan for next time.

OBJECTIVES

After reading this chapter and completing the learning activities for it, you should be able to:

1. Identify some of the current issues in physical education and health education that may impact the selection and use of technology.

2. Describe some popular uses for technology in physical education and health education.

3. Identify exemplary Internet sites for physical education and health.

4. Create instructional activities for physical education and health education that model successful integration strategies.

KEY TERMS

- accelerometers
- blood pressure devices
- body composition analyzer
- heart monitor
- nutritional analysis program
- pedometers
- spirometers

For more information on Key Terms, go to the *Key Terms* module for this chapter of the Companion Website at http://www.prenhall.com/roblyer.

INTRODUCTION

Today, the health of young people—and the adults they will become—is critically linked to the health-related behaviors they choose to adopt. Because strong evidence exists that participation in health and physical education classes can help develop healthy behaviors in children, many schools, like the one in the *Personal Fitness Plans You Can Live With* example at the beginning of this chapter, are trying to find ways in which all students can realize these benefits.

As the example shows, educational technology offers teachers valuable resources for informing and empowering students to make the right health choices. The most effective methods of instruction are student-centered approaches like the ones in *Personal Fitness Plans You Can Live With:* hands-on, cooperative learning activities, and activities that include problem solving and peer instruction to help students develop skills in decision making, communications, goal setting, resistance to peer pressure, and stress management (Kane, 1993; Seffrin, 1990). This chapter provides more details and examples of technology resources and integration strategies that teachers can use to help prepare students to lead longer and healthier lives.

ISSUES AND PROBLEMS IN PHYSICAL EDUCATION AND HEALTH EDUCATION

Physical Inactivity

Graham, Holt-Hale, and Parker (1998) point out that today's children are less physically active in part because they spend more of their free time on television and computer games, rather than outside in physical play. This society-wide trend affects both the motor development and health of our country's youth. Although technology may be partially responsible for the current decline in physical activity, it also holds the potential for motivating youngsters to increase their levels of physical activity. Several of the computer games available in arcades, such as *Downhill Skier, Dance Dance Revolution,* and golf games, require participants to be physically engaged in order to be successful in the game. However, this is not a substitute for mandatory physical education during school hours.

Instructional Time for Health and Physical Education

Schools currently are refocusing their priorities on issues such as meeting standards in content areas and increasing scores on state and national tests. The result is sometimes a lesser emphasis on health instruction and physical education. This is unfortunate, because three out of four deaths are due to preventable chronic conditions (U.S. Department of Health and Human Services, 1996a). In addition, cognitive functioning is related to proper nutrition

MAKING THE CASE FOR TECHNOLOGY INTEGRATION

Discuss these issues online with other students by selecting the *Making the Case* module for Chapter 14 of the Companion Website (http://www.prenhall.com/roblyer) or choose the *Message Board* module.

1. What type of support do you think the author is talking about in the following quote?: "Support is greatly needed if physical activity is going to be increased in a society as technologically advanced as ours. Most Americans today are spared the burden of excessive physical labor. Indeed, few occupations today require significant physical activity, and most people use motorized transportation to get to work and to perform routine errands and tasks" (Satcher, 1997, foreword).

   Is instructional technology part of the problem, part of the solution, or neutral? Is the problem likely to get worse or better? With the help of computer technology, more and more people are now working from their homes. Will this trend lead to more or less physical activity?

2. Is there a way to turn the passive activities discussed in the following quote into ones that require physical activity?: "Even leisure time is increasingly filled with sedentary behaviors, such as watching television, surfing the Internet, and playing video games" (Satcher, 1997, foreword).

   Can any of these activities be used to promote physical activity? What role can schools play in changing the amount of leisure time spent on sedentary activities?

and physical activity (Caine & Caine, 1995). Also, children's self-concept and self-esteem (Payne & Issacs, 1995), as well as their prosocial skills (Borba, 1989), are positively affected by their involvement in physical activities.

To achieve desired results, experts recommend the following: 50 hours of health instruction per school year, and 150 minutes of physical education instruction per week for grades K–5 and 225 minutes for grades 6–12. However, the actual amount of time contributed to health and physical education in most schools is far less. One solution may be the kind of technology-enabled curriculum integration shown in the *Personal Fitness Plans You Can Live With* example. Teachers can address several subject areas

Figure 14.1 NASPE Standards for Physical Education

1. Demonstrates competency in motor skills and movement patterns needed to perform a variety of physical activities.

2. Demonstrates understanding of movement concepts, principles, strategies, and tactics as they apply to the learning and performance of physical activities.

3. Participates regularly in physical activity.

4. Achieves and maintains a health-enhancing level of physical fitness.

5. Exhibits responsible personal and social behavior that respects self and others in physical activity settings.

6. Values physical activity for health, enjoyment, challenge, self-expression, and/or social interaction.

Source: Reprinted from *Moving into the Future: National Standards for Physical Education, 2nd Edition* (2004) with permission from the National Association for Sport and Physical Education, 1900 Association Drive, Reston, VA 20191-1599.

Figure 14.2 NASPE Standards for Health Education

1. Students will comprehend concepts related to health promotion and disease prevention.

2. Students will demonstrate the ability to access valid health information and health-promoting products and services.

3. Students will demonstrate the ability to practice health-enhancing behaviors and reduce health risks.

4. Students will analyze the influence of culture, media, technology, and other factors on health.

5. Students will demonstrate the ability to use interpersonal communication skills to enhance health.

6. Students will demonstrate the ability to use goal-setting and decision-making skills to enhance health.

7. Students will demonstrate the ability to advocate for personal, family, and community health.

Source: http://www.ericfacility.net/ericdigests/ed387483.html

simultaneously while allowing students to see the connections between what they learn in school and real-life situations. Technology resources improve communications among and the productivity of students and teachers; allow more hands-on, visual learning experiences; help motivate students to spend more time on activities; and serve as a platform for students' products.

Accuracy of Health and Physical Education Resources

To be information-literate, a person must be able to recognize when information is needed and know how to locate, evaluate, and use effectively the needed information. The national health standards speak directly to this issue. Because anyone can post anything on the Internet, students need to become more information literate so they can be good consumers of health and fitness products and information. Specifically, they must be able to differentiate between accurate and inaccurate information in the context of health and fitness education.

Addressing the Standards

School physical education has come far from its early emphasis on physical training and calisthenics. It evolved into sports education, then lifetime activities, and now its current focus is on health-related fitness, behavioral competencies, and motor skills needed for lifelong engagement in enjoyable physical activity. This current shift is due, in part, to the national physical education standards (see Figure 14.1), first introduced in 1995 and updated in 2004 by the National Association for Sport and Physical Education (NASPE). The NASPE national health education standards (see Figure 14.2) were also published in 1995 (American Alliance for Health, Physical Education, Recreation, and Dance). The focus of the health education standards is health literacy—the capacity of individuals to obtain, interpret, and understand basic health information along with the competence to use such information to enhance health.

Drawing on the findings from the School Health Policies and Programs Study (SHIPPS), Pate and Small (1995)

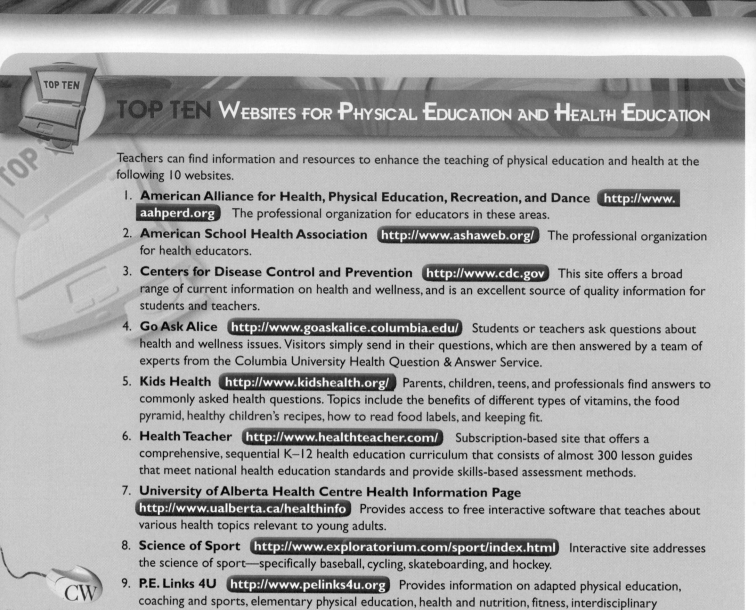

TOP TEN WEBSITES FOR PHYSICAL EDUCATION AND HEALTH EDUCATION

Teachers can find information and resources to enhance the teaching of physical education and health at the following 10 websites.

1. **American Alliance for Health, Physical Education, Recreation, and Dance** `http://www.aahperd.org` The professional organization for educators in these areas.

2. **American School Health Association** `http://www.ashaweb.org/` The professional organization for health educators.

3. **Centers for Disease Control and Prevention** `http://www.cdc.gov` This site offers a broad range of current information on health and wellness, and is an excellent source of quality information for students and teachers.

4. **Go Ask Alice** `http://www.goaskalice.columbia.edu/` Students or teachers ask questions about health and wellness issues. Visitors simply send in their questions, which are then answered by a team of experts from the Columbia University Health Question & Answer Service.

5. **Kids Health** `http://www.kidshealth.org/` Parents, children, teens, and professionals find answers to commonly asked health questions. Topics include the benefits of different types of vitamins, the food pyramid, healthy children's recipes, how to read food labels, and keeping fit.

6. **Health Teacher** `http://www.healthteacher.com/` Subscription-based site that offers a comprehensive, sequential K–12 health education curriculum that consists of almost 300 lesson guides that meet national health education standards and provide skills-based assessment methods.

7. **University of Alberta Health Centre Health Information Page** `http://www.ualberta.ca/healthinfo` Provides access to free interactive software that teaches about various health topics relevant to young adults.

8. **Science of Sport** `http://www.exploratorium.com/sport/index.html` Interactive site addresses the science of sport—specifically baseball, cycling, skateboarding, and hockey.

9. **P.E. Links 4U** `http://www.pelinks4u.org` Provides information on adapted physical education, coaching and sports, elementary physical education, health and nutrition, fitness, interdisciplinary secondary physical education, and technology in physical education. Also has links to other major physical education websites.

10. **Using Technology in Physical Education Newsletter** `http://www.pesoftware.com/technews/news.html` Newsletter provides physical educators and health educators with the latest information on using technology in physical education.

To visit these web links online, go to this text's Companion Website at http://www.prenhall.com/roblyer.

state: "Instruction practices in physical education often do not reflect the goals set by either the national health objectives or the National Physical Education Standards" (p. 312). This has not changed much since the introduction of the national standards. Although there has been some movement in certain areas of the country, there is certainly a need for greater implementation of the standards. Technology can play a role by making it easier to post and share key information. As health and physical educators share their successful standards-based curricula on the Internet, this may encourage broader implementation of standards. In addition, standards-based software now provides teachers with resources for increasing and measuring student learning related to standards.

Handling Controversial Health Issues

Controversial subject matter has proven to be another challenge for health education. Many special interest groups press for the inclusion of their particular issue, into the health education curriculum. But including too many such issues actually can water down a curriculum and make it less effective. One area of particular concern is human sexuality. Many experts believe information and guidance on sexual decisions are essential; others feel stu-

TECHNOLOGY-ENABLED PHYSICAL EDUCATION

Title: Integrating Technology into Middle School Physical Education

Content Area/Topic: Physical Fitness and Social Skills

Grade Level: 6–8

NETS for Students: Standards 3, 5, 6

Description: To make it possible for schools to spend needed time on physical education and health courses in grades 6–8, technology-based strategies can help teachers integrate these topics into other content areas to create interdisciplinary lessons. Technology can help make time spent on physical education and health more hands-on and productive.

Instruction: Students can keep personal fitness goals and achievements as part of their electronic portfolios; analyze and graph data from their uses of heart monitors; view videos that demonstrate model performances, various sports, and other motor activities to learn more about how the body works; and use the Internet to research sports and physical activities in other countries and historical periods. Another physical activity that is ideal as the basis for an interdisciplinary topic is orienteering. This is a combination of walking, running, and hiking while following a map and using a compass or GPS. Teachers can introduce the activity with a video such as *Finding Your Way in the Wild* (Quality Video) or software such as *Navigate!* (http://members.iinet.net.au/~glawford/navigate.html).

Assessment: These strategies will depend on teacher goals for the activities. Most plans call for students to complete portfolio components, which are then graded by rubric.

Source: Mohnsen, B. (2000). Vaughn, Nekomi, and Luis: What they were doing in middle school physical education. *Learning and Leading with Technology, 27*(5), 22–27.

---

dents should be taught that abstinence is the only choice and that teaching about a controversial subject tends to legitimize it in the mind of the student. Other controversial topics include date rape, suicide, drugs, violence, and character education. Technology resources such as videos and well-chosen websites can provide valuable insights on these topics as well as help to facilitate the logistics of instruction when only a subset of the total class is involved.

TECHNOLOGY INTEGRATION STRATEGIES FOR PHYSICAL EDUCATION AND HEALTH EDUCATION

This section is aligned with the national physical education (PE) and health education (HE) standards, as noted in parentheses in the following list:

1. Technology to Support Improvements in Fitness (PE 3, 4)

2. Technology to Develop and Improve Motor Skill Performance (PE 1, 2)

3. Technology to Improve Students' Beliefs and Interactions Related to Physical Activity (PE 5, 6)

4. Technology to Assess and Enhance Personal Health (HE 3, 6)

5. Technology to Support the Procurement of Valid Health Information (HE 1, 2, 4)

6. Technology to Influence Others' Health Behaviors (HE 5, 7)

7. Technology to Support Interdisciplinary Instruction.

Technology Integration Idea 14.1 illustrates how the following integration strategies can be implemented. For a summary of the strategies described here and technology resources that can help implement them, see Figure 14.3.

Supporting Improved Fitness

Technology devices and software are available to help analyze, monitor, and improve fitness. Exercise equipment, such as treadmills, stair steppers, and stationary bikes, meet the criteria of a technology device designed to improve fitness. Used in combination with monitors, these devices can show students the results of their efforts in terms of heart rate, speed, and power. The Life Cycle Rowers, for example, show a small boat moving across the

Figure 14.3 Summary of Technology Integration Strategies for Physical Education and Health Education

Technology Integration Strategies	Benefits	Sample Resources and Activities
Supporting improved fitness Courtesy of Polar USA. http://www.polarusa.com	• Devices help analyze, monitor, and improve fitness. • Displaying students' data on the Internet allows competition between students across the country. • Devices help monitor heart rate as students work toward fitness goals. • Helps students develop and track their fitness goals and plans.	• Treadmills, stair steppers, and stationary bikes • Heart monitors • Electronic portfolio and spreadsheet software
Developing and improving motor skill performance Courtesy of Seaside Software. http://www.sportscad.com/silverinfo.htm	• Displays model performances. • Supports self-analysis and monitoring of improvement. • Gives students visual feedback on performances. • Helps teachers organize data collection and report on students' progress.	• Instructional broadcasts on motor skills • Video cameras • Handheld computers • Biomechanical analysis programs: *SportsCAD Motion Analysis* http://www.sportscad.com
Shaping students' beliefs and interactions related to physical activity 	• Connects students of various backgrounds to allow interactions related to physical activity. • Students learn about the history of sports and dances.	• Televised shows and specials • Internet-based epals programs • Internet and electronic encyclopedias
Helping students assess and enhance personal health DINE Healthy Nutrient Analysis Software Program. Copyright 1994–2004 DINE Systems, Inc. 163 Brunswick Electric Rd. Whiteville, NC 28409; 800-688-1848. http://www.dinesystems.com/	• Guides students through the process of making changes to enhance their health.	• Nutritional analysis programs: *DINE Healthy* and *Pyramid Challenge* (DINE Systems) • Risk assessment programs
Helping students obtain valid health information Copyright 2005, A.D.A.M., Inc. All rights reserved. http://www.adam.com	• Provides current information for researching health topics.	• Internet sites: Web MD http://www.webmd.com • Software: *My Amazing Human Body* (DK Multimedia), *A.D.A.M.: The Inside Story* (A.D.A.M.)

Figure 14.3 (continued)

Technology Integration Strategies	Benefits	Sample Resources and Activities
Influencing health behaviors Courtesy of Science Kit, Inc. http://sciencekit.com	• Webquests allow students to collaborate on health-related issues. • Presents health issues in "real-life" settings to foster decision-making and critical thinking skills.	• Internet webquest sites: *Addiction* (http://technoteacher.com/ WebQuests/ADDICTION/). • Video-based simulations: *Science Sleuths* (Science Kit and Boreal Labs–http://sciencekit.com **Also see Technology Integration Idea 14.2:** Reinforcing Healthy Social Problem-solving
Supporting interdisciplinary instruction Math Health **Healthy Active Lifestyle** Physical Education Science Courtesy of Bonnie's Fitware, Inc.	• Shows relationships between physical education/health-related topics and other subject areas.	• **See Technology Integration Idea 14.1:** Integrating Technology into Middle School Physical Education

screen; the faster the student rows, the faster the boat moves. Connecting two Concept II rowers together provides the opportunity for indoor rowing races. Displaying the output of monitoring equipment to the Internet provides for competition between students across the country.

Electronic **blood pressure devices** (to monitor blood pressure), **body composition analyzers** (to determine the percent of body fat), **pedometers** (to monitor the number of steps one takes), **accelerometers** (to count calories, e.g., Cal Trac), and **spirometers** (to measure lung volume) are devices that assist with analyzing and monitoring fitness levels. Each device measures a different aspect of student health and fitness, allowing students to use their own bodies for data collection and analysis. The most popular device in this category is the **heart monitor** (e.g., Cardio Sport Ultima). Students wear the heart watches around their wrists while an elastic band holds the transmitters to their chests. (See Figure 14.4.) The transmitter senses the heartbeat from the heart's electrical impulses and transmits each beat to the wristwatch receiver through radio transmission. Younger children benefit from using the HeartTalker, where instead of reading their heart rates on a wristwatch receiver, they receive audio feedback regarding their heart rate and exercise time from headphones attached to the transmitter. Heart mon-

Figure 14.4 Student with Heart Monitor

itors are especially effective for providing students with feedback as to whether or not they are in their target heart rate zones and benefiting from the training effect for cardiorespiratory endurance.

Students also can be put in charge of their own learning along with the development of fitness goals and plans. *Health-Related Fitness Tutorial/Portfolio* (Bonnie's Fitware) guides students through the five areas of health-related fitness: flexibility, muscular strength, muscular endurance, body composition, and cardiorespiratory endurance. The electronic portfolio portion of this software allows students to enter fitness plans, exercises, drawings or video clips, journal entries, caloric input/output, and fitness scores, which are then analyzed by the software. **Nutritional analysis programs** (to analyze calorie intake and monitor portions of required food groups), fitness analysis programs, and spreadsheet applications also can be used to calculate and graph individual nutrition and fitness goals. *Muscle Flash* (Bonnie's Fitware), with grade-specific versions, teaches and quizzes students about the names, locations, functions, and exercises for a variety of muscles through a flash card simulation. The learning from this program allows students to select the appropriate exercise(s) for specific muscle groups.

Developing and Improving Motor Skill Performance

Technology can provide students with information, model performances, and feedback, along with opportunities for self-analysis and monitoring of improvement in the area of motor skill performance. In order for students to develop a new motor skill, they must first understand and observe a model performance. Instructional broadcasts on motor skills provide a model demonstration of the skill to be learned. Software (e.g., Bonnie's Fitware's *VolleyballComplete* and *Elementary Physical Education Dictionary*, Ball Hog's *Soccer*) also provides learners with model skill performances and a description of not only the *how*, but also the *why*. Knowing why a skill is performed in a certain manner is beneficial to the learning of new skills and, more significantly, to the transfer of that learning to new movement experiences.

Asking students to set personal goals and then monitoring their progress on motor skill acquisition is motivational to the student, but often a paperwork nightmare for a physical educator responsible for 200 to 600 students. Handheld computers help physical educators organize their data collection (e.g., grades, attendance, fitness scores) during the instructional period. Once the data have been transferred to a desktop or notebook computer, they can be analyzed and reported to students and parents in a variety of formats. Electronic portfolios (e.g., Bonnie's Fitware's *Physical Education Portfolio*) can put students in charge of collecting, recording, and analyzing their motor skill achievement, fitness performance, social interactions, and cognitive learning. (See Figure 14.5.) The electronic portfolios can be accessed using notebook, tablet, or even handheld computers.

Once students begin to practice motor skills, feedback becomes the significant component for perfecting performance. Digital video cameras record performance and allow for replay and analysis. The use of video is most effective when it is shown to the student immediately after the performance along with external verbal feedback and cues (Darden & Shimon, 2000; Doering, 2000). Video replay is best used with students beyond a beginner skill level. Students need some knowledge of the skill and some viable mental image of it in order to use the information these images provide. For students with advanced skills, replay also is useful for strategy and tactics. Because advanced movement is so fast and sometimes difficult to analyze at normal speed, slow motion replay and freeze-frame capabilities are essential.

Figure 14.5 **Student with Handheld Computer**

Figure 14.6 **Student with Video Camera**

To provide for student self-analysis, a digital video camera should be placed at one station in a learning circuit (e.g., for tennis skills). Each phase of the skill is modeled while students work in pairs to identify critical features, patterns, and concepts associated with the skill. (See Figure 14.6.) Then students rotate through the stations in small groups, with one group beginning at the digital camcorder station. One student hits the ball, the second student provides feedback, and the third person records the skill performance. The student-coach uses the first set of columns on a criteria sheet to provide specific feedback. On the rotation after the video station, the students review the images. The instant replay provides immediate feedback for the performer, who uses the second set of columns on the criteria sheet to self-assess performance.

Student projects can be used to assess and further develop students' understanding and performance of motor skills. All motor skills fall into a general movement pattern category (i.e., overhand pattern, kicking pattern). Understanding the relationship between skills using the same movement pattern helps when transferring knowledge and experience from one motor skill to another (i.e., overhand throw to volleyball serve). Students working in small groups can investigate one movement pattern and record their findings on video. Next they can visit other classes and record examples of their particular movement pattern. Each group then shares its video with the rest of the class.

The examples so far in this section have targeted standard 1; however, standard 2 also addresses motor skill improvement. Students must analyze their own movement performance using scientific principles of movement and create their own practice plan in order to improve performance. Physical educators often have believed that this learning would occur through the process of osmosis—simply participating in sport would transfer this learning to students. We now understand that for students to see

the connection between sports and science or sports and improvement, they must understand some basic cognitive concepts and principles.

Broadcasts, such as *SportsFigures* (ESPN), provide information on the science of sports. Each lesson includes step-by-step explanations of the scientific principles. ESPN has launched a companion website (http://www.sportsticker.com/sportsfigures) that is designed for teachers, students, and parents. It contains interactive components such as educational games, video clips, and curriculum information to support student learning.

Software packages such as *Biomechanics Made Easy* (Bonnie's Fitware) and *SimAthlete* (Bonnie's Fitware), provide reference information on the important biomechanical and motor learning concepts (e.g., goal setting, feedback, stability, force production). *Biomechanics Made Easy* then quizzes students on their understanding and application of the concepts while *SimAthlete* goes a step further by asking students to create a practice plan (coach) for different athletes. The better the practice plan, the better the athlete performs during competition. *Measurement in Motion* (Learning in Motion) and *Dart Trainer* (Dartfish) take biomechanical analysis to another level by encouraging open-ended exploration. The software packages use video clips (supplied by the teacher or captured using student subjects) and allow for ease of measurement and analysis of movement performance (e.g., ball rotation, limb speed).

Shaping Students' Beliefs and Interactions Related to Physical Activity

Standards 5 and 6 of the national physical education standards address primarily the affective domain. Although software to address this area is very limited, videos and the Internet can provide opportunities to address these areas. Televised shows, such as *The Wonder Years, Boston Public*, and after-school specials, often focus on social and self-esteem issues related to physical activity. In one of the *Wonder Years* episodes, a segment focused on picking teams in physical education. Physical educators use this clip as a journal writing prompt when asking students how they would feel if they were the last one picked for a team.

The Internet offers an ideal medium for connecting students with different backgrounds and beliefs and providing them with the opportunities for interactions related to physical activity. Many of us had pen pals when we were students. Today, our students have keypals (a.k.a. epals). Keypals are students who connect with one another via electronic mail. They can share ideas, concerns, physical education/activity experiences, information, written assignments, and research. Through these connections, they learn to accept individuals from other communities and cultures. Sites such as http://www.pesoftware.com/pepals.html or http://www.epals.com/, are available to help teachers get started with this type of activity. They can visit one of the sites to find other physical educators interested in teaming for this type of project.

Students also can access an array of individuals with knowledge and expertise related to physical education, sports, and fitness. Olympic athletes, professional athletes, biomechanists, medical doctors, exercise physiologists, and motor learning specialists can provide students with insights regarding "real-life" experiences related to physical activity. Bonnie's Fitware sponsors the Olympic Athlete Project (http://www.pesoftware.com/). This project began in 1995, when an Olympic rower was identified to share his trip to the Olympics with students. Steven Segaloff was a potential Olympic coxswain when he began communicating with students across the United States. He sent email messages every other week that dealt with his sport, his training program, the selection process, his relationship with the other rowers (teamwork), and his feelings about training and participating in the Olympics. Students, in turn, emailed back asking specific questions of interest to them.

An appreciation for a sport or dance can be enhanced through an understanding of its origins. The Internet and electronic encyclopedias provide students with access to a wealth of information including the history of sports and dances. However, it is important that students are prepared to use this research tool. Students must learn to double check all references, examine author credentials, and cite resources.

Helping Students Assess and Enhance Personal Health

When studying health, students are motivated when they can see a connection between what they are studying and their own bodies. When attempting to motivate individuals to change their lifestyles and adopt a wellness approach toward their health, information alone is not enough. Fortunately, software is available to guide students through the process of making changes. These programs (e.g., Ripple Effects' *Relate for Kids* and *Relate for Teens*) help students apply their knowledge to problem-solving situations. Record keeping, visual representation, and data analysis are all components of these programs.

Many nutritional analysis programs are currently available. These programs (e.g., DINE Systems' *DINE Healthy* and *Pyramid Challenge*) ask the user for age, weight, height, gender, and amount of physical activity, and then calculate the individual's nutritional needs. The user records the types and amounts of foods eaten daily, and the program creates a report that lists calories ingested, the nutrient values for all foods, and the total of all nutrients ingested. These reports then are used to determine if the student has met the recommended dietary allowances and whether the number of calories ingested was excessive. These programs expose poor nutritional and fitness behaviors through their analysis of daily food intake and physical activity. Appropriate menus and exercises are recommended for a healthier lifestyle. The software packages serve as personal trainers for fitness and nutrition.

Another type of program along these lines is the risk assessment program. These programs ask the user to input data regarding his or her lifestyle. Questions include height, weight, gender, age, cholesterol level, blood pressure, smoking habits, alcohol usage, physical activity habits, family medical history, nutritional information, and use of seat belts. Based on the data received, the program determines the individual's life expectancy, cardiovascular disease risk, and/or cancer risk. Several shareware programs on risk assessment are available, as well as web-based software at sites such as http://hin.nhlbi.nih.gov/atpiii/calculator.asp.

Helping Students Obtain Valid Health Information

Historically, the health education textbook has been the primary source of information and reading in a health education class. Today, students have access to a wide variety of Internet sites and software. As noted earlier, students need instruction on how to distinguish between accurate and inaccurate information.

KidsHealth (see Figure 14.7) is an example of a health-related site targeted at K–12 students. High-quality software includes *Body Fun* (Bonnie's Fitware) for elementary students and *BARNS Multimedia Series I* and *II* (Learning Multi-Systems) for middle and high school students. Chil-

Figure 14.7 KidsHealth Website

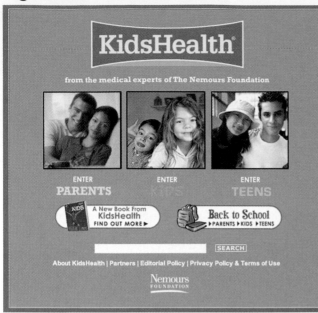

Source: Reprinted with permission. © 2004 www.KidsHealth.org

dren and teenagers can use these and other resources to research health topics, including the side effects of commonly used medicines or symptoms of major medical illnesses.

Influencing Health Behaviors

When dealing with all of the complex issues in health education, a mentoring relationship offers great potential for promoting self-analysis and metacognition on the part of the older student. Email and videoconferencing may also be used to set up online projects with other classes around the world. For example, fifth-grade classes in different parts of the world collaborate on studying local safety issues. When they complete their research, they collaborate on developing a web page that promotes environmental health. Students also are able to discuss the differences between various cultures with regard to subjects such as drug use or government-sponsored health care.

Using the webquest strategy (see http://edweb.sdsu.edu/webquest/webquest.html), students are given an authentic problem to solve along with web resources on the topic. Students typically work in collaborative teams. Each student explores the linked sites related to a specific role on the team. Students then teach what they have learned to the other team members. Finally, higher level questions guide students toward more challenging thinking and a deeper understanding of the topic being explored. An excellent example of a health webquest is *Addiction* (see http://technoteacher.com/WebQuests/ADDICTION/).

Video resources also are an efficient way to remove logistical hurdles when teaching health-related issues. Videos allow students to hear similar information and advice from a voice other than the teacher's. They also allow students to see health issues in "real-life" settings.

Some resources let students see the consequences of ill-advised choices, whether it be smoking, drugs, or poor nutrition. These resources include video-based simulations that foster decision-making and critical thinking skills. Simulation programs place students in situations where they have to apply their knowledge to solve medical or health mysteries. A popular simulation website, *Science Sleuths* (Science Kit and Boreal Labs), uses humorous mysteries to engage students in the process of problem solving and critical thinking. The mystery episodes are fictitious but introduce important health concepts and processes. Students can access video interviews, conduct science experiments, and examine photos, articles, charts, graphs, and much more. Topics related to health education include "Blood Components and Function," "Human Development and Heredity," and "The Nervous System."

Finally, simulations and diagnostic tools are available to help students think through health and social situations. Software available from Psychological Enterprises (http://www.eqparenting.com/ppsg.htm) helps students work through social decisions that can affect their physical and emotional health. For an example use of this product, see Technology Integration Idea 14.2.

Supporting Interdisciplinary Instruction

The popular opinion regarding interdisciplinary instruction for health and physical education is that these subject areas support learning in other subjects. However, the perspective of the health and physical educators is that interdisciplinary instruction requires a symbiotic relationship—where subject areas support each other. Mohnsen (2003) offers an example of an interdisciplinary health-related fitness unit in which the physical education teacher focuses on the benefits of physical training and conditioning and the health education teacher focuses on health issues related to diet and physical activity. The science teacher explores how the digestive system works and the mathematics teacher provides word problems on the input and output of calories. See Technology Integration Idea 14.1 earlier in this chapter for an example of an interdisciplinary lesson that integrates physical education, science, and math along with the use of computers. Technology teachers can help with these interdisciplinary units by providing Internet research support and multimedia project development tools that let students demonstrate their health and physical education learning.

TECHNOLOGY INTEGRATION IDEA 14.2

TECHNOLOGY-SUPPORTED HEALTH INSTRUCTION

Title: Reinforcing Healthy Social Problem-solving

Grade Level: K–6

Content Area/Topic: Health and Social Skills

NETS for Students: Standards 3, 5, 6

Description: The authors of this article (see source entry) say, "Social and emotional skills are learned skills, like riding a bike or tying your shoes" (p. 19).

Instruction: Begin by pretesting students with instruments such as the *Piers Harris* (to measure self-esteem), *Health Locus of Control* (to measure how much control students feel they have over health issues), and *Group Social Problem Solving Assessment* (to measure knowledge of social problem-solving strategies). Teach students concrete skills such as speaker power, listening position, keeping calm, active listening skills, and making new friends. (See source article for further information on these strategies.) This gives all students a common language for discussing social problems. Administer the PPSG to each student and, once students identify a problem, the software helps each of them work through the process of reflecting on feelings and setting a goal for solving the problem. The SDM/SPS program acts as a diagnostic tool and helps develop plans for improvement.

Assessment: After using these processes for at least 6 months, post-test each student. See the *Personal Problem Solving Guide* described at http://www.eqparenting.com/ppsg.htm

Source: Poedubicky, V., Brown, L. Hoover, H., & Elias, M. (2000–2001). Using technology to promote health decision making. *Learning and Leading with Technology, 28*(4), 18–21, 56.

INTERACTIVE SUMMARY

The following is a summary of the main points covered in this chapter. To see additional examples and information on these points, go to this textbook's Companion Website at http://www.prenhall.com/roblyer and click on the Chapter 14 Interactive Summary module to visit each of the recommended websites.

1. **Issues in physical education and health education** include physical inactivity; instructional time for health and physical education; accuracy of health and physical education resources; addressing the standards; and handling controversial health issues.

2. **Integration strategies for physical education and health education** are in seven general areas:

   - Supporting improved fitness (see http://www.sarkproducts.com/ for examples)

   - Developing and improving motor skill performance (see examples at http://www.sportscad.com/)

   - Shaping students' beliefs about physical activity

   - Helping students assess and enhance personal health (see http://www.dinesystems.com/ for examples)

   - Helping students obtain valid health information (see http://www.webmd.com/)

   - Influencing health behaviors (see sample webquest at http://technoteacher.com/WebQuests/ ADDICTION)

   - Supporting interdisciplinary instruction.

Online Activities

Visit this text's Companion Website at http://www.prenhall.com/roblyer to gain access to a variety of questions, activities, and exercises to help build your knowledge of this chapter's content.

Online Chapter 14 Self-Test

To review terms and concepts for this chapter, click on the Self-Test module for this chapter of the Companion Website.

Software Skill-Builder Tutorials

To access practical tutorial and skill-building activities to build skills using popular software and hardware, click on the Software Skill-Builder Tutorials module for this chapter of the Companion Website.

Web-Enrichment Activities

To complete activities that connect to chapter content and provide web-based resources, click on the Web-Enrichment Activities module for this chapter of the Companion Website.

TECHNOLOGY INTEGRATION WORKSHOP

THE TIP MODEL IN ACTION

Read each of the following scenarios related to implementing the TIP Model, and go to the Companion Website to answer the questions that follow it based on your Chapter 14 reading activities.

TIP Model Scenario #1   Ms. Hayward wants all of her physical education students to keep a "fitness portfolio." She wants them to enter weekly entries on what they have accomplished on their own fitness plans and on assigned exercises and activities, their entries on a fitness journal, and video clips of their performances. She wants them to be able to update it and share it easily with other students and their parents and friends.

     1.1 What technology-based strategies could Ms. Hayward use to address these needs?

     1.2 What would be the relative advantages of using these strategies?

     1.3 Why does Ms. Hayward want students be able to share the portfolio easily with parents and friends?

TIP Model Scenario #2   Whenever his tennis students are practicing various new skills he has just introduced, Mr. Larue takes videos of their performances with his digital camera. Later that day, he and the students look at their performances together and analyze how they could improve their techniques.

     2.1 What problem(s) does this technology-based strategy address?

     2.2 What is the relative advantage of using this strategy?

     2.3 What are two reasons Mr. Larue may want to use a digital video camera as opposed to a regular video camera to record students' performances?

TIP Model Scenario #3   Mr. Escarcega wants her students to be prepared for drug-related situations they may encounter outside school. She knows that it does no good to talk to them about what they should do in these situations. She has found a software package that includes a set of short videos, each with a different drug-related scenario. At the end of each scenario, students have an opportunity to choose from a list of responses and see what might happen after each choice.

     3.1 What problem(s) does this technology-based strategy address?

     3.2 What is the relative advantage of using this strategy?

     3.3 Should students work individually, in pairs, in small groups, or as a whole class on this activity? Explain.

TIP Model Scenario #4   Mr. Decker knows that his 10th- and 11th-grade students have and will have a lot of questions about issues related to drugs, sex, and domestic violence. They will be graduating soon, and he wants to make sure they know some of the places they can go for accurate, reliable information from health agencies and other authoritative sources. He decides to have them do an in-class scavenger hunt to locate answers to various questions by looking at some of the key sites.

     4.1 What problem(s) does Mr. Decker's technology-based strategy address?

     4.2 What is the relative advantage of using this strategy as opposed to just giving the students a list of the websites?

     4.3 Should students work individually, in pairs, in small groups, or as a whole class on this activity? Explain.

TIP Model Scenario #5   Mrs. Norgaard is a physical education teacher who wants each of her students to set fitness goals for themselves. She has students decide how many exercises of each kind they will do each week and what their target heart rate should be. She has them keep track of how well they have met their goals. However, keeping this information in the notebook she has set up for each class is becoming cumbersome and difficult to update. In addition, she cannot easily calculate averages across the class or how much a student has fallen short of or exceeded a goal.

     5.1 What technology-based strategy could Mrs. Norgaard use to address this need?

     5.2 What would be a good way to organize the ongoing task of entering and updating student information? Should Mrs. Norgaard do the updating or the students? Explain.

     5.3 What could Mrs. Norgaard do to help structure this activity to keep students on task?

TIE into Practice: Technology Integration Examples

The Technology Integration Example that opened this chapter (*Personal Fitness Plans You Can Live With*) showed how a teacher might have students create videos that depict healthy lifestyles. Having students use this strategy can be helpful in many kinds of health and physical education activities. With the knowledge you have gained from Chapter 14 do the following to explore this example:

1. Create part of a video example like the one described in the chapter. A sample frame from the video is shown here. **Create this sample video** in *iMovie* by following the *Hands-On with Technology* tutorial section on the DVD that accompanies this text.

2. Answer the following questions about the *Personal Fitness Plans You Can Live With* example:

   • Phase 1—Why would the use of videos be an especially powerful way to display this health-related information?

   • Phase 2—One of the desired outcomes identified for this project is to create a video of lifestyle recommendations for each example teenager. Create a rubric that the teachers might use to assess these videos. (*Hint:* Look at Kathy Schrock's Guide for Educators at http://school.discovery.com/schrockguide/assess.html to locate an existing rubric you can modify.)

   • Phase 3—What are the benefits of an interdisciplinary approach to this project? Why is this especially important when considering ways to teach physical education and health skills in today's schools?

   • Phase 4—Work and information from three different subject area classes must be coordinated so that one builds on the other. Name one way to facilitate

the sharing of these student products among the classes as students complete them.

   • Phase 5—One finding from the post-project assessment was that script writing took more time in the Technology Education class than originally anticipated. Can you think of a way to make this work go more quickly? (*Hint:* Script writing is an English/language arts skill.)

3. What NETS for Students skills would students learn by doing the *Personal Fitness Plans You Can Live With* project? (See front of book for a list of NETS for students.)

Technology Integration Lesson Planning

The *Technology Integration Workshop* DVD includes a set of technology integration ideas and links to online lessons, arranged as a searchable database. The DVD comes packaged in the back of this textbook. Click on the *Hands-On with Technology* section of the DVD and complete the following exercises.

1. Locate lesson ideas—The DVD has examples of lessons that use some of the integration strategies described in this chapter. Locate an example integration idea for each of these strategies.

2. Evaluate the lessons—Use the *Evaluation Checklist for a Technology-Integrated Lesson* (located on the DVD and the Companion Website) to evaluate each of these lessons.

3. Modify a lesson—Select one of the lesson ideas and adapt its strategies to meet a need in your own content area. You may choose to use the same approach in the original or adapt it to meet your needs.

4. Add descriptors—Create descriptors for your new lesson like those found on the database (e.g., grade level, content and topic areas, technologies used, relative advantage, objectives, NETS standards).

5. Add the new lesson —Add your modified lesson with all its descriptors to the lesson idea database.

For Your Teaching Portfolio

For this chapter's contribution to your teaching portfolio, add the following products you created in the Technology Integration Workshop:

   • The sample *iMovie* video you created

   • The evaluations you did using the *Evaluation Checklist for a Technology-Integrated Lesson*

   • The new lesson plan you developed, based on the one you found on the DVD.

Create this product using the *Hands-On with Technology* section of tutorial on the DVD.

Source: Sample iMovie Video.

CHAPTER 15

TECHNOLOGY IN SPECIAL EDUCATION

DAVE L. EDYBURN
UNIVERSITY OF WISCONSIN–MILWAUKEE

M. D. ROBLYER
UNIVERSITY OF MARYLAND UNIVERSITY COLLEGE

For most of us, technology makes things easier. For a person with a disability, it makes things possible.

Judy Heumann, Assistant Secretary, U.S. Department of Education,
Office of Special Education Programs

Based on: Judd-Wall, J. (1996). Curriculum blending: Computerized surveying activities for everyone. *Learning and Leading with Technology, 23*(8), 61–64.

Grade Level: All grade levels • Content Area/Topic: Research methods, data analysis, charting, and graphing • Length of Time: Three weeks

Phase 1: Determine relative advantage

Three of the students in Ms. Montoya's sixth-grade class had special needs. Dorothy had cerebral palsy and came to class in her motorized wheelchair. Although bright and enthusiastic, she had difficulty with fine-motor skills and could not write or use the computer keyboard and mouse. Ralph was a shy, sweet boy with mild mental deficits. Geraldo had hearing impairments and was reluctant to speak in class. Ms. Montoya made special efforts to involve Dorothy, Ralph, and Geraldo in all class activities and had shown the other students how to welcome them into their work and play. She consulted with the school district's Special Education Resource Office to obtain an alternate keyboard and input software for Dorothy and special speech development software for Geraldo. She tried several resources and strategies to help develop Ralph's reading skills and found that he especially liked working with interactive books. However, she wanted a class project that could involve all students and show that each one of them could make a valuable contribution to the work despite their varying talents and ability levels. She learned in a district workshop about curriculum blending or curriculum overlapping, the practice of having students at all ability levels (including those with physical or learning disabilities) work on the same activities, but grading them differently. She decided to do a curriculum blending project that involved having the class do a survey of students in the school. Dorothy and Geraldo and others would be put in charge of gathering the data using an alternative input and spoken word processor system recommended by the Special Education Resource Office. The system could voice the questions and students could enter responses directly onto a touch panel on the computer screen. Ralph could work in the group that did initial tasks in the data analysis, and the whole class could learn how to do research and ask different levels of "what if" questions from compiled data. She correlated several required math skills with these activities.

Phase 2: Decide on objectives and assessments

Ms. Montoya developed assignment sheets for each student that indicated which tasks they would be required to do and how they would be graded. The sheets were tailored to the ability and skill levels of each student. Although tasks were different, criteria were similar and included accomplishing all tasks, working with others in the group, and completing a required product. Ms. Montoya stated the outcome as follows:

- **Outcome:** Survey completion and data analysis.
- **Objective:** Students will complete each of their assigned tasks to complete the survey activity, analyze and display the data, and complete a bulletin board showing their work.
- **Assessment:** Checklist of survey/product tasks with points assigned to each task.

Phase 3: Design integration strategies

Ms. Montoya designed the following sequence of activities around a survey of the students in the school.

- **Week 1:** Introduce the survey project and train students. Give students the assignment sheets and discuss the purposes and uses of survey research. Work with them to design a simple "script" for the survey, enter it into the voice word processor, and show them how the input system works to collect data. Have them discuss methods of getting students to stop and complete the survey (e.g., offer them a sticker that says "I voted!" as some voting places offer on election days). Have students rehearse the sequence in advance, so it will move quickly when they actually begin the survey.
- **Week 2:** Do the survey. Select a location (e.g., near the library) for data collection. Ask Geraldo to be in charge of encouraging students who pass by to participate in the survey. Place Dorothy in charge of demonstrating how the system input works. To get the question presented, a student touches a question icon, and the computer gives a typed and a voice response that states the question. Then the student answers the question by touching answer icons.
- **Week 3:** As a whole class, show how to analyze the results and do a summary product (e.g., a bar graph) based

on the results. For example, ask students to calculate percentages (e.g., What percentage of the population is male? Female?) and query the data (Do male students tend to prefer a certain sport?). Have Ralph work the computer to sort and organize the responses for each query. Divide students into small groups and have them do their own queries and bar graphs. Have all students help prepare a bulletin board to post their findings for the school to see. Place pictures of students around the bulletin board, identifying the roles they played in the survey.

Phase 4: Prepare the instructional environment

Ms. Montoya worked closely with the special education personnel to set up the special computer system and learn how to use it. She had to obtain permission to have the "survey station" in the hall outside the library and asked the main office to publicize it in the morning announcements. She had to spend extra time with Geraldo and Ralph to prepare them for their roles.

Phase 5: Evaluate and revise

At the end of the unit, Ms. Montoya reviewed the project and reflected on its impact. Some of the questions she asked were as follows:

- Did students at all ability levels accomplish required tasks?
- Did students (including those with special needs) seem engaged in the learning?

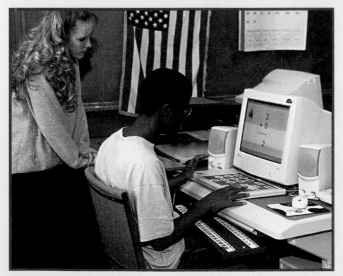

- Did students (including those with special needs) seem to acknowledge that all of them had made a valuable contribution to the class?
- Did the activities go smoothly with the alternative computer system?

Ms. Montoya was happy with how involved the students were in the survey. Parents of all three students with special needs came by to see the bulletin board and express their pride in their children's work. Ms. Montoya and the principal agreed they would have to work on locating the computer station so as not to disrupt hall traffic, since the "talking computer" had created quite a crowd. However, the principal also asked her to share her project with other teachers who had students with special needs.

OBJECTIVES

After reading this chapter and completing the learning activities for it, you should be able to:

1. Differentiate among the terms *impairment, disability,* and *handicap.*

2. Identify current issues affecting the acquisition and use of technology in special education.

3. Explore applications of assistive, instructional, and productivity technologies commonly used by students with disabilities and their teachers.

KEY TERMS

- alternative keyboards
- assistive technology
- closed-circuit television (CCTV)
- disability
- FM amplification systems
- handicap
- impairment
- inclusion
- joystick
- mainstreaming
- optical character recognition (OCR)
- screen readers
- sensory disabilities
- switches
- universal design

For more information on Key Terms, go to the *Key Terms* module for this chapter of the Companion Website at http://www.prenhall.com/roblyer.

INTRODUCTION

Education for students with special needs encompasses strategies for both those with physical and/or mental deficits and those with special gifts or talents. Although technology can be used to enhance education for both populations, this chapter addresses primarily applications for students with disabilities.

While the terms *impairment, disability,* and *handicap* are often used synonymously, differences among these concepts have important implications for the use of technology in classrooms. An **impairment** involves an abnormality or loss of function in a physical, anatomical, or psychological structure. Impairments to human function may be congenital (present at birth) or acquired through accident or disease. It is important not to make assumptions concerning a person's ability or limitations simply because he or she has an impairment.

When an impairment limits an individual from performing an activity in a manner normally expected for human beings (communicating with others, hearing, movement, manipulating objects, etc.), we refer to this as a **disability.** A student who has lost the function of his right arm has an impairment; this condition will have little or no impact on a variety of life functions. However, this student may encounter situations where the inability to use two arms places him at a disadvantage with others. A **handicap** arises when an individual is unable to fulfill a role due to an impairment or disability. It is critical to understand that a handicap is not a characteristic of an individual. Rather, a handicap results from the mismatch between one's abilities and the demands of an environment (Cook & Hussey, 1995).

In the United States, federal law recognizes several types of disabilities. Most citizens are likely to know one or more individuals whose life function has been affected by disability in some form: deaf, deaf-blind, hard of hearing, mental retardation, multihandicapped, orthopedically impaired, other health impaired, seriously emotionally disturbed, specific learning disability, speech impaired, or visually handicapped.

The fields of special education and rehabilitation have had a long-standing interest in technology. Historically, the emphasis on technology for individuals with disabilities has been thought of as **assistive technology,** that is, extending the abilities of an individual in ways that provide physical access (i.e., wheelchairs, braces) and sensory access (i.e., Braille, closed captioning). However, technology can also help address special teaching and learning needs. In this chapter we use the term *special education technology* to cover both dimensions of assistive technology and instructional technology.

Regardless of the specific application of technology, the general goal is always the same: to harness the potential of technology in ways that offer an individual with a disability increased opportunities for learning, productivity, and independence—opportunities that otherwise would not be available. In the next section, we explore several issues involved in capturing the potential of technology for individuals with disabilities.

ISSUES AND PROBLEMS IN SPECIAL EDUCATION

A number of issues affect the delivery of special education services. The following sections briefly identify five current issues that have an impact on uses of technology in special education.

Legal and Policy Directives

Special education, more than other areas of education, is governed by laws and policies. This means that teachers, administrators, and special education technology specialists must be well versed in federal and state laws, policies, and procedures. To learn more about the legal and policy foundations of the field of special education technology, consult the following resources: Blackhurst (1997), Blackhurst & Edyburn (2000), U.S. Department of Education (2000).

The following federal laws promote the use of technology by individuals with disabilities:

- The Technology-Related Assistance Act for Individuals with Disabilities (Public Law 100–407), passed in 1988, provides funding for statewide systems and services to provide assistive technology devices and services to individuals with disabilities.

- Reauthorization of the Individuals with Disabilities Education Act (IDEA) in 1997 (Public Law 105–17) mandates that every individualized education program (IEP) team "consider" assistive technology when planning the educational program of an individual with a disability. The most current reauthorization in 2004 contains no new technology information, but serves to reemphasize to schools the importance of academic achievement by students with disabilities and the need to help each student meet achievement goals.

Implications of the No Child Left Behind Act for Special Education

The No Child Left Behind (NCLB) Act is beginning to have a significant influence in special education, as it has in all other areas of education (see http://www.ataccess.org/resources/nochild.html). Perhaps one of the most important components of the law focuses on Annual Yearly Progress (AYP), which requires documentation that each school is meeting specific performance criteria the law has established. One benefit of these new AYP requirements is that they focus public attention education on the persistent underachievement of students with physical disabilities.

Need for Trained Personnel

Considerable effort has been devoted to identifying the knowledge and skills needed by teachers (Lahm & Nickels, 1999) and specialists (Lahm, 2000) to use technology in special education. Individuals can use the NETS competency statements to document their experience, knowledge, and skills in their own teaching portfolio. University teacher preparation programs and inservice workshop providers can review the NETS competency frameworks and align individual competency statements with specific courses and training events in order to communicate the specific outcomes participants will gain.

Despite efforts of most universities to improve the preparation of teachers to use technology in the classroom, most teachers begin their career with minimal experience in using technology in ways that (1) enhance their own productivity, (2) enhance the effectiveness of instruction and the success of all students, or (3) enable them to acquire and use assistive technology for students in need of performance support. The common three-credit course, first developed in the 1980s, continues to be the norm for preparing teachers; unfortunately, it is generally inadequate to exploit the power and possibilities that technology offers.

Another issue regarding the adequacy of personnel trained in special education technology centers on the use of interdisciplinary teams for evaluating the need for assistive technology and decision making in the selection of appropriate devices and services. The current assistive technology delivery system was originally developed to respond to the needs of students with low-incidence disabilities (approx. 1.4 million students in the United States). The sheer size of the high incidence population requires a rethinking of service delivery systems. The first step in accessing assistive technology services is not a referral for a comprehensive multidisciplinary evaluation (Edyburn, 2003). Instead, many students who have access to assistive technology do so as a result of advocacy efforts that challenge the system rather than through a systemic process that ensures all students in need of devices have them (Edyburn, 2000).

Requirements for Inclusive Classrooms

During the 1990s, a major change occurred in how special education services were delivered. Rather than placing

MAKING THE CASE FOR TECHNOLOGY INTEGRATION

Discuss these issues online with other students by selecting the *Making the Case* module for Chapter 15 of the Companion Website (http://www.prenhall.com/roblyer) or choose the *Message Board* module.

1. The following quote highlights critical professional development needs regarding using technology to enhance the academic performance of students with disabilities: "Given pressures exerted by regulations from IDEA and No Child Left Behind (2001), the need to develop specific methods that address general curriculum standards for special education students cannot be overstated. Special education professional training opportunities and experiences should be restructured to include methods that promote access to the general curriculum through the support possible by classroom uses of technology. This technology training must be curriculum specific, integrated across subject areas, and actively engage learners" (Puckett, 2004, p. 15).

   Do you feel you have adequate preparation to use technology to enhance the learning of all students in your classroom? In which areas do you feel most confident in your technology skills for differentiating instruction? In which areas do you feel most uncomfortable with your current skills and how might these deficits impact student achievement in specific content areas?

2. The following quote summarizes some of the current challenges associated with measuring the outcomes of assistive technology: "The continued scarcity of funding resources for assistive technology assessments, equipment, and training portends the need for predictive algorithms that can facilitate decision-making by practioners, reimbursement agencies, and consumers" (Lenker & Paquet, 2003, p. 13).

   What do these authors mean by "predictive algorithms"? What decision making can these algorithms help facilitate?

TOP TEN STRATEGIES FOR TECHNOLOGY IN SPECIAL EDUCATION

Take advantage of these 10 powerful strategies for using technology to enhance education for students with special needs.

1. **Use alternative keyboards such as Intellitools' IntelliKeys** — Students with limited manual dexterity need alternatives to the standard keyboard that let them use the computer independently.

2. **Use joysticks or switches instead of keyboards** — Students with severe physical disabilities need ways other than a keyboard to get input to the computer.

3. **Use text-to-speech products such as WizCom's Quicktionary pen** — These devices and materials assist students who have difficulty speaking.

4. **Provide a range of tools to support student writers** — Some students need simplified word processing tools like Tom Snyder's *Scholastic Keys,* or specialized word prediction word processors like Don Johnston's *Co:Writer.*

5. **Use digital cameras to capture images of objects and environments** — Students with cognitive disabilities sometimes need concrete examples as cues and prompts for learning.

6. **Use voice recognition software such as DragonTalk's Dragon Naturally Speaking** — Students who are unable to write by hand, who have illegible handwriting, or find handwriting extremely tedious can use this software to create text from their speech.

7. **Use talking word processors such as Don Johnston's Write:OutLoud** — Provides speech synthesis to allow students to hear what they have written.

8. **Use specialized calculators such as Programming Concepts' Coin-U-Lator®** — These handheld devices help students learn numerical concepts like making change.

9. **Use text-to-speech readers such as JAWS for Windows** — Students with visual disabilities can use these to have text read to them from a computer screen.

10. **Use optical character recognition (OCR) software or CCTV** — These strategies help enlarge text for students who are partially sighted.

students with disabilities in separate classrooms (self-contained special education) and allowing them to participate in selected classes in general education, a process called **mainstreaming,** efforts were made to include them in the general education classroom, an activity known as **inclusion.** This philosophical shift has been controversial. Nonetheless, students with disabilities now spend the majority of the school day in general education classrooms and receive a variety of support services (U.S. Department of Education, 2000).

Although students with disabilities have gained physical inclusion into general education, access to the general education curriculum is still limited. That is, without appropriate modifications, a student in a wheelchair cannot conduct the same science experiment as everyone else because his wheelchair cannot get close enough to the lab bench for the student to manipulate the chemicals and beakers. Likewise, when the bulk of subject matter content is contained in teacher-made materials and textbooks, a significant portion of the students do not have access to the information they are expected to learn (i.e., students who are blind, students with learning disabilities who cannot read at grade level). With the NCLB expectation that all students will achieve high academic standards, there is an urgent need for assistive technology to help students in the general education classroom succeed.

Universal Design for Learning

Principles of **universal design** have emerged from our understanding of the design of physical environments for individuals with disabilities. Perhaps the best example of the success of universal design principles is curb cuts. Originally designed to improve mobility for people with disabilities within our communities, curb cuts not only accomplish that, but also improve access for people with baby strollers, roller blades, bikes, etc. More recently, universal design concepts have been applied to computers in order to include disability accessibility software as part of the operating system so that access would be provided as the computer came out of the box (rather than require an individual to track down assistive technology specialists to make specialized modifications). Today, accessibility control panels are available on every computer.

In the past few years, a concerted effort has been made to apply universal design principles to learning. A leader in the area of universal design for learning has been the Center for Applied Special Technology (CAST). CAST feels universal design is a critical issue if students with disabilities are going to be able to access the general education curriculum. To learn more about universal design and access to the curriculum, visit the Center for Accessing the General Education Curriculum website at http://www.cast.org/naec/

Teachers working with students in inclusion settings face a relentless demand to modify curricular, instructional, and assessment materials. Modifications will always be necessary as a result of technology, media, and materials that are not designed with an understanding of the range of diversity found in every classroom. It is also important to note that modifications are always reactive. This means that students with disabilities often experience a delay in obtaining information that is readily available to their peers without disabilities. Universal design seeks to alter this paradigm by providing a new way of thinking about access that is proactive rather than reactive. For additional information about universal design, consult the references (Dolan, 2000; Edyburn, 2001; Grogan & Ruzic, 2000; Orkwis & McLane, 1998; Rose, 2000; Rose, Sethuraman, & Meo, 2000).

TECHNOLOGY INTEGRATION STRATEGIES FOR SPECIAL EDUCATION

This section provides information about general approaches to using assistive and instructional technology for students with special needs and describes specific products that are commonly integrated into curricula for helping achieve academic, behavioral, or social goals. Figure 15.1 summarizes all these strategies.

Foundations of Integration Strategies

Special educators must be concerned with two types of technology: assistive technology and instructional technology. Technology integration efforts must include both types of technology. Historically, the emphasis on technology for individuals with disabilities has been thought of as assistive technology. Indeed, the legal definition of assistive technology is considerably broad:

§300.5 Assistive technology device. As used in this part, *assistive technology device* means any item, piece of equipment, or product system, whether acquired commercially off the shelf, modified, or customized, that is used to increase, maintain, or improve the functional capabilities of a child with a disability. (Authority: 20 U.S.C. 1401(1))

The assistive technology evaluation process generally seeks to identify solutions on a continuum involving no-technology ("no-tech"), low-technology ("low-tech"), and advanced technology ("high-tech"). No-tech solutions are strategies such as teaching a person to use his or her body in a different manner to minimize the impact of an impairment (e.g., one-handed typing). The obvious advantage to solutions involving no technology is that they are available in any environment at any time. Low-tech solutions are generally considered to be nonelectrical. Personal word lists, highlighting markers, and organizing systems are all examples of low-technology solutions that can provide a person with appropriate levels of support to be successful in specific tasks. These solutions tend to be relatively inexpensive but quite flexible for enhancing individual performance. High-tech solutions are complex electrical or hydraulic systems (i.e., stair lift, powered wheelchair, voice-activated environmental control). Clearly, high-tech solutions tend to be the most costly and have the greatest number of restrictions regarding their use (i.e., user skill level, limited portability).

Professional practice in special education calls for the evaluation of potential solutions to begin with no-tech, and continue to low-tech, and then go to high-tech, as the needs dictate. For example, spelling words is most efficient when they are committed to memory. However, if a person displays persistent difficulty spelling from memory (no-tech), low-tech options like personal word lists or portable dictionaries may be helpful. High-tech solutions like electronic spelling checkers should be considered only after other options have proved less satisfactory because of the dependency on batteries, fragility, etc.

Two common approaches for technology use by individuals with disabilities involve remediation and compensation (King, 1999). Remediation involves helping an individual learn or improve performance, often the focus of education, training, and therapy. Compensation focuses using technology to accommodate difficulties performing specific tasks (i.e., providing for the use of a calculator in recognition that a child has been unable to learn the multiplication facts). Both approaches can be used when integrating technology into instruction or therapy.

General Integration Strategies for All Students

All of the technology integration strategies discussed in this book have important applications for students with disabilities. However, an essential consideration for all

Figure 15.1 Summary of Technology Integration Strategies for Special Education

Target Groups	Sample Technology Integration Strategies	Sample Resources and Activities
Students with mild and moderate to severe disabilities The Coin-U-Lator®. Courtesy of PCI Educational Publishing. http://www.specialed.net	**For individuals with mild cognitive disabilities:** • *Reading:* Use reading skill software, text-to-speech products, interactive storybooks. • *Writing:* Use voice recognition software and word prediction software. • *Mathematics:* Use graphing software, drills, games, and tutorials. **For individuals with moderate to severe cognitive disabilities:** • Software helps teach/reinforce functional skills (e.g., money management, daily living, employability). • Videos enhance acquisition, maintenance, and transfer of functional and community-based behaviors.	• WizCom's Quicktionary Reading Pen http://www.wizcomtech.com/ • Don Johnston's *Co:Writer* and *Write:OutLoud* http://donjohnson.com • DragonTalk's *Dragon Naturally Speaking* http://www.dragontalk.com/ • Freedom Scientific's WYNN word processing software http://www.freedomscientific.com • AbleNet, Inc. http://www.ablenetic.com • Attainment Company http://www.attainmentcompany.com
Students with physical disabilities Courtesy of Intellitools, Inc. http://www.intellitools.com/	• Provide alternative methods of accessing keyboard, mouse, and/or monitor. • Determine the best placement of adaptive technologies and provide training to ensure the student is able to operate it independently. • Monitor function to ensure maximum level of participation is obtained without undue physical demands.	• AbleNet, Inc. http://www.ablenetinc.com • Adaptivation, Inc. http://www.adaptivation.com • Enabling devices http://www.enablingdevices.com • Intelitools http://www.intellitools.com • ORCCA technology http://www.orcca.com
Students with sensory disabilities Courtesy of Dolphin Computer Access, Inc. http://www.dolphinuk.co.uk	**For individuals who are blind:** • Use canes and sensor technologies to assist movement. • Use text-to-Braille converters. • Use screenreaders. **For individuals who are visually impaired:** • Use closed-circuit television (CCTV) magnification systems. • Use built-in computer screen magnification control panels. **For individuals who are hearing impaired:** • Use FM amplification systems (assistive listening devices).	• Alva Access Group, Inc. http://www.aagi.com • Dolphin Computer Access, LLC. http://www.dolphinusa.com • Freedom Scientific Blind/Low Vision Group http://www.freedomscientific.com • TeleSensory http://www.telesensory.com • AudioEnhancement http://www.audioenhancement.com/

educators when planning for the needs of students with disabilities involves ensuring that the curriculum is accessible. When technology is used to make the curriculum accessible, students with disabilities have the same opportunities to learn as their peers without disabilities (Metheny, 2003; Scleef, 2003). Because some applications of technology in special education are commonly associated with specific disabilities, the following information will provide a brief overview of specific examples of technology used by people with disabilities.

Figure 15.1 (continued)

Target Groups	Sample Technology Integration Strategies	Sample Resources and Activities
At-risk students © 2005 Don Johnston Incorporated. http://www.donjohnston.com	• Locate software and websites that provide powerful and motivating opportunities to engage in learning activities. • Utilize electronic quizzes and other instructional materials that provide immediate feedback on performance.	• BrainPop http://www.brainpop.com • Don Johnston, Inc. http://www.donjohnston.com • Tom Snyder, Inc. http://www.tomsnyder.com
Students with gifts and talents Courtesy of Duke Talent Identification Program, Duke University. http://www.tip.duke.edu	• Locate starting point web pages to launch them into content with appropriate challenges • Provide tools for engaging in self-directed research • Provide tools such as multimedia presentations, web page design, and electronic portfolios to document learning experiences	• Duke TIP program http://www.tip.duke.edu/ • Hoagies' Gifted Education Page http://www.hoagiesgifted.org

Strategies for Students with Mild Disabilities

Mild disabilities are considered to be the most prevalent type of disability and include learning disabilities, serious emotional disabilities, and mental retardation. Current estimates indicate 3.8 million students, ages 6 to 21, have a mild disability (U.S. Department of Education, 2000), representing more than 71% of the students receiving special education services. Meese (2001) describes the following characteristics as being associated with mild disabilities: cognitive (i.e., intellectual ability, attentional deficits, memory and thinking skills), academic (i.e., reading, language arts, mathematics), and social-emotional.

Typically, the important issue for these students is not physical access to the technology, but reading, writing, memory, and retention of information. While these students often have some learning difficulties (e.g., inability to read at grade level), many have difficulty in learning in only one aspect of the curriculum. As a result, educators planning for the needs of students with mild disabilities often use productivity software, as well as other software materials and online resources that can be used with many low-performing students. (See Technology Integration Idea 15.1.) These may include materials for developing reading, writing, and mathematics skills. The key with all these uses is to balance remediation of skill deficits with activities that help develop more creative, higher level thinking skills.

Reading skills. A characteristic associated with many disabilities is difficulty in learning how to read and develop-ing grade-level reading skills. As a result, special education teachers tend to devote a great deal of time and energy to the teaching of reading and are likely to use a variety of software products to remediate students' reading abilities. Software products such as *Bailey's Book House* (Riverdeep), *JumpStart Kindergarten Reading* (Knowledge Adventure), and *Reader Rabbit* (Broderbund) are commonly used in classrooms where emergent readers are working on acquiring specific skills. Interactive storybooks are another commonly used resource. Text-to-speech products that help students with communications disabilities include CAST eReader (CAST), the Quicktionary Reading Pen (WizCom) shown in Figure 15.2, and *L&H Kurzweil 3000* (Lernout & Hauspie Speech Products). If teachers provide all instructional text in a digital format, students with disabilities and other struggling readers will be able to copy and paste the information into talking word processors and other text-to-speech software programs so they can listen to information they cannot read.

Writing skills. Many tools have been developed to support students who struggle in various phases of the writing process. For students who are unable to write by hand, who have illegible handwriting, or who find handwriting extremely tedious, voice recognition software such as Dragon Talk's *Dragon Naturally Speaking* may be an option. Some students who are slow typists or have difficulty spelling can benefit from word prediction software such as Don Johnston's *Co:Writer*, which offers word choices to complete the first few letters the student types.

TECHNOLOGY INTEGRATION IDEA 15.1

USING MULTIMEDIA TO HELP MEET STUDENTS' SPECIAL NEEDS

Title: A Multimedia Drivers' Study Guide for Students with Learning Disabilities

Content Area/Topic: Language arts: reading

Grade Level: 4–6

NETS for Students: Standards 3, 4, 6

Description: Many adolescents with learning disabilities are highly motivated to get their driver's license, but have difficulty with the written portion. This activity lets students use multimedia development software to create a guide that will help them study for this exam. Not only does the activity help them with language and study skills, it helps them use computers in a way that empowers them, instead of merely drilling or tutoring them. Divide the class into pairs of students, and give each a portion of the total booklet to analyze and present in the product. Students who are nonreaders or who have very low reading levels are paired with those who are better readers. When the entire product is completed, students present it to other classes and use it to study for the driver's examination.

Source: Speziale, M., & La France, L. (1992). Multimedia and students with learning disabilities. *The Computing Teacher,* 20(3), 31–34.

Figure 15.2   Quicktionary Reading Pen

Source: Courtesy of WizCom Technologies, Inc.

(See example in Figure 15.3.) Talking word processors, such as Don Johnston's *Write: OutLoud,* feature speech synthesis to allow students to hear what they have written. (See Figure 15.4.) *WYNN* (Freedom Scientific) is a specialized word processor that provides an array of support tools to students with learning disabilities. Finally, tools such as *Project Poster* (http://poster.hprtec.org/) and Tom Snyder's *Hollywood High* provide students with alternative writing environments that engage academically struggling students in the writing process in ways that traditional paper and pencil do not.

Math skills. Calculators are an important intervention for students with disabilities. A specialized calculator, the Coin-U-Lator® (Programming Concepts, Inc.), shown earlier in Figure 15.1, was developed to assist students having difficulty counting coins and making change. Other strategies have been developed around simple graphing software materials, as well as drills, games, and tutorials.

Strategies for Students with Moderate and Severe Disabilities

A variety of conditions may impair an individual's cognitive abilities. Such disabilities are often referred to as cognitive disabilities, developmental disabilities, or mental retardation. For individuals with moderate and severe cognitive disabilities, considerable effort is devoted to ensuring that they acquire daily living skills such as personal hygiene, shopping (Wissick, 1999b), and use of public transportation. In addition, software is available to help teach functional skills such as money management (Browder & Grasso, 1999), and employability skills (Fisher & Gardner, 1999) must also be taught. (See Technology Integration Idea 15.2.)

A promising line of research has focused on the creation of video-based instructional materials to enhance acquisition, maintenance, and transfer of functional and community-based behaviors (Mechling & Langone, 2000; Mechling, Gast, & Langone, 2002; Wissick, 1999a, 1999b).

TECHNOLOGY INTEGRATION IDEA 15.2

USING EMAIL AND DESKTOP PUBLISHING TO HELP MEET STUDENTS' SPECIAL NEEDS

Title: Teaching the Concept of Adaptation

Content Area/Topic: Language arts: reading

Grade Level: 10–12

NETS for Students: Standards 3, 4, 6

Description: Some students with mental deficits are successful in learning the mental and physical skills needed for careers in the food service industry. A key concept in their vocational training is learning to adapt what they learn in a lab setting to the varied situations they would encounter in the workplace. In this project, students learn this concept through a hands-on activity. The instructors begin by introducing the concept of adaptation by discussing the variations in hamburgers served in major fast-food restaurants. They talk about how workers at each location must prepare the same basic food (hamburger) according to that restaurant's recipes. After students have gathered email addresses from family and friends around the world, the instructor helps them compose an email message requesting favorite meatloaf recipes. As recipes come in, students use desktop publishing software to prepare a cookbook to compile them. They finish the project by preparing several of the recipes and talking about how people make meatloaf in so many different ways.

Source: Ervin, A. (2002). Meatloaf around the world. *Learning and Leading with Technology, 29*(5), 18–21, 62.

Figure 15.3 *Co: Writer* Word Prediction Word Processor

Source: Co:Writer is a copyright of Don Johnston, Incorporated. To purchase this product, contact Don Johnston, Incorporated, at 1-800-999-4660 (www.donjohnston.com).

Figure 15.4 *Write:OutLoud* Word Processor

Source: Write:OutLoud is a copyright of Don Johnston, Incorporated. To purchase this product, contact Don Johnston, Incorporated, at 1-800-999-4660 (www.donjohnston.com).

Teachers working with students with moderate and severe cognitive disabilities need to be familiar with an array of devices that provide an alternative means for accessing the computer since the typical keyboard may be problematic for many students. To simplify the physical or cognitive demands of interacting with the computer, **alternative keyboards,** such as the Intellikeys keyboard (Intellitools) (shown earlier in Figure 15.1) can be used to create customized keyboards. For instance, keys can be enlarged to provide more space for the student to press a key; keys that are not relevant for a given software program can be removed; multistep functions such as save, print, or quit can be programmed into a single key press. Companies such as AbleNet assist teachers in integrating the assistive technology into instruction.

Strategies for Students with Physical Disabilities

Physical disabilities typically impact a person's mobility and agility. Difficulties in motor movements may involve gross- or fine-motor movement and frequently exist concurrently with other disabilities. (See Figure 15.5.)

Adaptive input devices allow students with physical disabilities to use computers for learning.

Assistive technology for individuals with severe physical disabilities may take the form of a power wheelchair operated by a **joystick,** a device with a handle that moves in all directions. Joysticks can also control the movement of a cursor or pointer on a computer screen. To provide access to a computer, it is often necessary to offer an alternative to the typical keyboard. **Switches** are also commonly used for controlling and getting input to the computer as well as activating environmental control systems.

Assessing the need for assistive technology involves a team of specialists including occupational therapists, physical therapists, rehabilitation engineers, and assistive technology specialists. The goal is to identify appropriate tools for access and control that will allow the individual to function across environments: home, school, community, and eventually work.

Strategies for Students with Sensory Disabilities

Sensory disabilities involve impairments associated with the loss of hearing or vision. If there is a complete loss of vision, a person is considered blind. An individual is considered partially sighted if there is some visual acuity. Similarly, if there is a complete loss of hearing, a person is considered deaf. *Hearing impaired* is the term used to describe an individual with some hearing.

For the blind. For an individual who is blind, three kinds of technology facilitate independence and access to environments and information:

- **Canes and sensor technology**—These are used to provide the person with mobility and orientation information when navigating various environments.

- **Tools to convert printed information**—Other essential tools convert printed information into audio so that a person who is blind can gain information by listening rather than reading. This is accomplished through the use of a scanner, **optical character recognition (OCR)** software to scan and translate print into a word-processed file, and speech synthesis. It works by placing text material on the scanner and scanning the material scanned into the computer. The OCR software then converts the scanned information into text, and then the speech synthesis tools read the material read aloud. *L & H Kurzweil 3000* (Lernout & Hauspie Speech Products), and *Scan and Read Pro* (Premier Programming Solutions), are common text-to-speech systems used by individuals who are blind.

- **Screen readers**—**Screen readers** work as utility software, operating in the background of the computer operating system and reading any text that appears on the screen, for example, menus, text, web pages. (See Figure 15.6.) Examples of screen readers include *Hal Screen Reader* (Dolphin Computer Access), *Home Page Reader for Windows* (IBM Special Needs Systems), *JAWS for Windows* (Freedom Scientific), and *OutSPOKEN* (Alca Access Group).

For the partially sighted. Partially sighted individuals must have text information enlarged, or the contrast altered, in order to perceive printed information. When information is in printed form (e.g., books, magazines, flyers) a **closed-circuit television (CCTV)** magnification system can be used. CCTV is a video camera mounted on a frame with a television monitor. Users place materials on the desktop below the camera, set the desired magnification level and move the materials around as necessary such

Figure 15.5   Standing Wheelchair

Source: Courtesy of Johnson & Johnson.

Figure 15.6 JAWS Screen Reader

Source: Courtesy of Freedom Scientific.

that the information appears on the monitor in a size that can be read comfortably by the individual. Many partially sighted individuals can see print on a computer screen by simply activating the built-in screen magnification control panel. This function allows users to select the desired magnification of everything appearing on the screen. This not only helps people with disabilities but also those with failing eyesight associated with aging.

For the deaf. Individuals who are deaf often can use most technologies without significant modifications. However, one problematic area involves the use of audio feedback (e.g., error messages) and the reliance on sound in multimedia software. When designers provide essential information only in audio form, this information is inaccessible to deaf individuals. As a result, advocacy and design initiatives encourage all information to be available in multiple formats (e.g., error messages that produce an auditory signal as well as a message on the screen; multimedia software that includes closed captioning of audio tracks).

Individuals with hearing impairments need few modifications to be able to use computers. A new technology is finding increasing acceptance in classrooms: **FM amplification systems** (Easterbrooks, 1999). These systems involve the teacher wearing a wireless microphone, and students with hearing impairments and some students with learning disabilities involving auditory processing difficulties wearing receivers that amplify the teacher's voice and serve to focus attention. These devices are also referred to as assistive listening devices and are increasingly found in movie theaters as an accommodation for patrons of all ages.

Strategies for At-Risk Students

Students at risk for school failure are not considered disabled in the sense of the federal definition of disability. However, their lack of success in school often parallels the low performance of students with disabilities. The use of assistive technology by students with disabilities has helped the profession understand the types of academic challenges students face and the kinds of technology tools that allow them to be successful. The impact of NCLB may cause the profession to consider the application of these tools for other students who struggle to achieve in school. Figure 15.7 shows how selected assistive and instructional technology products can match the various needs of at-risk students.

Strategies for Students with Gifts and Talents

Heward (2000) says that, according to the Gifted and Talented Children's Act of 1978, gifted and talented students are those "possessing demonstrated or potential abilities that give evidence of high performance capability in such areas as intellectual, creative, specific academic or leadership ability, or in the performing or visual arts, and why by reason thereof require services or activities not ordinarily provided by the school (PL 95;-561, Title IX, Section 902)" (p. 534). The primary issue surrounding and shaping education for gifted students is how to identify students who merit these special "services or activities not ordinarily provided by the school." Heward gives a comprehensive discussion of these issues and describes criteria schools use to identify students who qualify as gifted and talented.

Heward (2000) also observes that " …the increasingly sophisticated use of technological tools and related methods will provide gifted students with greater connectivity and independence in the future" (p. 572). Citing work by Howell (1994), he finds that technology integration for gifted and talented students should revolve primarily around three strategies (p. 572):

- **Electronic communities** — Communicating with people from distant and differing cultures and languages encourages and provides new avenues for expression.
- **Research** — Using global resources (e.g., on the Internet) to research topics allows gifted students to explore ideas and events more quickly and in greater depth.
- **Interactive and multimedia presentations** — Developing presentations based on their research allows students to display their discoveries in ways that make them more independent learners.

Finally, when gifted students engage in cooperative group work on products such as websites and multimedia presentations, they are working in a motivational

Figure 15.7 Matching Technology Resources to the Needs of At-Risk Students

Learning Difficulties	Strategies
Difficulty remembering things to do, sequence of tasks	• Provide a reminder service: http://www.iping.com. • Use a specialized prompting device: Job Coach at http://www.attainmentcompany.com.
Inability to read and comprehend at grade level	• Provide digital text in a text-to-speech program: ReadPlease at http://www.readplease.com. • Provide instructional materials with multiple levels: http://www.windows.ucar.edu.
Difficulties in written expression	• Use a predictive word processor; e.g., *Co:Writer* (http://www.donjohnston.com) or *WordQ* (http://www.wordq.com). • Offer support for dictation: http://www.idictate.com.
Difficulties in math computations and concepts	• Use online calculators: WebMath at http://www.webmath.com • Use teaching tools such as Virtual Math Manipulatives at http://matti.usu.edu/nlvm/nav/vlibrary.html.
Lack of motivation to engage in school work	• Shift power and control for the student to take responsibility; e.g., clipping services like Crayon (http://crayon.net) to create their own newspaper or My.Yahoo (http://my.yahoo.com) to manage a personal calendar and to-do list. • Use TrackStar (http://hprtec.trackstar.org) to organize engaging instructional activities that parallel the curriculum.

environment in which they can learn important social skills required for them to be effective and productive in the world of work.

FINAL TIPS FOR TEACHERS

Teachers in non–special education classrooms face a constant challenge to meet the needs of students with disabilities. The following are suggestions for finding ways to apply the power of technology to meet these needs:

• Routinely use web accessibility checkers, like *Bobby*, to ensure that all web pages are accessible for students with sensory and physical disabilities—Web accessibility is a critical consideration for those designing instructional web pages as well as all of us who use them.

• Constantly be on guard for new solutions for academic performance problems—Resources such as Closing the Gap's *Solutions* database (http://www.closingthegap.com) provide an excellent tool for locating new tools for students with disabilities and other struggling students.

• Access professional development resources, such as Assistive Technology Training Online (http://atto.buffalo.edu), to support your continuing professional development. Regardless of how much time and energy you have devoted to learning about special education technology, there is always more to learn. Reserve some time to regularly update your knowledge and skills.

INTERACTIVE SUMMARY

The following is a summary of the main points covered in this chapter. To see additional examples and information on these points, go to this textbook's Companion Website at http://www.prenhall.com/roblyer and click on the Chapter 15 Interactive Summary module to visit each of the recommended websites.

1. **Issues in special education**—These include:
   • Legal and policy directives
   • Implications of the NCLB act for special education
   • Need for trained personnel
   • Require inclusive classrooms
   • Universal design for learning (see the Center for Accessing the General Education Curriculum).

2. **Strategies are described for integrating technology into instruction for all students with special needs, including students with:**
   • Mild disabilities (see Don Johnston's Co:Writer and Write: OutLoud)
   • Moderate and severe disabilities
   • Physical disabilities (see descriptions at AbleNet, Inc.)
   • Sensory disabilities (see products at Freedom Scientific)
   • At-risk behaviors/situations (see activities at BrainPop)
   • Gifts and talents.

Online Activities

Visit this text's Companion Website at http://www. prenhall.com/roblyer to gain access to a variety of questions, activities, and exercises to help build your knowledge of this chapter's content.

Online Chapter 15 Self-Test

To review terms and concepts for this chapter, click on the Self-Test module for this chapter of the Companion Website.

Software Skill-Builder Tutorials

To access practical tutorial and skill-building activities and to build skills using popular software and hardware, click on the Software Skill-Builder Tutorials module for this chapter of the Companion Website.

Web-Enrichment Activities

To complete activities that connect to chapter content and provide web-based resources, click on the Web-Enrichment Activities module for this chapter of the Companion Website.

TECHNOLOGY INTEGRATION WORKSHOP

CLIPS FROM THE CLASSROOM: LEARNING WITH TECHNOLOGY

Go to the *Technology Integration Workshop* DVD located in the back of this text and click on *Clips from the Classroom*. View the video clips listed below that support this chapter's content:

- SmartBoards *for Students with Hearing Impairments*.

Now, visit this text's Companion Website at http://www.prenhall.com/roblyer to answer questions and complete activities that will guide you in analyzing each clip.

THE TIP MODEL IN ACTION

Read each of the following scenarios related to implementing the TIP Model, and go to the Companion Website to answer the questions that follow it based on your Chapter 15 reading activities.

TIP Model Scenario #1
Ms. Cinqela has a student with cerebral palsy who cannot control her hands enough to write or use a computer keyboard. Ms. Cinqela believes her student is bright; she contributes some valuable things verbally and seems interested in everything they did. However, she is unable to complete most class assignments.

1.1 What technology-based strategies could Ms. Cinqela use to address these needs?

1.2 What would be the relative advantages of using these strategies?

1.3 Should Ms. Cinqela have her student with cerebral palsy work alone or with other students? Explain.

TIP Model Scenario #2
Mr. Allgood is a science teacher who has been assigned to teach a group of gifted students. The principal asked Mr. Allgood to create learning activities that would challenge and motivate these students to learn science and mathematics and offer a way they each could demonstrate individual learning using particular kinds of intelligence.

2.1 What technology-based strategy could Mr. Allgood use to carry out such a project?

2.2 What would be the relative advantage of using this strategy?

2.3 Describe how Mr. Allgood might manage this kind of activity in a classroom.

TIP Model Scenario #3
Mr. Bartle is a fifth-grade teacher who has three low-achieving students with very low mathematics test scores. It is clear that they each lack basic skills in math facts and operations. Mr. Bartle has no time to work with each of these students individually, but he knows they need practice in the skills they lack. They also need motivation to practice the skills, since each has failed frequently in previous classes.

3.1 What technology-based strategy could Mr. Bartle use to address these needs?

3.2 What would be the relative advantage of using these strategy?

3.3 Should these students work individually, in pairs, or as a small group on this activity? Explain.

TIP Model Scenario #4
Mr. Tindel is a seventh-grade social studies teacher who has two students with learning disabilities. Neither student can read or write very well. However, both have talents. One is an avid photographer, and the other likes to draw and paint. Mr. Tindel wants to create an activity that allows them to participate fully in classroom projects and have their talents recognized. He feels this recognition would help motivate them to spend time on other learning activities.

4.1 What technology-based strategy could Mr. Tindel use to address this need?

4.2 What would be the relative advantage of using this strategy?

4.3 How could Mr. Tindel determine whether or not these two students felt more positive about other class work as a result of participation in this activity?

TIP Model Scenario #5
Mr. Zircone is a fifth-grade teacher. He has a nonverbal student whose vocal cords were injured in a traffic accident. The student is very intelligent, but he is depressed and discouraged because he cannot communicate with his teachers or his classmates.

Mr. Zircone overheard some of the children referring to this student as "The Dummy." Mr. Zircone wants to find a way to allow this student to communicate in class to show the other students he is not a "dummy" and allow him to participate more fully in learning activities.

5.1 What technology-based tool could Mr. Zircone use to address this need?

5.2 What would be the relative advantage of using this tool?

5.3 Give an example of a learning activity in a content area (e.g., language arts, science, social studies) that would make use of this tool.

TIE INTO PRACTICE: TECHNOLOGY INTEGRATION EXAMPLES

The Technology Integration Example that opened this chapter (*Helping Students with Disabilities Blend In*) showed how teachers might have students with disabilities help complete a survey. To do the survey activity described in this lesson, the teacher has to create an online survey document using *Adobe Acrobat* software. With the knowledge you have gained from Chapter 15, do the following to explore this strategy:

1. Using *Adobe Acrobat* software, create a survey form like the example shown here. **Create this example collage** by using the *Hands-On with Technology* tutorial section on the DVD that accompanies this text.

2. Answer the following questions about the *Helping Students with Disabilities Blend In* example:

- Phase 1 — What is the relative advantage of the teacher using the alternative input and spoken word processor system for this survey activity?

- Phase 2 — To adapt classroom requirements to the capabilities of each student, the teacher creates a separate set of requirements for the students with disabilities. How does this kind of project make it more feasible to accomplish such adaptations?

- Phase 3 — Why is it important to give Ralph, Dorothy, and Geraldo highly visible roles in this project?

- Phase 4 — What other ways could Ms. Montoya have students use technologies to advertise the upcoming survey?

- Phase 5 — One of the end-of-project questions Ms. Montoya asked was if students acknowledged that each one had made an important contribution. How might she ascertain this?

Survey screen presented in *Adobe Acrobat*. (Create this product using the *Hands-On with Technology* tutorial section on the DVD.)

3. What NETS for Students skills would students learn by working on the *Helping Students with Disabilities Blend In* project? (See front of book for a list of NETS for students.)

TECHNOLOGY INTEGRATION LESSON PLANNING

The *Technology Integration Workshop* DVD includes a set of technology integration ideas and links to online lessons, arranged as a searchable database. The DVD comes packaged in the back of this textbook. Click on the *Hands-On with Technology* section of the DVD and complete the following exercises.

1. Locate lesson ideas — The DVD has several examples of lessons that use technology-based strategies to meet students' special needs, as described in this chapter. Locate an example integration idea for at least one of these strategies.

2. Evaluate the lessons — Use the *Evaluation Checklist for a Technology-Integrated Lesson* (located on the DVD and the Companion Website) to evaluate each of these lessons.

3. Modify a lesson — Select one of the lesson ideas and adapt its strategies to meet a need in your own content area. You may choose to use the same approach in the original or adapt it to meet your needs.

4. Add descriptors — Create descriptors for your new lesson like those found on the database (e.g., grade level, content and topic areas, technologies used, relative advantage, objectives, NETS standards).

5. Add the new lesson — Add your modified lesson with all its descriptors to the lesson idea database.

FOR YOUR TEACHING PORTFOLIO

For this chapter's contribution to your teaching portfolio, add the following products you created in the Technology Integration Workshop:

- The sample *Adobe Acrobat* survey you created using the tutorial
- The evaluations you did using the *Evaluation Checklist for a Technology-Integrated Lesson*
- The new lesson plan you developed, based on the one you found on the DVD.

GLOSSARY

accelerometer—A device that assists with analyzing and monitoring physical fitness levels by counting calories

Acceptable Use Policy (AUP)—An agreement created by a school or other educational organization that stipulates the risks involved in Internet use; outlines appropriate, safe student behavior on the Internet; asks students if they agree to use the Internet under these conditions; and asks if they agree to information about themselves being posted on the school's website

action research—According to Gay and Airasian, a process in which teachers collect evidence and make decisions about their own knowledge, performance, beliefs, and effects in order to understand and improve them

algorithm—A step-by-step solution to a problem (e.g., a programming problem)

alternative keyboard—Customized keyboards created for users with special needs (e.g., enlarging the keys to provide more space for the student to press a key; removing keys that are not relevant for a given software; programming multi-step functions like save, print, quit into a single key press)

American Council for the Teaching of Foreign Languages (ACTFL)—Professional organization for teachers of foreign languages

anchor—A link inserted on a web page to allow a link to that location from within the page

anchored instruction—Constructivist term for learning environments that reflect situated cognition, or instruction anchored in meaningful, real-life problems and activities

applet—A program that is written in the Java language and is designed to carry out a useful task on the Internet (e.g., showing a clock to tell the exact time)

applications programs—Computer software written to support tasks that are useful to a computer user (e.g., word processing) in contrast with systems software

applications software—(See applications programs.)

Archie—A program that allows users to locate a file on the Internet

ARPAnet—A network created in 1969 by the U.S. government–funded Advanced Research Projects Agency (ARPA) to enable communications among important defense sites in the event of a worldwide catastrophe such as a nuclear attack; later became the Internet

artificial intelligence (AI)—Computer programs that try to emulate the decision-making capabilities of the human mind

ASCII (American Standard Code for Information Interchange)—A standardized, commonly accepted format for representing data (e.g., characters and numbers) so that programs and files created with one program and stored in ASCII can be used by another program

assembler—A low-level programming language that uses mnemonic commands that are one step up in complexity from "machine language" (binary numbers)

assimilation—Piagetian view of how children learn by fitting new experiences into their existing view of the world

assistive technology—Devices that extend the abilities of an individual in ways that provide physical access (i.e., wheelchairs, braces) and sensory access (i.e., Braille, closed captioning)

asynchronous—Form of distance communications in which information and messages are left for the receiver to read later; contrasts with synchronous communications, in which information and messages are sent and received immediately

Audio Video Interleave (AVI) format—One of several digital formats for video that are able to be used with video editing software

authoring system—A program designed to help nonprogrammers write computer-based instructional programs (e.g., web pages or multimedia); can be either a high-level programming language or a series of nonprogramming prompts

automaticity—A level of skill that allows a person to respond immediately (i.e., automatically) with the correct answer to a problem

avatar—A graphic representation of a real person in cyberspace; a three-dimensional image that a person can choose to represent him or her in a virtual reality environment

avatar spaces—Multi-user dungeons (or dimensions or domains) or MUDs in which users can interact through their graphic representations (i.e., avatars)

backup copy—A copy of a disk that is made to guard against loss of files if an original disk is lost or destroyed

bar code—A set of lines that represents a number such as a UPC (Universal Product Code)

bar-code reader—A device that reads and interprets bar codes

BASIC (Beginners All-Purpose Symbolic Instruction Code)—A high-level programming language designed for beginning programmers; popular with early microcomputers in the 1980s

Basic Interpersonal Communications (BIC)—Social language, acquired mainly through verbal interactions in social settings

baud rate—The speed at which data are transmitted across communication lines between computers, measured in bits per second (bps); 1 baud = 1 bps

BB—(See bulletin board.)

binary—A condition of two possible states (e.g., on or off, 1 or 0). For computers, binary refers to the coding system that uses 1s and 0s

bit—A binary digit, either a 1 or a 0; several bits together (usually eight) make up a byte of computer storage that can hold a letter or a character

BitNet—An early network used primarily by higher education organizations; replaced by the Internet

blog—Short for "web log," a web page that serves as a publicly accessible location for discussing a topic or issue; began as personal journals and expanded to become public discussion forums in which anyone can give opinions on a topic

blood pressure devices—Devices that assist with analyzing and monitoring physical fitness levels by monitoring and reporting blood pressure

BMP—Stands for "bitmapped." Developed originally for use on Disk Operating System (DOS) and Windows-compatible computers, an image format used for drawn images, illustrations, clip art, or animations

body composition analyzer—A device that assists with analyzing and monitoring physical fitness levels by determining the percent of body fat

bomb—Condition in a computer when a program stops operating due to an error of some kind; also, to stop operating (See also logic bomb.)

Bookmark—In the *Netscape* browser, an Internet location or URL marked so that a user can return to it quickly; or the place so marked

Bookmarks file—In the *Netscape* browser, a set of Internet locations or URLs organized so that a user can return to them quickly (See also Favorites file.)

boot/boot up—To start up a computer system; a "cold boot" is turning on the device from a power switch; a "warm boot" is restarting from the keyboard without shutting off power

bps (bits per second)—The speed at which data are transmitted across communication lines between computers

browser—A software package (e.g., *Netscape, Internet Explorer, Safari*) that allows one to look at information on the Internet in graphic, rather than just text, format

bug—An error in a computer program caused either by faulty logic or incorrect program language syntax (named by early programmer and systems designer Grace Hopper, who found a moth in the machinery of a non-functioning computer)

bulletin board (BB)—A computer system set up to allow notices to be posted and viewed by anyone who has access to the network

button—A place on a computer screen, usually within a hypermedia program, that causes some action when the user clicks on it using a mouse; also called a hot spot or link

byte—A group of binary digits (bits) that represents a character or number in a computer system; designates a unit of computer storage (see also G, K, and M)

C—A structured programming language originally designed for use on the Unix operating system and widely used on today's microcomputers; current version is C++

CAI (computer-assisted instruction)—Software designed to help teach information and/or skills related to a topic; also known as instructional software or courseware

calculator-based lab (CBL)—Calculator with probes or sensors connected to it to allow gathering of numerical data

card—One frame or screen produced in a hypermedia program such as *HyperStudio* (several cards together make a stack)

CAT (computer-assisted testing)—Using a computer system to administer and score assessment measures; also, computer adaptive testing

CD-I (compact disc interactive)—A type of CD-ROM used on special players with built-in computer and TV capabilities

CD-ROM (compact disc—read only memory)—Removable computer storage medium that can store images and/or up to 250,000 pages of text

cell—In a spreadsheet, a row–column location that may contain numerical values, words, or character data, and formulas or calculation commands

Center for Applied Research in Educational Technology (CARET)—A funded project of the International Society for Technology in Education (ISTE) that has the most comprehensive review of research evidence available on the impact of technology in education (http://caret.iste.edu)

central processing unit (CPU)—The circuitry in a computer that processes programmed commands; it is composed of the controller, the arithmetic/logic unit (ALU), and internal memory

CGI (Common Gateway Interface)—An authoring specification on the Internet for how data will be collected at a website; CGI programs are written in a language such as PERL

charting/graphing tools—Software tools that automatically draw and print desired charts or graphs from data entered by users

chatroom—A location on the Internet set up to allow people to converse in real time by typing in messages or allowing their avatars to meet and "talk" to each other

chip—A piece of silicon inside a computer on which electronic circuits have been placed by depositing small paths of a metal such as aluminum; an integrated circuit

classical conditioning—Pavlovian view of learning as involuntary physical responses to outside stimuli (e.g., dogs salivate at the sight of a dog food can)

client—Programs like browsers and FTP software designed to carry out various activities for people to help them use the Internet

clip art—One or more pieces of professionally prepared art work, stored as files and designed to be inserted into a document or web page

clone—A computer designed to operate like another brand of computer, but usually not made by the same company as the original

closed circuit television (CCTV)—A magnification system in which a video camera is mounted on a frame with a television monitor. Users place materials on the desktop below the camera, set the desired magnification level, move the materials around as necessary, and information appears on the monitor in a size that can be read comfortably by an individual with visual impairments

CMI (computer-managed instruction) systems—Computer software systems designed to keep track of student performance data, either as part of CAI programs or by themselves

COBOL (Common Business Oriented Language)—A high-level language designed specifically for business applications

code—Lines of commands or instructions to a computer written in a certain language (e.g., BASIC or C++); the act of writing such instructions

Cognitive Academic Language Proficiency (CALP)—A complex level of human language that students must understand before they can benefit in a meaningful way from reading or engaging in academic discussions in the language; contrasts with Basic Interpersonal Communications (BICS)

cold boot—(See boot/boot up.)

command—One instruction to a computer written in a computer language

compiler—A computer program that converts all statements of a source program into machine language before executing any part of the program (in contrast with interpreter)

computer—Usually equivalent to computer system (See computer system); sometimes refers to the CPU part of the system

computer adaptive testing (CAT)—Computer software that continuously analyzes a student's test responses and presents more or less difficult questions based on the student's performance (See also CAT.)

computer-assisted design (CAD)—Software used by architects and others to aid in the design of structures such as houses and cars

computer-assisted instruction—(See CAI.)

computer-assisted testing—(See CAT.)

computerized kiln—Oven for firing ceramic products that uses computers to automatically set required temperature, monitor length of time, and begin the process of cooling down and shutting off

computer language—A communication syntax and vocabulary used to write computer programs

computer literacy—Term coined by Arthur Luehrmann in the 1960s to mean a set of basic abilities everyone should have with computer systems; now has variable meanings

computer-managed instruction systems—(See CMI.)

computer platforms—Types of computer systems identified by their operating systems, e.g., PCs with Windows operating systems or Macintoshes with Mac-OS operating systems

computer programs—(See software.)

computer system—A set of devices designed to work together to accomplish input, processing, and output functions in order to accomplish tasks desired by a user

concept mapping software—Tools designed to help people think through and explore ideas or topics by developing concept maps (i.e., visual outlines of ideas)

conferencing—Communication between people in two or more places made possible by computer systems connected by communication technologies

constructivist learning—Teaching/learning model based on cognitive learning theory; holds that learners should generate their own knowledge through experience-based activities rather than being taught it by teachers (See also directed instruction)

contingencies of reinforcement—According to learning theorist B. F. Skinner, experiences (positive reinforcement, negative reinforcement, punishment) that shape desired behavioral responses

control unit (controller)—The part of the computer system housed in the CPU that processes program instructions

cookie—A small piece of text transferred to a web browser through an Internet server for the purpose of tracking the Internet usage habits of the person using the browser

copy and paste—The act of copying text from one location in a document and inserting it in another location

course management system—An online collection of web course design and delivery tools; WebCT and BlackBoard are examples

courseware—Instructional software; computer software used to enhance or deliver instruction

cracker—A person who seeks to gain unauthorized access to a computer system for the purpose of stealing and corrupting data; a hacker

CRT (cathode ray tube)—A TV-like screen on which information from a computer system may be displayed; a monitor; a primary output device for a microcomputer system

cursor—A line, block, or underline, usually blinking, displayed on the computer screen to show where information may be inserted

cut and paste—The act of copying text from one location in a document, deleting it, and then inserting it in another location

data—Elements of information (e.g., letters, numbers, and words)

database—A collection of information systematized by computer software to allow storage and easy retrieval through keyword searching; the program designed to accomplish these tasks

database management system (DBMS)—Computer software designed to facilitate the use and updating of a collection of information in a database

data mining—The practice of collecting data from all the information available and searching it to see relationships among the data elements

data processing—Organizing and manipulating data for a specific purpose (e.g., to keep track of income and expenses, to maintain student records)

data warehouses—Central collection points for data collected through data mining (See also data mining.)

debug—To review a computer program and remove the errors or "bugs"

decoding—In reading, the act of "sounding out" words

desktop—The screen that appears first upon starting up a Macintosh computer or an MS-DOS computer with Windows; a graphic user interface (GUI) designed to make it easier for nontechnical people to use a computer

desktop publishing—Term coined in 1984 by the president of the Aldus Corporation to refer to the activity of using software to produce documents with elaborate control of the form and appearance of individual pages

desktop videoconferencing—A computer-to-computer form of live action, interactive, two-way video/audio; a typical desktop videoconferencing system has a video camera, microphone, and speakers at each workstation

Digital Divide—Term coined by Lloyd Morrisett, former president of the Markle Foundation, to mean a discrepancy in access to technology resources among socioeconomic groups

digital storytelling—Using images and audio to tell the stories of lives, events, or eras

digitized sound—Audible noises (e.g., music, voices) that are transferred to a computer storage medium by first encoding them as numbers

directed instruction—A teaching and learning model based on behavioral and cognitive theories; students receive information from teachers and do teacher-directed activities (See also constructivist learning.)

disability—Condition that occurs when an impairment limits an individual from performing an activity in a manner normally expected for human beings (communicating with others, hearing, movement, manipulating objects, etc.)

disaggregation—Taking student data from a general database and grouping it according to desired characteristics

disc—CD-ROMs, videodiscs, or other optical storage media, as opposed to magnetic storage (e.g., a floppy disk)

discovery learning—According to learning theorist Jerome Bruner, a more effective way of children learning concepts by discovering them during their interaction with the environment

disk—A computer storage medium on which data and programs are placed through a magnetic process (e.g., a floppy disk); contrasts with an optical storage medium or disc

disk drive—A device in a computer system used to store data on floppy disks or microdisks and retrieve data

diskette—(See disk.)

distance learning—A form of education in which some means, electronic or otherwise, is used to connect people with instructors and/or resources that can help them acquire knowledge and skills

distributed intelligence—(See shared intelligence.)

domain designator—A required part of a Uniform Resource Locator (URL) that indicates what kind of group owns the server; examples include ".edu," ".com," and ".org."

DOS (disk operating system)—The systems software that allows a computer to use applications programs such as word processing software; the operating system on IBM-type computers as opposed to those manufactured by Apple

dot-matrix printer—Output device that produces paper copy by placing patterns of dots on the paper to form letters

download—To bring information (e.g., text files, images) to a computer from the Internet or other network or from a computer to a disc

drill and practice—An instructional software function that presents items for students to work on (usually one at a time) and gives feedback on correctness; designed to help users remember isolated facts or concepts and recall them quickly

DVD (digital versatile disc)—A type of electronic storage medium that holds a minimum of 4.7 gigabytes of information

Dynamic HTML (DHTML)—Programming language that can allow the same URL to display a different page depending on conditions such as the time of day or the previous pages (See also HTML, URL.)

ebook—A flat panel computer display that is designed to resemble a book, but offers interactive graphics and searchable text features not possible in printed books; also an online text

educational technology—A combination of the processes and tools involved in addressing educational needs and problems, with an emphasis on applying the most current tools: computers and other electronic technologies

electronic bulletin boards—(See bulletin board.)

electronic field trip (virtual field trip)—Online activities in which students explore unique locations around the world and/or communicate with learners at those sites

electronic gradebook—Software designed to maintain and calculate student grades

electronic mail (email)—Messages sent via telecommunications from one person to one or more other people

electronic mentor—Subject matter expert who volunteers to work closely with students online

electronic outliner—Software features that automatically generate headings and subheadings from typed information

electronic portfolio—A collection of a person's work products over time, arranged so that he or she and others can see how skills have developed and progressed, and presented in an electronic format such as a website or multimedia product

electronic publishing—Activity when students submit their written or artistic products to a website

electronic slide shows—Sequences of frames shown in a linear way with presentation software (e.g., *PowerPoint*)

electronic whiteboard—A device connected to a computer to allow users at different sites to see what the instructor writes or draws during demonstrations; stores demonstrations as computer files

email—(See electronic mail.)

emoticon—A series of characters used together to convey emotion; for example, a sideways smiley face :-) designates a happy mood

English as a Second Language (ESL)—Designates a student who is learning English after achieving proficiency in another, native language

English Language Development (ELD)—A (lower) level of English proficiency that qualifies students to be sent from their home class into another class where instruction is geared to their specific level of performance

EPS—Stands for "Encapsulated PostScript," an image format that allows transfer of artwork between any software packages that use PostScript printing files

Ethernet—Type of local-area network (LAN) in which several data transmissions among network users can be sent at any given time (in contrast with token-passing networks, which allow only one transmission at a time)

Events of Instruction, Gagné's—The nine kinds of activities identified by learning theorist Robert Gagné as being involved in teaching and learning

expert system—A form of artificial intelligence (AI) that attempts to computerize human expertise

export—To save all or part of a document in a format other than that in which the program created it (e.g., as a text file) so it can be used by another program

Extensible Mark-up Language—(See XML.)

external storage—Devices outside the computer's internal circuitry that store information and/or data (in contrast with internal memory)

Favorites file—In the *Internet Explorer* browser, a set of Internet locations or URLs organized so that a user can return to them quickly (See also Bookmarks file.)

field—The smallest unit of information in a database

files—The products created by a database program; any collection of data stored on a computer medium

file server—In a local-area network (LAN), the computer that houses the software and "serves" it to the attached workstations

File Transfer Protocol—(See FTP.)

filtering software—Program stored on individual computers or on the school or district network in order to prevent access to Internet sites with inappropriate materials

firewall software—A system set up to prevent someone from going to certain locations on the Internet; may be implemented by keyword or by site name

flame—An email or newsgroup message that usually is emotional and often derogatory in nature

flash drive—(See jump drive.)

flat file database—Database program that creates single files (in contrast with a relational database)

floppy disk—(See disk.)

flowchart—A planning method that combines rectangles, diamonds, and other figures joined by arrows to show the steps of a problem solution in graphic form; used by programmers to show a program's logic and operation before it is coded into a computer language

FM amplification system—Resource for students with hearing impairments in which the teacher wears a wireless microphone and students with auditory processing learning disabilities wear receivers that amplify the teacher's voice and serve to focus attention

font—A type style used in a document (e.g., Courier, Palatino, or Helvetica)

footer—A line or lines in a document that can be set to repeat automatically at the bottom of each page; usually indicates a title and/or pagination (See also header.)

format—To prepare a disk to receive files on a computer; to initialize a disk; to design the appearance of a document (e.g., the font, type styles, type size), or the appearance so designed

forms makers—Software tools that create documents and web pages with "fillable" forms

formula—In a spreadsheet, commands used to do calculations on data

FORTRAN (FORmula TRANslator)—One of the earliest high-level computer languages; designed for mathematical and science applications

frame—Sections programmed to display on a web page; the contents of each frame are actually different web pages displayed on one screen

FTP (File Transfer Protocol)—On the Internet, a way of transferring files from one computer to another using common settings and transmission procedures; also, to transfer files

full immersion systems—Type of virtual reality (VR) system in which a user places a headset (e.g., goggles or a helmet) over the eyes to provide a channel through which the wearer "sees" (i.e., is immersed in) a computer-generated environment

full justification (also simply **justification**)—In word processing or desktop publishing, a type of text alignment in which text is both flush right on the right margin and flush left on the left margin (in contrast with right or left justified or centered)

fuzzy logic—A logic system in artificial intelligence (AI) designed to parallel the decision-making processes of humans by accounting for subjectivity and uncertainty

G (gigabyte)—Roughly 1 billion bytes of computer storage

game—(See instructional game.)

geocaching—An online activity in which students look at a database of caches at the geocaching website (http://www.geocaching.com), decide on a cache to hunt for, and use GPSs to help them locate it

geographic information system (GIS)—A computer system that is able to store in a database a variety of information about geographic locations and display the data in map form

GIF—Stands for "Graphics Interchange Format," an image format used for drawn images, illustrations, clip art, or animations

GIGO (garbage in/garbage out)—Popular term meaning that if the data that go into a computer are faulty or are badly organized, the result will also be inaccurate

gopher—An Internet storage and search system developed at the University of Minnesota and named after the school's mascot; most gopher servers are being converted to websites, which can be more easily accessed with Internet search engines

GPS (global positioning system)—An instrument that uses a worldwide radio-navigation system made possible by a bank of 24 satellites and their ground stations to pinpoint the exact geographic location where the GPS signal originates, cross-references it with mapping software, and shows the location to a user

gradebook —(See electronic gradebook.)

gradekeeping software—(See electronic gradebook.)

grammar checker—The part of the word processing software designed to check text for compliance with grammar and usage rules

graphic document makers—Software tools that simplify the activity of making highly graphic materials such as awards certificates and greeting cards by offering sets of clip art and pre-designed templates to which people add their own content

graphics tablet—Type of input device on which pictures are hand-drawn and transferred to the computer as files

graphic user interface (GUI, often pronounced "gooey")—Software that displays options to the user in graphic formats consisting of menus and icons, rather than text formats (e.g., the Macintosh and Windows desktops)

graphing calculator—A calculator with advanced functions and an LED display; allows users to enter equations and shows graphs that result from those equations

hacker—Computer user who demonstrates an unusual, obsessive interest in using the computer; a computer user who engages in unauthorized use of a computer system (See also cracker.)

handheld computer—A small, portable computing device. (See also personal digital assistant (PDA))

handicap—A condition that arises when an individual is unable to fulfill a role due to an impairment or disability

haptic interface—One of the devices (e.g., a data glove) that allow users to experience a full immersion virtual reality system by providing tactile or touch input

hard copy—A paper printout of a computer file from a printer, plotter, or other output device

hard disk (hard disk drive)—In a computer system, a secondary storage device, usually housed inside the computer, but can be external; holds up to several gigabytes of information

hardware—The devices or equipment in a computer system (in contrast with software or computer programs)

header—A line in a document that can be set to repeat automatically at the top of each page; usually indicates a title and/or pagination (See also footer.)

head-mounted display—In a full immersion virtual reality (VR) system, a headset that provides the sensory channel through which the wearer "sees" a computer-generated environment

heart monitor—Device consisting of a transmitter, which senses the heartbeat from the heart's electrical impulses, and a wristwatch receiver, which receives and records each beat through radio transmission from the transmitter

high-level language—Computer programming language (e.g., FORTRAN, BASIC, COBOL) designed with syntax and vocabulary like a human language so that less technical people can use it to write programs

hits—Pages or items listed as results of an Internet or database search

hot spot—(See button.)

HTML—Hypertext Markup Language; the primary authoring language used to develop web pages

HyperCard—Early authoring software designed for Macintosh systems to create hypermedia products called stacks, which consist of a series of frames or cards

hypermedia—Software that connects elements of a computer system (e.g., text, movies, pictures, and other graphics) through hypertext links

HyperStudio—A hypermedia authoring software based on an earlier system called *HyperCard*

hypertext—Text elements such as keywords that can be cross-referenced with other occurrences of the same word or with related concepts

Hypertext Transfer Protocol (http)—The first part of an Internet address

icon—On a computer screen, a picture that acts as a symbol for an action or item

IEP—Individual educational plan; the educational program required by law to be designed for each student with a disability

IEP generator—Software that assists teachers in preparing individual educational plans (IEPs) required by law for students with special needs by providing on-screen prompts that remind teachers of the required components in the plan

ILS—(See integrated learning system.)

image editing programs—Software tools used to enhance and format photos that are then imported into desktop publishing systems or web page products

image formats—Ways of storing digitized images for use in web pages and multimedia products, e.g., GIF, JPEG

image processing—Process of using a software package such as Adobe *Photoshop* to make changes to a digital image

impairment—An abnormality or loss of function in a physical, anatomical, or psychological structure; may be congenital (present at birth) or acquired through accident or disease

import—To bring into a document or all or part of another document that has been stored in another format. (See also export.)

inclusion—Activity in which students with disabilities are included in the general education classroom

information literacy—A set of skills defined by Johnson and Eisenberg as the "Big Six"; includes abilities to look for, evaluate, and use information from various sources; considered to be a subset of technological literacy

information service—A set of communications (e.g., email) and storage/retrieval options made available by a company such as America Online

Information Superhighway—A popular term with various meanings associated with the worldwide linkage of information; sometimes synonymous with the Internet

initialize—(See format.)

ink-jet printer—Type of output device that produces hard copy by directing a controlled spray of ink onto a page to form characters

input device—Any device in a computer system (e.g., keyboard, mouse) designed to get instructions or data from the user to the processing part of the system

inquiry-based learning—(See constructivist learning.)

instant messaging (IM)—A communications service that allows users to create a private chat room which only members of a mutually agreed-upon list may enter; the system alerts a user when someone from the IM list is online; IM also designates the act of instant messaging, as in "to IM"

instructional design—The structure and teaching approach of a given educational experience or material; the process used to create the structure and approach

instructional game—Type of software function designed to increase motivation by adding game rules to a learning activity

instructional software—Applications software that is designed specifically to deliver or assist with student instruction on a topic. (See also courseware.)

instructional technology—The subset of educational technology that deals directly with teaching and learning applications (as opposed to educational administrative applications)

integrated circuit—(See chip.)

integrated learning system (ILS)—Networked or online system that provides both computer-based instruction and summary reports of student progress

integrated packages—Software products (e.g., *Microsoft Works* and *AppleWorks*) that have several applications in a single package (e.g., word processing, database, spreadsheet, and drawing functions)

intelligent CAI—Computer-assisted instruction with software logic based on artificial intelligence (AI) principles

intensifier—In an email message, words and punctuation marks used to help convey meaning, e.g., LOL stands for "laugh out loud"; asterisks around a word indicate italics used for emphasis

interactive or dynamic geometry software—Programs that provide students with environments in which to make discoveries and conjectures related to geometry concepts and objects

interactive storybook—Software designed to display a story in any sequence selected by the person reading it

interactive video—Videodiscs that allow the user to control the order in and speed at which items from the disc are displayed on a screen. (In Level I, control is through a bar code reader or remote control; in Level III, control is through a menu on a computer screen.)

interface—Cables, adaptors, or circuits that connect components of a computer system; the on-screen method a person employs to use a computer (See also graphic user interface.)

internal memory—Integrated circuits inside a computer system designed to hold information or programs; ROM and RAM (in contrast with external storage)

Internet—A worldwide network that connects many smaller networks with a common set of procedures (protocols) for sending and receiving information

Internet Explorer—A popular browser software used to access the Internet

interoperability—The capability of wireless devices to communicate with each other and with many kinds of peripheral devices

interpreter—A computer program that converts program code into machine language and executes one statement of a source program before converting and executing the next (in contrast with compiler)

intranet—An internal network or a subset of the Internet, usually available only to the members of the organization that set it up

I/O (input/output)—The process of getting instructions and/or data into and out of a computer system; devices that perform both functions (e.g., disk drives)

IP (Internet Protocol)—A standard, agreed-upon way of coding and sending data across the Internet

ISDN (Integrated Services Digital Network)—A digital telecommunications system in which all types of data (e.g., video, graphics, text) may be sent over the same lines at very high speeds

ISP (Internet service provider)—A company or other organization (e.g., a university) that provides access to the Internet

Java—Originally called OAK, a high-level programming language developed by Sun Microsystems. An object-oriented language similar to C++, it has become popular for its ability to do interactive graphic and animation activities on web pages.

Java applets—Pre-developed applications created with the Java programming language; make possible web page features such as animations and special effects, graphics and buttons, interactive displays, web data collection forms; and chatrooms

joystick—Input device, used primarily with games, that moves on-screen figures or a cursor

JPEG (also JPG)—Stands for "Joint Photographic Experts Group", an image format used for photographs

jump drive—A small computer storage medium in cartridge form, it inserts into a USB port in a computer, thus making it easy transfer files from one computer to another; also called flash drive

justification—Arrangement of text in a word-processed or desktop-published document (See also full justification.)

K (kilobyte)—A unit of computer memory or disk capacity that is roughly equivalent to 1,000 bytes

keyboard—Any of a variety of input devices that have keys imprinted with letters, numbers, and other symbols in order to allow a user to enter information

keyboarding—The act of using a computer keyboard to enter information into a computer system; sometimes used to mean efficient, ten-finger typing as opposed to hunt-and-peck typing

keypals—Electronic penpals; people who correspond via email

LAN—(See local-area network.)

laptop computer—Small, stand-alone, portable personal computer system

laserdisc—(See videodisc.)

laser printer—An output device that produces hard copy by using a controlled laser beam to put characters on a page

LCD (liquid crystal display or diode) panel—A device consisting of light-sensitive material encased between two clear pieces of glass or plastic, designed to be placed on an overhead projector; projects images from the computer screen to a large surface

learning communities—Groups of people who "meet," usually via email, web pages, or other electronic means, to support each other's learning

learning hierarchies—According to learning theorist Robert Gagné, a set of building block skills a student must learn in order to learn a higher-order skill

light pen—Input device that allows a user to select items from a screen by sensing light on various points in the display

Likert scale—An assessment instrument consisting of a series of statements with which students indicate their degree of agreement or disagreement

link—Also known as a hot link or hot spot. On the Internet, a piece of text or an image that has been programmed into a web page to send the browser to another Internet location; in a multimedia product, a piece of text or an image that has been programmed to send the user to another location in the product

listserv (list)—On the Internet, a program that stores and maintains mailing lists and allows a message to be sent simultaneously to everyone on the list

local-area network (LAN)—A series of computers connected through cabling or wireless methods to share programs through a central file server computer

logic bomb—A type of computer virus that is set to be released or put into action at a certain time or when a certain event occurs (See also Trojan horse and worm.)

Logo—A high-level programming language originally designed as an artificial intelligence (AI) language but later popularized by Seymour Papert as an environment to allow children to learn problem-solving behaviors and skills

Logowriter—A word processing program that incorporates the logic and drawing capabilities of the Logo language

long-term memory (LTM)—According to information-processing learning theorists, one of the three kinds of memory or "stores" the brain uses to process information, much like a computer; LTM can hold information indefinitely after it is linked to prior knowledge already in LTM

low-level language—Programming language such as assembler designed for use by technical personnel on a specific type of computer (See also high-level language.)

M (megabyte)—A unit of computer memory or disk capacity that is roughly equivalent to 1 million bytes

machine language—Lowest level of computer programming language consisting of commands written in 1s and 0s

mainframe—Type of computer system that has several peripheral devices connected to a CPU housed in a separate device; has more memory and capacity than a microcomputer

mainstreaming—An activity in which students with disabilities participate in selected classes in general education

mark sense scanner—Input device that reads data from specially coded sheets marked with pencil

mastery learning—According to learning theorists Benjamin Bloom and B. F. Skinner, an instructional approach in which students learn a sequence of objectives that define mastery of the subject; students pass tests on each objective to demonstrate they have mastered a skill before proceeding to the next one

MBL (microcomputer-based laboratory)—A type of instructional software tool consisting of hardware devices (probes) and software (probeware) to allow scientific data to be gathered and processed by a computer

MECC—(See Minnesota Education Computing Corporation.)

media literacy—(See technological literacy.)

memory—Circuitry inside a computer or media such as disks or CD-ROMs that allows programs or information to be stored for use by a computer

menu—List of on-screen options available on a specific topic or area of a program or GUI

metropolitan-area network (MAN)—A network whose components are distributed over an area larger that a LAN but smaller than a WAN

microcomputer—Small, stand-alone computer system designed for use by one person at a time

minicomputer—A type of computer system in the range between microcomputers and mainframes. (In practice, minicomputers and mainframes are becoming indistinguishable.)

Minnesota Education Computing Corporation (MECC)—Originally established as the Minnesota Education Computing Consortium, one of the first organizations to develop and distribute instructional software (courseware) for microcomputers

modem—A device that changes (MOdulates) digital computer signals into analog frequencies that can be sent over a telephone line to another computer and changes back (DEModulates) incoming signals into ones the computer can use

monitor—An output device that produces a visual display of what the computer produces. (See also CRT.)

MOO (MUD object oriented)—A specific type of multiuser dungeon (MUD) system developed by Stephen White; see also MUD

morphing—Short for *metamorphosing*, refers to an animation technique in which one image gradually turns into another; also known as tweening

Mosaic—One of the first browser programs designed to allow Internet resources to be displayed graphically rather than just in text

motherboard—The main circuit board inside a microcomputer that holds all of the integrated circuits, chips, and connection slots for attaching additional circuit boards required to control peripheral devices (e.g., monitor, keyboard, disk drive)

Motion Picture Experts Group (MPEG)—A file format for storing and sending video sequences on a network

mouse—Input device that a computer user moves around on the table beside the computer in order to control a pointer on a screen, and presses down (clicks) in order to select options from the screen

MS-DOS (Microsoft Disk Operating System)—A type of systems software used on IBM and IBM-compatible computers

MUD—Multiuser dungeon (or dimension or domain); a location on the Internet where several users at a time can interact with each other's avatars (graphic representations of each other); see also MOO

multimedia—A computer system or computer system product that incorporates text, sound, pictures/graphics, and/or video

multiple intelligences—According to learning theorist Howard Gardner, nine different and relatively independent types of intelligence that may be fostered by differentiated instruction and assessment

Musical Educators National Conference (MENC)—Professional organization for music educators

Musical Instrument Digital Interface (MIDI)—A standard adopted by the electronic music industry for controlling devices that play music

Musical Instrument Digital Interface (MIDI) device—Equipment that works with specially designed software to allow a computer to control music-producing devices (e.g., sequencers, synthesizers)

music editor—Software that provides on-screen blank musical bars on which the user enters the musical key, time, and individual notes that constitute a piece of sheet music

music literacy—The ability to read standard music notation

music sequencer—Can be either software that supports the on-screen creation of music scores with several parts or tracks, or a hardware component of a music synthesizer workstation

music synthesizer—Music-making equipment controlled by a Musical Instrument Digital Interface (MIDI) device

National Education Technology Standards (NETS)—Benchmark technology skills created by the International Society for Technology in Education (ISTE) for teachers (NETS-T), students (NETS-S), and educational administrators (NETS-A)

netiquette—Etiquette guidelines for posting messages to online services, especially in email

Netscape Communicator—A popular browser software used to access the Internet

neural network—A type of AI program designed to work like a human brain and nervous system

No Child Left Behind (NCLB) Act of 2001—Federal law that put in place accountability measures of all U.S. students, teachers, and schools; requires schools to demonstrate adequate yearly progress (AYP) toward target goals, as demonstrated by test scores, attendance, and other quality indicators

node—One station or site on a computer network

notation software—Software that facilitates music making in the visual domain by allowing flexibility in music score and page setup, part extraction, text formatting, and other print-related issues

nutritional analysis program—Software that analyzes calorie intake and monitors portions of required food groups

objectivists—People who believe that knowledge has a separate existence outside human perception and that it must be transmitted through directed instructional methods, based on behavioral, cognitive-behavioral, and information processing theories

online—Being connected to a computer system in operation

operant conditioning—According to learning theorist B. F. Skinner, a way of shaping human behavior in which the consequences of people's past actions can act as stimuli to shape future behaviors

operating system—A type of software that controls system operation and allows the computer to recognize and process instructions from applications software such as word processing programs

optical character recognition (OCR)—Software that allows text to be scanned and placed in a word processing file

optical disc—Storage medium designed to be read by laser beam (e.g., CD-ROM, videodisc)

optical scanner—Input device that converts text and graphics into computer files

Orff instruments—Musical instruments developed for children by K. Maendler under the direction of composer Carl Orff; modeled after a wooden African instrument, they were specially designed to provide a successful and fun first experience with making music

outlining tools—Software designed to prompt writers as they develop outlines to structure documents they plan to write

output device—Any device in a computer system (e.g., monitor, printer) that displays the products of the processing part of the system

pagination—Automatic page numbering done by a word processing or desktop publishing program

password—A word or number designed to limit access to a system to authorized users only

PDA—(See personal digital assistant.)

pedometer—Device that assists with analyzing and monitoring physical fitness levels by monitoring the number of steps one takes

peripherals—Any hardware devices outside the CPU

PERL—Practical Extraction and Report Language; one of the programming languages (e.g., Java, C, Visual Basic) used to write Common Gateway Interface (CGI) programs that create "dynamic documents," or documents that allow interaction with users

personal computer (PC)—(See microcomputer.)

personal digital assistant (PDA)—A handheld computer that can function as a cellular phone, fax machine, and personal organizer; uses a stylus, keyboard, or voice recognition device for input

phishing—Sending an e-mail that falsely claims to be from a legitimate organization such as a credit card company in order to trick someone into giving private information (e.g., social security or driver license numbers) that can be used for identity theft. Also known as "brand spoofing" or "carding," it is a play on the word "fishing" since it involves sending email as bait to see who will "bite."

photo CD—A compact disc format designed by the Eastman Kodak Company to store and display photographs

PICT—Stands for "picture"; an image format developed originally for use on Macintosh computers

piracy—(See software piracy.)

pitch—The number of characters printed per inch, usually 10-pitch or 12-pitch

pixel—The smallest unit of light that can be displayed on a computer screen

PLATO (Programmed Logic for Automatic Teaching Operations)—One of the earliest computer systems (mainframe-based) designed for instructional use; developed by the University of Illinois and Control Data Corporation

plotter—An output device designed to make a paper copy of a drawing or image from a computer screen

plug-in—A program that adds a specific feature or service to a computer system; many types of audio and video messages are played through plug-ins

point size—A unit designating the height of a typeface character; 72 points = 1 inch

portable document format (PDF)—Format that allows documents to be seen and sent with all the formatting and design elements (e.g., margins, graphics) of the original document without requiring the desktop publishing or word processing software used to create it

presentation software—Programs designed to allow people to display pictures and text to support their lectures or talks

primary storage—(See internal memory.)

primitive—A simple command in the Logo programming language that does one operation (e.g., FORWARD)

printer—Output device that produces a paper copy of text and graphics from a computer screen

print graphics—Software designed to produce graphics on paper (e.g., cards, banners)

probeware—(See MBL.)

problem-based learning (PBL)—According to Sage (2000), learning organized around the investigation and resolution of an authentic, ill-structured problem

problem-solving software—Instructional software function that either teaches specific steps for solving certain problems (e.g., math word problems) or helps the student learn general problem-solving behaviors for a class of problems

program—(See software.)

programmed learning—Techniques for training and instruction based on learning theorist B. F. Skinner's reinforcement principles

prompt—On a computer screen, an indicator that the system is ready to accept input; can be any symbol from a C:\. to a ?

proportional spacing—Displaying text so that each character takes up a different amount of space depending on its width

public domain software—Uncopyrighted programs available for copying and use by the public at no cost

push technologies—A system set up to send out information whether or not anyone requests it. Some push systems are set up specifically to locate and return information with certain characteristics whenever it appears on the Internet

puzzle generator—Software tool that automatically formats and creates crossword puzzles, word search puzzles, and similar game-like activities, based on content entered by a user

***QuickTime*® movies**—Video sequences that may be viewed on a computer screen by a program designed by Apple Computer Company (i.e., *QuickTime*)

***QuickTime* VR Authoring Studio®**—Software that creates a type of virtual reality (VR) environment by using a series of photographs taken at 360 degrees around a pivotal point and "stitching" them together into a seamless panorama view

QWERTY keyboard—Traditional typewriter-like keyboard, so named because of the first six letters in the first line of a typewriter keyboard

radio frequency identification (RFID)—An electronic monitoring system that tracks the location of a person or object with an embedded computer chip and can update information on the chip; RFID devices are being field-tested to track student attendance, increase school security, and monitor the location of library resources

RAM (random access memory)—Type of internal computer memory that is erased when the power is turned off

record—In a database file, several related fields (e.g., all the information on one person)

relational database—Database program that can link several different files through common keyword fields

relative advantage—Term coined by Everett Rogers to refer to the perception by potential adopters of an innovation of the degree to which the new method or resource has advantages over the old one; major factor in determining whether the innovation is adopted

repurposing—Use of a program to show videodisc images in a different sequence from the one stored on the disc and for a purpose that may be different from what the developer of the disc intended

retrofit—Rewiring a building such as a school to permit networked communications

ROM (read-only memory)—Type of internal computer memory designed to hold programs permanently, even when the power is turned off

rubric—An assessment instrument designed to measure complex behaviors such as writing; consists of a set of elements that define the behavior and ratings that describe levels of performance for each element

sans serif typeface—Typeface in which letters have no small curves (serifs or "hands and feet") at the ends of the lines that make them up; usually used for short titles rather than the main text of a document

scaffolding—Term associated with learning theorist Vygotsky's belief that teachers can provide good instruction by finding out where each child is in his or her development and building on the child's experiences

scientific inquiry—The processes of approaching problems scientifically

screen reader—Utility software that operates in the background of the computer operating system, reading aloud any text that appears on the screen (e.g., menus, text, web pages)

search and replace (also find and replace)—A function in a program such as a word processing package that looks for all instances of a sequence of characters and/or spaces and replaces them with another desired sequence

search engine—An Internet software (e.g., Google) that helps people locate Internet sites and information related to a given topic

secondary storage—(See external storage.)

semantic differential—Type of assessment instrument in which students respond to a topic or question by checking a line between each of several sets of bipolar adjectives to indicate their level of feeling about the topic

sensory disabilities—Impairments associated with the loss of hearing or vision

sensory registers—According to information-processing learning theorists, the parts of the brain that receive information a person senses through receptors (i.e., eyes, ears, nose, mouth, and/or

hands) and, after a second or so, is either lost or transferred to short-term memory (STM) or working memory

sequencer—A device that facilitates music making in the aural domain by allowing users to record, edit, and play back digital audio and MIDI data

serif typeface—Typeface in which letters have small curves (serifs or "hands and feet") at the ends of the lines that make them up; usually used for the main text of a document

shared intelligence—A way of looking at intellect as residing in several persons, rather than in single individuals

shareware—Uncopyrighted software that anyone may use, but each user is asked to pay a voluntary fee to the designer

short-term memory (STM)—According to information-processing learning theorists, one of the three kinds of memory or "stores" the brain uses to process information, much like a computer; STM can hold information for about 5-20 seconds, after which it is either transferred to long-term memory (LTM) or lost

simulation—Type of software that models a real or imaginary system in order to teach the principles on which the system is based

site map—An at-a-glance guide to the contents of a website

situated cognition—Instruction that is anchored in experiences that learners consider authentic because they provide opportunities to emulate the behavior of adults

snail mail—Regular postal service mail, as opposed to email

social action project—Web-based project in which students are responsible for learning about and addressing important global social, economic, political, or environmental conditions

social activism—Characteristic agenda of renowned educator John Dewey that shaped his views about teaching and learning; resulted in the belief that social consciousness was the ultimate aim of all education, and learning was useful only in the context of social experience

social studies—According to the National Council for the Social Studies (NCSS), the integrated study of the social sciences and humanities to promote civic competence

software—Programs written in a computer language (in contrast with hardware or equipment)

software piracy—Illegally copying and using a copyrighted software package without buying it

software suite—Software sold as one package but containing several different, unintegrated programs such as Microsoft *Office*. (See also integrated packages.)

spam—Any unsolicited email or other messages, usually sent in large numbers to all users of a system; spam is the electronic equivalent of junk mail

speech synthesizer—An output device that produces spoken words through a computer program

spell checker—Part of a software package such as word processing or desktop publishing that looks for misspelled words and offers correct spellings

spirometer—A device that assists with analyzing and monitoring physical fitness levels by measuring lung volume

spreadsheet—Software designed to store data (usually, but not always, numeric) by row–column positions known as cells; can also do calculations on the data

sprite—Object in some versions of the Logo programming language that the user can define by color, shape, and other characteristics and then use to do animations on the screen

stack—A sequence of frames or cards in a *HyperStudio* multimedia product

statistical software packages—Software tools that help with qualitative data collection and analysis of student performance on tests by performing the calculations involved in any of these kinds of procedures

storyboard—A frame that serves as part of a planning blueprint from which a multimedia product or web page can be designed

streaming video/audio—A way of transmitting video or audio on the Internet so that it can be seen or heard as the file downloads

structured query language (SQL)—A type of high-level language used to locate desired information from a relational database

student information systems (SIS)—Networked software systems that help educators keep track of student, class, and school data (e.g., attendance, test scores) in order to maintain records and support decision making

student response systems (SIS)—(A.k.a., personal response systems or classroom response systems) a combination of handheld hardware and software that permits each student in the classroom to answer a question simultaneously and lets the teacher see and display a summary of results immediately

supercomputer—The largest of the mainframe computer systems with the greatest storage space, speed, and power

switches—Equipment to compress data in order for information to be transmitted at higher speeds [e.g., Asynchronous Transfer Mode (ATM) switches]; also devices that allow an alternative to the typical keyboard and thus allow easier input to the computer by a person with a disability

synchronous—Form of distance communications in which messages are sent and received immediately; contrasts with asynchronous communications, in which information and messages are left for the receiver to read later

synthesizer—Any of a series of output devices designed to produce sound, music, or speech through a computer program

SYSOP—The SYStem OPerator in a network; a person responsible for maintaining the software and activities on the network and assisting its users

systems approaches—Methods originated by educational psychologists such as Robert Gagné and Leslie Briggs, who applied principles from military and industrial training to developing curriculum and instruction for schools; methods used to create a carefully designed system of instruction or instructional design

systems software—Programs designed to manage the basic operations of a computer system (e.g., recognizing input devices, storing applications program commands)

tablet computer—A portable computer with the appearance of a writing tablet; has an LCD screen that allows handwritten entries using a special-purpose pen or stylus, digitizes the entries, and converts them to standard text through handwriting recognition technology

talking word processor—A software package that reads typed words aloud

Teachers of English for Speakers of Other Languages (TESOL)—The national organization for foreign language teachers; has established national standards for English language learners

technological literacy—Technical skills required for using information technology in education and the workplace

technology education—A view of technology in education that originated with industry trainers and vocational educators in the 1980s and is currently represented by the International Technology Education Association (ITEA); holds that (1) school learning should prepare students for the world of work in which they will use technology, and (2) vocational training can help teach all content areas such as math, science, and language

telecommunications—Communications over a distance made possible by a computer and modem or a distance learning system such as broadcast TV

telecomputing—Term coined by Kearsley to refer specifically to communications involving computers and modems

teleconferencing—People at two or more sites holding a meeting through computers and telephone lines

test generator—Software designed to help teachers prepare and/or administer tests

test item bank—Pre-made pools of questions that can be used by test generator software to create various versions of the same test

text messaging—Sending short text messages between devices such as cellular phones, handheld PDAs, or pagers

thesaurus—In word processing and desktop publishing, an optional feature that offers synonyms or antonyms for given words

TICCIT (Time-shared, Interactive, Computer-Controlled Information Television)—An early instructional computing system developed by Brigham Young University and the Mitre Corporation that combined television with computers

TIF—Stands for "Tagged Image File," an image format designed to allow exchange of image files among various software applications and computers

touch screen—Type of input device designed to allow users to make selections by touching the monitor

Trojan horse—Type of virus that gets into a computer by attaching to a legitimate program (See also logic bomb and worm.)

turtle—In the Logo programming language, the triangle-shaped object that can be programmed to move and/or draw on the screen

tutorial—Type of instructional software that offers a complete sequence of instruction on a given topic, including explanation, examples, embedded practice and feedback, and, usually, also assessment

tweening—(See morphing.)

universal design—Adjustments made to physical environments as a result of understanding the special needs of individuals with disabilities, e.g., curb cuts in sidewalks to allow wheelchair access

URL (Uniform Resource Locator)—A series of letters and/or symbols that acts as an address for a site on the Internet

USB—Stands for Universal Serial Bus; a location or port, usually in the back of a computer, to which devices such as cables and jump drives may be attached

variable—In programming languages, a name that stands for a place in computer memory that can hold one value

Veronica—On the Internet, a program that searches for files across gopher servers

videoconferencing—An online "meeting" between two or more participants at different sites using: a computer or network with appropriate software; video cameras, microphone, and speakers; and telephone lines or other cabling to transmit audio and video signals

videodisc (also laserdisc)—Now archaic, storage medium designed for storing pictures, video sequences, and movies

video editing software—Package such as *iMovie* that allows a user to make additions and changes to a selection of digital video

virtual field trip—(See electronic field trip.)

virtual manipulative—Software that students use to do simulated activities they used to do with real objects but which offers more flexibility than actual objects in the ways it can be used to illustrate concepts; often used in learning mathematics

virtual office—A space set up on a website to exchange documents and messages with colleagues working on the same activity

virtual reality (VR)—A computer-generated environment designed to provide a lifelike simulation of actual settings; often uses a data glove and/or headgear that covers the eyes in order to immerse the user in the simulated environment

virtual reality modeling language (VRML)—A programming language that allows the creation and display of 3-dimensional objects on a computer screen and allows users to have the illusion of moving around the objects

virtual system—An instructional environment in which the students learns through immersion in simulated or distance education experiences that take the place of face-to-face ones

virus—A program written with the purpose of doing harm or mischief to programs, data, and/or hardware components of a computer system. (See logic bomb, Trojan Horse, worm.)

virus protection software—Software put into place to protect computers from hackers and virus attacks. (See hacker, virus.)

visual literacy—A set of skills defined by Christopherson to include interpreting, understanding, and appreciating the meaning of visual messages; using visual messages to communicate; and using visual thinking to conceptualize solutions to problems; considered to be a subset of technological literacy

voice recognition—The capability provided by a computer and program to respond predictably to speech commands

VRML (Virtual Reality Modeling Language)—An authoring specification for displaying three-dimensional objects on the Internet

warm boot—(See boot/boot up.)

wearable systems—Computer components worn on one's body or clothing; usually accessed through voice recognition or other alternative input device

webbing software—(See concept mapping software.)

web browser—(See browser.)

webquest—A curriculum project in which students explore websites to find and analyze information on a topic

website—A location on the World Wide Web identified with a Uniform Resource Locator (URL); websites are physically located on a server connected to the Internet

whiteboard—(See electronic whiteboard.)

wide-area network (WAN)—An interconnected group of computers linked by modems and other technologies

window—A box in a graphic user interface that appears when one opens a disk or folder to display its contents

wireless connectivity—A computer network that reduces the number of required cables and allows greater freedom of movement by computer users; has one drop or cabled access point to the network through which many computer devices can access the network

word atlas—Electronic dictionaries and thesauruses that give pronunciations, definitions, and example uses for each word entry, and offer search and multimedia features similar to those of encyclopedias and atlases

word processing—An applications software activity that uses the computer for typing and preparing documents

word wraparound—In word processing, the feature in which text automatically goes to the next line on a page without the user pressing Return or Enter

worksheet—Another name besides "spreadsheet" for the product of a spreadsheet program

worksheet generator—Software tool that helps teachers produce exercises for practice (rather than for assessment) by prompting them to enter questions of various kinds

World Wide Web (WWW)—On the Internet, a system that connects sites through hypertext links; now often used as synonymous with "Internet"

worm—A type of virus that eats its way through (destroys) data and programs on a computer system. (See also logic bomb and Trojan horse.)

XML—Acronym for Extensible Mark-up Language, a language that describes the geometry and behavior of a virtual world or scene

zone of proximal development (ZPD)—Term coined by learning theorist Vygotsky to refer to the difference between two levels of cognitive functioning: adult or expert and child or novice

REFERENCES

Adams, C. (1998). Teaching and learning with SimCity 2000. *Journal of Geography, 97*(2), 47–55.

Adler, S. (2000). The ABCs of PDFs. *Technology & Learning, 21*(3), 41–46.

Albrecht, B., & Firedrake, G. (1997). New adventures in hands-on and far-out physics. *Learning and Leading with Technology, 25*(2), 34–37.

Alessi, S., & Trollip, S. (2001). *Multimedia for learning: Methods and development.* Needham Heights, MA: Allyn & Bacon.

Allen, D. (1993). Exploring the earth through software. Teaching with technology. *Teaching PreK-8, 24*(2), 22–26.

Alley, L., & Jansek, K. (2001). The ten keys to quality assurance and assessment in online learning. *Journal of Interactive Instructional Development, 13*(3), 3–18.

Alliance for Childhood. (1999). *Fool's gold: A critical look at computers and childhood.* Retrieved from http//www.allianceforchildhood.net/projects/computers/computers_reports.htm

American Alliance for Health, Physical Education, Recreation, and Dance. (1995). *National health education standards: Achieving health literacy.* Reston, VA: Author.

American Association for the Advancement of Science. (1989). *Science for all Americans.* Cary, NC: Oxford University Press.

American Association for the Advancement of Science. (1993). *Benchmarks for scientific literacy.* Cary, NC: Oxford University Press.

American Association of University Women. (2000). *Tech-savvy: Educating girls in the new computer age.* Washington, DC: Author. Retrieved from http://www.aauw.org/research/girls_education/techsavvy.cfm

Andaloro, G. (1991). Modeling in physics teaching: The role of computer simulation. *International Journal of Science Education, 13*(3), 243–254.

Anderson-Inman, L., & Zeitz, L. (1993). Computer-based concept mapping: Active studying for active learners. *The Computing Teacher, 21*(1), 6–8, 10–11.

Armstrong, S. (1999). *A framework for evaluating integrated learning systems/multimedia instructional systems.* Modesto, CA: California Instructional Technology Clearinghouse.

Arnett, P. (2000). Mastering reading and writing with technology. *Media & Methods, 37*(1), 12–14.

Assistive technologies. (2003). *eSchool News online, 5*(5). Retrieved from http://www.eschoolnews.org/news/showstory.cfm?ArticleID=3693

Atkinson, R., & Shiffrin, R. (1968). Human memory: A proposed system and its control processes. In K. Spence & J. Spence (Eds.), *The psychology of learning and motivation* (Vol. 2). New York: Academic Press.

Audet, R., & Ludwig, G. (2000). *GIS in schools.* Redlands, CA: Environmental Systems Research Institute.

Augmented reality soon could enhance learning. (2002). *eSchool News online, 6*(3). Retrieved from http://www.eschoolnews.org/news/showstory.cfm?ArticleID=4294

Ausubel, D. (1968). *Educational psychology: A cognitive view.* New York: Holt, Rinehart & Winston.

Baek, Y., & Layne, B. (1988). Color, graphics, and animation in a computer-assisted learning tutorial lesson. *Journal of Computer-Based Instruction, 15*(4), 31–35.

Bagui, S. (1998). Reasons for increased learning using multimedia. *Journal of Educational Multimedia and Hypermedia, 7*(1), 3–18.

Bailey, G., & Lumley, D. (1991). Supervising teachers who use integrated learning systems. *Educational Technology, 31*(7), 21–24.

Baines, L., & Stanley, G. (2000). We want to see the teacher. *Phi Delta Kappan, 82*(4), 327–330.

Bakas, C., & Mikropoulos, T. (2003). Design of virtual environments for the comprehension of planetary phenomena based on students' ideas. *International Journal of Science Education, 25*(8), 949–967.

Bangert-Drowns, R. (1993). The word processor as an instructional tool: A meta-analysis of word processing in writing instruction. *Review of Educational Research, 63*(1), 69–93.

Barab, S., Hay, K., & Barnett, M. (2000). Virtual solar system project: Building understanding through model building. *Journal of Research in Science Teaching, 37*(7), 719–756.

Barrett, H. C. (2000). Create your own electronic portfolio. *Learning and Leading with Technology, 27*(7), 14–21.

Bauer, J. F., & Anderson, R. S. (2001). A constructive stretch: Preservice teachers meet preteens in a technology-based literacy project. *Reading Online, 5*(5).

Baumbach, D., Christopher, T., Fasimpaur, K., & Oliver, K. (2004). Personal literacy assistants: Using handhelds for literacy instruction. *Learning and Leading with Technology, 32*(2), 16–21.

Beal, C., & Mason, C. (1999, January). Virtual fieldtripping: No permission notes needed. Creating a middle school classroom without walls. *Meridian Middle School Technologies Journal.* Retrieved November 1, 2004, from: http://www.ncsu.edu/meridian/jan99/vfieldtrip/

Bearden, D., & Martin, K. (1998). My make believe castle: An epic adventure in problem solving. *Learning and Leading with Technology, 25*(5), 21–25.

Beaton, A. E., et al. (1997–1998). Mathematics achievement in the middle school years, Mathematics achievement in the primary years, Mathematics achievement in the final year of secondary school. *IEA's Third International Mathematics and Science Study.* Chestnut Hill, MA: Boston College.

Becker, H. (1986a). *Instructional uses of school computers. Reports from the 1985 National Survey.* Issue No. 1. (ERIC Document Reproduction Service No. ED274319)

Becker, H. (1986b). *Instructional uses of school computers. Reports from the 1985 National Survey.* Issue No. 3. (ERIC Document Reproduction Service No. ED279303)

Becker, H. (1992). Computer-based integrated learning systems in the elementary and middle grades: A critical review and synthesis of evaluation reports. *Journal of Educational Computing Research, 8*(1), 1–41.

Becker, H. (1994). Mindless or mindful use of integrated learning systems. *International Journal of Educational Research, 21*(1), 65–79.

Becker, M., & Schuetz, J. (2003). An introduction to ground-water modeling using Virtual Reality Modeling Language (VRML). *Journal of Geoscience Education, 51*(5), 506–511.

Behrmann, M., & Jerome, M. (2002). Assistive technology for students with mild disabilities. *ERIC Digest.* (ERIC Document Reproduction Service No. ED463595)

Bender, P. (1991). The effectiveness of integrated computer learning systems in the elementary school. *Contemporary Education, 63*(1), 19–23.

Bennett, N., & Diener, K. (1997). Habits of mind: Using multimedia to enhance learning skills. *Learning and Leading with Technology, 24*(6), 18–21.

Benson, D. (1997). Technology training: Meeting teacher's changing needs. *Principal, 76*(3), 17–19.

Benton Foundation Communications Policy Program. (2002). *Great expectations: Leveraging America's investment in educational technology.* Washington, DC: Benton Foundation. Retrieved from http://www.benton.org/publibrary/e-rate/greatexpectations.pdf

Berkson, R., & Britsch, S. (1997). "I am that kid tha [sic] acts weird": Developing e-mail education in a third grade classroom. *Teaching Education, 8,* 97–104.

Bernard, R., Abrami, P., Lou, Y., Borokhovski, E. Wade, A., et al. (2004). How does distance education compare with classroom instruction? A meta-analysis of the empirical literature. *Review of Educational Research, 74*(3), 379–439.

Bernard, R., & Amundsen, C. (1989). Antecedents to dropout in distance education: Does one model fit all? *The Journal of Distance Education, 4*(2), 25–46.

Berson, I. R., & Berson, M. J. (2003). Digital literacy for cybersafety, digital awareness, and media literacy. *Social Education, 67*(3), 164–168.

Berson, M. (1996). Effectiveness of computer technology in the social studies. *Journal of Research on Computing in Education, 28*(4), 486–499.

Berson, M. J. (2004). Digital images: Capturing America's past with the technology of today. *Social Education, 68*(3), 214–219.

Berson, M. J., & Balyta, P. (2004). Technological thinking and practice in the social studies: Transcending the tumultuous adolescence of reform. *Journal of Computing and Teacher Education, 20*(4), 141–152.

Bertelsen, C. D., Kauffman, S., Howard, K., & Cochran, L. L. (2003, July/August). Web watch: Phonics websites. *Reading Online, 7*(1).

Biner, P. (1993). The development of an instrument to measure student attitudes toward televised courses. *The American Journal of Distance Education, 7*(1), 62–73.

Bitter, G., Camuse, R., & Durbin, V. (1993). *Using a microcomputer in the classroom* (3rd ed.). Boston: Allyn & Bacon.

Black, T. R. (1999). Simulations on spreadsheets for complex concepts: Teaching statistical power as an example. *Journal of Mathematics, Education, and Science Technology, 30*(4), 473–481.

Blackhurst, A. E. (1997). Perspectives on technology in special education. *Teaching Exceptional Children, 29*(5), 41–48.

Blackhurst, A. E., & Edyburn, D. L. (2000). A brief history of special education technology. *Special Education Technology Practice, 2*(1), 21–36.

Bloom, B. (1986). Automaticity. *Educational Leadership, 43*(5), 70–77.

Blosser, P. (1988). *Teaching problem solving—Secondary school science.* (ERIC Document Reproduction No. ED309049)

Bolliger, D., & Martindale, T. (2004). Key factors for determining student satisfaction in online courses. *International Journal on E-Learning, 3*(1), 61–67.

Borba, M. (1989). *Self-esteem builders resources.* Torrance, CA: Jalmar Press.

Borenstein, M. (1997). Mathematics in the real world. *Learning and Leading with Technology, 24*(7), 30–39.

Boulware, B., & Tao, L. (2002). E-mail: Instructional potentials and learning opportunities. *Reading and Writing Quarterly, 18*(3), 285–288.

Boxie, P., & Maring, G. H. (2001). Cybermentoring: The relationship between preservice teachers' use of online literacy strategies and student achievement. *Reading Online, 4*(10). Available at: http://www.readingonline.org

Boyd, J. (n.d.). *Myths, misconceptions, problems and issues in arts education.* Retrieved November 18, 2004, from http://www.qsa.qld.edu.au/

Boyle, T. (1997). *Design for multimedia learning.* London: Prentice Hall.

Bozeman, W. (1992). Spreadsheets. In G. Bitter (Ed.), *Macmillan encyclopedia of computers.* New York: Macmillan.

Bracy, G. (1992). The bright future of integrated learning systems. *Educational Technology, 32*(9), 60–62.

Branigan, C. (2000, December 4). Pennsylvania tests essay-grading computer program for its statewide exam. *eSchool News online, 3*(12). Retrieved from http://www.eschoolnews.com/news/showstory.cfm?ArticleID=1994

Brangian, C. (2002a). Study touts classroom benefits of handheld computers. *eSchool News online, 5*(5). Retrieved from http://www.eschoolnews.org/news/showstory.cfm?ArticleID=3693

Branigan, C. (2002b). Virtual reality gives these students a boost. *eSchool News online, 5*(9). Retrieved from http://www.eschoolnews.org/news/showstory.cfm?ArticleID=3961

Brangwin, N. (2002, Spring). Your personal cyberlibrarian. *Edutopia* (http://www.glef.org).

Browder, D. M., & Grasso, E. (1999). Teaching money skills to individuals with mental retardation: A research review with practical applications. *Remedial and Special Education, 20*, 297–308.

Brown, J. S., Collins, A., & Duguid, P. (1989). Situated cognition and the culture of learning. *Educational Researcher, 18*(1), 32–41.

Bruce, B. (2000). Dewey and technology. *The Journal of Adolescent and Adult Literacy, 42*(3), 222–226.

Bruner, J. (1973). *The relevance of education.* New York: W. W. Norton & Company.

Bruning, R., & Horn, C. (2000). Developing motivation to write. *Educational Psychologist, 35*(1), 25–37.

Brunner, C. (1996). Judging student multimedia. *Electronic Learning, 15*(6), 14–15.

Brush, T. (1998). Embedding cooperative learning into the design of integrated learning systems: Rationale and guidelines. *Educational Technology Research and Development, 46*(3), 5–18.

Brush, T., Armstrong, J., & Barbrow, D. (1999). Design and delivery of integrated learning systems: Their impact on student achievement and attitudes. *Journal of Educational Computing Research, 21*(4), 475–486.

Bryan, S. (2000, May 1). *SWAT savvy: A model for effect classroom technology using student experts.* Retrieved June 26, 2003, from http://www.techlearning.com/db_area/archives/WCF/archives/bryan.htm

Bull, G., Bull, G., & Bull, S. (2000). Java applets. *Learning and Leading with Technology, 27*(8), 42–54.

Bull, G., Bull, G., & Lewis, D. (1998). Introducing dynamic HTML. *Learning and Leading with Technology, 26*(2), 43–45.

Burrill, G. (1997). The NCTM standards: Eight years later. *School Science and Mathematics, 97*(6), 335–339.

Bush, V. (1986). As we may think. In S. Lambert & S. Ropiequet (Eds.), *CD-ROM: The new papyrus.* Redmond, WA: Microsoft Press. [Reprinted from *The Atlantic Monthly,* 1945, *176*(1), 101–108.]

CAI in music. (1994). *Teaching Music, 1*(6), 34–35.

Caine, R. N., & Caine, G. (1995). Reinventing schools through brain-based learning. *Educational Leadership, 52*(7), 43–47.

Caniglia, J. (1997). The heat is on: Using the calculator-based laboratory to integrate math, science, and technology. *Learning and Leading with Technology, 25*(1), 22–27.

Cann, A., & Seale, J. (1999). Using computer tutorials to encourage reflection. *Journal of Biological Education, 33*(3), 130–132.

Cannon, L. (2001). *National library of virtual manipulatives for interactive mathematics.* Retrieved January 5, 2001, from http://matti.usu.edu/nlvm/index.html

Carnine, D. (1993). Effective teaching for higher cognitive functioning. *Educational Technology, 33*(10), 29–33.

Carnine, D., Silbert, J., & Kameenui, E. (1997). *Direct instruction reading* (3rd ed.). Upper Saddle River, NJ: Merrill/Prentice Hall.

Carpenter, C. (1996). Online ethics: What's a teacher to do? *Learning and Leading with Technology, 23*(6), 40–41, 60.

Catchings, M., & MacGregor, K. (1998). Stoking creative fires: Young authors use software for writing and illustrating. *Learning and Leading with Technology, 25*(6), 20–23.

Cavallo, J. (2002, Fall). The virtual art museum. *Edutopia* (http://www.glef.org).

Cavanagh, S. (2204, November 10). NCLB could alter science teaching. *EdWeek, 24*(11), 1, 12–13. Retrieved November 15, 2004, from http://www.edweek.org

Center for Educational Policy Research. (2003). *Understanding university success: A report from the Standards for Success Project.* Eugene, OR: University of Oregon. Available from http://www.s4s.org/understanding.php

Chen, M. (2001, Winter). Project-based learning transforms curriculum and assessment. *Edutopia* (http://www.glef.org).

Cheng, H., Lehman, J., & Armstrong, P. (1991). Comparison of performance and attitude in traditional and computer conferencing classes. *The American Journal of Distance Education, 5*(3), 51–64.

Chrisman, G. (1992). Seven steps to ILS procurement. *Media and Methods, 28*(4), 14–15.

Christopherson, J. (1997). The growing need for visual literacy at the university. *Proceedings of the International Visual Literacy Association 1996 Annual Meeting,* Cheyenne, WY. (ERIC Document Reproduction No. ED408963)

Clark, J. (1996). Bells and whistles … but where are the references: Setting standards for hypermedia projects. *Learning and Leading with Technology, 23*(5), 22–24.

Clark, R. (1983). Reconsidering research on learning from media. *Review of Educational Research, 53*(4), 445–459.

Clark, R. (1985). Evidence for confounding in computer-based instruction studies: Analyzing the meta-analyses. *Educational Communications and Technology Journal, 33*(4), 249–262.

Clark, R. (1991). When researchers swim upstream: Reflections on an unpopular argument about learning from media. *Educational Technology, 31*(2), 34–40.

Clark, R. E. (1994). Media will never influence learning. *Educational Technology Research and Development, 42*(2), 21–29.

Clark, T. (2001, October). *Virtual schools: Trends and issues.* Report commissioned by the Distance Learning Resource Network, a WestEd Project. Cosponsored by the Centre for the Application of Information Technologies at Western Illinois University. Available from http://www.dlrn.org/trends.html

Clements, D. H. (1998). *From exercises and tasks to problems and projects: Unique contributions of computers to innovative mathematics education.* Retrieved January 3, 2001, from http://forum.swarthmore.edu/technology/papers/papers/clements/clements.html

Clinton, J. (1991). Decisions, decisions. *The Florida Technology in Education Quarterly, 3*(2), 93–96.

Cognition and Technology Group at Vanderbilt. (1990). Anchored instruction and its relationship to situated cognition. *Educational Researcher, 19*(6), 2–10.

Cognition and Technology Group at Vanderbilt. (1991, May). Integrated media: Toward a theoretical framework for utilizing their potential. *Proceedings of the Multimedia Technology Seminar,* Washington, DC.

Cohen, M., & Riel, M. (1989). The effect of distant audiences on children's writing: *American Educational Research Journal, 26*(2), 143–159.

Coiro, J. (2003). Reading comprehension on the Internet: Expanding our understanding of reading comprehension to encompass new literacies. *The Reading Teacher, 56*(5), 458–464.

Cole, J. (2004, April 2). Now is the time to start studying the Internet Age. *The Chronicle of Higher Education, 50*(30), B18.

Collis, B. (1990). *The best of research windows: Trends and issues in educational computing.* Eugene, OR: International Society for Technology in Education. (ERIC Document Reproduction No. ED323993)

Comer, R., & Geissler, C. (1998). *A methodology for software evaluation.* Paper presented at the 1998 meeting of the Society for Information Technology and Teacher Education, Washington, DC, March 10–14. (ERIC Document Reproduction No. ED421140)

Comer, S. (1999). Immersive imaging technology: VR for the web in academia. *Syllabus, 13*(1), 22–26.

Cook, A. M., & Hussey, S. M. (1995). *Assistive technologies: Principles and practice.* St. Louis, MO: Mosby.

Cordes, C., & Miller, E. (2000). *Fool's gold: A critical look and computers and childhood.* College Park, MD: Alliance for Childhood.

Corporation for Public Broadcasting. (2003). *Connected to the future: A report on children's Internet use from Corporation for Public Broadcasting.* Retrieved September 26, 2004, from http://cpb.org/ed/resources/connected

Coulter, B., Feldman, A., & Konold, C. (2000). Rethinking online adventures. *Learning and Leading with Technology, 28*(1), 42–47.

Coussement, S. (1995). *Educational telecommunication: Does it work? An attitude study.* (ERIC Document Reproduction No. ED391465)

Cradler, J. (2003). Technology's impact on teaching and learning. *Learning and Leading with Technology, 30*(7), 54–57.

Crews, K. (2003). Copyright and distance education: Making sense of the Teach Act. *Change, 35*(6), 34–39.

Cuban, L. (1986). *Teachers and machines: The classroom use of technology since the 1920s.* New York: Teachers College Press.

Cuban, L. (2001). *Oversold and underused.* Boston: Harvard University Press.

Cuban, L., Kirkpatrick, H., & Peck, C. (2001). High access and low use of technologies in high school classrooms: Explaining an apparent paradox. *American Educational Research Journal, 38*(4), 813–834.

Cummins, J. (1986). Empowering minority students: A framework for interaction. *Harvard Review, 50,* 18–36.

Curtis, M., Williams, B., Norris, C., O'Leary, D., & Soloway, E. (2003). *Palm handheld computers: A complete resource guide for teachers.* Eugene, OR: International Society for Technology in Education.

Cyrs, T. E. (1997). Competence in teaching at a distance. In T. E. Cyrs (Ed.), *Teaching and learning at a distance: What it takes to effectively design, deliver, and evaluate programs.* San Francisco: Jossey-Bass.

Dabbagh, N. (2001). Concept mapping as a mind tool for critical thinking. *Journal of Computing in Teacher Education, 17*(2), 16–23.

Darden, G., & Shimon, J. (2000). Revisit an "old" technology: Videotape feedback for motor skill learning and performance. *Strategies, 13*(4), 17–21.

Davydov, V. (1995). The influence of L. S. Vygotsky on education theory, research, and practice. *Educational Researcher, 24*(3), 12–21.

DeTure, M. (2004). Cognitive style and self-efficacy: Predicting student success in online distance education. *American Journal of Distance Education, 18*(1), 21–38.

Dille, B., & Mezack, M. (1991). Identifying predictors of high risk among community college telecourse students. *The American Journal of Distance Education, 5*(1), 24–35.

Dillon, A., & Gabbard, R. (1998). Hypermedia as an educational technology: A review of the quantitative research literature on learner comprehension, control, and style. *Review of Educational Research, 68*(3), 322–349.

Dillon, R. (1998). In the key of "see and hear": How students can learn to play the recorder by playing musical computers. *Learning and Leading with Technology, 26*(2), 15–17.

Dipinto, V., & Turner, S. (1995). Zapping the hypermedia zoo: Assessing the students' hypermedia projects. *The Computing Teacher, 22*(7), 8–11.

Dixon, J. K., & Falba, C. J. (1997). Graphing in the information age: Using data from the World Wide Web. *Mathematics Teaching in the Middle School, 2*(5), 298–304.

Doering, N. (2000). Measuring student understanding with a videotape performance assessment. *Journal of Physical Education, Recreation, and Dance, 71*(7), 47–52.

Dolan, B. (2000). Universal design for learning. *Journal of Special Education Technology, 15*(4), 44–51.

Dorsey, M., et al. (2001). An introduction to symmetry. Retrieved January 4, 2001, from http://www.geom.umn.edu/~demo5337/s97a/

Doty, D., Popplewell, S., & Byers, G. (2001). Interactive CD-ROM storybooks and young readers' reading comprehension. *Journal of Research on Computing in Education, 33*(4), 374–384.

Drier, H. (2001). *Collecting and numerically analyzing M&M's data.* Retrieved January 4, 2001, from http://curry.edschool.virginia.edu/teacherlink/math/activities/excel/M&Mnumerical/home.html

Dunham, P. H., & Dick, T. P. (1994). Research on graphing calculators. *Mathematics Teacher, 87,* 440–445.

Durden, W. (2001, October 19). Liberal arts for all, not just the rich. *Chronicle of Higher Education.* Available from http://chronicle.com

Dyrli, O. (1994). Riding the Internet schoolbus: Places to go and things to do. *Technology and Learning, 15*(2), 32–40.

Easterbrooks, S. (1999). Improving practices for students with hearing impairments. *Exceptional Children, 65,* 537–554.

Editors. (2003). Early reading software. *Technology & Learning, 23*(11), 32, 34, 36.

Educational Technology Magazine. (1991a, May). *31*(5). Special issue on constructivist versus directed approaches.

Educational Technology Magazine. (1991b, September). *31*(9). Special issue on constructivist versus directed approaches.

Edyburn, D. L. (2000). Assistive technology and students with mild disabilities. *Focus on Exceptional Children, 32*(9), 1–24.

Edyburn, D. L. (2001). Technology integration strategies: Universal design and technology integration, finding the connections. *Closing the Gap, 20*(1), 21–22.

Edyburn, D. L. (2003). Measuring assistive technology outcomes: Key concepts. *Journal of Special Education Technology, 18*(1), 53–55.

Eggen, P., & Kauchak, D. (2004). *Educational psychology: Windows on classrooms* (5th ed.). Upper Saddle River, NJ: Merrill/Prentice Hall.

Ehman, L., Glenn, A., Johnson, V., & White, C. (1992). Using computer databases in student problem solving: A study of eight social studies teachers' classrooms. *Theory and Research in Social Education, 20*(2), 179–206.

Eiser, L. (1988). What makes a good tutorial? *Classroom Computer Learning, 8*(4), 44–47.

EMC Corporation. (2003). *Fueling the pipeline: Attracting and educating math and science students.* Hopkinton, MA: Author. Retrieved November 15, 2004, from http://www.emc.com/about/emc_philanthropy/mmi/

Ervin, A. (2002). Meatloaf around the world. *Learning and Leading with Technology, 29*(5), 18–21, 62.

Estep, S., McInerney, W., & Vockell, E. (1999–2000). An investigation of the relationship between integrated learning systems and academic achievement. *Journal of Educational Technology Systems, 28*(1), 5–19.

Estes, C. (1994). The real-world connection. *Simulation and Gaming, 25*(4), 456–463.

Evans, R. (2004). *The social studies wars: What should we teach the children?* New York: The Teachers College Press.

Fabos, B., & Young, M. (1999). Telecommunication in the classroom: Rhetoric versus reality. *Review of Educational Research, 69*(3), 217–259.

Ferris, T. (1988). *Coming of age in the Milky Way.* New York: Doubleday.

Feurer, M., Towne, L., & Shavelson, R. (2002). Scientific culture and educational research. *Educational Researcher, 31*(8), 4–14.

Finzer, W., & Jackiw, N. (1998). Dynamic manipulation of mathematical objects. Retrieved January 5, 2001, from http://forum.swarthmore.edu/technology/papers/papers/s2k/

Fisher, S. K., & Gardner, J. E. (1999). Introduction to technology in transition. *Career Development for Exceptional Individuals, 22,* 131–151.

Flannery, M. (2004, February 22). FCAT puts less stress on study of history. *The Miami Herald.* Retrieved from http://www.miami.com.

Flores, A. (1998). *Electronic technology and NCTM standards.* Retrieved January 30, 2001, from http://forum.swarthmore.edu/technology/papers/papers/flores.html

Flowers, R. (1993). New teaching tools for new teaching practices. *Instructor, 102*(5), 42–45.

Forbes, L. S. (2004, October). Using Web-based bookmarks in K–8 settings: Linking the Internet to instruction. *The Reading Teacher, 58*(2), 148–153.

Forest, J. (1993). Music and the arts: Keys to a next-century school. *The Computing Teacher, 21*(3), 24–26.

Franklin, S. (1991). Breathing life into reluctant writers: The Seattle Public Schools laptop project. *Writing Notebook, 84*(4), 40–42.

Frederickson, S. (1997). Interactive multimedia storybooks. *Learning and Leading with Technology, 25*(1), 6–10.

Fulford, C., & Zhang, S. (1993). Perceptions of interaction: The critical predictor in distance education. *The American Journal of Distance Education, 7*(3), 8–21.

Funkhouser, C., & Dennis, J. (1992). The effects of problem-solving software on problem-solving ability. *Journal of Research on Computing in Education, 24*(3), 338–347.

Furger, R. (2002, Fall). A sampler of designs for teaching and learning. *Edutopia* (http://www.glef.org).

Furger, R. (2003, Fall). The write stuff. *Edutopia* (http://www.glef.org).

Furst-Bowie, J. (1997). Comparison of student reactions in traditional and videoconferencing courses in training and development. *International Journal of Instructional Media, 24*(3), 197–205.

Gagné, R. (1982). Developments in learning psychology: Implications for instructional design. *Educational Technology, 22*(6), 11–15.

Gagné, R. (1985). *The conditions of learning.* New York: Holt, Rinehart & Winston.

Gagné, R., Wager, W., & Rojas, A. (1981). Planning and authoring computer-assisted instruction lessons. *Educational Technology, 21*(9), 17–26.

Galas, P. (1998). From presentation to programming. *Learning and Leading with Technology, 25*(4), 18–21.

Gardiner, S. (2001). Cybercheating: A new twist on an old problem. *Phi Delta Kappan, 83*(2), 172–176.

Gauthier, S. (2004). GIS helps prepare students for emergencies. *Learning & Leading with Technology, 32*(3), 22–25.

Gay, L. R. (1993). *Educational research: Competencies for analysis and application* (4th ed.). Upper Saddle River, NJ: Merrill/Prentice Hall.

Gibbs, W., Graves, P., & Bernas, R. (2000). Identifying important criteria for multimedia instructional courseware evaluation. *Journal of Computing in Higher Education, 12*(1), 84–106.

Gibson, C., & Graf, A. (1992). Impact of adults' preferred learning styles and perception of barriers on completion of external baccalaureate degree programs. *Journal of Distance Education, 7*(1), 39–51.

Gill, B., Dick, W., Reiser, R., & Zahner, J. (1992). A new model for evaluating instructional software. *Educational Technology, 32*(3), 39–48.

Gitomer, D. H., Latham, A., & Ziomek, R. (1999). *The academic quality of prospective teachers: The impact of admissions and licensure testing.* Princeton, NJ: Teaching and Learning Division, Educational Testing Service.

Glasgow, J. (1996). Part I: It's my turn! Motivating young readers. *Learning and Leading with Technology, 24*(3), 20–23.

Glasgow, J. (1996–1997). Part II: It's my turn! Motivating young readers using CD-ROM storybooks. *Learning and Leading with Technology, 24*(4), 18–22.

Glasgow, J. (1997). Keep up the good work! Using multimedia to build reading fluency and enjoyment. *Learning and Leading with Technology, 24*(5), 22–25.

Gleeson, L. (1997). An interactive multimedia computer program on art history. In D. Gregory (Ed.) *New technologies in art education: Implications for theory, research, and practice.* Reston, VA: The National Art Education Association.

GLEF Staff. (2003, Spring). A passion for projects. *Edutopia* (http://www.glef.org).

Goldberg, A., Russell, M., & Cook, A. (2003). The effects of computers on student writing: A meta analysis of studies from 1992–2002. *Journal of Technology, Learning, and Assessment, 2*(1), 1–51.

Goldstein, L. (2002). Virtual reality researchers target special education classes. *Education Week, 22*(3), 8.

Gonsalves, D., & Lopez, J. (1998). Catch your students with microworlds games. *Learning and Leading with Technology, 26*(3), 19–21.

Goslee, S. (1998, June). *Losing ground bit by bit: Low-income communities in the information age.* Washington, DC: The Benton Foundation and the National Urban League. Available from http://www.benton.org/Library/Low-Income/home.html

Graham, G., Holt-Hale, S., & Parker, M. (1998). *Children moving: A reflective approach to teaching physical education.* Mountain View, CA: Mayfield Publishing Co.

Graham, R. (1994). A computer tutorial for psychology of learning courses. *Teaching of Psychology, 21*(2), 116–166.

Graham, R. (1998). A computer tutorial on the principles of stimulus generalization. *Teaching of Psychology, 25*(2), 149–151.

Grant, M. M. (2002). *Individual differences in constructionist learning environments: Qualitative inquiry into computer mediated learning artifacts.* Unpublished doctoral dissertation, The University of Georgia, Athens, GA.

Grogan, D., & Ruzic, R. (2000). Walking the walk: Universal design on the web. *Journal of Special Education Technology, 15*(3), 45–49.

Handler, M. (1992). Preparing new teachers to use technology: Perceptions and suggestions for teacher educators. *Computers in Education, 20*(2), 147–156.

Hanfland, P. (1999). Electronic portfolios. *Learning and Leading with Technology, 26*(6), 54–57.

Hardy, D. W., & Boaz, M. H. (1997). Learner development: Beyond the technology. In T. E. Cyrs (Ed.), *Teaching and learning at a distance: What it takes to effectively design, deliver, and evaluate programs.* San Francisco: Jossey-Bass.

Harp, L. (1996, October). The history wars: How technology changes everything. *Electronic Learning, 16,* 32–39.

Harris, J. (1985). Student writers and word processing. *College Composition and Communication, 36*(3), 323–330.

Harris, J. (1998a). Assistive annotations: The art of recommending web sites. *Learning and Leading with Technology, 25*(6), 58–61.

Harris, J. (1998b). *Virtual architecture: Designing and directing curriculum-based telecomputing.* Eugene, OR: International Society for Technology in Education.

Harris, J. (2000). Taboo topic no longer: Why telecollaborative projects sometimes fail. *Learning and Leading with Technology, 27*(5), 36–41.

Hartley, K. (2000). Online simulations. *Learning and Leading with Technology, 28*(3), 32–35.

Hartley, K., & Bendixon, L. (2001). Educational research in the Internet age: Examining the role of individual characteristics. *Educational Researcher, 30*(9), 22–26.

Hasselbring, T. (1988). Developing math automaticity in learning handicapped children. *Focus on Exceptional Children, 20*(6), 1–7.

Hasselbring, T., & Goin, L. (1993). Integrating technology and media. In E. Polloway & J. Patton (Eds.), *Strategies for teaching learners with special needs* (5th ed.). New York: Merrill.

Hauger, G. (2000). Instantaneous rate of change: A numerical approach. *The International Journal of Mathematical Education in Science and Technology, 31*(6), 891–897.

Hawisher, G. (1989). Research and recommendations for computers and compositions. In G. Hawisher & C. Selfe (Eds.), *Critical perspectives on computers and composition instruction.* New York: Teachers College Press.

Healy, J. (1998). *Failure to connect: How computers affect our children's minds—for better or worse.* New York: Simon & Schuster.

Helt, M. (2003). Writing the book on online literature circles. *Learning and Leading with Technology, 30*(7), 28–31, 58.

Henderson, L., Klemes, J., & Eshet, Y. (2000). Just playing a game? Educational simulation software and cognitive outcomes. *Journal of Educational Computing Research, 22*(1), 105–129.

Hermann, A. (1988). *Desktop publishing in high school: Empowering students as readers and writers.* (ERIC Document Reproduction No. ED300837)

Herrell, A., & Jordan, M. (2003). *Fifty strategies for teaching English language learners* (2nd ed.). Upper Saddle River, NJ: Merrill/Prentice Hall.

Heward, W. (2000). *Exceptional children: An introduction to special education* (6th ed.) Upper Saddle River, NJ: Prentice Hall.

Higgins, K., & Boone, R. (1993). Technology as a tutor, tools, and agent for reading. *Journal of Special Education Technology, 12*(1), 28–37.

Hill, J. R., Reeves, T. C., Grant, M. M., Wang, S. K., & Hans, S. (in press). Learning in a wireless environment: The success and challenges of ubiquitous computing in a school. In C. Vrasidas & G. V. Glass (Eds.), *Current perspective on applied information technologies: Preparing teachers to teach with technology* (Vol. II). Greenwich, CT: Information Age Publishing.

Hirsch, E. D. (2002). Classroom research and cargo cults. *Policy Review, 115.* Available from http://www.policyreview.org/OCT02/hirsch.html

Hoffenburg, H., & Handler, M. (2001). Digital video goes to school. *Learning and Leading with Technology, 29*(2), 10–15.

Hoffman, D., & Novak, T. (1998, April 17). Bridging the racial divide on the Internet. *Science, 280*(5362), 390–391.

Hoffman, J. L., & Lyons, D. L. (1997). Evaluating instructional software. *Learning and Leading with Technology, 25*(2), 52–56.

Howard, B. (2001, May 8). Lights! Camera! Learning curve! *PC Magazine.* Retrieved September 6, 2004, from http://www.pcmag.com/article2/0,1759,24860,00.asp

Howell, R. D. (1994). Technological innovations in the education of gifted and talented students. In J. L. Genschaft, M. Mirely, & C. L. Hollinger (Eds.), *Serving gifted and talented students.* Austin, TX: PRO-ED.

Hudgins, B. (2001). Leveraging handheld technology in the classroom. *T.H.E. Journal Online.* Retrieved from http://www.thejournal.com/magazine/vault/A3809.cfm

Humphries, D. (1989). A computer training program for teachers. In C. Selfe, D. Rodrigues, & W. Oates (Eds.), *Computers in English and the language arts.* Urbana, IL: National Council of Teachers of English.

International Reading Association. (2001). *Integrating literacy and technology in the curriculum: A position statement of the international reading association*. Newark, DE: Author.

International Society for Technology in Education. (2000). *National educational technology standards for students*. Eugene, OR: Author.

International Society for Technology in Education. (2002). *National educational technology standards for teachers: Preparing teachers to use technology*. Eugene, OR: Author.

Jacobsen, J., Moore, M., & Brown, L. (2002). Chemistry comes alive! *Journal of Chemical Education, 79*(11), 1381–1384.

Johnson, D. (2002). Web watch: Writing resources. *Reading Online, 5*(7).

Johnson, D. (2003). Choosing the right books for struggling readers. *Learning and Leading with Technology, 31*(1), 22–27.

Johnson, D., & Eisenberg, M. (1996). Computer literacy and information literacy: A natural combination. *Emergency Librarian, 23*(5), 12–16.

Johnson, D., & McLeod, S. (2004–2005). Get answers: Using student response systems to see students' thinking. *Learning and Leading with Technology, 32*(4), 18–23.

Johnson, D., & Zufall, L. (2004). Web watch—Not just for kids anymore: WebQuests for professional development. *Reading Online, 7*(5).

Kahn, J. (1997a). Scaffolding in the classroom: Using CD-ROM storybooks at a computer reading center. *Learning and Leading with Technology, 25*(2), 19, 19.

Kahn, J. (1997b). Well begun is half done: Teaching students to use concept-mapping software. *Learning and Leading with Technology, 24*(5), 39–40.

Kahn, J. (1998–1999). The same but different: The computer as an alternate medium. *Learning and Leading with Technology, 26*(4), 15–18.

Kajder, S., Bull, G., & Van Noy, E. (2004). A space for "writing without writing": Blogs in the language arts classroom. *Learning and Leading with Technology, 31*(6), 32–35.

Kajder, S., & Bull, G. (2003). Scaffolding for struggling students: Reading and writing with blogs. *Learning and Leading with Technology, 31*(2), 31–35.

Kajder, S., & Swenson, J. (2004). Digital images in the language arts classroom. *Learning and Leading with Technology, 31*(8), 18–21, 46.

Kane, W. M. (1993). *Step-by-step to comprehensive school health: The program planning guide*. Santa Cruz, CA: ETR Associates.

Karchmer, R. A. (2000). Using the Internet and children's literature to support interdisciplinary instruction. *The Reading Teacher, 54*(1), 100–104.

Karchmer, R. A. (2001a). Gaining a new, wider audience: Publishing student work on the Internet. *Reading Online, 4*(10). Available at http://www.readingonline.org

Karchmer, R. A. (2001b). The journey ahead: Thirteen teachers report how the Internet influences literacy and literacy instruction in their K–12 classrooms. *Reading Research Quarterly, 36*, 442–466.

Keizer, G. (1997). Which software works? *Family PC, 4*(5), 117–121.

Kennedy, D. (1995). Climbing the Tree of Mathematics. *Mathematics Teacher, 88*(6), 640–645.

Kimball, C., & Sibley, P. (1997–1998). Am I on the mark? Technology planning for the e-rate. *Learning and Leading with Technology, 25*(4), 52–57.

King, T. W. (1999). *Assistive technology: Essential human factors*. Boston: Allyn & Bacon.

Kinzer, C. K. (2003). The importance of recognizing the expanding boundaries of literacy. *Reading Online, 6*(10).

Kleiner, A., & Lewis, L. (2003). *Internet Access in U.S. public schools and classrooms: 1994–2002* (NCES Report No. 2004–011). Washington, DC: U.S. Department of Education, Institute of Education Science.

Klemm, W. (1998). Eight ways to get students more engaged in online conferences. *T.H.E. Journal, 26*(1), 62–64.

Klesius, J., Homan, S., & Thompson, T. (1997). Distance education compared to traditional instruction: The students' view. *International Journal of Instructional Media, 24*(3), 207–220.

Knee, R., Musgrove, A., & Musgrove, J. (2000). Lights, camera, action: Streaming video on your web site. *Learning and Leading with Technology, 28*(1), 50–53.

Knupfer, N., & McIsaac, M. (1989). Desktop publishing software: The effects of computerized formats on reading speed and comprehension. *Journal of Research on Computing in Education, 22*(2), 127–136.

Kozma, R. (1991). Learning with media. *Review of Educational Research, 61*(2), 179–211.

Kozma, R. (1994). Will media influence learning? Reframing the debate. *Educational Technology Research and Development, 42*(2), 5–17.

Kozma, R., Zucker, A., & Espinoza, C. (1998, October). *An evaluation of the virtual high school after one year of operation*. Arlington, VA: SRI International. Available from http://vhs.concord.org/

Kraemer, K. (1990). SEEN: Tutorials for critical reading. *Writing Notebook, 7*(3), 31–32.

Krashen, S. (1982). *Principles and practices in second language acquisition*. Oxford: Pergamon Press.

Kulik, J. (2003). *Effects of using instructional technology in elementary and secondary schools: What controlled evaluation studies say*. Arlington, VA: SRI International. Retrieved June 26, 2004, from http://www.sri.com/policy/csted/reports/sandt/it/Kulik_ITinK–12_Main_Report.pdf

Kurzweil, R. (2003). The end of handicaps. *eSchool News online, 6*(7). Retrieved from http://www.eschoolnews.org/news/showstory.cfm?ArticleID=4491

Kwajewski, K. (1997a). Memories in living color: Multimedia yearbooks. *Learning and Leading with Technology, 25*(2), 20–21.

Kwajewski, K. (1997b). Technology as a core value. *Learning and Leading with Technology, 24*(5), 54–56.

Labbo, L. D. (2004). Author's computer chair [Technology in Literacy Department]. *The Reading Teacher, 57*(7), 688–691.

Labbo, L. D., Eakle, A. J., & Montero, M. K. (2002). Digital language experience approach: Using digital photographs and software as a language experience approach innovation. *Reading Online, 5*(8).

Labbo, L. D., Leu, D. L., Kinzer, C. K., Teale, W. H., Cammack, D., et al. (2003). Teacher wisdom stories: Cautions and recommendations for using computer-relates technologies for literacy instruction [Technology in Literacy Department]. *The Reading Teacher, 57*(3), 300–304.

Labbo, L. D., Sprague, I., Montero, M. K., & Font, G. (2000). Connecting a computer center to themes, literature, and kindergartners' literacy needs. *Reading Online, 4*(1).

Ladelson, L. (1994). Calibrating probeware: Making in line. *The Computing Teacher, 21*(6), 46–47.

Lahm, E. A. (2000). Special education technology: Defining the specialist. *Special Education Technology Practice, 2*(3), 22–27.

Lahm, E. A., & Nickels, B. L. (1999). What do you know? Assistive technology competencies for special educators. *Teaching Exceptional Children, 32*(1), 56–63.

Lanham, R. (1995). *The electronic word: Democracy, technology, and the arts*. Chicago: University of Chicago Press.

Lary, L. (2004). Hide and seek: GPS and geocaching in the classroom. *Learning & Leading with Technology, 31*(6), 14–18.

Lemkuhl, M. (2002). Teaching ideas: Pen-pal letters: The cross-curricular experience. *The Reading Teacher, 55*(8), 720–729.

Lenker, J. A., & Paquet, V. L. (2003). A review of conceptual models for assistive technology outcomes research and practice. *Assistive Technology, 15,* 1–15.

Leu, D. J., Jr. (2002a). The new literacies: Research on reading instruction with the Internet. In A. E. Farstrup & S. J. Samuels (Eds.), *What research has to say about reading instruction* (3rd ed., pp. 310–336). Newark, DE: International Reading Association.

Leu, D. J., Jr. (2002b). Internet Workshop: Making time for literacy. *The Reading Teacher, 55*(5), 466–472.

Leu, D. J., Jr., & Kinzer, C. K. (2000). The convergence of literacy instruction with networked technologies for information and communication. *Reading Research Quarterly, 35,* 108–127.

Leu, D. J., Jr., & Leu, D. D. (2000). *Teaching with the Internet: Lessons from the classroom* (3rd ed.). Norwood, MA: Christopher-Gordon.

Lewis, P. (2001). *Spreadsheet magic: Forty lessons using spreadsheets to teach curriculum in K–8 classrooms.* Eugene, OR: International Society for Technology in Education.

Lewis, R. (1993). *Special education technology.* Pacific-Grove, CA: Brooks-Cole.

Lim, C. (2001). Computer self-efficacy, academic self-concept, and other predictors of satisfaction and future participation of adult distance learners. *The American Journal of Distance Education, 15*(2), 41–52.

Linn, R., Baker, E., & Betebenner, D. (2002). Accountability systems: Implications of requirements of the No Child Left Behind Act. *Educational Researcher, 31*(6), 3–16.

Litchfield, B. (1992). Science: Evaluation of inquiry-based science software and interactive multimedia programs. *The Computing Teacher, 19*(6), 41–43.

Litchfield, B. (1995). Helping your students plan computer projects. *The Computing Teacher, 22*(7), 37–43.

Lockard, J., & Abrams, P., (2001). *Computers for twenty-first century educators* (5th ed.). New York: Longman.

Lopez, S. (2000). Cat in the hat and all that. *Time Magazine, 156*(17), 6.

Loupe, D. (2001). Virtual schooling: A new dimension to learning brings new challenges for educators, *eSchool News, 4*(6), 41–47

Lowther, D. L., Ross, S. M., & G.M. Morrison (2003). When each one has one: The influences on teaching strategies and student achievement of using laptops in the classroom. *Educational Technology Research & Development, 51*(3), 23–44.

Lucas, G. (2003, Spring). Technology as a force for change. *Edutopia* (http://www.glef.org).

Ludlow, B. L. (1994). A comparison of traditional and distance education models. In *Proceedings of the Annual National Conference of the American Council on Rural Special Education,* Austin, TX. (ERIC Document Reproduction No. ED369599)

Machtmes, K., & Asher, J. W. (2000). A meta-analysis of the effectiveness of telecourses in distance education. *American Journal of Distance Education, 14*(1), 27–46. (ERIC Document Reproduction No. ED613342)

Mageau, T. (1990). ILS: Its new role in schools. *Electronic Learning, 10*(1), 22–24.

Mallott, R. (1993). The three-contingency model of performance management and support in higher education. *Educational Technology, 33*(10), 21–28.

Malone, T. (1980). *What makes things fun to learn? A study of intrinsically motivating computer games.* Palo Alto, CA: Xerox Palo Alto Research Center.

Mankus, M. L. (2000). *Using virtual manipulatives on the web to develop number sense.* NCTM Annual Meeting in Chicago. Available from http://mason.gmu.edu/~mmankus/talks/nctmch00. htm

Manouchehri, A., Enderson, M. C., & Pagnucco, L. A. (1998). Exploring geometry with technology. *Mathematics Teaching in the Middle School, 3*(6), 436–442.

Manouchehri, A., & Pagnucco, L. (1999–2000). Julio's run: Studying graphs and functions. *Learning and Leading with Technology, 27*(4), 42–45.

Maor, D. (1991, April). *Development of student inquiry skills: A constructivist approach in a computerized classroom environment.* Paper presented at the Annual Meeting of the National Association for Research in Science Teaching, Lake Geneva, WI, April 7–10, 1991. (ERIC Document Reproduction No. ED326261)

Margolis, J., & Fisher, A. (2002). *Unlocking the clubhouse: Women in computing.* Cambridge, MA: The MIT Press.

Maring, G. H., Boxie, P., & Wiseman, B. J. (2000). School-university partnership through online pattern books. *Reading Online, 4*(5).

Mark, M. (1996). *Contemporary music education* (3rd ed.). New York: Schirmer Books.

Martin, K., & Bearden, D. (1998). Listserv learning. *Learning and Leading with Technology, 26*(3), 39–41.

Matthews, M. S. (2000). Electronic literacy and the limited English proficient student. *Reading Online.* Available at http://www.readingonline.org/electronic/matthews

Mauricio, D. (2000). See Music Tech Ensemble information at http://hhs.suhsd.k12.ca.us/musictech/index.html

Mayer, R. (1997). Multimedia learning: Are we asking the right questions? *Educational Psychologist, 32*(4), 1–19.

Mayer, R., Fennell, S., & Farmer, L. (2004). A personalization effect in multimedia learning: students learn better when words are in conversational style rather than formal style. *Journal of Educational Psychology, 96*(2), 398–395.

Mayer, R., & Moreno, R. (1998). A split attention effect in multimedia learning: Evidence for dual processing systems in working memory. *Journal of Educational Psychology, 90*(2), 312–320.

Mayer, R., & Moreno, R. (2003). Nine ways to reduce cognitive load in multimedia learning. *Educational Psychologist, 38*(1), 43–52.

Mayes, R. (1992). The effects of using software tools on mathematics problem solving in secondary school. *School Science and Mathematics, 92*(5), 243–248.

McCarthy, R. (1998). Stop the presses: An update on desktop publishing. *Electronic Learning, 7*(6), 24–30.

McCoy, L. (1990). *Does the Supposer improve problem solving in geometry?* (ERIC Document Reproduction No. ED320775)

McCullen, C. (2001). Going the distance … with technology. *Technology & Learning, 21*(7), 45–47.

McGinley, R. (1991). Start them off with games! *The Computing Teacher, 19*(3), 49.

McGrath, D. (2004), Strengthening collaborative work. *Learning and Leading with Technology, 31*(5), 3–33.

McHenry, L., & Bozik, M. (1997). From a distance: Student voices from the interactive video classroom. *TechTrends, 42*(6), 20–24.

McNabb, M. (2001). In search of appropriate usage guidelines. *Learning and Leading with Technology, 29*(2), 50–54.

Mechling, L. C., Gast, D. L., & Langone, J. (2002). Computer-based video instruction to teach persons with moderate intellectual disabilities to read grocery aisle signs and locate items. *The Journal of Special Education, 35*(4), 224–240.

Mechling, L., & Langone, J. (2000). The effects of computer-based instructional program with video anchors on the use of photographs for prompting augmentative communication. *Education and Training in Mental Retardation and Developmental Disabilities, 35*(1), 90–105.

Meese, R. L. (2001). *Teaching learners with mild disabilities: Integrating research and practice.* Belmont, CA: Wadsworth/Thomson Learning.

Merrill, D., & Salisbury, D. (1984). Research on drill and practice strategies. *Journal of Computer-Based Instruction, 11*(1), 19–21.

Metheny, R. (2003). Pre-K 2003: Inclusive, not assistive technology. *Closing the Gap, 22*(5), 1, 24–25.

Microsoft, schools mull security improvements. (2003). *eSchool News online, 5*(8). Retrieved from http://www.eschoolnews.org/news/showstory.cfm?ArticleID=4582

Mikropoulos, T., Katsikis, A., & Nikolou, E. (2003). Virtual environments in biology teaching. *Journal of Biological Education, 37*(4), 176–181.

Miller, H. L. (1997). The New York City Public Schools Integrated Learning Systems Project. *International Journal of Educational Research, 27*(2), 91–183.

Mintz, R. (1993). Computerized simulation as an inquiry tool. *School Science and Mathematics, 93*(2), 76–80.

Mitchell, K., Finkelhor, D., & Wolak, J. (2001). Risk factors for and impact of online sexual solicitation of youth. *Journal of the American Medical Association, 285*(23), 3011–3014.

Moersch, C. (1995). Choose the right graph. *The Computing Teacher, 22*(5), 31–35.

Mohnsen, B. (2000). Vaughn, Nekomi, and Luis: What they were doing in middle school physical education. *Learning and Leading with Technology, 27*(5), 22–27.

Mohnsen, B. (2003). *Concepts and principles of physical education: What every student needs to know.* Reston, VA: National Association for Sport and Physical Education.

Molenda, M. (1991). A philosophical critique on the claims of "constructivism." *Educational Technology, 31*(9), 44–48.

Molnar, A. (1978). The next great crisis in American education: Computer literacy. *AEDS Journal, 12*(1), 11–20.

Moore, M. (1995). The death of distance. *The American Journal of Distance Education, 9*(3), 1–4.

Moore, M., Myers, R., & Burton, J. (1994). What multimedia might do … and what we know about what it does. In *Multimedia and learning: A school leader's guide.* Alexandria, VA: National School Boards Association.

Mora, J. K. (2000/2001). Responding to the demographic challenge: An Internet classroom for teachers of language-minority students. *Reading Online, 4*(5).

Moreno, R., & Mayer, R. (2002). Verbal redundancy in multimedia learning: When reading helping listening. *Journal of Educational Psychology, 94*(1), 156–163.

Morkes, J. & Nielson, J. (1997). *Concise, scannable, and objective: How to write for the Web.* Retrieved March 1, 2005, from http://www.useit.com/papers/webwriting/writing.html

Moskal, P., Martin, B., & Foshee, N. (1997). Educational technology and distance education in central Florida: An assessment of capabilities. *The American Journal of Distance Education, 11*(1), 6–22.

Moyer, P. S., Bolyard, J. J., & Spikell, M. A. (2002). What are virtual manipulatives? *Teaching Children Mathematics, 8*(6), 372–377.

Muckerheide, P., Mogill, A., & Mogill, H. (1999). In search of a fair game. *Mathematics and Computer Education, 33*(2), 142–150.

Muffoletto, R. (1994). Technology and restructuring education: Constructing a context. *Educational Technology, 34*(2), 24–28.

Muro, D. (1994). *The art of sequencing* [Video]. Miami, FL: CPP/Belwin.

Murray, C. (2003a, June). Budget ax falls on school tech programs. *eSchool News, 6*(6), 1, 29.

Murray, C. (2003b, November 18). Controversial radio ID tags keep track of kids. *eSchool News online, 6*(11).

Murray, T., et al. (1988). *An analogy-based computer tutorial for remediating physics misconceptions.* (ERIC Document Reproduction No. ED299172)

Music Educators National Conference. (1994). *Standards for arts education.* Reston, VA: Author. Retrieved March 16, 2005, from the Kennedy Center ArtsEdge website: http://artsedge.kennedy-center.org/teach/standards/

Music Educators National Conference. (2004). *Bridging the gap: Popular music and music education.* Reston, VA: Author.

Myers, J., & Beach, R. (2001). Hypermedia authoring as critical literacy. *Journal of Adolescent & Adult Literacy, 44*(6), 538–546.

Naisbitt, J. (1984). *MegaTrends.* New York: Warner Books.

Nathan, J. (1985). *Micro-myths: Exploring the limits of learning with computers.* Minneapolis, MN: Winston Press.

National Association for Sport and Physical Education. (2004). *Moving into the future: National standards for physical education* (2nd ed.). Reston, VA: Author.

National Council for Accreditation of Teacher Education. (1997). *Technology and the new professional teacher. Preparing for the 21st century classroom.* Washington, DC: Author.

National Council for the Social Studies. (1994). *Expectations of excellence: Curriculum standards for social studies.* Silver Springs, MD: Author.

National Council of Teachers of English & International Reading Association. (1996). *Standards for the English language arts.* Urbana, IL: Author.

National Council of Teachers of Mathematics. (2000). *Principles and standards for school mathematics.* Reston, VA: Author.

National Council of Teachers of Mathematics. (2001). *E-Example 5.4: Accessing and investigating data using the World Wide Web; E-Example 5.5: Collecting, representing, and interpreting data.* Retrieved January 5, 2001, http://standards.nctm.org/document/eexamples/chap5/5.4/index.htm and http://standards.nctm.org/document/eexamples/chap5/5.5/index.htm

National Research Council (1996). *National science education standards.* Washington, DC: National Academy Press.

Newman, J. (1988). Online: Classroom publishing. *Language Arts, 65*(7), 727–732.

Niemiec, R., & Walberg, R. (1989). From teaching machines to microcomputers: Some milestones in the history of computer-based instruction. *Journal of Research on Computing in Education, 21*(3), 263–276.

Norris, C., Sullivan, T., Poirot, J., & Soloway, E. (2003). No access, no use, no impact: Snapshot surveys of educational technology in K–12. *Journal of Research on Technology in Education, 36*(1), 15–27.

Norris, W. (1977). Via technology to a new era in education. *Phi Delta Kappan, 58*(6), 451–459.

Norvelle, R. (1992). Desktop publishing. In G. Bitter (Ed.), *Macmillan encyclopedia of computers.* New York: Macmillan.

O'Bannon, B., Krolak, B., Harkelroad, M., & Dick, D. (1999). Awesome graphics: Using *PhotoShop* for web graphics. *Learning and Leading with Technology, 26*(5), 54–57.

Oblender, T. (2002). A hybrid course model: One solution to the high online drop-out rate. *Learning and Leading with Technology, 29*(6), 42–46.

Odasz, F. (1999–2000). Collaborative Internet tools. *Learning and Leading with Technology, 27*(4), 11–15.

Office of Technology Assessment. (1995). *Teachers and technology: Making the connection* (OTA-EHR-616). Washington, DC: U.S. Government Printing Office.

Ohler, J. (1998). The promise of MIDI technology: A reflection on musical intelligence. *Learning and Leading with Technology, 25*(6), 6–15.

Okolo, C. (1992). The effect of computer-assisted instruction format and initial attitude on the arithmetic facts proficiency and continuing motivation of students with learning disabilities. *Exceptionality: A Research Journal, 3*(4), 195–211.

Oliver, H. (1994). Book review. Education and informatics worldwide: The state of the art and beyond. *Journal of Research on Computing in Education, 26*(2), 285–290.

Oppenheimer, T. (2003). *The flickering mind: The false promise of technology in the classroom and how learning can be saved.* New York: Random House.

Oravec, J. A. (2002). Bookmarking the world: Weblog applications in education. *Journal of Adolescent & Adult Literacy, 45*(7), 616–621.

Orkwis, R., & McLane, K. (1998). *A curriculum every student can use: Design principles for student access. OSEP topical brief.* Reston, VA: Council for Exceptional Children. Also available from http://www.cec.sped.org/osep/udsign.htm

Orman, E. (2003). Effect of virtual reality graded exposure on heart rate and self-reported anxiety levels of performing saxophonists. *Journal of Research in Music Education, 51*(4), 302–315.

Ormrod, J. (2001). *Educational psychology: Developing learners* (3rd ed.). Upper Saddle River, NJ: Merrill/Prentice Hall.

Osborn, V. (2001) Identifying at-risk students in videoconferencing and web-based distance education, *American Journal of Distance Education, 15*(1), 41–54.

Papert, S. (1980). *Mindstorms: Children, computers, and powerful ideas.* New York: Basic Books.

Papert, S. (1987). Computer criticism vs. technocentric thinking. *Educational Researcher, 16*(1), 22–30.

Parham, C. (2003). Virtual skies. *Technology and Learning, 24*(4), 34–35.

Parker, R. C. (1989). Ten common desktop design pitfalls. *Currents, 15*(1), 24–26.

Parmenter, B., & Burns, M. (2001). GIS in the classroom: Challenges, opportunities and alternatives. *Learning and Leading with Technology, 28*(7), 10–16.

Parmenter, B., & Burns, M. (2001). GIS in the classroom: Challenges, opportunities, and alternatives. *Learning and Leading with Technology, 28*(7), 10–17.

Pate, R. R., & Small, M. L. (1995). School physical education. *Journal of School Health, 65*(8), 312–317.

Paterson, W., Henry, J., & O'Quin, K. (2003). Investigating the effectiveness of an integrated learning system on early emergent readers. *Reading Research Quarterly, 38*(2), 172–207.

Payne, V. G., & Issacs, L. D. (1995). *Human motor development: A lifespan approach* (3rd ed.). Mountain View, CA: Mayfield Publishing Co.

Perkins, D. (1991). Technology meets constructivism: Do they make a marriage? *Educational Technology, 31*(5), 18–23.

Peterson, C., & Bond, N. (2004). Online compared to face-to-face teacher preparation for learning standards-based planning skills. *Journal of Research on Technology in Education, 36*(4), 345–360.

Phillips, D. C. (1995). The good, the bad, and the ugly: The many faces of constructivism. *Educational Researcher, 24*(7), 5–12.

Ploger, D., Rooney, M., & Klingler, L. (1996). Applying spreadsheets and draw programs in the classroom. *Tech Trends, 41*(3), 26–29.

Ploger, D., & Vedova, T. (1999). Programming dynamic charts in the elementary classroom. *Learning and Leading with Technology, 26*(5), 38–41.

Plymate, L. (1998). Is it linear? *Learning and Leading with Technology, 26*(1), 16–22.

Poedubicky, V., Brown, L., Hoover, H., & Elias, M. J. (2000). Using technology to promote health. *Learning and Leading with Technology, 28*(4), 18–21, 56.

Poock, M. (1998). The Accelerated Reader: An analysis of the software's strengths and weaknesses and how it can be used to best potential. *School Library Media Activities Monthly, 14*(9), 32–35.

Puckett, K. S. (2004). Project ACCESS: Field testing an assistive technology toolkit for students with mild disabilities. *Journal of Special Education Technology, 19*(2), 5–17.

Pugalee, D., & Robinson, R. (1998). A study of the impact of teacher training in using Internet resources for mathematics and science instruction. *The Journal of Research on Computing in Education, 31*(1), 78–88.

Quesada, A. (1998). The arts connection. *Technology and Learning, 19*(2), 52–58.

Randel, J., Morris, B., Wetzel, C., & Whitehill, B. (1992). The effectiveness of games for educational purposes: A review of recent research. *Simulation and Gaming, 23*(3), 261–276.

Rankin-Erickson, J., Wood, L., & Beukelman, D. (2003). Early computer literacy: First graders use the "talking" computer. *Reading Improvement, 40*(3), 132–144.

Readers' choice awards. (2004). *eSchool News, 7*(4), 32–33.

Reigeluth, C., & Schwartz, E. (1989). An instructional theory for the design of computer-based simulations. *Journal of Computer-Based Instruction, 16*(1), 1–10.

Reinking, D., McKeena, M. C., Labbo, L. D., & Kieffer, R. F. (eds.). (1998). *Handbook of literacy and technology: Transformations in a post-typographic world.* Mahwah, NJ: Erlbaum.

Reissman, R. (2000). Priceless gifts. *Learning and Leading with Technology, 28*(2), 28–31.

Reitsma, P. (1988). Reading practice for beginners: Effects of guided reading, reading-while-listening, and independent reading with computer-based speech feedback. *Reading Research Quarterly, 23,* 219–235.

Rembelinsky, I. (1997–1998). Us and them: Multimedia explorations of prejudice and intolerance in American history. *Learning and Leading with Technology, 25*(4), 42–47.

Renne, C. (2000). Taking shape: Linking geometry and technology. *Learning and Leading with Technology, 27*(7), 58–62.

Repp, R. (1999). The World Wide Web: Interfaces, databases, and applications to education. *Learning and Leading with Technology, 26*(6), 40–41, 60–61.

Revenaugh, M. (1997). *Productivity in the classroom.* Redmond, WA: Microsoft Corporation. Available from http://www.microsoft.com/education/k12/resource/lessons.htm

Richards, C., & Ridley, D. (1997). Factors affecting college students' persistence in online computer-managed instruction. *College Student Journal, 31,* 490–495.

Richards, J. (1992). Computer simulations in the science classroom. *Journal of Science Education and Technology, 1*(1), 67–80.

Riddle, J. (1990). *Measuring affective change: Students in a distance learning class.* Paper presented at the Annual Meeting of the Northern Rocky Mountain Educational Research Association, Greeley, CO. (ERIC Document Reproduction No. ED325514)

Rieber, L., Smith, L., & Noah, D. (1998). The value of serious play. *Educational Technology, 38*(6), 29–37.

Rifkin, J. (2000). *The age of access.* New York: Tarcher/Putnam.

Ringstaff, C., & Kelley, L. (2002). *The learning return on our technology investment: A review of findings from research.* San Francisco: WestEd RTEC. Available from http://www.wsetedrtec.org

Ringstaff, C., & Yocam, K. (1995). *Creating an alternative context for teacher development: The ACOT teacher development centers* (ACOT Report, H#18). Cupertino, CA: Apple Computer Co.

Ritchie, D., & Boyle, K. (1998). Finding the bucks for technology. *Learning and Leading with Technology, 26*(2), 46–50.

Robinson, R., & Roland, C. (1994). *Technology and arts education.* Tallahassee, FL: Florida Department of Education.

Roblyer, M. (1983). How to evaluate software reviews. *Executive Educator, 5*(9), 34–39.

Roblyer, M. (1990). The glitz factor. *Educational Technology, 30*(10), 34–36.

Roblyer, M. D. (1991). Electronic hands across the ocean: The Florida-England connection. *The Computing Teacher, 19*(5), 16–19.

Roblyer, M. (1992). Computers in education. In G. Bitter (Ed.), *Macmillan encyclopedia of computers*. New York: Macmillan.

Roblyer, M. D. (1996). The constructivist/objectivist debate: Implications for instructional technology research. *Learning and Leading with Technology, 24*(2), 12–17.

Roblyer, M. D. (1997). Technology and the oops! effect: Finding a bias against word processing. *Learning and Leading with Technology, 24*(7), 14–16.

Roblyer, M. D. (1998). Visual literacy: Seeing a new rationale for teaching with technology. *Learning and Leading with Technology, 26*(2), 51–54.

Roblyer, M. D. (1999). Our multimedia future: Recent research on multimedia's impact on education. *Learning and Leading with Technology, 26*(6), 51–53.

Roblyer, M. D. (2000). Digital desperation: Research reports on a growing technology and equity crisis. *Learning and Leading with Technology, 27*(8), 50–53, 61.

Roblyer, M. D. (2003a). Getting our NETS worth: The role of ISTE's National Educational Technology Standards (NETS). *Learning and Leading with Technology, 30*(8), 6–13.

Roblyer, M. D. (2003b). Virtual high schools in the United States: Current views, future visions. In Jo Bradley (Ed.), *The open classroom: Distance learning in and out of schools*. London: Kogan Page.

Roblyer, M. D. (2004). Virtual schools, real issues. *The International Principal, 8*(3). Retrieved September 28, 2004, from http://www.readnow.info/

Roblyer, M., Castine, W., & King, F. J. (1988). *Assessing the impact of computer-based instruction: A review of recent research*. New York: Haworth Press.

Roblyer, M. D., & Ekhaml, L. (2000). How interactive are your distance courses? A rubric for assessing interactivity in distance learning. *Online Journal of Distance Learning Administration, 3*(2). Available from http://www.westga.edu/~distance/summer32.htm

Roblyer, M. D., & Erlanger, W. (1998). Preparing Internet-ready teachers: Which methods work best? *Learning and Leading with Technology, 26*(4), 59–61.

Roblyer, M. D., & Marshall, J. (2002–2003). Predicting success of virtual high school distance learners: Preliminary results from an educational success prediction instrument (ESPRI). *Journal of Research on Technology in Education, 35*(2), 241–255.

Roblyer, M. D., & McKenzie, B. (2000). Distant but not out-of-touch: What makes an effective distance learning instructor? *Learning and Leading with Technology, 27*(6), 50–53.

Roblyer, M. D., & Wiencke, W. (2003). Design and use of a rubric to assess and encourage interactive qualities in distance courses. *The American Journal of Distance Education, 17*(2), 77–98.

Roblyer, M. D., & Wiencke, W. (2004). Exploring the interaction equation: Validating a rubric to assess and encourage interaction in distance courses. *The Journal of Asynchronous Learning Networks, 9*(1). Available from http://www.sloan-c.org/publications/jaln/index.asp

Rogers, E. (2004). *Diffusion of innovations*. New York: The Free Press.

Ronen, M. (1992). Integrating computer simulations into high school physics teaching. *Journal of Computers in Mathematics and Science Teaching, 11*(3–4), 319–329.

Rose, D. (2000). Universal design for learning. *Journal of Special Education Technology, 15*(1), 67–70.

Rose, D., Sethuraman, S., & Meo, G. J. (2000). Universal design for learning. *Journal of Special Education Technology, 15*(2), 56–60.

Rose, S. (1988). A desktop publishing primer. *The Computing Teacher, 15*(9), 13–15.

Ross, T. W., & Bailey, G. D. (1996). Creating safe Internet access. *Learning and Leading with Technology, 24*(1), 51–53.

Royer, R., & Royer, J. (2002). Developing understanding with multimedia. *Learning and Leading with Technology, 29*(7), 40–45.

Rubin, A. (undated). *Educational technology: Support for inquiry-based learning*. Retrieved November 15, 2004, from http://ra.terc.edu/publications/

Rudolph, T. (2004). *Technology strategies for music education*. Wyncote, PA: Technology Institute for Music Educators.

Rudolph, T., & Peters, K. (1996). The MIDI sequencer in the music classroom [Video]. Chicago: GIA Publications.

Russell, M., & Plati, T. (2000). *Mode of administration effects on MCAS composition performance for grades four, eight, and ten*. Retrieved February 1, 2001, from http://nbetpp.bc.edu/reports.html

Russell, T. L. (1992). Television's indelible impact on distance education: What we should have learned from comparative research. *Research in Distance Education, 4*(4), 2–4.

Russell, T. L. (1997). *The "no significant difference" phenomenon as reported in research reports, summaries, and papers*. Raleigh: Office of Instructional Telecommunications, North Carolina State University.

Saettler, P. (1990). *The evolution of American educational technology*. Englewood, CO: Libraries Unlimited.

Sage, S. (2000). A natural fit: Problem-based learning and technology standards. *Learning and Leading with Technology, 28*(1), 6–12.

Salisbury, D. (1990). Cognitive psychology and its implications for designing drill and practice programs for computers. *Journal of Computer-Based Instruction, 17*(1), 23–30.

Salpeter, J. (2004). Data mining with a mission. *Technology and Learning, 24*(8), 30–34.

Satcher, D. (1997). *Physical activity and health: A report of the surgeon general*. Washington, DC: U.S. Government Printing Office.

Scharf, E., & Cramer, J. (2002). Desktop poetry project. *Learning and Leading with Technology, 29*(6), 28–31, 50–51.

Schmar-Dobler, E. (2003). Reading on the Internet: The link between literacy and technology. *Journal of Adolescent & Adult Literacy, 47*(1), 80–85.

Scholten, B., & Whitmer, J. (1996). Hypermedia projects: Metastacks increase content focus. *Learning and Leading with Technology, 24*(3), 59–62.

Scleef, L. (2003). Inclusive school communities: Accessible learning environments for all. *Closing the Gap, 22*(3), 1, 14–15, 28.

Scot, T., & Harding, D. (2004). Splicing video into the writing process. *Learning and Leading with Technology, 32*(1), 26–31.

Seamon, D. (1999). Expanded description of SGML. *Learning and Leading with Technology, 27*(2), 39.

Seffrin, J. R. (1990). The comprehensive school health curriculum. *Journal of School Health, 60*(4), 151–156.

Sfard, A. (1998). One–two metaphors for learning and the dangers of choosing just one. *Educational Researcher, 27*(2), 4–13.

Shea, V. (2004). *Netiquette*. Available from http://www.albion.com/netiquette/book/index.html

Sheingold, K. (1991). Restructuring for learning with technology: The potential for synergy. *Phi Delta Kappan, 73*(1), 17–27.

Sherman, T. (1987–1988). A brief review of developments in problem solving. *Computers in the Schools, 4*(3–4), 171–178.

Shore, A., & Johnson, M. (1992). Integrated learning systems: A vision for the future. *Educational Technology, 32*(9), 36–39.

Simmons, P., & Lunetta, V. (1993). Problem-solving behaviors during a genetics computer simulation. *Journal of Research in Science Teaching, 30*(2), 153–173.

Simonson, M., Smaldino, S., Albright, M., & Zvacek, S. (2000). *Teaching and learning at a distance: Foundations of distance education*. Upper Saddle River, NJ: Merrill/Prentice Hall.

Simonson, M. R., & Thompson, A. (1994). *Educational computing foundations*. New York: Merrill.

Simpson, C. M. (2001). *Copyright for schools: A practical guide* (2nd ed.). Worthington, OH: Linworth Publishing.

Skipton, C. (1997, May 5). As the worlds turn: VRML authoring and modeling software. *New Media, 7*(6).

Smith, C. K. (1996). *Convenience vs. connection: Commuter students' views on distance learning*. Paper presented at the Annual Forum of the Association for Institutional Research, Albuquerque, NM. (ERIC Document Reproduction No. ED397725)

Smith, K. (1992). Earthquake! *The Florida Technology in Education Quarterly, 4*(2), 68–70.

Smith, R. A., & Sclafani, S. (1989). Integrated teaching systems: Guidelines for evaluation. *The Computing Teacher, 17*(3), 36–38.

Snyder, I. (1993). Writing with word processors: A research overview. *Educational Research, 35*(1), 49–68.

Solloway, S., & Harris, E. (1999). Creating community online. *Educom Review, 34*(2). Available from http://www.educause.edu/ir/library/html/erm99021.html

Soloman, G. (2001). Deconstructing a grant. *Technology & Learning, 21*(11), 44–52.

Spence, I., & Hively, W. (1993). What makes Chris practice? *Educational Technology, 35*(6), 5–23.

Speziale, M., & La France, L. (1992). Multimedia and students with learning disabilities. *The Computing Teacher, 20*(3), 31–34.

Stanton, D. (1992). Microcomputer-based labs. *Electronic Learning Special Edition (Buyers Guide), 12*(1), 16–17.

Steed, M. (2001). 3-D visualization: Using 3-D software to represent curricular concepts. *Learning and Leading with Technology, 29*(3), 14–20.

Stein, M., Silbert, J., & Carnine, D. (1997). *Designing effective mathematics instruction: Direct instruction mathematics* (3rd ed.). Upper Saddle River, NJ: Merrill/Prentice Hall.

Steinburg, R., & Oberem, G. (2000). Research-based instructional software in modern physics. *Journal of Computers in Mathematics and Science Teaching, 19*(2), 115–136.

Steinhaus, K. (1986–1987). Putting the music composition tool to work. *The Computing Teacher, 14*(4), 16–18.

Stemler, L. (1997). Educational characteristics of multimedia: A literature review. *Journal of Educational Multimedia and Hypermedia, 6*(3–4), 339–359.

Stephenson, N. (1993). *Snow crash*. New York: Bantam Books.

Stevenson, S. (2001). Discover and create your own field trips. *Multimedia Schools, 8*(4), 40–45.

Stokes, J. (1999). Problem solving software, equity, and allocation of roles. *Learning and Leading with Technology, 26*(5), 6–9, 30.

Stoll, C. (1999). *High-tech heretic: Why computers don't belong in the classroom and other reflections by a computer contrarian*. New York: Doubleday.

Strommen, E. (1994). Can technology change the test? *Electronic Learning, 14*(1), 44–53.

Stuhlmann, J. (1997). Butterflies! Using multimedia to capture a unique science project. *Learning and Leading with Technology, 25*(3), 22–27.

Sullivan, J. (1995). Exciting ways to use videodiscs. *Media and Methods, 31*(3), S8–S10.

Sumrall, W., & Forslev, W. (1994). Spreadsheet meteorology. *Science Scope, 18,* 36–38.

Sutherland, R. (1993). A spreadsheet approach to solving algebra problems. *Journal of Mathematical Behavior, 12*(4), 353–383.

Swain, M. (1993). The output hypothesis: Just reading and writing aren't enough. *The Canadian Modern Language Review, 50,* 158–164.

Swan, K., & Meskill, C. (1996). Using hypermedia in response-based literature classrooms: A critical review of commercial applications. *Journal of Research on Computing in Education, 29*(2), 167–192.

Taylor, D. (1989). Communications technology for literacy work with isolated learners. *Journal of Reading, 32*(7), 634–639.

Taylor, R. (1980). *The computer in the school: Tutor, tool, tutee*. New York: Teachers College Press.

Tennyson, R. (1990). Integrated instructional design theory: Advancements from cognitive science and instructional technology. *Educational Technology, 30*(7), 9–15.

Tergan, S. (1998). Checklists for the evaluation of education software: Critical review and prospects. *Innovations in Education and Training, 35*(1), 9–20.

Thatcher, M. (2003). Building 3-D worlds. *Technology and Learning, 24*(4), 34.

Thomerson, D., & Smith, C. (1996). Student perceptions of the affective experiences encountered in distance learning courses. *The American Journal of Distance Education, 10*(3), 37–48.

Thompson, G. (1990). How can correspondence-based distance learning be improved? A survey of attitudes of students who are not well disposed toward correspondence study. *Journal of Distance Education, 5*(1), 53–65.

Threlkeld, R., & Brzoska, K. (1994). Research in distance education. In B. Willis (Ed.), *Distance education: Strategies and tools*. Englewood Cliffs, NJ: Educational Technology Publications.

Tibbs, P. (1989). Video creation for junior high language arts. *Journal of Reading, 32*(6), 558–559.

Tinker, B., Staudt, C., & Walton, D. (2002). The handheld computer as field guide. *Learning and Leading with Technology, 30*(1), 36–41.

Tinker, R. (1998, Winter). Teaching and learning in the knowledge society. *The Concord Consortium Newsletter,* 1–2, 14.

Tolhurst, D. (1995). Hypertext, hypermedia, multimedia defined? *Educational Technology, 35*(2), 21–26.

Toomey, R., & Ketterer, K. (1995). Using multimedia as a cognitive tool. *Journal of Research on Computing in Education, 27*(4), 472–481.

Topping, K., & Paul, T. (1999). Computer-assisted assessment of practice at reading: A large scale survey using Accelerated Reader data. *Reading & Writing Quarterly, 15*(3), 213–232.

Torgeson, J. (1986). Using computers to help learning disabled children practice reading: A research-based perspective. *Learning Disabilities Focus, 1*(2), 72–81.

Torgeson, J., Waters, M., Cohen, A., & Torgeson, J. (1988). Improving sight word recognition skills in learning disabled children: An evaluation of three computer program variations. *Learning Disabilities Quarterly, 11,* 125–133.

Trend, D. (2001). *Welcome to cyberschool*. Lanham, MD: Rowman and Littlefield.

Trotter, A. (1991). In the school game, your options abound. *Executive Educator, 13*(6), 23.

Truett, C. (1993). CD-ROM storybooks bring children's literature to life. *The Computing Teacher, 21*(1), 20–21.

Tufte, E. (2003). *PowerPoint is evil. Power corrupts. PowerPoint corrupts absolutely. Wired Magazine,* Issue 11(9). Retrieved September 6, 2004, from http://www.wired.com/wired/archive/11.09/ppt2.html

Tumulty, K., & Dickerson, J. (1998). *Gore's costly high-wire act, 151*(20), 52–55.

Turkle, S. (2004, January 30). How computers change the way we think. *The Chronicle of Higher Education,* B26–B28.

Turner, J., & Paris, S. (1995). How literacy tasks influence children's motivation for literacy. *The Reading Teacher, 48,* 662–673.

Turner, S. V., & Dipinto, V. M. (1992). Students as hypermedia authors: Themes emerging from a qualitative study. *Journal of Research on Computing in Education, 25*(2), 187–199.

Tuthill, G., & Klemm, B. (2002). Virtual field trips: Alternatives to actual trips. *International Journal of Instructional Media, 29*(4), 453–468.

University of Delaware AUP website: http://www.ash.udel.edu/ash/teacher/AUP.html

U.S. Department of Education. (2000). *Twenty-second annual report to Congress on the implementation of the Individuals with Disabilities Education Act.* Washington, DC: Author. Available from http://www.ed.gov/offices/OSERS/OSEP/OSEP2000AnlRpt/

U.S. Department of Health and Human Services. (1996a). *Physical activity and health: A report of the Surgeon General.* Atlanta, GA: U.S. Department of Health and Human Services, Centers for Disease Control and Prevention, National Center for Chronic Disease Prevention and Health Promotion.

U.S. Department of Health and Human Services. (1996b). *Physical activity and health: Adolescents and young adults.* Atlanta, GA: U.S. Department of Health and Human Services, Centers for Disease Control and Prevention, National Center for Chronic Disease Prevention and Health Promotion.

U.S. Department of Labor. (1992). *SCANS (The Secretary's Commission on Achieving Necessary Skills) report.* Washington, DC: U.S. Government Printing Office.

Vaille, J., & Hall, J. (1998). *Guidelines for the evaluation of instructional technology resources.* Eugene, OR: International Society for Technology in Education.

van Buren, C., & Aufdenspring, D. (1998). Quilting our history: An integrated schoolwide project. *Learning and Leading with Technology, 26*(2), 22–27.

Van Dusen, L., & Worthen, B. (1995). Can integrated instructional technology transform the classroom? *Educational Leadership, 53*(2), 28–33.

van Hover, S., Swann, K. O., & Berson, M. J. (2004). Digital images in social studies curriculum. *Learning & Leading with Technology, 31*(8), 22–25.

Van Rossum, G. (2001). *Python language website.* Retrieved January 5, 2001, from http://www.python.org/

Viani, N. (2003–2004). The right write site. *Learning and Leading with Technology, 31*(4), 24–27.

Viau, E. (1998). Color me a writer: Teaching students to think critically. *Learning and Leading with Technology, 25*(5), 17–20.

Volker, R. (1992). Applications of constructivist theory to the use of hypermedia. *Proceedings of Selected Research Presentations at the Annual Convention of the AECT.* (ERIC Document Reproduction No. ED348037)

Vygotsky, L. S. (1962). *Thought and language.* Cambridge, MA: The MIT Press.

Walsh, J. (1999). Edison Project, now Edison Schools Inc., plans to go public. *Education Week, 19*(1), 6.

Walsh, T. (2001). SAMDADs for your classroom. *Learning and Leading with Technology, 28*(6), 32–35, 60.

Wang, A., & Newlin, M. (2000). Characteristics of students who enroll and succeed in web-based classes. *Journal of Educational Psychology, 92*(1), 137–143.

Watson, J. (1993). *Teaching thinking skills with databases.* Eugene, OR: International Society for Technology in Education.

Watt, D. (1992). Logo. In G. Bitter (Ed.). *Macmillan encyclopedia of computers.* New York: Macmillan.

Weinstein, P. (1999). Computer programming revisited. *Technology & Learning, 19*(8), 38–42.

Weizenbaum, J. (1976). *Computer power and human reason.* San Francisco: W. H. Freeman & Co.

Westbrook, T. (1997). Changes in students' attitudes toward graduate business instruction via interactive television. *The American Journal of Distance Education, 11*(1), 55–69.

Wetzel, K. (1993). Teacher educators' use of computers in teaching. *Journal of Technology and Teacher Education, 1*(4), 335–352.

White, M. (1992). Are ILSs good for education? *Educational Technology, 32*(9), 49–50.

Whitworth, S. A., & Berson, M. J. (2003). Computer technology in the social studies: An examination of the effectiveness literature (1996–2001). *Contemporary Issues in Technology and Teacher Education* [Online serial], *2*(4). Available from http://www.citejournal.org/vol2/iss4/socialstudies/article1.cfm

Wilkerson, T. (2001). Reading and writing the digital way. *Learning and Leading with Technology, 29*(3), 42–24, 60–61.

Wilkes, C., & Burnham, B. (1991). Adult learner motivations and electronic distance education. *The American Journal of Distance Education, 5*(1), 43–51.

Willinsky, J., & Bradley, S. (1990). Desktop publishing in remedial language arts settings: Let them eat cake. *Journal of Teaching Writing, 9*(2), 223–238.

Wissick, C. A. (1999a). Quickstarts: Developing functional literacy skills around food. *Special Education Technology Practice, 1*(3), 22–25.

Wissick, C. A. (1999b). Quickstarts: Let's go grocery shopping. *Special Education Technology Practice, 1*(4), 33–36.

Wood, D., Underwood, J., & Avis, P. (1999). Integrated learning systems in the classroom. *Computers and Education, 33*(2–3), 91–108.

Ybarra, R., & Green, T. (2003). Using technology to help ESL/EFL students develop language skills. *The Internet TESL Journal, 9*(3). Available from http://iteslj.org/

Young, J. (2000, October 6). Virtual reality on a desktop hailed as new tool in distance education. *The Chronicle of Higher Education,* p. A43.

Zemsky, R., & Massey, W. (2004). *Thwarted innovation: What happened to e-learning and why.* Philadelphia: The Learning Alliance at the University of Pennsylvania.

Zirkin, B., & Sumler, D. (1995). Interactive or non-interactive: That is the question!!! An annotated bibliography. *Journal of Distance Education, 10*(1), 95–112.

Zisow, Marcie A. (2001). Fundraising with technology. *Learning and Leading with Technology, 28*(4), 36–41.

Zucker, A., & Kozma, R. (2003). *The virtual high school: Teaching generation V.* New York: Teachers College Press.

Name Index

Estep, S., 105
Estes, C., 90
Evans, R., 353

Fabos, B., 252
Falba, C. J., 334
Farmer, L., 190
Fasimpaur, K., 300, 301
Feicht, L., 332
Feldman, A., 252
Fennell, S., 190
Feurer, M., 21
Finegan-Stoll, C., 342
Finkelhor, D., 23, 227
Firedrake, G., 177
Fisher, A., 22, 32
Fisher, S. K., 416
Flannery, M., 352
Flick, L., 340
Flowers, R., 94
Font, G., 291
Forbes, L. S., 298
Forest, J., 174
Forslev, W., 131
Foshee, N., 225
Franklin, S., 15
Frederickson, S., 184, 207
Fulford, C., 224
Funkhouser, C., 96
Furger, R., 15, 16, 17
Furst-Bowie, J., 224

Gabbard, R., 189
Gagné, R., 37, 41, 46, 77, 82, 84
Galas, P., 77
Galloway, C., 135
Gardiner, S., 13, 23, 32
Gardner, J. E., 416
Gast, D. L., 416
Gauthier, S., 361
Gay, L. R., 163
Geissler, C., 111
Gibbs, W., 193
Gibson, C., 223, 225
Gill, B., 108
Gitomer, D. H., 337
Glasgow, J., 192
Gleeson, L., 383
GLEF Staff, 17
Glenn, A., 139
Goin, L., 92
Goldberg, A., 122, 124
Goldberg, K., 134
Goldstein, L., 209
Gonsalves, D., 77
Goslee, S., 22
Graf, A., 223, 225
Graham, G., 394
Graham, R., 86
Grant, M. M., 297
Graves, P., 193
Green, T., 318
Greenman, M., 95
Grogan, D., 413

Hagins, C., 171
Hall, J., 105, 106, 111
Handler, M., 65, 203, 204
Hanfland, P., 28, 29
Hans, S., 297
Hardy, D. W., 224, 225
Harkelroad, M., 165
Harp, L., 355, 357
Harris, E., 244
Harris, J., 122, 221, 233, 252, 261
Hartley, K., 253, 255

Hasselbring, T., 82, 92
Hauger, G., 131, 132
Hawisher, G., 122, 124
Hay, K., 208
Healy, J., 13, 21
Helt, M., 297
Henderson, L., 95
Henry, J., 105
Hermann, A., 158
Herrell, A., 316
Heward, W., 419
Higgins, K., 82
Hill, J. R., 297, 300
Hirsch, E. D., 36, 41, 46
Hively, W., 41
Hoffenburg, H., 203, 204
Hoffman, B., 308
Hoffman, D., 22
Hoffman, J. L., 106, 111
Hofstetter, E., 178
Holt-Hale, S., 394
Homan, S., 224
Hoover, H., 404
Horn, C., 299
Howard, B., 203
Howard, K., 294
Howell, R. D., 419
Hudgins, B., 27
Hundley, S., 342
Hussey, S. M., 408

Insinnia, E., 288
International Reading Association, 290, 291, 292, 294
International Society for Technology in Education, 64
Issacs, L. D., 394

Jacobsen, J., 203
Jacobson, P., 91
Jansek, K., 243
Jernigan, J., 335
Jerome, M., 22
Johnson, D., 17, 165, 292, 294, 297, 299
Johnson, V., 139
Jordan, M., 316
Judd-Wall, J., 408

Kahn, J., 82, 169, 192, 195
Kajder, S., 240, 297, 298
Kameenui, E., 41
Kane, W. M., 394
Karchmer, R. A., 291, 298, 301
Katsikis, A., 208
Kauchak, D., 38, 44
Kauffman, S., 294
Keizer, G., 121
Kelly, L., 13, 21
Kennedy, D., 327
Kent School District, 57
Ketterer, K., 291
Kieffer, R. F., 291
Kimball, C., 62
King, F. J., 13
King, T. W., 413
Kinzer, C. K., 291
Kirkpatrick, H., 14, 65
Kleiner, A., 22
Klemes, J., 95
Klemm, B., 253
Klemm, W., 243
Klesius, J., 224
Klingler, L., 132
Knee, R., 272
Knupfer, N., 156, 158
Konold, C., 252

Kozma, R., 13, 21, 27, 221, 223, 225
Kraemer, K., 86
Krashen, S., 310, 311
Krolak, B., 165
Kulik, J., 104
Kurzweil, R., 27
Kwajewski, K., 62, 205

Labbo, L. D., 291, 299
Lach, C., 167
Ladelson, L., 176, 177
La France, L., 416
Lahm, E. A., 411
Langone, J., 416
Lanham, R., 373
Lary, L., 361
Latham, A., 337
Layne, B., 86
Lehman, J., 224, 225
Lemkuhl, M., 301
Lenker, J. A., 411
Leu, D. J., Jr., 291, 292, 294
Lewis, D., 268
Lewis, L., 22
Lewis, P., 131, 317
Lewis, R., 161
Lim, C., 225
Linn, R., 21
Litchfield, B., 106, 199, 200
Little, E., 167
Lockard, J., 111
Lopez, J., 77
Lopez, S., 176, 294, 297
Loupe, D., 221
Lowther, D. L., 300
Lucas, G., 17
Ludlow, B. L., 225
Ludwig, G., 348
Lumley, D., 100
Lunetta, V., 90
Lyons, D. L., 106, 111

MacGregor, K., 165
Machtmes, K., 223
MacLachlan, K. B., 237
Mageau, T., 106
Mallott, R., 41
Malone, T., 93
Mankus, M. L., 330
Manouchehri, A., 177, 333
Maor, D., 139
Marcovitz, D., 143
Margolis, J., 22, 32
Maring, G. H., 294
Mark, M., 377
Marshall, J., 221, 222, 224, 225
Martin, B., 225
Martin, K., 99
Martindale, T., 223
Mason, C., 356
Massey, W., 222
Mathematical Sciences Education Board, 331
Matthews, M. S., 292
Mauricio, D., 372
Mayer, R., 188, 190
Mayes, R., 98
McCarthy, R., 158
McCoy, L., 98
McCullen, C., 220
McGinley, R., 94, 96
McGrath, D., 256
McHenry, L., 224, 225
McInerney, W., 105
McIsaac, M., 156, 158
McKeena, M. C., 291
McKenzie, B., 225

McLane, K., 413
McLeod, S., 165
McNabb, M., 21, 32, 64, 222, 226
Mechling, L., 416
Meese, R. L., 415
Meo, G. J., 413
Merrill, D., 79, 82
Meskill, C., 188, 189
Metheny, R., 414
Mezack, M., 225
Mikropoulos, T., 208
Miller, E., 219
Miller, H. L., 105
Mintz, R., 90
Mitchell, K., 23, 227
Moersch, C., 167
Mogill, A., 94
Mogill, H., 94
Mohnsen, B., 209, 397, 403
Molenda, M., 37, 45
Molnar, A., 10, 23
Montero, M. K., 291
Moore, M., 186, 203, 219
Mora, J. K., 292
Moreno, R., 188, 190
Morgan, B., 335
Morkes, J., 298
Morris, B., 93
Morrison, G. M., 300
Moskal, P., 225
Moyer, P. S., 330
Muckerheide, P., 94
Muffoletto, R., 6
Muro, D., 372
Murray, C., 21, 25
Murray, T., 86
Musgrove, A., 272
Musgrove, J., 272
Music Educators National Conference, 371
Myers, J., 291
Myers, R., 186

Naisbitt, J., 13
Narhan, J., 154
National Association of Biology Teachers, 331
National Council for Teachers of English, 290, 291, 292, 294
National Council for the Accreditation of Teacher Education, 27, 53
National Council for the Social Studies, 350, 357
National Council of Teachers of Mathematics, 327, 330, 334
Nazzaro, D., 167
Newlin, M., 225
Newman, J., 158
Ng, K., 100
Nickels, B. L., 411
Nielson, J., 298
Niemiec, R., 9
Nikolou, E., 208
Noah, D., 95
Norris, C., 14, 22, 25
Norris, W., 10, 76
Norvelle, R., 156
Novak, T., 22

O'Bannon, B., 165
Oberem, G., 86
Oblender, T., 223
Odasz, F., 240
Ohler, J., 174, 376
O'Leary, D., 25
Oliver, H., 65
Oliver, K., 300, 301
Oppenheimer, T., 13–14, 21, 32
O'Quin, K., 105

Oravec, J. A., 298
Orkwis, R., 413
Orman, E., 209
Ormrod, J., 42, 44
Orrill, C., 135
Osborn, V., 225

Pagnucco, L., 177, 333
Papert, S., 10, 44, 77
Paquet, V. L., 411
Parham, C., 25
Paris, S., 301
Parker, M., 394
Parker, R. C., 158, 159
Parmenter, B., 178, 348
Pate, R. R., 395
Paterson, W., 105
Paul, T., 176
Payne, V. G., 394
Peck, C., 14, 65
Perkins, D., 106
Peters, K., 376, 377
Peterson, C., 223
Peterson, R., 258
Phillips, D. C., 37
Pilgrim, J., 279
Plati, T., 300
Ploger, D., 77, 132
Plymate, L., 177
Poedubicky, V., 404
Poirot, J., 14
Poock, M., 176, 294, 297
Popplewell, S., 192, 297
Puckett, K. S., 411
Pugalee, D., 139

Quesada, A., 383, 384

Randel, J., 93, 94
Rankin-Erickson, J., 297
Reeves, T. C., 297
Reigeluth, C., 89
Reinking, D., 291
Reiser, R., 108
Reissman, R., 127, 158, 159, 160, 258, 302
Reitsma, P., 294
Rembelinsky, I., 199
Renne, C., 332, 336
Repp, R., 269
Revenaugh, M., 136
Richards, C., 225
Richards, J., 90
Riddle, J., 225
Ridley, D., 225
Rieber, L., 95
Riel, M., 15
Rifkin, J., 21
Ringstaff, C., 13, 21, 65
Ritchie, D., 65, 66
Robinson, R., 139, 370
Roblyer, M. D., 9, 12, 13, 16, 17, 21, 22, 27, 65, 111, 124, 188, 199, 221, 222, 224, 225, 377
Rogers, E., 53
Rojas, A., 41, 77
Roland, C., 370
Ronen, M., 90
Rooney, M., 132
Rose, D., 413
Rose, S., 158
Ross, S. M., 300
Ross, T. W., 227
Rossum, V., 331
Royer, J., 199, 200, 201
Royer, R., 199, 200, 201
Rubin, A., 337

Rudolph, T., 372, 376, 377
Russell, M., 122, 124, 300
Russell, T. L., 223
Ruzic, R., 413

Saettler, P., 5, 6, 7, 8, 13
Sage, S., 253
Salisbury, D., 79, 82
Salpeter, J., 141
Satcher, D., 394
Scharf, E., 152, 159
Schmar-Dobler, E., 298
Scholten, B., 207
Schuetz, J., 209
Schwartz, E., 89
Sclafani, S., 105
Scleef, L., 414
Seale, J., 86
Seamon, D., 268
Seffrin, J. R., 394
Sethuraman, S., 413
Sfard, A., 36
Shavelson, R., 21
Shaw, D. B., 85
Shea, V., 239
Sheingold, K., 53
Sherman, T., 96
Shiffrin, R., 40
Shimon, J., 400
Sibley, P., 62
Silbert, J., 41
Simmons, P., 90
Simonson, M. R., 188, 220
Simpson, C. M., 64
Sims, J., 206
Skarecki, E., 288
Skipton, C., 269
Slater, T., 168, 259
Slattery, W., 342
Smaldino, S., 220
Small, M. L., 395
Smith, C., 225
Smith, C. K., 224
Smith, K., 90
Smith, L., 95
Smith, R. A., 105
Snyder, I., 122, 124
Solloway, S., 244
Soloman, G., 65, 66
Soloway, E., 14, 25
Spence, I., 41
Speziale, M., 416
Spikell, M. A., 330
Sprague, I., 291
Stanley, G., 45
Stanton, D., 176
Starr, B., 258
Staudt, C., 25
Steed, M., 208, 383, 384
Stein, M., 41
Steinburg, R., 86
Steinhaus, K., 174
Stemler, L., 189
Stephenson, N., 269
Stevenson, S., 208
Stokes, J., 99
Stoll, C., 13
Strommen, E., 165
Stuhlmann, J., 204, 207
Sullivan, T., 14
Sumler, D., 224
Sumrall, W., 131
Swain, M., 311, 313
Swan, K., 188, 189
Swann, K. O., 359
Swenson, J., 297, 298

SUBJECT INDEX

ISTE National Educational Technology Standards for Students

NETS for Students

Technology Foundation Standards for All Students

The technology foundation standards for students are divided into six broad categories. Standards within each category are to be introduced, reinforced, and mastered by students. These categories provide a framework for linking performance indicators within the Profiles for Technology Literate Students to the standards. Teachers can use these standards and profiles as guidelines for planning technology-based activities in which students achieve success in learning, communication, and life skills.

Technology Foundation Standards for Students

1. Basic operations and concepts
   - Students demonstrate a sound understanding of the nature and operation of technology systems.
   - Students are proficient in the use of technology.

2. Social, ethical, and human issues
   - Students understand the ethical, cultural, and societal issues related to technology.
   - Students practice responsible use of technology systems, information, and software.
   - Students develop positive attitudes toward technology uses that support lifelong learning, collaboration, personal pursuits, and productivity.

3. Technology productivity tools
   - Students use technology tools to enhance learning, increase productivity, and promote creativity.
   - Students use productivity tools to collaborate in constructing technology-enhanced models, prepare publications, and produce other creative works.

4. Technology communications tools
   - Students use telecommunications to collaborate, publish, and interact with peers, experts, and other audiences.
   - Students use a variety of media and formats to communicate information and ideas effectively to multiple audiences.

5. Technology research tools
   - Students use technology to locate, evaluate, and collect information from a variety of sources.
   - Students use technology tools to process data and report results.
   - Students evaluate and select new information resources and technological innovations based on the appropriateness for specific tasks.

6. Technology problem-solving and decision-making tools
   - Students use technology resources for solving problems and making informed decisions.
   - Students employ technology in the development of strategies for solving problems in the real world.